Lots of people think the best time to visit the **LINCOLN MEMORIAL (left)** is at night, when it's lit up and dramatic. Romantic, too. But I like visiting during the day—swallowed up in the crush of chattering international travelers and curious school children—and feeling oh-so-proud of being linked by nationality to this remarkable American, considered by many to be the country's greatest president.

On September 21, 2004, 25,000 Native Americans representing 400 tribes from all over the Western Hemisphere marched and danced down the National Mall—to the beat of drums and thunderous applause from more than 55,000 spectators—to herald the opening of the **NATIONAL MUSEUM OF THE AMERICAN INDIAN (above).** When you visit, be sure to admire every detail—from the windswept-look exterior to the Indian fry bread served in the museum cafe.

ARMANDO MARIN ZEPEDA
RANDALL C SHORT
JAMES W PETERSON
DENNIS C DURAND
ROY L MEADOWS
PHILIP D SHARP
LEROY J WESTRA
PAUL D CARTER
JOSEPH D ESPARZA
ROBERT L GREENSTREET
ROY IGNACIO
JERRY FOY
JOSEPH E SWEENEY
THOMAS W KNUCKEY
DONALD R MATHIS
MITCHELL O BARNES
JOSE MARIA R ARREDONDO
GARY J SHINN
ROY M SEABROOK
PAUL G MAGERS
AUGUSTUS ADAMS
JAMES R SAXON
DENNIS L MEDUNA
EDWARD A WERMAN
ANDREW C STRONG III
GEORGE H POTTS
JOSE ANGEL SANCHEZ
EDGAR D THOMAS
LEM CLARK
WILLIAM K TAYLOR
KIMBER L HALL
MARTIN E LOVING
WILLIAM J LAMMERS
EDMOND T BALLANCE
ANTHONY M EILERS
BERNARD BARNES
JOHN R MICKLE
MAURICE H BRYANT
THOMAS E EPPERSON
STEPHEN K MASDEN
JOHNNY ARTHUR
CARL W BREWSTER
LOYD E ROBINSON
STEVEN J ELLIS
CHARLES A SANCHEZ
GARY L WESTPHAL
JEFFREY D SCHUMACHER
EARL R LESTER Jr
DEE BERGERA
WILLIAM T WALSH
BILLY D PEDINGS
DANNY G STUDDARD
TERRY L KELLY
RAYMOND V DEBLASIO
ROGER E WITTE
RANDY V HINES
PAUL TRUJILLO
HENRY F DELLECKER
DANNY T JETT
HAROLD J RITCH
VINCENT P MARTIN Jr
CHARLES A POPPLETON
ROBERT R CHESSER
RONNIE SHARPE
JOHN W GEORGE
ROBERT D BEUTEL
JAMES H SPANN
BILLY RAY COFFEY
ARCHIE T LLOY
STEVEN J McDONALD
OSCAR PAULLEY Jr
WILLIAM D THOMPSON
ROBERT L WYNN

These are the words of my husband Jim, a veteran of the Vietnam War, to those who visit the **VIETNAM VETERANS MEMORIAL (left)**: Run your fingers over the names of the lost inscribed here. Observe the reflections of others tracing a particular name. Notice the impromptu memorials left along the wall—flowers, a set of dog tags, an old photo, a faded combat badge. And listen to the murmurs of other visitors in the procession past the wall, ongoing since November 13, 1982, when the memorial was dedicated.

Of all the war memorials, the **KOREAN WAR VETERANS MEMORIAL (above)**, dedicated in 1995, moves me the most on a visceral level. The lifelike statues of 19 men, weighed down by their gear, appear to be trudging through a field. Surrounded by juniper bushes (symbolic of Korea's rugged terrain) and covered in ponchos (a reminder of the foul weather they endured), they convey in their wary poses both cold fear and courage.

It can be hard to get through the doors of the Library of Congress, thanks to security procedures, but once you're in, patient volunteer docents treat you like you're the first one to ask how to get to the **READING ROOM OVERLOOK (left),** where to find the Gutenberg Bible, and how one registers to use the Reading Room. The best-kept secret is the lineup of engaging lectures, concerts, and films the Library hosts, mostly in the evenings; see the list on www.loc.gov.

"Meet you at the elephant." Translation: Meet you in the Rotunda of the **NATIONAL MUSEUM OF NATURAL HISTORY (below).** Washingtonians and visitors alike love these hard-to-miss museum landmarks as places to rendezvous and opportunities to marvel. This natural history museum is the largest in the world, with more than 126 million artifacts—including the legendary Hope Diamond—and yet it's only one of the Smithsonian Institution's 19 museums.

I would have preferred a museum that honored our soldiers by telling their stories, the way my dad recalls his time as a POW after being captured at the Battle of the Bulge. But the still powerful **NATIONAL WORLD WAR II MEMORIAL (above)** honors those who fought and died in the war with a pavilion of 56 granite pillars (one for each state and territory); 24 bas-relief panels illustrating scenes from the Atlantic and Pacific theaters; and a wall of 4,000 gold stars—one for each 100 soldiers who perished.

At the **WASHINGTON NATIONAL CATHEDRAL (right),** you can enjoy a picnic and get comfortable on the lawn of the Bishop's Garden. Inside this sixth largest cathedral in the world, you can admire the stained glass windows, stare up at the parade of state flags arrayed high up along the walls, and listen to an organ practice (every Mon and Wed 12:30–1pm).

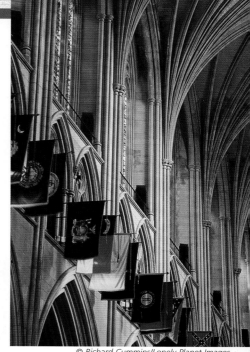

At **TRYST CAFÉ (above)** in Adams Morgan—
an eclectic, comfy coffeehouse/lounge—
patrons hook up to laptops, cellphones,
and lattes during the day, and connect
with each other, over cocktails, at night.
Tryst features free live jazz Monday
through Wednesday evenings.

Ballets grace the stage at the **KENNEDY
CENTER (right)**, along with the best opera,
orchestra, and theater performances. You'll
also find free concerts, affordable family
events, and $25-per-person jazz shows.
Above all, I love the center's festivals,
which range from American gospel music
to Arabian culture, in all its facets.

Everyone should join the crowds on the National Mall at least once for Independence Day. Among the festivities are a parade down Constitution Avenue and a reading of the Declaration of Independence in front of the National Archives. The day culminates in a **DISPLAY OF FOURTH OF JULY FIREWORKS,** lighting up the sky above the Washington Monument, exploding in time to the National Symphony renditions of "The 1812 Overture" and "Stars and Stripes Forever."

After dining at one of **GEORGETOWN**'s
(left) great restaurants or browsing in one
of its well-known shops, I like to stroll
though the neighborhood's quiet back
streets—where dollhouse-ish dwellings
and grande-dame mansions line up
behind brick sidewalks. Who lives here, I
wonder as I stroll by, and who lived here
200 years ago? And how ever do they fit
furniture through those narrow doors?

Traveling through **ROCK CREEK PARK**
(above)—whether on foot, bike, or by car—
one can reach the National Zoo, the
Kennedy Center, and neighborhoods
from Foggy Bottom and Georgetown all
the way to Cleveland Park and Chevy
Chase. It's a haven, beautiful in every
season, and it's the one place you'll see
Washingtonians of all stripes, unplugged
and relaxed.

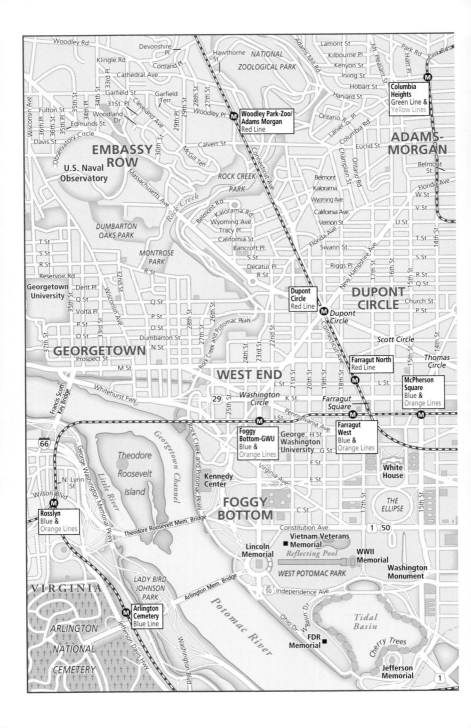

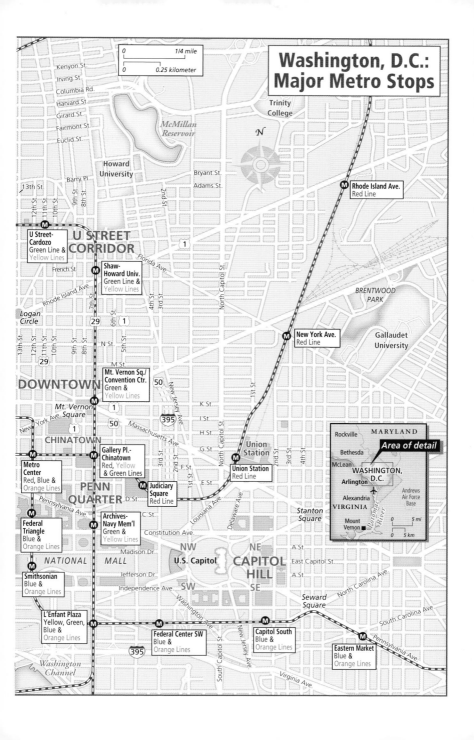

Washington, D.C.: Major Metro Stops

Kenyon St.
Irving St.
Columbia Rd.
Harvard St.
Girard St.
Fairmont St.
Euclid St.

McMillan Reservoir

Trinity College

N

Rhode Island Ave.
Red Line

Howard University

Bryant St.
Adams St.

13th St.
Barry Pl.
9th St.
8th St.

U Street-Cardozo
Green Line & Yellow Lines

U STREET CORRIDOR

French St.

Florida Ave.

Shaw-Howard Univ.
Green Line & Yellow Lines

BRENTWOOD PARK

Rhode Island Ave.

Logan Circle

29 1

4th St.
3rd St.

New York Ave.
Red Line

Gallaudet University

13th St.
12th St.
11th St.
10th St.
9th St.
8th St.
N St.

29

6th St.
5th St.

M St.

Mt. Vernon Sq./Convention Ctr.
Green & Yellow Lines

50 New Jersey Ave.

DOWNTOWN

1

50

Massachusetts Ave.

K St.

North Capitol St.

Mt. Vernon Square

1

I St.

395

1st St.

H St.

CHINATOWN

New York Ave.

Gallery Pl.-Chinatown
Red, Yellow & Green Lines

3rd St.
2nd St.

G St.

F St.

North Capitol St.

Union Station

Metro Center
Red, Blue & Orange Lines

Judiciary Square
Red Line

E St.

Union Station
Red Line

2nd St.
3rd St.
4th St.

PENN QUARTER

Pennsylvania Ave.

D St.

Federal Triangle
Blue & Orange Lines

Archives-Navy Mem'l
Green & Yellow Lines

C St.

Louisiana Ave.

Delaware Ave.

Stanton Square

Constitution Ave.

Madison Dr.

NATIONAL MALL

Smithsonian
Blue & Orange Lines

Jefferson Dr.

Independence Ave.

NW

U.S. Capitol

SW

NE

CAPITOL HILL

SE

East Capitol St.

A St.

A St.

Seward Square

North Carolina Ave.

Washington Ave.

L'Enfant Plaza
Yellow, Green, Blue & Orange Lines

South Carolina Ave.

395

Washington Channel

Federal Center SW
Blue & Orange Lines

South Capitol St.

New Jersey Ave.

Capitol South
Blue & Orange Lines

Eastern Market
Blue & Orange Lines

Pennsylvania Ave.

Virginia Ave.

Area of detail

Rockville
MARYLAND

Bethesda

McLean

WASHINGTON, D.C.

Arlington

Andrews Air Force Base

Alexandria
VIRGINIA

Mount Vernon

Potomac River

0   5 mi
0   5 km

0   1/4 mile
0   0.25 kilometer

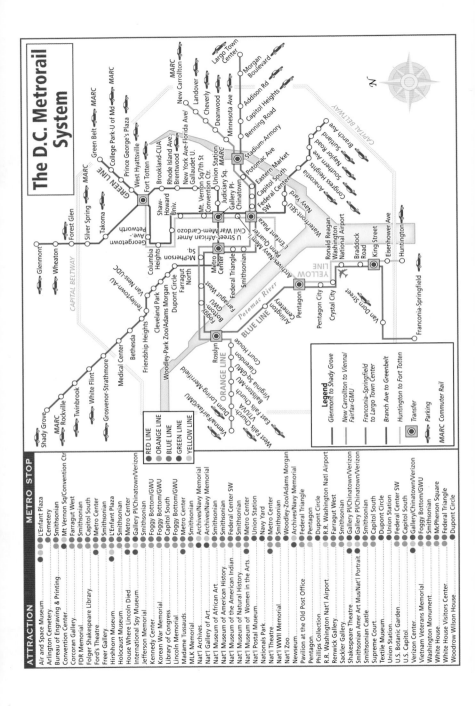

The D.C. Metrorail System

Legend

──	Glenmont to Shady Grove
──	New Carrollton to Vienna/Fairfax-GMU
──	Franconia–Springfield to Largo Town Center
──	Branch Ave to Greenbelt
──	Huntington to Fort Totten
◉	Transfer
🚗	Parking
🚂	MARC Commuter Rail

- ● RED LINE
- ● ORANGE LINE
- ● BLUE LINE
- ● GREEN LINE
- ● YELLOW LINE

ATTRACTION	METRO STOP
Air and Space Museum	L'Enfant Plaza
Arlington Cemetery	Cemetery
Bureau of Engraving & Printing	Smithsonian
Convention Center	Mt Vernon Sq/Convention Ctr
Corcoran Gallery	Farragut West
FDR Memorial	Smithsonian
Folger Shakespeare Library	Capitol South
Ford's Theatre	Metro Center
Freer Gallery	Smithsonian
Hirshhorn Museum	L'Enfant Plaza
Holocaust Museum	Smithsonian
House Where Lincoln Died	Metro Center
International Spy Museum	Gallery Pl/Chinatown/Verizon
Jefferson Memorial	Smithsonian
Kennedy Center	Foggy Bottom/GWU
Korean War Memorial	Foggy Bottom/GWU
Library of Congress	Capitol South
Lincoln Memorial	Foggy Bottom/GWU
Madame Tussauds	Metro Center
MLK Memorial	Smithsonian
Nat'l Archives	Archives/Navy Memorial
Nat'l Gallery of Art	Archives/Navy Memorial
Nat'l Museum of African Art	Smithsonian
Nat'l Museum of the American History	Smithsonian
Nat'l Museum of the American Indian	Smithsonian
Nat'l Museum of Natural History	Smithsonian
Nat'l Museum of Women in the Arts	Metro Center
Nat'l Postal Museum	Union Station
Nationals Park	Navy Yard
Nat'l Theatre	Metro Center
Nat'l WWII Memorial	Smithsonian
Nat'l Zoo	Woodley-Zoo/Adams Morgan
Newseum	Archives/Navy Memorial
Pavilion at the Old Post Office	Federal Triangle
Pentagon	Pentagon
Phillips Collection	Dupont Circle
R.R. Washington Nat'l Airport	R.R. Washington Natl Airport
Renwick Gallery	Farragut West
Sackler Gallery	Smithsonian
Shakespeare Theatre	Gallery Pl/Chinatown/Verizon
Smithsonian Amer Art Mus/Nat'l Portrait	Gallery Pl/Chinatown/Verizon
Smithsonian Castle	Smithsonian
Supreme Court	Capitol South
Textile Museum	Dupont Circle
Union Station	Union Station
U.S. Botanic Garden	Federal Center SW
U.S. Capitol	Capitol South
Verizon Center	Gallery/Chinatown/Verizon
Vietnam Veterans Memorial	Foggy Bottom/GWU
Washington Monument	Smithsonian
White House	McPherson Square
White House Visitors Center	Federal Triangle
Woodrow Wilson House	Dupont Circle

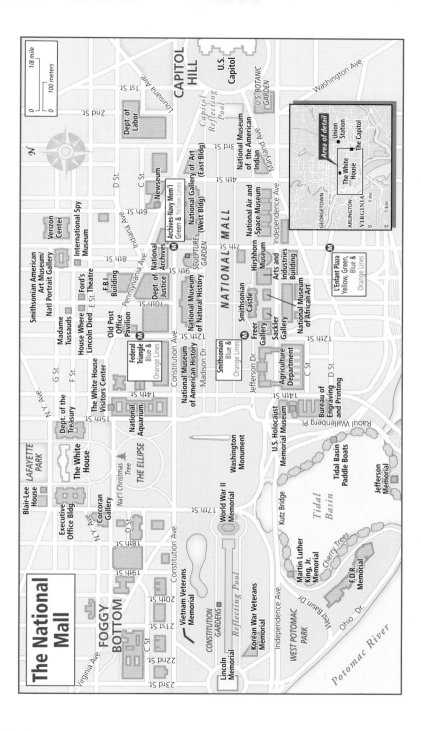

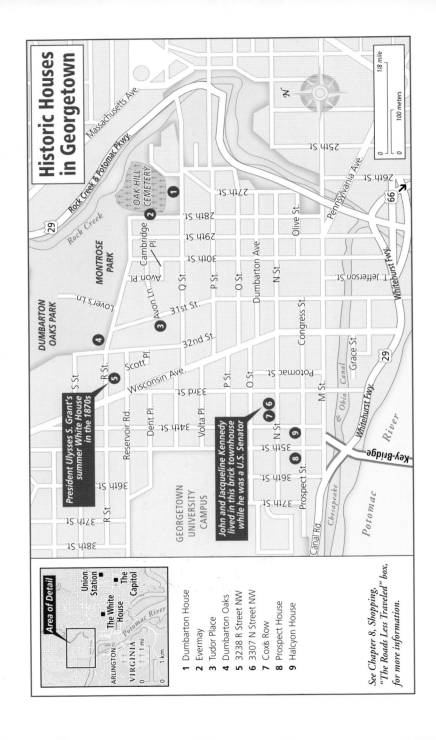

Historic Houses in Georgetown

Area of Detail

VIRGINIA
ARLINGTON

The White House
Union Station
The Capitol

Potomac River

0   1 km
0   1 mi

1 Dumbarton House
2 Evermay
3 Tudor Place
4 Dumbarton Oaks
5 3238 R Street NW
6 3307 N Street NW
7 Cox's Row
8 Prospect House
9 Halcyon House

See Chapter 8, Shopping, "The Roads Less Traveled" box, for more information.

President Ulysses S. Grant's summer White House in the 1870s

John and Jacqueline Kennedy lived in this brick townhouse while he was a U.S. Senator

OAK HILL CEMETERY

MONTROSE PARK

DUMBARTON OAKS PARK

GEORGETOWN UNIVERSITY CAMPUS

Rock Creek & Potomac Pkwy.

Massachusetts Ave.

Rock Creek

Chesapeake & Ohio Canal

Potomac River

Key Bridge

Whitehurst Fwy.

Whitehurst Fwy.

Canal Rd.

Reservoir Rd.

Wisconsin Ave.

Pennsylvania Ave.

T. Jefferson St.

Dumbarton Ave.

Lover's Ln.
Avon Ln.
Cambridge Pl.
Avon Pl.

S St.
R St.
Scott Pl.
Dent Pl.
Volta Pl.
P St.
O St.
N St.
M St.
Prospect St.
Grace St.

Q St.
P St.
O St.
Congress St.
Potomac St.

Olive St.

25th St.
26th St.
27th St.
28th St.
29th St.
30th St.
31st St.
32nd St.
33rd St.
34th St.
35th St.
36th St.
37th St.
38th St.

29
66
29

N

0   100 meters
0   1/8 mile

Frommer's®

Washington, D.C.
2010

by Elise Hartman Ford

WILEY
Wiley Publishing, Inc.

ABOUT THE AUTHOR

Elise Hartman Ford has been a freelance writer in the Washington, D.C., area since 1985. Her writing has appeared in the *Washington Post, Washingtonian* magazine, *Ladies Home Journal, National Parks* magazine, *National Geographic Traveler,* the travel website *Home & Abroad,* the London-based Bradman's *North America Guide, The Essential Guide to Business Travel,* and in other online and in-print national, regional, and trade publications. In addition to this guide, she is the author of *Night + Day D.C.,* a guidebook in the Cool Cities series published by ASDavis Media Group/PulseGuides.

Published by:

WILEY PUBLISHING, INC.

111 River St.
Hoboken, NJ 07030-5774

ISBN 978-0-470-47546-1

Editor: William Travis
Production Editor: Jonathan Scott
Cartographer: Roberta Stockwell
Photo Editor: Richard Fox
Production by Wiley Indianapolis Composition Services

Front cover photo: Iwo Jima Memorial © Photodisc / Superstock, Inc.
Back cover photo: Giant Panda at the National Zoo © Ken Ross / Viestiphoto.com

For information on our other products and services or to obtain technical support, please contact our Customer Care Department within the U.S. at 877/762-2974, outside the U.S. at 317/572-3993 or fax 317/572-4002.

Wiley also publishes its books in a variety of electronic formats. Some content that appears in print may not be available in electronic formats.

Manufactured in the United States of America

5   4   3   2   1

CONTENTS

4 SUGGESTED WASHINGTON, D.C., ITINERARIES   66

5 WHERE TO STAY   80

6 WHERE TO DINE   115

7 EXPLORING WASHINGTON, D.C.   163

8 SHOPPING   233

9 WASHINGTON, D.C., AFTER DARK   252

10 SIDE TRIPS FROM WASHINGTON, D.C.   272

11 FAST FACTS   289

INDEX   298

LIST OF MAPS

HOW TO CONTACT US

In researching this book, we discovered many wonderful places—hotels, restaurants, shops, and more. We're sure you'll find others. Please tell us about them, so we can share the information with your fellow travelers in upcoming editions. If you were disappointed with a recommendation, we'd love to know that, too. Please write to:

Frommer's Washington, D.C. 2010
Wiley Publishing, Inc. • 111 River St. • Hoboken, NJ 07030-5774

AN ADDITIONAL NOTE

Please be advised that travel information is subject to change at any time—and this is especially true of prices. We therefore suggest that you write or call ahead for confirmation when making your travel plans. The authors, editors, and publisher cannot be held responsible for the experiences of readers while traveling. Your safety is important to us, however, so we encourage you to stay alert and be aware of your surroundings. Keep a close eye on cameras, purses, and wallets, all favorite targets of thieves and pickpockets.

FROMMER'S STAR RATINGS, ICONS & ABBREVIATIONS

Every hotel, restaurant, and attraction listing in this guide has been ranked for quality, value, service, amenities, and special features using a **star-rating system.** In country, state, and regional guides, we also rate towns and regions to help you narrow down your choices and budget your time accordingly. Hotels and restaurants are rated on a scale of zero (recommended) to three stars (exceptional). Attractions, shopping, nightlife, towns, and regions are rated according to the following scale: zero stars (recommended), one star (highly recommended), two stars (very highly recommended), and three stars (must-see).

In addition to the star-rating system, we also use **six feature icons** that point you to the great deals, in-the-know advice, and unique experiences that separate travelers from tourists. Throughout the book, look for:

Finds	Special finds—those places only insiders know about
Fun Facts	Fun facts—details that make travelers more informed and their trips more fun
Moments	Special moments—those experiences that memories are made of
Overrated	Places or experiences not worth your time or money
Tips	Insider tips—great ways to save time and money
Value	Great values—where to get the best deals

The following **abbreviations** are used for credit cards:

AE	American Express	DISC	Discover	V	Visa
DC	Diners Club	MC	MasterCard		

TRAVEL RESOURCES AT FROMMERS.COM

Frommer's travel resources don't end with this guide. Frommer's website, **www.frommers. com,** has travel information on more than 4,000 destinations. We update features regularly, giving you access to the most current trip-planning information and the best airfare, lodging, and car-rental bargains. You can also listen to podcasts, connect with other Frommers.com members through our active-reader forums, share your travel photos, read blogs from guidebook editors and fellow travelers, and much more.

What's New in Washington, D.C.

OK, so let me ask you something, and I want you to be honest: Do you think Washington is cool? And now let me give you the correct answer: Washington is cool. And since we're both being straight with each other, I'll confess that, much as I'd like to think otherwise about my beloved city, this is something new. The signs are everywhere.

The numbers of hip hotels and restaurants in the capital have reached a tipping point. Among the latest: **The Four Seasons Hotel** (not new, but remodeled, and always D.C.'s very best, see p. 109), in Georgetown, debuted a Michael Mina **Bourbon Steak** restaurant (p. 153) in 2009 and it is now the hottest place in town. Gawkers, be gone. (So there I was, sipping a glass of wine in the Lounge at Bourbon Steak on a recent Sunday evening, when I glanced over and saw Brad Pitt quietly enjoying cocktails with his buds. We did the polite nod. Yeah, man, we're cool.)

A **W Hotel** (p. 91), that paradigm of hip, debuted in July 2009, presenting guests and D.C. with a goodie bag of chill treats, from its posh, year-round rooftop bar with an unparalleled view of the White House and the Washington Monument, to its **J&G Steakhouse** (the restaurant opened too late to be reviewed in this edition), compliments of the renowned Jean-Georges Vongerichten.

The luxury boutique hotel, **The Jefferson,** reclaims a top spot in D.C.'s hotel hierarchy, having re-opened in August 2009 (again, too late to be included in this edition), after a 2-year inside-out renovation. Interior decoration and amenities draw inspiration from items and interests that Thomas Jefferson brought home from France, fabrics to wines.

Celebrity chefs from the reality TV show circuit are also among us. José Andrés did a successful stint on Iron Chef of America, but "the face of Spanish food in America" is actually best known and recognized in culinary circles (he's always winning something in the annual James Beard Foundation awards) for his D.C. restaurants, **Oyamel** (p. 135) and **Zaytinya** (p. 137) among them. In 2010, expect his avant-garde, six-seat **minibar** (p. 128) restaurant (inside the restaurant (**Café Atlantico,** p. 128) to triple in size, and increase your chances of scoring a seat at the table. You'll still have to book a month in advance, though.

Top chef contestant Spike Mendelsohn, meanwhile, is being hailed as D.C.'s burger king, having opened **Good Stuff Eatery** (p. 124) to wildly enthusiastic reviews. At this writing, President Obama has not stopped by, but Michelle Obama and her staff have.

In the category of nightlife, where the hip quotient can make or break a place, a speakeasy in a nondescript building on happening 14th St. is creating its own buzz by accepting reservations for half of its 48 seats and keeping the door locked once it reaches that capacity. But it's not just the exclusive policy that attracts hipsters to **The Gibson** (p. 267)—it's the cozy, sexy atmosphere and the expert mixologist at the bar, using fresh ingredients and vintage recipes to concoct sensational cocktails.

Across town in the Atlas District, the **H St. Country Club** (p. 269) has finally opened, its success almost pre-ordained, thanks to seasoned owner Joe Englert's credentials (he operates other hot spots in town) and offbeat sense of entertainment. The Country Club is a bar where you can play skee ball, pool, shuffleboard, and putt-putt golf on a 9-hole course. Better yet, the Mexican food is great.

Washington's annual festivals, like the **Smithsonian Folklife Festival** and **National Cherry Blossom Festival** always attract record-breaking crowds and are generally and rightly regarded as must-do events. Lately, though, an assortment of less traditional and, yes, hipper, annual celebrations have popped up and are thriving on the cultural scene. In 2010, look for these cool amusements: In February and again in September, the city hosts **D.C. Fashion Week** (p. 30), an 8-day extravaganza featuring designers from around the world, parties, runway shows, and trunk shows at citywide venues, always culminating in an international couture fashion show held at the French Embassy. In June the **Duke Ellington Jazz Festival** takes over the city, with the biggest and best names in jazz performing in venues all over town. Come July, the fourth iteration of the **Capital Fringe Festival** (p. 32) celebrates experimental theater with 130 separate productions taking place at more than 14 venues daily for 18 days.

If hipness means fewer hassles, then the **Capitol Visitor Center** now makes a visit to the Capitol one of the hottest tickets around. First you go online to book your tickets, then you show up at the designated time in the immense, underground visitor center, get in the right line, and off you go. Hungry? Head to the 530-seat restaurant. Need to make a pit stop? You've got your pick of 26 restrooms. Need a refresher course on Congress and the Capitol? An exhibit tells you more than you can imagine. (Anyone who took a tour of the Capitol before December 2008, when bad weather, long waits for both tour passes and entry into the Capitol, hunger pangs, and dire bathroom emergencies were all part of the mix, will appreciate the new experience as nothing short of miraculous.)

Finally, if hipness is measured in the way identity and experience converge and reverberate in a particular place, then I can say that D.C.'s time has arrived. It's a bit hard to articulate, but you may feel it, too, in a shared sense of the city that emerges when you converse with strangers on the Metro, at a restaurant, in a museum, or even with fellow tourists and Secret Service agents during a tour of the White House.

Cool? Oh yeah, we're cool.

The Best of Washington, D.C.

Ain't nothin' like the real thing, baby. Isn't that what traveling is all about? Cellphone snapshots, tweets, YouTube videos, movies, television scenes, and of course, the written word, go only so far to reveal a place and its people to the interested party. There's simply no substitute for being here on the ground—seeing, hearing, tasting, feeling, and breathing it all in, gaining a true and personal understanding of a particular location, connecting with it, and by extension, widening one's frame of reference.

That's what I'm thinking as I stand on the steps of the **Lincoln Memorial,** relishing the moment, and the view, and the possibilities of this monumental day in the nation's capital. "It's often breezy here," I overhear a park ranger say, just as a gust lifts the cap off the head of the T-shirted tourist next to me. I reach for it, and then it's gone. I scan the landscape, across to the **Reflecting Pool** and beyond that to the **World War II Memorial** and then to the **Washington Monument,** presiding on its own hill nearly a mile away. Snaking my way left across the crowded steps, around the Buddhist monk in saffron robes aiming his cellphone camera at the marvelous view, through a throng of German visitors listening intently to their interpreter guide, I am able to spy the **Capitol,** lined up in the distance behind the Washington Monument.

A noisy commotion has broken out on a nearby street, and I observe a stream of black sedans and limos sweeping through an intersection cleared by police. "The President, out on an official visit," says someone behind me. It's my capless tourist, who thanks me for trying to catch his hat. He's from Louisiana, it turns out, which compels me to recommend a favorite restaurant, **Johnny's Half Shell** on Capitol Hill, for authentic tastes of New Orleans' gumbo, but also of our regional cuisine—crab imperial, crab cakes. He in turn enthuses about the free nightly concerts at the **Kennedy Center;** a zydeco band played there the night before, it seems.

"You know, we might be able to see the Kennedy Center from here," I say. And together we stroll to the back platform of the Lincoln Memorial to admire the gorgeous sight of the **Memorial Bridge** and the Potomac River, which swerves gracefully past the Kennedy Center and on to **Georgetown.** A handful of other tourists have migrated to this choice location, including a sunburned British family, whose patriarch is attempting to pose his brood for a family portrait.

In another few minutes my little band of tourists will rejoin the hordes of other sightseers visiting the **National Museum of American History,** boarding a tour bus, standing in line at the Capitol. And by day's end, back at the hotel, they will be regretting that they didn't wear sunscreen, or resolving to rise earlier tomorrow to secure a ticket to tour the **Newseum.**

I wish I could gather them around me before they go. I would tell them that Washington is a place of grand images, but also of remarkable words. They should note them everywhere, starting with the inscription of Lincoln's Gettysburg Address, right there in the memorial: "Four score and seven years ago, our fathers brought forth on this continent, a new nation, conceived in Liberty, and dedicated to the proposition that all men are created equal."

I would direct them to make time for visiting my favorite museum, the **Smithsonian American Art Museum,** conjoined with the **National Portrait Gallery**—in my favorite part of town—the Penn Quarter, to view the masterpieces like Howard Finster's folk art, William H. Johnson's scenes of African-American life, Louise Nevelson's sculptures, and portraits of national figures, Pocahontas to George Washington, Samuel Clemens (Mark Twain) to Katherine Hepburn. I would recommend that they then wander across the street to enjoy a cocktail at the popular wine bar/restaurant **Proof,** which overlooks the museum and the bustling downtown scene. And follow up that experience with dinner there or at the nearby joyful Mexican restaurant **Oyamel;** or its Asian neighbor, the ultra-sexy and newish **Sei;** or at a beloved Washington haunt, the **Tabard Inn,** in Dupont Circle. And top off the night at **Twins Jazz,** on U Street, for sounds of world-class, cool performances by jazz legends, or head up to **Madams Organ,** in Adams Morgan, for hot blues and Latin beats.

Finally, I would say, "Leave room for the chance encounter." In this city, whose population is as culturally diverse as those who tour here, you may find yourself forging connections with people from halfway around the world, or from your own hometown, and these experiences may prove your fondest memories of the city. As the nation's capital and the home of our democratic government, Washington, D.C., like no other city, holds a certain place in the world, as it represents all the freedoms and ideals that Americans hold dear. Against the backdrop of the **White House,** the **Capitol,** and the **Supreme Court;** in the corners of our national memorials and museums; within the shared experience of the music and food and theater and shops and parks and sights and sounds of our Washington neighborhoods, a little small talk between strangers creates opportunities for understanding differences. And that's the real thing, baby.

1 THE MOST UNFORGETTABLE TRAVEL EXPERIENCES

- **Watch the Supreme Court in Action:** Only in Washington can one watch and listen to the country's nine foremost legal experts nimbly and intensely dissect the merits of both sides of an argument, whose decisions can affect profoundly both a person and the nation. Think of the Supreme Court justices as a team representing the U.S. Constitution, and only in their chamber do you get to see them play. See p. 170.

- **View Washington Landmarks by Moonlight:** A must. There is nothing as spectacular as seeing the Lincoln Memorial illuminated at night, unless it's the sight of the White House, the Capitol, or the Washington Monument lit up after dark. Go by bus on Tourmobile or by bike via the Bike the Sites

service; both operations offer narrated day- and nighttime tours. See p. 177.

- **Visit Your Senator or Member of Congress:** Take advantage of your constituent status and stop by your senator's and/or representative's office on Capitol Hill to offer your two cents on current issues. Pick up passes to the Capitol's Senate and House chambers and attend a session to observe your elected politicians at work. Make sure you've reserved Capitol tour passes online and tour the Capitol. See p. 163.

- **Bicycle past the Potomac River and Around the Tidal Basin:** Rent a bike and ride the paved bike/walking path that extends 11 miles from the Lincoln Memorial to the Maryland border (through Rock Creek Park). Or head the other direction from the Lincoln Memorial, following the combination of street, sidewalk, and pathway that encircles the cherry tree–rimmed Tidal Basin. The Potomac River, Rock Creek, and spectacular Washington sites are on either side of you as you make your way. For a really long bike ride, follow the pathway past the Lincoln Memorial, cross the Arlington Memorial Bridge to the trail on the other side, and pedal the 19 miles to Mount Vernon. See p. 231 and 280.

2 THE BEST SPLURGE HOTELS

- **Mandarin Oriental,** 1330 Maryland Ave. SW, near National Mall (© **202/554-8588;** www.mandarinoriental.com/washington): This is the capital's swankiest hotel. You're away from it all but still within walking distance of Smithsonian museums. Its spa and restaurant are the crème de la crème, and guestroom designs follow the principles of Feng shui to attract good fortune. See p. 85.
- **Four Seasons,** 2800 Pennsylvania Ave. NW, Georgetown (© **202/342-0444;** www.fourseasons.com/washington): It's so nice to be loved, isn't it? And the Four Seasons staff make you feel that way, pampering you relentlessly and greeting you by name, remembering your likes and dislikes. Thanks to its second multimillion-dollar renovation in 4 years, hotel guest rooms are 50% larger and twice as inviting, suites are redone, and the new restaurant and lounge are now the scene-ist scenes in the city. See p. 109.
- **Willard InterContinental Washington,** 1401 Pennsylvania Ave. NW, Penn Quarter (© **202/628-9100;** www.washington.interconti.com): The Willard provided a temporary home for a president or two and continues to be a major gathering spot for capital powermongers. This homegrown, but worldclass, hotel has a historic bar, a Red Door Spa, a French café, and an enviable location. But if you're going to splurge, do it right and book a suite with a view of Pennsylvania Ave. See p. 92.

3 THE BEST MODERATELY PRICED HOTELS

- **The Dupont,** 1500 New Hampshire Ave. NW, Dupont Circle (© **202/483-6000;** www.doylecollection.com/dupont): A 2009 change of ownership and renovation has added élan to this property, which already had its location going for it: sitting on Dupont Circle, at the very heart of the fun neighborhood. Rooms are urban chic with wooden blinds on the windows, MP3 docking stations on desks, heated marble floors in bathrooms. Rates start at $189 for a double and can go up quite a bit from there, but still stay fairly reasonable for all that. See p. 104.
- **Georgetown Suites,** 1111 30th St. NW, Georgetown (© **202/298-1600;** www.georgetownsuites.com): The suites are large, light-filled, and cheery and the service welcoming in this greatvalue hotel. All sorts of lodging are available, from studio to penthouse, but all units have a full kitchen. And while hotels throughout the city increase their rates from year to year, Georgetown Suites' rates remain fairly constant, in the range of $155 for a studio to $425 for a town house. See p. 111.
- **Hampton Inn Washington, D.C. Convention Center,** 901 6th St. NW,

Penn Quarter (☎ **202/842-2500;** www.
washingtondc.hamptoninn.com): Close
to the convention center and the heart
of the Penn Quarter, this hotel, which
opened in 2005, still has a fresh feeling

about it. Rates start as low as $129 on
weekends, $201 weekdays. Included in
rates are use of the hotel's exercise room
and pool, and the daily hot breakfast.
See p. 93.

4 THE MOST UNFORGETTABLE DINING EXPERIENCES

- **Central Michel Richard,** 1001 Pennsylvania Ave. NW, Penn Quarter (☎ **202/
626-0015**): The rumor is that D.C.'s
favorite Frenchman, Michel Richard,
may be closing his bastion of creatively
fine French dining, Citronelle at the
end of 2009; should you find that Citronelle is still open, by all means, try to
book a table there (in the Latham
Hotel, 3000 M St. NW, (☎ **202-625-
2150**). Otherwise head instead to
Central, in the Penn Quarter. If the
ebullient chef is in the kitchen, you're
in for a special treat, since he usually
swings out for hellos. But you're in for a
treat either way. Richard's French takes
on American standards make for pure
deliciousness, from mac and cheese to
apple pan dowdy. And the lively atmosphere guarantees a wonderfully good
time. See p. 129.
- **Komi,** 1509 17th St. NW, Dupont
Circle (☎ **202/332-9200**): A dinner at
Komi restores one, thanks to creative—
but not too creative—dishes (grilled
asparagus with watercress and feta,
squab stuffed with foie gras and figs),
polished service, and a remarkably
relaxed atmosphere. And then there's
the chef, the unassuming Johnny
Monis, who somehow has figured this
all out at the tender age of 30 or so. See
p. 148.
- **CityZen,** 1330 Maryland Ave. SW, in
the Mandarin Oriental Hotel, near
National Mall (☎ **202/787-6868**):
Eric Ziebold is the chef here, having
previously served at the renowned

French Laundry, in Napa Valley. Washingtonians don't quite know what
they've done to deserve the culinary
gifts he bestows upon them: North
Carolina rainbow trout served with
petite red Russian kale and smoked
salmon roe emulsion, for example.
Bring a full wallet. See p. 120.
- **Bourbon Steak,** in the Four Seasons
Hotel, 2800 Pennsylvania Ave. NW,
Georgetown (☎ **202/944-2026**): D.C.'s
hottest new restaurant pulls in a stellar
crowd nightly. The tiered restaurant
allows for romance, partying, and business depending on whether you're seated
window-side overlooking the C&O
Canal, at tables near the open kitchen, or
in the centrally located booths. Beyond
the perfectly grilled steak, lobster pot
pie, French fries cooked in duck fat, and
roasted duck with foie gras are all getting
a lot of attention. Be sure to stop for a
drink before or after in the Lounge. See
p. 153.
- **Restaurant Eve,** 110 S. Pitt St., Old
Town Alexandria (☎ **703/706-0450**):
It's as hard to book a table here as at
CityZen in the District. Exotic drinks,
entrees such as bouillabaisse and butter-
poached halibut with lobster, and service that includes ironing tablecloths
between seatings, have drawn people
here from all over the area. Birthday or
not, order the "birthday cake" for dessert: delicious white cake layered and
iced with pink frosting and sprinkles.
Yum. See p. 286.

5 THE BEST THINGS TO DO FOR FREE

- **Peruse the Constitution:** Only in Washington and only at the National Archives will you ever be able to read the original documents that so well grounded this nation in liberty. Here, you'll find the Declaration of Independence, the Constitution of the United States, and the Bill of Rights—all on display behind glass. See p. 200.

- **People-Watch at Dupont Circle:** This traffic circle is also a park, an all-weather hangout for mondo-bizarre biker-couriers, chess players, street musicians, and lovers. Sit on a bench and watch the scenes around you. See p. 70.

- **Attend a Millennium Stage Performance at the Kennedy Center:** Every evening at 6pm, the Kennedy Center presents a free 1-hour concert performed by local, up-and-coming, national, or international musicians. This is a winner. After the performance, head through the glass doors to the terrace for a view of the Potomac River. See p. 254.

- **Groove to the Sounds of Live Jazz in the Sculpture Garden:** On summer's Friday evenings at the National Gallery of Art Sculpture Garden, you can dip your toes in the fountain pool and chill, as live jazz groups serenade you from 5 to 8pm. The jazz is free; the tapas and wine and beer served in the garden's Pavilion Café are not. See p. 202.

- **Pick a Museum (Just About), Any Museum:** That's the thing about Washington—because this is the U.S. capital, many of its museums are federal institutions, which means admission is free. The National Gallery of Art, the U.S. Botanic Garden, and the Smithsonian's 17 Washington museums, from National Air and Space to the Freer Gallery, are among the many spectacular free places to visit. See chapter 7.

6 THE BEST OUTDOOR ACTIVITIES

- **Ice Skate at the National Gallery:** The National Gallery of Art Sculpture Garden pool turns into an ice-skating rink in winter. So visit the Gallery, finishing up at the Sculpture Garden, where you can rent skates and twirl around on the ice, admiring sculptures as you go. Treat yourself to hot chocolate and sandwiches at the Pavilion Café in the garden. See p. 232.

- **Attend an Event on the Mall:** Think of the National Mall as the nation's public square, where something is always going on, whether it's a book festival in the fall, the splendid Independence Day celebration every Fourth of July, or soccer, baseball, even cricket games year-round. Pack a picnic and hold your own

little party. See p. 29 for a calendar of annual events.

- **View Washington from the Water:** Rent a paddle boat to skim the surface of the Tidal Basin for an hour, or cruise the Potomac River aboard one of several sightseeing vessels to relax from foot-weary travels. The paddle boats give you a remarkable view of the Jefferson Memorial; river cruises offer a pleasant interval for catching a second wind, as they treat you to a marvelous perspective of the city. See chapter 7.

- **Sit at an Outdoor Cafe and Watch the Washington World Go By:** The capital has plenty of places that offer front-row seats, from Capitol Hill's Johnny's Half Shell, with all its Hill traffic (and a bit

Site Seeing: The Best Washington, D.C., Websites

- **www.bnbaccom.com:** For those who prefer to stay in a private home, guesthouse, inn, or furnished apartment, this service offers more than 30 for you to consider.
- **www.bwiairport.com:** Ground transport, terminal maps, flight status, and airport facilities for Baltimore–Washington International Airport.
- **www.culturaltourismdc.org:** Cultural Tourism DC is a grass-roots, non-profit coalition of more than 200 arts, heritage, community, and cultural organizations collaborating to promote the less-known stories and attractions of Washington. The website lists tours, itineraries, calendars, and plenty of background information about historic and cultural sites that you won't find anywhere else.
- **www.dc.gov:** This is the city of Washington's website, full of details about both federal and local D.C., including history and tourism. Every day, the site lists a calendar of what's going on around town.
- **www.wdcahotels.com:** This nicely designed site recommends hotels suited for families, women, sightseers, or business travelers.
- **www.destinationdc.org:** Destination DC is the new name for the Washington, D.C. Convention and Tourism Corporation. This website leads you through various screens of information on what to see and do in D.C. and provides travel updates on security issues. You have to play around with the site a little to find all the information you need. Start by clicking on "Visiting" and take it from there, for tips on where to stay, dine, shop, and sightsee.
- **www.fly2dc.com:** In addition to its extensive information about airline travel in and out of Washington (and ground transportation from each airport), this site also offers fun articles about restaurants and things to do in D.C. The monthly print magazine version, *Washington Flyer*, is available free at Washington National and Dulles airports.
- **www.house.gov:** This is the site for the U.S. House of Representatives. Find out about the legislative process, what's going on in Congress, and what's going on with your own representatives—the site links you to the individual websites for each of the representatives.
- **www.kennedy-center.org:** Find out what's playing at the Kennedy Center and listen to live broadcasts through the Net.
- **www.metwashairports.com:** Ground transport, terminal maps, flight status, and airport facilities for Washington Dulles International and Ronald Reagan Washington National airports.
- **www.mountvernon.org:** Click on "Visit" for daily attractions at Mount Vernon and a calendar of events, as well as information on dining, shopping, and school programs. For a sneak preview, click on "Virtual Mansion Tour" to see images of the master bedroom, dining room, slave memorial, and the Washingtons' tomb.

- **www.nps.gov:** This National Park Service site includes links to some dozen memorials and monuments. When you click "DC" on the map, a listing of the capital's National Park sites appears, including the National World War II Memorial, Washington Monument, Jefferson Memorial, National Mall, Ford's Theatre, FDR Memorial, Lincoln Memorial, and Vietnam Veterans Memorial.
- **www.opentable.com:** This site allows you to make reservations at some of the capital's finest restaurants.
- **www.senate.gov:** In the U.S. Senate site, click on "Visitors" for an online virtual tour of the Capitol building and information about touring the actual Senate Gallery. It takes a few seconds for the images to download, but it's worth the wait to enjoy the panoramic video tour. Also, find out when the Senate is in session. The site connects you with the websites for each of the senators; you can use this site to e-mail your senator.
- **www.si.edu:** This is the Smithsonian Institution's home page, which provides information about visiting Washington and leads you to the individual websites for each Smithsonian museum.
- **www.visitdc.com:** Capitol Reservations, a 26-year-old company, represents more than 100 hotels in the Washington area, each of which has been screened for cleanliness, safety, and other factors. You can book your room online.
- **www.visitthecapitol.com:** The new Capitol Visitor Center's website posts the history of the Capitol and the center, discusses the art and architecture of the buildings and the legislative work that takes place within, and is the portal to the online reservation system for booking tours of the Capitol.
- **www.washingtonian.com:** The print magazine of the same name posts some of its articles here, including "What's Happening," a monthly guide to what's going on at museums, theaters, and other cultural showplaces around town, and a directory of reviews of Washington restaurants. The magazine really wants you to buy the print edition, though—for sale at bookstores, drugstores, and grocery stores throughout the area.
- **www.washingtonpost.com:** The *Washington Post*'s site is an extremely helpful source for up-to-date information on restaurants, attractions, shopping, and nightlife (as well as world news).
- **www.whitehouse.gov:** Click on "Tours & Events" to learn about visiting the White House and about upcoming public events. You'll find all sorts of links here, from a history of the White House, to archived White House documents, to an e-mail page you can use to contact the president or vice president. Twitter, Facebook, and other connections are all here.
- **www.wmata.com:** Timetables, maps, fares, and more for the Metro buses and subways that serve the Washington, D.C., metro area.

of the Capitol); to the Penn Quarter's Café du Parc, which looks down Pennsylvania Avenue to Hank's Oyster Bar, whose Dupont Circle perch is the perfect spot for watching a passing parade of live entertainment. See chapter 6.

7 THE BEST NEIGHBORHOODS FOR GETTING LOST

- **Go Behind the Scenes in Georgetown:** The truth is, you *want* to get lost in Georgetown because it's the side streets that hold the history and centuries-old houses of this one-time Colonial tobacco port. And not to worry, Georgetown is so compact, you're never very far from the main drags of M Street and Wisconsin Avenue. For a back-streets tour of Georgetown, see p. 234.
- **Spend the Day in Alexandria:** Just a short distance (by Metro, car, boat, or bike) from the District is George Washington's Virginia hometown. On and off the beaten track are quaint cobblestone streets, charming boutiques and antiques stores, 18th-century houses and other historic attractions, and fine restaurants. See p. 275.
- **Stroll Embassy Row:** Explore the neighborhood of Dupont Circle to view smaller embassies, then head northwest on Massachusetts Avenue to admire the larger ones. You'll walk along gorgeous tree-shaded streets lined with Beaux Arts mansions, many built by fabulously wealthy magnates during the Gilded Age. See p. 261 for information about how to see the interiors of some of these embassies.

8 THE BEST PLACES TO HANG WITH THE LOCALS

- **Shop at Eastern Market:** Capitol Hill is home to more than government buildings; it's a community of old town houses, antiques shops, and the veritable institution Eastern Market. (Although a fire in spring 2007 destroyed much of the historic interior, the market should be up and running by the time you read this.) Here, the locals barter and shop every Saturday and Sunday for fresh produce, baked goods, and flea-market bargains. See p. 242.
- **Pub- and Club-It in D.C.'s Hot Spots:** Join Washington's footloose and fancy-free any night of the week, but especially Thursday through Saturday, along U Street between 9th and 16th streets; in Adams-Morgan; and in the Penn Quarter as they start out or end up (mostly end up—clubs and bars are open late in these neighborhoods). See chapter 9 for bar and club suggestions.
- **Go for a Jog on the National Mall:** Lace up your running shoes and race down the Mall at your own pace, dodging tourists and admiring famous sites as you go. Your fellow runners will be buff military staff who've zoomed over from the Pentagon, speed-walking members of Congress, and a cross section of downtown workers doing their best to stave off the telltale pencil pusher's paunch. Distance from the foot of the Capitol to the Lincoln Memorial: 2 miles. See p. 176.
- **Take Tea at the Top of Washington National Cathedral:** Join a certain segment of Washington society (mostly women friends and moms and daughters) for tea and a tour. Tuesday and

Wednesday afternoons at 1:30pm you can tour the world's sixth-largest cathedral, then indulge in tea, scones, and lemon tarts served on the seventh floor of the West tower, whose arched windows overlook the city and beyond to Sugarloaf Mountain in Maryland. See p. 217.

9 THE BEST OFFBEAT EXPERIENCES

- **Listen to "Obama Mia" and "Help Me Fake It to the Right":** The Capitol Steps, a musical political satire troupe, performs these and other irreverent original tunes in skits that skewer politicians on both sides of the aisle. You can see them every weekend at the Ronald Reagan Building. See p. 258.

- **Salsa Up a Storm:** At Habana Village in Adams-Morgan, Lucky Bar near Dupont Circle, and other clubs and bars, you can take salsa and tango lessons, and then put your steps to the test on the dance floor. See p. 263.

- **Explore Washington from a Different Angle:** Sign up for a tour of Washington that follows a certain theme, such as Civil War landmarks, theater trails, places where Dickens stopped, or scandal-laced sites, to name just a few. Several companies offer offbeat kinds of tours. See p. 228.

- **Sample Offbeat but World-Class Cuisine:** At the minibar inside Café Atlantico, chef José Andrés concocts whimsical little tastes—like foie gras in a cocoon of cotton candy. Thirty or more tastes make an unforgettable meal for 12 lucky people (2 seatings of 6 people each—or, if Andrés has tripled the capacity, as planned, 36 people) per night. See p. 128.

Washington, D.C., in Depth

Allow me to introduce you to Washington, D.C. You may well have made her earlier acquaintance—so many people have. The city, after all, is America's capital, the seat of power for the world's most enlightened democracy, the home of the president of the United States, and to every embassy with whom the U.S. government maintains diplomatic relations.

So it's quite possible that you've been here before, and toured the Capitol, observed a session of Congress underway in the Senate or House gallery, or watched the Supreme Court justices argue a momentous case. Perhaps you strolled the perimeter of the White House or even arranged a group tour of the interior. You might have peered at the original Declaration of Independence on view in the National Archives or taken a walking tour through Georgetown's historic streets.

No? History and politics leave you cold, you say? Well then, you must have visited Washington to bask in its beauty—we *are* known for that, you know. No doubt you arrived in spring, to gaze at our famous blossoming cherry trees bordering the Tidal Basin. Or in autumn perhaps, when you probably rode a bike through the woodlands of Rock Creek Park, the National Park Service's oldest and largest urban park. In summer, I'm certain you would have found time to cruise the placid Potomac, the perfect, coolest vantage spot for admiring Washington's elegant cityscape. And in winter, surely, you went ice-skating on the rink in the National Gallery's Sculpture Garden, surrounded by remarkable sculptures close up, and famous landmarks in the landscape beyond.

And if you arrived in D.C. wanting none of that, or only some of that, you must have been here for arts and culture—our museums, performing arts centers, and restaurants are world-renowned, as I'm sure you are well aware. I can imagine you would have attempted to tackle every one of D.C.'s 16 Smithsonian museums, from the Freer Gallery to the American History Museum, or made sure to take in a ballet at the Kennedy Center. You may have stopped to enjoy a champagne cocktail at Proof, in the Penn Quarter, and a juicy steak at the Palm, near Dupont Circle.

You may have done all of these things and been to Washington many times, but still, I am sorry—or rather, overjoyed—to have to tell you, that no, you really don't know Washington. You couldn't possibly. You are not here right now, in this particular moment.

For never has there been a more exciting time to visit the nation's capital. A charismatic and brilliant new president is in the White House and a debonair young mayor is in charge of the city. The city's Penn Quarter, Dupont Circle, and Georgetown neighborhoods bustle with activity day and night. The U.S. Capitol Visitor Center is open on the Hill and the Martin Luther King, Jr., National Memorial is nearly ready to debut along the Tidal Basin, just off the National Mall. Celebrity chefs Alain Ducasse, Wolfgang Puck, Eric Ripert, Michael Mina, and Jean-Georges Vongerichten now have their own restaurants in Washington, dubbed "one of the most exciting restaurant cities on the East Coast" by *Travel + Leisure.*

Thrilling change and a renewed sense of purpose, both political and cultural, are in the air. Come, come to Washington, to re-visit places of old with fresh eyes, and to celebrate what's new.

1 LOOKING BACK AT WASHINGTON, D.C.

Like most cities, Washington, D.C.'s history is written in its landscape. Behold the lustrous Potomac River, whose discovery by Captain John Smith in 1608 led to settlement of the area, getting the story going. Notice the lay of the land: the 160-foot-wide avenues radiating from squares and circles, the sweeping vistas, the abundant parkland, very much as Pierre Charles L'Enfant intended when he planned the "Federal District" in 1791. Look around and you will see the Washington Monument, the U.S. Capitol, the Lincoln Memorial, the White House, and other landmarks, their very prominence in the flat, central cityscape attesting to their significance in the formation of the nation's capital.

But Washington's history is very much a tale of two cities. Beyond the National Mall, the memorials, and federal government buildings lies "D.C.," the municipality. Righteous politicians and others speak critically of "Washington," shorthand, we understand, for all that is wrong with government. They should be more precise. With that snide dismissal, critics dismiss, as well, the particular locale in which the capital resides. It is a place of vibrant neighborhoods and vivid personalities, a vaunted arts-and-culture scene, international diversity, rich African-American heritage, uniquely D.C. attractions and people—the very citizens who built the capital in the first place and have kept it running ever since.

EARLY DAYS

In the beginning, there were Indians. Of course. Captain John Smith may have been the first European to discover this waterfront property of lush greenery and woodlands, but the Nacotchtank and Piscataway tribes were way ahead of him. As Smith and company settled the area, they

---

Scandals

What is it about politicians and scandal? Examples throughout Washington's history suggest a mutual attraction. Consider these:

DNA tests have proven the sexual misconduct of the nation's third president, Thomas Jefferson, who fathered a child with his slave, Sally Hemings; and about 200 years later, of America's 42nd president, when the stain on the blue dress of White House intern Monica Lewinsky was indeed determined to be the remains of the president's semen.

In the famous Teapot Dome case of the early 1920s, the 29th president, Warren Harding, presided over a corrupt administration, several of whose members accepted bribes in return for helping private developers obtain federal oil fields. Other scandals surfaced after Harding's death, including the fact that the president had carried on several affairs while he was in the White House.

In 1979, John Jenrette, the Democratic congressman from South Carolina, was arrested on charges of corruption, but most people more readily remember him as the politician discovered having sex on the Capitol steps with his wife, Rita.

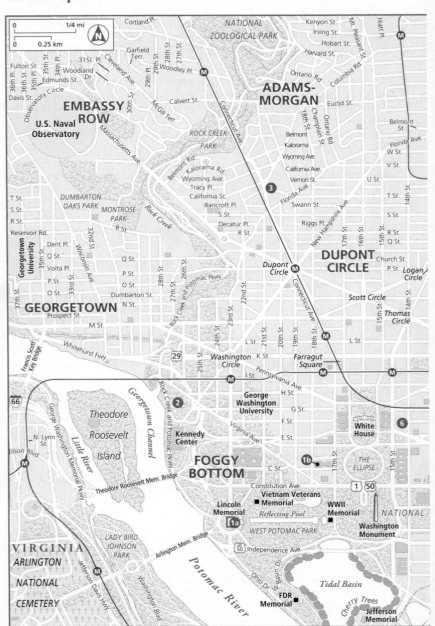

① Built in 1912, directly two miles west of the Capitol, the **Lincoln Memorial ①ₐ** honors our most inspiring president. Among the inspired was the Rev. Dr. Martin Luther King. Find the marked spot, 18 steps down from the chamber and you will be standing exactly where King stood on Aug. 28, 1963, when he delivered his remarkable "I Have a Dream" speech to the crowd of 200,000 people who had gathered here after "Marching on Washington" with King to pressure Congress to pass the Civil Rights Act.

The Lincoln Memorial was the site of another significant moment in civil rights history, on Easter Sunday, 1939, when contralto Marian Anderson sang to a crowd of 75,000 people on the memorial steps, after the Daughters of the American Revolution refused to allow the African-American to perform at their **Constitution Hall ①ᵦ**. First Lady Eleanor Roosevelt resigned her DAR membership over the incident. Eventually, Anderson did sing at Constitution Hall (in 1943 and again in 1952), and at the Lincoln Memorial a second time, in 1952.

② **The Watergate Building** looks harmless enough these days, despite the fact that the very word "Watergate" calls up its scandalous history. In June 1972, members of President Nixon's re-election staff broke into the Democratic National Committee's offices here, an act that eventually forced Nixon to resign. Two decades later, Pres. Clinton carried on an affair at the White House with a 20-something intern, who just happened to live at the Watergate.

③ **The Hilton Washington** was the scene of the attempted assassination of Pres. Reagan on March 30, 1981, when John Hinkley shot Pres. Reagan, his press secretary James Brady, a DC police officer, and a Secret Service agent. All survived.

④ President Lincoln was not so lucky. On April 14, 1865, John Wilkes Booth fatally shot Abraham Lincoln as the president sat in the "State Box" in **Ford's Theatre** watching a performance of "Our American Cousin." Visitors can view Lincoln's seat, but not sit there.

⑤ In the early to mid-20th century, U Street was known as the Black Broadway and the general area between 11th and 15th streets was the epicenter of a black cultural renaissance. At places like the **Lincoln Theatre ⑤ₐ** and the **Club Caverns ⑤ᵦ** (now Bohemian Caverns), African-Americans came to hear the music of Ella Fitzgerald, Cab Calloway, and most of all, DC native son Duke Ellington. Visit the re-born neighborhood today and you can follow in their footsteps, as you walk by **1212 T St. NW ⑤ᵪ**, where the Duke grew up; or take in a set at the Lincoln Theatre (p. 257), Bohemian Caverns (p. 261), or newer venues, like Twins Jazz (p. 262), always ending the night with a half-smoke at the decades-old Ben's Chili Bowl (p. 143).

⑥ Since its beginnings in 1850, and continuing on through its current incarnation (built on the site of the original in 1901), **The Willard Hotel** has always played a special role in the life of the capital. At least six presidents, from Zachary Taylor to Abraham Lincoln, lived at the Willard for a while. Julia Ward Howe composed "The Battle Hymn of the Republic" in it in 1861, and the Rev. Dr. Martin Luther King composed his "I Have a Dream" speech here in 1963. Stop in at the hotel to admire the ornate lobby and exquisite architecture, but don't leave without visiting the bar, the city's historic center of activity. Sip a mint julep, introduced here by statesman Henry Clay in 1850, and consider the tradition you're upholding: It was here that Washington Irving brought Charles Dickens for a brandy, Samuel Clemens (Mark Twain) imbibed bourbon with his pal, Nevada Sen. Stewart., and Nathaniel Hawthorne set up his base for covering the Civil War for the Atlantic Monthly magazine, writing ". . . for the conviviality of Washington sets in at an early hour, and, so far as I have had the opportunity to observe, never terminates at any hour."

disrupted the Indian ways of life and introduced European diseases. The Indians gradually moved away.

By 1751, Irish and Scottish immigrants had founded "George Town," named for the king of England and soon established as an important tobacco-shipping port. Several houses from those days still exist in Georgetown: the Old Stone House (on M St. NW), originally a woodworker's home from around the 1760s, operated by the National Park Service and open to the public; and a few magnificent ship merchants' mansions on N and Prospect streets, which, at the time, overlooked the Potomac River. (These are privately owned and not open to the public.)

BIRTH OF THE CAPITAL

After colonists in George Town and elsewhere in America rebelled against British rule, defeating the British in the American Revolution (1775–83), Congress, in quick succession, unanimously elected General George Washington as the first president of the United States, ratified a U.S. Constitution, and proposed that a city be designed and built to house the seat of government for the new nation and to function fully in commercial and cultural capacities. Much squabbling ensued. The North wanted the capital; the South wanted the capital. President Washington huddled with his secretary of state, Thomas Jefferson, and devised a solution that Congress approved in 1790: The nation's capital would be "a site not exceeding 10 miles square" located on the Potomac. The South was happy, for this area was nominally in their region; Northern states were appeased by the stipulation that the South pay off the North's Revolutionary War debt, and by the city's location, on the North-South border. Washington, District of Columbia, made her debut.

The only problem was that she was not exactly presentable. The brave new country's capital proved to be a tract of undeveloped wilderness, where pigs, goats, and cows roamed free, and habitable houses were few and far between. Thankfully, the city did have the masterful 1791 plan of the gifted but temperamental French-born engineer, Pierre Charles L'Enfant. Slaves, free blacks, and immigrants from Ireland, Scotland, and other countries strove to fulfill L'Enfant's remarkable vision, erecting first the White House (the city's oldest federal structure), then the Capitol, and other buildings. Gradually, the capital began to take shape, though too slowly perhaps for some. The writer Anthony Trollope, visiting in 1860, declared Washington "as melancholy and miserable a town as the mind of man can conceive."

WASHINGTON GROWS UP

During the Civil War the capital became an armed camp and headquarters for the Union Army, overflowing with thousands of followers. Parks became campgrounds; churches, schools, and federal buildings, including the Capitol and the Patent Office (now the National Portrait Gallery), became hospitals; and forts ringed the town. The population grew from 60,000 to 200,000, as soldiers, former slaves, merchants, and laborers converged on the scene. The streets were filled with the wounded, nursed by the likes of Walt Whitman, one of many making the rounds to aid ailing soldiers. In spite of everything, President Lincoln insisted that work on the Capitol continue. "If people see the Capitol going on, it is a sign we intend the Union shall go on," he said.

In the wake of the Civil War and President Lincoln's assassination, Congress took stock of the capital and saw a town worn out by years of war and awash in people, but still lacking the most fundamental facilities. The place was a mess. Members proposed moving the capital city elsewhere, perhaps to St. Louis or some other more centrally located city. A bilateral rescue of sorts arrived in the capital: in the development of a streetcar system that

Presidential Quotes

I greatly fear that my countrymen will expect too much from me.

—George Washington

I have an irrepressible desire to live till I can be assured that the world is a little better for my having lived in it.

—Abraham Lincoln

I'm asking you to believe. Not just in my ability to bring about real change in Washington . . . I'm asking you to believe in yours.

—Barack Obama

allowed the District's overflowing population to move beyond city limits, and in the persons of public works leaders, especially an official named Alexander "Boss" Shepherd, whose "comprehensive plan of improvement" at last incorporated the infrastructure so necessary to a functioning metropolis. Shepherd established parks, constructed streets and bridges, installed water and sewer systems and gas lighting, and just generally nudged the nation's capital closer to showplace design. Notable accomplishments included the completion of the Washington Monument finally in 1884 (only took 36 years) and the opening on the Mall of the first Smithsonian museum, in 1881.

WASHINGTON BLOSSOMS

With the streets paved and illuminated, the water running, streetcars and rail transportation operating, and other practical matters well in place, Washington, D.C., was ready to address its appearance. In 1900, as if on cue, a senator from Michigan, James McMillan, persuaded his colleagues to appoint an advisory committee to create "the city beautiful." This retired railroad mogul, with architectural and engineering knowledge, determined to complete the job that L'Enfant had started a century earlier. Using his own money, McMillan sent a committee that included landscapist Frederick Law Olmsted (designer of New York's Central Park),

sculptor Augustus Saint-Gaudens, and noted architects Daniel Burnham and Charles McKim, to Europe for 7 weeks to study the landscaping and architecture of that continent's great capitals.

"Make no little plans," Burnham counseled fellow members. "They have no magic to stir men's blood, and probably themselves will not be realized. Make big plans, aim high in hope and work, remembering that a noble and logical diagram once recorded will never die, but long after we are gone will be a living thing, asserting itself with ever growing insistency."

The committee implemented a beautification program that continued well into the 20th century, further enhanced by the efforts of a presidential Commission of Fine Arts, which positioned monuments and fountains throughout the city, and President Franklin Delano Roosevelt's Works Progress Administration, whose workers erected public buildings embellished by artists. The legacy of these programs is on view today, in the cherry trees along the Tidal Basin, the Lincoln Memorial at the west end of the Mall, the Arlington Memorial Bridge, the Library of Congress, Union Station, the Corcoran Gallery, and so many other sights, each in its perfect place in the city.

The American capital was coming into its own on the world stage, as well, emerging from the Great Depression, two world wars, and technological advancements in

Little-Known Facts

- Many, including Washington, District of Columbia, residents, wonder how the city wound up with such an unwieldy name. Here's how: President Washington referred to the newly created capital as "the Federal City." City commissioners then chose the names "Washington" to honor the president and "Territory of Columbia" to designate the federal nature of the area. Columbia was the feminine form of Columbus, synonymous in those days with "America" and all she stood for, namely liberty. The capital was incorporated in 1871, when it officially became known as Washington, District of Columbia.

- The distance between the Capitol, at one end of the National Mall, and the Lincoln Memorial at the other, is 2 miles. The circumference of the White House property, from Pennsylvania Avenue to Constitution Avenue and 15th Street to 17th Street is about $1^1/_2$ miles.

- Seventy percent of Washington, D.C., is national parkland, which makes the capital one of the "greenest" cities in the country. The biggest chunk is the 2,000-acre Rock Creek Park, the National Park Service's oldest urban park, founded in 1890.

- Every country that maintains diplomatic relations with the United States has an embassy in the nation's capital. Currently, the number of embassies comes to 184, mostly located along Massachusetts Avenue, known as Embassy Row, and other streets in the Dupont Circle neighborhood.

air and automobile travel, as a strong, respected, global power. More and more countries established their embassies here and the city's international population increased exponentially.

As did Washington's black population, which by 1950 was about 60% of the total. The capital became known as a hub of black culture, education, and identity, centered on a stretch of U Street NW, called "Black Broadway," where Cab Calloway, Duke Ellington, and Pearl Bailey often performed in speakeasies and theaters. (The reincarnated "U Street Corridor" or "New U" is now a diverse neighborhood of blacks, whites, Asians, and Latinos, and a major restaurant-and-nightlife destination.) Nearby, Howard University, created in 1867, distinguished itself as the nation's most comprehensive center for higher education for blacks.

On August 28, 1963, black and white Washingtonians were among the 200,000 who "Marched on Washington" and listened to an impassioned Rev. Dr. Martin Luther King, Jr., deliver his stirring "I Have a Dream" speech on the steps of the Lincoln Memorial, where 41 years earlier, during the memorial's dedication ceremony, black officials were required to stand and watch from across the road.

During the final decades of the 20th century, Washington experienced riots following the assassination of Dr. King, protests of the Vietnam War, and one political scandal after another, from Pres. Nixon's Watergate political debacle to D.C. Mayor Barry's drug and corruption problems, to Pres. Clinton's sexual shenanigans. And still, the city flourished. A world-class subway system opened, the Verizon Center debuted and transformed its aged downtown neighborhood into the immensely popular Penn Quarter, and the city's Kennedy Center, Shakespeare theaters, and other arts-and-culture venues came to world attention, receiving much acclaim.

Having begun the 20th century a backwater town, Washington finished the century a sophisticated city, profoundly shaken but not paralyzed by the September 11, 2001, terrorist attacks. Peace and prosperity have returned in the years since. The year 2010 glimmers with an "all things are possible" perspective, as the remarkably capable visionary, America's first African-American president, Barack Obama, continues to lead the country toward a renewal both of its essential spirit and its strong place in the world. Meanwhile, the District's young mayor, Adrian Fenty, does his energetic best for his hometown.

History informs one's outlook, but so does the present. Look again at the Potomac River and think of Captain John Smith, but observe the Georgetown University crew teams rowing in unison across the surface of the water, and tour boats traveling between Georgetown and Old Town Alexandria. As you traverse the city, admire L'Enfant's inspired design, but also enjoy the sight of the wonks and office workers, artists and students, and people of every possible ethnic and national background, making their way around town. Tour the impressive landmarks and remember their namesakes, but make time for D.C.'s homegrown attractions, whether a meal at a sidewalk cafe in Dupont Circle, jazz along U Street, a walking tour past Capitol Hill's old town houses, or a visit to an old church where those original immigrants once worshiped.

2 WASHINGTON, D.C., TODAY

Washington, D.C., is the capital of the United States and a city unto itself, and therein lies its charms, but also a host of complications, control of the city being the main issue. The District is a freestanding jurisdiction, but because it is a city with a federal overseer, and not a state, it has never been entitled to the same governmental powers as the states. For instance, Congress today, as it has from the beginning, supervises the District's budget and legislation. Originally, Congress granted the city the authority to elect its own governance, but rescinded that right in the late 1800s when the District overspent its budget in attempting to improve its services and appearance after the Civil War. The White House then appointed three commissioners, who ran D.C.'s affairs for nearly 100 years.

In 1972, the city regained the right to elect its own mayor and city council, but Congress retains control of the budget and the courts, and can veto municipal legislation. District residents can vote in presidential primaries and elections and they can elect a delegate to Congress, who introduces legislation and votes in committees, but who cannot vote on the House floor. This unique situation, in which residents of the District pay federal income taxes but don't have a vote in Congress, is a matter of great local concern. Among the ways that D.C. residents publicly protest the situation is by displaying license plates bearing the inscription "Taxation without Representation." (Perhaps 2010 will witness a turning point. Pres. Obama favors D.C. statehood and may help to bring this about.)

Another wrinkle in this uncommon relationship is the fact that Washington's economy relies heavily upon the presence of the federal government, which employs about 28% of D.C. residents, making it the city's single largest employer, and upon the tourism business that Washington, as the capital, attracts. Even as the city struggles toward political independence, it recognizes the economic benefits of the situation.

Does any of this affect you, as you tour the city this year? In a way, yes.

In 2010, you will find Washington, D.C., to be a remarkably vibrant city. But it wasn't always this way, and you should know a little bit of background. Fifteen, even 10 years ago, Washington wasn't so attractive. Tourists wanted to visit federal buildings, like the Capitol, the White House, and the Smithsonian museums, but stayed away from the dingy downtown and other off-the-Mall neighborhoods. The city had the potential for being so much more, and certain people, heroes, in my book, helped inspire action and brought about change themselves: Delegate Eleanor Holmes Norton, now in her tenth term in office, steadfastly fighting for state's rights and economic revival for the District; former Mayor Anthony Williams, who rescued the District's budget when his predecessor, the notorious, mismanaging Mayor Marion Barry brought the city to the brink of financial ruin; and the community-minded developers Abe and Irene Pollin, who used their own funds to finance the $200-million MCI sports center (now called the "Verizon Center") in the heart of town. Entrepreneurs started trickling in. Today, the wildly successful Verizon arena anchors the Penn Quarter neighborhood, utterly transformed and now one of the liveliest city centers in the country.

Revitalization continues to take root throughout the city, from southeast D.C., where a spanking-new baseball stadium, Nationals Ballpark, opened in March 2008, to the Columbia Heights enclave in upper northwest D.C., now a mélange of Latino culture, loft condominiums, and ethnic eateries. The city's evergreens, that is, the memorials and monuments, the historic neighborhoods, and the Smithsonian museums are unflaggingly popular.

But D.C. has its share of problems, some in fact deriving from the gentrification effort, like the displacement of residents from homes they can no longer afford in a newly improved but expensive neighborhood. Other problems are those that every municipality struggles with, namely how to provide healthcare, good schools, safe neighborhoods, adequate housing, and basic social services to all citizens.

Enter the dashing young Adrian Fenty, the city's mayor, who seems more than up to the task of improving the city and carrying it forward. In office since January 2007, Fenty has shown himself to be a hands-on, can-do administrator, and he needs that attitude as he governs this metropolis of almost 600,000 people.

The city he's managing has a diverse population: 56% African American and 8% Latino, with 12% being foreign-born, and 15% speaking a language other than English at home. There are slightly more female (53%) than male (46%) residents and the median age for the population is 35. The citizenry is well educated: 46% of D.C. residents have a bachelor's degree, while 19% have advanced degrees. Women residents stand out: 43.9% have a bachelor's degree or higher, the highest percentage in the nation.

As the son of a white mother and black father, native son Fenty is in tune with the city's diversity. But mostly, it's clear that he loves his city.

And so, it seems, do visitors, as statistics and surveys bear out: The latest figures show that D.C. welcomes 16 million visitors a year, 1.2 million of whom are international tourists. A 2008 *Outside* magazine rating of America's best towns for "civic

What Was That? An Abridged Dictionary of Political Lingo

Washington politicos have their own vernacular, most words relating to Capitol Hill business. Here are choice examples and their definitions, for you to recognize while you're in town, and to bandy about in conversation when you return home.

- **Boondoggle:** Also known as a junket: a trip by congressional members and/or staff in which leisure is more of a focus than business.
- **Call up a Bill:** To raise up a bill on the floor for immediate consideration.
- **Caucus:** An informal group of members sharing an interest in the same policy issues.
- **Filibuster:** A tactic used to extend the debate on a proposal in order to block its vote in Congress.
- **Gerrymander:** To manipulate the geographic shape of a congressional district for political purposes.
- **Log Rolling:** The process in which two dissimilar interests join to help pass pieces of legislation that on their own, neither interest could pass.
- **Mark-up:** The meeting of a congressional committee to review and amend the text of a bill before sending the bill for review by the full House or Senate.
- **PAC:** The name for special interest groups that are legally permitted to give money to candidates running for political office.
- **Platform:** A formal, written statement of the principles, objectives, and policies of a political party.
- **Whip:** As a verb, whip means to gather votes. As a noun, whip refers to the officers, one Republican, one Democrat in the House, and one Republican and one Democrat in the Senate, responsible for counting potential votes and for promoting party unity in voting. The political party in the majority determines whether the whip is the Majority Whip or the Minority Whip in the House and Senate.

re-invention and fresh ideas" places Washington, D.C., at the top of the list of ten. The 2007 *Places Rated Almanac* ranks Washington seventh on its list of "best places" in the country to live and work, a measure of the quality and abundance of such features as arts, jobs, recreation, and transportation.

And in a 2008 *Travel + Leisure–CNN Headline News* poll that asked travelers to rate 25 domestic urban destinations in various categories, the respondents named D.C. best in the nation for historical sites and monuments and for museums and galleries, making it the top choice overall as a cultural getaway.

Yes, Washington today is all that—and as you'll discover for yourself, a whole lot more.

3 WASHINGTON, D.C., IN POPULAR CULTURE: BOOKS, FILM & MUSIC

BOOKS

You can put yourself in the mood for a visit to Washington by reading a few of the great novels set in the capital, memoirs and histories by some of the city's more famous residents, and other guidebooks, whose topics supplement what you learn in these pages.

By far the most popular kind of Washington book being published these days is the insider's memoir, a genre unto itself. Why not start with President Barack Obama's own bestsellers, *The Audacity of Hope* and *Dreams from My Father?*

If you're looking for some insight into the previous administration, you've got a lot to choose from, including former Bush press secretary Scott McClellan's *What Happened: Inside the Bush White House and Washington's Culture of Deception;* former CIA director George Tenet's *At the Center of the Storm: My Years at the CIA;* and former Pentagon official Douglas Feith's *War and Decision: Inside the Pentagon at the Dawn of the War on Terrorism.*

Two memoir musts that reveal how the powerful operate in Washington are these two pre-Bush administration tales: *Personal History,* by the late Katharine Graham, who for many years was publisher of the *Washington Post;* and *Washington,* by Graham's close friend and colleague, Meg Greenfield, a columnist and editor at the *Washington Post* for more than 30 years.

Fiction lovers might pick up works by Edward P. Jones, the Pulitzer Prize-winning author whose short story collections, *Lost in the City* and *All Aunt Hagar's Children*, will take you beyond D.C.'s political and tourist personas, into the neighborhoods and everyday lives of African Americans; books by Ward Just, including his short-story collection, *The Congressman Who Loved Flaubert;* Ann Berne's *A Crime in the Neighborhood;* Marita Golden's *The Edge of Heaven;* Allen Drury's *Advise and Consent;* or one of the growing number of mysteries whose plot revolves around the capital, such as Margaret Truman's *Murder at the Smithsonian* or George Pelicanos's hard-core thrillers that, like Edward Jones's stories, take you to parts of the city you'll never see as a tourist: *Hell to Pay* and *King Suckerman,* are just two.

If you're keen on learning more about the history of the nation's capital, you might try Arthur Schlesinger's *The Birth of the Nation,* F. Cary's *Urban Odyssey,* David Brinkley's *Washington at War,* and Douglas E. Evelyn and Paul Dickson's *On This Spot,* which traces the history of the city by revealing exactly what took place at specific locations—"on this spot"—in years gone by, neighborhood by neighborhood.

And here's a special one I'll recommend: *The Great Decision: Jefferson, Adams, Marshall and the Battle for the Supreme Court,* by Cliff Sloan and David McKean, which tells the lively story of Marbury v. Madison, the case that established the precedent for the Supreme Court's authority in its role as the judicial branch of government. (Cliff's my brother-in-law.)

And for hilarious takes on the capital, read Christopher Buckley's *Washington Schlepped Here: Walking in the Nation's Capital,* an irreverent sendup of the city's most famous attractions and characters, its anecdotes all true. And don't miss Buckley's equally humorous Washington-based novels, *The White House Mess, No Way to Treat a First Lady,* and *Thank You for Smoking.*

FILMS

Hollywood has long used Washington as a setting and politicians as actors, so much so that some refer to D.C. as "Hollywood on the Potomac." Starting in 1915 with *Birth of a Nation,* the lineup includes *Mr. Smith Goes to Washington* (1939), *All the King's Men* (1949), *Advise and Consent* (1962), *All the President's Men* (1972), and *Wag the Dog* (1998). These represent only a fraction of the films based in Washington, whose popularity as a subject and location only grows and grows. Among recent releases and coming attractions are the following:

Farragut North, a political drama in which a young communications director works for an up-and-coming presidential candidate, stars George Clooney and Leonardo DiCaprio.

State of Play, an adaptation of the BBC miniseries by the same name, stars Russell Crowe, Ben Affleck, and Helen Mirren in a plot that involves investigative reporters trying to solve the murder of a congressman's mistress.

W, Oliver Stone's biopic, examines the life of George W. Bush.

Night at the Museum 2: Battle of the Smithsonian is a sequel to the blockbuster starring Ben Stiller.

Burn After Reading is a Coen Brothers production, which explains why it's described as a "dark comedy-thriller." George Clooney, Brad Pitt, and Frances McDormand star.

Get Smart, the Steve Carrell and Anne Hathaway comedy, is based on the classic television series.

Next time you're taking in a movie, note whether the film involves Washington at all, then look for shots of famous landmarks (that really is the Smithsonian's National Air and Space Museum seen in *Night at the Museum 2*). And when you're in Washington visiting, keep your eyes peeled for film crews as you tour the city,

and who knows? Maybe you'll end up in the film as an extra.

MUSIC

Washington's musical heritage is steeped in jazz and the legendary performances and compositions of native son Duke Ellington, who started his career playing in clubs along historic U St. NW. "Black Broadway" was the name given to this section of U Street, for Washingtonians Pearl Bailey, Jelly Roll Morton, and Shirley Horn, all performed here as well.

An annual, 10-day jazz festival in June pays tribute to the Duke, staging concerts in venues all over town. Year-round, the jazz scene lives on, along U Street, but also at clubs in every neighborhood, including, most notably, Blues Alley in Georgetown, where the biggest names in jazz take the stage, continuing the capital's most famous musical tradition.

More recently, a Washingtonian named Chuck Brown pioneered the birth of another music form, "go-go," a forerunner of rap; go-go blends African percussion with funk, jazz, and verbal interplay. Heard the tune "Bustin' Loose"? That's a Chuck Brown original, his first hit.

Other famous local musicians include big names on the rock scene, the Foo Fighter's Dave Grohl and members of the band O.A.R.; and on the opera front, the world-famous mezzo-soprano, Denyce Graves, who returns to perform here from time to time.

And Washington offers a distinctly American musical experience in its military bands, each representing the Air Force, Army, Navy, and Marine Corps, who play for free during the summer at designated locations throughout the city, and are known for their highly professional, wide-ranging performances.

This covers just the tip of the city's fabulous musical scene. For more information, see chapter 9.

Food writers outside the city like to talk about Washington's culinary scene as if it has newly come into its own. They're out of touch. The truth is that the capital has been cultivating an enviable stable of truly excellent restaurants gradually for about the last 10 years—and by "excellent," I don't necessarily mean fine dining/expensive. For example, old-timer **Jaleo's** (p. 133) specialty is its small plates of authentic Spanish tapas, priced at $5 to $10, while newcomer **Tackle Box** (p. 158) offers a full dinner of wood-grilled fresh fish and two delicious sides for a flat $13.

It *is* true that our restaurants keep getting better and better. As mentioned earlier, *Travel + Leisure* recently named D.C. "one of the most exciting restaurant cities on the East Coast," calling out **Founding Farmers** (p. 140) as one of its top 50 best

---

(Finds) **Ethnic Eating**

Locals and visitors both benefit from the capital's multicultural population and the resulting abundance of restaurants serving cuisine from around the world. If you want to taste the most authentic food available in the capital from a particular country, seek out one of the restaurants on the following list. Though hardly comprehensive, the list, at least, names reliable "real deals" for ethnic eats. If you don't see a mention of your favorite cuisine, for instance, Chinese, it's probably because the restaurants best representing that country have fled to the suburbs.

Belgian: How is it that Belgian cuisine has become such a hot commodity in the nation's capital? (There are at least four Belgian restaurants.) I have no idea. But for yummy tastes of lamb sausage, beef carbonade, and Belgian beers, and for a super fun time, try **Brasserie Beck** (p. 142).

Ethiopian: Washington is said to have more Ethiopian restaurants than any other American city. The preponderance of Ethiopian restaurants in the U Street Corridor has even lent the name "Little Ethiopia" to the area. **Etete,** 1942 9th St. NW (© **202/232-7600;** www.eteterestaurant.com), is recommended for its spicy stews and lentil-filled pastries *(sambusas),* to name just two good examples.

Greek: Washington has a few Greek restaurants now, but, as good as they are, I wouldn't call their food "traditional Greek." **Zorba's Café,** 1612 20th St. NW (© **202/387-8555**), in downtown D.C., is nothing if not classic Greek, from its bouzouki music to its grilled Greek sausages and ground beef and onion pie. Inexpensive, too.

Indian: This turns out to be a controversial category—everyone seems to have her own favorite Indian restaurant. I consulted the Indian Embassy, which declined to weigh in. So let's go with *Washingtonian* magazine's selection of **Heritage India** (p. 159), which the food critic describes as "Best for diners,

new restaurants in America. And our restaurants consistently receive AAA Five Diamond and James Beard Award Foundation distinctions.

All of this attention has encouraged several of the world's most esteemed chefs to establish restaurants in the capital, including Wolfgang Puck, whose the **Source** (p. 125) is in the Newseum; Eric Ripert and his **Westend Bistro** (p. 153) sits in the Ritz-Carlton Washington; Alain Ducasse, whose **Adour** is the St. Regis Hotel Washington's resident restaurant

(p. 137); Michael Mina, of **Michael Mina Bourbon Steak** (p. 153), is in the Four Seasons Hotel; and Jean-Georges Vongerichten's **J&G Steakhouse** takes a space in the W Hotel Washington.

Washingtonians are in the catbird's seat, licking their lips. Eating out is a way of life here, whether simply for the pleasure of it, or for business—the city's movers and shakers meet over breakfast, lunch, and dinner. When Congress passed a ban prohibiting members of Congress and their staffs from accepting gifts of any value,

including vegetarians, who savor the subtlety and elegance of refined Indian cooking."

Japanese: The city's oldest sushi restaurant is still the best: go to **Sushi-Ko** (p. 160), in Glover Park, for superb sushi and sashimi, but also for shrimp in tempura and other non-sushi, Japanese tastes.

Lebanese: Our **Lebanese Taverna** (p. 162) might be considered a national treasure, 2 decades old and still going strong. For the best, most authentic tastes of Lebanon, choose from the mezze dishes: hummus, baba ghanouj, taboulleh, and so on.

Mexican: Its owner chef is Spanish and the eatery is only a couple of years old, but Jose Andres's **Oyamel** (p. 135) is the uncontested place for true regional tastes of Mexico, from ceviche to avocado soup to chipotle-sauced meatballs.

Peruvian: Las Canteras (p. 145), in Adams-Morgan, is a pretty restaurant serving pleasurable, traditional Peruvian dishes, such as the seco de carne (a slow-cooked beef stew) and causa (a cake of yellowed potatoes layered with corned and shredded chicken).

Salvadoran: Salvadorans make up the largest immigrant population in the capital, and yet a good Salvadoran restaurant is hard to find. **El Tamarindo,** in Adams-Morgan, 1785 Florida Ave. NW (© **202/328-3660;** www.eltamarindodc.com) is your best bet for great pupusas, tamales, and other Salvadoran favorites. Plus, the place is open until 5am Friday and Saturday.

Spanish: No controversy here: **Jaleo** (p. 133), with its long list of classic tapas, is the hands-down best for casual Spanish fare, while the ornate **Taberna del Alabardero** (p. 139) is easily the top choice for upscale Spanish dining. (This is where King Juan Carlos and Queen Sophia dine when in Washington.)

including meals, restaurateurs feared that their clientele would stop going out to eat. But business is flourishing, it turns out, with congressional members and staff paying for themselves, if need be, and with corporate executives, lobbyists, and other professionals taking each other, but not elected politicians, out for a meal.

One other thing to note here: When Congress is in town, that is, not out on recess, restaurants are full and reservations are an absolute must. When Congress is in recess, in August, mid-December to January, and at other times, many restaurants, especially those close to Capitol Hill and in the downtown area, are so empty, it's creepy.

You have quite a number of restaurants from which to choose: 1,727, from delis to showplace dining rooms, according to the Restaurant Association of Metropolitan Washington. An immense variety of cuisines is on hand, representing the international population of the capital, including the diplomatic staffs of 184 foreign embassies and our immigrant communities from Ethiopia and El Salvador, especially, but from scores of other countries, as well (see the "Ethnic Eating" box, p. 24). A strong African-American presence means that the District has some delicious soul food eateries and our location in the Mid-Atlantic region near the Chesapeake Bay means that crabs are a favorite item here, served in soft-shell, hard-shell, soup, or cake form.

Currently, the capital is witnessing a variety of culinary trends, with wine bars (see chapter 9) and chocolate lounges (see chapter 6) proliferating and vegetarian options on the rise. Exotic drinks, such as fruit-infused martinis, are increasingly a draw at popular restaurants, many of which now include a bar lounge for those who want to unwind with a cocktail before dinner, or sip a nightcap afterward.

A growing concern about the environment is inspiring restaurants to pursue ecologically friendly policies, like the sustainable seafood restaurant **Hook** (p. 156), which serves only those varieties of fish that can reproduce at the rate they're being caught; or **Poste** brasserie (p. 131), which despite its downtown location, grows and harvests its own herbs, vegetables, and greens on-site for immediate use; or **Founding Farmers** (p. 140), owned by a collective of American farmers and designed to use natural and recyclable products, composting, and farm-to-table practices.

All in all, Washington's eating and drinking culture, already hot, keeps getting hotter.

Planning Your Trip to Washington, D.C.

The thing about Washington, D.C., is there's never a bad time of year to visit. Something's always going on, whether it's the Lighting of the National Christmas Tree in December, the Cherry Blossom Festival in spring, or the fabulous Independence Day parade and fireworks on the Fourth of July—not to mention a daily menu of live music and theater performances, restaurant openings, museum exhibits, sports events, and all of the activities associated with the capital's raison d'etre: White House administrating, Congress's legislating, and the Supreme Court's decision-making. If you're interested in soaking up the spirit of the city, any day of the year is your oyster.

But no matter when you go, you can help maximize the pleasure of your trip and minimize hassles by doing a certain amount of advance planning. Generally speaking, the earlier you book your room, the greater your chance of finding the best rate at your preferred hotel. The same goes for restaurant reservations; Washingtonians are a ravenous bunch, filling tables nightly throughout the city, recession or no recession, so if dining at a new hot spot or old favorite is important, call or book online now! You can even avoid lines at some sightseeing attractions by obtaining tickets months in advance (see Box, "Ways to Get Ahead," at the end of this chapter).

And then there are all those other tedious but crucial details to consider: the weather, what to wear, how much things cost, how best to travel here and get around once you arrive, what attractions are musts, what's new, what's closed—what's what!

Now that I've torqued you up, let me calm you down. Everything you need to know is illuminated in the following pages.

For additional help in planning your trip and for more on-the-ground resources in Washington, D.C., see chapter 11, "Fast Facts."

1 WHEN TO GO

The city's peak seasons generally coincide with two activities: the sessions of Congress and springtime—starting with the appearance of the cherry blossoms along the Potomac. Specifically, from about the second week in September until Thanksgiving, and again from about mid-January to June (when Congress is "in"), hotels are full with guests whose business takes them to Capitol Hill or to conferences. And mid-March through June traditionally is the most frenzied season, when families and school groups descend upon the city to see the cherry blossoms and enjoy Washington's sensational spring. Hotel rooms are at a premium and airfares tend to be higher. This is also a popular season for protest marches.

If crowds turn you off, consider visiting Washington at the end of August/early September, when Congress is still "out" and families return home to get their children back to school, or between Thanksgiving and mid-January, when Congress leaves again and many people are ensconced in their own holiday-at-home celebrations. Hotel rates are cheapest at this time, too, and many hotels offer attractive packages.

If you're thinking of visiting in July and August, be forewarned: The weather is very hot and humid. Despite the heat, Independence Day (July 4th) in the capital is a spectacular celebration. Summer is also the season for outdoor concerts, festivals, parades, and other events (see chapter 9 for details about performing arts schedules).

THE WEATHER

Check the Washington Post's website (www.washingtonpost.com) or the website for Washington, D.C.'s official convention and visitors corporation, Destination D.C. (www.destinationdc.org), for current and projected weather forecasts.

Season by season, here's what you can expect of the weather in Washington:

Fall: This is my favorite season. The weather is often warm during the day—in fact, if you're here in early fall, it may seem entirely *too* warm. But it cools off, even getting a bit crisp, at night. Washington trades its famous greenery for the brilliant colors of fall foliage, and the stream of tourists tapers off.

Winter: People like to say that Washington winters are mild—and sure, if you're from Minnesota, you'll find Washington warmer, no doubt. But D.C. winters can be unpredictable: bitter cold one day, an ice storm the next, followed by a couple of days of sun and higher temperatures. Pack for all possibilities.

Spring: Early spring weather tends to be colder than most people expect. Cherry blossom season, late March to early April, can be iffy—and very often rainy and windy. Then, as April slips into May, the weather usually mellows, and people's moods with it. Late spring is especially lovely, with mild temperatures and intermittent days of sunshine, flowers, and trees colorfully erupting in gardens and parks all over town. Washingtonians, restless after having been cooped up inside for months, sweep outdoors to stroll the National Mall, sit on a park bench, or laze away an afternoon at an outdoor cafe. Spring is a great time to enjoy D.C.'s outdoor attractions. But during this season, the city is also at its most crowded with visitors and school groups, here to view the blooming cherry blossoms or take advantage of spring breaks.

Summer: Anyone who's ever spent July and August in D.C. will tell you how hot and steamy it can be. Though the buildings are air-conditioned, many of Washington's attractions, like the memorials, monuments, and organized tours, are outdoors and unshaded, and the heat can quickly get to you. Make sure you stop frequently for drinks (vendors are plentiful), and wear a hat, sunglasses, and sunscreen. But if you can deal with all that, this is a good time to visit. Locals often go elsewhere on vacation, so the roads and attractions are somewhat less crowded. Best of all, hotels tend to offer their best rates in July and August.

Average Temperatures (°F/°C) & Rainfall (in inches) in Washington, D.C.

	Jan	Feb	Mar	Apr	May	June	July	Aug	Sept	Oct	Nov	Dec
Avg. High	44/5	46/8	54/12	66/19	76/25	83/29	87/31	85/30	79/26	68/20	57/14	46/8
Avg. Low	30/-1	29/-1	36/2	46/8	56/14	65/19	69/20	68/20	61/16	50/10	39/4	32/0
Rainfall (in.)	2.8	2.6	3.4	2.8	3.9	3.3	4	4.1	3.3	3	3	3.1

WASHINGTON, D.C., CALENDAR OF EVENTS

Washington's most popular annual events are the Cherry Blossom Festival in spring, the Fourth of July celebration in summer, and the lighting of the National Christmas Tree in winter. But some sort of special event occurs almost daily. For the latest schedules, check **www.destinationdc.org**, **www.nps.gov/ncro** (click on "Calendar of Events"), **www.culturaltourismdc.org**, **www.dc.gov**, and **www.washington post.com**.

For an exhaustive list of events beyond those listed here, check **http://events. frommers.com**, where you'll find a searchable, up-to-the-minute roster of what's happening in Washington (and other cities all over the world).

In the calendar below, I've done my best to accurately list phone numbers for more information, but the numbers seem to change constantly. If the number you try doesn't get you the details you need, call **Destination D.C.** at ✆ **202/789-7000.**

When you're in town, grab a copy of the *Washington Post,* especially the Friday "Weekend" section, or a copy of the monthly magazine, *Washingtonian,* whose "Where and When" section features that month's recommended goings-on around town.

For annual events in Alexandria, see p. 278.

JANUARY

Martin Luther King, Jr.'s, Birthday. Events include speeches by prominent leaders and politicians, readings, dance, theater, concerts and choral performances, and prayer vigils. On the Friday preceding the national holiday, the National Park Service holds a ceremony at the Department of Interior Building at 1849 C St. NW, attended by schoolchildren and open to the public; park rangers then transfer the wreath used during the ceremony to the Lincoln Memorial. Call ✆ **202/619-7222.** Third Monday in January.

FEBRUARY

Black History Month. Numerous events, museum exhibits, and cultural programs celebrate the contributions of African Americans to American life, including a celebration of abolitionist Frederick Douglass's birthday. For details, check the *Washington Post* or call the National Park Service at ✆ **202/ 619-7222.**

Chinese New Year Celebration. A friendship archway, topped by 300 painted dragons and lighted at night, marks Chinatown's entrance at 7th and H streets NW. The celebration begins the day of the Chinese New Year and continues for 10 or more days, with traditional firecrackers, dragon dancers, and colorful street parades. Some area restaurants offer special menus. For details, call ✆ **202/ 789-7000.** Early February.

Abraham Lincoln's Birthday. This day is marked by a wreath-laying and reading of the Gettysburg Address at noon at the Lincoln Memorial. Call ✆ **202/ 619-7222.** February 12.

George Washington's Birthday/President's Day. The city celebrates Washington's birthday in two ways: on the actual day, February 22, with a ceremony that takes place at the Washington Monument; and on the federal holiday, the third Monday in February, when schools and federal offices have off. Call ✆ **202/619-7222** for details. The occasion also brings with it great sales at stores citywide. (Also see chapter 10, "Side Trips from Washington, D.C.," for information about the bigger celebrations held at Mount Vernon and in Old Town Alexandria on the third Mon in Feb.)

International Food & Wine Festival. Now in its 11th year, this 2-day, annual event held at the Ronald Reagan Building and International Trade Center is the largest indoor wine festival in the Mid-Atlantic, with more than 200 international wineries participating, as well as food vendors and other merchants. Hefty admission price: $95 at the door. Call ℂ **800/343-1174** or go online, www.wine-expos.com/DC. Mid-February.

D.C. Fashion Week. This biennial event features designers from around the world. The 8-day extravaganza stages parties, runway shows, and trunk shows at citywide venues, always culminating in an international couture fashion show held at the French Embassy. Most events are open to the public, but may require a ticket. Call ℂ **202/271-7235** or look online, www.dcfashionweek.org. Mid-February and mid-September.

MARCH

Women's History Month. Various institutions throughout the city stage celebrations of women's lives and achievements. For the schedule of National Park Service events, check the calendar at www.nps.gov/ncro; for Smithsonian events, call ℂ **202/633-1000** or go online at www.si.edu; for other events, check the websites listed in the intro to this section.

St. Patrick's Day Parade. A big parade on Constitution Avenue NW, from 7th to 17th streets, with floats, bagpipes, marching bands, and the wearin' o' the green. For parade information, call ℂ **202/789-7000.** The Sunday before March 17.

Smithsonian Kite Festival. This event is delightful if the weather cooperates—an occasion for a trip in itself. Throngs of kite enthusiasts fly their unique creations on the grounds of the Washington Monument, and compete for ribbons and prizes. Now in its 44th year, the kite festival even has its own website: www.kitefestival.org. Visit the website or call ℂ **202/633-1000** or 633-3030 for details. To compete, just show up at the designated spot with your kite between 10am and noon and register. A Saturday in mid- or late March, or early April, but always at the start of the National Cherry Blossom Festival.

APRIL

National Cherry Blossom Festival. Washington's best-known annual event: a 2-week festival coinciding with the blossoming of more than 3,700 Japanese cherry trees by the Tidal Basin, on Hains Point, and on the grounds of the Washington Monument. Events take place all over town, including fireworks, concerts, special art exhibits, park ranger–guided talks and tours past the cherry blossom trees, and sports competitions. A grand parade caps the festival, complete with floats, marching bands, dancers, celebrity guests, and more. For information, call ℂ **877/44BLOOM** (442-5666) or go to www.nationalcherry blossomfestival.org. Also see "Potomac Park" on p. 222 for more information about the cherry blossoms. March 27 to April 11, 2010. National and local news programs monitor the budding.

White House Easter Egg Roll. The biggie for little kids under age 10. The annual White House Easter Egg Roll continues a practice begun in 1878. Entertainment on the White House South Lawn and the Ellipse traditionally includes appearances by costumed cartoon characters, clowns, musical groups (Fergie appeared last year, the Jonas Brothers the year before), egg-decorating exhibitions, puppet and magic shows, an Easter egg hunt and an egg-rolling contest. In 2009, President Obama inaugurated a new procedure for obtaining tickets, making tickets available for ordering online about 2 weeks ahead of Easter Monday (a few kinks still need to be worked out, however). Call ℭ **202/208-1631** for details or go online at www.whitehouse.gov/ eastereggroll, 2 or 3 weeks in advance of Easter. Easter Monday between 8am and 5pm.

African-American Family Day at the National Zoo. This tradition extends back to 1889, when the zoo opened. The National Zoo, 3001 Connecticut Ave. NW, celebrates African-American families the day after Easter with music, dance, Easter egg rolls, and other activities. Free. Call ℭ **202/633-1000** for details. Easter Monday.

Thomas Jefferson's Birthday. Celebrated at the Jefferson Memorial with wreaths, speeches, and a military ceremony. Call ℭ **202/619-7222** for time and details. April 13.

White House Spring Garden Tour. These beautifully landscaped creations are open to the public for free tours, 2 days only. Tickets are required. Call ℭ **202/208-1631** for details. Two days in mid-April.

Earth Day. 2010 marks the 40th anniversary of Earth Day and you can expect D.C.'s celebration, always significant, to be even more so. Official Earth Day is April 22; D.C. often marks the event on a Sunday close to that date. The National Mall is ground-zero for green-themed volunteer activities, campaigning, and live music performed by big names—Los Lobos and The Flaming Lips were two bands who played in the 2009 event. Call

ℭ **202-518-0044,** ext. 210; www.earth day.net. April 22.

Filmfest D.C. This annual film festival presents more than 100 works by filmmakers from around the globe. Screenings take place in movie theaters, embassies, and museums citywide. Tickets are usually $10 per movie and go fast; some events are free. Call ℭ **202/234-FILM** (3456) or check the website, www.filmfestdc.org. Ten days in April.

Smithsonian Craft Show. Held in the National Building Museum, 401 F St. NW, this juried show features one-of-a-kind limited-edition crafts by more than 120 noted artists from all over the country. There's an entrance fee of about $15 per adult each day, free for children 12 and under. No strollers. For details, call ℭ **888/832-9554** or 202/ 633-5006, or check the website, www. smithsoniancraftshow.com. Four days in late April.

MAY

Washington National Cathedral Annual Flower Mart. Now in its 71st year, the flower mart takes place on cathedral grounds, featuring displays of flowering plants and herbs, decorating demonstrations, ethnic food booths, children's rides and activities (including an antique carousel), costumed characters, puppet shows, and other entertainment. Admission is free. Call ℭ **202/ 537-3185** or go to www.cathedral.org (click on "All Hallows Guild") for details. First Friday and Saturday in May, rain or shine.

Georgetown Garden Tour. View remarkable private gardens in one of the city's loveliest neighborhoods. Admission ($30–$35) includes light refreshments. Some years there are related events such as a flower show at a historic home. Call ℭ **202/965-1950** or browse the website www.georgetowngardentour.com for details. Early to mid-May.

Memorial Day. Ceremonies take place at the Tomb of the Unknowns in Arlington National Cemetery (② **703/607-8000**), at the National World War II and Vietnam Veterans Memorial (② **202/619-7222**), and at the U.S. Navy Memorial (② **202/737-2300**). A National Memorial Day Parade marches from the Capitol, down Constitution Avenue, to the White House. On the Sunday before Memorial Day, the National Symphony Orchestra performs a free concert at 8pm on the West Lawn of the Capitol to honor the sacrifices of American servicemen and servicewomen (② **202/619-7222**). And one other thing: Hundreds of thousands of bikers from around the country roll into town in an annual tribute called "Rolling Thunder," to pay tribute to America's war veterans, prisoners of war, and those missing in action (**www.rollingthunder1.com**).

JUNE

Dupont-Kalorama Museum Walk Day. This 27th annual celebration welcomes visitors to nine museums and historic houses located in several charming, off-the-Mall neighborhoods. Free food, music, tours, and crafts demonstrations are on offer. Shuttle buses travel to each location. Call ② **202/667-0441**, ext. 35, or access the website, www.dkmuseums.com. First full weekend in June.

Smithsonian Folklife Festival. A major event reveling in both national and international traditions in music, crafts, food, games, concerts, and exhibits, staged the length of the National Mall. Each Folklife Festival showcases three or four cultures or themes; 2009 introduced those of African-American culture, music of the Americas, and Wales. All events are free; most events take place outdoors. Call ② **202/633-6440**, or check the website, www.folklife.si.edu, or the listings in the *Washington Post,* for details. For 10 days in late June and early July, always including July 4.

JULY

Independence Day. There's no better place to be on the Fourth of July than in Washington, D.C. The festivities include a massive National Independence Day Parade down Constitution Avenue, complete with lavish floats, princesses, marching groups, and military bands. A morning program in front of the National Archives includes military demonstrations, period music, and a reading of the Declaration of Independence. In the evening, the National Symphony Orchestra plays on the west steps of the Capitol with guest artists. And big-name entertainment precedes the fabulous fireworks display behind the Washington Monument. Check the website www.nps.gov/mall/july4 or call ② **202/619-7222** for details. July 4, all day.

Capital Fringe Festival. This event debuted in 2006 and celebrates experimental theater in the tradition of the original fringe festival held annually in Edinburgh, Scotland. With 130 separate productions taking place at more than 14 venues daily for 18 days, it adds up to about 600 individual performances in all. Local and visiting artists perform in theater, dance, music, and other disciplines. All tickets are $15, available online at www.capitalfringe.org, by calling ② **866/811-4111**, or at the Fort Fringe Box Office, 607 New York Ave. NW. The action centers on the Penn Quarter. Eighteen days starting July 9 or thereabouts.

AUGUST

Shakespeare Theatre Free for All. This free theater festival presents a different Shakespeare play each year for a 2-week run at the Sydney Harmon Hall theater, across from the Verizon Center, in the Penn Quarter. Tickets are required, but they're free. Call © 202/547-1122, or check the website, www.shakespeare theatre.org. Evenings, late August through mid-September.

SEPTEMBER

Labor Day Concert. The National Symphony Orchestra closes its summer season with a free performance at 8pm on the West Lawn of the Capitol; call © 202/619-7222 for details. Sunday before Labor Day. (*Rain date:* Same day and time at Constitution Hall or the Kennedy Center.)

Kennedy Center Open House Arts Festival. A daylong festival of the performing arts, featuring local and national artists on the front plaza and river terrace (which overlooks the Potomac), and throughout the stage halls of the Kennedy Center. Past festivals have featured the varied performances of the Suzanne Farrell Ballet Co., the Cirque du Soleil, pop rocker Ben Kweller, and Washington Opera soloists. Kids' activities usually include a National Symphony Orchestra "petting zoo," where children get to blow, blow, drum, or strum a favorite instrument. Admission is free, although you may have to stand in a long line for the inside performances. For details, call © 800/444-1324 or 202/467-4600, or access the website, www.kennedy-center.org. A Saturday or Sunday in early to mid-September.

Black Family Reunion. Performances, food, and fun are part of this 2-day celebration of the African-American family and culture, held on the Mall. Free. Check the website, www.ncnw. org/events/reunion.htm. Early to mid-September.

Adams-Morgan Day. Thousands turn out along 18th Street NW, Columbia Road NW, and other streets in this small multicultural neighborhood to revel in the music, art, dance, and cuisines of its residents. Check the website, adamsmorgandayfestival.com. Second Sunday in September.

Library of Congress National Book Festival. Co-sponsored by the Library of Congress and the First Lady, this festival welcomes at least 80 established authors and their many fans to the National Mall for readings, author signings, and general hoopla surrounding the love of books. Check www.loc.gov/bookfest, or call © 888/714-4696 for more information. A Saturday in late September.

OCTOBER

Marine Corps Marathon. Thirty thousand runners compete in this 26.2-mile race (the fifth-largest marathon in the United States). The 2010 race marks its 35th year. It begins at the Marine Corps Memorial (the Iwo Jima statue) and passes major monuments. Call © 703/432-1159 for details. Anyone can enter; register online at www.marinemarathon. com. Last Sunday in October.

Halloween. There's no official celebration, but costumed shenanigans seem to get bigger every year. Grownups trick or treat at embassies or participate in costumed pub crawls throughout the city. Giant block parties take place in the Dupont Circle neighborhood (including a Drag Queen High Heel race held the Tuesday before Halloween at 17th and Q streets) and in Georgetown. Check the *Washington Post* for special parties and activities. October 31.

NOVEMBER

Veterans Day. The nation's war dead are honored with a wreath-laying ceremony at 11am at the Tomb of the Unknowns in Arlington National Cemetery followed by a memorial service. The president of the United States or his stand-in officiates, as a military band performs. Wreath-laying ceremonies also take place at other war memorials in the city. Call ℂ **703/607-8000** for more information about Arlington Cemetery events and **202/619-7222** for information about war memorial events. November 11.

DECEMBER
Christmas Pageant of Peace/National Tree Lighting. At the northern end of the Ellipse, the president lights the national Christmas tree to the accompaniment of orchestral and choral music.

The lighting inaugurates the 4-week Pageant of Peace, a tremendous holiday celebration full of free activities, including musical performances, mostly of local school and church choruses, nightly on the Ellipse. (Brrrr!) Call ℂ **202/208-1631,** or check the website, www.nps.gov/whho/pageant.htm, for details; tickets are free but required to attend the tree-lighting ceremony. The tree-lighting ceremony takes place at 5pm on a day in early December, and the Pageant of Peace continues every night throughout the month.

2 ENTRY REQUIREMENTS

PASSPORTS

Virtually every air traveler entering the U.S. is required to show a passport. If you expect to stay for a maximum of 90 days, then you should make sure your passport is valid for six months past your final day here, unless your country has a specific agreement that provides an exception. (Quite a number of countries do have these exceptions, so it's worth checking on the http://travel.state.gov page, where you click on the "International" tab.)

All persons, including U.S. citizens, traveling by air between the United States and Canada, Mexico, Central and South America, the Caribbean, and Bermuda are required to present a valid passport. U.S. and Canadian citizens entering the U. S. at land and seaports of entry from within the western hemisphere will need to present government-issued proof of citizenship, such as a birth certificate, along with a government-issued photo ID, such as a driver's license. A passport is not required for U.S. or Canadian citizens entering by land or sea, but it is highly encouraged to carry one. Continue reading the next section on visas, and consult the "Passports" section in chapter 11 (p. 291).

VISAS

The U.S. State Department has a **Visa Waiver Program (VWP)** allowing citizens of the following countries to enter the United States without a visa for stays of up to 90 days: Andorra, Australia, Austria, Belgium, Brunei, Czech Republic, Denmark, Estonia, Finland, France, Germany, Hungary, Iceland, Ireland, Italy, Japan, Latvia, Liechtenstein, Lithuania, Luxembourg, Malta, Monaco, the Netherlands, New Zealand, Norway, Portugal, Republic of Korea, San Marino, Singapore, Slovakia, Slovenia, Spain, Sweden, Switzerland, and the United Kingdom. (**Note:** This list was accurate at press time; for the most up-to-date list of countries in the VWP, consult http://travel.state.gov/visa.) Even though a visa isn't necessary, in an effort to help U.S. officials check travelers against terror watch lists before they arrive at U.S. borders, visitors from VWP countries must register online through the **Electronic System for Travel Authorization (ESTA)** before boarding a plane or a boat to the U.S. Travelers will complete an electronic application providing basic personal and travel eligibility information. The Department of Homeland Security recommends filling out the form at least three days before traveling. Authorizations will be valid for up to two years or until the traveler's passport expires, whichever comes first. Currently, there is no fee for the online application. *Note:* Any passport issued on or after October 26, 2006, by a VWP country must be an **e-Passport** for VWP travelers to be eligible to enter the U.S. without a visa. Citizens of these nations also need to present a round-trip air or cruise ticket upon arrival. E-Passports contain computer chips capable of storing biometric information, such as the required digital photograph of the holder. If your passport doesn't have this feature, you can still travel without a visa if it is a valid passport issued before October 26, 2005, and includes a machine-readable zone, or between October 26, 2005, and October 25, 2006, and includes a digital photograph. For more information, go to http://travel.state.gov/visa. Canadian citizens may enter the United States without visas; they will need to show passports (if traveling by air) and proof of residence, however.

Citizens of all other countries must have (1) a valid passport that expires at least 6 months later than the scheduled end of their visit to the U.S., and (2) a tourist visa.

For information on obtaining a visa, see chapter 11, "Visas" (p. 293).

CUSTOMS
What You Can Bring into the U.S.

Every visitor more than 21 years of age may bring in, free of duty, the following: (1) 1 liter of wine or hard liquor; (2) 200 cigarettes, 100 cigars (but not from Cuba), or 3 pounds of smoking tobacco; and (3) $100 worth of gifts. These exemptions are offered to travelers who spend at least 72 hours in the United States and who have not claimed them within the preceding 6 months. It is forbidden to bring into the country almost any meat products

(including canned, fresh, and dried meat products such as bouillon, soup mixes, and so on). Generally, condiments including vinegars, oils, spices, coffee, tea, and some cheeses and baked goods are permitted. Avoid rice products, as rice can often harbor insects. Bringing fruits and vegetables is not advised, though not prohibited. Customs will allow produce depending on where you got it and where you're going after you arrive in the U.S. International visitors may carry in or out up to $10,000 in U.S. or foreign currency with no formalities; larger sums must be declared to U.S. Customs on entering or leaving, which includes filing form CM 4790. For details regarding U.S. Customs and Border Protection, consult your nearest U.S. embassy or consulate, or **U.S. Customs** (**www.customs.gov**).

What You Can Take Home from Washington, D.C.
For information on what you're allowed to bring home, contact one of the following agencies:

Canadian Citizens: Canada Border Services Agency (© **800/461-9999** in Canada, or 204/983-3500; www.cbsa-asfc.gc.ca).

U.K. Citizens: HM Customs & Excise at © **0845/010-9000** (from outside the U.K., 020/8929-0152), or consult their website at www.hmce.gov.uk.

Australian Citizens: Australian Customs Service at © **1300/363-263,** or log on to www.customs.gov.au.

New Zealand Citizens: New Zealand Customs, The Customhouse, 17–21 Whitmore St., Box 2218, Wellington (© **04/473-6099** or 0800/428-786; www.customs.govt.nz).

MEDICAL REQUIREMENTS
Unless you're arriving from an area known to be suffering from an epidemic (particularly cholera or yellow fever), inoculations or vaccinations are not required for entry into the United States.

GETTING TO WASHINGTON, D.C.

By Plane

Three airports serve the Washington, D.C., area. General information follows that should help you determine which airport is your best bet. See chapter 11, "Fast Facts," for the listing of airlines that travel to Washington, D.C., and their toll-free numbers and websites, p. 294.

A note for **international visitors**: Some large airlines offer transatlantic or transpacific passengers special discount tickets under the name **Visit USA**, which allows mostly one-way travel from one U.S. destination to another at very low prices. Unavailable in the U.S., these discount tickets must be purchased abroad in conjunction with your international fare. If Washington, D.C., is just one of the places you're visiting in the United States, you might want to check out the Visit USA program, which might prove the easiest, fastest, and cheapest way for you to see the country.

Ronald Reagan Washington National Airport (DCA) lies 4 miles south of D.C., across the Potomac River in Virginia, a trip of only a few minutes by car, 15 to 20 minutes by Metro in non-rush-hour traffic. Its proximity to the District and its direct access to the Metro rail system are reasons why you might want to fly into National.

Approximately 12 airlines serve this airport, which has nonstop flights to 69 U.S. cities, plus Nassau, Bermuda, Montreal, and Toronto. Nearly all nonstop flights are to and from cities located within 1,250 miles from Washington. The exceptions are flights between National and Phoenix, Denver, Las Vegas, Seattle, Los Angeles, and Salt Lake City. Among the airlines serving National Airport are **Air Canada, American, Continental,**

Delta, Northwest, United, and **US Airways,** and discount airlines **Frontier** and **AirTran.** Delta and US Airways operate shuttles that together offer hourly or nearly hourly flights between National and Boston's Logan Airport, and National and New York's LaGuardia Airport.

National Airport's traveler-friendly services include ticket counters that provide access to passengers with disabilities, more than 30 eateries (notably Legal Seafoods and hometown favorite Five Guys for burgers and fries), 30 shops (look for America! and the Smithsonian Museum Store for last-minute gifts), Wi-Fi service (rates vary depending on your choice of internet provider) throughout the airport, currency-exchange stations, commissioned artwork displayed throughout the terminals (go on a tour if your flight's been delayed), and climate-controlled pedestrian bridges that connect the terminal directly to the Metro station, whose Blue and Yellow lines stop here. The Metropolitan Washington Airports Authority oversees both National and Dulles airports, so the website is the same for the two facilities: www.mwaa.com. Check there for airport information, or call ℰ **703/417-8000.** For Metro information, call ℰ **202/637-7000.**

Washington Dulles International Airport (IAD) is 26 miles outside the capital, in Chantilly, Virginia, a 35- to 45-minute ride to downtown in non-rush-hour traffic. Of the three airports, Dulles handles more daily flights, with more than 30 airlines flying nonstop to 127 destinations, including 43 foreign cities. And though the airport is not as convenient to the heart of Washington as National, it's more convenient than BWI (see below), thanks to an uncongested airport access road that travels half the distance toward Washington.

Dulles is closing in on the completion of a decades-long expansion. By the time you read this, the airport should have debuted its underground airport train system and station, replacing the cumbersome mobile lounges that until now have transported most travelers to and from the main and midfield terminals. The project's other improvements include a pedestrian walkway between the main terminal and concourses A and B and, eventually, the addition of a fifth runway that will more than triple its annual passenger traffic to 55 million.

Among Dulles's major domestic airlines are **American, Continental, Delta, Northwest, United,** and **US Airways,** and discount airlines **AirTran, JetBlue, Southwest, Ted,** and **Virgin America.** The airport's major international airlines include **Aeroflot, Air Canada, British Airways, Aer Lingus, Air France, Lufthansa, Virgin Atlantic, ANA Airways,** and **Saudi Arabian Airlines.**

Dulles's many eateries and shops include Gordon Biersch Brewery and Restaurant, Five Guys for burgers and fries, Brooks Brothers clothiers, and the Smithsonian Museum Store. Like National, Dulles provides Wi-Fi service (rates vary depending on your choice of internet provider) throughout the airport and has several currency exchange stations and ATMs.

The airport's website is www.mwaa. com, and its information line is (C) **703/ 572-2700.**

Last but not least is **Baltimore–Washington International Thurgood Marshall Airport (BWI),** which is located about 45 minutes from downtown, a few miles outside of Baltimore. A vast expansion has added 11 gates to a newly improved concourse, skywalks from parking garages to terminals, and triple the number of parking spaces. One factor especially accounts for this tremendous growth, the same that recommends BWI to travelers: the major presence of **Southwest Airlines,** whose bargain fares and flights to nearly 40 cities seem to offer something for everyone.

(Southwest also serves Dulles Airport, but in a much smaller capacity.)

In all, about 14 airlines serve BWI, flying nonstop to 70 destinations, including five foreign cities. Major domestic airlines include **American, Continental, Delta, Northwest, United,** and **US Airways** and discount airlines **AirTran, Southwest,** and **USA 3000.** Major international airlines include **British Airways** and **Air Canada.**

Among BWI's on-site attractions are plenty of eateries, like Baltimore favorite, Obrycki's Restaurant, some shops, like America! and Godiva Chocolatier, currency exchange stations, ATMs, and Wi-Fi service ($8 a day) available throughout the airport.

Call (C) **800/435-9294** for airport information, or point your browser to www.bwiairport.com.

Getting into Town from the Airport

Each of the three airports offers similar options for getting into the city. Follow the signs to "ground transportation" and look for the banners or a staff representative of the service you desire. All three airports could really use better signage, especially because their ground transportation desks always seem to be located quite a distance from the gate at which you arrive. Keep trudging, and follow baggage claim signs, too, since ground transportation operations are always situated near baggage carousels.

TAXI SERVICE For a trip to downtown D.C., you can expect a taxi to cost anywhere from $10 to $20 for the 10- to 20-minute ride from National Airport; $50 to $60 for the 30- to 45-minute ride from Dulles Airport; and about $90 for the 45-minute ride from BWI.

SUPERSHUTTLE Vans ((C) **800/258-3826;** www.supershuttle.com) offer shared-ride, door-to-door service between the airport and your destination, whether in the District or in a suburban location. You make a reservation by phone or online and then proceed to the SuperShuttle desk in your airport to check in and be assigned to your bus. The only drawback to this service is the roundabout way the driver must follow, as he or she drops off or picks up other passengers en route. If you arrive after the SuperShuttle desk has closed, you can summon a van by calling customer service at ☏ **888/888-6025.** The 24-hour service bases its fares on zip code, so to reach downtown, expect to pay about $14, plus $10 for each additional person from National; $29, plus $10 per additional person from Dulles; and $37, plus $12 per additional person from BWI. If you're calling the SuperShuttle for a ride from a D.C. area location to one of the airports, you must reserve a spot at least 24 hours in advance.

LIMOUSINES Limousine service is the most costly of all options, with prices starting at $35 at National, $86 at Dulles, and $120 at BWI, for private car transportation to downtown D.C. For pickup from BWI, reserve passage by calling ☏ **800/878-7743** or 301/912-0000; or go online at www.rmalimo.com. For pickup from National or Dulles, try **Red Top Executive Sedan** (☏ **800/296-3300** or 703/522-3333; www.redtopcab.com). Or choose a limousine service from the list posted on Destination D.C.'s website, www.destinationdc.com. (Click on "Visiting," then "Browse DC," then "Interactive Visitors Guide," then the category "Transportation, Tours, and Neighborhoods," where you'll find a healthy selection of transportation services.

Free hotel/motel shuttles operate from all three airports to certain nearby properties. Best to inquire about such transportation when you book a room at your hotel.

Individual Transportation Options from Each Airport

FROM RONALD REAGAN WASHINGTON NATIONAL AIRPORT If you are not too encumbered with luggage, you should take **Metrorail** (☏ 202/637-7000) into the city. Metro's Yellow and Blue lines stop at the airport and connect via an enclosed walkway to level two, the concourse level, of the main terminal, adjacent to terminals B and C. If yours is one of the airlines that still uses the "old" terminal A (Spirit, AirTran, Midwest, Northwest), you will have a longer walk to reach the Metro station. Signs pointing the way can be confusing, so ask an airport employee if you're headed in the right direction; or, better yet, head out to the curb and hop a shuttle bus to the station, but be sure to ask the driver to let you know when you've reached the enclosed bridge that leads to the Metro (it may not be obvious, and drivers don't always announce the stops). **Metrobuses** (☏ 202/637-7000) also serve the area, should you be going somewhere off the Metro route. But Metrorail is fastest, a 15- to 20-minute non-rush-hour ride to downtown. It is safe, convenient, and cheap, costing $1.35 base fare and going up from there, depending on when (fares increase during rush hours) and where you're going.

If you're renting a car from an on-site **car-rental agency, Alamo** (☏ 888/215-0010), **Avis** (☏ 703/419-5815), **Budget** (☏ 703/419-1021), **Dollar** (☏ 800/800-4000), **Hertz** (☏ 703/419-6300), **National** (☏ 703/419-1032), or **Thrifty** (☏ 877/283-0898), go to level two, the concourse level, follow the pedestrian walkway to the parking garage, find garage A, and descend one flight. You can also take the complimentary Airport Shuttle (look for the sign posted at the curb outside the terminal) to parking garage A. If you've rented from off-premises agency **Enterprise** (☏ 703/553-7744), head outside the baggage claim area of your terminal, and catch the Enterprise shuttle bus.

To get downtown by car, follow the signs out of the airport for the George Washington Parkway, headed north toward Washington. Stay on the GW Parkway until you see signs for I-395 north to Washington. Take the I-395 north exit, which takes you across the 14th Street Bridge. Stay in the left lane crossing the bridge and follow the signs for Route 1, which will put you on 14th Street NW. (You'll see the Washington Monument off to your left.) Ask your hotel for directions from 14th Street and Constitution Avenue NW. Or take the more scenic route, always staying to the left on the GW Parkway as you follow the signs for Memorial Bridge. You'll be driving alongside the Potomac River, with the monuments in view across the river; then, as you cross over Memorial Bridge, you're greeted by the Lincoln Memorial. Stay left coming over the bridge, swoop around to the left of the Memorial, take a left on 23rd Street NW, a right on Constitution Avenue, and then, if you want to be in the heart of downtown, left again on 15th Street NW (the Washington Monument will be to your right).

FROM WASHINGTON DULLES INTERNATIONAL AIRPORT

The **Washington Flyer Express Bus** (© 888/927-4359; www.washfly.com) runs between Dulles and the West Falls Church Metro station, where you can board a train for D.C. In the airport, look for signs for the DULLES AIRPORT SHUTTLE, which leaves from Door 4 on the arrivals level. Buses to the West Falls Church Metro station run daily, every 30 minutes, and cost $10 one-way. (By the way, **"Washington Flyer"** is also the name under which the taxi service operates at Dulles.)

More convenient is the **Metrobus** service (no. 5A) that runs between Dulles (buses depart from curb 2E, outside the Ground Transportation area) and the L'Enfant Plaza Metro station, located near Capitol Hill and within walking distance of the National Mall and Smithsonian museums. The bus departs every 30 to 40 minutes weekdays, hourly on weekends; costs only $3.10; and takes about an hour.

If you are renting a car at Dulles, head down the ramp near your baggage claim area, and walk outside to the curb to look for your rental car's shuttle-bus stop. The buses come by every 5 minutes or so en route to nearby rental lots. These include **Alamo** (© 703/260-0182), **Avis** (© 703/661-3505), **Budget** (© 703/437-9373), **Dollar** (© 866/434-2226), **Enterprise** (© 703/661-8800), **Hertz** (© 703/471-6020), **National** (© 703/260-0182), and **Thrifty** (© 877/283-0898).

To reach downtown Washington from Dulles by car, exit the airport and stay on the Dulles Access Road, which leads right into I-66 east. Follow I-66 east, which takes you across the Theodore Roosevelt Memorial Bridge; be sure to stay in the center lane as you cross the bridge, and this will put you on Constitution Avenue (Rte. 29). Ask your hotel for directions from this point.

FROM BALTIMORE–WASHINGTON INTERNATIONAL AIRPORT

Washington's Metro service runs an Express Metro Bus ("B30") between its Metrorail Green Line Greenbelt station and BWI Airport. In the airport, head to the lower level and look for PUBLIC TRANSIT signs to find the bus, which operates daily, departs every 40 minutes, takes about 30 minutes to reach the station, and costs $3.10. At the Greenbelt Metro station, purchase a Metro fare card and board a Metro train, which will take you into the city. Depending on where you want to go, you can either stay on the Green Line train to your designated stop or get off at the Fort Totten Station to transfer to a Red Line train, whose stops include Union Station (near Capitol Hill) and various downtown locations. Transfers can be tricky, so you may want to ask a fellow passenger or a Metro attendant to make sure you're headed in the right direction.

You also have the choice of taking either an **Amtrak** (© 800/872-7245) or a **Maryland Rural Commuter** (MARC;

C 800/325-7245) train into the city. Both trains travel between the BWI Railway Station (*C* 410/672-6169) and Washington's Union Station (*C* 202/906-3260), about a 30-minute ride. Amtrak's service is daily (ticket prices range from $12 to $39 per person, one-way, depending on time and train type), while MARC's is weekdays only ($6 per person, one-way). A courtesy shuttle runs every 10 minutes or so between the airport and the train station; stop at the desk near the baggage-claim area to check for the next departure time of both the shuttle bus and the train. Trains depart about once per hour.

BWI operates a large off-site car-rental facility. From the ground transportation area, you board a shuttle bus that transports you to the lot. Rental agencies include **Alamo** (*C* 410/859-8092), **Avis** (*C* 410/859-1680), **Budget** (*C* 410/859-0850), **Dollar** (*C* 800/800-4000), **Enterprise** (*C* 800/325-8007), **Hertz** (*C* 410/850-7400), **National** (*C* 410/859-8860), and **Thrifty** (*C* 410/850-7139).

Here's how you reach Washington: Look for signs for I-195 and follow I-195 west until you see signs for Washington and the Baltimore–Washington Parkway (I-295); head south on I-295. Get off I-295 when you see the signs for Route 50/New York Avenue, which leads into the District, via New York Avenue. Ask your hotel for specific directions from New York Avenue NE.

Long-Haul Flights: How to Stay Comfortable

- Your choice of airline and airplane will definitely affect your legroom. Find more details about U.S. airlines at **www.seatguru.com**. For international airlines, the research firm Skytrax has posted a list of average seat pitches at **www.airlinequality.com**.
- Emergency exit seats and bulkhead seats typically have the most legroom.

Emergency exit seats are usually left unassigned until the day of a flight (to ensure that someone able-bodied fills the seats); it's worth checking in online at home (if the airline offers that option) or getting to the ticket counter early to snag one of these spots for a long flight. Many passengers find that bulkhead seating offers more legroom, but keep in mind that bulkhead seats have no storage space on the floor in front of you.

- To have two seats for yourself in a three-seat row, try for an aisle seat in a center section toward the back of coach. If you're traveling with a companion, book an aisle and a window seat. Middle seats are usually booked last, so chances are good you'll end up with three seats to yourselves. And in the event that a third passenger is assigned the middle seat, he or she will probably be more than happy to trade for a window or an aisle.
- To sleep, avoid the last row of any section or the row in front of an emergency exit, as these seats are the least likely to recline. Avoid seats near highly trafficked toilet areas. Avoid seats in the back of many jets—these can be narrower than those in the rest of coach. Or reserve a window seat so you can rest your head and avoid being bumped in the aisle.
- Get up, walk around, and stretch every 60 to 90 minutes to keep your blood flowing. This helps avoid **deep-vein thrombosis,** or "economy-class syndrome."
- Drink water before, during, and after your flight to combat the lack of humidity in airplane cabins. Avoid caffeine and alcohol, which will dehydrate you.
- If you're flying with kids, don't forget to carry on toys, books, pacifiers, and snacks and chewing gum to help them relieve ear pressure buildup during ascent and descent.

By Car

About one-fifth of leisure visitors to Washington arrive by plane, and if that's you, don't worry about renting a car. In fact, it's better if you don't, since the traffic in the city and throughout the region is absolutely abysmal, parking spaces are hard to find, garage and lot charges are exorbitant, and hotel overnight rates are even worse. Furthermore, Washington is amazingly easy to traverse on foot—so easy, in fact, that the Brookings Institution recently named it the most walkable city in the country. Our public transportation and taxi systems are accessible and comprehensive, as well.

But if you are like most visitors, you're planning on driving here, traveling on one of the following major highways: I-70 and I-270, I-95, and I-295 from the north; I-95 and I-395, Route 1, and Route 301 from the south; Route 50/301 and Route 450 from the east; and Route 7, Route 50, I-66, and Route 29/211 from the west.

No matter which road you take, there's a good chance you will have to navigate some portion of the **Capital Beltway** (I-495 and I-95) to gain entry to D.C. The Beltway girds the city, about 66 miles around, with more than 56 interchanges or exits, and is nearly always congested (especially during weekday morning and evening rush hours, roughly btw. 5:30–9:30am and 3–7pm). Drivers can get a little crazy, weaving in and out of traffic.

Get yourself a good map before you do anything else. **Destination D.C.**'s website, www.destinationdc.com, posts downloadable maps that are quite helpful. Another great source is the **American Automobile Association (AAA; ℂ 800/763-9900** for emergency road service and for connection to the mid-Atlantic office; www.aaa.com), which provides its members with maps and detailed Trip-Tiks that give precise directions to a destination, including up-to-date information about areas of construction. AAA also provides towing services should you have car trouble during your trip.

If you are driving to a hotel in D.C. or its suburbs, contact the establishment to find out the best route to the hotel's address and other crucial details concerning parking availability and rates.

The District is 240 miles from New York City, 40 miles from Baltimore, 700 miles from Chicago, 500 miles from Boston, and about 630 miles from Atlanta.

Car Rentals

If you need to rent a car while you're here, you have several options.

Residents and tourists alike seem to be turning to car-rental clubs that allow more flexible car-use arrangements, whether you need a car for an hour or for a month, with parking and other services included. One such company in Washington is **Zipcars** (ℂ **866/494-7227;** www.zipcar.com), which has a downtown office at 403 8th St. NW, entrance on 8th Street (ℂ **202/737-4900**), and pickup locations all over town.

Here's how it works: You apply and pay a membership fee or application fee ahead of time online, order the car online or by phone using a credit card, and establish exactly when and where you need a car. You receive a special card in the mail, which you use to activate the specific car you've reserved at the specific location, time, and day you've pre-arranged. The idea is that this special card unlocks the reserved car and you climb inside to retrieve the keys, following instructions you're given ahead of time. Zipcar's rates start at $9.25 an hour and this fee covers gas and insurance.

Or, you can go the usual route and rent a car from one of the major car-rental companies.

Car-rental rates can vary even more than airfares. Check out **Breezenet.com**, which offers domestic car-rental discounts with some of the most competitive rates around. Also worth visiting are Orbitz,

Hotwire.com, Travelocity, and Priceline. com, all of which offer competitive online car-rental rates.

If you're visiting from abroad and plan to rent a car in the United States, keep in mind that foreign driver's licenses are usually recognized in the U.S., but you should get an international one if your home license is not in English. International visitors should also note that insurance and taxes are almost never included in quoted rental car rates in the U.S. Be sure to ask your rental agency about additional fees for these. They can add a significant cost to your car rental.

For listings of the major car-rental agencies in Washington, please see the preceding section on airport car rentals, as well as chapter 11, "Fast Facts" (p. 296).

It helps to do your homework: Take the time to shop around and ask a few key questions and you might save hundreds of dollars:

- Are weekend rates lower than weekday rates? Ask if the rate is the same for pickup Friday morning, for instance, as it is for Thursday night.

- Is the weekly rate cheaper than the daily rate? Even if you need the car for only 4 days, it may be cheaper to keep it for 5.

- Does the agency assess a drop-off charge if you don't return the car to the same location where you picked it up? Is it cheaper to pick up the car at the airport or at a downtown location?

- Are special promotional rates available? If you see an advertised price in your local newspaper, be sure to ask for that specific rate; otherwise, you may be charged the standard cost. Terms change constantly.

- Are discounts available for members of AARP, AAA, frequent-flier programs, or trade unions?

- How much tax will be added to the rental bill? Local tax? State use tax? Local taxes and surcharges can vary

from location to location, even within the same car company, which can add quite a bit to your costs.

- What is the cost of adding an additional driver's name to the contract?

- How many free miles are included in the price? Free mileage is often negotiable, depending on the length of your rental.

- Are there extra charges if you're under 25? For instance, Avis tacks on an additional $25 per day for those 21 to 24, but does not set a maximum age requirement or extra charge. *Note:* All car rental agencies require drivers be at least 21.

Some companies offer "refueling packages," in which you pay for an entire tank of gas upfront. The price is usually fairly competitive with local gas prices, but you don't get credit for any gas remaining in the tank. If a stop at a gas station on the way to the airport will make you miss your plane, then by all means take advantage of the fuel purchase option. Otherwise, skip it.

For information on insurance, review your own car insurance policy and contact the **American Automobile Association (AAA; *C* 800/763-9900)** for advice and helpful information.

By Train

Amtrak (*C* **800/USA-RAIL;** www. amtrak.com) offers daily service to Washington from New York, Boston, and Chicago. Amtrak also travels daily between Washington and points south, including Raleigh, Charlotte, Atlanta, cities in Florida, and New Orleans. Amtrak's **Acela Express** trains offer the quickest service along the "Northeast Corridor," linking Boston, New York, Philadelphia, and Washington. The trains travel as fast as 150 mph, making the trip between New York and Washington in about 3 hours and 30 minutes and between Boston and Washington in about 7 hours. Amtrak runs fewer Acela trains on weekends, and honors passenger discounts, such as those for seniors and AAA members, only on weekend Acela travel.

Amtrak offers a smorgasbord of good-deal rail passes and discounted fares; although not all are based on advance purchase, you may have more discount options by reserving early. The bargain fares can be used only on certain days and hours of the day; be sure to find out exactly what restrictions apply. Tickets for children ages 2 to 15 cost half the price of a regular coach fare when the children are accompanied by a fare-paying adult. For more information, go to **www.amtrak.com** and click on the website's "Hot Deals" section, where you'll find assorted discount possibilities. *Note:* Amtrak requires reserved seating on its regional trains running between Boston and Newport News, Virginia, which means that every traveler is guaranteed a seat.

International visitors who plan to travel to other places in the country can buy a **USA Rail Pass,** good for 15 or 30 days of unlimited travel on **Amtrak.** The pass is available online or through many overseas travel agents. See Amtrak's website for the cost of travel within the western, eastern, or northwestern United States. Reservations are generally required and should be made as early as possible. Other rail passes are also available.

Amtrak trains arrive at historic **Union Station,** 50 Massachusetts Ave. NE (© 202/371-9441; www.unionstationdc.com), a short walk from the Capitol, across the circle from several hotels, and a short cab or Metro ride from downtown. Union Station is a turn-of-the-20th-century Beaux Arts masterpiece that was magnificently restored in the late 1980s. Offering a three-level marketplace of shops and restaurants, this stunning depot is conveniently located and connects with Metro service. Taxis are almost always available. (For more on Union Station, see chapters 7 and 8.)

By Bus

I would be negligent if I didn't mention the fact that bus travel between Washington, D.C., and New York City is now in vogue, thanks as much to the economy as to the rise of fabulously priced, comfortable, clean, and fast bus services between the two cities. **Greyhound** (© 800/231-2222; www.greyhound.com) travel is one thing, but, first, the D.C. bus depot, at 1005 First St. NE, is a pretty unsavory place to begin or end a journey, and second, the bus ride itself just does not compare with the one you experience on these new transports. Of course, Greyhound does travel to many more places than New York City.

But if NYC is your point of departure/arrival, check out one of these fleets: **Bolt-Bus (www.boltbus.com)**, which travels daily between D.C.'s Metro Center downtown and NYC's Penn Station or Chinatown, for $1-$23 each way; **Megabus** (© 877/462-6342;www.megabus.com), which travels between NYC's Penn Station and other locations, and D.C.'s Chinatown for $1–$21 each way; and, my personal favorite, **Vamoose Bus** (© 877/393-2828;www.vamoosebus.com), which travels between Rosslyn, Virginia's, stop near the Rosslyn Metro station and Bethesda, Maryland's stop near the Bethesda Metro station, and NYC's Penn Station, for $25 each way, with a coupon given at the end of each trip: collect four and ride one-way for free.

International visitors can obtain information about the **Greyhound North American Discovery Pass.** The pass, which offers unlimited travel and stopovers in the U.S. and Canada, can be obtained from foreign travel agents or through www.discoverypass.com.

GETTING AROUND

Washington is one of the easiest U.S. cities to navigate, thanks to its comprehensive public transportation system of trains and buses. Ours is the second-largest rail transit network and the fifth-largest bus network in the country. But because Washington is of manageable size and marvelous beauty, you may find yourself shunning transportation and choosing to walk.

City Layout

Washington's appearance today pays homage to the 1792 vision of French engineer Pierre Charles L'Enfant, who created the capital's grand design of sweeping avenues intersected by spacious circles, directed that the Capitol and the White House be placed on prominent hilltops at either end of a wide stretch of avenue, and superimposed this overall plan upon a traditional street grid. The city's quadrants, grand avenues named after states, alphabetically ordered streets crossed by chronologically ordered streets, and parks integrated with urban features are all ideas that started with L'Enfant. President George Washington, who had hired L'Enfant, was forced to dismiss the temperamental genius after L'Enfant apparently offended quite a number of people. But Washington recognized the brilliance of the city plan and hired surveyors Benjamin Banneker and Andrew Ellicott, who had worked with L'Enfant, to continue to implement L'Enfant's design.

The U.S. Capitol marks the center of the city, which is divided into **northwest (NW), northeast (NE), southwest (SW), and southeast (SE) quadrants.** Most, but not all, areas of interest to tourists are in the northwest. The boundary demarcations are often seamless; for instance, you are in the northwest quadrant when you visit the National Museum of Natural History, but by crossing the National Mall to the other side to visit the Freer Gallery, you put yourself in the southwest quadrant. Pay attention to the quadrant's geographic suffix; as you'll notice when you look on a map, some addresses—for instance, the corner of G and 7th streets—appear in all quadrants.

MAIN ARTERIES & STREETS From the Capitol, North Capitol Street and South Capitol Street run north and south, respectively. East Capitol Street divides the city north and south. The area west of the Capitol is not a street at all, but the National Mall, which is bounded on the north by Constitution Avenue and on the south by Independence Avenue.

The primary artery of Washington is **Pennsylvania Avenue,** which is the scene of parades, inaugurations, and other splashy events. Pennsylvania runs northwest in a direct line between the Capitol and the White House—if it weren't for the Treasury Building, the president would have a clear view of the Capitol—before continuing on a northwest angle to Georgetown, where it becomes M Street.

Pennsylvania Avenue in front of the White House—between 15th and 17th streets NW—remains closed to cars for security reasons but has been remade into an attractive pedestrian plaza, lined with 88 Princeton American Elm trees.

Constitution Avenue, paralleled to the south most of the way by Independence Avenue, runs east-west, flanking the Capitol and the Mall. If you hear Washingtonians talk about the "House" side of the Hill, they're referring to the southern half of the Capitol, the side closest to Independence Avenue, and home to Congressional House offices and the House Chamber. Conversely, the Senate side is the northern half of the Capitol, where Senate offices and the Senate Chamber are found, closer to Constitution Avenue.

Washington's longest avenue, **Massachusetts Avenue,** runs parallel to Pennsylvania (a few avenues north). Along the way, you'll find Union Station and then Dupont Circle, which is central to the area known as Embassy Row. Farther out are the Naval Observatory (the vice president's residence is on the premises), Washington National Cathedral, American University, and, eventually, Maryland.

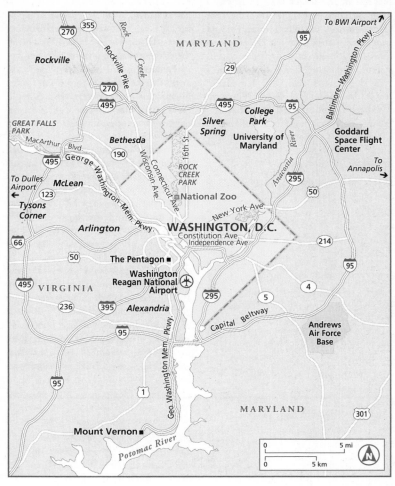

Connecticut Avenue, which runs more directly north (the other avenues run southeast to northwest), starts at Lafayette Square, intersects Dupont Circle, and eventually takes you to the National Zoo, on to the charming residential neighborhood known as Cleveland Park, and into Chevy Chase, Maryland, where you can pick up the Beltway to head out of town. Downtown Connecticut Avenue, with its chic-to-funky array of shops and clusters of top dollar-to-good value restaurants, is a good street to stroll.

Wisconsin Avenue originates in Georgetown; its intersection with M Street forms Georgetown's hub. Antiques shops, trendy boutiques, nightclubs, restaurants, and pubs all vie for attention. Wisconsin Avenue basically parallels Connecticut Avenue; one of the few irritating things about the city's transportation system is that the Metro does not connect these two major arteries in the heart of the city. (Buses do, and, of course, you can always walk or take a taxi from one avenue to the other; read about two supplemental bus systems, the Georgetown Metro Connection shuttle and the D.C. Circulator, below.) Metrorail's first stop on Wisconsin Avenue is in Tenleytown, a residential area. Follow the avenue north and you land in the affluent Maryland cities of Chevy Chase and Bethesda.

FINDING AN ADDRESS If you understand the city's layout, it's easy to find your way around. As you read this, have a map handy.

Each of the four corners of the District of Columbia is exactly the same distance from the Capitol dome. The White House and most government buildings and important monuments are west of the Capitol (in the northwest and southwest quadrants), as are major hotels and tourist facilities.

Numbered streets run north-south, beginning on either side of the Capitol with 1st Street. Lettered streets run east-west and are named alphabetically, beginning with

A Street. (Don't look for a B, a J, an X, a Y, or a Z St., however.) After W Street, street names of two syllables continue in alphabetical order, followed by street names of three syllables; the more syllables in a name, the farther the street is from the Capitol.

Avenues, named for U.S. states, run at angles across the grid pattern and often intersect at traffic circles. For example, New Hampshire, Connecticut, and Massachusetts avenues intersect at Dupont Circle.

With this in mind, you can easily find an address. On lettered streets, the address tells you exactly where to go. For instance, 1776 K St. NW is between 17th and 18th streets (the first two digits of 1776 tell you that) in the northwest quadrant (NW). *Note:* I Street is often written as "Eye" Street to prevent confusion with 1st Street.

To find an address on numbered streets, you'll probably have to use your fingers. For instance, 623 8th St. SE is between F and G streets (the sixth and seventh letters of the alphabet; the first digit of 623 tells you that) in the southeast quadrant (SE). One thing to remember: You count B as the second letter of the alphabet even

---

ⓘ Tips   Transit Tip

If you plan to use D.C.'s Metrorail and bus service a lot while you're here, you might want to do what most Washington commuters do: purchase a **SmarTrip** card, which is faster to use than a farecard—you just touch it to the target on a faregate inside a Metro station or farebox inside a Metrobus. The SmarTrip card also replaces the now obsolete paper transfers; when you transfer from Metrobus to Metrorail, or vice versa, you simply flash your SmarTrip card, which discounts your fare by 50¢. You can purchase SmarTrip cards for $30 ($25 travel value) online at www.wmata.com; for $5 (you'll need to add value to use it) at vending machines in certain Metro stations; and for $10 ($5 travel value) at WMATA headquarters (weekdays only), 600 5th St. NW, its sales office at Metro Center (weekdays only), 12th and F streets NW, or at one of many retail stores, like Giant or Safeway grocery stores. You can add value as needed at the passes/farecard vending machines in every Metro station, or even on a Metrobus, using the farebox. For more information, contact Metro (ⓒ **888/762-7874;** www.wmata.com).

To avoid risking the ire of commuters, be sure to follow these guidelines: Stand to the right on the escalator so that people in a hurry can get past you on the left. And when you reach the train level, don't puddle at the bottom of the escalator, blocking the path of those coming behind you; move down the platform. Eating, drinking, and smoking are strictly prohibited on the Metro and in stations.

though no B Street exists today (Constitution and Independence aves. were the original B sts.), but because there's no J Street, K becomes the 10th letter, L the 11th, and so on. To be honest, though, I don't know anyone who actually uses this method for figuring out an exact location.

By Public Transportation
Metrorail

The Metrorail system continues to be the best way to get around the city, in spite of the fact that on June 22, 2009, a horrific train crash on the Red Line track killed nine people and injured 80. The crash pointed up the fact, in the starkest of ways, that the 34-year-old system requires repairs. In fact, a $177 million rehabilitation project had already been planned for 2010 when the crash occurred. That work is underway now and will continue for many years on the Metro system's oldest line, the Red Line.

You should expect delays on the Red Line throughout the long period of repair and maintenance, as trains travel at reduced speeds and schedules are disrupted to allow for service. As a tourist, you may not notice or be as affected as regular commuters are, by these changes. For more information, contact **Washington Metropolitan Area Transit Authority (WMATA;** © **202/637-7000;** www. wmata.com). If you have concerns, you can always ride the buses (see information below), which will always be slower than the train system, but will get you wherever you want to go.

If you do ride Metrorail, try to avoid traveling during rush hour (Mon–Fri 5–9:30am and 3–7pm), since delays can be frequent, lines at farecard machines long, trains overcrowded, and Washingtonians at their rudest. You can expect to get a seat during off-peak hours (basically weekdays 10am–3pm, weeknights after 7pm, and all day weekends). All cars are air-conditioned and fitted with comfortable upholstered seats.

Metrorail's system of 86 stations and 106 miles of track includes locations at or near almost every sightseeing attraction; it also extends to suburban Maryland and northern Virginia. There are five lines in operation—Red, Blue, Orange, Yellow, and Green. The lines connect at several points, making transfers easy. All but Yellow and Green Line trains stop at Metro Center; all except Red Line trains stop at L'Enfant Plaza; all but Blue and Orange Line trains stop at Gallery Place/Chinatown. See the color map inside the back cover of this book.

Metro stations are indicated by discreet brown columns bearing the station's name and topped by the letter M. Below the M is a colored stripe or stripes indicating the line or lines that stop there. When entering a Metro station for the first time, go to the kiosk and ask the station manager for free, helpful brochures, including the *Metro System Pocket Guide.* It contains a map of the system, explains how it works, and lists the closest Metro stops to points of interest. The station manager can answer questions about routing or purchase of farecards. You can download a copy of the pocket guide and loads of information, including schedules, from Metro's website (www.wmata.com). The pocket guide is available in 7 languages besides English: French, Chinese, Japanese, Spanish, Korean, and German.

To enter or exit a Metro station, you need a computerized **farecard,** available at vending machines near the entrance. The machines take nickels, dimes, quarters, and bills from $1 to $20; they can return up to $4.95 in change (coins only). The vending machines labeled PASSES/FARE-CARDS accept both cash and credit cards. At this time, the minimum fare to enter the system is $1.35, which pays for rides to and from any point within 7 miles of boarding during nonpeak hours; during peak hours (Mon–Fri 5–9:30am and 3–7pm), $1.35 takes you only 3 miles. The maximum you will pay to the farthest destination is $4.50. Metro Authority is always contemplating a fare hike, though.

Once you're on the platform, you'll figure out your correct side of the track by finding your desired station stop on the list of upcoming stops posted on the brown pylon for trains headed in your direction. A display board overhead flashes the number of minutes anticipated before the next train pulls into the station. Lights embedded in the platform floor pulsate to alert you to the train's impending arrival. The only tricky part of traveling on Metro concerns transferring to a different line. Metro has eight transfer hubs, and probably the busiest hub is at Metro Center, where tracks crisscross on upper and lower levels and passengers can switch to a red, blue, or orange line train; read and follow the signs carefully, or ask someone for help, to make sure you get to the right track.

If you plan to take several Metrorail trips during your stay, put more value on the farecard to avoid having to purchase a new card each time you ride. For stays of more than a few days, your best value would be the **7-Day Fast Pass,** for $39 per person, which allows you unlimited travel; **1-Day Rail Passes** are available for $7.80 per person, allowing you unlimited passage for the day after 9:30am weekdays, or all day on Saturday, Sunday, and holidays. You can buy these passes online or at the Passes/Farecards machines in the stations. You can also purchase them at WMATA headquarters (weekdays only), 600 5th St. NW (✆ 202/637-7000; www.wmata.com), its sales office at Metro Center (weekdays only), 12th and F streets NW, or one of the retail stores, like Giant or Safeway grocery stores, where farecards are sold.

ⓘ Tips   Getting to Georgetown

Metrorail doesn't go to Georgetown, and though Metro buses do (the no. 30 line), the public transportation I'd recommend is that provided by two other bus systems, the **D.C. Circulator** (see p. 50 for more information about its services and the Georgetown route) and the **Georgetown Metro Connection shuttle,** which travels between the Rosslyn, Virginia, and Dupont Circle Metro stations, stopping at designated points in Georgetown along the way. The shuttle runs every 10 minutes from 7am to midnight Monday through Thursday, 7am to 2am Friday, 8am to 2am Saturday, and 8am to midnight Sunday. One-way fares cost $1, or 50¢ with a SmarTrip card. Look for the pretty blue school buses, stamped "Georgetown Metro Connection." See www.georgetowndc.com/getting-here for more information.

Other passes are available—see the box, "Transit Tip," above, check out the website or call the main number for further information.

Up to two children ages 4 and under can ride free with a paying passenger. Seniors (65 and older) and people with disabilities (with valid proof) ride Metrorail and Metrobus for a reduced fare.

When you insert your card in the entrance gate, the time and location are recorded on its magnetic tape, and your card is returned. Don't forget to snatch it up and keep it handy; *you have to reinsert your farecard in the exit gate at your destination,* where the fare will automatically be deducted. The card will be returned if there's any value left on it. If you arrive at a destination and your farecard doesn't have enough value, add what's necessary at the Exitfare machines near the exit gate.

Most Metro stations have more than one exit. To save yourself time and confusion, try to figure out ahead of time which exit gets you closer to where you're going. In this book, I include the specific exit you should use for every venue mentioned, including hotels, restaurants, and attractions. For instance, if you ride the Blue and Orange lines to the Smithsonian stop, you'll want to exit at the Mall to visit the museums, but exit at 12th St. and Independence Ave. SW if you're headed to the Mandarin Oriental Hotel.

Metrorail opens at 5am weekdays and 7am Saturday and Sunday, operating until midnight Sunday through Thursday, and until 3am Friday and Saturday. *Note:* The one exception is the stretch of the Yellow line between Mt. Vernon Square/7th Street–Convention Center, which does not operate during weekday rush hours, 5 to 9:30am and 3 to 7pm, but otherwise follows the same schedule as the rest of the system. Call ℭ **202/637-7000,** or visit www.wmata.com, for holiday hours and for information on Metro routes.

Metrobus

The **Metrobus** system encompasses 1,500 buses traveling 340 routes, making 12,000 stops, operating within a 1,500 square mile area that includes major arteries in D.C. and the Virginia and Maryland suburbs. The bus's destination appears above its windshield and on the boarding side of the vehicle.

Bus stops are identified by their red, white, and blue signs. However, the signs tell you only what buses pull into a given stop, not where they go. Furthermore, don't rely on the bus schedules posted at bus stops, which are sometimes out-of-date. Instead, for routing information, call ℭ **202/637-7000,** Monday through Friday 6am to 10:30pm, Saturday and Sunday 7am to 10:30pm. It's much faster and easier to obtain information and purchase farecards online, at www.wmata.com, but if you don't have access to a computer, call this same number to request a free map and time schedule, and any other information you need.

Base fare in the District is $1.35, $3.10 on express routes; there may be additional charges for travel into the Maryland and Virginia suburbs. Bus drivers are not equipped to make change, so be sure to carry exact change. If you'll be in Washington for a while and plan to use the buses a lot, consider buying a 1-week pass ($11), available online and also at the Metro Center station and other outlets. Also see the box, Transit Tip, above.

Most buses operate daily around-the-clock. Service is quite frequent on weekdays, especially during peak hours and less frequent on weekends and late at night.

Up to two children 4 and under ride free with a paying passenger on Metrobus, and there are reduced fares for seniors (ℭ **202/637-7000**) and people with disabilities (ℭ **202/962-1245** or 962-1100; see "Travelers with Disabilities" later in this chapter for transit information). If you leave something on a bus, on a train,

PLANNING YOUR TRIP TO WASHINGTON, D.C.

Tips **D.C. Circulator**

In addition to the Georgetown Metro Connection shuttle bus (p. 48), D.C. offers another fantastic supplemental bus system that is efficient, inexpensive, and convenient. The D.C. Circulator's fleet of air-conditioned red-and-gray buses travel five circumscribed routes in the city: the north-south route between the D.C. Convention Center and the waterfront (operates 7am–9pm daily); the east-west route between upper Georgetown and Union Station (operates 7am–9pm daily, with a special service added between upper Georgetown and the intersection of 17th and I streets NW, from 9pm to midnight Sun–Thurs, 9pm–2am Fri–Sat); the Smithsonian/National Gallery route (operates 10am–6pm weekends only), which simply loops around the Mall, from 4th Street to Independence Avenue, to 17th Street, to Constitution Avenue, and back around; the Union Station to Washington Navy Yard track (located near the Washington Nationals Ballpark, the service operates 6am–7pm weekdays, with extended hours on Nationals game days); and the route that travels between the Woodley Park/Adams-Morgan Metro station and the McPherson Square Metro station (operates 7am–midnight Sun–Thurs, 7am–3:30am Fri–Sat). Buses stop at designated points on their routes (look for the distinctive red-and-gold sign, often topping a regular Metro bus-stop sign) every 10 minutes. The fare at all times is $1 and you can order passes online, or pay upon boarding with exact change or with the use of a SmarTrip Metro card, or a D.C. Circulator pass purchased at a street meter near the bus stop. For easy and fast transportation in the busiest parts of town, you can't beat it. Call 𝒞 **202/962-1423** or go to www.dccirculator.com.

3

GETTING THERE & GETTING AROUND

or in a station, call Lost and Found Tuesday through Friday, 11am to 5pm, at 𝒞 **202/962-1195**.

By Car

Nearly 75% of all leisure visitors to the District arrive by car; but when you get here, my advice is to park your car and use your own feet, Metrorail, the Georgetown Shuttle, and the D.C. Circulator to get around.

If you must drive, be aware that traffic is always thick during the week, parking spaces are often hard to find, and parking lots are ruinously expensive. You can expect to pay overnight rates of at least $25 at hotels, hourly rates of $8 at downtown parking lots and garages, and flat rates starting at $20 in the most popular parts of town, like Georgetown and the Penn Quarter when there is an event at the

Verizon Center. If you're hoping to snag a metered space, better set out with a pocketful of quarters, since 25¢ buys you 15, sometimes 20, minutes.

Gasoline, as you're well aware, is expensive everywhere. In the District, I can tell you of two centrally located service stations that offer some of the best rates: the Sunoco White House, at 1442 U St. NW (at 15th St. NW) and the BP station at 1800 18th St. NW (at S St. NW). You'll know you've found either one when you see the number of cabbies pulling up to the pumps—always a good sign that the gas price is probably a better deal here than elsewhere. For a listing of other D.C. stations selling the cheapest gas, access the local AAA website, www.aaamidatlantic.com, and click on "Fuel Price Finder," under "Drive It," on the home page. From there, enter Washington, as the city, DC as the state, and the zip code of your hotel, say "20004," and you'll turn up names and locations of area service stations listed in order of gas prices, cheapest to most expensive. You don't have to be a member to use this service.

Watch out for **traffic circles.** The law states that traffic already in the circle has the right of way. No one pays any attention to this rule, however, which can be frightening (cars zoom into the circle without a glance at the cars already there). The other thing you'll notice is that while some circles are easy to figure out (Dupont Circle, for example), others are nerve-rackingly confusing (Thomas Circle, where 14th St. NW, Vermont Ave. NW, and Massachusetts Ave. NW come together, is to be avoided at all costs).

Sections of certain streets in Washington become **one-way** during rush hour: Rock Creek Parkway, Canal Road, and 17th Street NW are three examples. Other streets change the direction of some of their traffic lanes during rush hour: Connecticut Avenue NW is the main one. In the morning, traffic in four of its six lanes travels south to downtown, and in late afternoon/early evening, downtown traffic in four of its six lanes heads north; between the hours of 9am and 3:30pm, traffic in both directions keeps to the normally correct side of the yellow line. Lit-up traffic signs alert you to what's going on, but pay attention. Unless a sign is posted prohibiting it, a right-on-red law is in effect. The speed limit within city boundaries is usually 25 mph, up to 35 mph on some streets.

To keep up with street closings and construction information, go online to the

Washington Post's home page, at www. washingtonpost.com, and click on "Traffic," to learn about current traffic and routing problems in the District and suburban Maryland and Virginia. Another helpful source is a page on the D.C. government's website, www.dc.gov/closures, which identifies major street closures, traffic alerts, and construction in the city, though this info is not always current.

By Taxi

In May 2008, the D.C. taxicab system switched from charging passengers by geographical zones to charging passengers according to time- and distance-based meters. Cabbies protest that they are losing money using meters. Fares may increase, but at press time, fares began at $3, plus 25¢ per each additional $^{1}/_{6}$ mile, 25¢ per minute of wait time, and $1.50 per additional passenger. Other charges might apply, for instance, if you telephone for a cab, rather than hail one in the street, or for extra luggage or services. *Note:* Generally speaking, taxis accept only cash for payment, not credit cards.

Try **Diamond Cab Company** (© 202/387-6200) or **Yellow Cab** (© 202/544-1212).

Call © 202/645-6018 to inquire about fares within the District and © 202/331-1671 to find out the rate between any point in D.C. and an address in Virginia or Maryland. For more information about D.C. taxicabs than you could ever even guess was available, check out the D.C. Taxicab Commission's website, www. dctaxi.dc.gov.

---

4 MONEY & COSTS

The Value of U.S. Dollars vs. Other Popular Currencies

US$	Can$	UK£	Euro (€)	Aus$	NZ$
$1	$1.24	£.69	€.77	A$1.4	NZ$1.8

Frommer's lists exact prices in the local currency. The currency conversions quoted above were correct at press time. However, rates fluctuate, so before departing consult a currency exchange website such as www. oanda.com/convert/classic to check up-to-the-minute rates.

Anyone who travels to the nation's capital expecting bargains is in for a rude awakening, especially when it comes to lodging. Less expensive than New York and London, Washington, D.C.'s average daily hotel rates range from $157 per room per night in August, traditionally, D.C.'s slowest month, to a hefty $252 per room per night in October, reflecting the city's popularity as a top destination among U.S. travelers. D.C.'s restaurant scene is rather more egalitarian: heavy on the fine, top-dollar establishments, where you can easily spend $100 per person, but with plenty of excellent bistros and small restaurants offering great eats at lower prices. When it comes to attractions, though, the nation's capital has the rest of the world beat, since most of its museums and tourist sites offer free admission.

ATMS

Nationwide, the easiest and best way to get cash away from home is from an ATM (automated teller machine), sometimes referred to as a "cash machine" or "cashpoint." In Washington, D.C., ATMs are ubiquitous, in locations ranging from the National Gallery of Art's gift shop, to Union Station, to grocery stores. **MasterCard's** (*©* 800/424-7787; www.mastercard.com) Maestro and Cirrus, and **Visa's** (*©* 800/336-3386; www.visa.com) PLUS networks operate in D.C., as they do across the country. Go to your bank card's website or call one of your branches to find ATM locations in Washington. Be sure you know your personal identification number (PIN) and daily withdrawal limit before you depart. If your PIN is five or six digits, you should obtain a four-digit PIN from your local bank before you leave home, since the four-digit PINs are what most ATMs in Washington accept.

Note: Many banks impose a fee every time you use a card at another bank's ATM, and that fee is often higher for international transactions (up to $5 or more) than for domestic ones (where they're rarely more than $2). In addition, the bank from which you withdraw cash may charge its own fee. Visitors from outside the U.S. should also find out whether their bank assesses a 1% to 3% fee on charges incurred abroad.

CREDIT CARDS & DEBIT CARDS

Credit cards are the most widely used form of payment in the United States: **Visa** (Barclaycard in Britain), **MasterCard** (Eurocard in Europe, Access in Britain, Chargex in Canada), **American Express, Diners Club,** and **Discover.** They also provide a convenient record of all your expenses, and offer relatively good exchange rates. You can withdraw cash advances from your credit cards at banks or ATMs, but high fees make credit-card cash advances a pricey way to get cash.

It's highly recommended that you travel with at least one major credit card. You must have a credit card to rent a car, and hotels and airlines usually require a credit card imprint as a deposit against expenses.

ATM cards with major credit card backing, known as **"debit cards,"** are now a commonly acceptable form of payment in most stores and restaurants. Debit cards draw money directly from your checking account. Some stores enable you to receive cash back on your debit-card purchases as well. The same is true at most U.S. post offices.

What Things Cost in Washington, D.C.	US$	UK£*
Cup of coffee	2.00	1.37
Movie ticket	10.00	6.90
Taxi from Dulles	60.00	41.24
Subway fare	1.65	1.13
Moderate hotel rate	200.00	138.00

* Assuming a US$ to UK£ conversion rate of $1 =.69 UK£.

TRAVELER'S CHECKS

Travelers increasingly prefer to use credit cards and debit cards over traveler's checks, though traveler's checks are still accepted here. Foreign visitors should make sure that traveler's checks are denominated in U.S. dollars; foreign-currency checks are often difficult to exchange.

You can buy traveler's checks at most banks. Most are offered in denominations of $20, $50, $100, $500, and sometimes $1,000. Generally, you'll pay a service charge ranging from 1% to 4%.

The most popular traveler's checks are offered by **American Express** (© **800/ 221-7282** for cardholders—this number accepts collect calls, offers service in several foreign languages, and exempts Amex cardholders from the service fee); and **Visa** (© **800/732-1322**). Be sure to keep a copy of the traveler's checks' serial numbers separate from your checks in the event that they are stolen or lost. You'll get a refund faster if you know the numbers.

PREPAID TRAVEL CARDS

As traveler's checks go out of fashion, **prepaid traveler's check cards** are quickly taking their place. These are reloadable cards that work much like debit cards but aren't linked to your checking account.

AAA, which stopped selling traveler's checks in December 2007, now sells its own version of the prepaid travel card, called the **Visa Travel Money Card.**

Members can order the card online (www. aaa.com) or over the phone (© **866/674-9622**) for $4.95, or at a participating AAA office and retail location for up to $16.95. The pin-based card may be used at any ATM or for any purchase throughout the world, where Visa credit is accepted. A card can hold from $100 to $9,999 and AAA applies a $1.50 fee when you use your card at a U.S. ATM and a $3 fee for ATM transactions abroad; when you use your Money Card to pay for services, AAA does not charge a fee. Unlike banks, AAA does not stipulate a minimum age for a card user, which means a parent can purchase a card for a child who will be traveling.

AAA's downtown Washington office, open weekdays 9:30am to 5:30pm, at 1405 G St. NW, between 14th and 15th streets (© **202/481-6811**), sells these cards to members.

International travelers should know that U.S. money comes in paper bills, most commonly in $1 (a "buck"), $5, $10, and $20 denominations. There are also $2 bills (seldom encountered), $50 bills, and $100 bills (the last two are usually not welcome as payment for small purchases).

Coins come in seven denominations: 1¢ (1 cent, or a penny); 5¢ (5 cents, or a nickel); 10¢ (10 cents, or a dime); 25¢ (25 cents, or a quarter); 50¢ (50 cents, or a half dollar); the gold-colored Sacagawea coin, worth $1; and the rare silver dollar.

5 HEALTH

BEFORE YOU GO

Although it's not required of travelers, health insurance is highly recommended. Most health insurance policies cover you if you get sick away from home—but check your coverage before you leave.

International visitors should note that unlike many European countries, the United States does not usually offer free or low-cost medical care to its citizens or visitors. Doctors and hospitals are expensive, and in most cases will require advance payment or proof of coverage before they render their services. So, it's worth investing in a good travel and health insurance policy to make sure you're able to cover the costs of an accident, illness, or repatriation. Packages such as **Europ Assistance's "Worldwide Healthcare Plan"** are sold by European automobile clubs and travel agencies at attractive rates. **Worldwide Assistance Services, Inc.** (ℂ **800/ 777-8710;** www.worldwideassistance.com) is the agent for Europ Assistance in the United States.

Though lack of health insurance may prevent you from being admitted to a hospital in nonemergencies, don't worry about being left on a street corner to die: The American way is to treat you, and then bill you for it.

If you suffer from a chronic illness, consult your doctor before your departure. Pack **prescription medications** in your carry-on luggage, and carry them in their original containers with the pharmacy labels—otherwise they won't make it through airport security. Visitors from outside the U.S. should carry generic names of prescription drugs, if possible.

WHAT TO DO IF YOU GET SICK AWAY FROM HOME

Before you leave, you should talk to your local physician and ask for a referral in the D.C. area, should you need one. If your doctor isn't able to help, talk to the concierge or general manager at your hotel. Most hotels are prepared for just such medical emergencies and work with local doctors, who are able to see ill or injured hotel guests. You can also try the emergency room of any D.C. hospital, all of which have walk-in clinics for emergency cases that are not life-threatening. Turn to chapter 11, p. 291, to review insurance information to make sure your insurance policy covers you in any of these circumstances; and for lists of important **hot lines, hospitals,** and **emergency numbers**.

---

6 SAFETY

In the years following the September 11, 2001, terrorist attack on the Pentagon, the federal and D.C. governments, along with agencies such as the National Park Service, have continued to work together to increase security, not just at airports, but around the city, including government buildings, tourist attractions, and the subway. The most noticeable and, honestly, most irksome aspect of increased security at tourist attractions can be summed up in three little words: **waiting in line.**

Although visitors have always had to queue to enter the Capitol, the Supreme Court, and other federal buildings, now it can take more time to get through because of more intense scrutiny when you finally reach the door.

Besides lines, you may notice vehicle barriers in place at a wider radius around the Capitol building and new vehicle barriers and better lighting installed at the Washington Monument and at the Lincoln and Jefferson memorials. A new, tightly secured underground visitor center at the Capitol, which opened in late 2008, was built in great part, to safeguard members of Congress as well as all who work for them (see chapter 7, "Exploring Washington, D.C.," for more information about the center). Greater numbers of police and security officers are on duty around and inside government buildings, the monuments, and the Metro.

Just because so many police are around, you shouldn't let your guard down. Washington, like any urban area, has a criminal element, so it's important to stay alert and take normal safety precautions.

Ask your hotel front-desk staff or the city's tourist office if you're in doubt about which neighborhoods are safe. Read the section "The Neighborhoods in Brief," at the beginning of chapter 4, Suggested Washington, D.C., Itineraries, to get a better idea of where you might feel most comfortable.

Avoid deserted areas, especially at night, and don't go into public parks at night unless there's a concert or similar occasion that will attract a crowd.

Avoid carrying valuables with you on the street, and don't display expensive cameras or electronic equipment. If you're using a map, consult it inconspicuously—or better yet, try to study it before you leave your room. In general, the more you look like a tourist, the more likely someone will try to take advantage of you. If you're walking, pay attention to who is near you as you walk. If you're attending a convention or event where you wear a name tag, remove it before venturing outside. Hold on to your purse, and place your billfold in an inside pocket. In theaters, restaurants, and other public places, keep your possessions in sight.

Remember also that hotels are open to the public, and in a large hotel, security may not be able to screen everyone entering. Always lock your room door.

Be careful crossing streets, especially in the downtown area, and be even more cautious at rush hour. Though this may seem like obvious advice, it's worth a mention here, as there's been an alarming increase lately in the number of pedestrians being hit by cars and buses. Drivers in a hurry run red lights, turn corners too quickly, and so on, so be sure to take your time and check for oncoming traffic when crossing streets, and to use the crosswalks. If you're from Great Britain or Australia, remember to look to your left first, rather than to your right, on two-way streets.

7 SPECIALIZED TRAVEL RESOURCES

In addition to Washington's specific resources listed below, please visit **Frommers.com** for additional specialized travel resources.

GAY & LESBIAN TRAVELERS

Washington, D.C., has a large and vibrant gay and lesbian community and clearly welcomes gay and lesbian visitors, as evidenced by the fact that the city's convention and tourism bureau, Destination D.C., includes on its website, **www.destinationdc.org**, a link to information for the GLBT crowd: On the home page, click on "Visiting," then "Experience DC," then scroll to and click on "Pride in D.C." This special section covers the history of the gay rights movement in the capital; a calendar of noteworthy events, like the annual, weeklong Capital Pride Celebration held in June, complete with a street fair and a parade; and favorite-place recommendations made by local gays and lesbians. Better yet is Destination D.C.'s *GLBT Traveler's Guide,* which covers just about every aspect of the not-straight life in D.C. You can order the 65-page guide by calling Destination D.C.'s main number, ⓒ **202/789-7000,** or download it from the website.

When in Washington, you'll want to get your hands on the *Washington Blade* (ⓒ **202/797-7000;** www.washington blade.com), a comprehensive weekly newspaper distributed free at Metro stations and hundreds of other places throughout the city, including Kramerbooks, 1517 Connecticut Ave. NW. Every issue provides an extensive events calendar and a list of hundreds of resources, such as crisis centers, health facilities, switchboards, political groups, religious organizations, social clubs, and student activities; it puts you in touch with everything from groups of lesbian bird-watchers to the Asian Gay Men's Network. Gay restaurants and clubs are also listed and advertised.

Washington's gay bookstore, **Lambda Rising,** 1625 Connecticut Ave. NW (ⓒ **202/462-6969;** www.lambdarising. com), informally serves as an information source and gathering place for the gay community, which centers on the Dupont Circle neighborhood.

TRAVELERS WITH DISABILITIES

Washington, D.C., is one of the most accessible cities in the world for travelers with disabilities. It helps that it was here that Congress recognized and established the rights of the disabled when it passed the Americans with Disabilities Act in 1990, with amendments added in 2008. If you're not already familiar with the act and all that it entitles you, or if you want to learn more, access the website, **www.ada.gov**.

In the capital, you'll find that federal buildings, even the most historic and access-challenging, have been altered to conform to ADA requirements. So, the **Capitol,** the **White House,** the **Supreme Court,** and such national landmarks as the **Lincoln, Jefferson, FDR, Vietnam War,**

and **Korean War** memorials and the **Washington Monument** are each equipped to accommodate visitors with disabilities; many keep wheelchairs on the premises. There's limited parking for visitors with disabilities at some of these locations. Call ahead to these and other sightseeing attractions for accessibility information and special services.

But while government buildings and national attractions are easily accessible, private hotels, restaurants, clubs, and shops aren't always, since some seem to interpret ADA rules in ways that are often disabled-unfriendly. The best overall source of information about accessibility at specific Washington hotels, restaurants, shopping malls, and attractions is available from the nonprofit organization **Access Information.** You can read the information (including restaurant reviews) online at **www.disabilityguide.org,** or order a free copy of the *Washington, DC Access Guide* by calling ⓒ **301/528-8664,** or by writing to Access Information, 21618 Slidell Rd., Boyds, MD 20841. The information is not totally current, but you can find out more by calling or e-mailing the organization.

The **Washington Metropolitan Transit Authority** publishes accessibility information on its website **www.wmata.com,** or you can call ⓒ **202/962-1245** (TTY 202/628-8973) with questions about Metro services for travelers with disabilities, including how to obtain an ID card that entitles you to discounted fares. (Make sure that you apply at least 3 weeks ahead to allow enough time to obtain an ID card.) For up-to-date information about how Metro is operating on the day you're using it—to verify that the elevators are operating at the stations you'll be traveling to, for instance—call ⓒ **202/962-1212.**

Each Metro station is equipped with an elevator (complete with Braille number plates) to train platforms and extra-wide fare gates for wheelchair users; rail cars are fully accessible. Metro has installed punctuated rubber tiles leading up to the granite-lined platform edge to warn visually impaired Metro riders that they're nearing the tracks; barriers between rail cars prevent the blind from mistaking the gap for entry to a car. For the hearing-impaired, flashing lights indicate arriving trains; for the visually impaired, door chimes let you know when the train doors are closing. Train operators make station and onboard announcements of train destinations and stops, although the noise of the train and a less-than-perfect audio system often make these announcements unintelligible. Nearly all of the District's Metrobuses have wheelchair lifts and kneel at the curb, though they aren't always operating. The TTY number for Metro information is ✆ 202/638-3780.

Regular **Tourmobile** trams (p. 229) are accessible to visitors with disabilities. The company also operates special vans for immobile travelers, complete with wheelchair lifts. Tourmobile recommends that you call a day ahead to ensure that the van is available for you when you arrive. For information, call ✆ 703/979-0690, or go to www.tourmobile.com.

Major Washington museums, including all **Smithsonian museum buildings,** are accessible to wheelchair visitors. The Smithsonian has in place an accessibility program, the details of which you can learn about by calling ✆ 202/633-2921 or TTY 202/633-4353. Go online at www.si.edu/visit/visitors_with_disabilities.htm for more information, including downloadable maps that identify accessibility points throughout all Smithsonian buildings.

Washington theaters are handily equipped. Among the most accessible are these two:

The **John F. Kennedy Center for the Performing Arts** is fully accessible. The center provides headphones to hearing-impaired patrons at no charge. A wireless, infrared listening-enhancement system is available in all theaters. Some performances offer sign language and audio description. A public TTY is located in the lobby of the Family Theater near the entrance of the Hall of States, as well as on parking lot level A. Large-print programs are available at every performance; a limited number of Braille programs are available from the house manager. All theaters in the complex are wheelchair accessible. To reserve a wheelchair, call ✆ **202/416-8340.** For other questions regarding patrons with disabilities, including information about half-price tickets (you will need to submit a letter from your doctor stating that your disability is permanent), access the center's website, www.kennedy-center.org, or call the Office for Accessibility (✆ **202/416-8727**). The TTY number is ✆ **202/416-8728.**

The **National Theatre** is wheelchair accessible and features special performances of its shows for visually and hearing-impaired theatergoers. To obtain amplified-sound earphones for narration, simply ask an usher before the performance (you'll need to provide an ID). The National also offers a limited number of half-price tickets to patrons with disabilities who have obtained a Special Patron card from the theater, or who can provide a letter from a doctor certifying disability; you may receive no more than two half-price tickets. For details, call ✆ **202/628-6161,** or go the website, www.nationaltheatre.org.

For more on organizations that offer resources to travelers with disabilities, go to **Frommers.com**.

FAMILY TRAVEL

To locate accommodations, restaurants, and attractions that are particularly kid-friendly, refer to the "Kids" icon throughout this guide. Also be sure to see the "Especially for Kids" section on p. 226 of chapter 7.

Field trips during the school year and family vacations during the summer keep Washington, D.C., crawling with kids all year long. More than any other city, perhaps, Washington is crammed with historic buildings, arts and science museums, parks, and recreational sites to interest young and old alike. The Smithsonian Institution's family of 17 D.C. museums is a stellar example. First of all, the National Zoo is a Smithsonian entity. Enough said. But even the Smithsonian's grandiose museums on and off the National Mall are utterly kid-oriented. You can show up and be entertained, or check out the calendar ahead of time on the website: www.si.edu. Click on "Events" at the top of the page, and then check the box for "Kids and Families" displayed on the left-hand side of the screen. A long menu of options appears, from Indian dance performances at the National Museum of the American Indian, to Family Day activities scheduled at the National Postal Museum.

It's worth calling or checking websites in advance for the schedules of other attractions you're thinking of visiting. The fact that so many attractions are free is a boon to the family budget.

Hotels, more and more, are doing their part to make family trips affordable, too. At many lodgings, children under a certain age (usually 12) sleep free in the same room with their parents. (I've noted these policies in all the listings in chapter 5.) Hotel weekend packages often offer special family rates. See the "Family-Friendly Hotels" box on p. 91 for a rundown of the hotels that are most welcoming to young travelers.

Restaurants throughout the Washington area are growing increasingly family-friendly. Many provide kids' menus or charge less for children's portions. The best news, though, is that families are welcome at all sorts of restaurants these days and need no longer stick only to burger joints. See the "Family-Friendly Restaurants" box on p. 135 for a list of places kids will especially love.

Washington, D.C., is easy to navigate with children. The Metro covers the city, and it's safe. Children 4 and under ride free.

Also visit D.C.'s tourism website, www. destinationdc.org, click on "Experience DC," then scroll down and click on "Family," for some more family-related tourism hints. The *Washington Post* publishes a "Weekend" section every Friday that covers all possible happenings in the city, including family-friendly activities. If you arrive on a Friday, be sure to pick up a copy of the paper; otherwise, you can go online to www.washingtonpost.com, click on the "Going Out Guide" section, and then click on "This Weekend" in the browsing window to read what's up, entertainment-wise, in Washington.

Also look for *Frommer's Washington, D.C., with Kids,* which makes an excellent companion piece to this book, providing in-depth coverage of sightseeing with children in Washington.

SENIOR TRAVEL

Members of **AARP,** 601 E St. NW, Washington, DC 20049 (*©* **888/687-2277;** www.aarp.org), get discounts on hotels, airfares, and car rentals. AARP offers members a wide range of benefits, including *AARP The Magazine* and a monthly newsletter. Anyone over 50 can join.

With or without AARP membership, seniors often find that discounts are available to them at hotels, especially chain hotels such as the Hilton, so be sure to inquire when you book your reservation.

Venues in Washington that grant discounts to seniors include the Metro; certain theaters, such as the Shakespeare Theatre; and those few museums, like the Phillips Collection, that charge for entry. Each place has its own eligibility rules, including designated "senior" ages: The Shakespeare Theatre's is 60 and older, the Phillips Collection's is 62 and older, and the Metro discounts seniors 65 and older. See the "Getting Around" section earlier in this chapter for more information about the Metro, and refer to chapters 7 and 9 of this book for more information about the above-mentioned and other venues and their individual senior programs.

Many reliable agencies and organizations target the 50-plus market. **Elderhostel** (© 800/454-5768; www.elderhostel. org) arranges worldwide study programs for those age 55 and over. In 2009, Elderhostel hosted nearly 30 programs in Washington, D.C., ranging from 1 to 5 days in length and covering diverse topics—from espionage to historic neighborhoods.

Frommers.com offers more information and resources on travel for seniors.

AFRICAN-AMERICAN TRAVELERS

African Americans currently compose about 55% of the District's population, whose most notable residents are now, of course, our first African-American president, Barack Obama, and his family, Michelle, Malia, and Sasha Obama and family. But African Americans have long made their home in the nation's capital, richly contributing to the District's history, culture, personality, and identity. African-American museums, monuments, memorials, musical venues, and other landmarks all over town herald their achievements, individually or as a group. Naturally, all of this makes D.C. a compelling destination for African Americans or anyone interested in their culture. From the **Smithsonian Anacostia Neighborhood Museum and Center for African American History and Culture;** to Benjamin Banneker Park; to the **jazz clubs along U Street,** where Duke Ellington and Cab Calloway once catted; to the **African-American Civil War Memorial and Museum;** to the **Mary McLeod Bethune House,** Washington's black-American heritage is here to discover. Check out Destination D.C.'s website,

www.destinationdc.org, click on "Experience DC," and then scroll down and click on "African-American Experience" for an introduction to the city's historic black sites. Peruse Destination D.C.'s calendar for annual events, like the **Black Family Reunion** in September and the **Black History Month** activities in February. Browse the Cultural Tourism D.C. website, www. culturaltourismdc.org, to review its database of 200 sites on the **African American Heritage Trail.** (You can also order a copy of the booklet or find out where in Washington you can pick one up for free.) The Cultural Tourism D.C. site lists guided tours that follow an African-American theme, for instance the "Before Harlem, There Was U St. Tour," but you can also create your own tour with the information provided. Coming in 2011: the dedication of the **Dr. Martin Luther King, Jr., Memorial** on the National Mall.

STUDENT TRAVEL

When it comes to admission discounts in Washington, students rule. The one caveat: You must have a valid ID, although your current school ID should be good enough. For benefits that extend beyond reduced admission to D.C. attractions, you may want to consider obtaining an **International Student Identity Card (ISIC),** from the **International Student Travel Confederation (ISTC;** www.istc.org). ISTC was formed in 1949 to make travel around the world more affordable for students. Check out its website for comprehensive travel services information and details on how to get the ISIC, which qualifies students for substantial savings on rail passes, plane tickets, entrance fees, and more. It also provides students with basic health and life insurance and a 24-hour help line. The card is valid for a maximum of 18 months. You can apply for the card online or in person at **STA Travel** (© 800/ 781-4040 in North America; www. statravel.com), the biggest student travel

It's Easy Being Green

Here are a few simple ways you can help conserve fuel and energy when you travel:

- Each time you take a flight or drive a car greenhouse gases release into the atmosphere. You can help neutralize this danger to the planet through "carbon offsetting"—paying someone to invest your money in programs that reduce your greenhouse gas emissions by the same amount you've added. Before buying carbon offset credits, just make sure that you're using a reputable company, one with a proven program that invests in renewable energy. See "General Resources for Green Travel," box below.

- Whenever possible, choose nonstop flights; they generally require less fuel than indirect flights that stop and take off again. Try to fly during the day—some scientists estimate that nighttime flights are twice as harmful to the environment. And pack light—each 15 pounds of luggage on a 5,000-mile flight adds up to 50 pounds of carbon dioxide emitted.

- Where you stay during your travels can have a major environmental impact. To determine the green credentials of a property, ask about trash disposal and recycling, water conservation, and energy use; also question if sustainable materials were used in the construction of the property.

- At hotels, request that your sheets and towels not be changed daily. (Many hotels already have programs like this in place.) Turn off the lights and air-conditioner (or heater) when you leave your room.

- Use public transport where possible—trains, buses, and even taxis are more energy-efficient forms of transport than driving. Even better is to walk or cycle; you'll produce zero emissions and stay fit and healthy on your travels.

- If renting a car is necessary, ask the rental agent for a hybrid, or rent the most fuel-efficient car available. You'll use less gas and save money at the tank.

- Eat at locally owned and operated restaurants that use produce grown in the area. This contributes to the local economy and cuts down on greenhouse gas emissions by supporting restaurants where the food is not flown or trucked in across long distances.

agency in the world. STA has a Washington location, on the George Washington University campus, in the Marvin Center, at 800 21st St. NW (© 202/747-9772). If you're no longer a student but are still under 26, you can get an **International Youth Travel Card (IYTC)** from the same people, which entitles you to some discounts.

As important as discounts are, many student and 20-something entertainment options are available in D.C. Live music venues, from the 9:30 Club to the Black Cat, are nationally known and feature amazing acts nightly. Bars and clubs proliferate throughout the city, and many of them honor the traditional Thursday College Night. See chapter 9 for a rundown of possibilities.

8 SUSTAINABLE TOURISM

In some respects, Washington, D.C., has always been ahead of the curve when it comes to green-friendly endeavors. It was Pierre L'Enfant, in 1791, after all, whose vision for the city included a network of parks, an expansive "public walk," beautiful gardens and sweeping vistas. The capital today stays true to L'Enfant's plan, as anyone can see who has strolled the 2-mile long National Mall, biked through the 2,000-acre Rock Creek Park (the nation's oldest urban park), or picnicked on a verdant spot overlooking the Potomac River. The National Park Service maintains 70% of the city's land; when you count the parkland in the surrounding metropolitan area, the total exceeds 230,000 acres.

The capital continues to build upon its green foundation. Consider these facts:

Not only is D.C. the nation's most walkable city, but it also has the greatest number of walkable urban places per capita, according to the Brookings Institution. Biking, always popular here as recreation, is increasingly a transportation choice and the city has responded: the District recently added 40 new miles of bike lanes to city streets and has partnered with **Smart Bike DC** (www.smartbikedc. com), a self-service bike rental program, America's first, to avail Smart Bike subscribers (there's a $40 annual fee) of bikes, kept at stations throughout the city. By the time you read this, more than 500 bikes at 50 locations should be on hand.

D.C.'s excellent public transportation system (see "Getting Around" earlier in this chapter) provides another inducement for drivers to leave their cars behind, and the picture gets even better, when it comes to the many Metrobuses and D.C. Circulator buses that run on clean-burning natural gas.

The list goes on, whether we're talking about construction: Washington, D.C., was the first major city to require developers to adhere to guidelines established by the U.S. Green Building Council; hotel trends: most D.C. hotels are incorporating eco-friendly practices into their daily operations and many, like the **Willard Inter-Continental** (p. 92) and the **Hotel Palomar** (p. 103), go even further, adopting nearby parks, for instance, and helping to maintain them; or dining options: from **Hook** (p. 156), named as one of the country's top 10 eco-friendly restaurants by "Bon Appetit," to **Equinox** (p. 138), known as Michelle Obama's choice for celebrating her birthday, but also as a restaurant committed to using ingredients grown within 100 miles of the restaurant.

If participating in the environmental movement is important to you, you'll have countless opportunities to do so when you travel to the capital. To make it easy for you, I've included specific information about the eco-friendly practices of hotels, restaurants, and attractions in their descriptions within corresponding chapters.

9 STAYING CONNECTED

TELEPHONES AND CELLPHONES

If you are American and own a **cellphone,** bring your phone with you to D.C., making sure first, of course, that your

cellphone service does not charge excessively—or at all—for long-distance calls. In fact, if you are from outside the country and own an international cellphone with service that covers the Washington area,

General Resources for Green Travel

In addition to the resources for *Washington, D.C.* listed above, the following websites provide valuable wide-ranging information on sustainable travel. For a list of even more sustainable resources, as well as tips and explanations on how to travel greener, visit www.frommers.com/planning.

- **Responsible Travel** (www.responsibletravel.com) is a great source of sustainable travel ideas; the site is run by a spokesperson for ethical tourism in the travel industry. **Sustainable Travel International** (www.sustainable travelinternational.org) promotes ethical tourism practices, and manages an extensive directory of sustainable properties and tour operators around the world.
- In the U.K., **Tourism Concern** (www.tourismconcern.org.uk) works to reduce social and environmental problems connected to tourism. The **Association of Independent Tour Operators** (**AITO;** www.aito.co.uk) is a group of specialist operators leading the field in making holidays sustainable.
- In Canada, **www.greenlivingonline.com** offers extensive content on how to travel sustainably, including a travel and transport section and profiles of the best green shops and services in Toronto, Vancouver, and Calgary.
- In Australia, the national body which sets guidelines and standards for ecotourism is **Ecotourism Australia** (www.ecotourism.org.au). **The Green Directory** (www.thegreendirectory.com.au), **Green Pages** (www.thegreen pages.com.au), and **Eco Directory** (www.ecodirectory.com.au) offer sustainable travel tips and directories of green businesses.
- **Carbonfund** (www.carbonfund.org), **TerraPass** (www.terrapass.org), and **Carbon Neutral** (www.carbonneutral.org) provide info on "carbon offsetting," or offsetting the greenhouse gas emitted during flights.
- **Greenhotels** (www.greenhotels.com) recommends green-rated member hotels around the world that fulfill the company's stringent environmental requirements. **Environmentally Friendly Hotels** (www.environmentally friendlyhotels.com) offers more green accommodation ratings. The **Hotel Association of Canada** (www.hacgreenhotels.com) has a Green Key Eco-Rating Program, which audits the environmental performance of Canadian hotels, motels, and resorts.
- **Sustain Lane** (www.sustainlane.com) lists sustainable eating and drinking choices around the U.S.; also visit **www.eatwellguide.org** for tips on eating sustainably in the U.S. and Canada.
- For information on animal-friendly issues throughout the world, visit **Tread Lightly** (www.treadlightly.org). For information about the ethics of swimming with dolphins, visit the **Whale and Dolphin Conservation Society** (www.wdcs.org).
- **Volunteer International** (www.volunteerinternational.org) has a list of questions to help you determine the intentions and the nature of a volunteer program. For general info on volunteer travel, visit **www.volunteer abroad.org** and **www.idealist.org**.

bring that phone along. The point is, that hotels often charge outrageous fees for each long-distance or local call you make using the phone in your hotel room.

AT&T, Verizon, Sprint, and T-Mobile are among the cellphone networks operating in Washington, D.C., so there's a good chance that you'll have full coverage anywhere in the city—except, possibly on the subway, where Verizon is the sole provider of wireless service. You can expect reception to be generally excellent, but maybe not during certain special events, say, the inauguration of President Barack Obama, when cellphone use was off the charts and affected connections.

International visitors should check their **GSM (Global System for Mobile Communications) wireless network,** to see where GSM phones and text messaging work in the U.S.; go to the website www.t-mobile.com/coverage.

In any case, take a look at your wireless company's coverage map on its website before heading out. If you know your phone won't work here, or if you don't have a cellphone, you have several options:

You can **rent** a phone before you leave home from **InTouch USA** (✆ 800/872-7626 in the U.S., www.intouchusa.com or 703/222-7161 outside the U.S.).

You can use a **public pay telephone,** although these are increasingly hard to find. Many public pay phones at airports now accept American Express, MasterCard, and Visa credit cards. **Local calls** made from pay phones in most locales cost 35¢. (No pennies, please.)

You can **buy** a phone once you arrive. All three Washington-area airports sell cellphones and SIM cards. Look for the **Airport Wireless** shops at Dulles International Airport (✆ 703/661-0411), National Airport (✆ 703/417-3983), and BWI Airport (✆ 410/691-0262).

You can purchase a pay-as-you-go phone from all sorts of places, from Amazon.com to any Verizon store. In D.C.,

Verizon has a store at Union Station (✆ 202/682-9475) and another at 1314 F St. NW (✆ 202/624-0072), to name just two convenient locations.

Your final option is to buy **prepaid calling cards,** which are sold at convenience and grocery stores, post offices, and pharmacies, in denominations up to $50. These calling cards can be useful to anyone, but they come in handy especially if you're a traveler from abroad; the cards can be the least expensive way to call home.

Most long-distance and international calls can be dialed directly from any phone. **For calls within the United States and to Canada,** dial 1 followed by the area code and the seven-digit number. **For other international calls,** dial 011 followed by the country code (44 to the U.K., 61 to Australia, and 64 to New Zealand), the city code, and the number you are calling.

Calls to area codes **800, 888, 877,** and **866** are toll-free. However, calls to area codes **700** and **900** (chat lines, bulletin boards, "dating" services, and so on) can be very expensive—usually a charge of 95¢ to $3 or more per minute, and they sometimes have minimum charges that can run as high as $15 or more.

For **reversed-charge or collect calls,** and for person-to-person calls, dial the number 0 and then the area code and number; an operator will come on the line, and you should specify whether you are calling collect, person-to-person, or both. If your operator-assisted call is international, ask for the overseas operator.

For **local directory assistance** ("information"), dial 411; for long-distance information, dial 1, then the appropriate area code and 555-1212.

VOICE-OVER INTERNET PROTOCOL (VOIP)

If you have Web access while traveling, consider a broadband-based telephone service (in technical terms, **Voice-over Internet protocol,** or **VoIP**) such as Skype

Frommers.com: The Complete Travel Resource

Planning a trip or just returned? Head to **Frommers.com,** voted Best Travel Site by *PC Magazine*. We think you'll find our site indispensable before, during, and after your travels—with expert advice and tips; independent reviews of hotels, restaurants, attractions, and preferred shopping and nightlife venues; vacation giveaways; and an online booking tool. We publish the complete contents of over 135 travel guides in our **Destinations** section, covering over 4,000 places worldwide. Each weekday, we publish original articles that report on **Deals and News** via our free **Frommers.com Newsletters.** What's more, **Arthur Frommer** himself blogs five days a week, with cutting-edge opinions about the state of travel in the modern world. We're betting you'll find our **Events** listings an invaluable resource; it's an up-to-the-minute roster of what's happening in cities everywhere—including concerts, festivals, lectures, and more. We've also added weekly **podcasts, interactive maps,** and hundreds of new images across the site. Finally, don't forget to visit our **Message Boards,** where you can join in conversations with thousands of fellow Frommer's travelers and post your trip report once you return.

(www.skype.com) or Vonage (www.vonage. com), which allow you to make free international calls from your laptop or in a cybercafe. Neither service requires the people you're calling to also have that service (though there are fees if they do not). Check the websites for details.

INTERNET & E-MAIL
With Your Own Computer
More and more hotels, resorts, airports, cafes, and retailers are going Wi-Fi (wireless fidelity), becoming "hot spots" that offer free Wi-Fi access or charge a small fee for usage. Most laptops sold today have built-in wireless capability. To find public Wi-Fi hot spots in Washington, go to **www.jiwire.com**; its Hotspot Finder holds the world's largest directory of public wireless hot spots (201 in the center of Washington, last time I checked). Or, you could just head to your corner Starbucks, which has offered up free Wi-Fi service with its lattes for quite some time.

All of the D.C. hotels listed in chapter 5 offer Internet access.

Wherever you go, bring a **connection kit** of the right power and phone adapters, a spare phone cord, and a spare Ethernet network cable—or find out whether your hotel supplies them to guests.

Without Your Own Computer
Increasingly, hotels provide guests computer and Internet access on one or more computers in the hotel business center, often as a complimentary service. Both of D.C.'s **Embassy Suites Hotels,** the **Downtown** location and the **Convention Center** property (p. 105 and 92), are two examples.

All three D.C. airports offer Wi-Fi service, but, depending on your service provider, you may have to pay for it. Check out copy shops like **Kinko's** (FedEx Kinko's), which offers computer stations with fully loaded software (as well as Wi-Fi).

For help locating cybercafes and other establishments where you can go for Internet access, please see chapter 11 (p. 291).

Ways to Get Ahead

Popularity has its price, and in Washington that equals a lengthy wait in a long line for admission to its famous sites. Doesn't have to be that way, though: When you know generally the dates of your trip to Washington, call or e-mail in advance for desired tickets, passes, or reservations, and you might be able to visit places off-limits to the walk-up tourist and waltz through the door of A-list attractions, leaving the queues behind you. Follow this timeline to make sure you obtain tickets and reservations to those venues you most want to visit. Turn to the page numbers listed for specific information on how to proceed.

- **U.S. Capitol:** several days to 4 months ahead.
- **Washington National Cathedral Tour and Tea:** 5 to 6 months ahead of the desired date, p. 217.
- **White House Tours:** At least 2 months and as much as 6 months in advance, p. 172.
- **Washington Monument:** At least 1 day prior, as much as 6 months in advance, p. 178.
- **United States Holocaust Memorial Museum:** Two weeks ahead in spring and summer; the day before, otherwise, p. 203.
- **Theater Performances, Concerts, and Special Museum Exhibits:** As soon as you can.
- **Restaurant Reservations:** Two weeks ahead.

Suggested Washington, D.C., Itineraries

President Obama had been in office for less than a month when Washington's tourism bureau, Destination DC, posted an "Explore Obama's Backyard" itinerary on its website. (See www.destinationdc.org, then click on "Visiting," then "Browse DC," then go down the page to find "Sample Itineraries.") The tour follows in the Obamas' footsteps around the city, leading you to places they've been, from the Hay-Adams Hotel (p. 94), the Obamas' temporary home before they moved into the White House; to their favorite D.C. restaurants, like Ben's Chili Bowl and Equinox (p. 144 and 138); to the Kennedy Center (p. 214), where our first family attended a performance of the Alvin Ailey Dance Ensemble.

I gotta tell you: As the author of a guidebook to this city that I love, I am over the moon about the fact that President, Michelle, Malia, and Sasha Obama are not just living in the White House, but making themselves at home in Washington, and getting to know D.C. personally. Believe me, this is not typical First Family behavior. So go ahead if you want and follow that itinerary, which will have lengthened considerably, I imagine, by the time you read this.

Or follow one of my tours, each of which has been designed to introduce you to our beautiful American capital, a glorious city in its own right, and a hustling, bustling town.

But first, read the brief descriptions of D.C.'s neighborhoods, considering the individual appeal and attractions of each, as you get an overall sense of the place. Then, look over all three itineraries to see which one fits your personal agenda and schedule, allowing you the amount of time you'd like at each site. Call ahead and make sure the places on your desired itinerary are open. Be calm and flexible: Lines to enter public buildings are longer than ever, thanks to security clearance procedures and the capital's continuing popularity. Reserve spots on tours to avoid some of those waits, and book advance reservations at recommended restaurants, to make sure you get a table. Most important, don't be afraid to ask questions: The police on Capitol Hill, the National Park Service rangers on duty at the memorials, and the staff at all the museums know an awful lot—take advantage of their expertise.

1 THE NEIGHBORHOODS IN BRIEF

ADAMS-MORGAN Though this ever-trendy, multiethnic neighborhood is about the size of a postage stamp, it's crammed with boutiques, bars, clubs, and restaurants. Everything is located on either 18th Street NW or Columbia Road NW. You won't find any hotels here, but there are several nearby in the Dupont Circle and Woodley Park neighborhoods (see below). Parking during the day is okay, but difficult at night, especially weekends (a parking garage on Champlain St., just off 18th St., helps things a little). Luckily, you can easily walk (be alert—the neighborhood is edgy) to Adams-Morgan from the Dupont Circle or Woodley Park Metro stops, bus it, or take a taxi there. The weekend begins Thursday nights in the nightlife land of Adams-Morgan.

ATLAS DISTRICT The Atlas District, no more than a section of H Street NE, really, between 12th and 14th streets northeast of Union Station, is increasingly a nightlife and live music destination. A hardscrabble part of town by day, the Atlas District turns into a music and bar playground at night, especially Thursday through Saturday, as the city's thirsty scenemakers hit the street. There are no hotels, for now.

BARRACKS ROW Barracks Row, likewise, refers mainly to a single stretch of 8th Street SE, south of Pennsylvania Avenue, SE, but also to side streets occupied by Marine Corps Barracks since 1801, hence the name. Known for its lineup of shops, casual bistros, and pubs, Barracks Row's attractions continue to grow, in response to the 2008 opening of the Nationals baseball team's stadium, Nationals Park. The closest hotel for now is Capitol Hill Suites, which is 6 blocks away, at C and 2nd Street SE. Expect more hotels to blossom as part of Nationals Park development.

CAPITOL HILL Everyone's heard of "the Hill," the area crowned by the Capitol. The term, in fact, refers to a large section of town, extending from the western side of the Capitol to the D.C. Armory going east, bounded by H Street to the north and the Southwest Freeway to the south. It contains not only the chief symbol of the nation's capital, but the Supreme Court building, the Library of Congress, the Folger Shakespeare Library, Union Station, and Eastern Market. Much of it is a quiet residential neighborhood of tree-lined streets and Victorian homes. There

are a number of restaurants in the vicinity and a smattering of hotels, mostly close to Union Station. Keep to the well-lit, well-traveled streets at night, and don't walk alone—crime occurs more frequently in this neighborhood than in some other parts of town.

CLEVELAND PARK Cleveland Park, just north of Woodley Park, is an enclave of beautiful old houses with wraparound porches, found on picturesque streets extending off the main artery, Connecticut Avenue. With its own stop on the Red Line Metro system and a respectable number of excellent restaurants, Cleveland Park is worth visiting when you're near the zoo (just up the street) or in the mood for some fine cuisine and a sense of affluent D.C. neighborliness. Most hotels lie a short walk away in Woodley Park, and farther south into the city.

DOWNTOWN The area roughly between 6th and 21st streets NW going east to west, and M Street and Pennsylvania Avenue going north to south, is a mix of the Federal Triangle's government office buildings; K Street, ground zero for the city's countless law and lobbying firms; Connecticut Avenue restaurants and shopping; historic hotels; the city's poshest small hotels; **Chinatown;** the huge convention center; and the White House. You'll also find the historic **Penn Quarter,** D.C.'s hottest locale, which has continued to flourish ever since the 1997 opening of the Verizon Center (venue for Washington Wizards and Mystics basketball games, Capitals hockey games, and rock concerts). A number of off-the-Mall museums, like the mammoth Newseum, the International Spy Museum, and the Smithsonian's National Portrait Gallery and American Art Museum, are here. This is also where you'll find the hippest restaurants, boutique hotels, and nightclubs. The total downtown area takes in so many blocks and attractions that I've divided

4

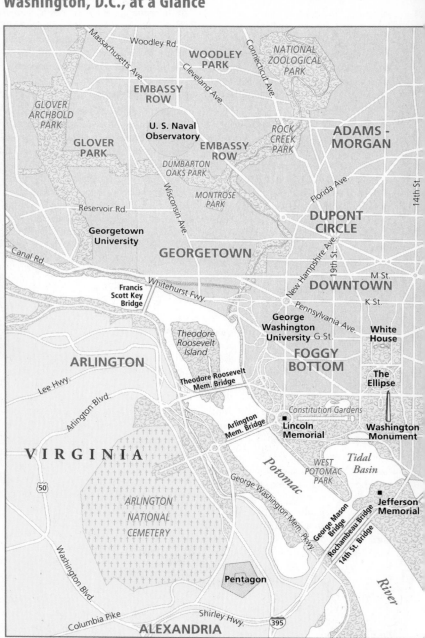

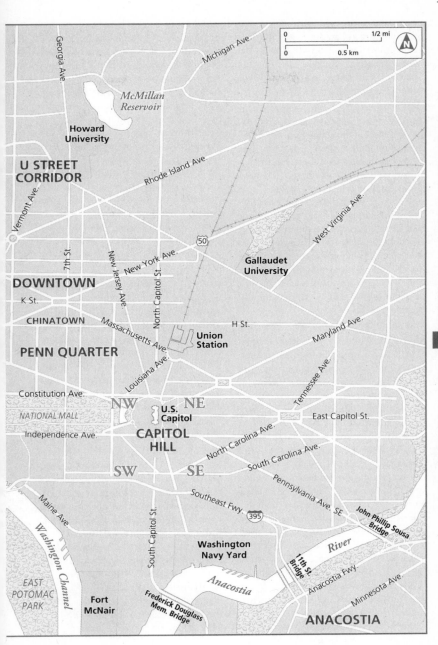

discussions of accommodations (chapter 5) and dining (chapter 6) into two sections: "**Midtown**," roughly the area west of 15th Street to 21st Street, and north of Pennsylvania Avenue to M Street; and "**Penn Quarter**," roughly east of 15th Street to 6th Street, and Pennsylvania Avenue north to New York Avenue.

DUPONT CIRCLE   One of my favorite parts of town, Dupont Circle, is fun day or night. It takes its name from the traffic circle minipark, where Massachusetts, New Hampshire, and Connecticut avenues collide. Washington's famous **Embassy Row** centers on Dupont Circle, and refers to the parade of grand embassy mansions lining Massachusetts Avenue and its side streets. The streets extending out from the circle are lively, with all-night bookstores, good restaurants, wonderful art galleries and art museums, nightspots, and Washingtonians at their loosest. It is also the hub of D.C.'s gay community. There are plenty of hotels.

FOGGY BOTTOM/WEST END   The area west of the White House, south of Dupont Circle, and east of Georgetown encompasses both Foggy Bottom and the West End. Foggy Bottom, located below, or south, of Pennsylvania Avenue, was Washington's early industrial center. Its name comes from the foul fumes emitted in those days by a coal depot and gasworks, but its original name, Funkstown (for owner Jacob Funk), is perhaps even worse. There's nothing foul (and not much funky) about the area today. The West End edges north of Pennsylvania Avenue, booming with the latest big-name restaurants and new office buildings. Together, the overlapping Foggy Bottom and West End neighborhoods present a mix of townhouse residences, George Washington University campus buildings, small- and medium-size hotels, several fine eateries, student bars, and the Kennedy Center, lining either side of Pennsylvania Avenue and its side streets beyond.

GEORGETOWN   This historic community dates from Colonial times. It was a thriving tobacco port long before the District of Columbia was formed, and one of its attractions, the Old Stone House, dates from pre-Revolutionary days. Georgetown action centers on M Street and Wisconsin Avenue NW, where you'll find the luxury Four Seasons hotel (and less expensive digs—see chapter 5), numerous boutiques (see chapter 8), chic restaurants, and popular pubs. Expect lots of nightlife here. But detour from the main drags to relish the quiet, tree-lined streets of restored Colonial row houses, stroll the beautiful gardens of Dumbarton Oaks, and check out the C&O Canal. Georgetown is also home to Georgetown University. Note that the neighborhood gets pretty raucous on the weekends, which won't appeal to everyone.

GLOVER PARK   Mostly a residential neighborhood, this section of town, just above Georgetown and just south of the Washington National Cathedral, is worth mentioning because of several good restaurants and bars located along its main stretch, Wisconsin Avenue NW. Glover Park sits between the campuses of Georgetown and American Universities, so there's a large student presence here. See chapter 5 for information about the Savoy Hotel, its only lodging.

THE MALL   This lovely, tree-lined stretch of open space between Constitution and Independence avenues, extending for 2^1/$_2$ miles from the Capitol to the Lincoln Memorial, is the hub of tourist attractions. It includes most of the Smithsonian Institution museums and several other notable sites. Tourists as well as natives—joggers, food vendors, kite flyers, and picnickers among them—traipse the 300-foot-wide Mall. Most hotels and restaurants are located beyond the Mall to the north, with a few located south of the Mall, across Independence Avenue.

U STREET CORRIDOR U St. NW and 14th St. NW form the crux of D.C.'s most diverse neighborhood, where blacks and whites mix more comfortably than anywhere else in the city. The quarter continues to rise from the ashes of the nightclubs and theaters located here decades ago when the performances of jazz and blues legends Duke Ellington, Louis Armstrong, and Cab Calloway gave the area the name "Black Broadway." Today, clubs like Twins Jazz and HR-57 honor that legacy, drawing jazz lovers, while the corridor's many clubs fill nightly with the city's young and restless. New restaurants (see chapter 6) and little shops (see chapter 8) proliferate. The Penn Quarter may be hot and high energy, but the U St. Corridor is hip and laid back. Go here to party, not to sleep—there are no hotels along this stretch.

WOODLEY PARK Home to Washington's largest hotel (the Marriott Wardman Park), Woodley Park boasts the National Zoo, many good restaurants, and some antiques stores. Washingtonians are used to seeing conventioneers wandering the neighborhood's pretty residential streets with their name tags still on.

2 THE BEST OF WASHINGTON IN 1 DAY

Note: *For this itinerary, it's best if you book tickets in advance for a Capitol tour and for a moonlight tour, and reserve a table in advance at Johnny's Half-Shell (see information below).*

The first two stops on this tour are the Capitol, which is open to visitors Monday through Saturday, and the Supreme Court, open only on weekdays. If you're here on a weekend, plan accordingly. If you're here on a weekday, let's be honest: When both the Supreme Court and Congress are in session, and you're hoping to attend both, and to tour the Capitol, you can expect those activities alone to take up the better part of a day. So I'm offering you some choices: Visit the Supreme Court *or* the Capitol, and continue with the itinerary as laid out; *or* hope for the best, attempt to take in both the Court *and* the Capitol, and work in other stops on this itinerary as you're able. It's possible, with everything working in your favor, to experience this itinerary in its entirety. But many factors will come into play: ebbs and flows of tourist seasons, interest in a particular case being argued in the Supreme Court, legislation up for a vote in the Senate or House, even the weather. And if you're traveling with children age 12 and under, that's another factor: Visit the Capitol and, if you want, do a tour of the Supreme Court, but do not try to attend a Supreme Court argument with young children. Rule of thumb: To be sure of attending a Supreme Court argument and touring the Capitol, be prepared to line up early (7:30am in high season) at the Supreme Court and order your tickets way in advance to tour the Capitol on your desired day. ***Start:*** *Metro on the Blue Line to Capitol South, or on the Red Line to Union Station.*

❶ The Capitol

The story of the design and construction of the Capitol is a tumultuous one, full of strong personalities and brave compromises—kind of like the history of the United States, actually. Startling truths abound, beginning with the fact that the most important U.S. building was designed in 1792 by a Scottish-trained physician from the British West Indies. William Thornton, the first architect of the Capitol, explained himself, "I lamented not having studied architecture and resolved to attempt that grand undertaking and study at the same time." Seventy years and three architects later, the Capitol completed its most notable feature, a 287-foot-high dome, made of two enormous cast-iron shells, one inside the other, with all the exterior trim, cornices, and columns painted to look like marble. Tilt your head all the way back to see the 19-foot-statue, *Freedom,* which was set in place atop the dome in December 1863, at the height of the Civil War—the same year that Abraham Lincoln issued his Emancipation Proclamation. See p. 163.

❷ Supreme Court

You don't have to be aware of the Supreme Court's schedule to know when a controversial case is up—you'll observe the line of hopeful visitors stretching across the Court's front plaza. You'll spot media types, too. The southwest corner of the plaza is a favorite location for TV correspondents to deliver on-camera reports; with the right angle, the shot captures the newsperson and the crowds of people in endless queues, framed against the backdrop of the Court's stately columned edifice and elaborate pediment inscribed with the words EQUAL JUSTICE UNDER LAW. See p. 170.

❸ Library of Congress

As the world's largest library, the Library of Congress commands an inventory of nearly 142 million items. In an enduring effort to share its wealth, the Library reaches into its pockets, so to speak, to pull out wondrous objects from one of its particular collections, and then mounts an exhibition to show them off. One example: An ongoing exhibit titled "Creating the United States," displays an assortment of artifacts that inform our understanding of the birth of our democracy, from an "original Rough Draught" of Thomas Jefferson's much marked-up Declaration of Independence, to early-18th-century hand-colored etchings conveying political satire, to a 1797 manuscript in George Washington's hand, outlining a plan of government for Virginia. The Library of Congress: not just for bibliophiles. See p. 214.

④ LE BON CAFÉ

Order a sandwich and try to snag a seat at one of the outside tables. Or better yet, get it to go, and proceed to your next destination, where an Elizabethan garden awaits you. ✆ 202/547-7200. See p. 124.

❺ Folger Shakespeare Library and Garden

If your timing is right (try before noon or after 1pm), you'll have the garden to yourself—to sit on a bench; munch on a picnic lunch; and relax amid the English ivy, rosemary, and lavender, all plantings true to Shakespeare's day. Positioned throughout the garden are statues of characters from eight of the Bard's plays. Stop inside to see "what's on" in the paneled, Tudor-style Great Hall, and check the calendar for plays being staged in the re-created Elizabethan Theatre. Attend an evening production, if you can; they're always a treat. See p. 205.

Note: If you're running out of time, skip the next stop and head straight to #7—unless you love flora, in which case, continue on to:

❻ U.S. Botanic Garden

At the foot of the Capitol grounds on the Independence Avenue side is this other garden—well, several gardens and plant collections, in fact—contained within a large greenhouse. Not much is asked of you here—you don't have to be a gardener to appreciate the beauty of orchids or the wonder of the "Musa Praying Hands" (it's in the banana family). Be sure to climb all the way up the stairs in the tallest part of the conservatory and look out: You'll have views of the Capitol and the neighborhood that I'll bet even most locals haven't discovered. See p. 221.

❼ National Gallery of Art and Sculpture Garden

The National Gallery's special exhibits are always amazing, so if there's one being staged, go, no matter who the artist. For

1 Capitol
2 Supreme Court
3 Library of Congress
4 Le Bon Café
5 Folger Shakespeare Library and Garden
6 U. S. Botanic Garden
7 National Gallery of Art
8 Johnny's Half Shell
9 Union Station
10 Moonlight Tour

example, head to the East Wing and go straight up to the tower to take a look at the latest show in a series that focuses on developments in art since the 1970s. The tower gets less traffic than other spots in the museum, mostly because not everyone's hip to it. (*FYI:* The Matisse cutouts that used to be on view here are now found on the concourse level.) From here, you'll want to high-tail it over to the West Wing, to view as much of the grand sculpture galleries, European paintings from the 13th to the 19th century, and modern artworks in the Sculpture Garden, as time allows. See p. 202.

If you're short on time or energy, take a taxi; otherwise walk the half-mile or so to Johnny's Half Shell.

8 JOHNNY'S HALF SHELL

Sit on the terrace in view of the Capitol or head inside to enjoy Johnny's particular conviviality and "Seafood Specialties, Strong Drinks," as the restaurant puts it. Never sampled a soft-shell crab? This is the place to try it, if in season. Non-seafood items are also available. Arrive weekdays 4:30 to 7:30pm and you'll be in time for happy hour, or Monday to Saturday 5 to 7pm, to enjoy the good value pretheater menu. From here, it's just a couple of blocks to Union Station, your next destination. ✆ **202/737-0400,** p. 121.

⑨ Union Station

This handsome structure is a major thoroughfare for commuters rushing for Metro and Amtrak trains, so watch out. The ticket kiosks for the various tour operations are at the front of the Main Hall, making them hard to miss; whether you've reserved space in advance (recommended) online or by phone, or you're just now purchasing your tickets, you'll need to stop by the booths to obtain the actual tour tickets. See p. 216.

⑩ Moonlight Tour

Tourmobile and Old Town Trolley offer nighttime tours of the memorials and the Washington Monument. Some consider this the most dramatic way to view the historic sites. After a full day of sightseeing, it is certainly the easiest and most relaxing way to get around. Both operations offer narrated tours, with stops (for 20 min. or so) at the Lincoln, FDR, Vietnam Veterans, and Jefferson memorials. But their specific fares, routes, and schedules differ. (Tourmobile's twilight tour, for instance, is a seasonal operation.) Hop aboard and enjoy the ride. See p. 229.

---

3 THE BEST OF WASHINGTON IN 2 DAYS

Note: For this itinerary, you should call in advance for restaurant and ticket reservations (see information below).

Your second day takes you to three powerhouse museums in the hopping Penn Quarter: the Newseum and the Smithsonian's National Portrait Gallery and American Art Museum, then across Pennsylvania Avenue to tour four more Smithsonian museums on the National Mall, before you finish up at the National Archives. (You will have passed some of these edifices the night before on your moonlight tour.) From there, you'll be ready to re-cross Pennsylvania Avenue to return to the Penn Quarter for cocktails and dinner. *Suggestion:* Purchase advance tickets to tour the Newseum to guarantee entry for the day and time you desire and to bypass lines. Start: *Metro on the Green or Yellow Line to Archives/Navy Memorial/Penn Quarter station; or on the Red Line to the Judiciary Square stop, exiting at 4th Street.*

---

❶ Newseum

This mammoth museum debuted April 11, 2008, and the word is "Wow!" Its glass-fronted, seven-story, block-long-and-wide building grabs your attention, vying with nearby notables, like the Capitol just up the avenue. Is it truly "the world's most interactive museum," as it proclaims? Maybe so: Fourteen galleries, 15 theaters, two broadcast studios, and 130 interactive stations invite visitors to explore 5 centuries of news history. You can put yourself in the reporter's seat in an interactive

newsroom, play the NewsMania game to test your knowledge of news events, or be "on the scene" at a dramatic moment in history, through an amazing 4-D theater experience that puts you virtually back in that moment. Awesome. See p. 211.

Walk one block over to 7th St. and follow 7th St. north to F St. to find the following museums.

❷ National Portrait Gallery &
❸ American Art Museum

Before this building was even finished, in 1867, it had already served as a Civil

Map Legend:

1. Newseum
2. National Portrait Gallery
3. Smithsonian American Art Museum
4. Zola
5. National Air and Space Museum
6. Freer Gallery
7. National Museum of American History
8. National Museum of Natural History
9. National Archives
10. Central Michel Richard

War hospital and as the site of Abraham Lincoln's second inaugural ball. Upon completion, the building housed patent offices, whose clerks eventually issued patents to Alexander Graham Bell, Thomas Edison, and 500,000 other inventors. The Smithsonian took over the Patent Office Building and remodeled it before opening two-museums-in-one in 1968.

Fast-forward to 2006, after an even more intense renovation to the museums, which just happened to coincide with the remarkable renewal taking place in the museums' surrounding Penn Quarter neighborhood.

The reopening of the National Portrait Gallery and the American Art Museum in July 2006 signified nothing less than a rebirth, and the city staged a celebration to herald this much-improved bastion of "American Originals." The museums and their vast displays do America proud, representing the nation's spirit and people at their best in every artistic genre, including presidential portraits, folk art, photographs, Latino art, African-American art, and paintings by the masters, from Gilbert Stuart to Georgia O'Keeffe to modernist Aaron Douglas. Go. See p. 199.

4

ZOLA
In the same building as the Spy Museum and across the street from the Smithsonian museums, Zola plays upon a sleuth theme in its decor. The food's for real, though, and highly recommended. ☎ **202/654-0999.** See p. 132. From here, you should re-trace your steps to Pennsylvania Ave., which you'll cross, continuing south across the National Mall to reach the Air and Space Museum.

❺ National Air and Space Museum

Nothing attests to human ingenuity better than this vast display of the machines we've created to fly through air and space. And yet, one of this museum's enduring attractions is something that puts those human accomplishments in perspective: The Albert Einstein Planetarium (you'll need a ticket to enter). It coaxes you to wonder about the dimensions of the universe and where it leads. See p. 189.

Follow Independence Ave. west to your next stop.

❻ Freer Gallery

This handsome building, with its Italian Renaissance architecture and arched courtyard, is devoted to Asian art, with one major exception: its Whistler holdings. Visit the spectacular Peacock Room, so called for the golden peacock feathers that Whistler painted upon the walls of the room, which was once part of a friend's London town house. The friend was most displeased, but today's gallerygoers are generally intrigued. Continue through other chambers of the gallery to admire ancient jade objects, early Buddhist sculpture, Islamic art, and a wealth of Asian works. See p. 188.

Cross to the other side of the Mall to find your next two museums.

❼ National Museum of American History

Across the Mall from the Freer lies this ponderous museum, newly reopened after a much-needed renovation. You won't have time to view everything on display in this fascinating tribute to American culture and history. But certain things you shouldn't miss: the magnificent, original Star-Spangled Banner, now on display in its own multistory, glass-paneled gallery; 10-foot-high, glass-paned artifact walls showcasing choice items from the museum's three-million-piece collection, from an 1815 tavern sign to Helen Keller's watch; and a favorite, Julia Child's kitchen, moved from the famous chef's home in Cambridge, Massachusetts, to its permanent niche here. See p. 191.

❽ National Museum of Natural History

This is yet another so-much-to-see, so-little-time venue, especially given the fact that this is the largest natural-history museum in the world. Do take a gander at the Hope Diamond and other gems and minerals, and don't miss the fossil collection and the dinosaur hall. But if your time is limited, visit the museum's two newest exhibits. The 23,000-square-foot Ocean Hall, the museum's largest permanent exhibit, aims to explain the essential connection between oceans and all life. Displays include a life-size replica of a North Atlantic whale and an 1,800-gallon-tank display of coral reef. Butterflies + Plants: Partners in Evolution is two exhibits in one. Partners in Evolution explores the relationship between plants and insects and animals, while the Butterfly Pavilion is aflutter with live and colorful butterflies, allowing visitors to walk in their midst, observing them straight on, not through glass. The Butterfly Pavilion is the Smithsonian's rare exhibit that charges admission. Tickets cost $5 for children, $6 for adults, every day but Tuesday, when admission is free but a timed ticket still necessary. See p. 195.

❾ National Archives

Area residents are slow to catch on, but the National Archives has gradually been transforming itself into a multimedia complex, mounting major exhibitions, screening documentaries, and hosting talks by contemporary authors. Its finest feature, however, will always be its display of the original Declaration of Independence, U.S. Constitution, and Bill of Rights. See p. 200.

🔟 CENTRAL MICHEL RICHARD

You've been on your feet all day! Treat yourself to a lobster burger, cassoulet, or steak au poivre, accompanied by an apricot sour or a glass of fine wine. Congratulate yourself if you've succeeded in booking a reservation (and reservations are a must) at perhaps the hottest restaurant in the city. As you'll discover, its popularity has as much to do with the party atmosphere as with the top-notch cuisine. ✆ **202/626-0015.** See p. 129.

---

4 THE BEST OF WASHINGTON IN 3 DAYS

Especially if you're traveling with children ages 11 and under, you might start Day 3 with a lively visit to the National Zoo. Otherwise, consider visiting the U.S. Holocaust Memorial Museum in the morning and then spend the afternoon taking a restorative stroll through some of D.C.'s loveliest quarters. Obtain admission tickets ahead of time for the museum, if possible; if not, you should plan to arrive early to wait in line. Start: Metro on the Red Line, exiting at the Woodley Park/Zoo/Adams-Morgan station to go to the National Zoo; Metro on the Blue Line to the Smithsonian stop, exiting at Independence Avenue and 12th Street SW, to visit the Holocaust Museum.

---

❶ National Zoological Park or ❷ U.S. Holocaust Memorial Museum

If you (or your children) want to get an early start on the day, the National Zoological Park, an off-the-Mall Smithsonian complex, opens at 6am, year-round. Make your way to the Asia Trail, whose winding path presents close-up sights of sloth bears sucking up termites, giant pandas frolicking in a waterfall, fishing cats caught in the act, and the assorted activities of clouded leopards and Japanese salamanders. Those three giant pandas remain the zoo's top draws, but the baby gorilla, born January 10, 2009, is pretty cute, too. See p. 197.

Fifteen years after its debut, crowds continue to tour the U.S. Memorial Holocaust Museum, especially its heart-tearing main exhibit. Some people also come here to do research: Open to the public without appointment is a library on the fifth floor, where you can look up information on a name, a town, or any subject to do with the Holocaust. The museum, meanwhile, is expanding its mission to include special exhibits on related events—firsthand accounts and photographs depicting the persecution and torture of the people of Darfur, Sudan, for instance. See p. 203.

From the Metro's Red Line National Zoo stop, take the Metro south one stop to the Dupont Circle station, exiting to Q St. From the Metro's Blue Line Smithsonian station, take the Metro to Metro Center and switch to the Red Line, going toward Shady Grove. Exit at Dupont Circle, exiting to Q St.

❸ Phillips Collection

This beautiful museum-mansion was expanded in 2006 to include a sculpture garden, a new cafe, an auditorium, a gallery devoted to the works of Mark Rothko, and a larger exhibit space for postwar contemporary art. Always keep an eye out for visitors' favorite pieces: Renoir's *Luncheon of the Boating Party;* numerous Bonnards; and, on display from time to time, a painting executed by founder Duncan Phillips's wife, Marjorie Phillips: *Night Baseball.* See p. 213.

---

4 **PIZZERIA PARADISO**

Open daily from lunch straight through to 10pm (Sun), 11pm (Mon–Thurs), or midnight (Fri–Sat), this cherished pizzeria expanded in 2009 to satisfy its steady stream of customers, who come for the pies that are several cuts above the average: cooked in an oak-burning oven and topped with your choice of 31 fresh ingredients, from pancetta to eggplant. ℂ **202/223-1245.** See p. 150.

---

5 **Embassy Row and Dupont Circle**
Stop in shops along Connecticut Avenue, and then follow side streets to discover boutiques, little art galleries, and quaint century-old town houses. If you look carefully, you'll start to notice that some of these buildings are actually embassies or historic homes. The most awesome embassies lie on Massachusetts Avenue, west of Dupont Circle. Flags and plaques clearly identify them. Turn onto S Street NW and look for no. 2340 to see where President Woodrow Wilson lived after he left the White House. Right next door is a cool little museum, the Textile Museum. Both the Woodrow Wilson House and the Textile Museum are worth touring if you have time. Embassies are rarely open to the public. See p. 78 and 70.

Walk, if you feel up to it, or take a taxi to the Kennedy Center.

6 **Kennedy Center**
Head to the Kennedy Center for the 6pm nightly free concert in the Grand Foyer (part of the center's Millennium Stage program). At concert's end, proceed through the glass doors to the terrace overlooking Rock Creek Parkway and the Potomac River, and enjoy the view. See p. 214.

Take a taxi or walk the half-mile or so to Georgetown.

7 **Georgetown**
Finish up the day with dinner and shopping in Georgetown, where stores and restaurants tend to stay open later than those in other parts of town. See p. 153 and 236.

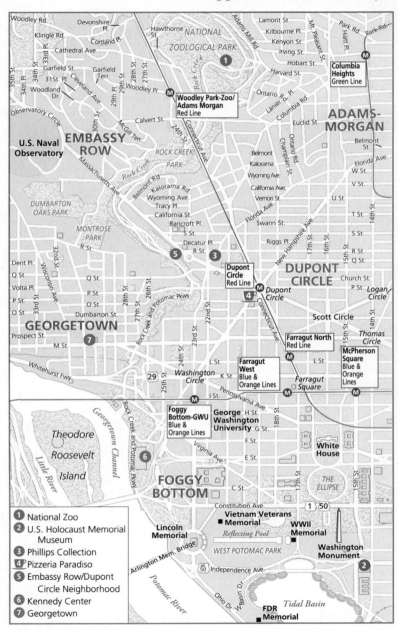

1 National Zoo
2 U.S. Holocaust Memorial Museum
3 Phillips Collection
4 Pizzeria Paradiso
5 Embassy Row/Dupont Circle Neighborhood
6 Kennedy Center
7 Georgetown

Where to Stay

What is a hotel but a temporary
home? And no matter how brief your stay,
you should feel welcome, relaxed, and
comfortable there. Beyond a basic level
establishing that the lodging is clean, well-
lit, and safe, offers good service and a snug
bed, the word "comfortable" means different things to different people. Size of
room, size of hotel, location, luxurious-
ness, ambience, clientele, kinds of amenities available both in the room and within
the hotel, and of course rates, are just some
of the elements that can turn you on or off
during a hotel stay. I've kept all this in
mind as I've visited and written about each
of the hotels included in this chapter.

If you have a favorite brand of hotel
chain, you're likely to find it represented in
Washington, D.C. The Hilton family of
Embassy Suites, Hampton Inn, and Hilton Garden Inn properties, offers good
value for both business and leisure guests;
the Marriott dynasty of 16 D.C. hotels
includes upscale Renaissances, extended-
stay Residence Inns, business-traveler
mainstay Courtyard by Marriott, and the
high-end traveler option, the JW Marriott;
and our all-American Hyatt, Sheraton,
and Omni brands offer a range, from the
luxurious Park Hyatt to the more practical
Four Points Sheraton.

International chains, like Ireland's gracious Doyle and France's chic Sofitel, are
here. So is Kimpton Group Hotels, the un-
chainlike chain, that now counts 11 hotels
in the D.C. area and continues to up the
ante on chicly whimsical lodging. Two of
the newest brands to debut here are the hip
Thompson Hotels Collection, in the form
of Donovan House (see "Midtown" section
of this edition), and W Hotels, whose W
Washington, D.C., property arrived in July
2009 (see Penn Quarter section).

Luxury lodging is big business in D.C.
The Four Seasons, two Ritz-Carltons, and
the Mandarin Oriental vie with each
other—and with three exquisite smaller
establishments, the Hay-Adams, the St.
Regis, and the Jefferson (reopened in 2009,
too late to be reviewed for this edition)—
for the patronage of the wealthy.

Washington also has quite a number of
beloved, homegrown accommodations,
from the romantic Swann House in the
Dupont Circle neighborhood to the
Georgetown Suites, always a remarkable
deal given its buzzing locale.

You'll find descriptions of 50 hotels and
inns within this chapter, along with tips
on choosing a neighborhood, getting the
best rate, landing the best room, and finding a place to stay when the whole city
seems booked.

CHOOSING A NEIGHBORHOOD

Most of Washington's hotels lie in the heart of downtown, near Dupont Circle, and in
the Foggy Bottom/West End areas, with a handful scattered in Georgetown, on Capitol
Hill, and northward on Connecticut Avenue. Each of these communities has its own
character, as detailed in the section "The Neighborhoods in Brief," in chapter 4.

If proximity to Capitol Hill is important to you, consider the cluster of hotels on the
north side of the Hill, close to Union Station and just off North Capitol Street. If you
want to be within a short walk of the National Mall, think about staying in either the
lah-di-dah Mandarin Oriental or the family-friendly Residence Inn, each just a couple of

blocks from the Smithsonian-lined Mall. Both the Capitol Hill and Mall-area properties are in the thick of things and convenient for sightseeing during the day, but can feel isolated at night—especially those near the Mall—when tourist sites and offices close and Hill staff, government office workers, and museumgoers go home. The hotels are not near residential areas, and restaurants and shops are few.

To take the pulse of the city as it goes about its business, stay in a downtown hotel. This is also where you should stay if you want to be able to walk to good restaurants, bars, and nightclubs. Divided into two sections here, Penn Quarter (btw. 6th and 15th sts. NW) and Midtown (btw. 15th and 21st sts. NW), Washington's downtown is bustling day and night all week long. Hotels in the downtown segment east of 15th Street are close to theaters and several museums; properties on or near Pennsylvania Avenue, like the Willard or the JW Marriott, are within walking distance of the National Mall and the White House. The Hotel Monaco, between 7th and 8th streets, is just a few blocks north of Pennsylvania Avenue, the Newseum, and the National Gallery. Downtown hotels west of 15th Street are also within a stroll of the White House, as well as some smaller museums, like Decatur House and the Renwick and Corcoran galleries.

If you prefer the feel of a residential neighborhood, look to hotels in Dupont Circle and Woodley Park. For a taste of campus life, you might choose lodging in Foggy Bottom; the accommodations near Pennsylvania Avenue and Washington Circle border George Washington University's widening campus. And if you're a serious shopper, Georgetown should be your top choice, with Dupont Circle as your second pick.

Within each neighborhood heading, this chapter further organizes hotels by rate categories, based on their lowest peak rates for standard double rooms: **Very Expensive** (from about $400 and up); **Expensive** (from about $250); **Moderate** (from about $175); and **Inexpensive** (anything under $175). But these categories are intended as a general guideline only—rates can rise and fall dramatically, depending on how busy the hotel is. It's often possible to obtain a special package or a better rate than the first rate quoted, as the next section explains.

SAVING ON YOUR HOTEL ROOM

The **rack rate** is the maximum rate that a hotel charges for a room. Hardly anybody pays this price, however, except during peak season. Every hotel usually offers ways for customers to pay a lower rate than the published rate. These general guidelines can help lower the cost of your room:

- **Ask about special rates or other discounts.** Always ask whether a room less expensive than the first one quoted is available, or whether any special rates apply to you. You may qualify for corporate, government, student, military, senior, or other discounts, and these can be substantial. Mention membership in AAA, AARP, frequent-flier programs, or trade unions, which may entitle you to special deals as well.
- **Dial direct.** When booking a room in a chain hotel, you'll often get a better deal by calling the individual hotel's reservation desk rather than the chain's main number. *Warning:* You'll want to confirm that you are talking to someone on-site at the hotel, even if you've dialed a local "202" phone number. Increasingly, chain hotels are outsourcing the bulk of their reservation bookings to regional offices, whose staff are simply not informed enough to answer basic questions about a particular hotel.
- **Book online.** Many hotels offer Internet-only discounts or supply rooms to Priceline, Travelocity, or Expedia at rates lower than the ones you can get through the hotel itself.
- **Remember the law of supply and demand.** Washington's downtown hotels are busiest during the week and when Congress is in session, so you can expect the best

discounts over the weekend and on holidays, when Congress heads out of town. Most hotels have high-season and low-season prices, and booking the day after high season ends can mean good deals.

- **Look into group or long-stay discounts.** If you come as part of a large group, you should be able to negotiate a bargain rate, because the hotel can then guarantee occupancy in a number of rooms. Likewise, if you're planning a long stay (at least 5 days), you might qualify for a discount. As a general rule, expect 1 night free after a 7-night stay.
- **Avoid excess charges and hidden costs.** D.C. hotels charge unbelievable rates for overnight parking—usually more than $25 a night—plus tax! So if you can avoid driving to D.C., you can save yourself parking expenses. Use your own cellphone, pay phones, or prepaid phone cards instead of dialing direct from hotel phones, which usually have exorbitant rates, as do the room's minibar offerings. Finally, ask about local taxes and service charges. The D.C. hotel sales tax is a whopping 14.5%, merchandise sales tax is 5.75%, and food and beverage tax is 10%, all of which can rapidly increase the cost of a room.
- **Book an efficiency room.** A room with a kitchenette allows you to shop for groceries and cook your own meals—a big money saver, especially for families on long stays.
- **Consider enrolling in hotel "frequent-stay" programs,** which aim to win the loyalty of repeat customers. Frequent guests can now accumulate points or credits to earn free hotel nights, airline miles, in-room amenities, merchandise, tickets to concerts and events, and discounts on sporting facilities. Perks are awarded not only by many chain hotels and motels (Hilton Honors and Marriott Rewards, to name two), but also by individual inns and B&Bs. Many chain hotels partner with other hotel chains, car-rental firms, airlines, and credit card companies to give consumers additional incentive to do repeat business.

LANDING THE BEST ROOM

Somebody has to get the best room in the house; it might as well be you. You can start by joining the hotel's frequent-guest program, which may make you eligible for upgrades. A hotel-branded credit card usually gives its owner "silver" or "gold" status in frequent-guest programs for free. Always ask about a corner room. They're often larger and quieter, with more windows and light; and they often cost the same as standard rooms. When you make your reservation, ask if the hotel is renovating; if it is, request a room away from the construction. Ask about nonsmoking rooms, rooms with views, rooms with twin, queen-, or king-size beds. If you're a light sleeper, request a quiet room away from vending machines, elevators, restaurants, bars, and dance clubs. Ask for one of the rooms that have been most recently renovated or redecorated. If you aren't happy with your room when you arrive, say so; most properties will try to accommodate you.

USING A LOCAL RESERVATIONS SERVICE

If you suffer from information overload and would rather someone else do the research and bargaining, you can always turn to one of the following reputable—and free!—local reservations services:

- **VisitDC.com** (© **800/VISIT-DC** [847-4832] or 202/452-1270; www.visitdc.com) will find you a hotel that meets your specific requirements and is within your price range. Formerly called Capitol Reservations, the 26-year-old service works with about 100 area hotels that have been screened for cleanliness, safe locations, and other desirability factors; you can check rates and book online.

- **WDCAHotels.com** (© 800/503-3330 or 202/289-2220; www.wdcahotels.com), formerly known as Washington, D.C., Accommodations, has been in business for 25 years and, in addition to finding lodgings, can advise you about transportation and general tourist information and even work out itineraries.
- **BedandBreakfastDC.com** (© 877/893-3233 or 413/582-9888; www.bedand breakfastdc.com), in business since 1978, works with more than 30 homes, inns, guesthouses, and unhosted furnished apartments to find lodging for visitors.

---

1 BEST HOTEL BETS

- **Best Historic Hotel:** The **Willard InterContinental** celebrated its 100th anniversary in 2006, as the "new" 12-story Willard, replacing the original, smaller "City Hotel" that existed here between 1816 and 1906. Whether known as the City or the Willard, the hotel has hosted nearly every U.S. president since Franklin Pierce in 1853, including two presidents who lived here for a time—Lincoln in 1861 and Calvin Coolidge in 1923. President Ulysses S. Grant liked to unwind with cigar and brandy in the Willard lobby after a hard day in the Oval Office, and literary luminaries like Mark Twain and Charles Dickens used to hang out in the Round Robin bar. The hotel continues to draw political, society, business, and cultural icons today. See p. 92.
- **Best Location:** Three contenders in three different locations win this category: For a true heart-of-the-city experience, the **Hotel Monaco** (p. 90) can't be beat. The hotel lies halfway between the White House and Capitol Hill, across the street from the Verizon Center and two Smithsonian museums, and in the middle of a neighborhood known for its many restaurants, shops, and clubs. If you desire proximity to the White House, no hotel gets closer than the **Hay-Adams** (p. 94), right across Lafayette Square from the Executive Mansion. And if you'd like to be within walking distance of both Capitol Hill and the National Mall, the **Residence Inn Capitol** (p. 88) is a good choice. Also see the **W Washington, D.C. Hotel,** described below, and on p. 91).
- **Best Trendy Hotel: Donovan House** (p. 96), which arrived in March 2008, and the **W Washington, D.C. Hotel** (p. 91), which debuted in July 2009, represent the ying and yang of trendiness. Donovan House's style is offbeat, with its cocoon spiral showers and leather-wrapped beds, rooftop bar, and "People Are Art" motif. The W Hotel is chicly trendy, from the Bliss Spa on the lower level, to the canopied rooftop bar overlooking the White House, and in between a Jean-Georges Vongerichten restaurant and *très moderne* guest rooms.
- **Best Place for a Romantic Getaway:** The posh **Ritz-Carlton Georgetown** (p. 110) in the heart of Georgetown is just enough off the beaten track to make you feel like you've really escaped; its small size, only 86 rooms, adds an air of intimacy. While the Ritz's spa, sexy bar, lovely rooms, and solicitous service may tempt you to stay put, it would be a shame to pass up the chance to stroll hand in hand along Georgetown's quaint streets to dine close by at one of the city's most romantic restaurants—1789 (p. 154) and La Chaumiere (p. 157) among them.
- **Best Washington Insider Hotel:** The **Willard** wins again. This is where the term "lobbyists" came into popular use, after all. When President Ulysses S. Grant enjoyed a brandy in the Willard lobby, he was often besieged by politicians and businessmen clamoring for his attention. "Lobbyists," Grant called them, making famous a term

someone else had coined. Lobbyists still come and go here, as do high-ranking government officials, television news anchors, and visiting heads of state. Be sure to duck your head into the Round Robin bar. See p. 92.

See p. 92.

 Tips **Staying Green in D.C.**

D.C. hotels are taking the green cause to heart, though with varying degrees of fervor. The Starwood Capital Group is planning to build a luxury, thoroughly organic, "green-minded" hotel, one of its "1 Hotels" in the West End, with a 2011 anticipated completion date, at which time the hotel will surely be included in these pages. Until then, you have many eco-conscious lodging options from which to choose. The following list, though not comprehensive, is a good starting point for assessing the level of ecological commitment at some D.C. hotels.

- **Four Seasons** (p. 109) has a behind-the-scenes program that directs various departments toward practices that conserve energy and reduce, reuse, and recycle, whenever possible. The hotel's "It Is Easy Being Green" program allows guests the option of keeping the same bed linens and towels during their stay. In addition, the hotel's Bourbon Steak restaurant (p. 153) cultivates its own herb garden on the property, for use in cooking.

- **All Kimpton Hotels in D.C.** participate in the chain's EarthCare program, which uses low-flow toilets, sinks, and shower heads; non-toxic cleaning agents; in-room recycle bins; and a service that allows guests to keep the same linens and towels during their stay, saving on water and energy use. Individual properties go a bit further; for instance, the Hotel Madera has an on-site hybrid car available for guest use and provides free parking to guests whose own cars are hybrids; the Hotel Palomar has adopted Dupont Circle, the central park around which traffic drives, and works with the National Park Service to keep it in fine green shape.

- **The Willard InterContinental** (p. 92) buys all of its electricity from such renewable energy sources as wind power. A hybrid car is available for guest transport. All of the hotel's light bulbs are now low-impact fluorescents. The hotel invests in local environmental causes, such as the cleanup of the much-polluted Anacostia River and maintenance of Pershing Park, across the street from the Willard. Read more about its program at www.willarddc.com/sd.

- **Phoenix Park Hotel** (p. 89) has a green procurement program, "Irish Green Goes Extreme," which includes recycling goods and purchasing recycled goods as much as possible; using energy-efficient light bulbs and sensors, timers, and non-toxic cleaning supplies; and installing low-flow shower heads, sinks, and toilets. The hotel also offers guests the option of keeping the same linens and towels during their stay to conserve water and energy, and reduce the use of detergents.

- All **Marriott properties,** in D.C. and elsewhere, have low-flow toilets and shower heads. The chain is moving toward replacing all standard light bulbs with fluorescent lighting and is partnering with Conservation International to determine ways to reduce its carbon footprint.

- **Best Inexpensive Hotel:** The boutique **Normandy Hotel**'s rates start at $99 and though they can go as high as $349, rates still tend to be less expensive here than at other D.C. hotels offering the same degree of personable service and chicness. Extras like an exercise room and pool are available at its sister hotel around the corner. A multitude of restaurants, bars, art galleries, and shops lie within walkable reach in the Dupont Circle and Adams-Morgan neighborhoods. See p. 100.

- **Best Service:** The **Four Seasons** (p. 109) staff pampers you relentlessly and greets you by name. The hotel also offers an "I Need It Now" program that delivers any of 100 or more left-at-home essentials (tweezers, batteries, cuff links, electric hair curlers, and so on) to you in 3 minutes, at no cost. And then there's the **Mandarin Oriental** (p. 85), where staffers speak in hushed tones, almost bowing; the spa features something called an amethyst steam room; and the very design of the hotel follows the principles of Feng shui, the better to attract good fortune.

- **Best Health Club:** The **Ritz-Carlton, Washington, D.C.**'s is still the best fitness center in the city. Its two-level, 100,000-square-foot Sports Club/LA boasts state-of-the-art weight-training equipment and free weights, two regulation-size basketball courts and four squash courts, an indoor heated swimming pool and aquatics pool with sun deck, all sorts of exercise and dance classes, personal trainers, the full-service Splash Spa and Roche Salon, and a restaurant and café. See p. 108.

- **Best Views:** The **Hay-Adams** has such a great, unobstructed view of the White House that the Secret Service comes over regularly to do security sweeps of the place. Ask for a room on the H Street side of the hotel, on floors six through eight. See p. 94. For a coveted overlook of Washington's famous cherry blossoms in spring or of the Tidal Basin and Jefferson Memorial year-round, stay at the **Mandarin Oriental,** specifying a room offering that particular view. See p. 85. And the new **W Washington, D.C. Hotel** is the only lodging whose views take in both the White House and the Washington Monument, from its rooftop bar as well as from specific guest rooms. See p. 91.

- **Best for Travelers with Disabilities:** The **Omni Shoreham Hotel** has 41 specially equipped rooms for guests with disabilities, about half with roll-in showers, and vibrating door knockers and pillows, and flashing lights to alert guests when fire alarms are sounding (all of these devices are available, but you must ask for them). The hotel carries copies of disabilityguide.org's *Access Entertainment* guide, which offers detailed information about how to travel around and enjoy D.C., if you have limited mobility. See p. 111.

2 CAPITOL HILL/THE MALL

VERY EXPENSIVE

Mandarin Oriental, Washington, D.C. ★★★ The location of this fabulously posh hotel is in a government-building neighborhood, a few blocks from the National Mall and Smithsonian museums, a short cab ride to the Capitol. By day, the location is ultra-convenient; at night, not at all. These streets are dark, not meant for strolling; and there's nothing to do.

Never mind. Once you're ensconced inside the Mandarin, you may have no inclination to leave. Rather than roam the neighborhood, you may enjoy rambling around the hotel's terraces of landscaped gardens, whose views of the Tidal Basin, marina, and Jefferson Memorial, are unmatched by any other D.C. hotel. In fact, a footbridge on the

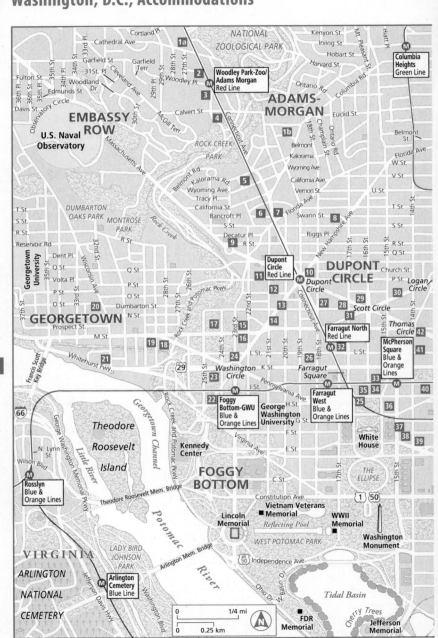

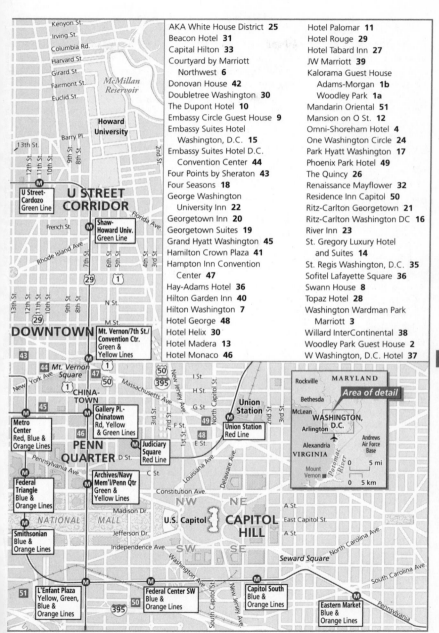

AKA White House District **25**
Beacon Hotel **31**
Capital Hilton **33**
Courtyard by Marriott
  Northwest **6**
Donovan House **42**
Doubletree Washington **30**
The Dupont Hotel **10**
Embassy Circle Guest House **9**
Embassy Suites Hotel
  Washington, D.C. **15**
Embassy Suites Hotel D.C.
  Convention Center **44**
Four Points by Sheraton **43**
Four Seasons **18**
George Washington
  University Inn **22**
Georgetown Inn **20**
Georgetown Suites **19**
Grand Hyatt Washington **45**
Hamilton Crown Plaza **41**
Hampton Inn Convention
  Center **47**
Hay-Adams Hotel **36**
Hilton Garden Inn **40**
Hilton Washington **7**
Hotel George **48**
Hotel Helix **30**
Hotel Madera **13**
Hotel Monaco **46**

Hotel Palomar **11**
Hotel Rouge **29**
Hotel Tabard Inn **27**
JW Marriott **39**
Kalorama Guest House
  Adams-Morgan **1b**
  Woodley Park **1a**
Mandarin Oriental **51**
Mansion on O St. **12**
Omni-Shoreham Hotel **4**
One Washington Circle **24**
Park Hyatt Washington **17**
Phoenix Park Hotel **49**
The Quincy **26**
Renaissance Mayflower **32**
Residence Inn Capitol **50**
Ritz-Carlton Georgetown **21**
Ritz-Carlton Washington DC **16**
River Inn **23**
St. Gregory Luxury Hotel
  and Suites **14**
St. Regis Washington, D.C. **35**
Sofitel Lafayette Square **36**
Swann House **8**
Topaz Hotel **28**
Washington Wardman Park
  Marriott **3**
Willard InterContinental **38**
Woodley Park Guest House **2**
W Washington, D.C. Hotel **37**

WHERE TO STAY

5

CAPITOL HILL/THE MALL

property actually crosses the water to deposit you on the lip of the Tidal Basin, within steps of the Jefferson—and in spring, in the midst of the famous blossoming cherry trees. Many consider the hotel's renowned **CityZen** restaurant (p. 120) the best in the city.

Hotel decor richly combines Asian and American traditions, with each guest room laid out in accordance with the principles of Feng shui. Guest rooms situated in the corner on each floor overlook both the city and the water, but all rooms are generously sized, measuring upward of 400 square feet. Triple-paned windows and a recycling program for guests are two aspects of the Mandarin's eco-friendly efforts.

1330 Maryland Ave. SW (at 12th St.), Washington, DC 20024. (C) **888/888-1778** or 202/554-8588. Fax 202/554-8999. www.mandarinoriental.com/washington. 400 units. $495–$695 double; $1,150–$8,000 suite. Children age 12 and under stay free in parent's room. For information about special packages, call the hotel directly or check the website. AE, DC, DISC, MC, V. Parking $38. Metro: Smithsonian (Independence Ave. & 12th St. SW exit). Pets under 40 lb. accepted, with certain restrictions. **Amenities:** 2 restaurants, 2 bars; babysitting; children's programs; concierge; concierge-level rooms; world class health club & full-service spa, with heated indoor pool, sauna & Jacuzzi; room service; complimentary Wi-Fi in public spaces. *In room:* A/C, TV/DVD, CD player, hair dryer, minibar, MP3 docking station, robes, Wi-Fi ($15/day).

EXPENSIVE

The Hotel George ★★   Behind a facade of stainless steel, limestone, and glass is one of Washington's hippest places to stay, and one within easy reach of both the Capitol and Union Station. Clientele leans toward powerbrokers and celebrities, who often meet with Washington's version of the same in the hotel's **Bistro Bis** restaurant (p. 121). Decor in the oversize guest rooms (around 260 square feet) is minimalist, all creamy white and modern, with fluffy vanilla-colored comforters resting on over-large beds. Like all Kimpton hotels, the George offers in-room spa services, reservable when you book your room. The smoke-free hotel has three one-bedroom suites. The George adheres to the Kimpton hotels' EarthCare program (for details, see "Staying Green in D.C." box).

15 E St. NW (at N. Capitol St.), Washington, DC 20001. (C) **800/576-8331** or 202/347-4200. Fax 202/347-4213. www.hotelgeorge.com. 139 units. Weekdays $289–$659 double; weekends $169–$349 double. Year-round $750–$1,050 suite. Children 17 and under stay free in parent's room. Rates include hosted evening wine hour. Ask about seasonal and corporate rates, and the "Hot Dates, Great Rates" deal. Extra person $25. AE, DC, DISC, MC, V. Parking $40 plus tax overnight. Metro: Union Station (Massachusetts Ave. NW exit). Pets accepted. **Amenities:** Restaurant, bar; children's amenity program; concierge; small exercise room w/steam rooms; room service. *In room:* A/C, TV, CD/DVD player, hair dryer, minibar, MP3 docking station, robes, umbrella, free Wi-Fi.

Residence Inn Capitol   Four Native American tribes are 49% owners of this hotel, which makes this the first multitribal partnership with nontribal partners on land off a reservation. During the day, you can easily walk to the Smithsonian National Museum of the American Indian and other Mall museums, as well as to Capitol Hill; at night, however, this part of town shuts down. Its proximity to the Hill and the Mall translates into a steady clientele of government employees and tourists.

Hotel features mimic the look of the Indian Museum. Guest rooms evince a Native American cultural motif through the use of etched-wood headboards, artwork, and other design elements. This is an all-suite hotel whose rooms are twice the size of standard hotel rooms, starting with the studio suites, and increasing in size from there. All units have fully equipped kitchens. The hotel's eco-friendly practices are too many to list here, but include generating 50% of its electricity from wind power, use of fluorescent lighting throughout the hotel, and carbon offset and guest recycling programs.

333 E St. SW (at 4th St.), Washington, DC 20024. (C) **800/331-3131** or 202/484-8280. Fax 202/554-0484. www.capitolmarriott.com. 233 suites. Peak: $359 studio, $379 1-bedroom suite, $399 2-bedroom suite.

Off-peak: $149 studio, $159 1-bedroom suite, $399 2-bedroom suite. Call about seasonal and long-term rates. Rates include hot breakfast daily, light dinner Mon–Wed, and grocery delivery service. AE, DC, DISC, MC, V. Parking $30. Metro: Federal Center Southwest or L'Enfant Plaza. Pets accepted for a fee. **Amenities:** Concierge; health club with fitness center, indoor pool, whirlpool, and sun deck; free Wi-Fi in public spaces. *In room:* A/C, TV, hair dryer, free Internet, full kitchen.

MODERATE

Phoenix Park Hotel ★   The Phoenix Park is one in a cluster of hotels across from Union Station and 2 blocks from the Capitol, making this a favorite of business folks here to meet with government officials. It's distinguished by its popular and authentic Irish pub, the **Dubliner** (p. 266), which helps set the tone of Irish hospitality for the entire property. A major renovation completed in 2007 re-did the guest rooms in sage, gold, or dusky rose hues, and added a pillow-topped mattress and high-definition, flatscreen TV. Irish decorative accents include linens and artwork. Rooms are all standard size, though of different configurations. Best rooms are on the top floors (the hotel has nine) facing Massachusetts Avenue, toward the North Capitol Street end, with views of the National Postal Museum and a smidgen of Union Station. Or book one of the six suites, available in one- or two-story units, with kitchenette, working fireplace, and spiral staircase. The Phoenix is big in the Green movement—read about it in the "Staying Green in D.C." box earlier in this chapter.

520 N. Capitol St. NW (at Massachusetts Ave.), Washington, DC 20001. ✆ **800/824-5419** or 202/638-6900. Fax 202/393-3236. www.phoenixparkhotel.com. 149 units. Peak $149–$489 double; Off-peak $99–$299 double; year-round from $699 suite. Extra person $30. Children 16 and under stay free in parent's room. AE, DC, DISC, MC, V. Parking $40. Metro: Union Station (Massachusetts Ave. NW exit). **Amenities:** Irish pub; small exercise room; room service. *In room:* A/C, TV, hair dryer, minibar, free Wi-Fi.

Tips   ## When All Else Fails

If your luck and time are running out and you still haven't found a place to stay, these ideas are worth a try:

- **Call one of the free reservations services** at the beginning of this chapter, including the Bed & Breakfast Accommodations service. Talk to someone "on location" who can work with you to find a place.
- **Check out the Vacation Rental by Owner website, www.vrbo.com**, and enter "Washington" as your city to read about furnished apartments for rent around the city.
- **Consider house swapping.** Try **HomeLink International** (Homelink.org), the largest and oldest home-swapping organization, founded in 1953, with more than 13,000 listings worldwide ($110 for a yearly membership). **www.homexchangevacation.com** and **InterVac.com** are also reliable.
- **Call Washington's tourism bureau, Destination D.C.** (✆ **202/789-7000**), and ask the tourist rep for the names and numbers of any **new or about-to-open hotels.** If the rep isn't sure, ask her to check with the marketing director. Up-and-coming hotels may have available rooms, for the simple reason that few people know about them.
- **Consider lodging outside the city.** See separate box in this chapter, "Inside and Outside the Beltway, Beyond-D.C. Hotel Options," p. 113.

3 PENN QUARTER

VERY EXPENSIVE

Hotel Monaco Washington D.C. ★★   Museum-like in appearance, the Monaco occupies a four-story, all marble mid-19th-century building, half of which was designed by Robert Mills, the architect for the Washington Monument. The other half was designed by Thomas Walter, one of the architects for the U.S. Capitol. The halves connect seamlessly, enclosing a landscaped courtyard.

Spacious guest rooms measure about 400 square feet and feature vaulted ceilings and long windows hung with charcoal-and-white patterned drapes. Eclectic furnishings include neoclassical armoires and three-legged desks. (The hotel's historic status precludes it from installing closets; hence, the armoires, which some guests say are too small.) Recently re-vamped décor marries gold, espresso, and deep red colors.

Interior rooms overlook the courtyard and the restaurant, **Poste** (p. 131); exterior rooms view city sights, the higher up the better. The interior rooms on the first floor are somewhat subterranean (a window close to the ceiling lets in some light). Best rooms are the 32 Monte Carlos, which are nearly twice the standard size, but cost just an extra $30; located on the second and third floors, these rooms have huge windows, letting in amazing light and overlooking great sights. When you stay at the Monaco, you're not just downtown, you're part of the scene.

700 F St. NW (at 7th St.), Washington, DC 20004. ✆ **800/649-1202** or 202/628-7177. Fax 202/628-7277. www.monaco-dc.com. 184 units. Weekdays $369–$609 double, $509–$1,200 suite; weekends $169–$369 double, $269–$800 suite. Extra person $20. Children 17 and under stay free in parent's room. Rates include complimentary organic coffee in morning and a hosted evening wine hour. AE, DC, DISC, MC, V. Parking $34. Metro: Gallery Place (7th and F sts. NW exit). Pets welcome—they get VIP treatment, with their own registration cards at check-in, maps of neighborhood fire hydrants and parks, and gourmet puppy and kitty treats. **Amenities:** Restaurant, bar; children's amenity program; concierge; spacious fitness center w/flatscreen TVs; room service. *In room:* A/C, TV w/pay movies, CD player, hair dryer, minibar, robes, free Wi-Fi.

JW Marriott Hotel on Pennsylvania Avenue ★   A $40 million renovation completed in 2009 has transformed this 25-year-old property into a thoroughly modern Marriott. Changes include leather-wrapped columns and flat-screen TV-covered media walls in the atrium lobby, and a plug-in technology panel in each guest room that allows guests to split the TV screen and simultaneously watch TV and check email..

The hotel is primely located on Pennsylvania Avenue near theaters, the White House, the National Mall, and restaurants. Ask for a room on floors 3 through 15 facing Pennsylvania Avenue for views of the avenue and of the Washington Monument beyond. Floors 7 and 12 on the Pennsylvania Avenue side have balconies; floors 14 and 15 are the concierge level. Politicos and corporate types fill the hotel on weekdays, families take over on weekends. Like all Marriott properties, this one participates in eco-friendly practices by offering guests carbon offset options and by replacing toilet paper, towels, pens, and other supplies with environmentally better alternatives, to name just two initiatives.

1331 Pennsylvania Ave. NW (at E St.), Washington, DC 20004. ✆ **800/228-9290** or 202/393-2000. Fax 202/626-6991. www.marriott.com/wasjw. 772 units. Peak (Feb 23–Jun 27) $399–$489; Off-peak (Jun 28–Feb 22) $279–$489 double; year-round from $650 suites. Extra person free. AE, DC, DISC, MC, V. Valet parking $39. Metro: Metro Center (13th St. NW exit). **Amenities:** 2 restaurants, Starbucks; concierge; executive-level rooms; extensive health club w/full fitness center, indoor swimming pool, whirlpool, and sauna; room service. *In room:* A/C, TV, hair dryer, Internet ($13/day), minibar.

Family-Friendly Hotels

Embassy Suites Hotel Washington, D.C. (p. 105) Close to both a Red line and a Blue line Metro station (the zoo is on the Red line; the Smithsonian museums are on the Blue line) and within walking distance of Georgetown, this hotel lets your kids sleep on the pullout sofa in the separate living room. Rooms have some kitchen facilities, but the complimentary breakfast in the atrium is unbelievable. There are also an indoor pool and a free game room. For all of the same reasons, but a different location (within walking distance of Penn Quarter attractions), also consider the **Embassy Suites Hotel D.C. Convention Center** (p. 92).

Four Seasons (p. 109) Spare the parent and spoil the child at this luxurious hotel, whose amenities for kids includes age-appropriate snacks and amusements, from fuzzy duckies and coloring books and crayons for the under-6 bunch, to Fandex and *Teen Vogue* for teenagers. The hotel's Georgetown location makes it a good choice for teens, especially if they like to shop; its location on the C&O Canal recommends it for family hikes along the towpath. And the nearby waterfront offers fun for all in the form of narrated cruises along the Potomac. (The Four Seasons does have its own pool, but it's a lap pool and not particularly kid-friendly.)

Omni Shoreham Hotel (p. 111) Adjacent to Rock Creek Park, the Omni is within walking distance of the zoo and Metro and is equipped with a large outdoor pool and kiddie pool. Children receive a goodie bag at check-in, and the concierge has a supply of board games (no charge to borrow, just remember to return).

W Washington, D.C. Hotel ★★ The W wants to blow you away (you, the hotel guest, and all who drop by), and it doesn't mess around. Its posh, year-round rooftop bar is unique in serving unbeatable views of the White House and the Washington Monument, alongside that dry martini. Its Sweat fitness center offers similar landmark sights, as you work out on treadmill, elliptical, or bike. The hotel claims the capital's only Bliss Spa, known for its over-the-top treatments, "peeling groovy" to "hangover herbie" facials, and the unending brownie buffet. A wine bar opens to a sidewalk terrace on Pennsylvania Ave. Renowned Jean-Georges Vongerichten is the chef behind the hotel's J&G Steakhouse; make your reservation now. Guest rooms are of varying configurations and cross ultra-modern, ice-white furnishings with antique gold and pinstriped accents. Best are those that wrap around the corner of the hotel, where 15th Street meets Pennsylvania Avenue The Living Room (lobby, to you and me), with grand arches reaching two stories high, nearly touching the ornate cornices, is a splendid reminder of the fact that this used to be the Hotel Washington, a historic property whose original architectural features the W has taken pains to preserve. The W, with wine bar, spa, rooftop bar, and foodie restaurant is an in-town destination as well as hotel, so if that aspect appeals, consider a stay.

15th St. and Pennsylvania Ave. NW, Washington, DC 20004. ✆ **202/661-2400** or 877/WHOTELS. Fax 202/661-2425. www.whotels.com/washingtondc. 317 units. $469–$699 double; $1,000–$10,000 suites. Base rate allows up to 4 people in room. Book online for best offers and rates. AE, DC, DISC, MC, V. Parking

$40. Metro: Metro Center (13th St. NW exit). Dogs and cats under 40 lb. and service dogs welcome, with $25 charge plus non-refundable $100 cleaning fee. **Amenities:** Restaurant, 4 bars; concierge; state-of-the-art, fully equipped fitness center; room service; over-the-top spa with retail store; free Wi-Fi in lobby. *In room:* A/C, TV/DVD, CD player, hair dryer, minibar, MP3 docking station, Wi-Fi ($15/day).

Willard InterContinental Washington ★★★ This is one of D.C.'s finest hotels, and certainly its most famous. Its magnificent lobby and grand Willard Room (until recently the hotel's main restaurant, now a special event space) are favorite settings for movie directors; its illustrious history includes the fact that two presidents (Lincoln in 1861, Coolidge in 1923) lived here for a while: the Willard warrants visiting, even if you don't stay here. But if you do stay here, you'll find you're perfectly situated near the White House, Smithsonian museums, excellent restaurants, and theaters.

Standard-size guest rooms present a handsome decor, heavy on reproduction Federal- and Edwardian-style furnishings. (Decor may have changed by the time you read this, following a 2009 renovation.) The rooms with the best views are the oval suites overlooking Pennsylvania Avenue to the Capitol and the rooms fronting Pennsylvania Avenue. Rooms facing the courtyard are the quietest.

The Willard's designation as a National Historic Landmark in 1974 and magnificent restoration in the 1980s helped revitalize Pennsylvania Avenue and this part of town. Stop in at the Round Robin Bar for a mint julep (introduced here), and listen to barman Jim Hewes spin tales about all the people who have stopped or stayed here, from Mark Twain to Bill Clinton. Or check out the Willard's Scotch bar, added in 2009, featuring one of the largest single malt whiskey collections in the region.

Although the Willard's main clientele are heads of state and corporations doing business with various government agencies, the hotel attracts nearly as many getaway travelers, who appreciate the new Red Door Spa, charming **Café du Parc** (p. 129), and schedule of seasonal festivities (Christmas caroling, a cherry blossom-themed afternoon tea in spring).

The Willard has won several awards recognizing its sustainability program; read about it in the "Staying Green in D.C." box earlier in this chapter.

1401 Pennsylvania Ave. NW (at 14th St.), Washington, DC 20004. ✆ **800/827-1747** or 202/628-9100. Fax 202/637-7326. www.washington.interconti.com. 332 units. Peak (Mar 1–Jun 30 and Sept 13–Dec 31) weekdays from $599, weekends from $339 double; Off peak (Jan 1–Feb 28 and Jul 1–Sept 12) weekdays from $299, weekends from $229 double. Suites from $479 off-peak to $849 peak. Ask about special promotions and packages. AE, DC, DISC, MC, V. Parking $35. Metro: Metro Center (13th St. NW exit). Small pets accepted. **Amenities:** Cafe w/seasonal terrace, 2 bars, tearoom; babysitting; children's programs; concierge; thoroughly equipped and luxurious Red Door health club & spa w/steam room, Jacuzzi, sauna; room service. *In room:* A/C, TV, CD player, fridge, hair dryer, minibar, MP3 docking station, robes, Wi-Fi ($4.95/hr. to $11/24 hr.).

EXPENSIVE

Embassy Suites Hotel D.C. Convention Center ★ (Kids) Business is booming in Washington; and this hotel is booming along with it, thanks to its clever location a short walk from both the convention center and the heart of the Penn Quarter. The hotel often sells out—with families during extended school breaks, and with conventioneers at other times. The suites average 550 square feet in size, each with the living room and bedroom separated by the bathroom. Decor is fresh and upbeat, employing light woods, earth tones, and glass accents. Each living room has a pullout sofa. Common areas in the hotel are also attractive, from the glass- and wood-paneled, six-story-high atrium, to the restaurant, in whose sunroom a stunning complimentary breakfast is served daily. The hotel hosts a nightly, complimentary cocktail reception in the two-level bar. The hotel's exercise room and pool are on the second floor, where wide windows overlook D.C.'s downtown. Embassy Suites recycles bottles and paper as part of its sustainability program.

900 10th St. NW (btw. New York Ave. and K St. NW), Washington, DC 20001. ⓒ **800/EMBASSY** (362-2779) or 202/739-2001. Fax 202/739-2099. www.washingtonconventioncenter.embassysuites.com. 384 units. Peak weekdays $279–$399, weekends $199–$279 double; Off-peak weekdays $229–$329, weekends $159–$209 double. Extra person $25. Children 17 and under stay free in parent's room. Book online or call direct for best rates. AE, DC, DISC, MC, V. Valet parking $34. Metro: Metro Center (11th St. NW exit). **Amenities:** Restaurant, bar; concierge; fitness center with cardio equipment, free weights, indoor pool, and whirlpool; free Internet use in business center. *In room:* A/C, TV w/pay movies, fridge, hair dryer, Internet ($9.95/day), microwave, MP3 docking station.

Grand Hyatt Washington ★   With its room count of 888, the Grand Hyatt is the largest hotel near the convention center, 3 blocks away. The hotel lies between Capitol Hill and the White House, 2 blocks from the Verizon Center.

Guest rooms are average size, measuring 325 square feet, and feature a contemporary look of dark hardwood furniture and hues of brown and gold. Rooms with interior views overlook the hotel atrium; otherwise, rooms offer city views. Every guest room has a "Grand Bed," a 13-inch-thick pillowtop mattress, triple-sheeted and covered with a fluffy white duvet instead of a bedspread. The Regency Club (12th) floor is the VIP level; guests here pay an extra $60 for premium services, including access to the fitness and health club and to the 12th-floor lounge, where food and beverages are available. The fitness club is state-of-the-art, offering cardio and weight equipment; spa treatment rooms; Pilates, yoga, and aerobics classes; and massages. With total fitness in mind, this hotel is entirely smoke free, including its guest rooms. The hotel participates in a recycling program and offers guests the option of re-using linens and towels during stays of more than a day.

1000 H St. NW (at 10th St. NW), Washington, DC 20001. ⓒ **800/233-1234** or 202/582-1234. Fax 202/637-4781. www.grandhyattwashington.com. 888 units. Weekdays $199–$429 double; weekends $129–$199 double; $450–$2,500 suite. Extra person $25. Children 17 and under stay free in parent's room. Ask about special promotions and packages. AE, DC, DISC, MC, V. Valet parking $30; self-parking $24. Metro: Metro Center (11th St. NW exit). **Amenities:** 4 restaurants, 2 bars, Starbucks; concierge; executive-level rooms; health club, lap pool, steam and sauna rooms, aerobics, and spa (hotel guests pay $10 per room per day for club use); room service. *In room:* A/C, TV w/pay movies, hair dryer, minibar, MP3 docking station, Wi-Fi ($10/day or $5/hr.).

MODERATE

Hampton Inn Washington, D.C., Convention Center ★   This 13-story hotel, which opened in 2005, is 2 blocks from the convention center, within walking distance of Penn Quarter restaurants and attractions. (Though not technically "in" the Penn Quarter, the hotel lies close enough to be included.) From the saltwater aquarium on display in the airy lobby to guest rooms that feature a charcoal and chocolate-brown color scheme, fluffy duvets, ergonomic chairs, and lapboard bed trays, this Hampton Inn is a cut above the standard for this particular Hilton brand. Ask for a corner room on the Massachusetts Avenue side, high up, for best city views. In addition to standard king- and queen-size-bed rooms, the hotel has 10 studio suites, 11 two-room suites, and 20 king study suites (the suite holds both a king-size bed and a sofa bed).

901 6th St. NW (at Massachusetts Ave.), Washington, DC 20001. ⓒ **800/HAMPTON** (426-7866) or 202/842-2500. Fax 202/842-4100. www.washingtondc.hamptoninn.com. 228 units. Weekdays $201–$349 double; weekends $129–$199 double; $249–$329 suite. Extra person $10. Children 17 and under stay free in parent's room. Rates include "Hot Breakfast Buffet." AE, DC, DISC, MC, V. Parking $28 plus tax. Metro:

Gallery Place/Chinatown (7th and H sts. NW exit) or Mount Vernon Square/Convention Center. **Amenities:** Concierge; cardio fitness center w/indoor pool and spa. *In room:* A/C, TV w/pay movies, fridge, hair dryer, microwave, MP3 docking station, free Wi-Fi.

Hilton Garden Inn, Washington, D.C. Downtown   The Hilton Garden Inn, Washington, D.C. Downtown is across the street from Metro's Blue Line McPherson Square station (and three stops from the Smithsonian museums station), within a short walk of the White House. Rooms are spacious with either king-size or double beds and are designed for comfort. Each room has a cushiony chair with an ottoman and a large desk with an ergonomic chair and adjustable lighting; a dial on the side of the mattress allows guests to adjust its firmness. Guests can connect a personal laptop or MP3 player to the room's flatscreen LCD HDTV. Best for space and views are rooms facing 14th Street, at the front of the hotel. The hotel's 24-hour pantry sells essentials; the 24-hour business center allows free use of computer, faxing, and copying services. All but 14th-floor guest rooms are smoke free. Each of the hotel's 20 suites holds a small pullout sofa in the living room. Recent renovations completely re-did the restaurant, lobby and lounge, and updated the fitness center with new Precor fitness equipment, free weights, and a weight center.

815 14th St. NW (btw. H and I sts.), Washington, DC 20005. (© **877/782-9444** or 202/783-7800. Fax 202/783-7801. www.washingtondcdowntown.stayhgi.com. 300 units. Weekdays $209–$349 double, $409 suite; weekends $109–$149 double, $179 suite. Extra person $10. No more than 4 people per room. Children 17 and under stay free in parent's room. AE, DC, DISC, MC, V. Parking $30. Metro: McPherson Square (Franklin Sq./14th St. NW exit). **Amenities:** Restaurant, bar w/fireplace; 24-hr. fitness center w/ indoor pool; room service. *In room:* A/C, TV w/pay movies, fridge, hair dryer, microwave, free Wi-Fi.

4 MIDTOWN

VERY EXPENSIVE

Hay-Adams ★★★   In its 82-year history, the Hay-Adams has welcomed the world's most illustrious, from Amelia Earhart in 1928 to a certain family named Obama in January 2009, in the days leading up to the presidential inauguration. And it's no wonder that the Obamas made the Hay-Adams their temporary home. First off, the hotel lies just across Lafayette Square from the White House. In fact, the hotel's first-floor dining room and guest rooms on the sixth through eighth floors on the H Street side of the hotel overlook Lafayette Square, the White House, and the Washington Monument. Rooms facing 16th Street overlook the 1815 St. John's Episcopal Church, known as the "church of the presidents," where the Obamas sometimes attend services, as well.

Beyond its superb location and views, this classic D.C. hotel is boutique in size, comfortably sophisticated, and grandly gracious. It consistently wins awards such as its "Most Excellent Hotel in the United States and Canada" rating by *Condé Nast Johansens* in 2009.

Built in the late 1920s, the hotel's original ornate plaster moldings, ornamental fireplaces, walnut-paneled lobby, and high ceilings are still in place. Guest rooms average 385 square feet in size and present an elegant decor of sage green, off-white, beige, and gold toile fabrics; custom European linens; and marble bathrooms with brass fixtures.

The hotel has about 14 one-bedroom suites and seven junior suites. Stop in at the Off the Record bar for a drink and the chance of spying a big name in the media or administration—who knows? Maybe even the President himself.

One Lafayette Square (at 16th and H sts. NW), Washington, DC 20006. © **800/853-6807** or 202/638-6600. Fax 202/638-2716. www.hayadams.com. 145 units. Weekdays $415–$1,000 double; weekends $329–$789 double, from $799 junior suite, from $1,099 1-bedroom suite. 3rd person $30. Children 17 and under stay free in parent's room. AE, DC, DISC, MC, V. Valet parking $40. Metro: Farragut West (17th St. NW exit). Pets under 25 lb. accepted. **Amenities:** Restaurant, bar; concierge; access to local health club ($15 per day); room service. *In room:* A/C, TV w/pay movies, Bose CD player with CD assortment, hair dryer, minibar, robes, slippers, umbrella, free Wi-Fi.

Sofitel Lafayette Square, Washington, D.C. ★★

The Sofitel, like the Hay-Adams Hotel, borders Lafayette Square and is just minutes from the White House.

This early-20th-century building's distinctive façade includes decorative bronze corner panels, bas-relief sculptural panels at ground-floor level, and a decorative 12th-floor balcony. Inside, hotel staff dressed in designer uniforms greet you with *"Bonjour!"*—a hint that the French company Accor Hotels owns the Sofitel. Noted French designer Pierre-Yves Rochon styled the interior; the hotel's restaurant, Ici, serves French bistro fare.

Because of the corner location and exceptionally large windows, guest rooms are bright with natural light, and second- and third-floor rooms facing 15th or H Street boast windows that extend nearly from floor to ceiling. Rooms average 350 square feet in size, and each room sports elegantly modern decor that includes a long desk, plasma-screen TV, creamy duvet on a king-size bed (about 17 rooms have two double beds), a much-marbled bathroom, fresh flowers, and original artwork. Recycling and water conservation programs are among several of Sofitel's eco-friendly practices.

806 15th St. NW (at H St.), Washington, DC 20005. © **800/763-4835** or 202/737-8800. Fax 202/730-8500. www.sofitelwashingtondc.com. 237 units. Peak: Weekdays $295–$500 double; weekends $155–$400 double; from $495 suite; Off peak: $155–$225 double. For lowest rates at any time, call directly to the hotel and ask about specials or packages; also check out the website. Extra person $20. Children 12 and under stay free in parent's room. AE, DC, DISC, MC, V. Parking $40. Metro: McPherson Square (Vermont Ave. NW/White House exit). Pets accepted with prior approval. **Amenities:** Restaurant, bar; concierge; state-of-the-art fitness center; room service; library w/books about D.C. and Paris. *In room:* A/C, TV w/pay movies, CD player, hair dryer, minibar, MP3 docking station, robes, slippers, Wi-Fi ($9.95/day).

The St. Regis Washington, D.C. ★★

A glance to the right as you enter or leftward as you exit the St. Regis confirms that you can only be in Washington, D.C.: That's the White House, all right, staring back at you from the end of 16th Street. A 16-month, multimillion-dollar renovation completed in 2008 touched up the ornate lobby, but otherwise thoroughly re-designed the hotel's interior. Already-elegant guest rooms are more so now, with built-in, handcrafted armoires hiding the TV, minibar, wine fridge, drawers, and closets. Rooms are larger, too, measuring 350 to 470 square feet. Add plumped-up beds and sofas; golden sienna, sage, and rust tones; and antiqued desks and tables, and you've got an especially lovely place to stay the night. Don't miss ultra-cool amenities, like the television embedded behind the bathroom mirror—the picture appears within the glass. The hotel's 25 suites offer individually designed, ultra-deluxe rooms, one-bedrooms, and junior suites. The cherry on top is the new restaurant, Alain Ducasse's **Adour** (see p. 137).

926 16th and K St. NW, Washington, DC 20006. © **202/638-2626** or 866/716-8116. Fax 202/638-4231. www.stregis.com/washington. 175 units. Peak $375–$845 double; junior suite $575–$1,495; specialty suite from $3,400; 1-bedroom suite $635–$3,200. Check the website or call for holiday, off-peak, and promotional rates. 3rd person $75. Children 12 and under stay free in parent's room. AE, DC, DISC, MC, V. Valet parking $45. Metro: Farragut West (17th St. NW exit) or Farragut North (K St. NW exit). Pets under 25 lb. allowed for $100 nonrefundable fee, plus $25 per day. **Amenities:** Restaurant, bar; babysitting; signature butler service; children's programs; concierge; exercise room; room service. *In room:* A/C, TV w/pay

movies, Bose radio, DVD/CD player, fridge, hair dryer, minibar, MP3 docking station, robes, slippers, umbrella, Wi-Fi ($13/day).

EXPENSIVE

Capital Hilton ★ Located just 2 blocks from the White House, the hotel has hosted 13 presidents since it opened in 1943. Unfortunately, the hotel's historic stature translated into "old in appearance," for a while there. But now the Capital Hilton is in the midst of a major renovation scheduled for completion by year's end 2010. Among much needed improvements are new landscaping and porte-cochere lighting at the 16th Street main entrance and the replacement of the Capital City Club & Spa's old exercise machines with state-of-the-art Precor equipment. (The club's K St.-front location will not change, so you'll still be able to work your buns off while watching the downtown Washington scene; nor will the cost change: Use of the club is free to certain Hilton HHonors guests and $10/day, $25/maximum, for longer stays, for others.) Best change of all is the sophisticatedly fresh look of guest rooms, courtesy of handsome new mahogany finishes, recessed panels, Williamsburg and Federal-style color palettes, black-and-white photographs of D.C. landmarks, and brushed nickel finishes. Corner rooms on the 16th Street side are the most spacious and offer the best city sights; a handful present a partial view of the White House. Business travelers appreciate the concierge floors (its higher floors, 10, 11, 12, and 14, also mean better views) and extensive facilities. A number of suites are available, including three with outdoor patios. The Capital Hilton is very eco-friendly; two of many examples: the hotel offers guests the option to use the same bed linens and towels for longer than overnight stays, and the hotel is committed to the Hilton chain's goal of reducing energy consumption by 10–20% by 2014.

1001 16th St. NW (btw. K and L sts.), Washington, DC 20036. (©) **800/HILTONS** (445-8667) or 202/393-1000. Fax 202/639-5784. www.capital.hilton.com. 544 units. Peak: $269–$499 double; Off-peak $139–$199 double; $45 more for Executive units; $219–$459 minisuite. Extra person $25. Children 18 and under stay free in parent's room. Weekend packages and other discounts available. AE, DC, DISC, MC, V. Parking $40. Metro: Farragut North (K St. NW exit) or McPherson Square (Vermont Ave./White House exit). Pets under 75 lb. allowed for non-refundable $75 fee. **Amenities:** Restaurant, bar; concierge; concierge-level rooms; 10,000-sq.-ft. health club & spa; room service. *In room:* A/C, TV w/pay movies, hair dryer, MP3 docking station; Wi-Fi ($13/day).

Donovan House ★★ Managed by trendy Thompson Hotels, Donovan House gets high marks for hipness, starting with the lobby: an arty chandelier/sculpture, buzzing bar scene, Italian leather chairs, and a banquette nook set in the wall endow a nightclub vibe. Ditto the guest rooms; the same ergonomic designer chairs in coffee, plum, and olive contrast with snow-white dressers and walls. A brown leather strip acts as a headboard for the bed and extends up to and across the ceiling. The pristine bathroom features a snail-like shower stall, whose cylindrical shape protrudes into the guest room—its opaque walls ensure the shower-er is not on show. "People are art" is the theme, so mirrors take the place of artwork. Floor-to-ceiling windows overlook Thomas Circle, nearby landmark churches, and cityscapes. The best spot for great views, though, is the seasonal rooftop pool and bar. Seventeen one-bedroom suites are available.

1155 14th St. NW (at Thomas Circle NW), Washington, DC 20005. (©) **800/383-6900** or 202/737-1200. Fax 202/521-1410. www.thompsonhotels.com. 193 units. Weekdays $249–$499 double; weekends $179–$459 double; from $449 suite. 3rd person $30. Children 17 and under stay free in parent's room. AE, DISC, MC, V. Valet parking $35. Metro: McPherson Sq. (Franklin Sq./14th St. NW exit). **Amenities:** Restaurant (Asian-themed), 2 bars; concierge; state-of-the-art fitness center; rooftop pool; room service. *In room:* A/C, TV w/pay movies, hair dryer, minibar, MP3 docking station, robes, Wi-Fi ($10/day).

Hamilton Crowne Plaza ★   This well-placed hotel is situated midway between the two sections of downtown: the K Street side and the revitalized Penn Quarter neighborhood surrounding the Verizon Center. The hotel's restaurant is especially popular with office workers at weekday lunch, thanks to a generous buffet of soups, salads, and rotisserie items for $19. Guest rooms feature dark-wood armoires and headboards and comfortable accommodations like the seven-layer bed. Rooms are rather small; so those with king-size beds feel a bit tight, those with two double beds a little roomier. K Street-side rooms overlook Franklin Park, and those on the upper floors offer views of the city skyline. In keeping with the times, the hotel has a designated "women's floor," accessible only to those with a special elevator key. The newly upgraded fitness center offers cardiovascular machines with built-in televisions, treadmills, and elliptical equipment.

1001 14th St. NW (at K St.), Washington, DC 20005. ✆ **800/2-CROWNE** (227-6963) or 202/682-0111. Fax 202/682-9525. www.hamiltonhoteldc.com. 318 units. Weekdays $119–$389 double, suites $300–$800; look for much lower rates on weekends. Extra person $20. Children 17 and under stay free in parent's room. AE, DC, DISC, MC, V. Parking $33. Metro: McPherson Square (Franklin Sq./14th St. NW exit). Pets accepted. **Amenities:** Restaurant (American), bar, Starbucks; concierge; executive-level rooms; fully equipped fitness center; room service. *In room:* A/C, TV w/pay movies, CD player, hair dryer, robes, Wi-Fi ($13/day).

Renaissance Mayflower ★★   The Mayflower is steeped in history: When it opened in 1925, it was the site of Calvin Coolidge's inaugural ball. President-elect FDR and family lived in room nos. 776 and 781 while waiting to move into the White House; this is where he penned the words, "The only thing we have to fear is fear itself."

Guest rooms feature silvery-green bed coverings, embroidered drapes, silk wall coverings, pillowtop mattresses, and sink-into armchairs. Each guest room has its own marble foyer, high ceiling, combination of reproduction and contemporary furnishings, and Italian marble bathroom. The Mayflower has a club level on the eighth floor, as well as 74 executive suites.

In the hotel's lovely Café Promenade, lawyers and lobbyists continue to gather for weekday power breakfasts. At cocktail time, the clubby, mahogany-paneled Town and Country Lounge is a favorite spot for locals, thanks to complimentary hors d'oeuvres and bartender Sambonn Lek's magical martinis.

1127 Connecticut Ave. NW (btw. L and M sts.), Washington, DC 20036. ✆ **800/228-7697** or 202/347-3000. Fax 202/776-9182. www.renaissancemayflower.com. 657 units. Weekdays $299–$519 double, $499–$599 suites; weekends $179–$299 double, $499–$599 suites. Rates include complimentary coffee service in Lobby Court. No charge for extra person in room. AE, DC, DISC, MC, V. Parking $39. Metro: Farragut North (L St. NW exit). Pets under 100 lb. allowed for flat $100 fee. **Amenities:** Restaurant, lobby café/lounge, bar; concierge; concierge-level rooms; fitness center; Internet ($13/day); room service. *In room:* A/C, TV w/pay movies, hair dryer, Internet ($13/day), minibar, robes.

MODERATE

Four Points by Sheraton, Washington, D.C. Downtown ★   This contemporary property offers complimentary Internet access, a 650-square-foot fitness center, and an unbeatable location close to both the convention center and the Verizon Center. Add in reasonable rates and fine hotel amenities and you've got a good choice for both business and leisure visitors.

A refurbishment in 2006 added lots of earth tones, leather, tweeds, and modern furniture, contributing to the overall stylish, retro look you see in the guest rooms. Bedding was changed, too, and now features the "Four Points" custom-designed, multilayered, pillowtop mattress. Guests have a choice of rooms with two double beds or one king-size bed. Corner rooms (there are only about 10) are a little more spacious than others. **Be forewarned:** These book first, so they are seldom available. While guest rooms offer city views, the rooftop pool presents a wider vista of the city.

1201 K St. NW (at 12th St.), Washington, DC 20005. © **888/481-7191** or 202/289-7600. Fax 202/349-2215. www.fourpoints.com/washingtondcdowntown. 265 units. Peak: $195–$450 double; Off-peak: $109–$265 double. Extra person $20. Children 12 and under stay free in parent's room. AE, DC, DISC, MC, V. Parking $35. Metro: McPherson Square (Franklin Sq./14th St. NW exit) and Metro Center (12th and G sts. exit). **Amenities:** Restaurant; bar; executive-level rooms; fitness center; indoor heated pool on rooftop; room service; free Wi-Fi in public spaces. *In room:* A/C, TV, hair dryer, free Internet.

Hotel Helix ★   A recent sprucing up refreshed decor throughout the hotel, but you can still expect to see eye-popping patterns and bright colors. Guest rooms have a minimalist feel; the platform bed is placed behind sheer drapes in an alcove (in the king deluxe rooms), leaving the two-person settee, a triangular desk, and the flatscreen TV out in the open. Roomiest are the 18 suites, each with a separate bedroom and slate-blue sectional sofas in the living room. Specialty rooms include "Eats" rooms, which have Italian cafe tables, bar stools, and a fully equipped kitchenette; kid-friendly "Bunk" rooms that have a separate bunk bed area with TV/DVD player combo; a "Flex" room that has a StairStepper; and "Zone" rooms equipped with a plasma-screen TV, high-tech stereo system, lava lamp, and lounge chair. The Helix Lounge is popular with locals, especially from May to October, when its outdoor patio is open.

1430 Rhode Island Ave. NW (btw. 14th and 15th sts.), Washington, DC 20005. © **800/706-1202** or 202/462-9001. Fax 202/332-3519. www.hotelhelix.com. 178 units. Weekdays and weekends $149–$329 double; specialty rooms: add $30 to double rate; suites: add $100 to double rate. Best rates usually Fri-Sun. Extra person $20. Children 17 and under stay free in parent's room. Rates include hosted evening "bubbly hour" (champagne). AE, DC, DISC, MC, V. Parking $33. Metro: McPherson Square (Vermont St. NW/White House exit). Pets welcome. **Amenities:** Bar/cafe; babysitting; exercise room; room service. *In room:* A/C, TV/DVD, CD player, fridge, hair dryer, minibar, free Wi-Fi.

Hotel Rouge ★   Shades of red are everywhere: in the staff's red-striped shirts, in the accent pillows on the retro furniture, and in the artwork. Rouge guest rooms have deep crimson drapes at the window and a floor-to-ceiling red "pleather" headboard for your comfortable, white-with-red-piping duvet-covered bed. The dressing room holds an Orange Crush–colored dresser, where the built-in minibar holds such red goodies as Hot Tamales candies, red wax lips, and Red Bull. Rooms are spacious enough to easily accommodate several armchairs and a large ottoman (in shades of red and gold), a number of funky little lamps, a huge mahogany-framed mirror leaning against a wall, and a 10-foot-long mahogany desk. Fifteen specialty guest rooms include "Chill Rooms," which have a chaise longue and a little sitting-room area, DVD player, and PlayStation and Wii; and "Chow Rooms," which have a microwave and refrigerator.

1315 16th St. NW (at Massachusetts Ave. NW and Scott Circle), Washington, DC 20036. © **800/738-1202** or 202/232-8000. Fax 202/667-9827. www.rougehotel.com. 137 units. Weekdays and weekends $149–$359 double; add $40 to reserve a specialty room. Best rates available on the website and by calling the 800 number and asking for promotional price. Extra person $20. Rates include complimentary bloody marys and cold pizza weekend mornings 10–11am and hosted evening wine hour weeknights 5–6pm. Children 17 and under stay free in parent's room. AE, DC, DISC, MC, V. Parking $33. Nonsmoking property. Metro: Dupont Circle (South, 19th St. NW exit). Pets welcomed and pampered. **Amenities:** Restaurant/bar; children's amenity program; modest-size fitness center; room service. *In room:* A/C, TV w/pay movies, CD/DVD player, hair dryer, minibar, robes, free Wi-Fi.

The Quincy ★ ⟨**Value**⟩   The Quincy went upscale in a renovation completed in 2007, adding pillowtop mattresses, sectional sofas, flatscreen TVs, complimentary high-speed

Internet access, and double-paned windows to all rooms. It remains a good value for all that it offers. (Another example is the free access it gives guests to the nearby, full-service Bally's Fitness Center.) The top-to-bottom transformation evinces a "conservative contemporary" decor, so that the overall design is brighter and very 21st century. Suites are large and comfortable; about 28 are equipped with full kitchens, while the rest have wet bars (minifridge, microwave, and coffeemaker). The Quincy has direct access to **Mackey's,** an Irish pub right next door, and to **Recessions,** a lounge on the lower level serving American/Mediterranean cuisine.

Lots of extended-stay guests and repeat customers bunk here and are often rewarded for it with goodies in the room or complimentary room upgrades.

1823 L St. NW, Washington, DC 20036. ✆ **800/424-2970** or 202/223-4320. Fax 202/293-4977. www.thequincy.com. 99 suites. Weekdays $169–$269; weekends $99–$189 year-round. Discounts available for long-term stays. Children 17 and under stay free in parent's room. AE, DC, DISC, MC, V. Parking $28 (in adjoining garage). Metro: Farragut North (L St. NW exit). Pets under 25 lb. accepted for $150 nonrefundable deposit. **Amenities:** Restaurant, bar; concierge; free passes to the well-equipped Bally's Fitness Center nearby; room service. *In room:* A/C, TV w/pay movies, fridge, hair dryer, microwave, free Wi-Fi.

---

5 ADAMS-MORGAN

Note: The hotels listed here are situated just north of Dupont Circle, more at the mouth of Adams-Morgan than within its actual boundaries.

EXPENSIVE

Hilton Washington ★ (**Kids**) This sprawling hotel, built in 1965, occupies 5.5 acres. By the time you read this, the hotel will have undergone a top-to-bottom renovation, leaving no room, no surface, no space untouched. Specifically, you can count on: a saline-treated outdoor pool; bedrooms brought up to date with granite bathrooms, ergonomic chairs, dark-wood furnishings, textured wall coverings, and Hilton Serenity beds; finer amenities, like Crabtree & Evelyn soaps; and state-of-the-art technology throughout the hotel.

What won't change, however, is the neighborhood. Embassies, great restaurants, and museums are just a stroll away. The hotel's vast conference facilities, though much improved, will remain vast and will still offer one of the largest hotel ballrooms on the East Coast (it accommodates more than 4,000). And the hotel's position halfway up a hill overlooking the city means that if you stay in a southside guest room on the fifth floor or higher, you'll have panoramic views of the capital.

The Hilton caters to corporate groups, some with families in tow (during the summer, the reception desk gives families a complimentary gift and lends them board games—ask for the "Vacation Station" perk), and is accustomed to coordinating meetings for thousands of attendees.

1919 Connecticut Ave. NW (at T St.), Washington, DC 20009. ✆ **800/HILTONS** (445-8667) or 202/483-3000. Fax 202/232-0438. www.washington.hilton.com. 1,070 units. Weekdays and weekends $119–$319 double; $30 more for executive rooms. Look for deals on the website or by calling Hilton's 800 number. Extra person $25. Children 18 and under stay free in parent's room. AE, DC, DISC, MC, V. Valet parking $33, self-parking $28. Metro: Dupont Circle (North, Q St. NW exit). Pets under 75 lb. allowed for a flat $75 fee. **Amenities:** Restaurant coffee kiosk, 2 bars; concierge; concierge-level rooms; extensive health club; seasonal outdoor pool; room service. *In room:* A/C, TV w/pay movies, hair dryer, Internet ($12/day), MP3 docking station.

Courtyard by Marriott Northwest Across Connecticut Avenue from the enormous Hilton Washington is this much smaller property that, like the Hilton, sits on an incline, so overlooks the city from certain rooms. Its interior has a European feel and a well-heeled appearance. Crystal chandeliers hang in the lobby and in the restaurant, and you may hear an Irish lilt from time to time (the hotel is one of three in Washington owned by the Doyle Collection Group, an Irish hotelier company). Guests tend to linger in the comfortable lounge off the lobby, where coffee is available all day.

A recent $6.5 million refurbishment replaced nearly everything in the guest rooms, which now present a comfortable and bright decor that includes cherry furniture, plush carpeting, and 25-inch TVs. All rooms have floor-to-ceiling windows, but those facing Connecticut Avenue on the sixth to ninth floors present wide-sweeping views of the city, some with views of the Washington Monument, in the distance. Especially nice are the 15 executive rooms, which are a little larger and are equipped with marble bathrooms, fax machines, and robes.

1900 Connecticut Ave. NW (at Leroy Place), Washington, DC 20009. ℂ **888/236-2427** or 202/332-9300. Fax 202/319-1793. www.doylecollection.com/courtyard or www.marriott.com. 147 units. $99–$349 double. Extra person $15. Children 17 and under stay free in parent's room. For the best deals, call direct to the hotel or go to the website. AE, DC, DISC, MC, V. Parking $28. Metro: Dupont Circle (North, Q St. NW exit). **Amenities:** Restaurant, bar; small exercise room; outdoor pool (seasonal); room service; free Wi-Fi in lobby. *In room:* A/C, TV w/pay movies, hair dryer, free Internet.

INEXPENSIVE

Kalorama Guest House This San Francisco–style B&B has two locations: a set of Victorian town houses in Adams-Morgan and two houses in nearby Woodley Park (see "Woodley Park," later in this chapter). As of 2007, all of the guest rooms at both locations have new beds.

The cozy common areas and homey guest rooms are furnished with finds from antiques stores, flea markets, and auctions. Rooms offer either double or queen-size beds. The Mintwood Place town house also has an efficiency apartment with a kitchen, telephone, and TV; one small two-room apartment with a kitchen, cable TV, and telephone; and four suites (two, two-bedroom and two "executive" suites, in which the living room and bedroom are together). At the Adams-Morgan location, unit #3 is notable for having a twin bed in one room, a full size in the other, and a large screened-in porch overlooking Kalorama Park. Each location serves an expansive complimentary breakfast. Guests have access to laundry and ironing facilities, a refrigerator, a TV, and a phone. Free Wi-Fi access is available in all of the rooms.

1854 Mintwood Place NW (btw. 19th St. and Columbia Rd.), Washington, DC 20009. ℂ **800/974-6450** or 202/667-6369. Fax 202/319-1262. www.kaloramaguesthouse.com. 29 units, 15 with private bathroom. $89–$119 double with shared bathroom; $119–$139 double with private bathroom. Extra person $10. Rates include expansive breakfast. AE, DISC, MC, V. Very limited parking $15 plus tax. Metro, Woodley Park location: Woodley Park–Zoo. Adams-Morgan location: Dupont Circle (North, Q St. NW exit). Kids 6 and older only. **Amenities:** Washer/dryer; common fridge; common TV. *In room:* A/C, free Wi-Fi access.

The Normandy Hotel ★ ⒻⒾⓃⒹⓈ This gracious hotel is a gem—a small gem, but a gem nonetheless. It lies on a very quiet street surrounded by handsome residences, the embassies of Afghanistan, Syria, Senegal, and the Alliance Francaise. But you're only a short walk from great restaurants, bars, clubs, shops, galleries, and the Dupont Circle Metro stop, to get you anywhere else you want to go. A renovation in 2009 transformed

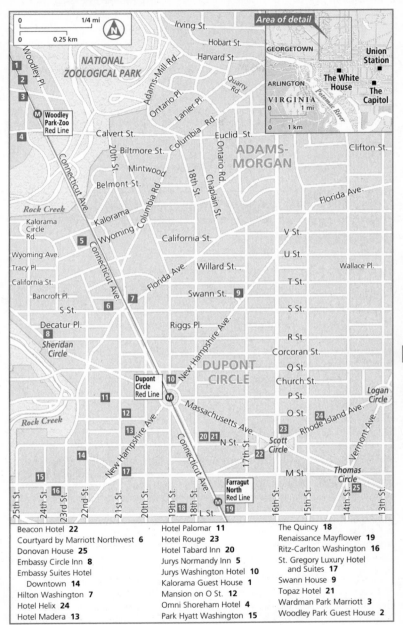

Beacon Hotel **22**
Courtyard by Marriott Northwest **6**
Donovan House **25**
Embassy Circle Inn **8**
Embassy Suites Hotel
Downtown **14**
Hilton Washington **7**
Hotel Helix **24**
Hotel Madera **13**

Hotel Palomar **11**
Hotel Rouge **23**
Hotel Tabard Inn **20**
Jurys Normandy Inn **5**
Jurys Washington Hotel **10**
Kalorama Guest House **1**
Mansion on O St. **12**
Omni Shoreham Hotel **4**
Park Hyatt Washington **15**

The Quincy **18**
Renaissance Mayflower **19**
Ritz-Carlton Washington **16**
St. Gregory Luxury Hotel
and Suites **17**
Swann House **9**
Topaz Hotel **21**
Wardman Park Marriott **3**
Woodley Park Guest House **2**

the six-story hotel from old-fashioned to chic. Guest rooms look utterly different, decorated as they are in charcoal and ivory toile wallcoverings and drapes, raspberry velvet-cushioned slipper chairs, boxy lamps, and variegated marble-walled bathrooms. Rooms are small, with best ones overlooking the tree-lined Wyoming Avenue. The Normandy's public spaces are improved, as well, with the lounge now a plushly comfortable place to sit by the fire in winter or enjoy a good breakfast in the morning. With embassies for neighbors, the hotel hosts many embassy-bound guests. You may discover this for yourself on a Tuesday evening, when guests gather in the lounge, conservatory, and garden patio for complimentary wine and cheese.

2118 Wyoming Ave. NW (at Connecticut Ave.), Washington, DC 20008. ✆ **800/424-3729** or 202/483-1350. Fax 202/387-8241. www.doylecollection.com/normandy. 75 units. $99–$349 double, but call or go online for best deals, which can fall well below that $349 rate. Extra person $20. Children 12 and under stay free in parent's room. AE, DC, DISC, MC, V. Limited parking $28. Metro: Dupont Circle (North, Q St. NW exit). **Amenities:** Access to the neighboring Courtyard by Marriott Northwest's pool and exercise room; free Wi-Fi in public spaces. *In room:* A/C, TV, DVD, fridge, hair dryer, free Wi-Fi.

6 DUPONT CIRCLE

VERY EXPENSIVE

The Mansion on O Street ★★ (Finds)   A legend in her own time, H. H. Leonards Spero operates this Victorian property, made up of five interconnecting four- and five-story town houses. It's a museum, an event space, a private club, and a hotel.

Guest rooms will blow you away. Most breathtaking is the two-level Log Cabin loft suite, with Remington sculptures, a bed whose headboard encases an aquarium, and an eco-friendly bathroom with sauna. The Art Deco–style penthouse takes up an entire floor, with large living room, two bathrooms, a bedroom, and a kitchen; it has its own security cameras and elevator. The mansion also has conference spaces; 32 far-out bathrooms; 18 fireplaces; and art, antiques, and books everywhere (everything is for sale). Be sure to look for the electric guitars displayed throughout the mansion, each signed by a famous musician, some, like Sean Ono Lennon, who have stayed here. It's possible to rent the entire mansion or a portion of it. Full business services are available. Don't miss the mansion's Sunday brunch featuring jazz or gospel music, or regularly scheduled evening performances by big names on the local music scene.

2020 O St. NW (btw. 20th and 21st sts.), Washington, DC 20036. ✆ **202/496-2000.** Fax 202/833-8333. www.omansion.com. 23 units, all with private bathrooms. $350–$850 double; $550–$2,000 suites. Non-profit, group, government, and long-term rates available. Rates include continental breakfast. AE, DC, DISC, MC, V. Parking $25 by reservation. Metro: Dupont Circle (South, 19th St. NW exit). **Amenities:** Babysitting, children's programs, concierge, free passes to Sports Club/LA health club at the nearby Ritz-Carlton; Jacuzzi; sauna; room service. *In room:* A/C, TV, MP3 docking station, robes, free Wi-Fi.

EXPENSIVE

Beacon Hotel and Corporate Quarters ★   Opened in 2005, the Beacon attracts a lively local gathering in its bar and grill, right off the lobby, which adds to the overall genial ambience of the hotel. All rooms are furnished with flatscreen TVs and contemporary touches, like down-filled duvets and large leathery-looking headboards. The best rooms are in the "turret": the one-bedroom suites, one per floor, that perch in the corner of the building. But the New York–style junior suites offer a great deal: Each suite's compact kitchen includes a dishwasher, fridge, stovetop, microwave, and cabinets. Add **103** the roomy living room with a sleep sofa and you've got a good home base—for both corporate folks on business and families on holiday. The hotel's seasonal 10th-floor bar is open Wednesday to Saturday and offers views of the Dupont Circle neighborhood, the boulevards of the city, and—come the Fourth of July—the fireworks on the Mall.

1615 Rhode Island Ave. NW (at 17th St.), Washington, DC 20036. ℭ **800/821-4367** or 202/296-2100. Fax 202/331-0227. www.beaconhotelwdc.com. 199 units. Peak season: $329–$529 weekdays, $129–$309 weekends; Off peak: $199–$289 weekdays, $109–$189 weekends. Ask for AAA or AARP discounts or check the website for best rates; always ask for promotional rates. Extra person $20, up to 3 adults maximum per room. Children 13 and under stay free in parent's room. AE, DC, DISC, MC, V. Parking $29 weekdays, discounted on weekends; no oversize SUVs, buses, conversion vans. Metro: Dupont Circle (South, 19th St. NW exit). **Amenities:** Restaurant, 2 bars (1 is seasonal rooftop bar); in-house cardio fitness center, plus free access to nearby, fully equipped YMCA w/indoor pool; room service. *In room:* A/C, TV w/ pay movies, fridge, hair dryer, robes, Wi-Fi ($13/day).

Hotel Palomar Washington, D.C. ★★
If you prefer a hotel to be more than simply a place to sleep, you'll love the Palomar. This Kimpton hotel lies in the heart of the fun Dupont Circle neighborhood, full of art galleries, boutiques, and excellent restaurants; and it regularly invites local artists to pop in for the evening wine hour. The Palomar fancies itself a kind of art gallery, from its displays of handcrafted decorative arts in the lobby, to the splashes of mulberry and magenta, zebrawood, and faux-leather finishes in the guest rooms. These are spacious rooms, averaging 520 square feet!, and comfortably appointed, some with a maneuverable, oversize elliptical desk, an ergonomic mesh chair, and some with an undulating chaise longue. The bathrooms hold granite-topped vanities and L'Occitane bath products. Specialty rooms include 18 "Tall" rooms (the beds are 90-in. kings) and 8 "Motion" rooms (each comes with in-room exercise equipment). Ask for an executive king room with floor to ceiling windows overlooking P Street for best in-the-neighborhood experience.

2121 P St. NW (at 21st St.), Washington, DC 20037. ℭ **877/866-3070** or 202/448-1800. Fax 202/448-1801. www.hotelpalomar-dc.com. 335 units. Sun–Thurs $299–$599 double, Fri–Sat $189–$399 double; from $600 suite. Book online for best rates. Extra person $20. Children 17 and under stay free in parent's room. AE, DC, DISC, MC, V. Parking $38. Metro: Dupont Circle (South, 19th St. NW exit). Pets welcome. **Amenities:** Restaurant, bar/lounge; children's amenity program; concierge; fitness center, outdoor (seasonal) lap pool w/sun deck and private cabanas; room service. *In room:* A/C, TV w/pay movies, CD/DVD players, hair dryer, minibar, MP3 docking station, robes, umbrella, free Wi-Fi.

St. Gregory Luxury Hotel and Suites ★
Open since June 2000, the St. Gregory is an affordable luxury property, whose $3-million sprucing-up in 2006–07 pushed decor toward a comfortably contemporary and sexy look. Wingback chairs, soft benches in place of coffee tables, high-backed sofas, oversize silk-fabric-covered slipper chairs, and multilayered mattresses are just some of the fresh appointments. Flatscreen TVs are in the rooms; flat-panel TVs are in the suites.

Most of the rooms are one-bedroom suites with separate living room and bedroom. For privacy and views, choose one of the 16 "sky" suites on the top three floors, each with terrace and city overlooks. Of the 100 suites, 85 have pantry kitchens, including microwaves, ovens, and full-size refrigerators.

The St. Gregory offers special rates to long-term and government guests, and to those from the diplomatic community. If you don't fall into one of those categories, check the hotel's website for great deals.

2033 M St. NW (at 21st St.), Washington, DC 20036. ✆ **800/829-5034** or 202/530-3600. Fax 202/466-6770. www.stgregoryhotelwdc.com. 154 units. Weekdays $329–$489 double or suite; weekends $139–$309 double or suite. Extra person $20. Children 13 and under stay free in parent's room. Ask about discounts, long-term stays, AAA and AARP rates, and packages. AE, DC, DISC, MC, V. Parking $25 weekdays, discounted price on weekends (garage has maximum 6-ft. clearance). Metro: Dupont Circle (South, 19th St. NW exit). **Amenities:** Restaurant, coffee bar, bar/lounge; babysitting; concierge; concierge-level rooms; state-of-the-art fitness center, as well as access (for $20 fee) to the nearby and larger Sports Club/LA health club at the Ritz-Carlton; room service. *In room:* A/C, TV w/pay movies, fridge, hair dryer, Wi-Fi ($11/day).

Swann House ★ (Finds)   This stunning 1883 mansion, poised prominently on a corner 4 blocks north of Dupont Circle, has nine exquisite guest rooms. Renovations completed in 2009 focused on bathrooms; 4 rooms now have whirlpool tubs. Hard to say which is the prettiest, but I do love the Blue Sky Suite, covered in blue-and-white toile, with the original rose-tiled working fireplace, a queen-size bed and daybed, a sitting room, and a gabled ceiling. The most romantic room might be Il Duomo, with Gothic windows, a cathedral ceiling, a working fireplace, and a turreted bathroom with angel murals, a claw-foot tub, and a rain shower head. There are three suites. You'll want to spend some time on the main floor of the mansion, which has 12-foot ceilings, fluted woodwork, inlaid wood floors, a turreted living room, a columned sitting room, and a sunroom leading through three sets of French doors to the garden and pool. Check the inn's website for rate specials. Swann House is doing its eco-friendly part, using "green" cleaning products and switching to energy efficient light bulbs. This is a no-smoking property.

1808 New Hampshire Ave. NW (btw. S and Swann sts.), Washington, DC 20009. ✆ **202/265-4414.** Fax 202/265-6755. www.swannhouse.com. 9 units, all with private bathroom (3 with shower only). $165–$385 depending on unit and season. 2-night minimum weekends, 3-night minimum holiday weekends. Extended-stay and government rates available. Extra person $35. Rates include expanded continental breakfast. AE, DISC, MC, V. Limited off-street parking $14. Metro: Dupont Circle (North, Q St. NW exit). No children 12 and under. **Amenities:** Outdoor pool; free Wi-Fi. *In room:* A/C, TV, CD player, hair dryer, MP3 docking station, robes, free Wi-Fi.

MODERATE

The Dupont Hotel ★ (Value)   This hotel gets high marks for convenience (it's right on Dupont Circle), service, and comfort. Formerly the Jurys Washington Hotel, this property's 2009 change of ownership and top-to-bottom renovation added a ninth floor (the club level) and a duplex Presidential Suite (only such in the city), and put an urban-chic spin on guest room appearance and amenities. Striped carpeting, leather headboards, and dark woods and fabrics lend rooms an overall handsome and streamlined look—a look, actually, that applies throughout the hotel, including bar, restaurant, and lobby. Bathrooms have heated marble floors; toilet and shower (no tubs here) are separated by glass partition, while the sink and vanity lie outside the bathroom in an alcove. Despite its prime location in a sometimes-raucous neighborhood, the hotel is designed to guard against rude intrusions, its guest rooms insulated from the noise. But if you want to see what's going on out there, ask for a room overlooking Dupont Circle. Streets lined with cafes, bookstores, galleries, bars, and boutiques surround the hotel.

1500 New Hampshire Ave. NW (across from Dupont Circle), Washington, DC 20036. ✆ **877/587-9787** or 202/483-6000. Fax 202/328-3265. www.doylecollection.com/dupont. 327 units. From $189 double; from $289 suite. Extra person $20. Children under 18 stay free in parent's room. AE, DC, DISC, MC, V. Parking $32 plus tax. Metro: Dupont Circle (either exit). Dogs 20 lb. or under allowed, with flat $150 non-refundable fee. **Amenities:** Restaurant, bar; babysitting; children's programs; concierge; concierge-level rooms; state-of-the-art fitness center with cardio and weight machines; room service. *In room:* A/C, TV w/pay movies, hair dryer, minibar, MP3 docking station, robes, slippers, free Wi-Fi.

Embassy Circle Guest House ★ This delightful, turn-of-the-20th-century mansion, whose owners also own the lovely Woodley Park Guest House (p. 113), is an upscale and sophisticated inn, reflecting its Embassy Row neighborhood of enchanting chancelleries and embassies, a brief walk from Dupont Circle cafes, bars, and galleries. Guests are welcome to enjoy complimentary wine and snacks each evening and breakfast in the elegantly furnished parlor and dining room, respectively. Guest rooms take their decorative cues and their names from the antique Persian carpet displayed in each. So room no. 124, the Pearl Gazvin, presents the carpet of that name and a creamy, tranquil space to complement it. The Red Kashan carpet adds vivid color to its namesake, room no. 111, further enhanced by the room's colorful paintings and furnishings. As at the Woodley Park Guest House, all of the Embassy Circle's artworks are original pieces created by artists who have stayed there. The inn also has an elevator, a rare feature of older buildings, and one that comes in handy for guests with heavy luggage or disabilities.

2224 R St. NW (at Massachusetts Ave. NW), Washington, DC 20008. ✆ **877/232-7744** or 202/232-7744. www.dcinns.com. 11 units, each with private bathroom. $180–$280 double. Rates include continental breakfast and wine and snacks. AE, DISC, MC, V. Limited parking; call for specific dates and information. Metro: Dupont Circle (North, Q St. NW exit). (Well-behaved) children 12 and older. **Amenities:** Impromptu dinner parties, at the whim of the owner or even guests. *In room:* A/C, free Wi-Fi.

Embassy Suites Hotel Washington, D.C. ★ (Kids) This well-placed hotel offers great value within walking distance of Georgetown and Dupont Circle. A tropical eight-story atrium is the setting for an ample complimentary breakfast every morning and complimentary cocktails and light snacks every evening.

Every unit is a two-room suite. The living room holds a full-size sofa bed, 32-inch plasma TV, easy chair, and table and chairs. The bedroom lies at the back of the suite, overlooking a quiet courtyard or the street. A king-size bed or two queen-size beds, TV, armchair, and bureau furnish this space. Between the living room and the bedroom are the bathroom, a small closet, and a microwave and mini-fridge. Request a room on the eighth or ninth floor for views of Georgetown and beyond; request an "executive corner suite" for a slightly larger unit.

Another plus: free Internet use available at nine mobile kiosks throughout the public area and at three business center computers.

1250 22nd St. NW (btw. M and N sts.), Washington, DC 20037. ✆ **800/EMBASSY** (362-2779) or 202/857-3388. Fax 202/293-3173. www.washingtondc.embassysuites.com. 318 suites. Peak $269–$329; Off peak $169–$259 double. Rates include full breakfast and evening reception. Ask for AAA discounts or check the website for best rates. Extra person $20 weekdays, $25 weekends. Children 18 and under stay free in parent's room. AE, DC, DISC, MC, V. Parking $31. Metro: Dupont Circle (19th St. exit) or Foggy Bottom. **Amenities:** Restaurant; bar; concierge; state-of-the-art fitness center w/indoor pool, whirlpool, and sauna; mobile and free Internet kiosks in public area and business center; room service. *In room:* A/C, TV w/pay movies; fridge; hair dryer, microwave; Wi-Fi ($12/day).

Hotel Madera ★ The Hotel Madera fancies itself a kind of eco-conscious *pied-à-terre* for travelers. Guest rooms are large, with those on the New Hampshire Avenue side offering balconies and city views. If you have trouble sleeping, ask for a higher-up room on this side, because you're directly over the entrance to the restaurant, **Firefly.** Rooms at the back of the house on floors 6 through 10 have views of Rock Creek Park and the Washington National Cathedral. All rooms are comfortable and furnished with beds whose headboards are giant dark-wood panels inset with a patch of vibrant blue padded mohair. Other distinct touches: pillows covered in animal print or satiny fabrics, grass cloth–like wall coverings, and black granite with chrome bathroom vanities. This Kimpton hotel's "specialty" rooms include "Snack" rooms (studio with kitchenette and grocery shopping service), "Tranquility" rooms (with personal massage chair), and "Cardio" rooms (with treadmill, exercise bike, or elliptical steps).

1310 New Hampshire Ave. NW (btw. N and O sts.), Washington, DC 20036. ⓒ **800/430-1202** or 202/296-7600. Fax 202/293-2476. www.hotelmadera.com. 82 units. Weekdays and weekends $149–$439 double; add $40 to the going rate for a specialty room. For best rates, call direct to the hotel or go to its website. Extra person $20. Children 17 and under stay free in parent's room. Rates include hosted evening wine hour. AE, DC, DISC, MC, V. Parking $36 plus tax. Metro: Dupont Circle (South, 19th St. NW exit). Pets welcome. **Amenities:** Restaurant/bar; babysitting; bikes; children's amenity program; concierge; access to the posh Sports Club/LA health club at the nearby Ritz-Carlton ($15 per guest per day); room service. *In room:* A/C, TV w/pay movies, CD/DVD player, hair dryer, minibar, MP3 docking station, robes, umbrella, free Wi-Fi.

Hotel Tabard Inn   If you favor the offbeat and personal over cookie-cutter chains, try the Tabard. Named for the hostelry in Chaucer's *Canterbury Tales,* the Tabard is the oldest continuously operating hotel in the city, having opened in 1917. Initially, the Tabard occupied a single Victorian town house, but expanded in 1920 to encompass the town houses on either side of it. The trio of joined Victorians has operated as an inn ever since.

The heart of the ground floor is the dark-paneled lounge, with worn furniture, fireplace, the original beamed ceiling, and bookcases. Washingtonians come here for drinks, jazz on Sundays, or to linger before or after dining in the charming **Tabard Inn** restaurant (p. 106).

From the lounge, the inn leads you up and down stairs, along dim corridors, and through nooks and crannies to guest rooms furnished with antiques and flea-market finds. Perhaps the most eccentric room is the spacious top-floor "penthouse," which has skylights, exposed brick walls, an ample living room, and the feel of a New York City loft. Quaint as it appears, the Tabard is progressive when it comes to going green: its rooves are planted with herb and rose gardens (the Tabard's restaurant uses the fresh herbs in its cooking; see p. 149 for the restaurant review) and solar panels provide the inn with hot water heating.

The inn is not easily accessible to guests with disabilities.

ⓜ Moments   All That Jazz

For a pleasurable evening's entertainment, you sometimes need look no further than the bar/lounge or in-house restaurant of your own or a nearby hotel. The genre is usually jazz, the performers are top-notch, and the admission is free. So if it's a Sunday night, you might want to plant yourself in the paneled parlor of the **Hotel Tabard Inn** (p. 106) to listen to bassist Victor Dvoskin play world-class jazz, often accompanied by a guitarist. Weeknights, locals crowd into the **Renaissance Mayflower** hotel's (p. 97) fabled Town & Country Lounge for happy hour to imbibe bartender Sambonn Lek's legendary cocktails, gobble complimentary hors d'oeuvres, and enjoy the jazz and other standards turned out by the resident pianist. And every single night, starting at 9pm, the **Phoenix Park Hotel's** (p. 89) Dubliner restaurant is the place to be if you enjoy hoisting a pint to the tune of "Danny Boy" and rowdier Irish ballads, performed live by musicians with such names as "Conor Malone" and "Andy O'Driscoll."

1739 N St. NW (btw. 17th and 18th sts.), Washington, DC 20036. (℃) **202/785-1277.** Fax 202/785-6173. **107** www.tabardinn.com. 40 units, 27 with private bathroom (6 with shower only). $113–$160 double with shared bathroom; $158–$218 double with private bathroom. Extra person $15. Rates include continental breakfast. AE, DC, DISC, MC, V. Limited street parking, plus 1 parking garage on N St. Metro: Dupont Circle (South, 19th St. exit). Small and confined pets accepted for a $20 fee. **Amenities:** Restaurant w/lounge (free live jazz Sun evenings); free access to nearby YMCA (w/extensive facilities that include indoor pool, indoor track, and racquetball/basketball courts); fax and hair dryer available at front desk; free computer access in lobby. In room: A/C, free Wi-Fi.

Topaz Hotel ★ A whimsical decor rules in the guest rooms, where a refurbishment completed in 2007 transformed rooms with splashes of emerald, sapphire, ruby, and other jewel tones on wallpaper, down comforter, armoire, and armchair. The rooms are unusually large, averaging 400 square feet; half have an alcove with a desk and a separate dressing room. The Topaz pursues a sort of New Age wellness motif; note the smooth "energy" stones and horoscope placed upon your pillow. You have the option to book a specialty room: either an "Energy" guest room, which includes a piece of exercise equipment (an elliptical or a stationary bike), fitness magazines, and TV with VCR and CD player; or a "Yoga" room, which comes with an exercise mat, an instructional tape, padded pillows, special towels, and yoga magazines.

The Topaz lies on a quiet residential street whose front-of-the-house windows overlook picturesque town houses.

1733 N St. NW (right next to the Tabard Inn [see above] btw. 17th and 18th sts.), Washington, DC 20036. (℃) **800/775-1202** or 202/393-3000. Fax 202/785-9581. www.topazhotel.com. 99 units. Weekdays and weekends $149–$369 double; add $40 to rate for specialty rooms. It is very likely that you can get a much lower rate by calling direct to the hotel or by booking a reservation online. Extra person $25. Children 17 and under stay free in parent's room. Rates include complimentary morning Power Hour, serving energy potions. AE, DC, DISC, MC, V. Parking $35. Metro: Dupont Circle (North, Q St. NW exit). Pets welcome. **Amenities:** Bar/restaurant; babysitting; bikes; children's amenity program; concierge; access to nearby health club ($5 per guest); room service. In room: A/C, TV w/pay movies, CD/DVD player, hair dryer, minibar, MP3 docking station, robes, free Wi-Fi.

7 FOGGY BOTTOM/WEST END

VERY EXPENSIVE

Park Hyatt, Washington, D.C. ★★ This luxury hotel features spacious lodging, from the "Park" room, at 408 square feet, to the "Park Deluxe" room, which measures 618 square feet. Wood-slat blinds are on the windows, puffy down duvets cover the beds, and decorative features include coffee-table books on American culture, like Annie Leibowitz's photo portraits of American musicians. The flatscreen television in the Park Deluxe rooms pivots in the wall to present an antique chessboard on its reverse side (decorative, not functional). Creamy yellow leather chairs are actually rockers. Bathrooms are spa-like, with floor, ceiling, and walls of dark gray limestone. Everything is out in the open, from the deep soaking marble tub to its adjoining shower.

Don't miss the hotel's Tea Cellar, complete with a tea humidor for storing the cellar's collection of rare and single estate teas, and the restaurant, the **Blue Duck Tavern** (see p. 151), which serves food that's out of this world.

1201 24th St. NW (at M St.), Washington, DC 20037. (℃) **800/778-7477** or 202/789-1234. Fax 202/419-6795. www.parkhyattwashington.com. 216 units. From $350 Park Room double, from $450 Park Deluxe double; from $750 suites. For best rates, go to the hotel's website or call the main reservation number. Extra person $60. Children 16 and under stay free in parent's room. Families should ask about the family plan. AE, DC, DISC, MC, V. Parking $35 plus tax. Metro: Foggy Bottom. Pets welcome, with $150 fee per stay. **Amenities:** Restaurant, bar/lounge, tea cellar; bikes; concierge; fitness center w/whirlpool and indoor pool; room service; free Wi-Fi in public areas. *In room:* A/C, TV, fridge, hair dryer, minibar, robes, Wi-Fi ($9.95/day).

The Ritz-Carlton, Washington, D.C. ★★★   Doormen greet you effusively when you arrive, and poised young women in the bar swan around, gracefully serving you your cocktail. The Ritz staff is always looking after you.

Some guest rooms overlook the hotel's peaceful landscaped courtyard; rooms on the outside perimeter view the West End's cityscape. Deluxe rooms are spacious (standard guest rooms average 450 square feet) and richly furnished with decorative inlaid wooden furniture, a comfy armchair and ottoman, and pretty artwork. Large marble bathrooms offer ample counter space, separate bathtub and shower stall, and the toilet in its own room behind a louvered door. The clock radio doubles as a CD player, and the phone features a button for summoning the "technology butler" (a complimentary, 24/7 service for guests with computer questions). For a $15 fee, guests may use the two-level, 100,000-square-foot **Sports Club/LA,** the best hotel health club in the city. The hotel's **Westend Bistro by Eric Ripert** (see p. 153) is one of the hottest restaurants in town.

1150 22nd St. NW (at M St.), Washington, DC 20037. ✆ **800/241-3333** or 202/835-0500. Fax 202/835-1588. www.ritzcarlton.com/hotels/washington_dc. 300 units. Weekday from $649 double, from $749 suite; weekend from $349 (on occasion, $249) double, from $449 suite. No charge for extra person in the room. Ask about discount packages. AE, DC, DISC, MC, V. Valet parking $28. Metro: Foggy Bottom. Pets accepted and pampered (no fee). **Amenities:** Restaurant, bar/lounge; bikes; concierge; concierge-level rooms; health club & spa (the best in the city; see above); room service. *In room:* A/C, TV w/pay movies, CD/DVD player, fridge, hair dryer, minibar, robes, umbrella, Wi-Fi ($9.95/day).

MODERATE

George Washington University Inn   Kennedy Center performers, corporate folks, visiting professors, and parents of GW students are frequent guests at this hotel owned by George Washington University.

Rooms are a little larger and corridors are a tad narrower than those in a typical hotel, and each room includes a roomy dressing chamber. More than one-third of the units are one-bedroom suites. These are especially spacious, with living rooms that hold a sleeper sofa and a TV hidden in an armoire (there's another in the bedroom). The suites, plus the 16 efficiencies, have kitchens. The spaciousness and the kitchen facilities make this a popular choice for families and for long-term guests.

The hotel is located in a lovely neighborhood, close to Georgetown, the Kennedy Center, and downtown. Mention your affiliation with George Washington University, if you have one, and you may receive a special "GWU" rate.

824 New Hampshire Ave. NW (btw. H and I sts.), Washington, DC 20037. ✆ **800/426-4455** or 202/337-6620. Fax 202/298-7499. www.gwuinn.com. 95 units. Weekdays $159–$269 double, $179–$289 efficiency, $199–$309 1-bedroom suite; weekends $109–$209 double, $139–$229 efficiency, $169–$249 1-bedroom suite. Children 12 and under stay free in parent's room. AE, DC, DISC, MC, V. Limited parking $30. Metro: Foggy Bottom. **Amenities:** Restaurant, bar; complimentary passes to nearby fitness center; room service. *In room:* A/C, TV w/pay movies, fridge, hair dryer, microwave, robes, slippers, umbrella, free Wi-Fi.

One Washington Circle Hotel   The George Washington University owns this hotel, whose corporate and family clientele like the outdoor pool, in-house restaurant, prime location near Georgetown and the Metro, and the full kitchen with oven, microwave, and refrigerator (about 10% of rooms have kitchenettes). Five types of suites are available, ranging in size from 390 to 710 square feet. The one-bedroom suites have a sofa bed and dining area; all rooms are spacious, evince a contemporary look, and have walk-out balconies, some overlooking the Circle and its statue of George Washington. Guest rooms have double-paned windows, which help keep the sounds of the city at bay; for quietest rooms of all, ask to stay on the L Street side.

Call the hotel directly for best rates; mention a GWU affiliation if you have one and you may receive a discount.

One Washington Circle NW (btw. 22nd and 23rd sts. NW), Washington, DC 20037. © **800/424-9671** or 202/872-1680. Fax 202/887-4989. www.thecirclehotel.com. 151 units. Weekdays $159–$299 smallest suites, $199–$339 largest suites; weekends $109–$199 smallest suites, $159–$239 largest suites. Call hotel to get best rates. Extra person $20. Children 12 and under stay free in parent's room. AE, DC, MC, V. Parking $30. Metro: Foggy Bottom. **Amenities:** Restaurant, bar; fitness center; outdoor pool; room service; free Wi-Fi. *In room:* A/C, TV w/pay movies, CD player, hair dryer, free Internet, full kitchens (in 90% of suites, w/oven, fridge, microwave), robes.

The River Inn ★ Finds   The River Inn is a sweet little secret that lies on a quiet residential street of town houses near both the Kennedy Center and Georgetown. Guest rooms feature pillowtop mattresses on beds; comfortable armchairs with soft leather footstools; ebony armoires; coppery gold, rust, and brown tones; and a cool chaise longue that unfolds into a sofa bed. Suites have all this, plus a dressing room and a separate, well-equipped kitchen. All but 31 suites combine the bedroom and living-room areas, and include an oversize desk that doubles as a workspace and dining table in a corner off the kitchen. Those 31 suites are roomy one-bedrooms, with an expansive living room (with sleep sofa) and a separate bedroom that holds a king-size bed and a second TV. Best are the suites on the upper floors, offering views of the Potomac River and from some (no. 804, for example) the Washington Monument.

924 25th St. NW (btw. K and I sts.), Washington, DC 20037. © **800/424-2741** or 202/337-7600. Fax 202/337-6520. www.theriverinn.com. 125 units. Peak weekdays $219–$299 double, $269–$349 1-bedroom suite; Off-peak weekdays $159–$199 double, $209–$249 1-bedroom suite; Peak weekends $149–$199 double, $199–$249 1-bedroom suite; Off-peak weekends $99–$149 double, $149–$199 1-bedroom suite. Extra person $20. Children 17 and under stay free in parent's room. AE, DC, DISC, MC, V. Parking $30. Metro: Foggy Bottom. Pets welcome for nonrefundable $150 fee. **Amenities:** Restaurant, bar; bikes; concierge; small fitness center; room service. *In room:* A/C, TV w/pay movies, fridge, hair dryer, microwave, MP3 docking station, robes, slippers, umbrella, free Wi-Fi.

8 GEORGETOWN

VERY EXPENSIVE

Four Seasons ★★★ Kids   The Four Seasons is absolutely the best hotel in Washington. The kind of service you receive from staff, porter to cleaning crew, is unparalleled; the hotel keeps track of repeat guests' preferences and trains staff to recognize guests and greet them by name. The concierge team knows its stuff. Clientele draws from the world's wealthiest and most distinguished, Hollywood actors to Middle East statesmen. Recent renovations updated the entire "west wing," whose rooms measure anywhere from 625 to 4,000 square feet; added 11 new rooms; completely transformed the lobby and public spaces; and debuted the immediately popular restaurant, Michael Mina's Bourbon Steak (see review in dining chapter, p. 153). Located at the mouth of Georgetown, the hotel's original (east) wing holds spacious guest rooms (from 380 to 1,270 square feet) designed by Pierre-Yves Rochon, with custom-crafted furniture and color schemes of either celadon or purple. Most rooms have sleeper sofas. Bathrooms are prettily turned out in pear- and maple-wood accents, with a deep soaking tub separate from the shower.

2800 Pennsylvania Ave. NW (which becomes M St. a block farther along), Washington, DC 20007. ℂ 800/332-3442 or 202/342-0444. Fax 202/944-2076. www.fourseasons.com/washington. 222 units. Weekdays $545–$795 double, $950–$12,500 suite; weekends from $395 double, from $525 suite. Extra person $50. Children 18 and under stay free in parent's room. AE, DC, DISC, MC, V. Parking $47. Metro: Foggy Bottom. Pets accepted, up to 15 lb. **Amenities:** 2 restaurants, bar; bikes; children's amenities program; concierge; extensive state-of-the-art fitness club & spa w/personal trainers, lap pool, facials, and synchronized massage (2 people work on you at the same time); room service. *In room:* A/C, TV w/pay movies, CD/DVD player, hair dryer, minibar, MP3 docking station, robes, Wi-Fi ($12/day).

The Ritz-Carlton Georgetown, Washington, D.C. ★★★   This Ritz is exclusively small, designed like a sophisticated refuge in the middle of wild and woolly Georgetown. It's especially favored by privacy-seeking celebrities and romancing couples. Look for the 130-foot-high smokestack to guide you to the hotel, which is built on the site of a historic incinerator and incorporates the smokestack into the design and overall theme. The lobby's front brick wall is original to the incinerator, the restaurant's name is "Fahrenheit," the bar's is "Degrees," and the signature drink is the "Fahrenheit 5 Martini." Guest rooms lie one level below the lobby, accessible by an elevator that requires a key card to operate, so anyone visiting you must either be escorted by you or a staff person. Rooms are very large (averaging 450 square feet), decorated in shades of moss green, gold, and a burnt red, with lots of dark-wood furniture and accents. The bathroom, like those at all Ritz-Carltons, is sublime: spacious, with marble vanity, separate tub and shower, fancy wood shelving. More than one-third of the rooms are one-bedroom suites.

3100 South St. NW (at 31st St., btw. K and M sts.), Washington, DC 20007. ℂ 800/241-3333 or 202/912-4100. Fax 202/912-4199. www.ritzcarlton.com/hotels/georgetown. 86 units. Weekdays from $699 double, from $799 suite; weekends from $499 double ($399 on occasion), from $599 suite. No charge for extra person in the room. Check website or 800 number for weekend packages and specials. AE, DC, DISC, MC, V. Valet parking $32. Metro: Foggy Bottom. Small (under 30 lb.) pets accepted (no fee). **Amenities:** Restaurant, bar; bikes; concierge; state-of-the-art fitness center & spa; room service. *In room:* A/C, TV w/pay movies, CD/DVD player, hair dryer, minibar, robes, umbrella, Wi-Fi ($9.95/day).

EXPENSIVE

Georgetown Inn   This hotel is in the thick of Georgetown. Come the third weekend in May, the hotel is full of the proud parents of students graduating from blocks-away Georgetown University. (The hotel books up 2 years in advance for graduation weekend.) Its location is what best recommends the hotel, so if you're a shopper, visiting the university, or conducting business in Georgetown, this is a good pick.

A million-dollar renovation completed in 2006 refurbished the hotel without changing its general style: traditional American, heavy on the dark woods with pretty sage-green accents. About one-third of the rooms hold two beds, the others have a king- or queen-size bed. Ask for an "executive room" if you'd like a sitting area with pullout sofa. Best are the 10 one-bedroom suites, in which bedroom and large living room are separate. The bathrooms have only showers (some also have bidets), no tub.

1310 Wisconsin Ave. NW (btw. N and O sts.), Washington, DC 20007. ℂ 800/368-5922 or 202/333-8900. Fax 202/333-8308. www.georgetowninn.com. 90 units. Peak: $239–$499 double weekdays, $199–$409 double weekends; Off peak: from $159 double weekdays, from $149 double weekends; suites from $299. Ask about promotional rates. Extra person $20. Children 12 and under stay free in parent's room. AE, DC, DISC, MC, V. Valet parking $32 plus tax. Metro: Foggy Bottom. **Amenities:** Restaurant, bar; small exercise room, plus complimentary pass to nearby, more extensive sports club; room service. *In room:* A/C, TV w/ pay movies, hair dryer, Wi-Fi ($11/day).

Georgetown Suites ★ (**Value**)   This hotel was designed to meet the needs of business travelers on extended visits, but its casual atmosphere and kitchen suites work well for families, too. The hotel offers a good deal: friendly service; clean, bright, and spacious lodging; and up-to-date amenities. It has two locations within a block of each other. The main building is on quiet, residential 30th Street, steps away from Georgetown's action. The Harbor Building, on 29th Street, is situated next to Whitehurst Freeway and across from the Washington Harbor complex, so is a bit noisier.

Accommodations at both locations have living rooms, dining areas, and fully equipped kitchens, bedding with fluffy duvets, and HDTV flatscreen televisions. Half are studios (550 square feet), half are one-bedroom suites (800 square feet). The biggest and best suites are the three two-level, two-bedroom town houses attached to the main building. Also recommended are two penthouse suites, which have their own terraces overlooking Georgetown rooftops.

1111 30th St. NW (just below M St.) and 1000 29th St. NW (at K St.), Washington, DC 20007. (✆) **800/348-7203** or 202/298-1600. Fax 202/333-2019. www.georgetownsuites.com. 220 units. Weekdays $155 studio, $215 1-bedroom suite; weekends $155 studio, $185 1-bedroom suite. Penthouse suites from $350; town houses from $425. Rollaway or sleeper sofa $10 extra. Rates include continental breakfast. AE, DC, DISC, MC, V. Limited parking $20. Metro: Foggy Bottom. **Amenities:** Executive-level rooms; small exercise room; business center w/computers and free Wi-Fi. *In room:* A/C, TV, CD player, hair dryer, full kitchen (w/ fridge, coffeemaker, microwave, and dishwasher), free Wi-Fi.

---

9 WOODLEY PARK

EXPENSIVE

Omni Shoreham Hotel ★ (**Kids**)   This is Woodley Park's *second* biggest hotel, although with 834 rooms, the Omni Shoreham is still about 500 short of the behemoth Wardman Park Marriott (see listing). And it's all the more appealing for it, since it's not quite so overwhelming as the Marriott. Its design—wide corridors, vaulted ceilings and archways, and arrangements of pretty sofas and armchairs in the lobby and public spaces—endows the Shoreham with the air of a grand hotel. The Omni rightfully boasts its status as the city's largest AAA four-diamond hotel, as well as its membership in Historic Hotels of America. Guest rooms evince a certain elegance and are twice the size of your average hotel room. The hotel sits on 11 acres overlooking Rock Creek Park and beyond—you can spot the Washington Monument from some rooms.

Built in 1930, the Shoreham has been the scene of inaugural balls for every president since FDR. Do you believe in ghosts? Ask about room no. 870, the haunted suite (available for $3,000 a night).

2500 Calvert St. NW (near Connecticut Ave.), Washington, DC 20008. (✆) **800/843-6664** or 202/234-0700. Fax 202/265-7972. www.omnishorehamhotel.com. 834 units. $199–$359 double; suites from $350 and way up. Call the hotel directly for best rates. Extra person $30. Children 17 and under stay free in parent's room. AE, DC, DISC, MC, V. Valet parking $30; self-parking $23. Metro: Woodley Park–Zoo. Pets allowed under 25 lb., $50 cleaning fee. **Amenities:** Restaurant, bar/lounge; children's amenities program; concierge; fitness center ($10/day, $18/stay per person) w/heated outdoor pool, separate kids' pool, and whirlpool, and spa services by appointment; room service. *In room:* A/C, TV w/pay movies, hair dryer, robes, free Wi-Fi.

Washington Wardman Park Marriott Hotel ★   This is Washington's biggest hotel, resting on 16 acres just down the street from the National Zoo and several good restaurants. Its size and location (the Woodley Park–Zoo Metro station is literally at its doorstep) make it a good choice for conventions, tour groups, and individual travelers. The hotel's atrium is often a-swirl with activity as meeting goers and soiree attendees make their way to their various events.

The hotel's oldest section, built in 1918, houses about 100 rooms, each with high ceilings, ornate crown moldings, and an assortment of antique French and English furnishings. The main building completed a major renovation of all guest rooms in 2008, updating their look and furnishings by adding multilayered, Marriott-brand bedding, flatscreen TVs, and long desks with high-backed chairs. The overhaul also installed all new, state-of-the-art equipment in the fitness center and vastly improved the in-house restaurant, now called the Stone's Throw. Harry's Bar, meanwhile, serves well as a comfortable place to have a drink after your meeting.

2660 Woodley Rd. NW (at Connecticut Ave. NW), Washington, DC 20008. © **800/228-9290** or 202/328-2000. Fax 202/234-0015. www.marriotthotels.com/wasdt. About 1,300 units. Weekdays $309 double; weekends $119–$289 double; $350–$2,500 suite. Children 17 and under stay free in parent's room. AE, DC, DISC, MC, V. Valet parking $37; self-parking $32. Metro: Woodley Park–Zoo. Pets under 20 lb. accepted, but charges may apply; call for details. **Amenities:** Restaurant, 2 bars; babysitting; concierge; concierge-level rooms; well-equipped fitness center w/outdoor heated pool and sun deck; room service. *In room:* A/C, TV w/pay movies, hair dryer; Internet ($13/day).

INEXPENSIVE

In addition to the Woodley Park Guest House, listed below, you might consider the Woodley Park location of the **Kalorama Guest House,** at 2700 Cathedral Ave. NW (entrance on 27th St.; © **800/974-9101** or 202/328-0860; fax 202/328-8730; www.kaloramaguesthouse. com), which has 18 units, 12 with private bathrooms. Rates are $89 for a double with a shared bathroom, $119 to $139 for a double with private bathroom, and include an expansive breakfast. A communal television and telephone are available in the parlor; individual guest rooms do not provide TV or telephone at this location. Free Wi-Fi access is available in all the rooms of the main house. Best room at this location is unit #14, which has a queen-size bed and a sitting area with sleeper sofa. Very limited parking (only two spots) is available for $15 plus tax, and the Woodley Park–Zoo Metro stop is nearby. See p. 100 for the full listing for the main location of the Kalorama Guest House in Adams-Morgan for more information.

(**Finds**) **Extended Stays in the Heart of the City**

Travelers to Washington, D.C., who plan to visit for a week or longer should know about the centrally located **AKA White House District** apartment/hotel (1710 H St. NW; © **202/904-2500;** www.stayaka.com). The D.C. location is one of 10 AKA properties (most are in NYC), all of which offer luxuriously furnished one- and two-bedroom apartments that are available for per-night rates (a minimum of 4–7 nights is generally required) or negotiated lease terms for extended stays. Federal employees will be happy to learn that AKA accepts the government's per-diem rate. Check out the website to see for yourself some of the property's fine appointments and amenities, including fully equipped kitchens, stylish decor, free Wi-Fi, on-site fitness center, washer/dryer (in each apartment), and complimentary continental breakfast. K Street law offices, the White House, the Smithsonian's Renwick Gallery, and excellent restaurants, like the Taberna del Alabardero, are just some of the property's notable neighbors.

Tips **Inside and Outside the Beltway, Beyond-D.C. Hotel Options**

Normally, I don't like to recommend hotel options outside the capital, since I believe that to get a real sense of a place, you need to wake up in it. Circumstances sometimes dictate otherwise, however. If you have an early flight to catch and want to be close to the airport, or if you're having a hard time finding available and/or affordable rooms at D.C. hotels, look to the following options. In northern Virginia, Route 1, also known as "Jefferson Davis Highway" within Crystal City limits, is lined with hotels for every budget, though most are aimed at the high-end traveler. Crystal City and its Northern Virginia neighbors are also prime locations if you want to stay near Ronald Reagan Washington National Airport, which is less than a mile away. (National Airport, by the way, is only 4 miles from downtown Washington.) So, whether you're looking for vacancies or affordable lodging, or simply want to guarantee a free shuttle and a quick trip between your hotel and National Airport, go to the Metropolitan Washington Airports Authority website (www.mwaa.com), click on "Travel Tips," under the National Airport section, and then click on "Local Hotels," in the Local Tourism section on that page to discover a long listing of hotels. One of the closest to the airport is the **Crystal City Marriott** (1999 Jefferson Davis Hwy.; ✆ **703/413-5500**).

Likewise, if you want to stay as close as possible to Washington Dulles International Airport, refer to the same website, but click on the Travel Tips line in the Dulles box, then the Local Hotels line within Local Tourism. Of the hotels listed, one is actually located on airport property: the **Washington Dulles Marriott** (45020 Aviation Dr.; ✆ **703/471-9500**).

Finally, the Baltimore–Washington International Thurgood Marshall Airport's website, www.bwiairport.com, directs you to its list of nearby hotels: Click on "To and From BWI," and then "Hotels and Services Near BWI." As at Dulles Airport, only one of the many hotels listed is located on BWI airport property: the **Four Points by Sheraton** (7032 Elm Rd.; ✆ **410/859-3300**).

WHERE TO STAY

5

WOODLEY PARK

Woodley Park Guest House This charming, 16-room B&B offers clean, comfortable, and cozy lodging; inexpensive rates; a super location; and a personable staff. Guests hail from around the globe, a fact which inspired the owners to add a globe to the breakfast room; people sitting across the table from each other in the morning often go over to the globe and point out exactly where they live: the Arctic Circle, Brazil, Seattle.

Special features of the guesthouse include a wicker-furnished, tree-shaded front porch; exposed, century-old brick walls; beautiful antiques; and original art. (The innkeepers buy works only from artists who have stayed at the guesthouse.) Rooms have either one or two twins, one double, or one queen-size bed. The guesthouse benefits from its proximity to the Marriott Wardman Park Hotel, where airport shuttles and taxis are on hand. The Woodley Park–Zoo Metro stop, good restaurants, Rock Creek Park, and the National Zoo are all a short walk away. See the Dupont Circle section to read about the owners' other property, the **Embassy Circle Guest House** (p. 105).

114 2647 Woodley Rd. NW (at Connecticut Ave. NW), Washington, DC 20008. 📞 **866/667-0218** or 202/667-0218. Fax 202/667-1080. www.dcinns.com. 16 units, 12 with private bathroom (shower only), 4 singles, with shared bathroom. $120–$135 single with shared bathroom; $150–$225 double with private bathroom. Rates include continental breakfast. AE, MC, V. Limited on-site parking $18, plus tax. Metro: Woodley Park–Zoo. (Well-behaved) children 12 and over. **Amenities:** Free Wi-Fi. *In room:* A/C, free Wi-Fi.

Where to Dine

D.C. diners these days obsess after—are you ready?—cupcakes, wine bars, steak, organic produce, celebrity chefs, and chocolate, though not necessarily in that order. From **Georgetown Cupcake** to **Sweetgreen** salads, **Bourbon Steak** to **Cork Restaurant and Wine Bar,** and **CoCo. Sala Chocolate Lounge** to **Alain Ducasse Adour,** the capital's newest dining options represent intriguing trends.

Bigger than all of those, of course, is the current penchant for following the culinary trail laid by our diner-in-chief. President Barack Obama and First Lady Michelle Obama do the city proud, eating one day at the lovely, upscale **Equinox,** the next at downhome **Ben's Chili Bowl,** clearly enjoying the fruits of D.C. restaurant tables.

So what's your pleasure?

This chapter presents you with choices from as many different tastes, budgets, and styles as our pages allow, about 100 restaurants in all.

Read through the descriptions; if a place beckons, call ahead for **reservations,** especially for Saturday night. Most restaurants are affiliated with an online reservation service called **www.opentable.com,** so you can also reserve your table online.

If you wait until the last minute to make a reservation, expect to dine really early, say 5:30 or 6pm, or after 9:30pm. Or you can sit at the bar and eat, which can be more of a culinary treat than you might imagine; some of the best restaurants, including Palena, Marcel's, and Corduroy, offer a reasonably priced bar menu. See "A Seat at the Bar," p. 159.

Better yet, consider a restaurant that doesn't take reservations. At places like Oyamel and Pesce, where the atmosphere is casual, the wait can become part of the experience. The food is worth standing in line for.

Few places require men to wear a jacket and tie; I've made a special note in the listings for those places that do. If you're driving, call ahead to inquire about valet parking, complimentary or otherwise—on Washington's crowded streets, this service can be a true bonus.

I've listed the closest Metro station to each restaurant only when it's within walking distance of that restaurant. The closest Metro stop to Georgetown is the Blue Line's Foggy Bottom station; from there you can walk or catch the D.C. Circulator bus on Pennsylvania Avenue, up the street from the Metro station.

ABOUT THE PRICES

I've selected a range of menus and prices in the major "restaurant" neighborhoods of Washington. Restaurant groupings are first by location, then alphabetically in each price category. Keep in mind that the price categories refer to dinner prices, but some very expensive restaurants offer affordable lunches, early-bird dinners, tapas, or bar meals. The prices within each review refer to the cost of individual entrees, not the entire meal. I've used the following price categories: **Very Expensive** (entrees at dinner average more than $30); **Expensive** ($20–$30); **Moderate** ($10–$19); and **Inexpensive** ($10 and under).

- **Best for Romance:** The upscale, downtown **Taberna del Alabardero** (p. 139) is perfect for old-fashioned romantics looking for a hushed atmosphere, formal service, Old World decor of rich reds and ornate design, and authentic, first-class Spanish cuisine. If a trendy, sexy scene and exotic tastes are more your style, consider the Penn Quarter's softly lit **Rasika** (p. 136), whose hot Indian food spices up the night. And then there's **Cashion's Eat Place** (p. 145), a cozy neighborhood joint in Adams-Morgan; sit in the intimate, somewhat-private bar area, a step up and overlooking the main dining room, and enjoy American comfort food.

- **Best for Business: Charlie Palmer Steak** (p. 120), conveniently located within a walk of the Capitol, is a favorite spot for expense-account lobbyists and lawyers. They enjoy its great bar, fine cuts of steak, private rooms, and cleverly laid out seating that allows for discreet conversations. And then there's the **Caucus Room** (p. 125), where there's always a whole lot of handshaking going on.

- **Best for Regional Cuisine:** The **Blue Duck Tavern** (p. 151) pays homage to the tastes of various American regional cuisines by stating the provenance of each dish on the menu. The seasonal farm vegetables might hail from the Tuscarora Co-op in Pennsylvania, the duck from Crescent Farms in New York. **Johnny's Half Shell** (p. 121), meanwhile, is the place to go for superb Eastern Shore delicacies: crab cakes, crab imperial, and soft-shell crab. While Washington doesn't have its own cuisine, per se, its central location within the Mid-Atlantic/Chesapeake Bay region gives it license to lay claim to these local favorite foods. And nobody does 'em better than Johnny's.

- **Best Haute Cuisine:** Two restaurants stand out in this category: **CityZen** (p. 120) and **Komi** (p. 148). Chef Eric Ziebold came to CityZen from the renowned French Laundry in Napa Valley; his culinary skills can take a simple mushroom and transform it (fry it, add truffles) into a spiritual experience. Likewise, Komi, anointed D.C.'s top restaurant by *Washingtonian* magazine, shows off the genius of young chef Johnny Monis, whose gastronomic masterpieces often hint of Greek tastes.

- **Best All-Around for Fun and Food:** José Andrés offers excellent choices at either end of the spectrum: **Oyamel,** where everyone's slurping foam-topped margaritas and savoring small plates of authentic Mexican food; and **minibar,** the six-seat dining spot within the lively restaurant Café Atlantico (p. 128), where Andrés has fun whipping up 30 to 40 small concoctions, like foie gras in cotton candy, for $120 per person. A few blocks away, **Central** (p. 129) makes everybody happy with its convivial atmosphere and Michel Richard's take on French bistro and American classics, from mussels in white wine to fried chicken. And if the ebullient Michel Richard is in the house, the place rocks.

- **Best French Cuisine:** You can go in two directions here. For exquisite, upscale French cuisine, consider Michel Richard's upscale restaurant, **Citronelle** (p. 153), Robert Wiedemaier's **Marcel's** (p. 152), and Frank Ruta's **Palena** (p. 160). Not only are these the best French restaurants, but they are among the top 10 restaurants in the city, period. For French classics with Moulin Rouge ambience, check out **La Chaumiere** (p. 157), whose nightly specials and rustic decor have been attracting regulars for more than 30 years.

- **Best Italian Cuisine: Tosca** (p. 128) is a winner, serving fine and unusual dishes derived from the chef's northern Italian upbringing. At **Obelisk** (p. 148), chef/owner

Peter Pastan continues to do what he's always done, craft elegantly simple and delicious food in a pleasantly sparse room.

- **Best Pizza:** At **Pizzeria Paradiso,** peerless chewy-crusted pies are baked in an oak-
  burning oven and crowned with delicious toppings; you'll find great salads and sandwiches on fresh-baked focaccia here, too. See p. 150.
- **Best for "Taste of Washington" Experience:** Eat lunch at the **Monocle** (p. 122) and
  you're bound to see a Supreme Court justice, congressman, or senator dining here, too.
  For some down-home and delicious Washington fun, sit at the counter at **Ben's Chili
  Bowl** (p. 144), and chat with the owners and your neighbor over a chili dog or plate
  of blueberry pancakes. The place is an institution, and you can stop by anytime—it's
  open for breakfast, lunch, and dinner.

2 RESTAURANTS BY CUISINE

American/New American

Acadiana ★ (Penn Quarter, $$$,
   p. 128)
Ben's Chili Bowl (U Street Corridor, $,
   p. 144)
BLT Steak ★★ (Midtown, $$$$,
   p. 138)
Blue Duck Tavern ★★ (West End,
   $$$$, p. 151)
Bourbon Steak ★★ (Georgetown,
   $$$$, p. 153)
Café Saint-Ex ★ (U St. Corridor, $$,
   p. 143)
Cashion's Eat Place ★★ (Adams-
   Morgan, $$$, p. 145)
The Caucus Room ★★ (Penn Quar-
   ter, $$$$, p. 125)
Charlie Palmer Steak ★★ (Capitol
   Hill, $$$$, p. 120)
CityZen ★★★ (Capitol Hill, $$$$,
   p. 120)
Clyde's of Georgetown (Georgetown,
   $$, p. 157)
Corduroy ★★ (Midtown, $$$, p. 141)
Cork ★★ (U St. Corridor, $$, p. 143)
Creme Café ★ (U St. Corridor, $$,
   p. 143)
DC Coast ★ (Midtown, $$$, p. 141)
Equinox ★★ (Midtown, $$$$, p. 138)
Good Stuff Eatery (Capitol Hill, $,
   p. 124)

The Jockey Club ★★ (Dupont Circle,
   $$$$, p. 147)
Johnny's Half Shell ★★ (Capitol Hill,
   $$$, p. 121)
Kinkead's ★★ (Foggy Bottom, $$$$,
   p. 151)
Komi ★★★ (Dupont Circle, $$$$,
   p. 148)
Le Bon Café (Capitol Hill, $, p. 124)
Marvin ★ (U St. Corridor, $$, p. 144)
Mendocino Grille and Wine Bar ★
   (Georgetown, $$$, p. 156)
The Monocle (Capitol Hill, $$$,
   p. 122)
Next Door (U St. Corridor, $$, p. 144)
Old Ebbitt Grill (Penn Quarter, $$,
   p. 134)
The Oval Room ★ (Midtown, $$$,
   p. 141)
Palena ★★★ (Cleveland Park, $$$$,
   p. 160)
Poste ★ (Penn Quarter, $$$, p. 131)
Proof ★★ (Penn Quarter, $$$,
   p. 131)
PS7's ★★ (Penn Quarter, $$$, p. 131)
1789 ★★ (Georgetown, $$$$, p. 154)
Sonoma ★ (Capitol Hill, $$, p. 124)
Sweetgreen (Dupont Circle,
   Georgetown, $, p. 150)
Tabard Inn ★ (Dupont Circle, $$$,
   p. 149)

Key to Abbreviations: $$$$ = Very Expensive $$$ = Expensive $$ = Moderate $ = Inexpensive

Vidalia ★★ (Midtown, $$$$, p. 139)
Westend Bistro by Eric Ripert ★ (West End, $$$, p. 153)
Zola ★ (Penn Quarter, $$$, p. 132)

Asian Fusion

Café Asia (Midtown, $, p. 142)
Sei ★★ (Penn Quarter, $$, p. 136)
The Source ★★ (Penn Quarter, $$$$, p. 125)
Teaism (Dupont Circle, $, p. 150)
TenPenh ★ (Penn Quarter, $$$, p. 132)
Zengo ★ (Penn Quarter, $$$, p. 132)

Austrian

Leopold's Kafe & Konditorei ★ (Georgetown, $$, p. 157)

Barbecue

Old Glory Barbecue (Georgetown, $$, p. 158)

Belgian

Belga Café ★ (Capitol Hill, $$$, p. 120)
Brasserie Beck ★★ (Midtown, $$, p. 142)
Marvin ★ (U St. Corridor, $$, p. 144)

Chinese

Ching Ching Cha (Georgetown, $, p. 158)
Tony Cheng's Seafood Restaurant (Penn Quarter, $, p. 137)

Ethiopian

Etete ★ (U St. Corridor, $, p. 145)
Meskerem (Adams-Morgan, $, p. 147)

French

Adour ★★ (Midtown, $$$$, p. 137)
Bistro Bis ★ (Capitol Hill, $$$, p. 121)
Bistro D'Oc ★ (Penn Quarter, $$, p. 133)
Bistrot Lepic ★ (Georgetown, $$$, p. 154)

Café du Parc ★ (Penn Quarter, $$$, p. 129)
Central ★★★ (Penn Quarter, $$$, p. 129)
La Chaumiere ★★ (Georgetown, $$, p. 157)
Marcel's ★★★ (Foggy Bottom, $$$$, p. 152)
Michel Richard Citronelle ★★★ (Georgetown, $$$$, p. 153)
Montmartre ★ (Capitol Hill, $$, p. 124)
Palena ★★★ (Cleveland Park, $$$$, p. 160)
Westend Bistro by Eric Ripert ★ (West End, $$$, p. 153)

Greek

Komi ★★★ (Dupont Circle, $$$$, p. 148)
Zaytinya ★★ (Penn Quarter, $$, p. 137)

Indian

Bombay Club ★★ (Midtown, $$, p. 141)
Indique ★ (Cleveland Park, $$, p. 161)
Heritage India ★ (Glover Park, Dupont Circle, $$, p. 159)
Rasika ★★ (Penn Quarter, $$, p. 136)

Italian

Cafe Milano ★ (Georgetown, $$$, p. 156)
D'Acqua ★ (Penn Quarter, $$$, p. 130)
Matchbox ★ (Penn Quarter, $$, p. 134)
Obelisk ★★★ (Dupont Circle, $$$$, p. 148)
Pizzeria Paradiso ★ (Dupont Circle, $, p. 150)
Potenza (Penn Quarter, $$, p. 136)
Posto ★ (U St. Corridor, $$, p. 144)
Tosca ★★★ (Penn Quarter, $$$$, p. 128)

Japanese

Kaz Sushi Bistro ★ (Foggy Bottom, $$$, p. 152)

Sei ★★ (Penn Quarter, $$, p. 136)

Sushi-Ko ★ (Glover Park, $$, p. 160)

Latin American

Café Atlantico ★★ (Penn Quarter, $$$, p. 128)

Ceiba ★ (Penn Quarter, $$$, p. 129)

Las Canteras ★ (Adams-Morgan, $$, p. 145)

Lauriol Plaza (Adams-Morgan, $$, p. 147)

Oyamel ★★ (Penn Quarter, $$, p. 135)

Zengo ★ (Penn Quarter, $$$, p. 132)

Mexican

Lauriol Plaza (Adams-Morgan, $$, p. 147)

Oyamel ★★ (Penn Quarter, $$, p. 135)

Rosa Mexicano ★ (Penn Quarter, $$$, p. 132)

Middle Eastern

Lebanese Taverna (Woodley Park, $$, p. 162)

Zaytinya ★★ (Penn Quarter, $$, p. 137)

Peruvian

Las Canteras ★ (Adams-Morgan, $$, p. 145)

Pizza

Matchbox ★ (Penn Quarter, $$, p. 134)

Pizzeria Paradiso ★ (Dupont Circle, $, p. 150)

Potenza ★ (Penn Quarter, $$, p. 136)

Posto ★ (U St. Corridor, $$, p. 144)

Seafood

D'Acqua ★ (Penn Quarter, $$$, p. 130)

Hank's Oyster Bar ★ (Dupont Circle, $$, p. 149)

Hook ★ (Georgetown, $$$, p. 156)

Johnny's Half Shell ★★ (Capitol Hill, $$$, p. 121)

Legal Sea Foods ★ (Midtown, $$, p. 131)

Kinkead's ★★ (Foggy Bottom, $$$$, p. 151)

Oceanaire Seafood Room ★ (Penn Quarter, $$$, p. 130)

Pesce ★ (Dupont Circle, $$$, p. 149)

The Prime Rib ★★ (Midtown, $$$$, p. 138)

Tackle Box ★ (Georgetown, $, p. 158)

Tony Cheng's Seafood Restaurant (Penn Quarter, $, p. 137)

Southern/Southwestern

Acadiana ★ (Penn Quarter, $$$, p. 128)

Creme Café ★ (U St. Corridor, $$, p. 143)

Marvin ★ (U St. Corridor, $$, p. 144)

Next Door ★ (U St. Corridor, $$, p. 144)

Vidalia ★★ (Midtown, $$$$, p. 139)

Spanish

Jaleo ★ (Penn Quarter, $$, p. 133)

Lauriol Plaza (Adams-Morgan, $$, p. 147)

minibar ★★★ (Penn Quarter, $$$$, p. 128)

Taberna del Alabardero ★★ (Midtown, $$$$, p. 139)

Steak

BLT Steak ★★ (Midtown, $$$$, p. 138)

Bourbon Steak ★★ (Georgetown, $$$$, p. 153)

The Caucus Room ★★ (Penn Quarter, $$$$, p. 125)

Charlie Palmer Steak ★★ (Capitol Hill, $$$$, p. 120)

The Palm ★ (Dupont Circle, $$$$, p. 148)

The Prime Rib ★★ (Midtown, $$$$, p. 138)

Café Asia (Midtown, $, p. 142)
Teaism (Dupont Circle, $, p. 150)

Turkish

Zaytinya ★★ (Penn Quarter, $$, p. 137)

3 CAPITOL HILL

For information on eating at the Capitol and other government buildings, see the box titled "Views with a Meal," on p. 122.

VERY EXPENSIVE

Charlie Palmer Steak ★★ STEAK   Washington restaurant critics give CP high marks, both for its steaks and for its seafood entrees, like the butter-braised Maine lobster. Beef predominates, from the excellent wagyu sirloin to the perfectly done, dry-aged rib-eye. A dessert must: the chocolate hazelnut pyramid. The only steakhouse on Capitol Hill, CP Steak is more elegant than one might expect. Its dining room has three fireplaces, deep-cushioned couches, and intimate seating areas. It's a place to see and be seen—in big groups, preferably. Guests use a Palm Pilot-ish device to scroll through wine list selections from the 10,000-bottle inventory; a sommelier is on hand for consultation. The restaurant advertises that it overlooks the Capitol, but views are seasonal: In winter, you'll see more of the Capitol than you do in summer, when only the Capitol dome and the grounds are visible.

101 Constitution Ave. NW (at Louisiana Ave.). ✆ 202/547-8100. www.charliepalmer.com/Properties/CPSteak/DC. Reservations recommended. Lunch entrees $13–$39; prix-fixe lunch $25; dinner entrees $23–$61. AE, MC, V. Mon–Fri 11:30am–2:30pm and 5:30–10pm; Sat 5–10:30pm. Metro: Union Station (Massachusetts Ave. exit).

CityZen ★★★ NEW AMERICAN   Chef Eric Ziebold, winner of the 2008 James Beard Foundation's "Best Chef for the Mid-Atlantic Region" award, continues to fill tables nightly at CityZen and garner AAA five-diamond ratings annually. Located in the deluxe Mandarin Oriental Hotel, CityZen's dining room is temple-like: cathedral ceiling, dimly lit, with a coterie of acolytes flitting back and forth between tables and kitchen. The entire menu changes every 3 weeks, but you can always expect heavenly tastes, whether from an *amuse-bouche* of fried mushroom with truffle butter or a grilled pork jowl with marinated French green lentils. Between courses, waitstaff bring little refreshments, such as olive oil custard topped with infused butter. The restaurant's 500-plus-bottle wine selection concentrates on Bordeaux, Burgundy, and California Cabernet.

As mentioned in the review of the Mandarin Oriental Hotel (p. 85), the hotel is in an odd neighborhood. Enjoy a drink first on the hotel terrace or in CityZen's handsome bar (with its amazing "wall of fire"). ***Note:*** You can also dine fabulously and less expensively at the bar (p. 159).

In the Mandarin Oriental Hotel, 1330 Maryland Ave. SW (at 12th St.). ✆ **202/787-6868.** www.mandarinoriental.com/washington (then click on "Dining"). Reservations required. Sportswear, shorts, and denim discouraged. Prix-fixe $80 for 3-course menu; 6-course tasting menus $95 (vegetarian) and $110. AE, DC, DISC, MC, V. Tues–Thurs 6–9:30pm; Fri–Sat 5:30–9:30pm. Metro: Smithsonian (12th St./Independence Ave. exit).

EXPENSIVE

Belga Café ★ BELGIAN   Belga Café is located on a street called "Barracks Row," named for the Marine Corps barracks bordering the street to the east. This is one of those

D.C. neighborhoods that's been here forever—the Marine Barracks and the Navy Yard, just blocks away, sprouted 200 years ago—but now is being revitalized by merchants and the city, especially with the new, nearby presence of Nationals Ballpark, the Washington Nationals baseball stadium.

Enjoy sitting at the outdoor cafe on a fine spring day or inside the bustling, noisy, European-ish dining room. Everything's a waffle at brunch and lunch, meaning many of the sandwiches—croque-monsieur to hamburger—are served on *wafel* (waffled) bread. The menu lists each dish's Flemish name first, followed by the translation: *warme bloemkool soep* (cream of cauliflower soup), *vlaamse stoverij* (beef stew). My favorites? Belgian fries, beers (several on tap, another 30 or so in bottles), the mussels, and the *eendenborst,* which is duck breast à l'orange with duck confit.

514 8th St. SE (at Pennsylvania Ave.). (℅ **202/544-0100.** www.belgacafe.com. Reservations accepted. Brunch and lunch entrées $8.50–$24; dinner entrees $19–$29. AE, DC, DISC, MC, V. Lunch Mon–Thurs 11:30am–3pm, Fri 11:30am–5:30pm; brunch Sat 9am–5:30pm, Sun 9am–5pm; dinner Sun 5–9:30pm, Mon–Thurs 5:30–10pm, Fri–Sat 5:30–11pm. Metro: Eastern Market.

Bistro Bis ★ FRENCH BISTRO   The chic Hotel George is the home of this inconsistent, though mostly fine, French restaurant. The chef/owner, Jeff Buben, and his wife, Sallie, also run **Vidalia** (p. 139). You can sit at tables in the always-loud bar area, on the balcony overlooking the bar, at leather banquettes in the main dining room, or, in warm weather, on the sidewalk cafe. The menu covers French classics like bouillabaisse, boeuf bourguignon, and steak frites, endowed with Buben's own twist: Seared scallops Provençal comes with the anticipated tomatoes, garlic, and olives, but also an eggplant custard. Many items, including the sea scallops and the steak frites, appear on both the lunch and dinner menus but are considerably cheaper at lunch. Look around the dining room for nightly news types, since Bis's proximity to the Capitol make it a must-stop for movers and shakers, at all three meals.

15 E St. NW. (℅ **202/661-2700.** www.bistrobis.com. Reservations recommended. Breakfast $9–$14; brunch entrees $14–$20; lunch entrees $15–$24; dinner entrees $24–$33. AE, DC, DISC, MC, V. Daily 7–10am, 11:30am–2:30pm, and 5:30–10:30pm. Metro: Union Station.

Johnny's Half Shell ★★ (**Finds**) AMERICAN/SEAFOOD   Good restaurants are sparse in this neighborhood near Union Station and the Senate side of the Capitol, which partly explains why Johnny's, like the nearby Bistro Bis (see above), is always jumping. Mostly, though it's a matter of a good vibe—there's a healthy bar scene here—and unbeatable regional cuisine.

If you've heard of Eastern Shore fare, but don't know what that means, come here and try farm-raised chicken with old-fashioned slippery dumplings, or the crabmeat imperial with a salad of *haricots verts*, tomatoes, and shallots. If sautéed soft-shell crabs are on the menu, get them. Oysters and Wellfleet clams on the half shell are always available, of course.

Johnny's also runs the weekday Mexican takeout, *Taqueria Nacional* (℅ **202/737-7070**), which serves tacos, scrambled eggs, and waffles at breakfast and five varieties of soft tacos at $2.50 each, plus a daily $5.50 special, for lunch. Just look for the line leading beyond and to the right of Johnny's main entrance.

400 N. Capitol St. NW (at E St.). (℅ **202/737-0400.** www.johnnyshalfshell.net. Reservations recommended. Breakfast $7–$13; lunch entrees $8.25–$33; dinner entrees $18–$33. AE, MC, V. Mon–Fri 7–9:30am (*taqueria* 7–9am) and 11:30am–2:30pm (*taqueria* 11am–3pm); Mon–Sat 5–10pm; happy hour Mon–Fri 4:30–7:30pm. Metro: Union Station (Massachusetts Ave. exit).

Views with a Meal

Is there anything more wonderful than discovering that the attraction you are currently visiting also offers an excellent repast? Most tourist sites provide sustenance of some sort, generally humdrum in taste and high in price. Very few establishments proffer a delightful setting and food that's a real pleasure to eat. At the pinnacle of my list in Washington, D.C., are the **National Gallery of Art**'s restaurants, and in particular the **Sculpture Garden Pavilion Café** (© **202/289-3360**). You can sip a glass of wine and savor Cuban panini (roasted pork with crinkle-cut pickles, mustard, ham, cheese, and onions on Cuban bread), sitting inside in the glass pavilion in winter or on the terrace in warm weather, in view of sculpture, the landscaped garden, and grand sights of Washington, D.C. The gallery's **Cascades** and the **Garden Café** (© **202/712-7460**) are worthy second choices, offering a wide range of appetite-pleasers and really lovely surroundings. *FYI:* The Garden Café might be your first choice when its menu is tied to a particular exhibit, as it was recently when local chef celeb José Andrés created a special café menu of tapas and other Spanish dishes, inspired by the museum's exhibit of Spanish still life paintings.

Four other eateries are worth special mention: The **National Museum of the American Indian's Mitsitam Café** (© **202/633-1000**) seeks to educate as well as please the palate, since its menu represents traditional dishes from various Native American regions. Examples include cedar-planked juniper salmon from the Pacific Northwest, buffalo burgers from the Great Plains, and, a favorite, fry bread from all over. The **International Spy Museum's Spy City Café** (© **202/654-0995**) is one of the rare museum eateries to open early—8am weekdays and 10am weekends—and is rightly famous for its cleverly named hot dogs, like the Red Square Dog. The petite **Café** (© **202/387-2151**, ext. 351), in the **Phillips Collection**, is operated by the clever eco-friendly vendor operation, On the Fly, which sells tasty sandwiches, salads, soups, and small plates made from locally grown ingredients. Firehook Bakery, beloved for its sandwiches on thick breads and for its selection of delicious desserts operates the cafe at the **National Building Museum.** The **Newseum**'s separately owned but in-house restaurant is the exceptional **the Source** (© **202/637-6100**), Wolfgang Puck's three-level, glass-fronted, crowd-attracting eatery serving Asian-influenced cuisine.

The Monocle (Finds) AMERICAN   A Capitol Hill institution, the Monocle has been around since 1960. At this men-in-suits place, the litter of briefcases resting against the too-close-together tables can make for treacherous navigating. But you might want to take a look at whose briefcase it is you're stumbling over, for its proximity to both the Supreme Court and the Capitol guarantees that the Monocle is the haunt of Supreme Court justices and members of Congress. At lunch you'll want to order the hamburger, which is excellent; the tasty federal salad (field greens and tomatoes tossed with balsamic

Finally, you just can't beat the atmosphere (political) and value (cheap) of the all-American food served in certain dining rooms on Capitol Hill. Keep these places in mind while touring the Hill; but always call ahead, since these restaurants sometimes close to the public.

For a most exclusive experience, try to dine in the **House of Representatives Restaurant** (also called the "Members' Dining Room") in Room H118, at the south end of the Capitol (*C* **202/225-6300**). You are always welcome (after you've gone through security, of course) in the eateries located in the Capitol office buildings across the street from the Capitol. These are quite affordable—your meal isn't taxed, for one thing. You'll be surrounded by Hill staffers, who head to places like the immense, full-service **Rayburn House Office Building Cafeteria** (*C* **202/225-7109**), which is in Room B357, in the basement of the building, at 1st Street and Independence Avenue SW. Adjoining the cafeteria is a carryout that sells pizza and sandwiches. In the basement-level **Longworth Building Cafeteria,** Independence Avenue and South Capitol Street SE (*C* **202/225-0878**), you can grab a bite from a fairly nice food court. Other options include the Russell Carryout and the Cannon Carryout, both in the basement of the Cannon Building. All of these eateries are open weekdays only. The carryouts stay open until late afternoon, while the other dining rooms close at 2:30pm.

The new **Capitol Visitors Center's** (*C* **202/593-1785**) large dining hall is open 8:30am to 4pm Monday through Saturday, seats 400 people, and serves "meals and snacks that reflect the diverse bounty of America," which translates into the usual hamburgers and hot dogs, croissants and bagels, pizza and pasta, but also specialty sandwiches associated with different pockets of the country, like the New England lobster roll and the Philly cheese steak. Check it out.

Right across the street from the Capitol is the **Supreme Court's Cafeteria** (*C* **202/479-3246**), where you may spy a famous lawyer or member of the press, but not any of the justices, who have their own dining room; the cafeteria is open weekdays, 7am to 4pm.

vinaigrette); or the white-bean soup when it's on the menu. At dinner, consider the roasted oysters, the pork-rib chop with Pommery mustard sauce, or "Crab Conrad," a lump crab dish that owner John Valanos created to honor his father, Conrad Valanos, who opened the Monocle in 1960.

107 D St. NE. *C* **202/546-4488.** www.themonocle.com. Reservations recommended. Lunch entrees $9.95–$26; dinner entrees $17–$35. AE, DC, DISC, MC, V. Mon–Fri 11:30am–midnight; Sat 5–11pm. Closed Saturday nights Jun–Labor Day and for 2 weeks preceding Labor Day. Metro: Union Station (Massachusetts Ave. exit).

Montmartre ★ FRENCH   Montmartre's ambience is warmed by its decor—pale yellow-orange walls, exposed-wood ceiling, cozy bar, and old wooden tables, all fronted by a sidewalk cafe open in warm weather. It's very much a neighborhood spot. The owners here are French, and Montmartre is their little French restaurant offering big French pleasures: chicory salad tossed with goat cheese and croutons, chestnut soup, pistou, potato gratin, flatiron beef with Jerusalem artichokes, seared monkfish wrapped in smoked bacon, and calves' liver sautéed with smothered onions. Desserts, like the pear marzipan tart, don't disappoint.

327 7th St. SE. ✆ **202/544-1244.** Reservations recommended. Brunch $8.95–$17; lunch and dinner entrees $18–$21. AE, DC, MC, V. Tues–Fri 11:30am–2:30pm; Sat–Sun 10:30am–3pm; Mon–Fri 5:30–10pm; Sat 5:30–10:30pm; Sun 5:30–9pm. Metro: Eastern Market.

Sonoma ★ AMERICAN   Oenophiles and lounge lovers have equal reason to visit Sonoma, since the restaurant offers 40 wines by the glass from its inventory of 200 Californian wines, as well as a lively lounge scene on the second floor. (Families with small children should look elsewhere.) Plates of charcuterie, artisanal cheeses, and pizzas are for sharing, while a menu of "firsts" offers pastas and "seconds" lists meat and seafood dishes. Try a small plate of the charcuterie, then follow it up with a house-made goat cheese ravioli and the coffee-glazed Duroc baby back ribs. The smart-looking Sonoma stands out on this stretch of Pennsylvania Avenue, where most of its neighbors are coffeehouses and bars. The long, narrow dining room often fills up with a drinking crowd waiting for a table in the evening. That's when you'll want to head upstairs and check out the lounge, which has a fireplace and overlooks Pennsylvania Avenue.

223 Pennsylvania Ave. SE (at 2nd St. SE). ✆ **202/544-8088.** www.sonomadc.com. Reservations recommended. Lunch and dinner entrees $11–$34. AE, DC, DISC, MC, V. Mon–Fri 11:30am–2:30pm; Mon–Thurs 5:30–10pm; Fri–Sat 5:30–11pm; Sun 5:30–9pm. Metro: Capitol South.

INEXPENSIVE

Good Stuff Eatery ★ BURGERS   Top chef contestant Spike Mendelsohn is as much a master of celebrity fanfare as divine burgers. Winner of Rachael Ray's 2009 Burger Bash and assorted other kudos, Mendelsohn's burgery is also a player in the ongoing Obama burger wars, with the Prez choosing local chain Five Guys and other D.C. burger establishments and Michelle Obama and her staff heading here (in fairness, Michelle Obama has also tried Five Guys). Bottom line: If you're a fan of hamburgers, you gotta try one of these. Most people buy burgers to go, but you can dine in, upstairs, where beers and flatscreen TVs are added distractions. My personal faves are the Big Stuff Bacon Meltdown, made with Applewood smoked bacon, and the toasted marshmallow milkshake. There are also hefty salads and sides.

323 Pennsylvania Ave. NW (at 3rd St.). ✆ **202/543-8222.** www.goodstuffeatery.com. Reservations not accepted. Burgers $5.49–$7.79; milkshakes and sundaes $4.39–$5.25. AE, DISC, MC, V. Mon–Sat 11:30am–11pm. Metro: Capitol South.

Le Bon Café (Finds) AMERICAN/CAFE   Pennsylvania Avenue on Capitol Hill is a stretch of been-around-a-while pubs, coffeehouses, bakeries, and the occasional fine-dining establishment. The Capitol looms over the neighborhood, whose other big buildings hold the Library of Congress and Senate and House offices. Government edifices aside, this part of town is mostly a residential village, enlivened by the presence of young staffers who swarm here for lunch, dinner, coffee, or a drink. One of my favorite lunchtime eateries is the tiny Le Bon Café, whose menu is short but sweet: homemade pumpkin gingerbread and scones, smoked turkey club sandwich on farm bread, grilled salmon Niçoise salad, and the like. And it's cheap: The most expensive single item is that salmon salad for $9.85. Seating inside is minimal, with most people grabbing food to go; in pleasant weather, you can sit at outdoor tables. *FYI:* Pete's Diner and Carryout, right next door, also attracts a loyal Hill following with its low prices and burgers-and-fried-chicken menu; so stop there if you've got a greasy spoon kind of appetite.

210 2nd St. SE (at Pennsylvania Ave. SE). (C) **202/547-7200.** Breakfast items $2.25–$5; salads/sand-wiches/soups $3.85–$9.85. AE, DISC, MC, V. Mon–Fri 7am–3:30pm; Sat–Sun 8am–3pm. Metro: Capitol South.

4 DOWNTOWN, PENN QUARTER

VERY EXPENSIVE

The Caucus Room ★★ STEAK   Washington's powerful people like steakhouses. See for yourself. At lunch and dinner, the dining room is a true Washington scene, with all that this entails: a sprinkling of congressmen and -women, television newscasters, and corporate VIPs throughout the main dining room; lots of backslapping and shaking of hands; and meetings taking place behind closed doors (the restaurant has a number of private dining rooms).

Besides the steaks, favorite entrees include the crab cakes (the pass/fail test for a D.C. restaurant) and seared fish. A recent preparation was seared rockfish, sesame crusted and served with Asian vegetables. Even side dishes, like the creamed spinach and the horse-radish-spiked mashed potatoes, are winners.

After you finish your main course, lean back against the leather banquette and dis-creetly search for famous faces as you enjoy dessert, maybe a crème brulee or slice of key lime pie. *Tip:* Best time to be here is when Congress is in session; otherwise, you'll find the Caucus Room fairly deserted.

401 9th St. NW (at D St.). (C) **202/393-1300.** www.thecaucusroom.com. Reservations recommended. Lunch items $15–$59; dinner entrees $32–$59. AE, DC, DISC, MC, V. Mon–Fri 11:30am–2:30pm; Mon–Sat 5:30–10pm. Metro: Navy/Archives or Gallery Place (9th St. exit).

The Source ★★ ASIAN FUSION/AMERICAN   Even if you didn't know the Source was a Wolfgang Puck establishment, you would have to register its L.A.-cool vibe. Like the Newseum, in which the Source resides, the two-level restaurant is glass-fronted, attracting all who happen by. Background music veers from David Bowie to Indian trance. Hostesses look like models in their sexy black dresses and heels. And the place is extremely loud, whether in the downstairs lounge, where a young hip crowd gathers day and night, or up that long marble staircase to the main dining room, where the lighting is dim and the mood vibrant. The big news here is the food is really, really good. Though Puck himself is not in the kitchen, his inspiration is apparent in every dish. Do try the "tiny dumplings," my favorite item on the menu. Go on from there to lacquered duck, or the short ribs, and end with the chocolate purse for dessert.

575 Pennsylvania Ave. NW (in the Newseum). (C) **202/637-6100.** www.wolfgangpuck.com/restaurants. Reservations recommended. Lounge entrees $12–$16; lunch entrees $14–$29 or prix fixe $35; dinner entrees $26–$60. AE, DC, DISC, MC, V. Mon–Fri 11:30am–2pm; Mon–Thurs 5:30–10pm; Fri–Sat 5:30–11pm.

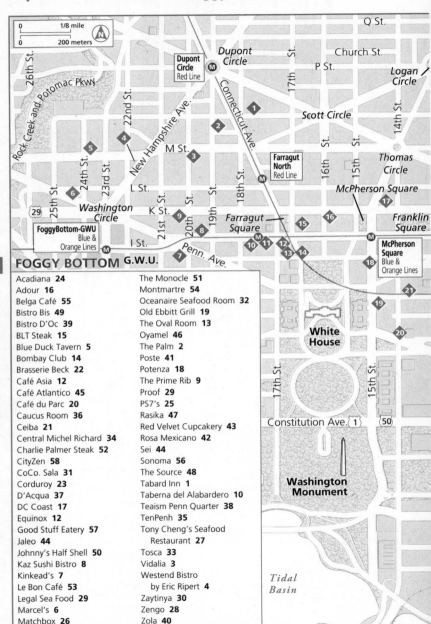

WHERE TO DINE

6

DOWNTOWN, PENN QUARTER

Acadiana **24**
Adour **16**
Belga Café **55**
Bistro Bis **49**
Bistro D'Oc **39**
BLT Steak **15**
Blue Duck Tavern **5**
Bombay Club **14**
Brasserie Beck **22**
Café Asia **12**
Café Atlantico **45**
Café du Parc **20**
Caucus Room **36**
Ceiba **21**
Central Michel Richard **34**
Charlie Palmer Steak **52**
CityZen **58**
CoCo. Sala **31**
Corduroy **23**
D'Acqua **37**
DC Coast **17**
Equinox **12**
Good Stuff Eatery **57**
Jaleo **44**
Johnny's Half Shell **50**
Kaz Sushi Bistro **8**
Kinkead's **7**
Le Bon Café **53**
Legal Sea Food **29**
Marcel's **6**
Matchbox **26**

The Monocle **51**
Montmartre **54**
Oceanaire Seafood Room **32**
Old Ebbitt Grill **19**
The Oval Room **13**
Oyamel **46**
The Palm **2**
Poste **41**
Potenza **18**
The Prime Rib **9**
Proof **29**
PS7's **25**
Rasika **47**
Red Velvet Cupcakery **43**
Rosa Mexicano **42**
Sei **44**
Sonoma **56**
The Source **48**
Tabard Inn **1**
Taberna del Alabardero **10**
Teaism Penn Quarter **38**
TenPenh **35**
Tony Cheng's Seafood
  Restaurant **27**
Tosca **33**
Vidalia **3**
Westend Bistro
  by Eric Ripert **4**
Zaytinya **30**
Zengo **28**
Zola **40**

Tosca ★★★ NORTHERN ITALIAN   Washington probably has more Italian restaurants than any other kind of ethnic eatery. Nevertheless, Tosca remains one of the finest in the city, when it comes to fine *ristorantes italiano*.

Tosca's interior of pale pastels, thick carpeting, and heavy drapes creates a hushed atmosphere, a suitable foil to the rich food. Even when there's a crowd, Tosca doesn't get too noisy—the restaurant's designers kept acoustics in mind. The menu, meanwhile, emphasizes the cooking of the Lake Como region of Italy. Recommended dishes include a grilled rack of veal with a mix of wild mushrooms and a roasted Mediterranean sea bass with balsamic vinegar sabayon and sautéed spinach with pine nuts and raisins. Tosca has something for everyone, including simply grilled fish accompanied by organic vegetables for the health-conscious, and desserts such as tiramisu or ricotta-and-goat-cheese fritters for those with a sweet tooth. *Tip:* Also read about Tosca's new sibling, the casual Italian restaurant, **Posto**, at 14th and P streets.

1112 F St. NW. Ⓒ **202/367-1990.** www.toscadc.com. Reservations recommended. Lunch entrees $14–$23; dinner entrees $24–$42; pretheater menu $35; tasting menus $70–$95. AE, DISC, MC, V. Mon–Fri 11:30am–2:30pm; Mon–Thurs 5:30–10:30pm; Fri–Sun 5:30–11pm. Metro: Metro Center (12th and F sts. exit).

EXPENSIVE

Acadiana ★ SOUTHERN   This glass-walled triangle-shaped restaurant lies close to the convention center, so if you're attending an event there, you might be interested to know that Acadiana's bar stays open straight through from lunch to dinner and offers a menu of appetizers, like mini pulled-pork sandwiches on biscuits and crispy catfish, as well as Sazeracs, mint juleps, and other pick-me-ups. The restaurant's high ceilings, ornate chandeliers, and oversize urns and other features fit with the over-the-top atmosphere that prevails. This is New Orleans central, right here. New Orleanians say the cuisine's the real thing, starting with the biscuits, served with a pepper jelly and cream cheese condiment; continuing on to deviled eggs, charbroiled oysters, and crabmeat and artichoke gratin starters; and even further to jambalaya, étouffée, red snapper in an almondine sauce, and barbecue shrimp. Service is excellent.

901 New York Ave. NW (at 9th St.). Ⓒ **202/408-8848.** www.acadianarestaurant.com. Reservations recommended. Bar items $5–$13; lunch entrees $12–$28; dinner entrees $21–$29. AE, DC, DISC, MC, V. Mon–Fri 11:30am–2:30pm; Mon–Thurs 5:30–10:15pm; Fri–Sat 5:30–10:30pm; Sun 11am–2:30pm and 5:30–9:15pm; bar stays open 11am to closing daily. Metro: Mount Vernon Sq./7th St. Convention Center.

Café Atlantico ★★ (Finds) LATIN AMERICAN   Born in Spain in 1969, the award-winning José Andrés, dubbed the "boy wonder of culinary Washington" by the *New York Times*, began his career in D.C. about 2 decades and many kitchens ago. Besides Atlantico, Andrés is behind the success of Jaleo (p. 133), Zaytinya (p. 137), and Oyamel (p. 135; as well as his new restaurant in L.A., The Bazaar). He has received highest praise for **minibar** ★★★ , a dining experience within Café Atlantico, where he concocts 30 to 40 small creations, from foie gras in a cocoon of cotton candy to pineapple ravioli, for six people per seating, Tuesday to Saturday, at 6 and 8:30pm. The gourmet adventure costs $120 per person, not including wine, tax, and tip, and requires a reservation that's best made a month in advance.

The main restaurant of Café Atlantico, meanwhile, rocks on. The colorful three-tiered bistro is a Penn Quarter hot spot, where *caipirinhas* and *mojitos* are the cocktails of choice and guacamole made tableside is a must. Check out the ceviche; Cornish hen wrapped in bacon served with deconstructed mole sauce; and seared scallops with coconut crispy rice and ginger, squid, and squid-ink oil; though the menu frequently changes, you're sure to find these or their equivalent listed. *Note:* A planned top-to-bottom renovation may have changed these particulars, or even closed the restaurant temporarily, by the time you read this review.

405 8th St. NW (at D St. NW). ✆ **202/393-0812.** www.cafeatlantico.com. Reservations recommended. Lunch entrees $13–$15; dinner entrees $20–$28; pretheater menu $35 (nightly 5–6:30pm); Latino dim sum brunch (Sat–Sun): you can choose a la carte items ($2–$8 each), pay $25 for a vegetarian all-you-can-eat meal, or $35 for a deluxe version. AE, DC, DISC, MC, V. Tues–Fri 11:30am–2:30pm; Sat–Sun brunch 11:30am–2:30pm; Sun and Tues–Thurs 5–10pm; Fri–Sat 5–11pm. Bar stays open late on weekends. Metro: Archives–Navy Memorial or Gallery Place/Verizon Center (7th and F sts. exit).

Café du Parc ★ FRENCH BRASSERIE

Although Washington has only recently come into its own as a great restaurant destination, the city has always been known for its excellent French establishments. That tradition continues as more French eateries come on board, including the Willard Hotel's delightful Café du Parc, the hotel's only restaurant, now that the famed Willard Room is used only for private events. The sunny two-level bistro overlooks Pershing Park and offers courtyard seating during clement weather—and the terrace is where you want to be when it's nice out. Renowned Michelin-starred chef Antoine Westermann oversees the menu and has dispatched his own assistants to staff the cafe; you can watch them at work in the open kitchen on the second floor. The dishes are redolent of Paris—*les tomates farcies aux legumes* (tomatoes stuffed with vegetables), *choucroute alsacienne* (sauerkraut with pork and sausages), and the *pâté en croûte* (pastry-wrapped terrine of veal, pork, and foie gras, cooked with wine and Armagnac). Francophiles find it a must, though most dine here at lunch, when the ambience is decidedly livelier than later in the day. You can carry out certain items daily until 5pm.

1401 Pennsylvania Ave. NW, part of the Willard InterContinental Washington Hotel (at 14th St.). ✆ **202/942-7000.** www.cafeduparc.com. Reservations accepted. Breakfast $5.50–$14; lunch entrees $20–$25; dinner entrees $19–$29. AE, DC, DISC, MC, V. Mon–Fri 6:30–10:30am, noon–2:30pm, and 5:30–10pm; Sat–Sun 7–11am, noon–2:30pm, and 6–10pm; limited menu daily 2–5:30pm; carryout daily until 5pm. Metro: Metro Center (13th St. exit) or Federal Triangle.

Ceiba ★ CONTEMPORARY LATIN AMERICAN

Ceiba is the creation of Jeff Tunks, the chef maestro behind TenPenh, DC Coast, and Acadiana (p. 132, 141, and 128). Here at Ceiba, Tunks works his magic on ceviches, offering four variations—grouper, shrimp, tuna, and striped bass—which you may order individually or as a sampler, as well as on other authentic Latin dishes, like the Veracruz-style red snapper, topped with tomatoes, capers, olives, and jalapeños. As is true at all Tunks establishments, fulsome drinks are integral to the experience. The ones offered here go down nicely: mojitos, mango margaritas, and pisco sours, as well as fine wines from Argentina and Chile. If you're stopping in for a quick fix, the bar menu complements those cocktails with tastes of pork pupusas, conch fritters, ceviches, and assorted others; each item is reasonably priced from $9 to $16. For best ambience, try for a table in the main dining room, to your right as you enter.

701 14th St. NW. ✆ **202/393-3983.** www.ceibarestaurant.com. Reservations recommended. Lunch entrees $13–$16; dinner entrees $14–$29. AE, DC, DISC, MC, V. Mon–Fri 11:30am–2:30pm; Mon–Thurs 5:30–10:30pm; Fri–Sat 5:30–11pm. Bar weekdays 11:30am–closing; Sat 3pm–closing. Metro: Metro Center (13th and G sts. exit).

Central Michel Richard ★★★ FRENCH BISTRO

Named "best new restaurant" by the James Beard Foundation in 2008, Central makes you feel good as soon as you walk through the door. It's a French-American brasserie with a *joie de vivre* ambience and a menu full of precociously re-created American and French classics. A lobster burger is layered with scallop mousse, macaroni and cheese is creamy with sour cream as well as cheeses, the fried chicken is an ungreasy version lightly dusted with bread crumbs. On and on it goes, the names of French dishes ping-ponging with American, hanger steak and onion soup to apple pan dowdy and banana split. The french fries, a country unto themselves, are perfection. The genius here is Michel Richard, who opened Central in 2007 to entice diners with affordable but grand cuisine. The Frenchman, who has lived in the U.S. for nearly 40 years, has a special fondness for his adopted country and it shows in both the menu and the ambience. Richard is best known for his ultra-expensive, wildly innovative Citronelle, which many consider the city's best restaurant; Richard has transferred his upscale cuisine talents to a new restaurant that should have opened in the Ritz-Carlton Hotel Tysons Corner, in suburban Virginia, by the time you read this. But rest assured: Central is staying put.

1001 Pennsylvania Ave. NW (at 11th St.). ✆ **202/626-0015.** www.centralmichelrichard.com. Reservations recommended. Lunch entrees $14–$33; dinner entrees $16–$33. AE, DC, DISC, MC, V. Mon–Fri 11:45am–2:30pm; Mon–Thurs 5–10:30pm; Fri–Sat 5–11pm; Sun 5–9:30pm. Metro: Metro Center (12th and F sts. exit).

D'Acqua ★ ITALIAN/SEAFOOD D'Acqua's window-fronted dining room overlooks the Navy Memorial and courtyard, as well as a slice of Pennsylvania Avenue; its seasonal sidewalk seating allows you to feel a part of the capital's bustling scene—during the day, especially. Decorative elements inside convey an Italian coastal feel thanks to a colorful palette of Tuscan gold and Mediterranean blue. The expansive L-shaped bar terminates at one end in a display of that day's fresh fish options. You select your fish, then request that it be grilled, oven-roasted, or salt-crust baked. The menu also offers a variety of its own meat, fish, and pasta preparations, like the delicious *triangoli di pesce,* which is seafood and porcini ravioli with lemon and marjoram sauce. D'Acqua offers nearby Tosca (p. 128) some competition for excellent Italian cuisine in this part of town, but D'Acqua might be the better choice if you're after fresh fish, an Italian accent, and a less formal atmosphere.

801 Pennsylvania Ave. NW (at 8th St.). ✆ **202/783-7717.** www.dacquadc.com. Reservations accepted. Lunch entrees $14–$23; dinner entrees $18–$34; bar menu $8–$9. AE, MC, V. Mon–Fri 11:30am–11pm; Sat 5–11pm; Sun 5–10pm. Metro: Gallery Place/Chinatown (7th and F sts. exit) or Archives/Navy Memorial.

Oceanaire Seafood Room ★ SEAFOOD The Oceanaire is a good spot for a lively party, with its red-leather booths, Art Deco decor, long bar, and festive atmosphere. It would be hard to get romantic or serious about business here—there's just too much to distract you, like the sight of mile-high desserts en route to another table. Oceanaire serves big portions of everything (including cocktails, another reason to bring a bunch of friends here). True to the restaurant's proclamation, "Fresh fish flown in daily from around the world!", the menu's daily catches are global offerings: grilled Hawaiian ono wahoo, Tasmanian ocean trout, Costa Rican mahimahi, and so on. These are usually served simply grilled or broiled. The waitstaff excel at explaining the tastes and textures of everything on the menu, so don't hesitate to ask. Two of the best entrees are the crab cakes, which are almost all lump crabmeat, and the shellfish platter, a fresh, chilled selection of oysters, lobster, shrimp, crab, and mussels, with hot matchstick fries alongside it all. The dozen varieties of oysters are fresh and plump. If you want to start with a salad, consider the BLT, which is just like eating a bacon-lettuce-tomato sandwich without the toast.

1201 F St. NW. ✆ **202/347-2277.** www.theoceanaire.com. Reservations recommended. Lunch entrees $20–$30; dinner entrees $20–$50. AE, DC, DISC, MC, V. Mon–Thurs 11:30am–10pm; Fri 11:30am–11pm; Sat 5–11pm; Sun 5–9pm. Metro: Metro Center (12th and F sts.).

Poste ★ NEW AMERICAN   This lovely brasserie lies within one of Washington's coolest hotels, the Monaco. You find its separate entrance via an arched carriageway that leads to a stone-paved courtyard, where the restaurant sets up tables in warm weather. Inside, past a small bar-lounge, is the dining area, which includes an exhibition kitchen, banquettes, and a quieter back room. Poste chef Robert Weland has established himself well, settling into a pleasant culinary groove that wins praise from local critics and diners. Weland uses seasonal local ingredients to create modern American fare heavily influenced by traditional French cuisine. At lunch that means a croque-monsieur is made with Virginia ham and Gruyère on brioche; at dinner, your selections may include French onion soup, herbed fresh ricotta ravioli, red wine–braised rabbit, steak frites, and boeuf bourguignon. Desserts, too, blend French and American tastes; try the chocolate *pot de crème* (custard), which lists chili (!) as an ingredient. A wine list of 100 California and French bottles offers nearly 30 wines by the glass.

555 8th St. NW, in the Hotel Monaco. ℂ **202/783-6060.** www.postebrasserie.com. Reservations recommended. Breakfast $8–$15; brunch $11–$20; lunch entrees $13–$26; dinner entrees $26–$42 (most are less than $30); pretheater menu $35. AE, DC, DISC, MC, V. Mon–Fri 7–10am and 11:30am–2:30pm; Sat–Sun 8am–2pm; Mon–Thurs 5–10pm; Fri–Sat 5–10:30pm; Sun 5–9pm. Bar daily 11:30am–closing. Metro: Gallery Place/Verizon Center (7th and F sts. exit).

Proof ★★ NEW AMERICAN   Proof plays up its superb location in the Penn Quarter, directly across the street from the Smithsonian American Art Museum/National Portrait Gallery. The restaurant's windowed front overlooks the stately building, while inside Proof, monitors over the bar flash images of works of art displayed in the museum. Message: Visit the museum, if you haven't already.

Meanwhile, you're in for a food and drink treat in the wine-centric Proof. Put yourself in your waiter's hands, as we did, and you will likely end up happy. We enjoyed rabbit terrine, pork rillettes, salmon flatbread (a little like small pizzas), heirloom tomatoes, short smoked black pearl salmon, topped off with toffee pudding cake and a trio of sorbets for dessert. Portions are manageable, the dishes delicious. And absolutely put yourself in sommelier Sebastian Zutant's capable hands. Zutant, who is charmingly, graciously cool, knows his stuff and directs diners to those wines that will suit individual budgets and tastes.

775 G St. NW (at 8th St.). ℂ **202/737-7663.** www.proofdc.com. Reservations recommended. Lunch entrees $13–$23; dinner entrees $21–$24. AE, MC, V. Mon–Fri 11:30am–2pm; Mon–Wed 5:30–10pm; Thurs–Sat 5:30–11pm; Sun 5–9:30pm. Metro: Gallery Place/Chinatown (9th and G sts. exit).

PS7's ★★ NEW AMERICAN   Chef Peter Smith opened PS7's in 2006 after many years working the kitchen at the award-winning Vidalia (p. 139). His culinary artistry is on excellent display here, but first you must navigate the fey menu, which organizes foods in categories of "Cool" (salads and such), "Hot" (soups and pastas), "Aqua" (fish), and "Terra" (meats). And though the portions are small, the food is rich . . . and delicious. We liked the beef shortrib and tenderloin with pomme frites, tuna sliders (bites of tuna tartare on sesame-seed buns), and spring rolls. The dining room is elegantly modern, with floor-to-ceiling windows, lots of dark wood, and hues of charcoal, brown, and blue. The restaurant also has an expansive bar/lounge, whose menu features several items from the main menu—including those tuna sliders and spring rolls. But the lounge seating can make noshing problematic, so stand for a drink and then head to the dining room for a proper tuck-in.

777 I St. NW (at 8th St.). ℂ **202/742-8550.** www.ps7restaurant.com. Reservations accepted. Lunch entrees $7.50–$19; dinner entrees $21–$27. AE, DC, MC, V. Mon–Fri 11:30am–2:30pm; Mon–Thurs 5:30–10pm; Fri–Sat 5:30–10:30pm; lounge menu available Mon–Fri all day, Fri–Sat 5:30pm–closing. Metro: Gallery Place/Chinatown (H and 7th sts. exit).

Rosa Mexicano ★ MEXICAN It's a chain, but hey, so what? Most of its other locations are in the Big Apple. This one stands out in the nation's capital for its sensational decor: a beautiful blue glass-tiled wall, over which flows a veil of water; 14-foot-high ceilings; and full-wall windows overlooking the hottest crossroads in town, at 7th and F streets, across from the Verizon Center. The place is popular. *Washington Flyer* magazine reports that Rosa serves "13,000 margaritas and 4,500 orders of guacamole every month." Trust those numbers, because both the guacamole and the margs are super. Other tasty items include quesadillas, grilled beef short ribs, and the *queso fundido* (melted cheese). Like a growing number of restaurants throughout the city, Rosa Mexicano's bar stays open from lunch until closing, even when the dining room shuts down. So if you're hungry or thirsty between lunch and dinner, stop in at the bar to consume your share of this month's quota of 13,000 margaritas and 4,500 orders of guacamole.

575 7th St. NW (at F St.). ✆ **202/783-5522.** www.rosamexicano.com. Reservations recommended. Brunch $9–$16; lunch entrees $10–$19; dinner entrees $14–$28. AE, DISC, MC, V. Mon–Wed 11:30am–10:30pm; Thurs–Fri 11:30am–11:30pm; Sat 11am–11:30pm; Sun 11am–10:30pm. Metro: Gallery Place/Verizon Center (7th and F sts. exit).

TenPenh ★ ASIAN FUSION The atmosphere is lively, and the food here stellar. TenPenh has a separate, loungey, hard-to-leave bar; but the dining room itself is inviting, with soft lighting, comfortable booths, and an open kitchen. Jeff Tunks, the man also behind DC Coast, Ceiba, and Acadiana (p. 141, 129, 128), presents translations of dishes he's discovered in travels throughout Asia: crispy whole fish; Chinese-style smoked lobster (also available at DC Coast); wok-seared calamari; and dumplings filled with steamed shrimp and chives. In spring, look for soft-shell crab on the menu. Spring is when the sidewalk tables open up, too; and you can sit outside on a warm day and take in the sights of the capital as you finish your meal with warm upsidedown banana cake. For post-lunch munchies, sit at the bar and order little things, like tuna sliders or lamb pot stickers, $8-$23.

1001 Pennsylvania Ave. NW (at 10th St.). ✆ **202/393-4500.** www.tenpenh.com. Reservations recommended. Lunch entrees $13–$18; dinner entrees $15–$28. AE, DISC, MC, V. Mon–Fri 11:30am–2:30pm; Mon–Thurs 5:30–10:30pm; Fri–Sat 5:30–11pm. Sun 5:30–9:30pm. Bar weekdays 2:30pm–closing; Sat 5:30pm–closing. Metro: Archives–Navy Memorial.

Zengo ★ LATIN/ASIAN FUSION Downstairs is the lounge, a pulsing after-work destination for a multiethnic cross section of Washington professionals. Men and women in suits balance small plates of tapas on their laps or lean back upon the puffy, low-slung sofas and ottomans to drink Zengo's signature mojitos and margaritas. Up two intimidating flights of wide, marble steps lies the dining room, which is just as popular; it features a ceviche bar, a glass-enclosed private dining room, and tables scattered throughout the large room, with some overlooking 7th Street. Latin-Asian cuisine might be an unusual concept, but D.C. diners are nothing if not intrepid. And it turns out that bravery isn't necessary anyway, since ceviches, sushi rolls, and dim sum appetizers marry Asian and Latin tastes quite nicely, whether in a Thai chicken empanada or a won ton taco. Entrées, like the wok-roasted scallops or the twice-cooked pork carnitas with kaboch squash puree, prove the same.

781 7th St. NW (at H St.). ✆ **202/393-2929.** www.modernmexican.com. Reservations recommended. Lunch entrees $14–$24; dinner entrees $16–$26. AE, MC, V. Mon–Fri 11:30am–3pm; Sun–Thurs 5–10pm; Fri–Sat 5–11:30pm. Metro: Gallery Place/Verizon Center (either exit).

Zola ★ AMERICAN Zola prepares "straight ahead American" cuisine, with a few twists. Count on deliciousness: a simple mushroom crepe, lobster "mac and cheese," or grilled lamb burger at lunch; the tangy sherry-lacquered skate wing or the vegetarian-friendly cauliflower-stuffed zucchini tart at dinner, with such sweets as key lime cheese-cake for dessert. Zola is a cleverly designed restaurant, trading on its location next to the International Spy Museum for a decor that includes red-velvet booths, backlit panels of coded KGB documents, and a center-pivoted swinging wall/door that's like something straight out of the TV show *Get Smart*. Zola, in its superb downtown location, has become a popular place for the young and single to hang. Servers are friendly. A $30 pretheater menu, available nightly 5 to 7pm, offers great value. Don't miss Zola Wine Kitchen, just around the corner (see p. 251).

800 F St. NW (at 8th St.). (©) **202/654-0999.** www.zoladc.com. Reservations recommended. Lunch entrees $12–$21; dinner entrees $17–$29; pretheater prix-fixe menu $30. AE, DC, DISC, MC, V. Mon–Thurs 11:30am–10pm; Fri 11:30am–11pm; Sat 5–11pm; Sun 5–9pm; bar stays open later. Metro: Gallery Place/Chinatown (7th and F sts. exit).

MODERATE

Bistro D'Oc ★ FRENCH   Grab your best girl or guy and duck in here at lunch to sit at a table set against the storefront window. Watch busloads of tourists waiting in line to enter Ford's Theater across the street before turning your attention to the meal: croque-monsieur, the *potage parisien* (potato and leek soup with Gruyère and croutons), or per-haps a salad of avocado, beets, and celeriac rémoulade. As you sup, the chef might emerge from the kitchen to chat in French with regulars, or to greet friends stopping in to say hello. From time to time, the place may erupt in more French, much commotion, and many kisses. You and your companion enjoy each other's company and the French-ness of the restaurant, with its orangey red-washed walls and Provençal tablecloths. If you're here at dinner, choose the hanger steak and *pommes frites,* mussels in cream sauce, cas-soulet, or just about anything representing the tastes of Languedoc, in southwestern France. An extensive wine list includes selections from the Languedoc region.

518 10th St. NW (btw. E and F sts. NW). (©) **202/393-5444.** www.bistrodoc.com. Reservations recommended. Lunch and brunch entrees $12–$18; dinner entrees $14–$23; daily pretheater (5:30–7pm) and post-theater (9–10pm) menu $22. AE, DC, DISC, MC, V. Mon–Sat 11:30am–2:30pm; Sun 11:30am–4pm (brunch); Mon–Thurs 5:30–10pm; Fri–Sat 5:30–11pm; Sun 4–8:30pm. Metro: Metro Center (12th and F sts. exit).

Jaleo ★ (Finds) SPANISH   Jaleo's dining room fills and empties each evening according to the performance schedule of the Shakespeare Theater next door. Lunchtime always draws a crowd from nearby office buildings and the Hill. This restaurant and executive chef/partner José Andrés (see Café Atlantico for more about Andrés) may be credited with initiating the tapas craze in Washington, where it remains popular 17 years after Jaleo debuted. Though the menu offers a handful of entrees (available only after 5pm), you really want to consider those tapas—60 at last count. These include a very simple but not-to-be-missed grilled bread layered with a paste of fresh tomatoes and topped with anchovies, date and bacon fritters, a skewer of grilled chorizo sausage atop garlic mashed potatoes, and gazpacho. Paella is among the few heartier entrees (it feeds two to four). Spanish wines, sangrias, and sherries are available by the glass. The casual-chic interior focuses on a large mural of a flamenco dancer inspired by John Singer Sargent's painting *Jaleo.*

480 7th St. NW (at E St.). (©) **202/628-7949.** www.jaleo.com. Reservations accepted at lunch and on a limited basis for dinner. Lunch and dinner entrees $8.50–$19; tapas $5–$13; pre-theater (Tues–Sun 5–7pm) $25. AE, DC, DISC, MC, V. Sun–Mon 11:30am–10pm; Tues–Thurs 11:30am–11:30pm; Fri–Sat 11:30am–midnight. Metro: Archives or Gallery Place (7th and F sts. exit).

Legal Sea Foods ★ (**Kids**) SEAFOOD   This location of the famous Boston-based, family-run seafood empire is situated in the very heart of the Penn Quarter, directly across the street from the Verizon Center, where crowds throng for big-name concerts and basketball and hockey games. Before and after those events, you'll often find fans here, drawn to Legal's fresh seafood, comfortable atmosphere, and lively bar scene. An expansion in January 2009 added a racetrack-shaped bar, more seating in the dining room, and a nautical decor.

Legal's buttery-rich clam chowder is a classic. Critics praise the fluffy pan-fried Maryland lump crab cakes served with mustard sauce. You can have one of eight or so varieties of fresh fish grilled or opt for one of Legal's specialty dishes, like the baked Boston scrod or the New England fried clams. Other pluses: The restaurant offers a gluten-free menu for the allergic, and an unusual, award-winning kids' menu of steamed lobster, popcorn shrimp, and the like, each served with fresh fruit and vegetable.

704 7th St. NW (btw. G and H sts.). ℂ 202/347-0007. www.legalseafoods.com. Reservations recommended, especially at lunch. Lunch entrees $11–$37; dinner entrees $16–$37. AE, DC, DISC, MC, V. Mon–Thurs 11am–11pm; Fri–Sat 11am–midnight; Sun noon–10pm. Metro: Gallery Place/Chinatown (either exit).

Matchbox ★ PIZZA/AMERICAN   This skinny, three-level town house in Chinatown is a grazing ground for twenty-somethings, who show up at all hours and every meal, happy hour to weekend brunch. Since Matchbox accepts limited reservations (see below), you often have to wait in the rowdy bar until a table frees up, so families, be forewarned. Wood-fired brick ovens bake the thin pizza crust at temperatures as high as 900°F. My favorite is the "prosciutto white," which is topped with prosciutto, kalamata olives, fresh garlic, ricotta cheese, fresh mozzarella, and extra-virgin olive oil; but you can request your own set of toppings, from smoked bacon to artichoke hearts. Matchbox also serves super salads (the chopped salad is my favorite: diced tomatoes, crispy bacon, hair-thin "pasta ringlets," and greens in a creamy herb vinaigrette), appetizers, sandwiches, and entrees (the honey-glazed pecan-crusted chicken is a keeper). Matchbox now has a second location in the Barracks Row section of Capitol Hill, 521 8th St. SE (ℂ **202/548-0369**).

713 H St. NW. ℂ 202/289-4441. www.matchboxdc.com. Reservations for parties of 6 or more, Sun–Thurs only. Pizzas and sandwiches $11–$21; lunch and dinner entrees $14–$29; brunch entrees $6–$14. AE, DC, DISC, MC, V. Mon–Fri 11am–closing; Sat–Sun 10am–closing. Metro: Gallery Place/Chinatown (H and 7th sts. exit).

Old Ebbitt Grill AMERICAN   You won't find this place listed among the city's best culinary establishments, but you can bet it's included in every tour book. It's an institution. The original Old Ebbitt was established in 1856, around the corner at 14th and F streets. The Grill moved to this location in 1983, bringing much of the old place with it. Among its artifacts are a walrus head bagged by Teddy Roosevelt, antique gas chandeliers, and antique beer steins. The overall feel is of an early 20th century saloon.

Tourists and office people fill the Ebbitt during the day, but flirting singles take it over at night. You'll generally have to wait for a table if you don't reserve ahead. The waiters are friendly and professional in a programmed sort of way; service could be faster. Menus change daily but always include certain favorites: burgers, trout Parmesan (Virginia trout dipped in egg batter and Parmesan cheese, flash fried), crab cakes, and oysters—Old Ebbitt's raw bar is its saving grace when all else fails. Aside from the fresh oysters, the tastiest dishes are usually the seasonal ones; fresh ingredients make all the difference.

675 15th St. NW (btw. F and G sts.). ℂ 202/347-4800. www.ebbitt.com. Reservations recommended. Breakfast $9.95–$14; brunch $5.95–$27; lunch and dinner entrees $13–$27; raw bar $8.95–$21. AE, DC, DISC, MC, V. Mon–Fri 7:30am–1am; Sat–Sun 8:30am–1am. Bar open until 2am Sun–Thurs, 3am Fri–Sat. Metro: Metro Center (13th and F sts. exit).

(Kids) **Family-Friendly Restaurants**

Nearly every restaurant welcomes families these days, starting, most likely, with the one in your hotel. What you need to know, mom and dad, is that many Washington restaurants are playgrounds for the city's vast population of young professionals. For example, I would love to recommend Matchbox, which serves an excellent pizza and other items kids love; but its reservations-only-for-six-or-more policy means that you and your little darlings are going to be waiting for your table (and there's almost always a wait) either in the jumping-all-day bar or out on the street in the middle of Chinatown. So read over this chapter and choose a place that sounds like its food, fun, and flexibility factors suit your family. Also consider dining early and getting a table away from the bar scene. Chinese restaurants and museum cafes are always a safe bet, and so are these:

Lebanese Taverna (p. 162)   Its location down the hill from the National Zoo and its voluminous menu (including items marked for "the little ones") make the Taverna attractive to mom, dad, and the whole caboodle. Around for nearly 2 decades, the Taverna has fallen off the radar of food critics pursuing the latest greatest craze. But locals continue to favor the place, and the result is that the owners keep opening new locations—there are five now.

Legal Sea Foods (p. 134)   Believe it or not, this seafood restaurant has won awards for its kids' menu. It features the usual macaroni and cheese and hot dogs, but it also offers kids' portions of steamed lobster; fried popcorn shrimp; a small fisherman's platter of shrimp, scallops, and clams; and other items, each of which comes with fresh fruit, fresh vegetables, and a choice of rice, mashed potatoes, or french fries. Prices range from $1.95 to $17.

Old Glory Barbecue (p. 158)   A boisterous, laid-back place where the waiters are friendly without being patronizing. Go early, since this is one of those restaurants that becomes a bar mob scene as the evening progresses. There is a children's menu, but you may not need it—the barbecue, burgers, muffins, fries, and desserts are so good that everyone can order from the main menu. Kids' meals are a flat $5.95 per child except on Sunday and Monday, 5–7pm, when kids 10 and under eat FREE! (Offer limited to two children per $10 adult entrée purchased.)

Oyamel ★★ LATIN AMERICAN/MEXICAN   José Andrés, the 40-ish Spaniard who has wowed us repeatedly as chef at Jaleo, Café Atlantico, Zaytinya, and minibar, does it again, even better, at Oyamel. With its limited reservations policy meant to encourage spontaneous walk-ins, open-all-day hours, menu of antojitos priced below $10 each (the menu also lists some entrees), hearty cocktails, and exuberant atmosphere, Oyamel serves as the ultimate chill pill for the capital's hungry and stressed-out wonks. Order the Oyamel margarita, which is topped with salt-air foam, and the table-made guacamole (ask for the spiciest version, which is still not that spicy). Consider the specials, like the beer-battered soft-shell crab (only $10!) served with a mango-roasted corn salsa. The menu features items you won't find at other D.C. Mexican cantinas, like the "*cochinita pibil con cebolla en escabeche*" (Yucatan-style pit-barbecued pork with pickled red onion and Mexican sour orange); try the taco version at only $3.50. With its lively bar scene and prime corner location in the heart of the Penn Quarter, Oyamel is always hopping.

401 7th St. NW (at D St.). (*C*) **202/628-1005.** www.oyamel.com. Limited reservations. Small plates and tacos $3–$12; lunch and dinner entrees $9–$19; brunch entrees $6–$9. AE, DC, DISC, MC, V. Sun–Mon 11:30am–10pm; Tues–Thurs 11:30am–11:30pm; Fri–Sat 11:30am–midnight. Metro: Gallery Place/Chinatown (7th and F sts. exit) or Archives/Navy Memorial.

Potenza ★ ITALIAN   This restaurant, named after the owner's grandmother, born in southern Italy, Potenza has that authentic Italian connection going for it, which is evident in the Tuscan bean soup; the spicy duck sausage pizza; the guinea hen with apples, chestnuts, and figs; and its specialty dishes. Just as authentic but more familiar-sounding items are on the menu, too, like bruschetta and manicotti. All delicious. Potenza has a very easygoing ambience and is perfect, in fact, as a place to duck in to, when taking a break from touring—the White House is just across the street and the National Mall is half a mile or so down 15th Street. The restaurant is open all day and includes a bakery and bar. *FYI:* As reasonably priced as the entrees are, it's the cost of the drinks that may throw you off the budgetary rails—my husband's martini cost $11, my manicotti $12.

1340 H St. NW (15th St.). (*C*) **202/638-4444.** www.potenzadc.com. Reservations accepted. Brunch, lunch, and dinner entrees $12–$26. AE, DC, DISC, MC, V. Sun 10am–10pm; Mon–Thurs 11:30am–10pm; Fri–Sat 11:30am–11pm. Metro: Metro Center (13th St. exit) or McPherson Sq.

Rasika ★★ INDIAN   This sexy-cool restaurant opened in December 2005 and immediately started to attract Washington glitterati, diplomats, administration stars, current and past, and the city's young sophisticates, always hanging out in the lounge. Soft lighting, cinnamon-and-spice tones, silk panels, and dangling glass beads contribute a rich and sensuously attractive feeling to the dining room and its adjoining lounge. Everyone's drinking martinis, usually the clove or the pomegranate. As for the food, it's divine. Try the crispy spinach, ginger scallops, tandoori salmon, black cod, or lobster masala.

633 D St. NW (at 7th St.). (*C*) **202/637-1222.** www.rasikarestaurant.com. Reservations recommended. Lunch and dinner entrees $14–$28; pretheater menu $30. AE, DC, DISC, MC, V. Mon–Fri 11:30am–2:30pm; Mon–Thurs 5:30–10:30pm; Fri 5:30–11pm; Sat 5–11pm. Lounge stays open throughout the day serving light meals. Metro: Archives/Navy Memorial or Gallery Place/Verizon Center (7th and F sts. exit).

Sei ★★ JAPANESE   This very sleek, rapture-in-white dining room is one of D.C.'s latest hot spots. A long communal table sits just beneath the sushi bar, and couples tend to migrate here, filling up the seats like it's the front row in front of the stage. Well, the sushi chefs *are* fun to watch. Meanwhile, directly across the room from the sushi bar, partly obscured by a partition, is the lounge, where more couples and young singlets mingle, drinking sake and potent signature drinks, like the Apple Blossom martini. Sushi lovers and others can find happiness here. I like something called the fish and chips roll, which wraps flounder, malt vinegar, and skinny potato strings together; the wasabi guacamole (as spicy as you want it to be), the Asian pork tacos (see: not everything is sushi); and the foie gras sushi. (I rest my case.)

444 7th St. NW (at E St.). (*C*) **202/783-7007.** www.seirestaurant.com. Reservations accepted. Small plates and sushi $5–$15. AE, DC, DISC, MC, V. Mon–Fri 11:30am–2:30pm; Mon–Thurs 5:30pm–midnight; Fri–Sat 5:30pm–1am; Sun 5–10pm. Metro: Gallery Place/Verizon Center (7th and F Sts. exit)

Zaytinya ★★ GREEK/TURKISH/MIDDLE EASTERN How popular is Zaytinya? Well, the restaurant serves, on average, 750 people per night during the week and 1,000 per night on weekends. It's big and it's busy and it always has been. Executive Chef José Andrés is behind it all. (See review of Café Atlantico, p. 128.)

Its limited reservations policy means that Zaytinya's bar scene is often rollicking, since that's the obvious place to wait for a table. Once seated, your waiter will explain that the wine list, like the mezze dishes, are a mixture of Greek, Turkish, and Lebanese specialties; and inform you that the word "Zaytinya" is Turkish for "olive oil." The few entrees are fine, but little dishes even better: zucchini-cheese cakes, which come with a caper and yogurt sauce; the carrot-apricot-pine nut fritters served with pistachio sauce; *fattoush,* or salad of tomatoes and cucumbers mixed with pomegranate reduction and crispy pita-bread croutons; and shrimp with tomatoes, onions, ouzo, and kefalograviera cheese. Finish with the seductive Turkish coffee chocolate cake.

701 9th St. NW (at G St.). ✆ **202/638-0800.** www.zaytinya.com. Limited reservations. Mezze items $5.50–$12; lunch and dinner entrees $6.50–$13; brunch items $5.95–$6.95. AE, DC, DISC, MC, V. Sun–Mon 11:30am–10pm; Tues–Thurs 11:30am–11:30pm; Fri–Sat 11:30am–midnight. Metro: Gallery Place/China-town (9th St. exit).

INEXPENSIVE

Tony Cheng's Seafood Restaurant CHINESE/SEAFOOD The best of the Washington area's Chinese restaurants are not in the city at all, but in the suburbs. The increasingly shrinking Chinatown has several. Tony Cheng's is the most presentable of Chinatown's eateries, and it's also a good choice if you like Cantonese specialties and spicy Szechuan and Hunan cuisine. Downstairs is the Mongolian Barbecue eatery, where you can order an $18-per-person, all-you-can-eat spread of foods you select for the chef to barbecue over a huge grill. The second-floor Tony Cheng's Seafood Restaurant has been here for decades. It has earned a reputation for its Cantonese roast duck (see it for yourself before ordering, since it is displayed in a case at the back of the restaurant); lobster or Dungeness crab, stir-fried and served with either ginger and scallions or black-bean sauce; and Szechuan crispy beef, to name just a few. Dim sum is available at lunch daily, but during the week you order items off the menu, rather than from rolling carts.

619 H St. NW (btw. 6th and 7th sts.). ✆ **202/842-8669** (Mongolian Barbecue) and **202/371-8669** (Sea-food Restaurant). www.tonychengrestaurant.com. Reservations recommended. Mongolian Barbecue $18 all-you-can-eat. Seafood restaurant lunch entrees $10–$15; dinner entrees $15–$25; dim sum items $3.50–$5.50 each. AE, MC, V. Sun–Thurs 11am–11pm; Fri–Sat 11am–midnight. Metro: Gallery Place/Chi-natown (7th and H sts. exit).

5 MIDTOWN

VERY EXPENSIVE

Adour ★★ FRENCH This is D.C.'s satellite restaurant in the galaxy of famed French chef/restaurateur Alain Ducasse. Foodies will know right away that the cuisine will be top-notch and that ingredients like black truffles, foie gras, Armagnac, and rose blossom will feature prominently. For all of its exquisiteness, Adour is comfortable, not precious. The dining room's modern decor features creamy leather banquettes as well as standalong tables and recessed nooks, high ceilings, and wine vaults that serve as walls. On the menu are dishes that show off the talent in the kitchen: sweetbreads, Riviera-style John Dory with baby fennel, and pressed foie gras with organic chicken and black truffle condiment. No matter what you order for dessert, say the baba au rhum or the apple soufflé, your table always receives a sendoff plate of dainty raspberry and chocolate macaroon cookies.

923 16th St. NW (at K St.). In the St. Regis Hotel. ☎ **202/509-8000**. www.adour-washingtondc.com. Reservations recommended. Breakfast entrees $7–$29; dinner entrees $25–$46; tasting menu $95. AE, DC, DISC, MC, V. Mon–Fri 7–10am; Sat–Sun 7am–noon; Tues–Thurs 5:30–10pm; Fri–Sat 5:30–10:30pm. Metro: Farragut West (17th St. exit) or Farragut North (K St. exit).

BLT Steak ★★ STEAK   BLT Steak is a younger, hipper cut of beeferie than one usually associates with Washington steakhouses. The restaurant, with its expansive bar, suede seats, large and airy room, and soul-music sound system, is a popular stamping ground for young professionals on weeknights and sees a steady stream of power brokers at all times. (BLT lies on a street btw. the White House and the K Street corridor of law firm and lobbyist offices.) The BLT stands not for bacon, lettuce, and tomato, but for Bistro Laurent Tourondel, the chef, whose other BLTs are located in New York City, San Juan, and assorted other hot spots. A meal begins with a basket of enormous, complimentary Gruyère popovers and a little pot of country pâté. Menu recommendations include the raw bar offerings, hanger steak, the American wagyu rib-eye (if you don't mind paying $92 for your entree!), blue cheese Tater Tots, onion rings, any of the salads, and the souffléd crepe with ricotta cheese for dessert.

1625 I St. NW (at 17th St.). ☎ **202/689-8999**. www.bltsteak.com. Reservations accepted. Lunch entrees $16–$49; dinner entrees $28–$49 (prices go as high as $92 for wagyu beef). AE, DC, DISC, MC, V. Mon–Fri 11:30am–2:30pm; Mon–Thurs 5:30–11pm; Fri–Sat 5:30–11:30pm. Metro: Farragut West (17th St. exit) or Farragut North (K St. exit).

Equinox ★★ NEW AMERICAN   Everyone seems to love Equinox, whose proximity to the White House guarantees a high-and-mighty clientele, including the Obamas, who celebrated Michelle Obama's birthday here a week before the presidential inauguration (both the President and Mrs. Obama ordered the striploin steak). Regulars appreciate that Equinox is not splashy in any way—it's just a pretty, comfortable restaurant serving creatively delicious American food. You'll eat all your vegetables here, because as much care is taken with these garnishes as with the entree itself, whether it's forest mushrooms with applewood bacon or white-bean ragout. Consider ordering additional side dishes, like the baked truffled macaroni and cheese. The home runs, of course, are the entrees. Standouts have included pan-roasted Alaska halibut with artichoke ragout; crab cakes made with lump crab mixed with capers, brioche bread crumbs, mayonnaise, and lemon-butter sauce; and veal strip loin with crispy sweetbreads and potato mousseline.

818 Connecticut Ave. NW. ☎ **202/331-8118**. www.equinoxrestaurant.com. Reservations recommended. Lunch entrees $19–$24; dinner entrees $29–$38; 4 tasting menus, from the $65 vegetarian to the 6-course $89. AE, DC, DISC, MC, V. Mon–Fri 11:30am–2pm; Mon–Thurs 5:30–10pm; Fri–Sat 5:30–10:30pm; Sun 5–9pm. Metro: Farragut West (17th St. exit).

The Prime Rib ★★ STEAK/SEAFOOD   The 34-year-old Prime Rib has plenty of competition in D.C., but it makes no difference. Beef lovers still consider this The Place. Male beef lovers, anyway: The Prime Rib has a definite men's club feel about it, with brass-trimmed black-paneled walls, leopard-skin carpeting, and comfortable black-leather chairs and banquettes. Waiters are tuxedoed, and a pianist at the baby grand plays show tunes and Irving Berlin classics at lunch; at dinner, a bass player joins the pianist.

The meat is from the best grain-fed steers and has been aged for 4 to 5 weeks. Steaks and cuts of roast beef are thick, tender, and juicy. In case you had any doubt, the Prime Rib's prime rib is the best item on the menu—juicy, thick, top-quality meat. For less carnivorous diners, there are about a dozen seafood entrees, including an excellent crab imperial. Mashed potatoes are done right, as are the fried potato skins; but I recommend the hot cottage fries.

2020 K St. NW. © **202/466-8811.** www.theprimerib.com. Reservations recommended. Jacket and tie required for men at dinner. Lunch entrees $12–$32; dinner entrees $22–$45. AE, DC, MC, V. Mon–Thurs 11:30am–3pm and 5–10:30pm; Fri 11:30am–3pm and 5–11pm; Sat 5–11pm; bar stays open throughout the day Mon–Fri. Metro: Farragut West (18th St. exit).

Taberna del Alabardero ★★ (Finds) SPANISH   Dress up to visit this fine restaurant, whose red walls, carved white cornices, tufted banquettes, and little sculpted cherubs add up overall to romance. You'll receive royal treatment from the Spanish staff, who are accustomed to attending to the real thing—Spain's King Juan Carlos and Queen Sofia have dined here. The Taberna is also a favorite of dignitaries attending meetings at the nearby World Bank and International Monetary Fund. The Spanish government recognized the Taberna as "the best Spanish restaurant outside Spain."

Order a plate of tapas to start: lightly fried calamari, shrimp in garlic and olive oil, artichokes sautéed with thin smoky serrano ham, and marinated mushrooms. Although the a la carte menu changes with the seasons (look for the duck breast with sweet vinegar sauce in spring), several paellas are always available, including the rich and flavorful seafood paella served on saffron rice. The Taberna also offers vegetarian lunch and dinner menus. The wine list features a selection of 315 wines, some American, but mostly Spanish. Good deal: Weekdays 3 to 6:30pm, tapas are half-price at the bar.

1776 I St. NW (entrance on 18th St. NW). © **202/429-2200.** www.alabardero.com. Reservations recommended. Jacket and tie for men suggested. Tapas $9–$20; lunch entrees $24–$36; dinner entrees $30–$39. AE, DC, DISC, MC, V. Mon–Fri 11:30am–2:30pm; Mon–Sat 5:30–10:30pm. Metro: Farragut West (18th St. exit).

Vidalia ★★ AMERICAN/SOUTHERN   Vidalia frequently wins prestigious culinary kudos from food critics, most recently capturing a 7th best D.C. restaurant rating from *Washingtonian* magazine. You'll understand why when you dine here. Vidalia's cuisine marries tastes of various regions of the South, with an emphasis on New Orleans. Featured dishes might include a roasted young pig with braised savoy cabbage or rockfish filet with succotash and turnip greens. A signature entree is scrumptious sautéed shrimp on a mound of creamed grits and caramelized onions with tasso ham in a cilantro butter sauce. Corn bread and biscuits with apple butter are served at every meal. Vidalia is known for its lemon chess pie and pecan pie, but always check out alternatives, which might be an apple napoleon or caramel cake. Vidalia offers an extensive wine list; at least 30 are offered by the glass, in both 3-ounce and 6-ounce pours.

If you're hesitant to dine at a restaurant that's down a flight of steps from the street, your doubts will vanish as soon as you enter Vidalia's tiered dining room. There's a party going on down here. Arrive between 5:30 and 7pm weeknights and you'll get in on the extremely popular wine tastings in the cozy wine bar. The chef sends out little canapés, like miniature BLTs; and both the wine tastings and the hors d'oeuvres are complimentary!

1990 M St. NW. © **202/659-1990.** www.vidaliadc.com. Reservations recommended. Lunch entrees $14–$23; dinner entrees $24–$35. AE, DC, DISC, MC, V. Mon–Fri 11:30am–2:30pm; Mon–Thurs 5:30–10pm; Fri–Sat 5:30–10:30pm; Sun 5:30–9:30pm. Metro: Dupont Circle (19th St. exit)

Tips **Dining Green in D.C.**

As the debut of the White House Kitchen Garden demonstrated in March 2009, the First Family is committed to the "green" movement's emphasis on organic gardening, eco-friendly farming, reliance on locally grown produce, and healthy eating. All the White House chef has to do is walk out to the garden to pluck fresh vegetables and herbs for immediate use in cooking for the Obamas. The White House kitchen is in good company throughout the city, where restaurants big and small, inexpensive and super pricey, are totally into earth-wholesome and healthy practices of energy and design, and the greenest of ways to grow, obtain, prepare and replenish ingredients for their meals. Here are but a few examples:

- **Bourbon Steak** (p. 153) Following in the White House's footsteps, the Four Seasons Hotel's popular restaurant introduced its on-site 500-square-foot herb and vegetable garden in June 2009. An Amish farm provided the 400 plants, which represent 62 varieties of produce, all of which are used in Michael Mina's dishes....and cocktails! Can't get more local than this. And it's all organically grown, no pesticides used.
- **Equinox** (p. 138) Chef Todd Gray uses community-farmed organic ingredients that are grown within 100 miles of the restaurant, whenever possible.
- **Sweetgreen** (p. 150) This Green Restaurant Association-Certified Green eatery powers its restaurants entirely from wind energy obtained through carbon offsets. Nearly all packaging is biodegradable, including the menu, which has been implanted with seeds, for you to pass it forward, planting the menu in the ground, and sprouting a sweetgreen something or other yourself. Healthy salads and frozen yogurts are the deal here, and all are made fresh.
- **Hook Restaurant** (p. 156) Its commitment to the "sustainable" movement means that Hook's chef shops for locally farmed produce and that the menus are printed on 100% post-consumer recycled paper, but most of all, that this seafood restaurant procures and serves only those varieties of fish that can reproduce at the rate at which they're caught. Right next door is Hook's inexpensive sibling, Tackle Box (p. 158), which follows the same eco-friendly practices.
- **Founding Farmers Restaurant** (1924 Pennsylvania Ave. NW, ℂ 202/822-8783, www.wearefoundingfarmers.com) Alas, you won't find this new restaurant included in the guidebook, but only for lack of space; look for it in next year's edition. And do seek it out while you're in D.C., if the following information appeals: Owned by a collective of American farmers, the restaurant is LEED Gold-certified for its Leadership in Environmental and Energy Design, and Green Restaurant-certified, as well. Ingredients used are sustainably farmed, locally sourced, and organically grown.

Corduroy ★★ AMERICAN   For many years, this restaurant was hidden inside the Four Points Sheraton Hotel. When chef Tom Power moved his operation in 2008 to a historic town house in the up-and-coming convention center neighborhood, he had no trouble enticing his fan base to follow him. He continues to attract new fans, as well, in this easier-to-find location, where the rooms are cozy and the kitchen is on display. Winning dishes here include pan-roasted duck with fig sauce, red snapper bisque, duck egg and leg salad, and for dessert, pistachio bread pudding or strawberry tart with strawberry creamsicle. *FYI:* Corduroy hosts a pleasant happy hour 5 to 7pm, with specially priced drinks and a small menu of big tastes available; during this same time, a 3-course, $30 prix fixe menu is also on offer.

1122 9th St. NW. ℭ **202/589-0699.** www.corduroydc.com. Reservations recommended. Dinner entrees $20–$38. AE, DC, DISC, MC, V. Mon–Sat 5:30–10:30pm. Metro: Mt. Vernon Sq./7th St./Convention Center.

DC Coast ★ NEW AMERICAN   The dining room is sensational: two stories high, with glass-walled balcony, immense oval mirrors hanging over the bar, and a full-bodied stone mermaid poised to greet you at the entrance. Gather at the bar first to feel a part of the loud and trendy scene and to nosh on bar menu treats ($10–$15), perhaps the fried oysters or a luscious flatbread pizza. Chef Jeff Tunks, the chef behind TenPenh, Ceiba, and Acadiana (p. 132, 129, and 128), started his dynasty with DC Coast, which opened in 1998. Here, Tunks fuses the coastal cuisines of the Mid-Atlantic, Gulf, and West Coast. Almost always on the menu are his Chinese-style smoked lobster with crispy fried spinach, pan-roasted sea scallops or grouper, and the porcini-crusted fish filet encrusted with braised mushrooms. Seafood is a big part of the menu, but there are a handful of meat dishes too; try the pork chop with snap pea ragout.

1401 K St. NW. ℭ **202/216-5988.** www.dccoast.com. Reservations recommended. Lunch entrees $13–$25; dinner entrees $22–$29. AE, DC, DISC, MC, V. Mon–Fri 11:30am–2:30pm; Mon–Thurs 5:30–10:30pm; Fri–Sat 5:30–11pm; Sun 5:30–9:30pm. Bar weekdays 2:30pm–closing; Sat 5:30pm–closing. Metro: McPherson Square (14th St./Franklin Sq. exit).

The Oval Room ★ NEW AMERICAN   The Oval Room is a local favorite, another winner for owner Ashok Bajaj, who also owns the Bombay Club (p. 141) right across the street and Rasika (p. 136) in the Penn Quarter. Current chef Tony Conti previously served as executive sous chef for Jean-Georges Vongerichten in New York. His reasonably priced modern American cuisine offers ricotta gnocchi, caramelized beef tenderloin, crispy striped bass, and the like. The Oval Room is a handsome restaurant, with contemporary art hanging on its pale green walls. Its atmosphere is congenial, not stuffy, no doubt because the bar area separating the restaurant into two distinct rooms sends cheerful sounds in either direction. In case you haven't made the connection, the Oval Room is a short walk from the White House.

800 Connecticut Ave. NW (at Lafayette Sq.). ℭ **202/463-8700.** www.ovalroom.com. Reservations recommended. Lunch entrees $7–$24; dinner entrees $16–$34; pretheater dinner (5:30–6:30pm) $35. AE, DC, DISC, MC, V. Mon–Fri 11:30am–3pm; Mon–Thurs 5:30–10pm; Fri–Sat 5:30am–10:30pm. Metro: Farragut West (17th St. exit).

MODERATE

Bombay Club ★★ (Finds) INDIAN   Twenty years old and still going strong is the delightful Bombay Club. A recent sprucing up added punches of pink in the decor and surprising new tastes in the menu: a kebab of ground duck is flavored with chilies and ginger; eggplant is roasted in a tandoor oven, then combined with sautéed onions, ginger, and yogurt. Yum.

But Bombay Club favorites remain: the ultra fiery green chili chicken ("not for the fainthearted," the menu warns); tandoori entrees (a food that has been marinated, then grilled, and baked in a clay oven), including the chicken tandoori, which is marinated in an almond, cashew, yogurt, ginger, and garlic dressing; and the delicately prepared lobster Lababdar. The Bombay Club is known for its vegetarian offerings (try the black lentils cooked overnight on a slow fire) and for its Sunday champagne brunch, which offers a buffet of fresh juices, fresh baked breads, and assorted Indian dishes. Patrons are as fond of the service as the cuisine; waiters seem straight out of *Jewel in the Crown,* attending to your every whim. This is one place where you can linger over a meal as long as you like.

815 Connecticut Ave. NW. © **202/659-3727.** www.bombayclubdc.com. Reservations recommended. Entrees $11–$32; Sun brunch $20. AE, DC, DISC, MC, V. Mon–Fri and Sun brunch 11:30am–2:30pm; Mon–Thurs 5:30–10:30pm; Fri–Sat 5:30–11pm; Sun 5:30–9pm. Metro: Farragut West (17th St. exit).

Brasserie Beck ★★ BELGIAN   This place hasn't stopped rocking since the doors opened in April 2007. Beck's, named for chef Robert Wiedmaier's younger son (as Wiedmaier's fine dining establishment, Marcel's, p. 152, is named for Beck's older brother), is one of the city's best bistros and hot spots. The bar scene explains part of Beck's popularity, seating 21 people at its huge marble-and-walnut bar and handling many more beyond that. Restaurant design also plays its part; Beck's features an attractive open kitchen of glass, steel, and cobalt-blue tiles, and the overall feel of a large train station, with large round clocks on display beneath 22-foot-high ceilings. But in the end it comes down to the food, and here, Beck's pegs it: Belgian tastes of in-house-cured salmon, beef carbonnade, steamed mussels served three ways, frites, duck confit, lamb sausage, and the list goes on. Beer-lover's bonus: a large assortment of Belgian beers on tap and by the bottle.

1101 K St. NW (at 11th St.). © **202/408-1717.** www.beckdc.com. Reservations recommended. Lunch entrees $14–$29; dinner entrees $16–$32; brunch entrees $14. AE, DC, DISC, MC, V. Mon–Thurs 11:30am–11pm; Fri 11:30am–11:30pm; Sat 5pm–1:30am; Sun 11:30am–9pm. Metro: Metro Center (11th and G sts. exit, with a few blocks' walk from there).

INEXPENSIVE

Café Asia ASIAN FUSION   It's easy to miss Café Asia, nestled as it is between hair salons and offices on I Street right near the White House. The restaurant has three levels to it, set within an atrium. From street level, walk downstairs to the main dining room.

The menu here is Pan-Asian: Chinese, Indonesian, Japanese, Thai. If your waitress steers you to something "interesting," you can take that to mean "spicy," like the Indonesian fried rice, which is "more interesting than Chinese." (Yeah—it's got chilies in it, for one thing.) For Americanized, tamed-down food, stick with the teriyaki and satays. If you like hot stuff, try the *nasi uduk,* an Indonesian coconut rice platter with spicy beef, crispy anchovies, pickled vegetables, and other tastes. Another winner is the *ikan pepes,* which is Indonesian grilled fish filet with spicy turmeric sauce, fresh basil, and lemon grass, wrapped in banana leaves. Café Asia also serves delicious sushi. Young professionals throng Café Asia's happy hour, Monday through Saturday from 4 to 7:30pm, when nigiri sushi is available for $1.25 per piece and select draft beers are sold for $2.50.

1720 I St. NW. © **202/659-2696.** www.cafeasia.com. Reservations accepted. Lunch and dinner entrees $9–$16. AE, DISC, MC, V. Sun–Thurs 11am–10pm; Fri–Sat 11am–midnight. Metro: Farragut West (17th St. exit) or Farragut North (K St. exit).

MODERATE

Café Saint-Ex ★ AMERICAN   There goes the neighborhood, only we're talking gentrification here. Café Saint-Ex was an early trendsetter in helping transform this worn residential area. The precious restaurant/bar wins stars from food critics and attracts legions of hungry Washingtonians as well as enterprising restaurateurs after the same success (see other restaurants listed in the section). This part of D.C. is changing, no doubt about it; if you're intrigued, Café Saint-Ex is worth investigating. Named for author/aviator Antoine de Saint-Exupéry, the dining room builds on the flight idea with black-and-white photos of pilots and aviation memorabilia. Regulars crow about the charming atmosphere and certain items on the menu, like the roast chicken; the grilled mahimahi; and the beets, grapefruit, and feta cheese salad. Personally, I love the fried green tomato BLT. D.C. hipsters stay on or arrive later to get in on Saint's nightlife scene, which features a DJ spinning hip-hop or indie tunes downstairs at Gate 54.

1847 14th St. NW, btw. S and T sts. ✆ 202/265-7839. www.saint-ex.com. No reservations (this policy may change). Lunch and brunch entrees $8–$11; dinner entrees $10–$24; pretheater menu $32. AE, MC, V. Sun and Tues–Thurs 11am–1:30am; Mon 5pm–1:30am; Fri–Sat 11am–2:30am. Metro: U St.–Cardozo (13th St. exit).

Cork ★★ AMERICAN   Cozy Cork is wowing wine lovers and small-plate munchers in its perch on the increasingly popular 14th Street. The crowd draws from the neighborhood, which means you'll see 20-somethings to 60-somethings, and sundry unclassifiable sorts. Ambience is both cheery and hip. The small plates are meant to be shared, which adds to the overall conviviality. It's just impossible to be unhappy when sharing yummy bites of "chianti salami," or pan-crisped brioche sandwich of prosciutto, fontina, and Path Valley egg; or the french fries. Of course, the wine pairings may have something to do with the good vibe, too. (Cork is also a wine bar.) For such a small restaurant, Cork offers a lot of variety, including in seating: you can sit on the patio in fine weather, in the front room at tables or the bar, or in the tiny backroom with views of the kitchen.

1720 14th St. NW (at S St.). ✆ 202/265-2675. www.corkdc.com. Reservations accepted only for pretheater dining, 5:30–6:30pm. Entrees $5–$15. AE, MC, V. Sun and Tues–Wed 5pm–midnight; Thurs–Sat 5pm–1am. Metro: U St./Cardozo (13th St. exit)

Creme Café and Lounge ★ AMERICAN/SOUTHERN   Long a nightlife destination, the U and 14th streets crossroads is now turning into a favorite restaurant scene, too. But not every new eatery fits with the urban, often edgy, neighborhood vibe. Crème, on the other hand, arrived about 5 years ago and settled right in. The cafe is a cross between upscale and down-home. First off, it's Creme, as in *cream*, not crème, as in *them*. On the menu are fare like shrimp and grits, pork and beans. But these are a twist on your grandmother's versions—hearty and delicious, but more sophisticated. The beans are no ordinary canned baked beans, but a mélange of cannellini and fava beans. Like everyplace else on U Street, Creme gets noisy and crowded as the night goes on, but try to stick around long enough for dessert. The coconut cake's my favorite—and everyone else's, too, it seems.

1322 U St. NW (at 14th St.). ✆ 202/234-1884. Reservations suggested. www.cremedc.com. Dinner entrees $9–$22; brunch entrees $9–$16. AE, DC, DISC, MC, V. Sun–Thurs 6–10:30pm; Fri–Sat 6–11:30pm; brunch Sat–Sun 11am–3pm. Metro: U St.–Cardozo.

Marvin ★ AMERICAN/BELGIAN   Marvin is two things, a bistro and a bar/lounge. But the nightclub scene is on the second level (see p. 269), so the bistro works on its own as a place to stop for a bit of Belgian fare and/or soul food. Named for homeboy Marvin Gaye, who lived for a while in Belgium, Marvin's menu features mussels in wine, ratatouille, big burgers, and fried chicken. Marvin might be the noisiest and liveliest place in town. Its servers are among the friendliest. So take a party here and have fun—just make sure you've made reservations or you'll never get in.

2007 14th St. NW (at U St.). ⓒ 202/797-7171. www.marvindc.com. Reservations accepted. Entrees $14–$28. AE, DISC, MC, V. Mon–Thurs 5:30pm–2am; Fri–Sat 5:30pm–3am; Sun 11am–3am. Metro: U St./Cardozo (13th St. exit)

Next Door AMERICAN/SOUTHERN   As in next door to Ben's (see below). So popular has Ben's grown in its 50 years of feeding barflies at 3am and presidents at noon, that the chili dog place has spawned this more genteel brother, and the best news for some is that this restaurant has a bar. A celebrity chef has already come and gone, but that's OK, the menu of American, and especially Southern, tastes continues to please, no matter who's in the kitchen. Next Door tends to keep its front door open, attracting all and sundry in to sit at its long bar or at hightop tables just to the left of the bar. A quieter dining room lies at the very back. We can attest to the excellence of the shrimp, biscuits, and gravy; the chili fries; and the brioche French toast. The short ribs and the fried chicken are also getting good reviews.

1211 U St. NW (at 14th St.). ⓒ 202/667-8880. www.bensnextdoor.com. Reservations accepted. Brunch entrees $9–$16; dinner entrees $10–$33 (most are under $20). AE, DISC, MC, V. Mon–Thurs 5pm–2am; Fri 5pm–3am; Sat 11am–3am; Sun 11am–2am. Metro: U St./Cardozo (13th St. exit).

Posto ★ ITALIAN   Posto is located along a theater-filled stretch of 14th Street (Studio Theatre is right next door; see p. 256), so it's a popular spot for the theater-bound, especially since Posto has become rather expert at feeding them quickly and sending them off fat and happy. As those patrons exit stage left, new ones quickly fill the room in their place. It's a big room, too, with a lot going on: a couple of long communal tables, an open kitchen, a glassfront that opens to sidewalk tables, and eager-to-please waiters dressed in black t-shirts and pants hurrying between tables and kitchen. The aroma of pizzas cooking in the wood-fired oven greets you as you enter—the pizza picante, with spicy salami, sausage, tomato and mozzarella is a winner. But don't think Posto is simply a pizzeria; this sibling of Tosca (see p. 128) serves excellent pastas, like the tortelli prepared with ricotta and mushroom ragu; and non-pasta main courses, like the "guance," which is braised veal cheeks served with sautéed spinach and garlic mashed potatoes.

1515 14th St. NW (at P St.). ⓒ 202/332-8613. www.postodc.com. Reservations not accepted. Entrees $11–$22. AE, MC, V. Mon–Thu 5:30–10:30pm; Fri–Sat 5:30–11:30pm; Sun 5–10pm. Metro: U St./Cardozo (13th St. exit).

INEXPENSIVE

Ben's Chili Bowl ⟨Moments⟩ AMERICAN   If you don't know about Ben's, you don't know nothin', man. Ben's is a veritable institution, a mom-and-pop place where everything looks (formica counters, red bar stools, and a Motown-playing jukebox), tastes, and probably even costs pretty much the same as when the restaurant opened in 1958. Ben's has won James Beard Foundation recognition as an "American Classic," and praise from President Obama, who ate here with D.C. Mayor Adrian Fenty 2 weeks before the presidential inauguration (catch the video on Ben's website). Bill Cosby's been coming here so long, Ben's has named a chili half-smoke after him.

The most expensive item on the menu is the veggie-burger sub for $8.15. Of course, the chili, cheese fries, and half-smokes are recommended, but so are the breakfast items: Try the salmon cakes, grits, scrapple, or blueberry pancakes (available during breakfast hours only). Everyone turns up here, from folks in the neighborhood on their way to work, to weekend nightclubbers who stream ravenously out of nearby nightclubs at 2 or 3am.

1213 U St. NW. ✆ **202/667-0909.** www.benschilibowl.com. Reservations not accepted. Entrees $2.50–$8.15. No credit cards. Mon–Thurs 6am–2am; Fri 6am–4am; Sat 7am–4am; Sun 11am–8pm. Metro: U St.–Cardozo (13th St. exit).

Etete ★ ETHIOPIAN   Widely regarded as D.C.'s best Ethiopian restaurant—this is no small thing in a city that has so many—Etete, which means "mama" in Amharic, is actually the nickname of the proprietress and chef, who is known for her sambusas (lentil-filled pastries), spicy stews, in meat and vegetarian options. Though Etete has long catered to D.C.'s large Ethiopian community, the bistro also has developed quite a following among the urban hipsters who live nearby or pop in here late at night for an inexpensive and delicious meal between flights of barhopping. Etete has a full bar.

1942 9th St. NW (at T St.). ✆ **202/232-7600.** www.eteterestaurant.com. Reservations accepted. Entrees $10–$15. AE, MC, V. Daily 11am–1am. Metro: U St./Cardozo (13th St. exit).

7 ADAMS-MORGAN

EXPENSIVE

Cashion's Eat Place ★★ (Finds) AMERICAN   Cashion's Eat Place is very much a neighborhood restaurant—easy, warm, comfortable—that also just happens to serve out-of-this-world cuisine. Owner/chef John Manalatos likes to incorporate a little hint of his Greek heritage in his dishes, which change daily. A recent menu listed eight entrees, including a braised leg of young rabbit with celery root gratin, and roasted garlic-scented lamb chops. An "after dark" menu of six to eight items, from leek tarte to bovine burger, is served Friday and Saturday nights from midnight to 2am. Sunday brunch is popular, too; you can choose from breakfast fare (cornmeal waffles) or heartier items (grilled Alaskan scallops).

The charming dining room curves around the slightly raised bar. In warm weather, the glass-fronted Cashion's opens invitingly to the sidewalk and its tables. Tables at the back offer a view of the small kitchen. In winter, ask for a table away from the front door, which lets in a blast of cold air with each new arrival.

1819 Columbia Rd. NW. ✆ **202/797-1819.** www.cashionseatplace.com. Reservations recommended. Brunch $9.50–$14; dinner entrees $19–$30. AE, MC, V. Tues 5:30–10pm; Wed–Sat 5:30–11pm; Sun 11:30am–2:30pm and 5:30–10pm. Metro: Woodley Park/Adams-Morgan, with a walk.

MODERATE

Las Canteras ★ LATIN AMERICAN/PERUVIAN   Traditional and contemporary Peruvian dishes are on the menu at this affordable restaurant in the heart of Adams-Morgan, including three versions of *ceviche* (fish marinated in lime juice); *causa* (a dish made with mashed potatoes stuffed with chicken); and quinoa salad, which tosses the quinoa (grain) with chickpeas, tahini, and lime juice. Las Canteras is a pretty restaurant, decorated with colorful Peruvian fabrics, handcrafted wrought-iron chandeliers, and photographs of Machu Picchu and other Andean landmarks. Head here Tuesday through Thursday night at 5pm for the early-bird special, a three-course meal for $24.

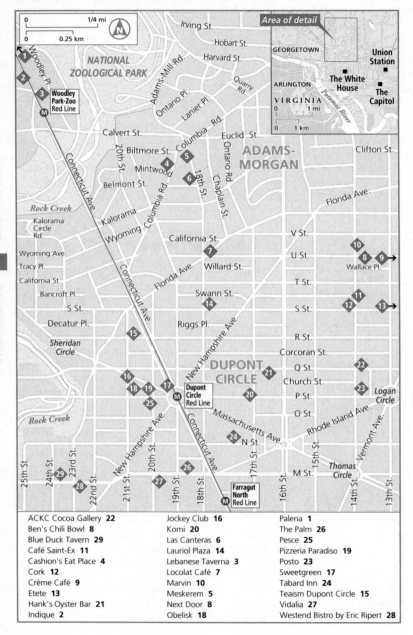

ACKC Cocoa Gallery **22**	Jockey Club **16**	Palena **1**
Ben's Chili Bowl **8**	Komi **20**	The Palm **26**
Blue Duck Tavern **29**	Las Canteras **6**	Pesce **25**
Café Saint-Ex **11**	Lauriol Plaza **14**	Pizzeria Paradiso **19**
Cashion's Eat Place **4**	Lebanese Taverna **3**	Posto **23**
Cork **12**	Locolat Café **7**	Sweetgreen **17**
Crème Café **9**	Marvin **10**	Tabard Inn **24**
Etete **13**	Meskerem **5**	Teaism Dupont Circle **15**
Hank's Oyster Bar **21**	Next Door **8**	Vidalia **27**
Indique **2**	Obelisk **18**	Westend Bistro by Eric Ripert **28**

2307 18th St. NW (at Kalorama St.). ☎ **202/265-1780.** www.lascanterasdc.com. Lunch and dinner **147** entrees $11–$18. AE, DC, MC, V. Tues–Sun 11am–3pm; Tues–Thurs and Sun 5–10pm; Fri–Sat 5–11pm. Metro: Woodley Park/Adams-Morgan, with a walk.

Lauriol Plaza MEXICAN/SPANISH/LATIN AMERICAN   This place is large (it seats 330) but immensely popular; so despite its size, you may still have to wait for a table. Lauriol Plaza looks like a factory from the outside, but inside it's stunning. You have a choice of sitting at sidewalk tables, on the rooftop deck, or in the two-tiered dining room with its large mural of a Spanish fiesta on one wall and windows covering another. Try the margaritas, *carne asada* (grilled meat) fajitas, and tasty *camarones diablo* (six broiled jumbo shrimp seasoned with spices). Anything mesquite grilled is sure to please. Servings seem as large as the restaurant. Sunday brunch draws singles from the Dupont Circle neighborhood. With so many diners here, Lauriol Plaza is a good place to people-watch.

1835 18th St. NW. ☎ **202/387-0035.** www.lauriolplaza.com. Reservations accepted only for dining in the main dining room before 5pm. Entrees $6.50–$18. AE, DC, DISC, MC, V. Sun–Thurs 11:30am–11pm; Fri–Sat 11:30am–midnight. Metro: Dupont Circle.

INEXPENSIVE

Meskerem ETHIOPIAN   Washington is known for its Ethiopian restaurants, notably in the 9th and U streets area, where you will find at least 10 cafes offering authentic Ethiopian cuisine and traditional musical entertainment. But Meskerem in Adams-Morgan was one of the first Ethiopian restaurants and remains among the best, especially for newcomers to the food.

Diners share large platters of food, scooping it up with a sourdough crepelike pancake called *injera* (no silverware here). You'll notice a lot of *watt* dishes, which refers to the traditional Ethiopian stew, made with your choice of beef, chicken, lamb, or vegetables, in varying degrees of hot and spicy; the *alicha watts* are milder and more delicately flavored. You might share an entree—perhaps *yegeb kay watt* (succulent lamb in thick, hot *berbere* sauce)—along with a sampler platter of five vegetarian dishes, served with tomato and potato salads. Some combination platters comprise an array of beef, chicken, lamb, and vegetables. There's a full bar, and the wine list includes Ethiopian honey wine and beer.

2434 18th St. NW. ☎ **202/462-4100.** www.ethiopianrestaurant.com. Reservations recommended. Lunch and dinner entrees $6.50–$15. AE, DC, MC, V. Sun–Thurs 11am–midnight; Fri–Sat 11am–2am. Bar stays open later Fri–Sat.

---

8 DUPONT CIRCLE

VERY EXPENSIVE

The Jockey Club ★★ AMERICAN   The Jockey Club first opened on the eve of President John F. Kennedy's inauguration in 1961 and immediately attracted the city's and the country's movers and shakers, from Lauren Bacall to Nancy Reagan. Nearly 50 years later, after closing in 2001, the restaurant is back with a vengeance, thanks to a grand renewal. Decorators purposefully have re-fashioned The Jockey Club in an updated version of its old look, opening up the room more but keeping the red leather banquettes, carved walnut furnishings, and art nouveau lighting fixtures. The famously gracious maitre'd, Martin Garbisu, is back. And the menu still serves Jockey Club classics, like the Dover sole meuniere, the beef sirloin au poivre, and the Maine lobster thermidor, along with more contemporary fare, like the blackened rib-eye steak There are still many in Washington with fond memories of the Jockey Club, and you will find them here, only now you'll find the newest generation of movers and shakers dining here, too.

2100 Massachusetts Ave. NW (at 21st St.). Inside the Fairfax at Embassy Row Hotel. © **202/835-2100.** www.thejockeyclub-dc.com. Reservations recommended. Lunch entrees $16–$24; dinner entrees $24–$49; pre-theater menu $$35. AE, DC, DISC, MC, V. Mon–Fri 6:30–11:30am; Mon–Sat 11am–2pm, Sun 11am–3pm; Mon–Thu 5:30–10pm; Fri–Sat 5:30–10:30pml Sun 5–9pm. Metro: Dupont Circle (either exit).

Komi ★★★ (Finds) NEW AMERICAN/GREEK   In 2009, *Washingtonian* magazine named Komi the city's best restaurant. Thirty-something chef/owner Johnny Monis looks a bit like Johnny Depp and cooks like nobody's business. You may see him at the back of the restaurant in the half-exposed kitchen. As young as he is, Monis knows what he wants and continues to fiddle with his menu and dining room to achieve it. In this intimate, comfortably attractive shotgun-length dining room Monis sends out his superb Greek-influenced dishes. These include the *mezethakia* sampler course, perhaps crispy artichoke, smoked prosciutto, fava beans, and aged pecorino cheese; the *macaronia* second course, which offers a choice of six or so pasta dishes, like the ravioli of local beets with feta or Gorgonzola raviolini with pears and almonds; and the third-course entrees, which might include a *bronzini* (Mediterranean sea bass) roasted in the oven in parchment paper, or the slow-roasted local Iberian pig. Greek-style doughnuts are always an option for dessert. Servers are some of the most efficient but charming staff in the city.

1509 17th St. NW (near P St.). © **202/332-9200.** www.komirestaurant.com. Reservations required. Tues–Sat $90–$125 per person for the tasting menu. AE, DC, DISC, MC, V. Tues–Sat 5:30–9:45pm. Metro: Dupont Circle (Q St. exit).

Obelisk ★★★ ITALIAN   Obelisk is one of the city's most consistently excellent restaurants. Service and food are simply superb. In this pleasantly spare room that seats only 36, the walls are decorated with 19th-century French botanical prints and Italian lithographs. Obelisk serves sophisticated Italian cuisine made of the freshest-possible ingredients. Each night, diners are offered two or three choices for each of five courses. Dinner might begin with an antipasti misti of zucchini fritters, deep-fried risotto croquettes, and garbanzo beans with tuna in olive oil; followed by sweetbread and porcini ravioli with sage butter; and then an artfully arranged dish of grilled stuffed quail and duck sausage with spinach, or black bass with peppers, fennel, and green sauce . . . or whatever the chef has been inspired to create. A cheese course and dessert follow. Breads and desserts are all baked in-house. Pastan's carefully crafted wine list represents varied regions of Italy, as well as California vintages.

2029 P St. NW. © **202/872-1180.** Reservations required. Fixed-price 5-course dinner Tues–Thurs $70, Fri–Sat $75. MC, V. Tues–Sat 6–10pm. Metro: Dupont Circle.

The Palm ★ (Finds) STEAK   The Palm is one in a chain of 25 locations that started 84 years ago in New York—but here in D.C., it feels like an original. The Washington Palm is 38 years old; though recently renovated and expanded to include a glass-enclosed veranda, its walls are still covered with the caricatures of regulars, the famous and the not-so-famous. If you think you see Chris Matthews at a table, you're probably right. You can't go wrong with steak, whether it's the 36-ounce dry-aged New York strip or sliced in a steak salad. Oversize lobsters are a specialty, and certain side dishes are a must: creamed spinach, onion rings, palm fries (something akin to deep-fried potato chips), and hash browns. You can order half-portions of these, so you have no excuse but to order at least one. Several of the longtime waiters like to kid with you a bit, but the service is always fast.

1225 19th St. NW. (© **202/293-9091**. www.thepalm.com. Reservations recommended. Lunch entrees $15–$20; dinner entrees $27–$64 (most items are in the neighborhood of $30–$39). AE, DC, MC, V. Mon–Fri 11:45am–10pm; Sat 5:30–10pm; Sun 5:30–9:30pm. Metro: Dupont Circle (19th St./South exit).

EXPENSIVE

Pesce ★ SEAFOOD Tables are close together and every table is full—that's Pesce, where a no-reservations policy and a reliably pleasing menu means that there's usually a line. A large blackboard displays a long list of daily specials: monkfish roasted with celery, apples, and duck jus; lobster risotto; grilled whole flounder; scallops; and soft-shell crabs were among recent options. Owner Regine Palladin is a vibrant and gracious presence in the 17-year-old restaurant, originally opened by her husband, the world-renowned chef, Jean-Louis Palladin, who died in 2001. Pesce draws a wide swath of Washingtonians, from the secretary of state to NPR correspondents to locals from the neighborhood, everyone ready for a convivial time and good eats. Its unflagging popularity is the reason that Pesce moved to a larger space, just up the block, in August 2009.

2002 P St. NW (near 20th St.). (© 202/466-3474. www.pescebistro.com. Reservations accepted at lunch and for parties of 6 or more at dinner. Lunch $12–$22; dinner entrees $20–$26. AE, DC, DISC, MC, V. Mon–Fri 11:30am–2:30pm; Mon–Thurs 5:30–10pm; Fri–Sat 5:30–10:30pm. Metro: Dupont Circle (19th St./South exit).

Tabard Inn ★ AMERICAN In spite of the fact that this restaurant lies inside the Hotel Tabard Inn (see description in chapter 5), the Tabard Inn is largely a beloved local spot. Saturday and Sunday brunch is a tradition for bunches of friends and families, weekday lunch pulls in the staff from surrounding embassies and association offices, and dinner seats couples, business partners, and Washingtonians meeting pals in town for meetings. The fetchingly homey main dining room holds wooden tables, hanging plants, a black-and-white tile floor, and windows overlooking a brick-walled garden. The kitchen smokes its own salmon (as it has for 27 years); cures its own pastrami, tasso ham, and prosciutto; and bakes its own bread and pastries, so these items are awfully good. Everything's good, though; and everything's fresh, from the oysters delivered straight from the coast of Maine to the grilled Hereford rib-eye steak, served with Gorgonzola new gold potatoes, broccolini, and bordelaise sauce.

1739 N St. NW (at 17th St., in the Hotel Tabard Inn). (© **202/331-8528**. www.tabardinn.com. Reservations recommended. Breakfast entrees $6.50–$19; lunch and brunch entrees $11–$17; dinner entrees $23–$32. AE, DC, DISC, MC, V. Mon–Fri 7–10am and 11:30am–2:30pm; Sat 8–9:45am; Sun 8–9:15am; Sat brunch 11am–2:30pm; Sun brunch 10:30am–2:30pm; Sun–Thurs 6–9:30pm; Fri–Sat 6–10pm. Metro: Dupont Circle (19th St./South exit).

MODERATE

Hank's Oyster Bar ★ SEAFOOD Deep in the heart of Dupont Circle is this lively, laid-back hangout, fronted by a sidewalk cafe in warm weather. Decor inside is cozy and casual, with exposed brick walls and pipes and a mix of seating at the bar, tall round tables, and the usual wooden rectangles. You want to order the specials at Hank's, which on a recent night included a sautéed soft-shell crab in citrus butter, and pan-roasted halibut with tomato-lemon relish. Signature dishes feature classics like popcorn shrimp and calamari, and, of course, fresh oysters served on the half shell, fried, or in a po' boy. Hank's easy atmosphere puts you in a good mood and gives you a merry send-off when you've got a fun night on the town planned. Hank's has a second location, in Old Town Alexandria, at 1026 King St. (© **703/739-4265**).

1624 Q St. NW (at 17th St.). ℂ **202/462-4265**. www.hanksdc.com. Reservations not accepted. Dinner entrees $13–$23; brunch entrees $6–$23. AE, MC, V. Sun–Tues 5:30–10pm; Wed–Sat 5:30–11pm; Sat–Sun 11am–3pm. Metro: Dupont Circle (Q St. exit).

INEXPENSIVE

Pizzeria Paradiso ★ PIZZA/ITALIAN   In spite of awesome competition, this is still the best pizza place in the city. An oak-burning oven turns out exceptionally doughy but light-crusted pizzas, with choices ranging from the plain Paradiso, which offers chunks of tomatoes covered in melted mozzarella, to the robust Siciliana, a blend of nine ingredients including eggplant and red onion. Or you can choose your own toppings from a list of 31. As popular as the pizzas are the panini of homemade focaccia, stuffed with marinated roasted lamb and vegetables and other fillings, and the salads, such as the panzanella (thick crusts of bread with chopped zucchini and peppers tossed with balsamic vinegar and olive oil). In 2009, Paradiso moved up the street to this twice-the-size location and added a Birerria Paradiso, like the one its Georgetown sister Paradiso has, at 3282 M St. NW (ℂ **202/337-1245**). If Dupont's Birerria is anything like Georgetown's (dubbed "one of the best pubs in the region" by *Washingtonian* magazine), you can expect spirited good times with that pizza.

2003 P St. NW. ℂ **202/223-1245**. www.eatyourpizza.com. Reservations not accepted. Pizzas $9.95–$19; sandwiches and salads $5.25–$8.95. DC, DISC, MC, V. Mon–Thurs 11:30am–11pm; Fri–Sat 11:30am–midnight; Sun noon–10pm. Metro: Dupont Circle (19th St./South exit).

Sweetgreen SALAD/YOGURT   Three Georgetown University students tired of searching for "fast-casual and healthy" food options in Georgetown decided to create their own, and thus the first Sweetgreen takeout was born in summer 2007, in the heart of their old neighborhood (3333 M St. NW; ℂ **202/337-9338**). All three of their current locations (there likely will be more by the time you read this) serve a winning, green, healthy and delicious set of salad and frozen yogurt choices. You can choose a signature salad, like the Parisien (baby arugula with roasted turkey breast, brie, pears, toasted almonds, topped with champagne vinaigrette and served with warm bread), an "old school" salad, like Caesar or cobb, or make your own. The frozen yogurt is unflavored but you can add toppings. Nearly all packaging is biodegradable, including the menu, which has been implanted with seeds, for you to pass it forward, planting the menu in the ground, and sprouting a sweetgreen something or other yourself.

1512 Connecticut Ave. NW (at Dupont Circle). ℂ **202/387-9338**. www.sweetgreen.com. Reservations not accepted. Salads $8–$9; yogurt $4–$6. AE, DC, DISC, MC, V. Daily 11am–10pm. Metro: Dupont Circle (either exit).

Teaism Dupont Circle (Finds) ASIAN FUSION   Occupying a turn-of-the-20th-century neoclassical building on a tree-lined street, Teaism has a lovely rustic interior. A display kitchen and tandoor oven dominate the sunny downstairs room, which offers counter seating along a wall of French windows that open in warm weather. Upstairs seating is on banquettes and small Asian stools at handcrafted mahogany tables.

The impressive tea list comprises close to 30 aromatic blends, most of them from India, China, and Japan. On the menu is light Asian fare served on stainless-steel plates or in lacquer lunchboxes (one Japanese bento box holds teriyaki salmon, cucumber-ginger salad, a scoop of rice with seasoning, and fresh fruit—all for $8.75). Dishes include Thai chicken curry with sticky rice, buffalo burger with Asian slaw, and a portobello and goat cheese sandwich. Baked jasmine crème brûlée and salty oat cookies are favorite desserts. Teaism is also popular at breakfast, when ginger scones and cilantro eggs and sausage are on tap. *Note:* Other locations include **Teaism Lafayette Square,** 800 Connecticut Ave. NW (𝒞 **202/835-2233**), near the White House, and **Teaism Penn Quarter** ★, 400 8th St. NW (𝒞 **202/638-6010**), which is the only branch that serves beer, wine, and cocktails.

2009 R St. NW (btw. Connecticut and 21st sts.). 𝒞 **202/667-3827.** www.teaism.com. All menu items $2–$10. DISC, MC, V. Mon–Thurs 8am–10pm; Fri 8am–11pm; Sat 9am–11pm; Sun 9am–10pm. Metro: Dupont Circle (Q St. exit).

9 FOGGY BOTTOM/WEST END

VERY EXPENSIVE

Blue Duck Tavern ★★ CONTEMPORARY AMERICAN   In this light-filled space, where modern American materials, like stainless steel and polished glass, mesh with classic features, like dark oak and blue burlap, chef Brian McBride, likewise combines traditional and state-of-the-art cooking methods and equipment to prepare exquisite, one-of-a-kind dishes, using the freshest produce, meats, and seafood from local and regional artisans and purveyors. The menu identifies the farm or other source of the prime ingredients for each dish. Recent home runs included white asparagus with periwinkles and crispy pancetta, crispy breast of guinea hen leg roulade, jumbo lump crab cakes with rémoulade sauce, and the baked rice with homemade andouille. The housemade steak fries are in a class of their own. Save room for dessert, like the chocolate cake flamed in bourbon, accompanied by a scoop of ice cream that you'll see hand-cranked minutes before it's delivered to your table. The wine list features 60 American wines and 300 from around the world.

1201 24th St. NW (at M St. NW), in the Park Hyatt Washington Hotel. 𝒞 **202/419-6755.** www.blueduck tavern.com. Reservations recommended. Breakfast $5–$16; brunch entrees $12–$28; lunch entrees $15–$28; dinner entrees $15–$50 (most in $25 range). AE, DC, DISC, MC, V. Daily 6:30–10:30am, 11:30am–2:30pm, and 5:30–10:30pm. Metro: Foggy Bottom or Dupont Circle (19th St./South exit).

Kinkead's ★★ SEAFOOD   Open since 1983, Kinkead's remains a reliable place to go for festive atmosphere and great, possibly the best, seafood in the city. Award- winning chef/owner Bob Kinkead orchestrates the action from his second floor kitchen, in this three-tier, 220-seat townhouse. Best seat: the booth named after the late, irreplaceable master journalist, R. W. Apple, who used to dine here; the booth is tucked into a corner of the lively bar area, rather private even though you're in the thick of things. The worst seat in the house: anywhere in the "atrium," the area that extends outside the doors of the restaurant into an indoor mall.

Kinkead's menu (which changes daily) features primarily seafood, but always includes at least one beef and one poultry entree. Among the favorite dishes are the fried Ipswich clams; cod topped with crab imperial; clam chowder; and pepita-crusted salmon with shrimp, crab, and chilies. Chef Kinkead piles on appetizing garnishes—that crab-crowned cod, for instance, comes with sweet potato purée and ham-laced spoon bread. The wine list comprises more than 300 selections.

2000 Pennsylvania Ave. NW. 𝒞 **202/296-7700.** www.kinkead.com. Reservations recommended. Lunch entrees $18–$27; dinner entrees $22–$34; light fare $9–$27. AE, DC, DISC, MC, V. Mon–Fri 11:30am–2:30pm; Sun–Thurs 5:30–10pm; Fri–Sat 5:30–10:30pm (light fare served weekdays 2:30–5:30pm). Metro: Foggy Bottom.

ⓥ Value Pretheater Dinners = Great Deals

Some of Washington's finest restaurants make you an offer you shouldn't refuse: a three-course dinner for just a little bit more than the cost of a typical entree. It's the pretheater dinner, available in the early evening on certain nights at certain restaurants; and while your choices may be limited, your meal will undoubtedly be delicious.

At one end of the spectrum is **Marcel's** ★★ (p. 152), whose $52 fixed-price includes any three courses from the regular menu, perhaps an arugula salad with caramelized shallots to start; an entree, like pan-seared Norwegian salmon; and a dessert, perhaps crème brûlée or chocolate terrine. Marcel's offers this menu nightly from 5:30 to 7pm or so and throws in complimentary limo service to and from the Kennedy Center, returning you to the restaurant after the show for the dessert portion, if you haven't already consumed it.

Café Atlantico's ★★ (p. 128) pretheater menu allows you three courses for $35: soup or salad to start, salmon with a Veracruz sauce, or a similar choice for the main course, and sorbet or warm chocolate cake to finish. The restaurant's pretheater menu is available nightly between 5 and 6:30pm.

Other restaurants in this chapter that offer a pretheater menu include **Ceiba** ★★ (p. 129), **Rasika** ★★ (p. 136), **1789** ★★★ (p. 154), and **Café Saint-Ex** ★ (p. 143).

Marcel's ★★★ FRENCH Chef Robert Wiedmaier's vivid style and cuisine are firmly on display here, with French dishes that include nods to his Belgian training: duck breast with baby turnips, rose lentils, and Calvados sauce, or venison with ragout of winter mushrooms and Madeira sauce. Those in the know order the *boudin blanc* sausage with chestnut puree, said to be out of this world. Desserts usually include such seasonal tarts as spring pear tart with raspberry coulis.

Service and ambience are rather formal in this dining room, whose French country decor includes panels of rough stone framed by rustic shutters and antique hutches displaying Provençal pottery. To the right of the exhibition kitchen is the more casual wine bar, which has its own menu (the full dinner menu is also available at some tables) and lovely live jazz Tuesday through Saturday year-round. Marcel's offers seating on the patio—right on Pennsylvania Avenue—in warm weather. See information about Marcel's grand pretheater dinner, in the box that follows.

2401 Pennsylvania Ave. NW. ⓒ **202/296-1166.** www.marcelsdc.com. Reservations recommended. Tasting menus: 4-course $75, 5-course $90, 7-course $125 (any dish on the menu may be ordered individually); pretheater dinner 5:30–7pm (including round-trip limo to/from Kennedy Center) $52. AE, MC, V. Sun 5:30–9:30pm; Mon–Thurs 5:30–10pm; Fri–Sat 5:30–11pm. Metro: Foggy Bottom.

EXPENSIVE

Kaz Sushi Bistro ★ JAPANESE Amiable chef/owner Kazuhiro ("Kaz") Okochi introduced Washington to sushi long ago, at a restaurant called Sushi-Ko (p. 160). Since 1999, Kaz has run his sushi bistro in this handsome town house. Aficionados vie for one of the six chairs at the bar to watch Kaz and his staff do their thing, especially at lunch, when fellow diners are likely to be Japanese men in Washington on business and young

Washingtonians. Besides sushi, Kaz is known for his seared scallops with lemon salt, Asian-style tender short ribs, and for his bento boxes, offering exquisite tastings of pan-seared salmon, spicy broiled mussels, and the like. This is also the place for premium sakes and a large selection of teas.

1915 I St. NW. ✆ **202/530-5500.** Reservations recommended. www.kazsushibistro.com. Sushi a la carte $4–$10; lunch entrees $13–$22; dinner entrees $16–$32. AE, DC, DISC, MC, V. Mon–Fri 11:30am–2pm; Mon–Sat 6–10pm. Metro: Farragut West.

Westend Bistro by Eric Ripert ★ FRENCH-AMERICAN   If you're going to use your name as part of your restaurant's name, you'd better be great. Apparently, Eric Ripert's (of New York City's esteemed Le Bernardin) name was enough to create a stampede of curious foodies when the bistro opened in November 2007. (The truth is, of course, that Ripert is not actually in the kitchen.) Its success continues. Me? I don't think the bistro is all that. The straightahead menu ranges from a classic burger to fish stew to roasted rack of lamb to pasta Bolognese. We were fairly satisfied but not overwhelmed by our burger, macaroni and cheese, flatiron steak, and arugula salad. So maybe we were expecting too much. Perhaps we should have chosen Ripert's signature dishes of salmon rillettes and the seafood stew. Expect crowds weeknights and Saturdays; it's much quieter Sundays.

1190 22nd St. NW (in the Ritz-Carlton Washington Hotel). ✆ **202/974-4900.** www.westendbistrodc. com. Reservations recommended. Lunch entrees $14–$29; dinner entrees $16–$33. AE, DC, DISC, MC, V. Mon–Fri 11:30am–2:30pm; Sun–Thurs 5:30–10pm; Fri–Sat 5:30–11pm. Metro: Foggy Bottom/West End.

10 GEORGETOWN

VERY EXPENSIVE

Bourbon Steak ★★★ STEAK   If you want to be in the hippest dining room in D.C., book your reservation for Bourbon Steak today. After yet another of its multimillion-dollar remodelings, the Four Seasons has moved its new primary restaurant upstairs to street level, where it belongs, placing it back and center of the property, overlooking the C&O Canal. To reach it, you must first thread your way past the vintage Ferraris and Rolls Royces jamming up the driveway, then enter the hotel and keep on going in a straight line, past the dueling reception desks, until you reach, first the Lounge, then the restaurant. Everyone is here: Angelina, Andrea Mitchell, Oprah, Owen Wilson, Senator Mark Warner. And now you. Pat yourself on the back: You have arrived. So sit down and get to it: the duck topped with seared foie gras, lamb loin with pomegranate marinade, lobster pot pie, and Japanese Kobe steak. Delicious. From the staff in the open kitchen, to the tables for two and four and eight, to the partiers out in the lounge, everyone's having a good time. That's really what it's all about here: great food, good stories, and fun. Enjoy.

2800 Pennsylvania Ave. NW (at 28th St.). Inside the Four Seasons Hotel. ✆ **202/944-2026.** www.four seasons.com. Reservations recommended. Lunch entrees $12–$32; dinner entrees $14–$48. AE, DC, DISC, MC, V. Mon–Fri 11:30am–2:30pm; Sun–Thu 6–10pm; Fri–Sat 5:30–10:30pm. Metro: Foggy Bottom, then either walk or ride the DC Circulator bus.

Michel Richard Citronelle ★★★ INNOVATIVE FRENCH   Food critics continue to name Citronelle as among D.C.'s best restaurants. It's my own personal favorite. And yet, there's a chance the restaurant may have closed by the time you read this; chef/owner Michel Richard is said to be contemplating shutting the doors on Citronelle so he can focus on opening a new restaurant in the Ritz-Carlton Hotel, in Tysons Corner,

Virginia. If Citronelle still exists by the time you read this, and you care about creatively delicious French cuisine, do try to book a table there. You're in for a (very expensive) treat. The ebullient Richard produces masterpieces in every form: from appetizers like the fricassee of escargots, an eggshell filled with caviar, sweetbreads, porcinis, and crunchy pistachios, to entrees like the crispy lentil-coated salmon or squab leg confit with macaroni gratin and black truffles. Each presentation is a work of art, with swirls of colorful sauce surrounding the main event. If you're passionate about food, you may want to consider dining at the chef's table in the kitchen, so you can watch Richard at work. This will cost you: $350 per person, with a minimum of six people and maximum of eight, is the stated price, but that's to give you a ballpark idea; call for more exact information.

Citronelle's decor is also breathtaking and includes a wall that changes colors, a state-of-the-art wine cellar (a glass-enclosed room that encircles the dining room, displaying its 8,000 bottles and a collection of 18th- and 19th-c. corkscrews), and a Provençal color scheme of mellow yellow and raspberry red.

Michel Richard's richly layered chocolate "bar" with sauce noisette (hazelnut sauce) is recommended for dessert, if available. Citronelle's extensive wine list offers about 20 premium by-the-glass selections, but with all those bottles staring out at you from the wine cellar, you may want to spring for one. Also consider dining at Richard's French/American bistro, **Central** (p. 129), 2008 winner of the James Beard Award for "Best New Restaurant." Central offers a less expensive, less elaborate, but every bit as delicious meal.

In the Latham Hotel, 3000 M St. NW. © **202/625-2150.** www.citronelledc.com. Reservations required. Jacket required, tie optional for men at dinner. Open for dinner only. Fixed-price 3-course dinner $105; 9-course tasting menu $190 per person or $280 with wine pairings; bar/lounge entrees $16–$42. AE, DC, MC, V. Tue–Sat 6–10pm.

1789 ★★ AMERICAN This 48-year-old restaurant near Georgetown University draws from its upper crust neighborhood of media types, socialites, politicians, and corporate execs. The menu changes daily but is consistent in offering savory and rich American fare, like the rack of lamb with charred onion puree and pickled radishes, or the thick pork chop served with blackeyed peas and applewood-smoked bacon, or my favorite, Carolina grouper with crispy soft-shell crab.

The 1789 has a reputation for romance, making it an excellent destination for hand-holding couples. The five dining rooms, especially those on the first floor, are cozy dens, with a homey decor that includes historical prints on the walls, silk-shaded brass oil lamps on tables, and, come winter, fires crackling in the fireplaces. So put on your best duds and be prepared for a relaxing meal with only the food and your dinner companion to distract you. The formal but cozy restaurant occupies two floors (three, if you count the room reserved for private parties) of a Federal town house near Georgetown University.

The $35, three-course pretheater menu is available nightly until 6:45pm; the same deal is available after 9pm Sunday through Thursday and after 10pm Friday and Saturday nights.

1226 36th St. NW. © **202/965-1789.** www.1789restaurant.com. Reservations recommended. Jacket required for men. Entrees $29–$38; fixed-price pretheater menu $35. AE, DC, DISC, MC, V. Mon–Thurs 6–10pm; Fri 6–11pm; Sat 5:30–11pm; Sun 5:30–10pm.

EXPENSIVE

Bistrot Lepic & Wine Bar ★ FRENCH Bistrot Lepic is the real thing—a charming French restaurant that seems plucked right off a Parisian side street. The atmosphere is bustling and cheery, and you hear a lot of French spoken—not just by the waiters, but

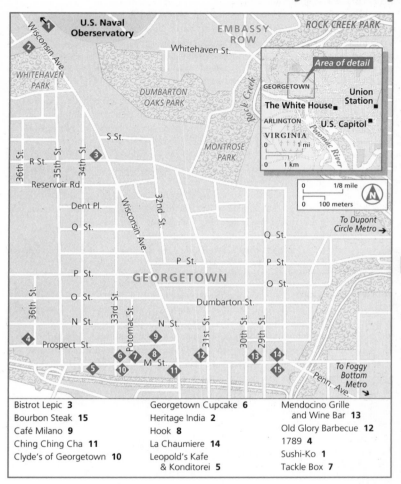

WHERE TO DINE

6

GEORGETOWN

Bistrot Lepic **3**	Georgetown Cupcake **6**	Mendocino Grille and Wine Bar **13**
Bourbon Steak **15**	Heritage India **2**	Old Glory Barbecue **12**
Café Milano **9**	Hook **8**	1789 **4**
Ching Ching Cha **11**	La Chaumiere **14**	Sushi-Ko **1**
Clyde's of Georgetown **10**	Leopold's Kafe & Konditorei **5**	Tackle Box **7**

also by customers. The Bistrot is a neighborhood place, and you'll often see diners waving hellos across the room to each other or even table-hopping. This is traditional French cooking, updated. The seasonal menu offers such entrees as grilled rainbow trout with tomatoes, capers, and olives; beef medallions with polenta and shiitake mushroom sauce; and sautéed sea scallops with ginger broccoli mousse. Depending on the season, specials might turn up rare tuna served on fennel with citrus vinaigrette or grouper with a mildly spicy lobster sauce upon a bed of spinach.

In its 15 years, the restaurant has made some changes to accommodate its popularity, including turning the upstairs into an Asian-accented wine bar and lounge (p. 270).

Come here to hang out, sip a glass of wine, and munch on offerings from the wine bar menu, where the most expensive item is the $14 terrine of homemade foie gras, or specialties of the house from the regular menu. The wine bar hosts complimentary wine tastings every Tuesday 6 to 8pm.

1736 Wisconsin Ave. NW. © **202/333-0111.** www.bistrotlepic.com. Reservations recommended. Lunch entrees $14–$19; 2-course ($20) and 3-course ($25) prix-fixe lunch menus Mon–Thurs also available; dinner entrees $16–$26. AE, DC, DISC, MC, V. Daily 11:30am–2:30pm; Sun–Mon 5:30–9:30pm; Tues–Thurs 5:30–10pm; Fri–Sat 5:30–10:30pm. Wine bar daily 5:30pm–midnight.

Cafe Milano ★ ITALIAN   The beautiful-people factor rises exponentially here as the night wears on. Cafe Milano has long been a magnet for Washington's famous, attractive, and powerful—and for visiting Hollywood and international celebrities. But this restaurant/nightclub/bar also serves good food. Salads are big, pasta servings are small, and fish and meat entrees are just the right size. We had the endive, radicchio, and arugula salad topped with thin sheets of Parmesan cheese; a *panzanella* salad of tomatoes, potatoes, red onion, celery, and cucumber basking in basil and olive oil; *cappellacci* (round ravioli) pockets of spinach and ricotta in cream sauce; sautéed sea bass on a bed of vegetables with lemon chive sauce; and the Santa Babila pizza, which has tomatoes, fresh mozzarella, oregano, and basil on a light pizza crust. All were delicious. Cafe Milano opens to a sidewalk cafe during the warm months. A bevy of good-humored waiters takes care of you.

3251 Prospect St. NW. © **202/333-6183.** www.cafemilano.net. Reservations recommended. Lunch and dinner entrees $15–$45 (most entrees are $20–$35). AE, DC, DISC, MC, V. Sun–Tues 11:30am–11pm; Wed–Sat 11:30am–midnight (bar menu served until midnight Mon–Tues, until 1am Wed–Sat).

Hook ★ SEAFOOD   Situated near the busy Georgetown intersection of M Street and Wisconsin Avenue, Hook can be as noisy inside as out, when there's a full house, which is quite often. The bar at the front offers a good view of the passing menagerie; beyond the bar is the minimalist all-white dining room, with the semi-open kitchen pulling up the rear. Hook is committed to the "sustainable" movement, which means that the chef shops for locally farmed produce and that the menus are printed on 100% post-consumer recycled paper, to give just two examples. But Hook's real "hook" is sustainable, in-season seafood, so you can expect the blackfin tuna that arrives with the crème fraîche and potato purée on your plate to have been pulled from the water sometime within the preceding 24 hours. Be sure to order one of pastry chef Heather Chittum's lovely desserts, from warm madeleine cookies to an inventive carrot cake.

3241 M St. NW (btw. Wisconsin Ave. and 33rd St.). © **202/625-4488.** www.hookdc.com. Reservations recommended. Brunch, lunch, and sunset menu (Sat–Sun 2:30–5:30pm) entrees $10–$16; dinner entrees $26–$29. AE, DC, DISC, MC, V. Sat–Sun 11am–10pm; Tues–Fri 11:30am–2:30pm; Mon–Tues 5–10pm; Wed–Fri 5–11pm.

Mendocino Grille and Wine Bar ★ AMERICAN   As its name suggests, you should come here to enjoy West Coast wine, along with contemporary American cuisine and a California-casual ambience. Most of the 200-or-so bottles on the wine list are California vintages, with some from Washington State and Oregon, too. California-casual doesn't mean cheap, though: Bottles range from $33 to $600, although most fall in the $50 to $60 range. The restaurant offers 20 wines by the glass, in different sizes, the better for tastings; and many of these run between $8 and $11 each.

Fresh ingredients predominate, whether it's an entree of olive oil–poached king salmon with sweet-and-sour red onions or South Carolina quail stuffed with pheasant sausage and accompanied by Brussels sprouts and roasted figs.

Rough-textured slate walls alternate with painted patches of Big Sur sky to suggest a West Coast winery in California's winegrowing region. Regulars from the neighborhood congregate nightly down the length of the handcrafted cherry-wood bar.

2917 M St. NW. (✆) **202/333-2912.** www.mendocinodc.com. Reservations recommended. Dinner entrees $12–$37. AE, DC, DISC, MC, V. Sun–Thurs 5:30–10pm; Fri–Sat 5:30–11pm.

MODERATE

Clyde's of Georgetown AMERICAN   Clyde's has been a favorite watering hole for an eclectic mix of Washingtonians since 1963. You'll see university students, Capitol Hill types, affluent professionals, Washington Redskins, romantic duos, and ladies out for lunch. Theme park–ish in decor, its dining areas include a cherry-paneled front room with oil paintings of sport scenes, as well as an atrium with vintage model planes dangling from the glass ceiling and a 16th-century French limestone chimney piece in the large fireplace.

Clyde's is known for its burgers, chili, and crab cake sandwiches. Appetizers are a safe bet, and Clyde's take on the classic Niçoise (chilled grilled salmon with greens, oven-roasted roma tomatoes, green beans, and grilled new potatoes in a tasty vinaigrette) is also recommended. Sunday brunch is a tradition, so popular that the brunch is offered on Saturday as well. The menu is reassuringly familiar—steak and eggs, omelets, waffles—with an assortment of sandwiches, burgers, and salads thrown in. Among bar selections are about 10 draft beers. Bottles of wine are half-price on Sundays until 10:30pm.

Clyde's also has a Penn Quarter location, **Clyde's of Gallery Place,** at 707 7th St. NW ((✆) **202/349-3700**). See its listing in chapter 9, p. 266.

3236 M St. NW. (✆) **202/333-9180.** www.clydes.com. Reservations recommended. Lunch and brunch entrees $9.50–$17; dinner entrees $13–$24 (most under $15); burgers and sandwiches (except for crab cake sandwich) $10 or less. AE, DC, DISC, MC, V. Mon–Thurs 11:30am–midnight; Fri 11:30am–1am; Sat 10am–1am; Sun 9am–midnight (Sat–Sun brunch until 4pm).

La Chaumiere ★★ FRENCH   After 33 years, La Chaumiere is still going strong. This rustically handsome dining room centers on a large hearth, which makes it an especially welcoming place in winter. Year-round, the restaurant fills up with locals who know the specials by heart; if it's Tuesday, that means "crabe en chemise" is on the menu: crepes filled with crabmeat, mushrooms, and champagne sauce. La Chaumiere prepares the full range of French classics just right, whether it's cassoulet or a chocolate soufflé. The service is warm but professional. The diners who gather here are a motley bunch, alike at least in their love of this kitchen's authentic French cooking.

2813 M St. NW (at 28th St.). (✆) **202/338-1784.** www.lachaumieredc.com. Reservations accepted. Lunch entrees $13–$18; dinner entrees $15–$30 (most are under $20). AE, MC, V. Mon–Fri 11:30am–2:30pm; Mon–Sat 5:30–10:30pm.

Leopold's Kafe & Konditorei ★ (**Finds**) AUSTRIAN   If you find yourself at the western end of Georgetown, caught in the maze of high-end shops collectively known as Cady's Alley, you owe it to yourself to track down Leopold's and treat yourself to a delicious taste of Sacher torte or veal schnitzel. This may be the only place in Washington that serves Austrian food; it is certainly one of the most adorable eateries, with its whimsically modern furniture and bright whites punched up with orange. The customers represent a cross section of Washington, from chic to bohemian, and offer an intriguing picture to contemplate as you sip your Viennese coffee and enjoy your *apfelstrudel.* At brunch, order the lemon soufflé pancakes. The cafe offers a full bar.

3315 Cady's Alley, no. 213 (off of M St. NW). (Find the passageway at 3318 M St., btw. 33rd and 34th sts., and walk back to Leopold's.) (✆) **202/965-6005.** www.kafeleopolds.com. Reservations not accepted.

Breakfast items $1.75–$10; lunch and dinner entrees $13–$22. AE, DISC, MC, V. Sun–Tues 8am–10pm; Wed 8am–11pm; Thurs–Sat 8am–midnight.

Old Glory Barbecue (Kids) BARBECUE   Raised wooden booths flank one side of the restaurant; an imposing, old-fashioned dark-wood bar with saddle-seat stools extends down the other. Background music is recorded swing music during the day, more mainstream music into the night. Old Glory boasts the city's "largest selection of single-barrel and boutique bourbons" and a rooftop deck with outdoor seating and views of Georgetown.

After 9pm or so, the two-story restaurant becomes packed with the hard-drinkin' young and restless. In early evening, though, Old Glory is prime for anyone—singles, families, or an older crowd—although it's almost always noisy. Come for the messy, tangy, delicious spareribs; hickory-smoked chicken; tender, smoked beef brisket; or marinated, wood-fired shrimp. Six sauces are on the table, the spiciest being the vinegar-based East Carolina and Lexington. The complimentary corn muffins and biscuits; side dishes of collard greens, succotash, and potato salad; and desserts like apple crisp and coconut cherry cobbler all hit the spot. See "Family-Friendly Restaurants" box, p. 135.

3139 M St. NW. ℂ **202/337-3406.** www.oldglorybbq.com. Reservations accepted. Lunch and dinner entrees $7.95–$25; brunch $15 per person. AE, DC, DISC, MC, V. Sun 11am–2am (brunch from 11am–3pm); Mon–Thurs 11:30am–2am; Fri–Sat 11:30am–3am.

INEXPENSIVE

Ching Ching Cha (Finds) CHINESE/JAPANESE   Located just below M Street, this sky-lit tearoom offers a pleasant respite from the crowds. You can sit on pillows at low tables or on chairs set at rosewood tables. Choices are simple: individual items like a tea-and-spice boiled egg, puff pastry stuffed with lotus-seed paste, or five-spice peanuts. Most typical is the $12 "tea meal," which consists of miso soup, your choice of three marinated cold vegetables, rice, and your choice of the featured meal, whether curry chicken, salmon with mustard-miso sauce, or steamed teriyaki-sauced tofu. Emphasis is really on the tea, of which there are 70 choices, including several different green, black, medicinal, and oolong teas, plus a Fujian white tea and a ginseng brew.

1063 Wisconsin Ave. NW. ℂ **202/333-8288.** www.chingchingcha.com. Reservations not accepted. All food items $4–$12; pot of tea $6–$20. AE, DISC, MC, V. Tues–Sat 11am–9pm; Sun 11am–7pm.

Tackle Box ★ SEAFOOD   What a delicious deal: your choice of crisped scallops, shrimp, calamari, clams, or oysters, or wood-grilled fresh fish, from tilapia to rainbow trout, plus two sides (whether fries, grilled asparagus, or assorted other options) for a total of $13. Tackle Box and **Hook** (p. 156), right next door, share the same owners, eco-friendly prac-tices, and passion for top-notch food. Dine in and you'll sit at picnic tables in a lobster buoy-bedecked room, in view and smelling range of the wood-grilling kitchen. No liquor license (Tackle Box hopes to acquire one soon.) means you might want to do takeout to your hotel or house to enjoy your feast with a bottle of wine or beer.

3245 M St. NW. ℂ **202/337-TBOX** (8269). www.tackleboxrestaurant.com. All items $2–$19. AE, DC, MC, V. Daily 11am–11pm. Metro: Foggy Bottom, with a walk or ride aboard the D.C. Circulator.

11 GLOVER PARK

The D.C. Circulator buses travel through Georgetown as far as Whitehaven Street, just a little bit short (south) of Glover Park; you can walk it easily, but it is all uphill. Regular Metro buses (the no. 30 series) travel to Glover Park. Perhaps the easiest thing to do is take a taxi.

Heritage India ★ INDIAN   This elegant two-story dining room caters to those with
sophisticated tastes for Indian food. You'll find all the standards here: tandoori dishes,

A Seat at the Bar

Dining out in Washington can be many things: a culinary adventure, a happy
pastime, a chance to transact business, a romantic interlude . . . and a competitive sport. Most restaurants require reservations, and in this cutthroat
town, all the best seem always to be booked. Oh pooh! What's a hungry, reser-
vation-less, good-food lover to do? Head to the bar, of course. In an effort to
please those who haven't managed to reserve a table in their main dining
rooms, but who nevertheless hope to sample some of their food, glorious food,
a number of the city's top restaurants have started serving modified versions
of their regular menus at the bar. The experience often proves more intimate
and convivial than that in the main dining room, and here's the kicker: it's
always less expensive. Consider these:

At **Palena,** 3529 Connecticut Ave. NW (℃ **202/537-9250**), you sit on comfy
stools and in booths in the bar area at the front of the house and enjoy chef
Frank Ruta's exquisitely prepared Kobe beef cheeseburger with brioche bun
and *sottocenere* (a creamy Italian cheese with black truffles), pastas, roasted
chicken, a charcuterie plate, a plate of french fries, fried lemons (don't knock
'em 'til you try 'em) and onion rings, all perfectly done—and everything costing
less than $20. This bar area is known as **Palena's Café,** to distinguish it from the
formal dining room beyond. You can also choose from the main dining room
menu here, but most people are happy with the cafe menu.

Ceiba, in the Penn Quarter, offers a sweet deal at the bar, on the early side,
from 3–6pm, and late-night, 9:30 to closing, when you can order $5 signature
cocktails (and the mojitos here may be the best in the city) and items from the
bar menu, from guacamole to empanadas, at half their usual $10–$16 price.

CityZen, in the Mandarin Oriental Hotel, 1330 Maryland Ave. SW (℃ **202/
787-6868**), offers perhaps the most jaw-dropping bar meal: Chef Eric Ziebold's
three-course tasting menu in his main dining room costs $80; at the bar, Zie-
bold's edited version goes for $45 to $50. The chef does not present a set bar
menu but pulls one or two choices from each course on offer that night, so you
can be sure you're dining on the same heavenly fare as those seated at tables:
maybe a pickled shad with braised celery and potato crisps, or braised shoat
shoulder with English peas. And the service is sublime.

Other bar scenes to recommend: **Marcel's** (p. 152), whose wine bar menu
ranges from a gratin of endive for $13 to beef carbonade, in $15 and $28 por-
tions (Marcel's also features live jazz in the wine bar nightly); **Bistrot Lepic**
(p. 154), whose second floor is a wine bar (p. 270), offering both bar item menus
and specialties of the house; and **Corduroy** (p. 141), whose nightly 5–7pm, $30
three-course bar menu features whatever the chef is inclined to serve that
night, but is always guaranteed to please the palate.

lamb vindaloo, and vegetarian entrees, such as the *palak makai* (herbed spinach), and vegetable fritters, each dish carefully prepared and seasoned. Service could be better, but the overall experience is rewarding. A second Heritage India is located in the Dupont Circle neighborhood, 1337 Connecticut Ave. NW (② **202/331-1414**), a "brasserie and lounge," whose menu includes contemporary Indian cuisine. Small plates of samosas, pakoras, and kabobs go down nicely with a cocktail; that's what the younger crowd comes here for, along with the dishes served at the original location and some more intriguing dishes, such as the hummus made with roasted garlic and black beans, and the tandoori-smoked mozzarella.

2400 Wisconsin Ave. NW (near Calvert St.). ② **202/333-3120.** www.heritageindiaofgeorgetown.com. Reservations accepted. Lunch entrees $7.95–$13; dinner entrees $10–$25. AE, DC, DISC, MC, V. Daily 11:30am–2:30pm and 5:30–10:45pm.

Sushi-Ko ★ JAPANESE   Sushi-Ko was Washington's first sushi bar when it opened 34 years ago, and it remains the best. The sushi chefs are fun to watch—try to sit at the sushi bar; if you do, ask chef Koji Terano to serve you his choice selections. You can expect superb sushi and sashimi standards, as well as daily specials, like a sea trout napoleon (diced sea trout layered btw. rice crackers), flounder sashimi with a black truffle sauce, and the delicately fried soft-shell crab (in season, spring and summer). Another option to capture the full range of tastes here: Order a bunch of the "small dishes," like the grilled baby octopus with mango sauce, or asparagus with smoked salmon and mustard dashi sauce. The tempuras and teriyakis are also excellent. And there's a long list of sakes, as well as burgundy wines and Japanese beer.

2309 Wisconsin Ave. NW. ② **202/333-4187.** www.sushikorestaurants.com. Reservations recommended. Entrees $10–$28. AE, MC, V. Tues–Fri noon–2:30pm; Mon–Thurs 6–10:30pm; Fri 6–11pm; Sat 5:30–11pm; Sun 5:30–10pm.

12 WOODLEY PARK & CLEVELAND PARK

VERY EXPENSIVE

Palena ★★★ NEW AMERICAN/FRENCH   One Metro stop past the Woodley Park–Zoo station takes you out of downtown and into the residential neighborhood of Cleveland Park. Palena is worth the trip.

Palena is the creation of former White House chef, Frank Ruta, who worked at the White House in the 1980s. Ruta turns out modern American dishes, infused with French and Italian influences, such as Portuguese sardines in puff pastry, cod roasted in lavender-infused olive oil, and Dover sole filet stuffed with porcini and pan-roasted with artichokes and endive. Dinner concludes with complimentary caramels to accompany your dessert choice, whether a fresh sorbet, cheesecake, bread pudding, or some other offering. This is an elegant restaurant with an old-world feel. Because of its immediate and sustained success, it's sometimes hard to get a reservation, but worth trying for. Or you can dine in the always jammed cafe/bar (see "A Seat at the Bar," above). Palena's Café, which is the name for the front of the house, is open Tuesday through Saturday and sometimes on Monday nights, serving the bar/cafe menu (diners can also choose from the main menu).

3529 Connecticut Ave. NW. ② **202/537-9250.** www.palenarestaurant.com. Reservations required for the main dining room but not accepted for the café. Fixed-price menus $58 (3-course), $67 (4-course), and $76 (5- to 6-course). Café menu items $10–$18. AE, DC, DISC, MC, V. Tues–Sat 5:30–10pm. Metro: Cleveland Park (exit to the east side of Connecticut Ave.).

Chocolate Lounges and Cupcake Shops

Busted! Washingtonians are finally exposed for what we are: all chocoholics and sweet cake addicts. An explosion of chocolate lounges and cupcake shops has forced us to come clean. You'll see us standing in line at various favorite places throughout the city, licking our lips in anticipation of our next indulgence. If you answer to the same passion, join the queue at one of these five places:

ACKC Cocoa Gallery, at 1529C 14th St. NW (📞 **202/387-COCO;** www.the cocoagallery.com). Part cafe, art gallery, and chocolate shop, ACKC is a delightful place for a chocolate break. Its eight versions of cocoa are named for some favorite femmes, including the Marilyn, Audrey, Lucy, and Liz. The shop also sells artisanal chocolates, made fresh daily by hand.

CoCo. Sala, 929 F St. NW (📞 **202/347-4265;** www.cocosala.com). This chocolate lounge and boutique is a sweet refuge in the heart of the Penn Quarter, dispensing coffees, cocoas, and small plates of light fare throughout the day. Dessert cocktails and chocolate-spiked liqueurs are on tap into the wee hours. See description in the nightlife chapter, p. 266.

Georgetown Cupcake, 1209 Potomac St. NW (📞 **202/333-8448;** www. georgetowncupcake.com). Two sisters, 12 flavors daily, darling designs and packaging, and the best cupcakes. That about sums it up. Truth is, Georgetown Cupcake pretty much launched the current cupcake craze. Locals vote the chocolate ganache the best cupcake in the city; I love the lemon cupcake with lemon cream cheese frosting.

Locolat Café, 1781 Florida Ave. NW (📞 **202/518-2570;** www.belgiumlocolat. com). The Adams-Morgan-based Locolat was already a Belgian chocolate confiserie when it launched its cafe with sidewalk seating. Chocoholics can sip chocolate-enhanced coffee and hot cocoas, and savor an assortment of cakes, Belgian waffles, pastries, and created-on-the-premises chocolate bonbons.

Red Velvet Cupcakery, 675 E St. NW (📞 **202/347-7895;** www.redvelvetcup cakery.com). Located in the heart of the Penn Quarter, Red Velvet stays open until 1am! Friday and Saturday nights (11pm other nights), happy to accommodate the bar and club crowd when a yen for a sweet something hits. Also serves hot chocolate to go.

MODERATE

Indique ★ INDIAN   When it first opened in 2006, Indique was a prime hot spot for hipsters. Things have settled down since then, or more likely, the young and the restless have moved on to another, more of-the-moment restaurant. But Indique still thrives in this upscale residential community of old streets lined with towering trees and Victorian houses, drawing people from the neighborhood, mostly wonks, intellects, journalists, and their families. Pomegranate martinis are ever popular, as are these very good Indian specialties: Cornish hen curry, vegetable samosas, and tandoori shrimp. Its authentic cuisine from different regions in India, from the curries and tandoori specialties of northern Italy to the appams and ishtews of southwestern India, attracts visiting dignitaries from India and Indian food-informed Washingtonians.

3512-14 Connecticut Ave. NW (btw. Porter and Ordway sts.). © **202/244-6600.** www.indique.com. Reservations accepted. Lunch entrees $9–$11; dinner entrees $11–$21. AE, DC, DISC, MC, V. Daily noon–3pm; Sun–Thurs 5:30–10:30pm; Fri–Sat 5:30–11pm. Metro: Cleveland Park (exit to west side of Connecticut Ave.).

Lebanese Taverna (Kids) MIDDLE EASTERN This family-owned restaurant, which opened in 1990, is known for its friendly service and basic but satisfying Lebanese cuisine. The taverna fronts on Connecticut Avenue, which makes its patio a favorite spot in pleasant weather. Inside, the dining room's domed ceiling and soft lighting gives it the feel of an inner courtyard. Lebanese music plays in the background and mouthwatering smells emanate from the wood-burning oven, where pita breads and appetizers bake. What you want to order are the mezze dishes: hummus, tabbouleh, baba ghanouj, stuffed grape leaves, cheese pastries, couscous, and pastry-wrapped spinach pies *(fatayer bi sabanikh)*, enough for dinner for a couple or as hors d'oeuvres for more. Also consider entrees, such as the roasted half chicken wrapped in bread and served with garlic purée. The wealth of meatless dishes will delight vegetarians, while rotisserie items, especially the chicken and the chargrilled kabobs of chicken and shrimp, will please all others.

2641 Connecticut Ave. NW. © **202/265-8681.** www.lebanesetaverna.com. Reservations recommended. Mezze items $5–$11; lunch and dinner entrees $8–$25 (most $15–$17). AE, DC, DISC, MC, V. Mon–Fri 11:30am–2:30pm; Sat noon–3pm; Mon 5:30–10pm; Tues–Thurs 5:30–10:30pm; Fri–Sat 5:30–11pm; Sun noon–9pm. Metro: Woodley Park–Zoo (take south exit on Connecticut Ave.).

7

Exploring Washington, D.C.

Into its 67 square miles, Washington, D.C., packs a walloping number of must-see attractions, starting with the capital triumvirate of the **White House,** the **Capitol,** and the **Supreme Court.** Add in a national park full of presidential memorials; museums both large, like the **National Air and Space Museum,** and small, like the **Textile Museum;** an outstanding zoo; the nation's oldest botanic garden; biking along the Potomac River; ice skating in a sculpture garden—well, the long and short of it is you're in for a fascinating, fun-filled time as you reconnect with your inner patriot, satisfy your hunger for art, and recreate on national parkland.

If you'd like some help figuring out a workable scenario, see chapter 4, "Suggested Washington, D.C., Itineraries," which offers 1-, 2-, and 3-day scenarios for tackling the town. Otherwise, peruse this chapter, see what strikes your fancy, put on some good walking shoes, and head out.

1 THE THREE HOUSES OF GOVERNMENT

The buildings housing the executive, legislative, and judicial branches of the U.S. government remain among the most visited sites in Washington. All three—the White House, the Capitol, and the Supreme Court—are stunning to behold and experience, and offer fascinating lessons in American history and government. Although these landmarks are not as freely open to the public as they were before the terrorist attacks of September 11, 2001, all three do allow tours.

The Capitol ★★★   The Capitol is as majestic up close as it is from afar. For 135 years it sheltered not only both houses of Congress, but also the Supreme Court and, for 97 years, the Library of Congress as well. When you tour the Capitol, you'll learn about America's history as you admire the place in which it unfolded. Classical architecture, interior embellishments, and hundreds of paintings, sculptures, and other artworks are integral elements of the Capitol. The hour-long tour (see procedures below) starts in the Capitol Visitor Center, where you watch a 13-minute orientation film, then takes you to the Rotunda, National Statuary Hall, down to the Crypt and back to the Visitor Center. (Get a jump on information about the history and art of the Capitol by going to www.visitthecapitol.gov and clicking on "About the Capitol," then the link "Learn More" about the Capitol, and then "Evolution of the Capitol." The architect of the Capitol's website, www.aoc.gov, is even more informative.

The **Rotunda**—a huge 96-foot-wide circular hall capped by a 180-foot-high dome—is the hub of the Capitol. The dome was completed, at Lincoln's direction, while the Civil War was being fought: "If people see the Capitol going on, it is a sign we intend the Union shall go on," said Lincoln. Ten presidents have lain in state here, with former president Ronald Reagan being the most recent; when Kennedy's casket was displayed,

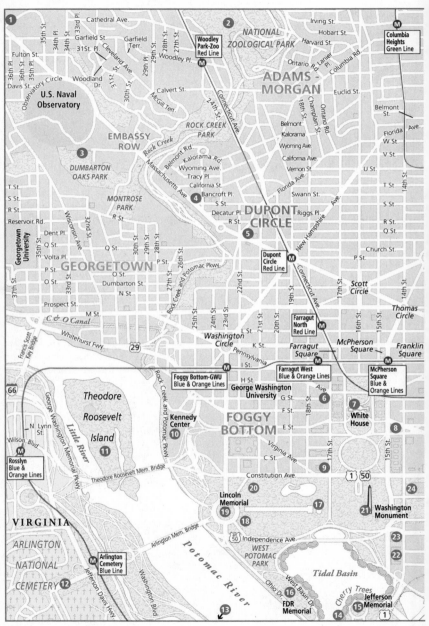

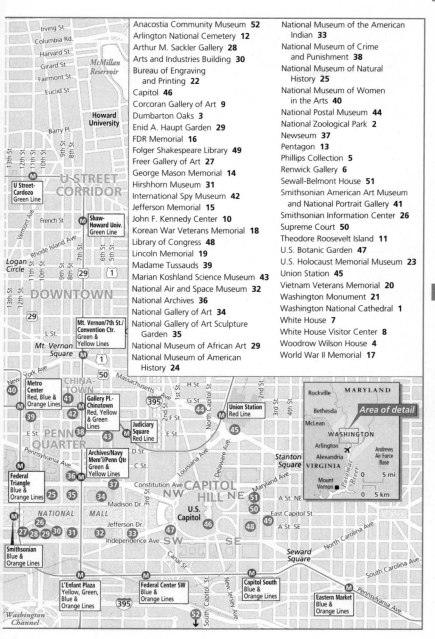

Anacostia Community Museum **52**
Arlington National Cemetery **12**
Arthur M. Sackler Gallery **28**
Arts and Industries Building **30**
Bureau of Engraving and Printing **22**
Capitol **46**
Corcoran Gallery of Art **9**
Dumbarton Oaks **3**
Enid A. Haupt Garden **29**
FDR Memorial **16**
Folger Shakespeare Library **49**
Freer Gallery of Art **27**
George Mason Memorial **14**
Hirshhorn Museum **31**
International Spy Museum **42**
Jefferson Memorial **15**
John F. Kennedy Center **10**
Korean War Veterans Memorial **18**
Library of Congress **48**
Lincoln Memorial **19**
Madame Tussauds **39**
Marian Koshland Science Museum **43**
National Air and Space Museum **32**
National Archives **36**
National Gallery of Art **34**
National Gallery of Art Sculpture Garden **35**
National Museum of African Art **29**
National Museum of American History **24**

National Museum of the American Indian **33**
National Museum of Crime and Punishment **38**
National Museum of Natural History **25**
National Museum of Women in the Arts **40**
National Postal Museum **44**
National Zoological Park **2**
Newseum **37**
Pentagon **13**
Phillips Collection **5**
Renwick Gallery **6**
Sewall-Belmont House **51**
Smithsonian American Art Museum and National Portrait Gallery **41**
Smithsonian Information Center **26**
Supreme Court **50**
Theodore Roosevelt Island **11**
U.S. Botanic Garden **47**
U.S. Holocaust Memorial Museum **23**
Union Station **45**
Vietnam Veterans Memorial **20**
Washington Monument **21**
Washington National Cathedral **1**
White House **7**
White House Visitor Center **8**
Woodrow Wilson House **4**
World War II Memorial **17**

> ## Heads Up
>
> Nine years after September 11, 2001, security measures continue to be fine-tuned and implemented. You may see wide swaths of construction underway on the plazas fronting government buildings, like that outside the National Mall entrance to the National Museum of American History, as workers install the 50-foot setback now required for all federal structures. Certain visitor precautions remain in place at many Washington, D.C., attractions. What that means is that you may have to stand in line to enter a museum or federal building. At many tourist sites, like the Smithsonian's National Air and Space Museum and National Museum of Natural History, and at most government buildings, staff search handbags, briefcases, and backpacks, and, at some sites, require you to walk past metal detectors. During the busy spring and summer seasons, you may be queuing outside as you wait your turn to pass through security. So pack your patience, but otherwise carry as little as possible, and certainly no sharp objects. Museums and public buildings rarely offer the use of lockers.

the line of mourners stretched 40 blocks. On rare occasions, someone other than a president, military hero, or member of Congress receives this posthumous recognition. In October 2005, Congress paid tribute to Rosa Parks by allowing her body to lie in state here, the first woman to be so honored. (Parks was the black woman who in 1955 refused to relinquish her seat to a white man on a Montgomery, Alabama, bus, thereby helping to spark a civil rights movement.)

Embracing the Rotunda walls are eight immense oil paintings commemorating great moments in American history, such as the presentation of the Declaration of Independence and the surrender of Cornwallis at Yorktown. In the dome is an allegorical fresco masterpiece by Constantino Brumidi, *The Apotheosis of Washington,* a symbolic portrayal of George Washington surrounded by Roman gods and goddesses watching over the progress of the nation. Brumidi was known as the "Michelangelo of the Capitol" for the many works he created throughout the building. (Take another look at the dome and find the woman directly below Washington; the triumphant *Armed Freedom* figure is said to be modeled after Lola Germon, a beautiful young actress with whom the 60-year-old Brumidi conceived a child.) Beneath the dome is a *trompe l'oeil* frieze depicting major developments in the life of America, from Columbus's landing in 1492 to the birth of the aviation age in 1903. Don't miss the sculptures in the Rotunda, including: a pensive Abraham Lincoln; a dignified Rev. Dr. Martin Luther King, Jr.; a ponderous trinity of suffragists Elizabeth Cady Stanton, Susan B. Anthony, and Lucretia Mott; and newly added in June 2009, a bronze statue of President Ronald Reagan, looking characteristically genial and confident.

The **National Statuary Hall** was originally the chamber of the House of Representatives. In 1864, it became Statuary Hall, and the states were invited to send two statues each of native sons and daughters to the hall. There are 100 statues in all, New Mexico completing the original collection with its contribution in 2005 of Po'Pay, a Pueblo Indian, who in 1680 led a revolt against the Spanish that helped to save Pueblo culture. (Stay tuned: The District of Columbia hopes to honor two of its own homegrown heroes with statues, despite the fact that Congress, as yet, refuses to recognize D.C. as a state.) States do have the prerogative to replace statues with new choices, which is what Alabama

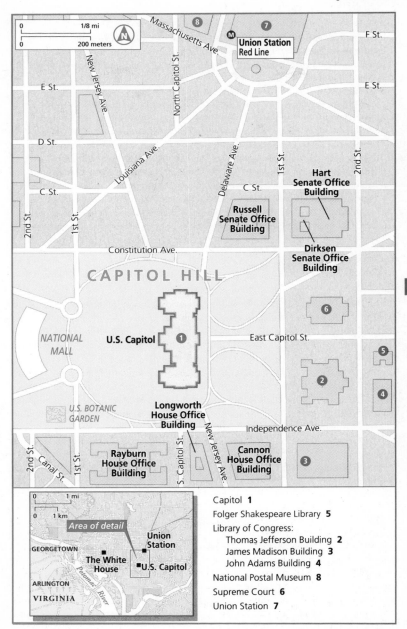

Capitol **1**

Folger Shakespeare Library **5**

Library of Congress:
  Thomas Jefferson Building **2**
  James Madison Building **3**
  John Adams Building **4**

National Postal Museum **8**

Supreme Court **6**

Union Station **7**

Call Ahead

Here's a crucial piece of advice: **Call the places you plan to tour each day before you set out.** Many of Washington's government buildings, museums, memorials, and monuments are open to the general public nearly all the time—except when they're not.

Because buildings like the Capitol, the Supreme Court, and the White House are offices as well as tourist destinations, the business of the day always poses the potential for closing one of those sites, or at least sections, to sightseers. There's also the matter of maintenance. The steady stream of visitors to Washington's attractions necessitates ongoing caretaking, which may require closing an entire landmark, or part of it, to the public, or putting in place new hours of operation or procedures for visiting. Finally, Washington's famous museums, grand halls, and public gardens double as settings for press conferences, galas, special exhibits, festivals, and even movie sets. You might arrive at, say, the National Air and Space Museum on a Sunday afternoon, only to find some or all of its galleries off-limits because a movie shoot is underway. (Have you seen *Night at the Museum 2: Battle of the Smithsonian*, by the way?) Want to avoid frustration and disappointment? Call ahead.

did in 2009, putting Helen Keller in and removing one of congressman Jabez Lamar Monroe Curry. Because of space constraints, only 38 statues or so reside in the Hall, with 24 now placed in the Visitor Center and the remaining scattered throughout the corridors of the Capitol. Statues include Ethan Allen, the Revolutionary War hero who founded the state of Vermont, and Missouri's Thomas Hart Benton—not the 20th-century artist famous for his rambunctious murals, but his namesake and uncle, who was one of the first two senators from Missouri and whose antislavery stance in 1850 cost him his Senate seat. Nine women are represented, including Montana's Jeannette Rankin, the first woman to serve in Congress and, as previously mentioned, Helen Keller; both of these statues are located in the Visitor Center's Emancipation Hall.

The **Crypt** of the Capitol lies directly below the Rotunda and is used mainly as an exhibit space.

In slow seasons, usually fall and winter, your public tour may include a visit to the **Old Supreme Court Chamber,** which has been restored to its mid-19th-century appearance. The Supreme Court met here from 1810 to 1860. Busts of the first four chief justices are on display—John Marshall, John Rutledge, John Jay, and Oliver Ellsworth—and so are some of their desks, believed to have been purchased in the 1830s. The justices handed down a number of noteworthy decisions here, including that of *Dred Scott v. Sandford*, which denied the citizenship of blacks, whether slaves or free, and in so doing precipitated the nation's Civil War.

You will not see them on your tour, but the **south and north wings** of the Capitol hold the House and Senate chambers, respectively. The House of Representatives chamber is the largest legislative chamber in the world, and the setting for the president's annual State of the Union addresses. (See the information below about watching Senate and House activity.)

Procedures for Touring the Capitol: Tours of the Capitol are free and take place year-round, Monday through Saturday between 8:50am and 3:20pm. Capitol Guide Service Guides lead the general public tours, which usually include 40 or 50 people at a time and last 50 to 60 minutes. You and everyone in your party must have a **timed pass,** which you must order online at www.visitthecapitol.gov. You can also contact your representative or senator in Congress and request passes for constituent tours, which are usually limited to groups of 15 and conducted by congressional staff, who may take you to notable places in the Capitol beyond those seen on the general public tour. A limited number of same-day passes are available daily from the tour kiosks on the east and west fronts of the Capitol and at the information desks on the lower level of the visitor center. During peak spring and summer sessions, you should order tickets at least 2 weeks in advance. No matter what, call © **202/225-6827** in advance of your visit; that way you'll know for sure whether the Capitol is open. The Capitol has quite a list of items it prohibits, and you can read the list online at www.visitthecapitol.gov or listen to a recitation by calling the number above. Everything from large bags of any kind to food and drink is included; leave everything possible back at the hotel.

Procedures for Visiting the House Gallery or Senate Gallery: Try to visit when both the Senate and House are **in session** ★★★. In fact, the Senate Gallery is open to visitors only when it is in session, but the House Gallery is open to visitors whether or not it is in session. (Children 5 and under are not allowed in the Senate gallery.) You must have a separate pass, one for each gallery. Once obtained, the passes are good through the

The Capitol Visitor Center

Until the Capitol Visitor Center opened in November 2008 (after 7 years of construction), visitors to the Capitol had to wait outside in long lines in all kinds of weather, first to obtain tour passes and then to actually enter the Capitol. It was miserable. The simultaneous opening of the center and inauguration of an online tour reservation system makes a visit to the Capitol a joy, by comparison. (Read the information in the text below to find out the procedures for obtaining passes and for touring the Capitol.)

What you should know about the Capitol Visitor Center is this: the enormous, 4,000-person capacity center is underground, which means that as you approach the East Front of the Capitol, you won't actually see it. But look for signs and the sloping set of steps on either side of the Capitol's central section, leading down to the center's entrances. Once inside, you'll pass through security screening and then enter the two-level chamber. If you have time before or after your tour, you'll find plenty to do here. (Most visitors, however, find it works better to explore the Center after touring the Capitol.) You can admire the 24 Statuary Hall statues scattered throughout and tour Exhibition Hall, which is a mini-museum of historic document displays; check out interactive kiosks that take you on virtual tours of the Capitol, filling you in on history, art, and architecture; and marvel at exhibits that explain the legislative process. Emancipation Hall is the large central chamber where you line up for tours; this is also where the 26 restrooms and 530-seat restaurant are. The Visitor Center is open Monday through Saturday, year-round, from 8:30am to 4:30pm.

remainder of the Congress. You can obtain visitor passes at the offices of your representative and senator, or in the case of District of Columbia and Puerto Rico residents, from the office of their delegate to Congress. To find out your member's office location, go online at www.house.gov or www.senate.gov and follow the links to your state's representatives' or senators' information; or call © **202/225-3121** to speak to a Capitol operator.

Contrary to popular belief, members of Congress do not have their main offices inside the Capitol building itself. Many of the senior ranking members have Capitol "hideaways," which are exactly what they sound like: places out of the fray where they can take care of business without interruption. The main, staffed offices of Congressional representatives and delegates are in House buildings on the south side, or Independence Avenue side, of the Capitol; senators' main, staffed offices are located in Senate buildings on the north side, or Constitution Avenue side, of the Capitol. If you need help or directions, just ask one of the many Capitol Hill police officers in the area. You should be able to pick up passes to both the Senate and House galleries in one place, at either your representative's office or your senator's office. (**Note:** International visitors can obtain both House and Senate gallery passes by presenting a passport or a valid driver's license with photo ID to staff at the House and Senate Appointments desks on the upper level of the Visitor Center, near the main entrance.) Visit the Capitol's website, **www.aoc.gov**, the Visitor Center website, **www.visitthecapitol.gov**, or call your senator or congressperson's office for more exact information about obtaining passes to the House and Senate galleries.

You'll know that the House and/or the Senate is in session if you see flags flying over their respective wings of the Capitol (**Remember:** House, south side; Senate, north side), or you can check the weekday "Today in Congress" column, online only, in the *Washington Post,* for details on times of the House and Senate sessions and committee hearings. This column also tells you which sessions are open to the public. Or again, access the Capitol's website, **www.aoc.gov**, for information about the history, art, and construction of the Capitol building; and **www.house.gov** and **www.senate.gov** for an in-depth education on the legislative process; schedules of bill debates in the House and Senate, committee markups, and meetings; and links to connect to your Senate or House representative's page.

Capitol and Capitol Visitor Center: On East Capitol St. (at 1st St. NW). © **202/225-6827** (recording), **202/593-1768** (Capitol Guide Service Office), **202/225-3121** (Capitol operator). www.visitthecapitol. gov, www.aoc.gov, www.house.gov, www.senate.gov. Free admission. Year-round Mon–Sat 8:30am–4:30pm, with first tour starting at 8:50am and last tour starting at 3:20pm. Closed for tours Sun and Jan 1, Thanksgiving, and Dec 25. Parking at Union Station or on neighborhood streets. Metro: Union Station (Massachusetts Ave. exit) or Capitol South (to walk to the Capitol Visitor Center located on the East Front of the Capitol).

The Supreme Court of the United States ★★★ The highest tribunal in the nation, the Supreme Court is charged with the power of "judicial review": deciding whether actions of Congress, the president, the states, and lower courts, in other words, of all branches of government and government officials, are in accordance with the Constitution, and with applying the Constitution's enduring principles to novel situations and a changing country. Arguably the most powerful people in the nation, the Court's chief justice and eight associate justices hear only about 75 to 100 of the most vital cases of the 8,000 to 9,000 petitions for *writ certiorari* submitted to the Court each year. The Court's rulings are final, reversible only by an Act of Congress.

Hard to believe, but the Supreme Court—in existence since 1789—did not have its own building until 1935. The justices met in New York, Philadelphia, and assorted nooks of the Capitol (see the Capitol's write-up above) until they finally got their own place. Architect Cass Gilbert designed the stately Corinthian marble palace that houses the Court today. Best known for his skyscrapers, like New York's 761-foot-high Woolworth Building, Gilbert was an interesting choice for the Supreme Court commission in a city where Congress restricts building height to 160 feet.

You'll have plenty of time to admire the exterior of this magnificent structure if you're in town when the Court is in session and decide to try **seeing a case being argued** ★★★ because—yup, you guessed it—you have to wait in line (sometimes for hours) on the front plaza of the building. But do try! The experience is totally worth the wait. People queue in every city for tickets to concerts and sports events. But only in Washington does a wait in line grant one the privilege of watching and listening to the country's nine foremost legal experts nimbly and intensely dissect the merits of both sides of an argument, whose decisions can affect profoundly both the person and the nation. The standing-in-line itself brings with it the same sort of thrill that builds in collective anticipation of a great performance.

Here's what you need to know: Starting the first Monday in October and continuing through late April, the Court "sits" for 2 weeks out of every month to hear two to four arguments each day, Monday through Wednesday, from 10am to noon and from 1 to 2 or 3pm. You can find out the specific dates and names of arguments in advance by calling the Supreme Court (© **202/479-3211**) or by going to the website, **www.supremecourtus. gov**, where the argument calendar and the "Merits Briefs" (case descriptions) are posted.

Plan on arriving at the Supreme Court at least 90 minutes in advance of a scheduled argument during the fall and winter, and as early as 3 hours ahead in March and April, when schools are often on spring break and students lengthen the line. (Dress warmly; the stone plaza is exposed and can be witheringly cold.) Controversial cases also attract crowds; if you're not sure whether a particular case has created a stir, call the Court information line to reach someone who can tell you. The Court allots only about 150 first-come, first-served seats to the general public, but that number fluctuates from case to case, depending on the number of seats that have been reserved by the lawyers arguing the case and by the press. The Court police officers direct you into one line initially; when the doors finally open, you form a second line if you want to attend only 3 to 5 minutes of the argument.

The justices may release opinions throughout the term, on every third Monday during the Supreme Court term and on argument days (if any opinions are ready). The opinions are delivered before the arguments begin. Mid-May to late June, you can attend brief sessions (about 15 min.) at 10am on Monday, when the justices release remaining orders and opinions for the term. Again, you must stand in line on the front plaza to enter the building.

Leave your cameras, recording devices, and notebooks at your hotel; they're not allowed in the courtroom. ***Note:*** But *do* bring quarters. Security procedures require you to leave all your belongings, including outerwear, purses, books, sunglasses, and so on, in a lower-level checkroom where there are coin-operated lockers that accept only quarters.

Once inside, pay close attention to the many rituals. At 10am, the marshal announces the entrance of the justices, and all present rise and remain standing while the justices take their seats (in high-backed, cushioned swivel chairs, by the way) following the chant: "The Honorable, the Chief Justice and Associate Justices of the Supreme Court of the United States. Oyez! Oyez! Oyez! All persons having business before the Honorable, the Supreme Court of the United States, are admonished to draw near and give their attention, for the Court is now sitting. God save the United States and this Honorable Court!" Unseen by the gallery is the "conference handshake"; following a 19th-century tradition symbolizing a "harmony of aims if not views," each justice shakes hands with each of the other eight when they assemble to go to the bench. The Court has a record before it of prior proceedings and relevant briefs, so each side is allowed only a 30-minute argument.

When the Court is not in session, you can tour the building and attend a **free lecture** in the courtroom about Court procedure and the building's architecture. Lectures are given every hour on the half-hour from 9:30am to 3:30pm. After the talk, explore the Great Hall and go down a flight of steps to see the **24-minute film** on the workings of the Court. Allow about an hour to tour. A gift shop and a public cafeteria are open to the public.

One 1st St. NE (btw. E. Capitol St. and Maryland Ave. NE). ⓒ **202/479-3000.** www.supremecourtus.gov. Free admission. Mon–Fri 9am–4:20pm. Closed all federal holidays. Metro: Capitol South or Union Station.

The White House ★★★ It's amazing when you think about it: This house has served as residence, office, reception site, and world embassy for every U.S. president since John Adams. The White House is the only private residence of a head of state that has opened its doors to the public for tours, free of charge. It was Thomas Jefferson who started this practice, which is stopped only during wartime. See the box "How to Arrange a White House Tour," below.

An Act of Congress in 1790 established the city, now known as Washington, District of Columbia, as the seat of the federal government. George Washington and city planner Pierre L'Enfant chose the site for the President's House and staged a contest to find a builder. Although Washington picked the winner—Irishman James Hoban—he was the only president never to live in the White House. The structure took 8 years to build, starting in 1792, when its cornerstone was laid. Its facade is made of the same stone that was used to construct the Capitol. The mansion quickly became known as the "White House," thanks to the limestone whitewashing applied to the walls to protect them, later replaced by white lead paint in 1818. In 1814, during the War of 1812, the British set fire to the White House, gutting the interior; the exterior managed to endure only because a rainstorm extinguished the fire. What you see today is Hoban's basic creation: a building modeled after an Irish country house (in fact, Hoban had in mind the house of the Duke of Leinster in Dublin).

Note: Tours of the White House exit from the North Portico. Before you descend the front steps, look to your left to find the window whose sandstone still remains unpainted as a reminder both of the 1814 fire and of the White House's survival.

Alterations over the years have incorporated the South Portico in 1824, the North Portico in 1829, and electricity in 1891, during Benjamin Harrison's presidency. In 1902, repairs and refurnishings of the White House cost nearly $500,000. No other great change took place until Harry Truman's presidency, when the interior was completely renovated after the leg of Margaret Truman's piano cut through the dining room ceiling. The Trumans lived at Blair House across the street for nearly 4 years while the White House interior was shored up with steel girders and concrete.

In 1961, First Lady Jacqueline Kennedy spearheaded the founding of the White House Historical Association and formed a Fine Arts Committee to help restore the famous rooms to their original grandeur, ensuring treatment of the White House as a museum of American history and decorative arts. "It just seemed to me such a shame when we came here to find hardly anything of the past in the house, hardly anything before 1902," Mrs. Kennedy observed.

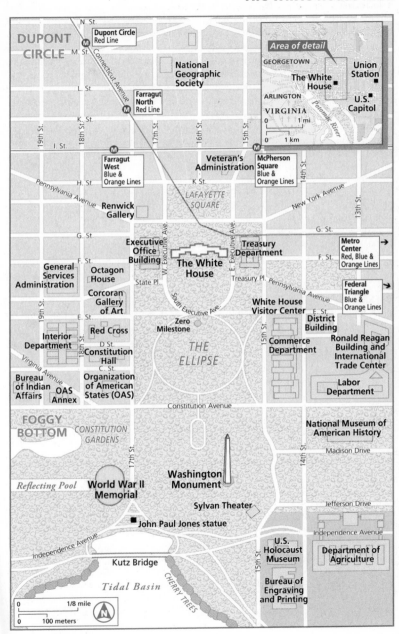

DUPONT CIRCLE

N. St.

Dupont Circle
Red Line

M. St.

Connecticut Avenue

National Geographic Society

L. St.

Farragut North
Red Line

K. St.

19th St.
18th St.
17th St.
16th St.
15th St.

I. St.

Farragut West
Blue & Orange Lines

Veteran's Administration

McPherson Square
Blue & Orange Lines

14th St.

Pennsylvania Avenue

H. St.

K St.

LAFAYETTE SQUARE

New York Avenue

13th St.

Renwick Gallery

G. St.

G. St.

Executive Office Building

W. Executive Ave.

E. Executive Ave.

Treasury Department

Metro Center
Red, Blue & Orange Lines →

General Services Administration

F. St.

The White House

F. St.

Octagon House

State Pl.

Treasury Pl.

Pennsylvania Avenue

Federal Triangle
Blue & Orange Lines →

Corcoran Gallery of Art

South Executive Ave.

White House Visitor Center

E. St.

District Building

19th St.

E. St.

Red Cross

Zero Milestone

15th St.

Commerce Department

Ronald Reagan Building and International Trade Center

Interior Department

18th St.

D St.

THE ELLIPSE

Constitution Hall

C. St.

Virginia Avenue

Organization of American States (OAS)

Bureau of Indian Affairs

OAS Annex

Labor Department

Constitution Avenue

FOGGY BOTTOM

CONSTITUTION GARDENS

National Museum of American History

17th St.

14th St.

Madison Drive

Reflecting Pool

World War II Memorial

Washington Monument

Jefferson Drive

Sylvan Theater

John Paul Jones statue

Independence Avenue

Independence Avenue

U.S. Holocaust Museum

Department of Agriculture

Kutz Bridge

15th St.

CHERRY TREES

Tidal Basin

Bureau of Engraving and Printing

0   1/8 mile
0   100 meters

N

Area of detail

GEORGETOWN

The White House

Union Station

ARLINGTON

VIRGINIA

U.S. Capitol

Potomac River

0   1 mi
0   1 km

Every President and first family put their own stamp on the White House. President and Michele Obama have installed in their private residence artworks on loan from the Hirshhorn Museum and from the National Gallery of Art, and are in the process of choosing works to hang in the public rooms of the White House. (Changing the art in the public rooms requires approval from the White House curator and the Committee for the Preservation of the White House.) Michele Obama has planted a vegetable garden on the White House grounds and the President plans to add a basketball court.

Highlights of the public tour include the **Gold-and-White East Room,** the scene of presidential receptions, weddings (Lynda Bird Johnson, for one), major presidential addresses, and other dazzling events. This is where the president entertains visiting heads of state and the place where seven of the eight presidents who died in office (all but Garfield) laid in state. It was also where Nixon resigned. The room's early-18th-century style was adopted during the Theodore Roosevelt renovation of 1902; it has parquet Fontainebleau oak floors and white-painted wood walls with fluted pilasters and classical relief inserts. Note the famous Gilbert Stuart portrait of George Washington that Dolley Madison saved from the British torch during the War of 1812. The portrait is the only object to have remained continuously in the White House since 1800 (except during times of reconstruction).

You'll visit the **Green Room,** which was Thomas Jefferson's dining room but today is used as a sitting room. Mrs. Kennedy chose the green watered-silk-fabric wall covering. In the **Oval Blue Room,** decorated in the French Empire style chosen by James Monroe in 1817, presidents and first ladies have officially received guests since the Jefferson administration. It was, however, Van Buren's decor that began the "blue room" tradition. The walls, on which hang portraits of five presidents (including Rembrandt Peale's portrait of Thomas Jefferson and G. P. A. Healy's of Tyler), are covered in reproductions of early-19th-century French and American wallpaper. Grover Cleveland, the only president to wed in the White House, was married in the Blue Room. This room was also where the Reagans greeted the 52 Americans liberated after being held hostage in Iran for 444 days, and every year it's the setting for the White House Christmas tree.

The **Red Room,** with its red satin-covered walls and Empire furnishings, is used as a reception room, primarily for afternoon teas. Several portraits of past presidents and a Gilbert Stuart portrait of Dolley Madison hang here. Dolley Madison used the Red Room for her famous Wednesday-night receptions.

From the Red Room, you enter the **State Dining Room.** Modeled after late-18th-century neoclassical English houses, this room is a superb setting for state dinners and luncheons. Below G. P. A. Healy's portrait of Lincoln is an inscription written by John Adams on his second night in the White House (FDR had it carved into the mantel): "I Pray Heaven to Bestow The Best of Blessings on THIS HOUSE and on All that shall here-after Inhabit it. May none but Honest and Wise Men ever rule under this Roof."

Note: Even if you have successfully reserved a White House tour for your group, you should still call ✆ **202/456-7041** before setting out in the morning, in case the White House is closed on short notice because of unforeseen events. If this should happen to you, you should make a point of walking by the White House anyway, since its exterior is still pretty awe-inspiring. Stroll past it on Pennsylvania Avenue, down 15th Street past the Treasury Building, and along the backside and South Lawn, on E Street.

1600 Pennsylvania Ave. NW (visitor entrance gate at E St. and E. Executive Ave.). ✆ **202/456-7041** or 202/208-1631. www.whitehouse.gov. Free admission. Tours for groups of 10 or more who have arranged the tour through their congressional offices. Metro: Federal Triangle.

(Tips) How to Arrange a White House Tour

The White House allows groups of 10 or more to tour the White House, Tuesday through Saturday, from 7:30am to 10am, and at other times, as well, depending on the President's schedule; if the President is out of town, it's possible that more tours will be allowed past the usual 10am cutoff time. Tours are self-guided and most people take no more than an hour to go through. You must have a reservation to tour the White House. At least 2 months and as far as 6 months in advance of your trip, call your senator's or representative's office with the names of the people in your group and ask for a specific tour date. The tour coordinator consults with White House on availability and, if your date is available, contacts you to obtain the names, birth dates, Social Security numbers (for those 14 and older), and other information for each of the people in your party. The Secret Service reviews the information and clears you for the tour, putting the names of the people in your group on a confirmed reservation list; you'll receive a confirmation number and the date and time of your tour usually about 1 month in advance of your trip. On the day of your tour, call ✆ **202/456-7041** to make sure that the White House is still open that day to the public. Then off you go, to the south side of East Executive Avenue, near the Southeast Gate of the White House, with photo IDs for everyone in your party who is 15 or older. Be sure to arrive about 15 minutes before your scheduled tour time.

Do not bring the following prohibited items: backpacks, book bags, handbags, or purses; food and beverages; strollers; cameras; videorecorders or any type of recording device; tobacco products; personal grooming items, from cosmetics to hairbrushes; any pointed objects, whether a pen or a knitting needle; aerosol containers; guns; ammunition; fireworks; electric stun guns; maces; martial arts weapons/devices; or knives of any description. Cellphones are okay, but not the kind that are also cameras. The White House does not have a coat-check facility, so there is no place for you to leave your belongings while you go on the tour. There are no public restrooms or telephones in the White House, and picture taking and videotaping are prohibited. **Best advice:** Leave everything but your wallet back at the hotel.

If your party numbers fewer than 10 people, go ahead and contact your member's office anyway. I've discovered that White House tour coordinators in congressional offices are sometimes willing and able to get you on a tour list, whether or not you have the official 10-person count, due to cancellations and schedule changes.

The White House Visitor Center The Visitor Center opened in 1995 to provide extensive interpretive data about the White House (and to serve as a ticket-distribution center, though that function has been suspended). It is run under the auspices of the National Park Service and the staff is well-informed. A 30-minute video about the White House provides interior views of the presidential precincts (it runs continuously throughout the day). Pick up a copy of the National Park Service's brochure on the White House, which tells you a little about what you'll see in the eight or so rooms you tour and a bit about the history of the White House. The White House Historic Association runs a small shop here. Before you leave the Visitor Center, take a look at the exhibits, which include information about the architectural history of the White House; portrayals by photographers, artists, journalists, and political cartoonists; anecdotes about first families (such as the time prankster Tad Lincoln stood in a window above his father and waved a Confederate flag at a military review); details about what goes on behind the scenes, focusing on the vast staff of servants, chefs, gardeners, Secret Service people, and others who maintain this institution; highlights of notable White House ceremonies and celebrations, from a Wright Brothers' aviation demonstration in 1911 to a ballet performance by Baryshnikov during the Carter administration; and photographs of the ever-changing Oval Office as decorated by administrations from Taft to Obama.

1450 Pennsylvania Ave. NW (in the Dept. of Commerce Building, btw. 14th and 15th sts.). ℂ **202/208-1631.** Free admission. Daily 7:30am–4pm. Closed Jan 1, Thanksgiving, and Dec 25. Metro: Federal Triangle.

2 THE NATIONAL MALL & MEMORIAL PARKS

The National Park Service refers to the national parkland that extends from the Capitol to the Potomac River, encompassing the memorials, Washington Monument, National Mall, and West and East Potomac parks as the **National Mall and Memorial Parks.** The National Mall and Memorial Parks has its own telephone number, ℂ **202/485-9880,** and website, www.nps.gov/nama.

THE NATIONAL MALL

As part of his vision for Washington, Pierre L'Enfant conceived of the National Mall as a bustling ceremonial avenue of embassies and other distinguished buildings. Today's 2-mile, 700-acre stretch of land extending westward from the Capitol reflecting pool to the Lincoln Memorial fulfills that dream to some extent. Ten Smithsonian buildings (see next section, "The Smithsonian Museums," p. 185), plus the National Gallery of Art and its Sculpture Garden, a stray government building (Dept. of Agriculture), and the U. S. Botanic Garden stake out the Mall's northern border along Constitution Avenue and southern border along Independence Avenue. Elm trees shade the pebbled walkways paralleling Jefferson and Madison drives. Tourists and locals crisscross the Mall as they visit the Smithsonian museums, hustle to work, pursue exercise, participate in whatever festival, event, or demonstration is taking place on the Mall that day, or simply go for a stroll, just as L'Enfant envisioned, perhaps.

What L'Enfant did not foresee was the toll that all of this activity might take on this piece of parkland. When you visit the Mall these days, you might be dismayed to see an expanse of browned grass instead of green, crumbling walkways, and an overall worn appearance. The National Park Service maintains the land but can't keep pace with the rate of needed repair and preservation, mostly because Congress won't authorize the necessary funds. The National Park Service is at work on a plan for the future of the National Mall (see www.nps.gov/nationalmallplan), as is the Trust for the National Mall, www.nationalmall.org, the Park Service's official fundraising partner. A third organization called the National Coalition to Save Our Mall (www.savethemall.org), made up of professional and civic groups as well as assorted concerned artists, historians, and residents, is also lobbying Congress for more support for the Mall's upkeep and improvements, including the addition of a 24/7 National Mall Welcome Center. These organizations don't necessarily agree on their visions for the Mall. Stay tuned.

The National Mall and Memorial Parks' major memorials honor esteemed presidents, war veterans, founding fathers, and, by the end of 2010, a civil rights leader. On November 13, 2006, thousands attended the official groundbreaking for the National Mall's newest memorial, the **Martin Luther King, Jr., National Memorial,** with many more anticipated for the memorial's dedication tentatively planned for late 2010. Located on a 4-acre parcel at the intersection of West Basin Drive and Independence Avenue, adjoining the Tidal Basin and adjacent to the FDR Memorial, and positioned in a direct line with the Lincoln and Jefferson memorials, the King Memorial pays tribute to the Baptist minister. Dr. King's commitment to nonviolence and direct action to force social change, and his efforts and compelling speeches profoundly moved the country toward that achievement—before King was assassinated at the age of 39 on April 4, 1968.

All of these memorials are located in picturesque **West Potomac Park** (p. 222 for full details on the park and its famous **cherry blossoms**), which lies at the western end of the Mall, where it borders the Potomac River and encircles the Tidal Basin. Unfortunately, none of the memorials lies directly on a Metro line, so you can expect a bit of a walk from the specified station.

The easiest thing to do, if you're up to it, is to walk from one landmark to the next. I've organized just such a tour, detailed below. Or, you can go by **Tourmobile** (p. 229), which continually picks up and discharges passengers at each of these sites throughout the day and allows you to purchase a ticket in advance or as you board, whichever works for you. Still another alternative is to bike the sites. See suggested bike-rental locations listed on p. 231. Every memorial site has a bike rack.

Touring the Memorials on Foot

I've designed—and tested—the following walking tour of the memorials, ordering the stops in a sequence that I believe makes most sense in terms of logistics and geography. The beauty of it is that you can easily tinker with this tour to suit your own purposes. The Washington Monument is the only site that has limited hours and requires a ticket; otherwise, the memorials are open 24 hours to the public, which means that you can follow this tour at 5am or 5pm, at 2 in the morning or 2 in the afternoon. Some believe the best time to visit the memorials is at night, when they're illuminated in all their imposing white-stone glory and the crowds have thinned. Use common sense, though. The memorials may be lit up, but not necessarily the lanes and pathways leading to them.

Before you start the tour, here's what you need to know:

- Dress for the weather: light clothing, shades, and sunscreen in summer; a hat, gloves, and warm jacket in winter. The Washington Monument and the memorials are mostly set in wide-open spaces, with little to no protection from the elements.
- The National Park Service manages all of these properties and maintains information about each of them, including upcoming events, at **www.nps.gov/nama**. Scroll down the page to click on the names of sites.
- Park rangers are on hand from 8am to 11:30pm year-round, except at the Washington Monument, which closes at 5pm Labor Day to Memorial Day and at 10pm Memorial Day to Labor Day.
- Restrooms are located inside the ranger lodge/ticket kiosk at the bottom of the hill from the Washington Monument; in the basements of the Jefferson and Lincoln memorials; at the back of the information and gift shop of the FDR Memorial; and

in a building beyond the National World War II Memorial information lodge. Visitors to the George Mason Memorial use the restrooms at the Jefferson Memorial; visitors to the Korean War Memorial and the Vietnam Veterans War Memorial use the restrooms at the Lincoln Memorial.

- Eat well before you head off on the tour. The National Park Service prohibits food and drink inside all of the memorials and at the Washington Monument. It allows refreshment kiosks and vendors, but only at a distance. Refreshment and souvenir kiosks are located across 15th Street from the Washington Monument's ticket booth; on Daniel Chester French Drive between the Lincoln Memorial and the Korean War Memorial; on Henry Bacon Drive across the street from the Vietnam Veterans Memorial, with another on the other side of the memorial; and in front of the Jefferson Memorial. These are rudimentary services, selling beverages, sandwiches, ice cream and the like, just enough to refresh you if you're feeling faint.
- The tour will take about 3 to 4 hours and cover 3 to 4 miles.
- Best times to take the tour: weekdays and evenings to avoid crowds, early or late in summer to avoid the heat; anytime otherwise.

This tour starts at the Washington Monument on 15th Street NW and ends at the National World War II Memorial on 17th Street NW.

Starting out: Take the Metro to Metro Center (13th and G sts. exit) and walk west 2 blocks to 15th Street NW. Have breakfast, lunch, or dinner at the **Old Ebbitt Grill** (p. 134), which opens early and stays open late. Then walk about ¹/₂ mile to the Washington Monument.

Note: I've included nearest Metro information for each site, in case you choose not to walk this tour.

Washington Monument ★★★ (Kids)

The idea of a tribute to George Washington first arose 16 years before his death, at the Continental Congress of 1783. But the new nation had more pressing problems and funds were not readily available. It wasn't until the early 1830s, with the 100th anniversary of Washington's birth approaching, that any action was taken.

Then there were several fiascoes. A mausoleum was provided for Washington's remains under the Capitol Rotunda, but a grandnephew, citing Washington's will, refused to allow the body to be moved from Mount Vernon. In 1830, Horatio Greenough was commissioned to create a memorial statue for the Rotunda. He came up with a bare-chested Washington, draped in classical Greek garb. A shocked public claimed he looked as if he were "entering or leaving a bath," and so the statue was relegated to the Smithsonian. Finally, in 1833, prominent citizens organized the Washington National Monument Society. Treasury Building architect Robert Mills's design was accepted.

The cornerstone was laid on July 4, 1848; and for the next 37 years, watching the monument grow, or not grow, was a local pastime. Declining contributions and the Civil War brought construction to a halt at an awkward 150 feet (you can still see a change in the color of the stone about halfway up). The unsightly stump remained until 1876, when President Grant approved federal moneys to complete the project. Dedicated in 1885, it was opened to the public in 1888.

Visiting the Washington Monument: A series of security walls encircles the Washington Monument grounds, a barrier to vehicles but not people; the National Park Service has gone to a good bit of trouble to incorporate these 33-inch-high walls into a pleasing landscape design. Please be aware that large backpacks and open containers of food or drink are not allowed inside the monument; small sealed containers are okay.

You'll need a ticket (see information below), and then you pass through a small screening facility before entering the monument's large elevator, which whisks you upward for 70 seconds.

Reaching the top, you'll be standing in the highest tip of the world's tallest free-standing work of masonry. The Washington Monument lies at the very heart of Washington, D.C., landmarks, and its 360-degree views are spectacular. Due east are the Capitol and Smithsonian buildings; due north is the White House; due west are the World War II and Lincoln memorials (with Arlington National Cemetery beyond); due south is the Jefferson Memorial, overlooking the Tidal Basin and the Potomac River. "On a clear day, you can see west probably 60 miles, as far as the Shenandoah Mountains," says National Park Service spokesperson Bill Line. Like being at the center of a compass, the monument provides a marvelous orientation to the city.

> **Impressions**
>
> *May the spirit which animated the great founder of this city descend to future generations.*
> —John Adams

The glass-walled elevator slows down in its descent, to allow passengers a view of some of the 192 carved stones inserted into the interior walls that are gifts from foreign countries, all 50 states, organizations, and individuals. One stone you usually get to see is the one given by the state of Alaska in 1982—it's pure jade and worth millions. There are stones from Siam (now Thailand), the Cherokee Nation, the Vatican, and the Sons of Temperance, to name just a few.

Allow half an hour here, plus time spent waiting in line. A concession stand is open at the corner of 15th Street and Madison Drive NW.

Ticket Information: Admission to the Washington Monument is free, but you still have to get a ticket. The ticket booth is located in the Monument Lodge, at the bottom of the hill from the monument, on 15th Street NW between Madison and Jefferson drives. It opens daily at 8:30am. Tickets are often gone by 9am, so plan to get there by 7:30 or 8am, especially in peak season. The tickets grant admission at half-hour intervals between the stated hours on the day you visit. If you want to get tickets in advance, call the National Park Reservation Service (© **877/444-6777**) or go to www.recreation.gov. The tickets themselves are free, but you'll pay $1.50 per ticket, plus $2.85 for shipping and handling, if you're ordering 10 or more days in advance; otherwise, you pick up the tickets at the "will call" window at the ticket kiosk. To make sure that you get tickets for your desired date, reserve these tickets at least 2 weeks in advance. You can order up to six tickets.

Directly south of the White House, on 15th St. (btw. Madison Dr. and Constitution Ave. NW). © **202/426-6841.** www.nps.gov/wamo. Free admission. Labor Day–Memorial Day 9am–4:45pm, Memorial Day–Labor Day 9am–10pm. Last elevators depart 15 min. before closing (arrive earlier). Closed Dec 25, open until noon July 4th. Limited parking. Metro: Smithsonian (Mall/Jefferson Dr. exit), then a 10-min. walk, or take Tourmobile or the D.C. Circulator (takes you close though not directly to it).

Return to 15th Street and head up the hill, crossing Independence Avenue SW and following the signs for the Jefferson Memorial. You'll pass the U.S. Holocaust Memorial Museum on your left, the Tidal Basin and pedal boats on your right. This will be your single longest walk on the tour—about a mile or less. Go around the bend to find the:

Jefferson Memorial ★★   President John F. Kennedy, at a 1962 dinner honoring 29 Nobel Prize winners, told his guests that they were "the most extraordinary collection of talent, of human knowledge, that has ever been gathered together at the White House, with the possible exception of when Thomas Jefferson dined alone." Jefferson penned the Declaration of Independence and served as George Washington's secretary of state, John Adams's vice president, and America's third president. He spoke out against slavery, although, like many of his countrymen, he kept slaves himself. He also established the University of Virginia and pursued wide-ranging interests, including architecture, astronomy, anthropology, music, and farming.

Franklin Delano Roosevelt, a great admirer of Jefferson, spearheaded the effort to build him a memorial, although the site choice was problematic. The Capitol, the White House, and the Mall were already located in accordance with architect Pierre L'Enfant's master plan for the city, and there was no spot for such a project that would maintain L'Enfant's symmetry. So the memorial was built on land reclaimed from the Potomac River, now known as the Tidal Basin. Roosevelt laid the cornerstone in 1939 and had all the trees between the Jefferson Memorial and the White House cut down so that he could see the memorial every morning.

The memorial is a columned rotunda in the style of the Pantheon in Rome, whose classical architecture Jefferson himself introduced to this country (he designed his home, Monticello, and the earliest University of Virginia buildings in Charlottesville). On the Tidal Basin side, the sculptural group above the entrance depicts Jefferson with Benjamin Franklin, John Adams, Roger Sherman, and Robert Livingston, all of whom worked on drafting the Declaration of Independence. The domed interior of the memorial contains the 19-foot bronze statue of Jefferson standing on a 6-foot pedestal of black Minnesota granite. The sculpture is the work of Rudolph Evans, who was chosen from more than 100 artists in a nationwide competition. Jefferson is depicted wearing a fur-collared coat given to him by his close friend, the Polish general Tadeusz Kosciuszko. If you follow Jefferson's gaze, you see that, sure enough, the Jefferson Memorial and the White House have an unimpeded view of each other.

Rangers present 20- to 30-minute programs throughout the day as time permits. Twenty to 30 minutes is sufficient time to spend here.

On Ohio Dr. SW, at the south shore of the Tidal Basin (in West Potomac Park). (C) **202/426-6841**. www.nps.gov/thje. Free admission. Ranger on duty daily 9:30am–11:30pm, except Dec 25. Limited parking. Metro: Smithsonian (12th St./Independence Ave. exit), with a 20- to 30-min. walk, or take Tourmobile.

Follow the memorial's front path back out to East Basin Drive, turn right and go around the bend to the:

George Mason Memorial   This memorial honors George Mason, author of the Virginia Declaration of Rights, which had much to do with the establishment of the United States Bill of Rights. Dedicated on April 9, 2002, the memorial consists of a bronze statue of Mason, set back in a landscaped grove of trees and flower beds (lots and lots of pansies), arranged in concentric circles around a pool and fountain. Mason appears in 18th-century garb, from buckled shoes to tricorn hat, seated on a marble bench, but leaning backward on one arm and gazing off in the general direction of the Washington Monument. Two stone slabs are inscribed with some of Mason's words, like these, referring to Mason's rejection of slavery, "that slow Poison, which is daily con-taminating the Minds & Morals of our People." Wooden benches at the site present a pleasant opportunity to learn about Mason and take a break before moving on. **Note:** The memorial is easy to miss, since it does not lie on the Tidal Basin path. As you approach the Jefferson Memorial from the direction of the FDR Memorial, or as you approach the FDR Memorial from the direction of the Jefferson, you'll come to the bridge that arches over the inlet leading from the Tidal Basin to the Potomac River; look straight across from the bridge, and there you'll see it.

At East Basin and Ohio Dr. SW (btw. the Jefferson and FDR memorials). ☏ **202/426-6841.** www.nps.gov/ gemm. Free admission. Always open, though rangers generally are not posted here. To find out more about George Mason, visit the Jefferson Memorial, a 5-min. walk away, across the street, on the Tidal Basin, where a park ranger is on duty 9:30am–11:30pm. Limited parking. Metro: Smithsonian (12th St./ Independence Ave. exit), with a 25-min. walk, or take Tourmobile.

Recross East Basin Drive to find the opening that leads to the Tidal Basin pathway. Follow the path about 5 minutes, enjoy the spectacular view of the Tidal Basin and the capital's skyline, until you see the sign for the FDR Memorial. You'll be entering the memorial the back way, but go ahead and follow the lane and then walk all the way through to the entrance of the:

Franklin Delano Roosevelt Memorial ★★ The FDR Memorial has proven to be one of the most popular of the presidential memorials since it opened in 1997. Its popularity has to do as much with its design as the man it honors. This $7^1/_2$-acre outdoor memorial stretches out, rather than rising up, across the stone-paved floor. Granite walls define the four "galleries," each representing a different term in FDR's presidency from 1933 to 1945. Architect Lawrence Halprin's design includes waterfalls, sculptures (by Leonard Baskin, John Benson, Neil Estern, Robert Graham, Thomas Hardy, and George Segal), and Roosevelt's own words carved into the stone.

One drawback of the FDR Memorial is the noise. Planes on their way to or from nearby Reagan National Airport zoom overhead, and the many displays of cascading water can sound thunderous. When the memorial first opened, adults and children alike arrived in bathing suits and splashed around on warm days. Park rangers don't allow that anymore, but they do allow you to dip your feet in the various pools. A favorite time to visit is at night, when dramatic lighting reveals the waterfalls and statues against the dark parkland.

Conceived in 1946, the FDR Memorial had been in the works for 50 years. Part of the delay in its construction can be attributed to the president himself. FDR had told his friend Supreme Court Justice Felix Frankfurter, "If they are to put up any memorial to me, I should like it to be placed in the center of that green plot in front of the Archives Building. I should like it to consist of a block about the size [of this desk]." In fact, such a plaque sits in front of the National Archives Building. Friends and relatives struggled to honor Roosevelt's request to leave it at that, but Congress and national sentiment overrode them.

As with other presidential memorials, this one opened to some controversy. Advocates for people with disabilities were incensed that the memorial sculptures did not show the president in a wheelchair, which he used after he contracted polio. President Clinton asked Congress to allocate funding for an additional statue portraying a wheelchair-bound FDR. You will now see a small statue of FDR in a wheelchair, placed at the very front of the memorial, to the right as you approach the first gallery. Step inside the gift shop to view a replica of Roosevelt's wheelchair, as well as one of the rare photographs of the president sitting in a wheelchair. The memorial is probably the most accessible tourist attraction in the city; as at most of the National Park Service locations, wheelchairs are available for free use on-site.

If you don't see a posting of tour times, look for a ranger and request a tour; the rangers are happy to oblige. Thirty minutes is sufficient time to allot here.

On West Basin Dr., alongside the Tidal Basin in West Potomac Park (across Independence Ave. SW from the Mall). ☏ **202/426-6841.** www.nps.gov/frde. Free admission. Ranger on duty daily 9:30am–11:30pm, except for Dec 25. Limited parking. Metro: Smithsonian (12th St./Independence Ave.), with a 30-min. walk, or take Tourmobile.

Return to the Tidal Basin path and turn left toward the Lincoln Memorial. As you come up to the street, you'll see the plaque, and perhaps actual construction of the memorial to the Rev. Dr. Martin Luther King, Jr., Walk to the traffic light and cross Independence Avenue. Turn right and walk a short distance to the clearing that leads you back to the D.C. War Memorial, which Pres. Herbert Hoover dedicated in 1931. Continue to the walkway behind the memorial and turn left to follow the main lane toward the Lincoln Memorial. But first, you'll come upon the:

Korean War Veterans Memorial ★   This privately funded memorial, founded in 1995, honors those who served in Korea, a 3-year conflict (1950–53) that produced almost as many casualties as Vietnam. It consists of a circular "Pool of Remembrance" in a grove of trees and a triangular "Field of Service," highlighted by lifelike statues of 19 infantrymen, who appear to be trudging across fields. A 164-foot-long black-granite wall depicts the array of combat and support troops that served in Korea (nurses, chaplains, airmen, gunners, mechanics, cooks, and others); a raised granite curb lists the 22 nations that contributed to the UN's effort there; and a commemorative area honors KIAs, MIAs, and POWs. Plan to spend 15 minutes for viewing.

Southeast of the Lincoln Memorial, on the Independence Ave. SW side of the Mall. ℂ **202/426-6841.** www.nps.gov/kowa. Free admission. Ranger on duty daily 9:30am–11:30pm except Dec 25. Limited parking. Metro: Foggy Bottom, with 30-min. walk, or take Tourmobile.

Next, tour the:

Lincoln Memorial ★★★ Ⓚ̲ⓘⓓⓢ   This beautiful and moving tribute to the nation's 16th president attracts millions of visitors annually. Like its fellow presidential memorials, the Lincoln was a long time in the making. Although it was planned as early as 1867—2 years after Lincoln's death—Henry Bacon's design was not completed until 1912, and the memorial was dedicated in 1922.

The neoclassical temple-like structure, similar in architectural design to the Parthenon in Greece, has 36 fluted Doric columns representing the states of the Union at the time of Lincoln's death, plus two at the entrance. On the attic parapet are 48 festoons symbolizing the number of states in 1922, when the monument was erected. Hawaii and Alaska are noted in an inscription on the terrace. Due east is the Reflecting Pool, lined with American elms and stretching 2,000 feet toward the Washington Monument and the Capitol beyond.

The memorial chamber has limestone walls inscribed with the Gettysburg Address and Lincoln's Second Inaugural Address. Two 60-foot-high murals by Jules Guerin on the north and south walls depict, allegorically, Lincoln's principles and achievements. On the south wall, an Angel of Truth freeing a slave is flanked by groups of figures representing Justice and Immortality. The north-wall mural portrays the unity of North and South and is flanked by groups of figures symbolizing Fraternity and Charity. Most powerful, however, is Daniel Chester French's 19-foot-high seated statue of Lincoln, which disappears from your sightline as you get close to the base of the memorial, then emerges slowly into view as you ascend the stairs.

Lincoln's legacy has made his memorial the site of numerous demonstrations by those seeking justice. Most notable was a peaceful demonstration of 200,000 people on August 28, 1963, at which the Rev. Dr. Martin Luther King, Jr., proclaimed, "I have a dream." Look for the words "I have a dream. Martin Luther King, Jr., The March on Washington for Jobs and Freedom, August 28, 1963," inscribed and centered on the granite step, 18 steps down from the chamber. The inscription, which the National Park Service added in July 2003, marks the precise spot where King stood to deliver his famous speech. On January 18, 2009, the memorial served joyful purpose as a stage for scores of entertainers, Bruce Springsteen to Beyoncé, as they celebrated in song the upcoming presidential inauguration of Barack Obama, with the president-elect, his family, and a hundred thousand friends and supporters in attendance.

Rangers present 20- to 30-minute programs as time permits throughout the day. Thirty minutes is sufficient time for viewing this memorial.

On the western end of the Mall, at 23rd St. NW (btw. Constitution and Independence aves.). ℂ **202/426-6842**. www.nps.gov/linc. Free admission. Ranger on duty daily 9:30am–11:30pm except Dec 25. Limited parking. Metro: Foggy Bottom, then a 30-min. walk, or take Tourmobile, or catch the D.C. Circulator to 17th and Constitution and walk from there.

Walk from the Lincoln Memorial toward the reflecting pool, but turn left and proceed toward the information kiosk, then right, to follow the path that leads to the Vietnam Veterans Memorial. You pass first a life-size sculpture of three Vietnam soldiers by Frederick Hart. Near the statue, a flag flies from a 60-foot staff. Another sculpture, the Vietnam Veterans Women's Memorial, *depicts three servicewomen tending a wounded soldier. Continue until you reach the:*

Vietnam Veterans Memorial ★★

The Vietnam Veterans Memorial is possibly the most poignant sight in Washington: two long, black-granite walls in the shape of a V, each inscribed with the names of the men and women who gave their lives, or remain missing, in the longest war in American history. Even if no one close to you died in Vietnam, it's wrenching to watch visitors grimly studying the directories to find out where their loved ones are listed, or rubbing pencil on paper held against a name etched into the wall. The walls list close to 60,000 people, most of whom died very young.

Because of the raging conflict over U.S. involvement in the war, Vietnam veterans had received almost no recognition of their service before the memorial was conceived by Vietnam veteran Jan Scruggs. The nonprofit Vietnam Veterans Memorial Fund raised $7 million and secured a 2-acre site in tranquil Constitution Gardens to erect a memorial that would make no political statement about the war and would harmonize with neighboring memorials. By separating the issue of the wartime service of individuals from the issue of U.S. policy in Vietnam, the VVMF hoped to begin a process of national reconciliation.

Yale senior Maya Lin's design was chosen in a national competition open to all citizens 18 and over years of age. Erected in 1982, the memorial's two walls are angled at 125 degrees to point to the Washington Monument and the Lincoln Memorial. The walls' mirror-like surfaces reflect surrounding trees, lawns, and monuments. The names are inscribed in chronological order, documenting an epoch in American history as a series of individual sacrifices from the date of the first casualty in 1959. The National Park Service continues to add names as Vietnam veterans die eventually of injuries sustained during the war. A movement is underway to create a visitor center for the Vietnam Veterans Memorial on the plot of land across Henry Bacon Drive from the memorial.

You should allow about 20 to 30 minutes here.

Be sure to seek out the knowledgeable park rangers if you have any questions.

Northeast of the Lincoln Memorial, east of Henry Bacon Dr. (btw. 21st and 22nd sts. NW, on the Constitution Ave. NW side of the Mall). ℂ **202/426-6841**. www.nps.gov/vive. Free admission. Ranger on duty daily 9:30am–11:30pm except Dec 25. Limited parking. Metro: Foggy Bottom, with 25-min. walk, or take Tourmobile, or catch the D.C. Circulator to 17th and Constitution and walk from there.

Now, turn back toward the reflecting pool and follow the shaded lane about half a mile east, making sure to walk as far as 17th Street, to visit the:

National World War II Memorial ★★   When this memorial was dedicated on May 29, 2004, 150,000 people attended: President Bush; members of Congress; Marine Corps General (retired) P. X. Kelley, who chaired the American Battle Monuments Commission, the group that spearheaded construction of the memorial; actor Tom Hanks and now-retired news anchor Tom Brokaw, both of whom had been active in eliciting support for the memorial; and last, but most important, thousands of World War II veterans and their families. These legions of veterans, some dressed in uniform, many wearing a cap identifying the name of the veteran's division, turned out with pride, happy to receive the nation's gratitude, 60 years in the making, expressed profoundly in this memorial.

Designed by Friedrich St. Florian and funded mostly by private donations, the memorial fits nicely into the landscape between the Washington Monument grounds to the east and the Lincoln Memorial and its reflecting pool to the west. St. Florian purposely situated the 7¹/₂-acre memorial so as not to obstruct this long view down the Mall. Fifty-six 17-foot-high granite pillars representing each state and territory stand to either side of a central plaza and the Rainbow Pool. Likewise, 24 bas-relief panels divide down the middle so that 12 line each side of the walkway leading from the entrance at 17th Street. The panels to the left, as you walk toward the center of the memorial, illustrate seminal scenes from the war years as they relate to the Pacific theater: Pearl Harbor, amphibious landing, jungle warfare, a field burial, and so on; the panels to the right are sculptured scenes of war moments related to the Atlantic theater: Rosie the Riveter, Normandy Beach landing, the Battle of the Bulge, the Russians meeting the Americans at the Elbe River. Architect and sculptor Raymond Kaskey sculpted these panels based on archival photographs.

Large open pavilions stake out the north and south axes of the memorial, and semicircular fountains create waterfalls on either side. Inscriptions at the base of each pavilion fountain mark key battles. Beyond the center Rainbow Pool is a wall of 4,000 gold stars, one star for every 100 soldiers who died in World War II. People often leave photos and mementos around the memorial, which the National Park Service gather up daily for an archive. If you are lucky, you will have the chance to talk to World War II veterans here to tour the memorial. For compelling, firsthand accounts of World War II experiences, combine your tour here with an online visit to the Library of Congress's Veterans History Project, at www.loc.gov/vets; see the Library of Congress entry later in this chapter for more information.

From the 17th Street entrance walk south around the perimeter of the memorial to reach a ranger station, where there are brochures as well as registry kiosks for looking up names of veterans. Better information and faster service is available online at www.wwii memorial.com.

On 17th St., near Constitution Ave. NW. ☎ **800/639-4WW2** (4992) or 202/426-6841. www.nps.gov/wwii. Free admission. Ranger on duty daily 9:30am–11:30pm, except Dec 25. Limited parking. Metro: Farragut West, Federal Triangle, or Smithsonian, with a 20- to 25-min. walk, or take Tourmobile, or catch the D.C. Circulator.

Reward yourself. From here, you can catch a ride on the D.C. Circulator bus, which stops at the corner of 17th Street and Constitution Avenue NW. Take it to, say, Constitution Avenue and 7th Street NW, where it's a short walk up to Pennsylvania Avenue NW and the Penn Quarter neighborhood—and lots of restaurants.

3 THE SMITHSONIAN MUSEUMS

Our Smithsonian museums are justly famous. Collectively known as the "Smithsonian Institution," these 19 museums, nine research centers, and the National Zoological Park comprise the world's largest museum complex. Twenty-five million people visit the Smithsonians annually. The Smithsonian's collection of nearly 137 million objects spans the entire world and all of its history, its peoples and animals (past and present), and our attempts to probe into the future.

So vast is the collection that Smithsonian museums display only about 1% or 2% of the collection's holdings at any given time. Artifacts range from a 3.5-billion-year-old fossil to inaugural gowns worn by the first ladies. Thousands of scientific expeditions sponsored by the Smithsonian have pushed into remote frontiers in the deserts, mountains, polar regions, and jungles.

Individually, each museum is a powerhouse in its own field: The National Museum of Natural History and the National Air and Space Museum are the most visited of the Smithsonians, each seeing seven million people come through its doors in 2008, according to the latest figures available. The National Air and Space Museum maintains the world's largest collection of historic aircraft and spacecraft. The Smithsonian American Art Museum is the nation's first collection of American art and one of the largest in the world. And so on.

Washington lays claim to 17 Smithsonian museums and the National Zoo. (The other two museums, the Cooper-Hewitt, National Design Museum and the National Museum of the American Indian's George Gustav Heye Center, are in New York City.) Of these, 10 are on the Mall (see earlier section on **"The National Mall & Memorial Parks"** for more information about the Mall, p. 176). The institution is planning to open at least one more Smithsonian museum, the National Museum of African American History and Culture, adjacent to the Washington Monument, bounded by Constitution Avenue NW, Madison Drive NW, and 14th and 15th streets NW; completion of the museum is a long way off.

Smithsonian Information Center ("the Castle")   Make this your first stop, and enter through the Enid A. Haupt Garden (see the "Parks & Gardens" section, later in this chapter) for a pleasurable experience. Built in 1855, this Norman-style red-sandstone building, popularly known as "the Castle," is the oldest building on the Mall.

The main information area here is the Great Hall, where a 24-minute video overview of the institution runs throughout the day in two theaters. There are two large schematic models of the Mall (as well as a third in Braille), which allow visitors to locate nearly 100 popular attractions and Metro and Tourmobile stops.

The entire facility is accessible to persons with disabilities, and information is available in a number of foreign languages. The information desk's volunteer staff can answer questions and help you plan a Smithsonian sightseeing itinerary. Most of the museums are within easy walking distance of the facility.

While you're here, notice the charming vestibule, which has been restored to its turn-of-the-20th-century appearance. It was originally designed to display exhibits at a child's eye level. The gold-trimmed ceiling is decorated to represent a grape arbor with brightly plumed birds and blue sky peeking through the trellis. This is also where the Castle Cafe is located; though the items are awfully pricey, you can't beat the convenience and the fact that it's open at 8:30am. So why not grab a cup of joe and a muffin, then settle

The Smithson Behind the Smithsonian

You must be wondering by now: How did the Smithsonian Institution come to be? It's rather an unlikely story. It's all because of the largesse of a wealthy English scientist named James Smithson (1765–1829), the illegitimate son of the duke of Northumberland. Smithson willed his vast fortune to the United States, to found "at Washington, under the name of the Smithsonian Institution, an establishment for the increase and diffusion of knowledge." Smithson never explained why he left this handsome bequest to the United States, a country he had never visited. Speculation is that he felt the new nation, lacking established cultural institutions, most needed his funds.

Smithson died in Genoa, Italy, in 1829. Congress accepted his gift in 1836; 2 years later, half a million dollars' worth of gold sovereigns (a considerable sum in the 19th c.) arrived at the U.S. Mint in Philadelphia. For the next 8 years, Congress debated the best possible use for these funds. Finally, in 1846, James Polk signed an act into law establishing the Smithsonian Institution and authorizing a board to receive "all objects of art and of foreign and curious research, and all objects of natural history, plants, and geological and mineralogical specimens . . . for research and museum purposes." In 1855, the first Smithsonian building opened on the Mall, not as a museum, but as the home of the Smithsonian Institution. The red sandstone structure suffered a fire and several reconstructions over the years, to serve today as the Smithsonian Information Center, known by all as "the Castle."

Private donations have swelled Smithson's original legacy many times over. Although the Smithsonian acquires approximately 70% of its yearly budget from congressional allocations, the institution depends quite heavily on these moneys from private donors, especially since many of the museums are undergoing or in need of renovation. In a sign of the times, and due to the need of the Smithsonian for larger contributions, the institution has imposed an admission fee for the first time ever (for one museum's exhibit only): $6 to enter the Butterfly Pavilion at the National Museum of Natural History (p. 195). General admission to the rest of the museum, and to all other Smithsonian museums, remains free.

To find out information about any of the Smithsonian museums, call (✆ **202/633-1000** or TTY 633-5285. The information specialists who answer are very professional and always helpful. The Smithsonian museums also share a website, **www.si.edu**, which helps get you to their individual home pages.

yourself outside on a bench in the Enid A. Haupt Garden with your guidebook and maps to plan your day. Ask about castle and garden tours.

1000 Jefferson Dr. SW. ✆ **202/633-1000.** Daily 8:30am–5:30pm (info desk 9am–4pm). Closed Dec 25. Metro: Smithsonian (Mall exit).

Anacostia Community Museum This museum is inconveniently located, but that's because it was initially created in 1967 as a neighborhood museum (which makes it unique among the Smithsonian branches). It's devoted to the African-American experience, focusing on Washington, D.C., and the Upper South. The permanent collection includes about 6,000 items, ranging from videotapes of African-American church services to art, sheet music, historical documents, textiles, glassware, and anthropological objects, dating from the early 1800s. In addition, the Anacostia produces a number of shows each year and offers a comprehensive schedule of free educational programs and activities in conjunction with exhibit themes. Allow about an hour here.

1901 Fort Place SE (off Martin Luther King, Jr., Ave.). ℭ **202/633-4820.** http://anacostia.si.edu. Free admission. Daily 10am–5pm. Closed Dec 25. Metro: Take a Green line train traveling in the direction of Anacostia; get off at the Anacostia station and head to the exit marked "Local," turn left after exiting, then take a W2 or W3 bus on Howard Rd. directly to the museum.

Arthur M. Sackler Gallery ★   Asian art is the focus of this museum and the neighboring Freer (together, they form the National Museum of Asian Art in the United States). The Sackler opened in 1987, thanks to Arthur M. Sackler's gift of 1,000 priceless works. Since then, the museum has received 11th- to 19th-century Persian and Indian paintings, manuscripts, calligraphies, miniatures, bookbindings from the collection of Henri Vever, and art collector Robert O. Muller's entire collection of 4,000 Japanese prints and archival materials.

Your visit begins in the entrance pavilion, where a series of rotating installations, collectively titled "Perspectives," showcases the works of contemporary artists from Asia and the Asian Diaspora. The Sackler is preparing you to appreciate the less familiar aspects of Asian art and culture.

The Sackler's permanent collection displays Khmer ceramics; ancient Chinese jades, bronzes, paintings, and lacquerware; 20th-century Japanese ceramics and works on paper; ancient Near Eastern works in silver, gold, bronze, and clay; stone and bronze sculptures from South and Southeast Asia; and a sumptuous graphic arts inventory covering a century of work by Japanese master printmakers. Supplementing the permanent collection are traveling exhibitions from major cultural institutions in Asia, Europe, and the United States. In the past, these have included such wide-ranging areas as 15th-century Persian art and culture, photographs of Asia, and art highlighting personal devotion in India. A visit here is an education in not just Asian decorative arts, but also in antiquities.

To learn more, arrive in time for a highlights tour, offered at 12:15pm most days except Wednesday. Allow at least an hour to tour the Sackler on your own.

Also enlightening, and more fun, are the public programs that both the Sackler and the Freer Gallery frequently stage, such as performances of contemporary Asian music, tea ceremony demonstrations, and Iranian film screenings. Most are free, but you might need tickets; for details, call the main information number or check out the website. In 2009, the Freer and Sackler galleries inaugurated a program called "Asia After Dark," which copies the one hosted by the Hirshhorn Museum (see below), and is aimed at young hipsters. Staged two evenings a year, 6:30–11:30pm, the programs charge $18 admission and include tours of both the Freer and Sackler, cocktails, and DJ-spun music. For information, go online to www.asia.si.edu/asiaafterdark/default.asp.

The Sackler is part of a museum complex that houses the National Museum of African Art and the S. Dillon Ripley Center. It shares its staff and research facilities with the adjacent Freer Gallery, to which it is connected via an underground exhibition space.

1050 Independence Ave. SW. ℭ **202/633-4880.** www.asia.si.edu. Free admission. Daily 10am–5:30pm. Closed Dec 25. Metro: Smithsonian (the Mall/Jefferson Dr. exit).

Arts and Industries Building   The building is closed for an extensive renovation. Completed in 1881 as the first U.S. National Museum, this red-brick and sandstone structure was the first Smithsonian museum on the Mall. President Garfield's Inaugural Ball took place here. (It looks quite similar to the Castle, so don't be confused; from the Mall, the Arts and Industries Building is the one on the left.) From 1976 to the mid-1990s it housed exhibits from the 1876 U.S. International Exposition in Philadelphia—a celebration of America's centennial that featured the latest advances in technology.

Weather permitting, a 19th-century **carousel** operates across the street, on the Mall.

900 Jefferson Dr. SW (on the south side of the Mall). www.si.edu/ai.

Freer Gallery of Art ★★   Charles Lang Freer, a collector of Asian and American art from the 19th and early 20th centuries, gave the nation 9,000 of these works for his namesake gallery's 1923 opening. Freer's original interest was American art, but his good friend James McNeill Whistler encouraged him to collect Asian works as well. Eventually the latter became predominant. Freer's gift included funds to construct a museum and an endowment to add to the Asian collection, which now numbers more than 26,000 objects and spans 6,000 years. It includes Chinese and Japanese sculpture, lacquer, metalwork, and ceramics; early Christian illuminated manuscripts; Iranian manuscripts, metalwork, and miniatures; ancient Near Eastern metalware; and South Asian sculpture and paintings.

The Freer is mostly about Asian art, but it also displays some of the more than 1,200 American works (the world's largest collection) by **Whistler.** Most remarkable and always on view is the famous **Harmony in Blue and Gold, the Peacock Room.** Originally a dining room designed for the London mansion of F. R. Leyland, the Peacock Room displayed a Whistler painting called *The Princess from the Land of Porcelain.* But after his painting was installed, Whistler was dissatisfied with the room as a setting for his work. When Leyland was away from home, Whistler painted over the very expensive leather interior and embellished it with paintings of golden peacock feathers. Not surprisingly, a rift ensued between Whistler and Leyland. After Leyland's death, Freer purchased the room, painting and all, and had it shipped to his home in Detroit. It is now permanently installed here. Other American painters represented in the collections are Thomas Wilmer Dewing, Dwight William Tryon, Abbott Handerson Thayer, John Singer Sargent, and Childe Hassam. You could spend a happy 1 to 2 hours here.

The Freer Gallery is an oasis on the Mall, especially if you arrive here after visiting its voluminous and crowded sisters, the Natural History, American History, and Air and Space museums. Housed in a grand granite-and-marble building that evokes the Italian Renaissance, the pristine Freer has lovely sky-lit galleries. The main exhibit floor galleries encircle a beautiful landscaped courtyard, complete with loggia and central fountain. If the weather's right, it's a pleasure to sit out here and take a break from touring. An underground exhibit space connects the Freer to the neighboring Sackler Gallery, and both museums share the **Meyer Auditorium,** which is used for free chamber music concerts, dance performances, Asian feature films, and other programs. Inquire about these, as well as children's activities and free tours given daily, at the information desk.

Jefferson Dr. SW at 12th St. SW (on the south side of the Mall). ℭ **202/633-4880.** www.asia.si.edu. Free admission. Daily 10am–5:30pm. Closed Dec 25. Metro: Smithsonian (Mall/Jefferson Dr.).

Hirshhorn Museum and Sculpture Garden ★★   This museum of modern and contemporary art is named after Latvian-born Joseph H. Hirshhorn, who, in 1966, donated his vast collection—more than 4,000 drawings and paintings and 2,000 pieces of sculpture—to the United States "as a small repayment for what this nation has done for me and others like me who arrived here as immigrants." The Hirshhorn opened in 1974 to display these works, adding 5,500 more bequeathed by Hirshhorn in 1981, upon his death. The Hirshhorn's current inventory numbers about 11,500.

Constructed 14 feet aboveground on sculptured supports, the doughnut-shaped concrete-and-granite building stands 82 feet high and measures 231 feet in diameter. The cylindrically shaped building encloses a hollow core, where a fountain spouts water five stories high. The building's light and airy interior holds three levels of galleries, each following a circular route that makes it easy to see every exhibit without getting lost in a honeycomb of galleries. Natural light from floor-to-ceiling windows makes the inner galleries the perfect venue for regarding sculpture—second only to the beautiful tree-shaded sunken **Sculpture Garden** ★ across the street (don't miss it). Make your way to the third-floor oculus and you'll be rewarded with a dramatic view of the National Mall.

A rotating show of about 600 pieces is on view at all times. The collection features just about every well-known 20th-century artist and touches on most of the major trends in Western art since the late 19th century, with particular emphasis on our contemporary period. Among the best-known pieces are Rodin's *Monument to the Burghers of Calais* (in the Sculpture Garden), Hopper's *First Row Orchestra,* de Kooning's *Two Women in the Country,* and Warhol's *Marilyn Monroe's Lips.*

Pick up a free calendar when you enter to find out about free films, lectures, concerts, and temporary exhibits. Some of these events are quite popular. For instance, the Hirshhorn hosts Hirshhorn After Hours three or four times a year, and it's always a sellout. Twenty-somethings especially love to attend the function, which takes place from 8pm to midnight and combines socializing with art, music or other performance, and cocktails. The $18 tickets are available in advance online, www.hirshhorn.si.edu/afterhours, or by calling ✆ **202/633-4629.** Docents give impromptu, free, 30-minute tours to anyone who stops by the information desk, noon to 4pm daily.

Independence Ave. at 7th St. SW (on the south side of the Mall). ✆ **202/633-4674.** www.hirshhorn.si. edu. Free admission. Museum daily 10am–5:30pm. Sculpture Garden daily 7:30am–dusk. Closed Dec 25. Metro: L'Enfant Plaza (Smithsonian Museums/Maryland Ave. or Smithsonian exit).

National Air and Space Museum ★★ (Kids) The National Air and Space Museum has two locations: its flagship museum on the National Mall and a second facility, the **Steven F. Udvar-Hazy Center,** located on the grounds of Washington-Dulles International Airport.

Let's start with this one, the original, ever-popular Air and Space Museum on the Mall. The museum, now in its 34th year, chronicles the story of the mastery of flight, from Kitty Hawk to outer space. It holds the largest collection of historic aircraft and spacecraft in the world, about 50,000—so many, in fact, that the museum is able to display only about 10% of its artifacts at any one time, hence the opening of the Udvar-Hazy Center in 2003.

During the tourist season and on holidays, arrive before 10am to make a beeline for the film ticket line when the doors open. The not-to-be-missed **IMAX films** ★ shown here are immensely popular, and tickets to most shows sell out quickly. You can purchase same-day tickets by phone or in person at the Lockheed Martin IMAX Theater box office on the first floor, or in advance online up to 24 hours before showtime. Surcharges apply to phone and online orders. Two or more films play each day, most with aeronautical or space-exploration themes; *To Fly* and *3D Sun* are two that were running in 2009, along with the feature film that has made the museum famous, *Night at the Museum: Battle of*

Tickets for feature films cost $12.50 for adults, $11 for children ages 2 to 12, and $11.50 for ages 60 or older; otherwise prices are $8.75 for adults, $7.25 for children, and $7.75 for seniors; they're free for children 1 and under. You can also see IMAX films most evenings after the museum's closing; call for details (© **877/932-4629**).

You'll also need tickets to attend a show at the **Albert Einstein Planetarium** ★, which creates "an astronomical adventure." Projectors display space imagery upon a 70-foot-diameter dome, making you feel as if you're traveling in 3-D through the cosmos. The planetarium's newest feature is the 23-minute **Cosmic Collisions,** which takes you on a trip through time and space, where you encounter cosmic collisions and hypersonic impacts as narrated by Robert Redford. Tickets are $8.75 for adults, $7.25 for ages 2 to 12, $7.75 for ages 60 or older.

Among the 22 exhibitions on display throughout the museum is one that children especially love: **How Things Fly,** which includes wind and smoke tunnels, a boardable Cessna 150 airplane, and dozens of interactive exhibits that demonstrate principles of flight, aerodynamics, and propulsion. All the aircraft are originals. Kids also flock to the walk-through **Skylab orbital workshop,** part of the **Space Race** exhibition on the first floor. Both children and adults stand in line to take their turn on the museum's **Flight Simulators.** (The Udvar-Hazy Center has several, too.) You'll have a choice of experiencing a simulated ride or an interactive simulated piloting. For the interactive simulation, you are strapped in and given a joystick, and for about 5 minutes you'll truly feel as if you are in the cockpit and airborne, maneuvering your craft up, down, and upside-down on a wild adventure, thanks to virtual reality images and high-tech sounds. The ride simulator costs $7, the interactive simulator costs $8. To board the ride simulators, children must measure 42 inches unless accompanied by an adult, and must measure 48 inches to go it alone on the interactive simulators.

Other galleries highlight the solar system, U.S. manned spaceflights, sea-air operations, and aviation during both world wars. **Explore the Universe** presents the major discoveries that have shaped the current scientific view of the universe; it illustrates how the universe is taking shape, and probes the mysteries that remain. Hundreds of space and aircraft artifacts dangle before your eyes everywhere you look, but don't miss the **1903 Flyer,** hanging in the exhibit called **The Wright Brothers and the Invention of the Aerial Age.** In late 2007, the museum debuted **America by Air,** an exhibit that covers an expanded history of commercial air travel.

The museum's cafeteria, the Wright Place, offers food from three popular American chains: McDonald's, Boston Market, and Donatos Pizzeria. Its three-level, 12,000-square-foot shop is the largest Smithsonian store.

At the Udvar-Hazy Center you'll find two hangars—one for aviation artifacts, the other for space artifacts—and a 164-foot-tall observation tower for watching planes leave and arrive at Dulles Airport. The center's James S. McDonnell Space Hangar stretches the length of three football fields and stands 10 stories high, the better to house the enormous *Enterprise,* NASA's first space shuttle; the tiny "Anita," a spider carried on Skylab inside a bottle for web formation experiments; the manned maneuvering unit used for the first untethered spacewalk; a full-scale prototype of the Mars Pathfinder Lander; and Pegasus, the first aircraft-launched rocket booster to carry satellites into space. Eventually, the gallery will hold more than 200 aircraft and 135 spacecraft. The center will also serve as the Air and Space Museum's primary restoration facility, and the public will be able to watch specialists at work. This location also shows IMAX films.

On Independence Ave. SW, btw. 4th and 7th sts. (on the south side of the Mall, with entrances on Jefferson Dr. or Independence Ave.). ✆ **202/633-1000** (for both locations), or 877/932-4629 for IMAX ticket information. www.nasm.si.edu. Free admission. Both locations daily 10am–5:30pm. The Mall museum often stays open until 7:30pm in summer, but call to confirm. Free 1¹/₂-hr. highlight tours daily at 10:30am and 1pm. Closed Dec 25. Metro: L'Enfant Plaza (Smithsonian Museums/Maryland Ave. exit) or Smithsonian (The Mall/Jefferson Dr. exit). The Udvar-Hazy Center is located at 14390 Air and Space Museum Pkwy., Chantilly, VA.

National Museum of African Art ★   Founded in 1964, and part of the Smithsonian since 1979, the National Museum of African Art moved to the Mall in 1987 to share a subterranean space with the Sackler Gallery (see above) and the Ripley Center. Its aboveground domed pavilions reflect the arch motif of the neighboring Freer Gallery of Art (see above).

The museum collects and exhibits ancient and contemporary art from the entire African continent and rotates displays of its 9,100-piece permanent collection. The museum's contemporary African art collection comprises the largest public holding in the United States. Among the museum's holdings are the **Eliot Elisofon Photographic Archives,** encompassing 80,000 photographic prints and transparencies and 120,000 feet of film on African arts and culture. A small, ongoing permanent exhibit of ceramic arts displays 14 traditional and contemporary pieces from the museum's 140-works collection. Most exciting is the Walt Disney–Tishman African Art collection, which the Walt Disney World Company donated to the museum in 2005. Its Tishman collection of 525 objects represents every area of Africa, dating from ancient to contemporary times and spanning art forms from textiles to jewelry. A rotating selection of at least 60 works are permanently on display in the museum.

Inquire at the desk about special exhibits, workshops (including excellent children's programs), storytelling, lectures, docent-led tours, films, and demonstrations. A comprehensive events schedule provides a unique opportunity to learn about the diverse cultures and visual traditions of Africa. Plan on spending a minimum of 30 minutes here.

950 Independence Ave. SW. ✆ **202/633-4600.** http://africa.si.edu. Free admission. Daily 10am–5:30pm. Closed Dec 25. Metro: Smithsonian.

National Museum of American History ★★★ **Kids**   As a bastion of U.S. culture and history, this museum tells America's story in terms of everyday life. Its objects can evoke feelings of awe (the desk on which Thomas Jefferson wrote the Declaration of Independence), affection (Dorothy's ruby slippers), or connection (Julia Child's kitchen). And some things here—the museum's ultimate possession, the huge **original Star-Spangled Banner** ★★★, for example—evoke all three emotions at once.

A grand renovation completed in November 2008 has much improved the museum. A skylight lightens up the place and a redesign creates better openness and flow; both rid the building of its old stifling sense of cluttered crowded-ness. Better yet, the museum brings American history to full-blooded life by staging entertainments in different locations throughout the day. The Mall-level's newly carved-out atrium is one perfect spot—we enjoyed performances of professional singers belting out American standards, like *Somewhere Over the Rainbow* and *Oklahoma*—and the East Wing's third floor space in front of the Clara Barton Red Cross ambulance is another—here, we listened to a man dressed in World War II army fatigues read a letter written by a soldier to his family back home.

Museum Exhibits Scheduled for 2010

The following listings, though hardly comprehensive, should give you an idea about 2010's upcoming or current shows at major Washington museums. Because schedules sometimes change, it's always a good idea to call ahead. See individual entries in this chapter for phone numbers and addresses.

Anacostia Community Museum "The African Presence in Mexico" (Nov 8, 2009–Jul 4, 2010). Paintings and artifacts examine the history, culture, and art of Afro-Mexicans.

Freer Gallery "The Texture of Night: James McNeill Whistler" (through June 2010). Fifteen moonlit landscapes in small scale works on paper, plus one oil, that represent Whistler's main focus throughout the 1870s.

Hirshhorn Museum and Sculpture Garden "Yves Klein" (Feb 17, 2010–May 23, 2010). The first American perspective in nearly 30 years of this French artist's work, who believed in the transformative power of art, and expressed it in performance art, music, and in his fire paintings and air architecture artworks.

National Gallery of Art "In the Darkroom: Photographic Processes" (Oct 25, 2009–Mar 14, 2010). Ninety photographs arranged chronologically and taken from the permanent collection, the exhibit traces major technological advancements in photography, from those of the inventor of photography, William Henry Fox Talbot, in 1843, to Polaroid prints by Andy Warhol.

National Museum of Natural History "Since Darwin: The Evolution of Evolution" (Sep 12, 2009–Jul 18, 2010). A celebration of the 200th anniversary of Darwin's birth and the 50th anniversary of the publication of his book on the origin of the species, using specimens from the museum's collections.

The piece de resistance of the museum always has been the original 30×34-foot wool and cotton Star Spangled Banner, which Francis Scott Key observed the morning of September 14, 1814, when he spied this very flag waving above Fort McHenry in Baltimore's harbor, at the height of the War of 1812. Key's emotion at the sight moved him to pen the poem that, when put to music, eventually became the U.S. national anthem. Thanks again to the renovation, the carefully preserved flag now rests in its own dimly lit, no, make that almost completely dark, multistory gallery, on view through an enormous windowfront. The gallery lies on the second floor behind the atrium wall, whose abstract depiction of the flag is meant to lead you to the exhibit entrance. (If you are like me, you might not catch on; just look for the straightforward signs showing you where to enter.) Take the time to examine the artifacts on display, like the piece of burned timber from the torched White House, and to read about the flag's seamstress, professional flagmaker Mary Pickersgill, who sewed the flag in 6 weeks with the help of her daughter, nieces, and a maid.

You'll notice another renovation improvement on the museum's first and second floors: the 10-foot-high "artifact walls" displaying assorted pieces from the museum's three-million-object collection.

But many of the museum's pre-renovation attractions remain.

National Postal Museum "Delivering Hope: FDR & Stamps of the Great Depression" (Jun 9, 2009–Jun 6, 2010). Stamp collector FDR changed the look of stamps to convey messages of hope, optimism, and solidity of the federal government.

Phillips Collection "Georgia O'Keeffe: Abstraction" (Feb 6, 2010–May 9, 2010). Seventy paintings and drawings, plus close-up photos of the artist by Alfred Stieglitz. Exhibit focuses on origins and range of O'Keefe's abstractions over the course of her career.

Renwick Gallery "The Art of Gaman: Arts and Crafts from the Japanese Internment Camps, 1942-1946" (Mar 5, 2010–Aug 1, 2010). Exhibit of artifacts and photos that show arts and crafts made by interred Japanese, in illustrating the Japanese concept of "gaman," which means "to bear the seemingly unbearable with dignity and patience."

Smithsonian American Art Museum "Alexis Rockman: A Fable for Tomorrow" (Nov 19, 2010–May 8, 2011). Eighty paintings and works on paper trace Rockman's artistic development as a depicter of the natural world using varied sources, including botanical illustrations, museum dioramas, and 19th-century landscapes.

Textile Museum "Designing Women of Postwar Britain: Their Art and the Modern Interior (May 15, 2010–Sep 12, 2010). Three women designers in particular transformed the artistic revolution in postwar Britain, incorporating colors and themes of bold artists, like Calder and Miro, into households.

On the third floor lies the exhibit **The American Presidency: A Glorious Burden,** which explores the power and meaning of the presidency by studying those who have held the position. Continue on this floor to the exhibit **The Price of Freedom: Americans at War,** which examines major American military events and explores the idea that America's armed forces reflect American society. Among the items on display here are George Washington's commission from Congress as commander in chief of the Continental Army and the uniform jacket that Andrew Jackson wore during the Battle of New Orleans in the War of 1812.

One of the most popular exhibits on the second floor is **First Ladies: Political Role and Public Image,** which displays the first ladies' gowns and tells you a bit about each of these women. Following that, find the exhibit called **Within These Walls . . . ,** which interprets the rich history of America by tracing the lives of the people who lived in a 200-year-old house transplanted from Ipswich, Massachusetts.

First-floor exhibits explore the development of farm and power machinery. A temporary exhibit whose popularity may make it a permanent display is ***Bon Appétit!* Julia Child's Kitchen at the Smithsonian,** a presentation of the famous chef's actual kitchen from her home in Cambridge, Massachusetts. When she moved to California in late 2001, Child donated her kitchen and all that it contained (1,200 items in all) to the museum. Most of these are on display, vegetable peeler to kitchen sink. Also look here for **America on the Move,** which details the story of transportation in America since 1876: 300 artifacts displayed within period settings. And if you enjoy science explained in personal terms, head to the **Hall of Invention** to discover the people behind inventions such as the Kevlar vest and the telephone.

Best to start your tour at the Welcome Center on the second floor to figure out how you'd like to proceed. Inquire about highlight tours and daily performances, as well as films, lectures, concerts, and hands-on activities for children and adults. Be sure to visit the museum's gift shops and dining options, also revamped during the remodeling.

On Constitution Ave. NW, btw. 12th and 14th sts. NW (on the north side of the Mall, with entrances on Constitution Ave. and Madison Dr.). ☎ **202/633-1000.** www.americanhistory.si.edu. Free admission. Daily 10am–5:30pm. Closed Dec 25. Metro: Smithsonian or Federal Triangle.

National Museum of the American Indian ★ **Kids** The National Museum of the American Indian officially opened on September 21, 2004, having taken 5 years and $219 million to construct. Outside and in, this museum is strikingly handsome. Its burnt-sand-colored exterior of Kasota limestone wraps around the undulating walls of the museum, making the five-story building a standout among the many white-stone structures on the National Mall. Its interior design incorporates themes of nature and astronomy. For instance, the Potomac (a Piscataway word meaning "where the goods are brought in") is a rotunda that serves as the museum's main gathering place; it is also "the heart of the museum, the sun of its universe" (as noted in the museum's literature). Measuring 120 feet in diameter, with an atrium rising 120 feet to the top of the dome overhead, the Potomac is the central entryway into the museum, a venue for performances, and a hall filled with celestial references, from the equinoxes and solstices mapped on the floor beneath your feet to the sights of sky visible through the oculus in the dome above your head.

A gift shop, a theater, and the museum's excellent restaurant, Mitsitam, occupy most of the remaining space on the first floor. A second shop and the museum's main galleries lie upstairs on the second and third levels. Three permanent exhibits, "Our Universes: Traditional Knowledge Shapes Our World," "Our Peoples: Giving Voice to Our Histories," and "Our Lives: Contemporary Life and Identities," use videos, interactive technology, and displays of artifacts to help you learn about Native cosmologies, history, and contemporary cultural identity, both of Native Americans as a group and within certain individual tribes. An exhibit called "Window on the Collections: Many Hands, Many Voices" displays 3,500 objects behind glass; a computer kiosk in front of each case allows the museumgoer to zoom in and learn more about a particular item on view. These precious wood and stone carvings, masks, pottery, feather bonnets, and so on are a fraction of the 800,000 objets d'art amassed by a wealthy New Yorker named George Gustav Heye (1874–1957). Heye founded the New York Museum of the American Indian, this museum's predecessor.

The National Museum of the American Indian does not provide much direction to self-guided touring, which tends to leave visitors at a loss as to how to proceed through the museum. Faced with the vast display of objects and with galleries that have no obvious beginning or end, tourists wander around, adopting a scattershot approach to the information, emerging eventually with more of an impression than with a coherent understanding of the Indian experience, and overwhelmed by the variety and number of artifacts and details. Perhaps that's intentional. Best advice? Stop at the Welcome Desk when you enter to sign up for a highlights tour.

National Museum of Natural History ★★★ (Kids)   Stop outside first, on the 9th
Street side of the building, to visit the **butterfly garden.** Four habitats—wetland,
meadow, wood's edge, and urban garden—are on view, designed to beckon butterflies
and visitors alike. The garden is at its best in warm weather, but it's open year-round.
(And if you like that, you're going to love the museum's new Butterflies and Plants
exhibit, which includes a Butterfly Pavilion—keep reading!)

Now go inside. Children often refer to this Smithsonian showcase as "the dinosaur
museum," because of the dinosaur hall, or as "the elephant museum," since a huge **African bush elephant** is the first thing you see in the Rotunda when you enter from the
Mall. Whatever you call it, the National Museum of Natural History is the largest of its
kind in the world and one of the most visited museums in Washington. It contains more
than 126 million artifacts and specimens, everything from Ice Age mammoths to the
legendary Hope Diamond.

In late 2008, the museum debuted a brand-new, 22,000-square-foot **Ocean Hall,** the
largest, most diverse exhibit of its kind in the world. Designed by the same firm that
created the exhibits and spaces of the highly interactive International Spy Museum, the
hall includes collections and state-of-the-art technology to demonstrate our oceans'
essential role in life on earth. Look for a model of a 45-foot-long North American right
whale and a 1,500-gallon coral reef aquarium with more than 70 live animals and 674
specimens. November 2009 brought the opening of **Origins: What Does It Mean to Be
Human?** It focuses on the story of human origins and probes the ecological and genetic
connection that humans have had with the natural world.

Meanwhile, the museum's long-popular permanent exhibits continue:

If you have children, you might want to make your first stop the first-floor **Discovery
Room,** which is filled with creative hands-on exhibits "for children of all ages." Call
ahead or inquire at the information desk about hours. Also on this floor is the **Kenneth
E. Behring Hall of Mammals.** Set in the restored west wing and boasting up-to-date
lighting and sound, the Hall of Mammals features interactive dioramas that explain how
mammals evolved and adapted to changes in habitat and climate over the course of millions of years. At least 274 taxidermied mammals, from polar bear to tiger, are on display,
along with a dozen mammal fossils. From time to time, the hall erupts with animal
sounds, all part of exhibit wizardry that helps make this a lifelike experience.

Other Rotunda-level displays include the **fossil collection,** which traces evolution
back billions of years and includes a 3.5-billion-year-old stromatolite (blue-green algae
clump) fossil—one of the earliest signs of life on earth—and a 70-million-year-old dinosaur egg. **Ancient Seas and Ice Age** features a 100-foot-long mural depicting primitive
whales, a life-size walk-around diorama of a 230-million-year-old coral reef, and more
than 2,000 fossils that chronicle the evolution of marine life. The **Dinosaur Hall** displays giant skeletons of creatures that dominated the earth for 140 million years before
their extinction about 65 million years ago. Mounted throughout the Dinosaur Hall are
replicas of ancient birds, including a life-size model of the *Quetzalcoatlus northropi,* which
lived 70 million years ago, had a 40-foot wingspan, and was the largest flying animal ever.
Also residing above this hall is the jaw of an ancient shark, the *Carcharodon megalodon,*
which lived in the oceans 5 million years ago. A monstrous 40-foot-long predator
with teeth 5 to 6 inches long, it could have consumed a Volkswagen Bug in one gulp.

7

(Tips) Eating on the Fly

Washington has plenty of street vendors planted near various attractions, but none are remarkable for their food. Enter **On the Fly,** www.dconthefly.com, the lime-colored, eco-friendly, bug-shaped smartkarts with wings that sell fast- and fresh food prepared by locally famous eateries, like Teaism and Julia's Empanadas. Look for these zero-emission, plug-in trucks at choice locations throughout the city, including at 12th St. and Madison Dr. NW, near the American History Museum; on the National Mall near the Smithsonian Castle; and at the corner of 7th St. and Jefferson Dr. SW, near the Hirshhorn Museum. Hours vary, prices are cheap: typically $3 to $6.

Elsewhere on this floor is **African Cultures,** which presents the people, cultures, and lives of Africa through photos, videos, and more than 400 objects.

Upstairs lies another exhibit popular among the under-10 crowd: the **O. Orkin Insect Zoo** ★, where kids enjoy looking at tarantulas, centipedes, and the like, and crawling through a model of an African termite mound. Right next door is **Butterflies and Plants: Partners in Evolution** ★, a 4,000-square-foot exhibit that illustrates the evolving relationship between butterflies and plants over millions of years. The exhibit includes a walk-through, 1,400-square-foot Butterfly Pavilion featuring live butterflies and plants. *Note:* The museum charges a $6 fee for admission to the pavilion portion of the exhibit.

Ever a big draw is the **Janet Annenberg Hooker Hall of Geology, Gems, and Minerals** ★, which showcases the Hope Diamond; the 23.1-carat Burmese Carmen Lucia ruby, one of the largest and finest rubies in the world; and other treasures of the National Gem Collection. Besides staring spellbound at priceless jewelry, you can learn all you want about earth science, from volcanology to the importance of mining. Interactive computers, animated graphics, and a multimedia presentation of the "big picture" story of the earth are some of the things that have moved the exhibit and the museum a bit further into the 21st century.

Don't miss the Samuel C. Johnson **IMAX theater** with a six-story-high screen for 2-D and 3-D movies (*Dinosaurs: Giants of Patagonia* and the feature film, *Night at the Museum: Battle of the Smithsonian,* were among those shown in 2009), a six-story Atrium Cafe with a food court, and expanded museum shops. The museum also offers the small **Fossil Café,** located within the Fossil Plants Hall on the first floor. In this 50-seat cafe, the tables' clear plastic tops are actually fossil cases that present fossilized plants and insects for your inspection as you munch away on smoked turkey sandwiches, goat-cheese quiche, and the like.

The theater box office is on the first floor of the museum; you can purchase tickets by phone (© **202/633-4629** or 877/932-4629), online, or at the box office at least 30 minutes before the screening. The box office is open daily from 9:45am to the last show. Films are shown continuously throughout the day. Ticket prices are $8.75 for adults, $7.25 for children (2–12), and $7.75 for seniors 60 or older; tickets for feature films cost $13 for adults, $11 for children, and $12 for seniors.

National Postal Museum ★   This museum remains a hit, especially for families, but anyone might spend a pleasant hour here. Bring your address book, and you can send postcards to the folks back home through an interactive exhibit that issues a cool postcard and stamps it. That's just one feature that makes this museum visitor-friendly. Many of its exhibits involve easy-to-understand activities, like postal-themed video games.

The museum documents America's postal history from 1673 (about 170 years before the advent of stamps, envelopes, and mailboxes) to the present. (Did you know that a dog sled was used to carry mail in Alaska until 1963, when it was replaced by an airplane?) In the central gallery, suspended from the 90-foot-high atrium ceiling, are three planes that carried mail in the early decades of the 20th century. These, along with a railway mail car, an 1851 mail/passenger coach, and a replica of an airmail beacon tower, are all part of the **Moving the Mail** exhibit, recently augmented by **On the Road.** This new exhibit explores the history of such city mail vehicles as the 1931 Ford Model A mail truck on display. **Customers and Communities** traces the evolution of mail delivery as it expanded to reach growing populations in both rural areas and the cities. In **Binding the Nation,** historic correspondence illustrates how mail kept families together in the developing nation. Several exhibits deal with the famed Pony Express, a service that lasted less than 2 years but was romanticized to legendary proportions by Buffalo Bill and others. In the Civil War section you'll learn about Henry "Box" Brown, a slave who had himself "mailed" from Richmond to a Pennsylvania abolitionist in 1856. The **Art of Cards and Letters** gallery displays rotating exhibits of personal (sometimes wrenching, always interesting) correspondence taken from different periods in history, as well as greeting cards and postcards. In addition, the museum houses a vast research library for philatelic researchers and scholars, a stamp store, and a museum shop. Inquire about free walk-in tours at the information desk.

Opened in 1993, this off-the-Mall Smithsonian museum occupies the lower level of the palatial Beaux Arts quarters of the Old City Post Office Building, which was designed by architect Daniel Burnham and is situated next to Union Station.

2 Massachusetts Ave. NE (at 1st St.). *C* **202/633-5555.** www.postalmuseum.si.edu. Free admission. Daily 10am–5:30pm. Closed Dec 25. Metro: Union Station.

National Zoological Park ★★ (Kids)   The zoo's biggest draw remains the three **giant pandas:** Mei Xiang and Tian Tian and their offspring, Tai Shan, born July 9, 2005. But don't stop there.

Established in 1889, the National Zoo is home to about 400 species—some 2,400 animals—many of them rare and/or endangered. A leader in the care, breeding, and exhibition of animals, it occupies 163 beautifully landscaped and wooded acres and is one of the country's most delightful zoos. You'll see cheetahs, zebras, camels, elephants, tapirs, antelopes, brown pelicans, kangaroos, hippos, rhinos, giraffes, apes, and, of course, lions, tigers, and bears.

Enter the zoo at the Connecticut Avenue entrance; you'll be right by the Education Building, where you can pick up a map and find out about feeding times and any special activities. Note that from this main entrance, you're headed downhill; the return uphill

EXPLORING WASHINGTON, D.C.

7

THE SMITHSONIAN MUSEUMS

> **Fun Facts** **Early Risers?**
>
> Zoo grounds open daily at 6am, which might be too early for a lot of tourists, but not for families whose young children like to rise at the crack of dawn. You know who you are. If you find yourselves trapped and restless in the hotel room, hop on the Red Line Metro, which opens at 5am weekdays, 7am Saturday and Sunday (or drive—no problem parking at that hour), get off at the Woodley Park–Zoo station, and walk up the hill to the zoo. Lots of animals are outdoors and on view. A Starbucks, which opens at 6am Monday to Saturday and 6:30am Sunday, is directly across from the zoo's entrance on Connecticut Avenue. Good morning.

walk can prove trying if you have young children and/or it's a hot day. But the zoo rents strollers, and snack bars and ice-cream kiosks are scattered throughout the park.

The zoo animals live in large, open enclosures—simulations of their natural habitats—along easy-to-follow paths. The **Olmsted Walk** winds from the zoo's Connecticut Avenue entrance all the way to the zoo's end, at Rock Creek Park. Two paths stem off the central Olmsted Walk: the **Valley Trail,** leading to seals, sea lions, beavers, the bald eagle refuge, and other North American mammals and birds; and the **Asia Trail,** which takes you past sloth bears, frolicking giant pandas, fishing cats, clouded leopards, and Japanese salamander. You can't get lost, and it's hard to miss a thing. Be sure to catch **Amazonia,** where you can hang out for an hour peering up into the trees and still not spy the sloth. (Do yourself a favor and ask the attendant where it is.) You'll notice construction underway for the **Elephants Trails,** a new permanent exhibit that will provide an improved elephant habitat, including exercise trails; it won't be complete until 2011.

If your children are ages 3 to 8, don't miss the **Kids' Farm** at the very bottom of the zoo. Ducks, chickens, goats, cows, and miniature donkeys are among the animals kids can observe up close. Children might also enjoy the vegetable garden and pizza sculpture.

The zoo offers several dining options, including the Mane Restaurant, the Panda Café, and a number of snack stands. Other facilities include stroller-rental stations, a number of gift shops, a bookstore, and several paid-parking lots. The lots fill up quickly, especially on weekends, so arrive early or take the Metro.

3001 Connecticut Ave. NW (adjacent to Rock Creek Park). (© 202/633-4800. www.nationalzoo.si.edu. Free admission. Apr–Oct (weather permitting) grounds daily 6am–8pm, animal buildings daily 10am–6pm; Nov–Mar grounds daily 6am–6pm, animal buildings daily 10am–4:30pm. Closed Dec 25. Metro: Woodley Park–Zoo or Cleveland Park.

Renwick Gallery of the Smithsonian American Art Museum ★ **Finds** A department of the Smithsonian American Art Museum (though located nowhere near it), the Renwick Gallery is a showcase for American creativity in crafts and decorative arts, housed in a historic mid-1800s landmark building of the French Second Empire style. It's located on the same block as the White House, just across Pennsylvania Avenue. The original home of the Corcoran Gallery (which now lies a short walk away, down 17th Street), it was saved from demolition by First Lady Jacqueline Kennedy in 1963, when she recommended that it be renovated as part of the Lafayette Square restoration. In 1965, it became part of the Smithsonian and was renamed for its architect, James W. Renwick, Jr., who also designed the Smithsonian Castle.

On view on the first floor are temporary exhibits of American crafts and decorative arts. On the second floor, the museum's rich and diverse displays boast changing crafts exhibits and contemporary works from the museum's permanent collection, such as Larry Fuente's *Game Fish* or Wendell Castle's *Ghost Clock*. Also on the second floor is the **Victorian Grand Salon,** styled in 19th-century opulence and worth a visit on its own merits: Its 40-foot-high laylight (a skylight unexposed to the outside) and its wainscoted rose walls covered in framed paintings evoke a 19th-century picture gallery. Tour the entire gallery for about an hour, rest for a minute, and then go on to your next destination.

The Renwick offers a comprehensive schedule of crafts demonstrations, lectures, and musical performances. Also check out the museum shop near the entrance for books on crafts, design, and decorative arts, as well as craft items, many of them for children. *Note:* The main branch of the Smithsonian American Art Museum (below) is located at 8th and F streets NW, in the Penn Quarter neighborhood.

1661 Pennsylvania Ave. NW (at 17th St. NW). ✆ **202/633-2850.** http://americanart.si.edu. Free admission. Daily 10am–5:30pm. Closed Dec 25. Metro: Farragut West or Farragut North.

Smithsonian American Art Museum and National Portrait Gallery ★★★

This historic landmark building houses two Smithsonian museums, the Smithsonian American Art Museum and the National Portrait Gallery. The structure itself is magnificent. Begun in 1836 and completed in 1868 to serve as the nation's Patent Office, it is the third-oldest federal building in the capital. With immense porticoes and columns on the outside, and colonnades, double staircases, vaulted galleries, and skylights inside, the museum captures your attention, no matter how or where you stand to look at it. The building occupies an entire city block, from 7th to 9th streets and from F to G streets.

As for the art presented throughout these three levels: It's like a shot in the arm for America. You will see here the faces of America's founding fathers and mothers, great American heroes and cultural icons, and scenes from American history and way of life, from the moment this country's story began 400 years ago: here an Edward Hopper, there a Gilbert Stuart, now a portrait of Samuel Clemens (Mark Twain), and on to contemporary art by Sean Scully.

Together, the Portrait Gallery and the American Art Museum display nearly 2,000 works from their permanent collections. The galleries flow one into another, so you may not always realize that you have stepped from an American Art wing into the Portrait Gallery wing—nor is it necessary to notice. Just wander and enjoy: the folk art, introductory "American Experience" landscapes and photographs, special exhibits, American Origins portraits, and other works on the first floor; portraits of America's presidents, an exhibit on "The Presidency and the Cold War," graphic arts, and American art through 1940 on the second floor; and art since 1945 and portraits of 20th-century Americans on the third floor. Expect to be dazzled by the creations of such American masters as Winslow Homer, Georgia O'Keeffe, David Hockney, Robert Rauschenberg, Thomas Cole, Andrew Wyeth, Mary Cassatt, and so many others. In addition, don't miss the two-level Lunder Conservation Center, where you'll be able to watch conservators working to preserve art pieces, and the Luce Foundation Center for American Art, which stores another 3,300 objects in such a way that they remain on view to the public. Finally, check out the museum's super-cool, year-round enclosed courtyard cafe. ***Please note:*** The Smithsonian American Art Museum and National Portrait Gallery are located near the National Mall, but not on it; they're across from the Verizon Center in the heart of the Penn Quarter neighborhood.

8th and F sts. NW. ✆ **202/633-1000.** www.reynoldscenter.org. Free admission. Daily 11:30am–7pm. Closed Dec. 25. Metro: Gallery Place/Chinatown.

4 OTHER ATTRACTIONS ON OR NEAR THE MALL

Bureau of Engraving & Printing   This is where they will literally show you the money. A staff of 2,200 works round-the-clock, Monday through Friday, churning it out at the rate of about $750 million a day. Everyone's eyes pop as they walk past rooms overflowing with new greenbacks. But the money's not the whole story. The bureau prints security documents for other federal government agencies, including military IDs and passport pages.

Many people line up each day to get a peek at all the moola, so arrive early, especially during the peak tourist season.

To save time and avoid a line, consider securing VIP, also called "congressional," tour tickets from your senator or congressperson; write or call at least 3 months in advance for tickets. These tours take place at 8:15am and 8:45am year-round, with additional tours added in the summer.

Tickets for general-public tours are generally not required from September to February; simply find the visitors entrance at 14th and C streets. March through August, however, every person taking the tour must have a ticket. To obtain a ticket, go to the ticket booth on the Raoul Wallenberg (formerly 15th St.) side of the building and show a valid photo ID. You will receive a ticket specifying a tour time for that same day and be directed to the 14th Street entrance of the bureau. You are allowed as many as four tickets per person. The ticket booth opens at 8am and closes when all tickets are dispersed for the day.

The 45-minute guided tour begins with a short introductory film. Large windows allow you to see what goes into making paper money: the inking, stacking of bills, cutting, and examination for defects. Most printing here is done from engraved steel plates in a process known as intaglio; it's the hardest to counterfeit, because the slightest alteration will cause a noticeable change in the portrait in use. Additional exhibits display bills no longer in circulation and a $100,000 bill designed for official transactions. (Since 1969, the largest denomination printed for the general public is $100.)

After you finish the tour, allow time to explore the **Visitor Center,** open from 8:30am to 3:30pm (until 7:30pm in summer), with additional exhibits and a gift shop where you can buy bags of shredded money, uncut sheets of currency in different denominations, and copies of such historic documents as the Gettysburg Address.

14th and C sts. SW. ⓒ 800/874-2330. www.moneyfactory.gov. Free admission. Sept–Mar Mon–Fri 9–10:45am and 12:30–2pm (last tour begins at 1:40pm); Apr–Aug 9–10:45am, 12:30–3:45pm, and 5–7pm. Closed Dec 25–Jan 1 and federal holidays. Metro: Smithsonian (Independence Ave. exit).

National Archives   ★The Rotunda of the National Archives displays the country's most important original documents: the Declaration of Independence, the Constitution of the United States, and the Bill of Rights (collectively known as the Charters of Freedom), as part of its exhibit, "The National Archives Experience." Fourteen document cases trace the story of the creation of the Charters and the ongoing influence of these fundamental documents on the nation and the world. A restoration of Barry Faulkner's two larger-than-life murals brings the scenes to vivid life. One mural, titled *The Declaration of Independence,* shows Thomas Jefferson presenting a draft of the Declaration to John Hancock, the presiding officer of the Continental Congress; the other, titled *The Constitution,* shows James Madison submitting the Constitution to George Washington

and the Constitutional Convention. Be sure not to miss viewing the original 1297
Magna Carta, on display as you enter the Rotunda; the document is one of only three or
four known to exist, and the only original version residing permanently in the United
States.

Public Vaults is an exhibit that features interactive technology and displays of documents and artifacts to explain the country's development in the use of records, from
Indian treaties to presidential websites. You can listen to recorded voices of past presidents as they deliberated over pressing issues of the time, and you can scour newly declassified documents. During the day, the William C. McGowan Theater continually runs
dramatic films illustrating the relationship between records and democracy in the lives of
real people, and at night it serves as a premier documentary film venue for the city. The
Lawrence F. O'Brien Gallery rotates exhibitions of Archives documents.

As a federal institution, the National Archives is charged with sifting through the
accumulated papers of a nation's official life—billions of pieces a year—and determining
what to save and what to destroy. The Archives' vast accumulation of census figures,
military records, naturalization papers, immigrant passenger lists, federal documents,
passport applications, ship manifests, maps, charts, photographs, and motion picture
film (and that's not the half of it) spans 2 centuries. Anyone age 16 and over is welcome
to use the National Archives center for genealogical research. Call for details.

The National Archives building itself is worth an admiring glance. The neoclassical
structure, designed by John Russell Pope (also the architect of the National Gallery of Art
and the Jefferson Memorial) in the 1930s, is an impressive example of the Beaux Arts
style. Seventy-two columns create a Corinthian colonnade on each of the four facades.
Great bronze doors mark the Constitution Avenue entrance, and four large sculptures
representing the Future, the Past, Heritage, and Guardianship sit on pedestals near the
entrances. Huge pediments crown both the Pennsylvania Avenue and Connecticut Avenue entrances to the building. Allow about 90 minutes to view everything.

700 Pennsylvania Ave. NW (btw. 7th and 9th sts. NW; tourists enter on Constitution Ave., researchers on
Pennsylvania Ave.). ☎ **202/357-5000.** www.archives.gov. Free admission. March 15 to Labor Day daily
10am–7pm; day after Labor Day to Mar 14 daily 10am–5:30pm. Call for research hours. Closed Dec 25.
Metro: Archives–Navy Memorial.

National Gallery of Art ★★★   This museum is such a treasure. Housing one of
the world's foremost collections of Western paintings, sculpture, and graphic arts, from
the Middle Ages into the 21st century, the National Gallery has a dual personality. The
original West Building, designed by John Russell Pope (architect of the Jefferson Memorial and the National Archives), is a neoclassical marble masterpiece with a domed
rotunda over a colonnaded fountain and high-ceilinged corridors leading to delightful
garden courts. At its completion in 1941, the building was the largest marble structure
in the world. It was a gift to the nation from financier/philanthropist Andrew W. Mellon,
who also contributed the nucleus of the collection, including 21 masterpieces from the
Hermitage, two Raphaels among them. The modern East Building, designed by I. M. Pei
and opened in 1978, is composed of two adjoining triangles with glass walls and lofty
tetrahedron skylights. The pink Tennessee marble from which both buildings were constructed was taken from the same quarry; it forms an architectural link between the two
structures.

Only a small percentage of the National Gallery's collection of 109,000 works is on
display at one time. The Gallery's permanent collection offers reason enough to visit, but
its mounted exhibitions make this museum a further must; they're always fantastic. See

the box "Museum Exhibits Scheduled for 2010," earlier in this chapter, for a small preview of a coming exhibit at the Gallery.

The West Building: From the Mall entrance, you can stop first at the **Art Information Room** to design your own tour on a computer, if you like. But don't spend too much time here. Step into the gorgeous Rotunda, which leads right and left of you to light-filled halls punctuated with sculpture; off these long corridors stem intimate **painting galleries** organized by age and nationality. To your left, as you face away from the Mall, are works by the older masters, from 13th-century Italians to 16th-century Germans. To your right are their younger counterparts, from 18th- and 19th-century French and Spanish artists to later works by British and American artists. These are creations by El Greco, Bruegel, Poussin, Vermeer, Van Dyck, Rubens, Fra Angelico, Gilbert Stuart, Winslow Homer, Constable, Turner, Mary Cassatt—you name it. The only Leonardo da Vinci painting in the Western Hemisphere hangs here, his *Ginevra de' Benci,* just another masterpiece among this bevy of masterpieces.

Descend the grand marble staircase to the ground floor, where the museum's **sculpture galleries** are columned, vaulted, and filled with light. Highlights here range from Chinese porcelain to Renaissance decorative arts to 46 wax statuettes by Degas to Honoré Daumier's entire series of bronze sculptures, including all 36 of his caricatured portrait busts of French government officials.

The **National Gallery Sculpture Garden** ★, just across 7th Street from the West Wing, takes up 2 city blocks and features open lawns; a central pool with a spouting fountain (the pool turns into an ice rink in winter); an exquisite glassed-in pavilion housing an excellent cafe; 17 sculptures by renowned artists like Roy Lichtenstein and Ellsworth Kelly (and Scott Burton, whose *Six-Part Seating* you're welcome to sit upon) and a Paris Metro sign; and informally landscaped shrubs, trees, and plants. It continues to be a hit, especially in warm weather, when people sit on the wide rim of the pool and dangle their feet in the water while they eat their lunch. Friday evenings in summer, the gallery stages live jazz performances here.

The East Building: This wing is a showcase for the museum's collection of 20th-century art, including works by Picasso, Miró, Matisse, Pollock, and Rothko; for an exhibit called **Small French Paintings,** which I love; and for the gallery's special exhibitions. But chances are, the first thing you'll notice in this wing is the famous, massive aluminum **Alexander Calder mobile** dangling in the seven-story sky-lit atrium. And here's a tip that lots of people don't know: If you make your way to the tippy-top of the East Wing, whether by elevator or stairs, you reach a level that's actually named the "Tower," the tiny setting for the gallery's ongoing series of shows highlighting artistic developments since 1970. In 2009, the Tower featured the comics- and politics-influenced paintings and drawings by American artist Philip Guston. (For anyone who remembers that the Tower was the longtime home for four Matisse cutouts, no worries; you will now find the cutouts displayed on the Concourse level of the East Wing, Mon–Sat 10am–3pm and Sun 11am–4pm.).

Altogether, you should allow at least 2 hours to tour the gallery, but you won't see everything here.

Pick up a floor plan and calendar of events at an information desk to find out about National Gallery exhibits, films, tours, lectures, and concerts. Immensely popular is the gallery's Sunday concert series, now in its 68th year, with concerts performed most Sunday evenings, October through June, at 6:30pm in the beautiful garden court of the West Building. Admission is free and seating is on a first-come basis; my suggestion is to tour the gallery in late afternoon, lingering until 6pm, when the galleries close and the queuing begins in the Rotunda. The concerts feature chamber music, string quartets, pianists, and other forms of classical music performances. Call © **202/842-6941.**

The gallery conducts school tours, wide-ranging introductory tours, and tours in several languages. The gift shop is a favorite. You'll also find several pleasing dining options—among them the concourse-level Cascade Café, which has multiple food stations; the Garden Café, on the ground floor of the West Building; and best of all, the sculpture garden's Pavilion Café (see information in chapter 6, "Views with a Meal," for more details.

On Constitution Ave. NW btw. 3rd and 7th sts. NW (on the north side of the Mall). © **202/737-4215.** www.nga.gov. Free admission. Gallery: Mon–Sat 10am–5pm; Sun 11am–6pm. Sculpture Garden: Memorial Day to Labor Day Mon–Thurs and Sat 10am–7pm, Fri 10am–9:30pm, Sun 11am–7pm; Labor Day to Memorial Day Mon–Sat 10am–5pm, Sun 11am–6pm. Closed Dec 25 and Jan 1. Metro: Archives/Navy Memorial, or Gallery Place/Verizon Center (Arena/7th and F sts. exit).

United States Holocaust Memorial Museum ★★   More than 28 million people from 132 countries have visited this museum since it opened in 1993, and the museum continues to be a top draw. In the busiest months, March through August, if you arrive without a reserved ticket specifying an admission time, you may have to wait in a lengthy line (see "Holocaust Museum Touring Tips," below).

Before you visit the museum, you might want to access its website, www.ushmm.org, and download copies of the Visitors Guide and the Permanent Exhibition Guide. These are also available at the museum, of course.

As you enter the museum, you may find the noise and bustle of so many visitors disconcerting, or at odds with the experience you expect is coming. But things settle down as you start the tour. When you enter, you will be issued an identity card of an actual victim of the Holocaust; at several points in the tour, you can find out the location and status of the person on your card—by 1945, 66% of those whose lives are documented on these cards were dead.

From its collection of more than 12,700 artifacts, the museum has organized some 900 items and 70 video monitors to reveal the Jewish experience in three parts: Nazi Assault, Final Solution, and Last Chapter. The tour begins on the fourth floor, where exhibits portray the events of 1933 to 1939, the years of the Nazi rise to power. On the third floor (documenting 1940–44), exhibits illustrate the narrowing choices of people caught up in the Nazi machine. You board a Polish freight car of the type used to transport Jews from the Warsaw ghetto to Treblinka and hear recordings of survivors telling what life in the camps was like.

 Holocaust Museum Touring Tips

Because so many people want to visit the museum (it has hosted as many as 10,000 visitors in a single day), tickets specifying a visit time (in 15-min. intervals) are required during the busiest months, March through August. Reserve as many as 40 tickets in advance via Tickets.com (© **800/400-9373;** www.tickets.com) for a small fee. If you order well in advance, you can have tickets mailed to you at home. You can also get as many as 20 same-day tickets (if available) at the museum beginning at 10am daily (lines form earlier, usually around 8am).

The second floor recounts a more heartening story: It depicts how non-Jews throughout Europe, by exercising individual action and responsibility, saved Jews at great personal risk. Denmark—led by a king who swore that if any of his subjects wore a yellow star, so would he—managed to hide and save 90% of its Jews. Exhibits follow on the liberation of the camps, life in Displaced Persons camps, emigration to Israel and America, and the Nuremberg trials. At the end of the permanent exhibition is a most compelling and heartbreaking hour-long film called *Testimony*, in which Holocaust survivors tell their stories. The tour concludes in the hexagonal Hall of Remembrance, where you can meditate and light a candle for the victims. The museum notes that most people take 2 to 3 hours on their first visit; many people take longer.

In addition to its permanent and temporary exhibitions, the museum has a Resource Center for educators, which provides materials and services to Holocaust educators and students; an interactive computer learning center; and a registry of Holocaust survivors, a library, and archives, which researchers may use to retrieve historical documents, photographs, oral histories, films, and videos.

The museum recommends not bringing children 11 and under; for older children, it's advisable to prepare them for what they'll see. You can see some parts of the museum without tickets, including two special areas on the first floor and concourse: **Daniel's Story: Remember the Children** and the **Wall of Remembrance** (Children's Tile Wall), which commemorates the 1.5 million children killed in the Holocaust, and the **Wexner Learning Center.** There's a cafeteria and museum shop on the premises.

100 Raoul Wallenberg Place SW (formerly 15th St. SW; near Independence Ave., just off the Mall). © 202/488-0400. www.ushmm.org. Free admission. Daily 10am–5:20pm, staying open later in peak seasons. Closed Yom Kippur and Dec 25. Metro: Smithsonian (12th St. and Independence Ave. SW exit).

5 MORE MUSEUMS

The Corcoran Gallery of Art ★★ This elegant art museum, a stone's throw from the White House, is a favorite party site in the city, hosting everything from inaugural balls to wedding receptions.

The first art museum in Washington, the Corcoran Gallery was housed from 1869 to 1896 in the red-brick and brownstone building that is now the Renwick. The collection outgrew its quarters and was transferred in 1897 to its present Beaux Arts building, designed by Ernest Flagg.

The collection, shown in rotating exhibits, focuses chiefly on American art. A prominent Washington banker, William Wilson Corcoran was among the first wealthy American collectors to realize the importance of encouraging and supporting this country's artists. Enhanced by further gifts and bequests, the collection comprehensively spans American art from 18th-century portraiture to 20th-century moderns like Nevelson, Warhol, and Rothko. Nineteenth-century works include Bierstadt's and Remington's imagery of the American West; Hudson River School artists; expatriates like Whistler, Sargent, and Mary Cassatt; and two giants of the late 19th century, Homer and Eakins.

The Corcoran is not exclusively an American art museum. On the first floor is the collection from the estate of Sen. William Andrews Clark, an eclectic grouping of Dutch and Flemish masters, European painters, French Impressionists, Barbizon landscapes, Delft porcelains, a Louis XVI *salon dore* (an extravagant room with gilded ornaments and paneling) transported in toto from Paris, and more. Clark's will stated that his diverse collection, which any curator would undoubtedly want to disperse among various museum departments, must be shown as a unit. He left money for a wing to house it, and the new building opened in 1928. Don't miss the small walnut-paneled room known as "Clark Landing," which showcases 19th-century French Impressionist and American art; a room of exquisite Corot landscapes; another of medieval Renaissance tapestries; and numerous Daumier lithographs donated by Dr. Armand Hammer. Allow an hour for touring the collection.

Pick up a schedule of events or check the website for information about temporary exhibits, gallery talks, concerts, art auctions, and more. There is some street parking.

The Corcoran Café is open Wednesday to Sunday 10am to 3pm staying open on Thursday until 8pm; call ℭ **202/639-1786** for more information. The Corcoran has a nice gift shop.

500 17th St. NW (btw. E St. and New York Ave.). ℭ **202/639-1700**. www.corcoran.org. $10 general admission, $8 for seniors, military, and students; admission fee may be higher for special exhibits. Always free for children 6 and under. Wed and Fri–Sun 10am–5pm; Thurs 10am–9pm. Closed Monday, Tuesday, Dec 25 and Jan 1. Metro: Farragut West (17th St. exit) or Farragut North (K St. exit).

Folger Shakespeare Library (Finds) ★ "Shakespeare taught us that the little world of the heart is vaster, deeper, and richer than the spaces of astronomy," wrote Ralph Waldo Emerson in 1864. A decade later, Amherst student Henry Clay Folger was profoundly affected by a lecture Emerson gave similarly extolling the Bard. Folger purchased an inexpensive set of Shakespeare's plays and went on to amass the world's largest (by far) collection of the Bard's works, today housed in the Folger Shakespeare Library. By 1930, when Folger and his wife, Emily, laid the cornerstone of a building to house the collection, it comprised 93,000 books, 50,000 prints and engravings, and thousands of manuscripts. The Folgers gave it all as a gift to the American people. The library opened in 1932.

The building itself has a marble facade decorated with nine bas-relief scenes from Shakespeare's plays; it is a striking example of Art Deco classicism. A statue of Puck stands in the west garden. An **Elizabethan garden** on the east side of the building is planted with flowers and herbs of the period. Most remarkable here are eight sculptures, each depicting figures from a particular scene in a Shakespeare play. Each work is welded onto the top of a pedestal, on which are inscribed the play's lines that inspired the sculptor, Greg Wyatt. These statues are half the size of those that Wyatt created for the Great Garden at New Place in Stratford-upon-Avon, England. Inquire about guided tours scheduled at 10 and 11am on every third Saturday from April to October. The garden is also a quiet place to have a picnic.

The facility, which houses some 256,000 books, 116,000 of which are rare (pre-1801), is an important research center not only for Shakespearean scholars, but also for those studying any aspect of the English and continental Renaissance. A multimedia computer exhibition called *The Shakespeare Gallery* offers users a close-up look at some of the Folgers' treasures, as well as Shakespeare's life and works. And the oak-paneled **Great Hall,** reminiscent of a Tudor long gallery, is a popular attraction for the general public. On display are rotating exhibits from the permanent collection: books, paintings, playbills, Renaissance musical instruments, and more. Plan on spending at least 30 minutes here.

At the end of the Great Hall is a theater designed to suggest an Elizabethan inn-yard where plays, concerts, readings, and Shakespeare-related events take place (see chapter 9 for details).

201 E. Capitol St. SE. ℭ **202/544-4600**. www.folger.edu. Free admission. Mon–Sat 10am–5pm. Free walk-in tours Mon–Fri at 11am and 3pm, and on Sat at 11am and 1pm. Closed federal holidays. Metro: Capitol South or Union Station.

Museums of Special Interest

To the right person, with a specific interest, these lesser-known museums can be more than fascinating. Don't try to drop in without calling because most are not open daily, and some require appointments.

Anderson House, 2118 Massachusetts Ave. NW (② 202/785-2040; www.hereditary.us/cin_anderson.htm): A century-old, 50-room mansion of amazing design and impressive art and furnishings. The mansion is headquarters for the Society of the Cincinnati, which was founded in 1783 by Continental officers (including George Washington) who had served in the American Revolution. Metro: Dupont Circle (Q St. exit).

Art Museum of the Americas ★, 201 18th St. NW, within the Organization of American States (② 202/458-6016; www.museum.oas.org): From 80 to 200 works by contemporary Latin and Caribbean artists, on display from the museum's permanent collection. An Aztec garden and a second gallery in adjoining OAS building. Metro: Farragut West (17th St. exit), then walk south about six blocks.

Daughters of the American Revolution (DAR) Museum, 1776 D St. NW (② 202/879-3241; www.dar.org/museum): Early American furnishings and decorative arts. Metro: Farragut West (17th St. exit), then walk south about 5 blocks.

Decatur House ★, 1610 H St. NW at Lafayette Park (② 202/842-0920; www.decaturhouse.org): Historic house museum with permanent collection of Federalist and Victorian furnishings. Metro: Farragut West (17th St. exit).

Frederick Douglass National Historic Site, 1411 W St. SE (② 202/426-5961; www.nps.gov/frdo): Last residence of the famous African-American 19th-century abolitionist. Metro: Anacostia, then catch bus no. B2, which stops by the house.

Hillwood Museum and Gardens, 4155 Linnean Ave. NW (② 202/686-5807; www.hillwoodmuseum.org): Magnificent estate of Marjorie Merriweather Post, who collected art and artifacts of 18th-century France and Imperial Russia. Formal gardens, grand rooms, high tea. Metro: Van Ness (exit east on Connecticut Ave.).

Hillyer Art Space, 9 Hillyer Court NW (② 202/338-0680; www.artsandartists.org/artspace.php): This new, hip little two-room gallery is an arm of International Arts & Artists and displays works of both regional and international artists in its mission to "increase cross-cultural understanding and exposure to the arts internationally." Metro: Dupont Circle (Q St. exit).

Interior Department Museum, 1849 C St. NW (② 202/208-4743; www.doi.gov/interiormuseum): Permanent exhibits relating to the work of agencies that fall within the Interior Department's jurisdiction: national parks, land management, Indian affairs, fish and wildlife services, environmental protection. Metro: Farragut West (18th St. exit), then walk about 6 blocks south.

Kreeger Museum ★, 2401 Foxhall Rd. NW (② 202/337-3050; www.kreegermuseum.org): This museum in a residential neighborhood is a treasure-trove of art from the 1850s to the 1970s, including Impressionist paintings and the works of many American artists. No Metro; take a cab.

Mary McLeod Bethune Council House National Historic Site, 1318 Vermont Ave. NW (☎ 202/673-2402; www.nps.gov/mamc): Last residence of African-American activist/educator Bethune, who was a leading champion of black and women's rights during FDR's administration. Metro: McPherson Square (Franklin Sq./14th St. exit).

National Building Museum, 401 F St. NW (☎ 202/272-2448; www.nbm.org): Housed within a historic building is this fine museum devoted to architecture, building, and historic preservation. Metro: Judiciary Square (F St. exit).

National Geographic Museum, 17th and M streets NW. (☎ 202/857-7588; www.nationalgeographic.com/museum): Rotating exhibits related to exploration, adventure, and earth sciences, using interactive programs and artifacts. Metro: Farragut North (Connecticut Ave. and L St. exit).

Old Stone House, 3051 M St. NW (☎ 202/426-6851; www.nps.gov/olst): A 1765 structure said to be the oldest in D.C. still standing on its original foundations. Colonial appearance, English garden. Metro: Foggy Bottom, with a 15-minute walk.

Sewall-Belmont House, 144 Constitution Ave. NE (☎ 202/546-1210; www.sewallbelmont.org): A must for those interested in women's history, the historic house displays memorabilia of the women's suffrage movement, which got its start here. Metro: Union Station.

State Department Diplomatic Reception Rooms, 2201 D St. NW (entrance on 23rd St. NW; ☎ 202/647-3241; https://receptiontours.state.gov): This is a fine-arts tour of rooms that serve as our country's main stage for international diplomacy. The rooms house a premier collection of Early American paintings, furniture, and decorative arts, dating from 1740. Metro: Foggy Bottom.

Textile Museum ★, 2320 S St. NW (☎ 202/667-0441; www.textilemuseum.org): Historic and contemporary handmade textile arts, housed in historic John Russell Pope mansion. Metro: Dupont Circle, Q Street exit, then walk a couple of blocks up Massachusetts Avenue until you see S Street. A second location is located at 421 7th St. NW. Metro: Gallery Place/Verizon Center (7th and F sts. exit).

United States Navy Memorial and Naval Heritage Center, 701 Pennsylvania Ave. NW (☎ 202/737-2300; www.lonesailor.org): Plaza honors men and women of the U.S. Navy; museum features interactive video kiosks used to learn about Navy ships, aircraft, and history. Metro: Archives–Navy Memorial.

Woodrow Wilson House, 2340 S St. NW (☎ 202/387-4062; www.woodrowwilsonhouse.org): The former home of this president, preserved the way it was when he lived here in the 1920s. Docents guide visitors on hour-long tours, pointing out noteworthy objects and telling stories about the 28th president. Metro: Dupont Circle, Q Street exit, then walk a couple of blocks up Massachusetts Avenue until you reach S Street.

Ford's Theatre and Lincoln Museum (**Kids**) On April 14, 1865, President Abraham Lincoln was in the audience at Ford's Theatre, one of the most popular playhouses in Washington. Everyone was laughing at a funny line from Tom Taylor's celebrated comedy, *Our American Cousin,* when John Wilkes Booth crept into the president's box, shot the president, and leapt to the stage, shouting, *"Sic semper tyrannis!"* ("Thus ever to tyrants!"). With his left leg broken from the vault, Booth mounted his horse in the alley and galloped off. Doctors carried Lincoln across the street to the house of William Petersen, where the president died the next morning.

The theater was closed after Lincoln's assassination and used as an office by the War Department. In 1893, 22 clerks were killed when three floors of the building collapsed. It remained in disuse until the 1960s, when it was remodeled and restored to its appearance on the night of the tragedy.

A much-needed renovation of the theater was completed in 2009, just in time to celebrate the bicentennial of Lincoln's birthday on February 12. Among the improvements: enhanced acoustics, better seating, a remodeled lobby and dressing rooms—enhancements that don't change the essential historic nature of the theater. The President's Box is still on view, and no, you are not allowed to enter it and sit where Lincoln sat. Ford's remains a working theater, so be sure to consider attending a play: *The Rivalry,* by Norman Corwin, which re-creates the debates that Lincoln engaged in with Stephen Douglas; and the musical, *Little Shop of Horrors,* are two productions scheduled for the 2010 season.

Free tours of the theater take place daily, 9am to 5pm, but tickets are required. Order the tickets online, for a small processing fee, or pick up same-day passes at the theater. Tours include either a National Park Service Ranger's interpretive program or a mini-play, each designed to educate the audience about the Civil War in Washington and the events of April 14, 1865. Only the final tours of the day allow visitors to walk through the theater on their own.

The tiny Lincoln Museum on the level below the theater was still under renovation at press time. By the time you read this, the museum should have re-opened and been incorporated into your tour. Also visit the Petersen House across the street.

517 10th St. NW (btw. E and F sts.). (©) **202/426-6925.** www.fords.org. Daily 9am–5pm. Free tours offered on the hour, throughout the day. Metro: Metro Center (11th and G sts. exit).

The House Where Lincoln Died (the Petersen House) (**Kids**) After Lincoln was mortally wounded at Ford's Theatre, the doctors attending him had him carried out into the street, where boarder Henry Safford, standing in the open doorway of his rooming house, gestured for them to bring the president inside. So Lincoln died in the home of William Petersen, a German-born tailor. Now furnished with period pieces, the dark, narrow town house looks much as it did on that fateful April night. It takes about 5 minutes to troop through the building. You'll see the front parlor where an anguished Mary Todd Lincoln spent the night with her son, Robert. In the back parlor, Secretary of War Edwin M. Stanton held a cabinet meeting and questioned witnesses. From this room, Stanton announced at 7:22am on April 15, 1865, "Now he belongs to the ages." Lincoln died, lying diagonally because he was so tall, on a bed the size of the one in the room. (The Chicago Historical Society owns the actual bed and other items from the room.) In 1896, the government bought the house for $30,000, and it is now maintained by the National Park Service.

516 10th St. NW. (©) **202/426-6924.** Free admission. Daily 9am–5pm. Closed Dec 25. Metro: Metro Center.

International Spy Museum ★★ (Kids) A visit here begins with a 5-minute briefing **209** film, followed by a fun indoctrination into "Tricks of the Trade." Interactive monitors test one's powers of observation and teach you what to look for when it comes to suspicious activity. In addition to surveillance games, this first section displays trick equipment (such as a shoe transmitter used by Soviets as a listening device and a single-shot pistol disguised as a lipstick tube) and runs film in which spies talk about bugging devices and locks and picks. You can watch a video that shows individuals being made up for disguise, and you can crawl on your belly through ductwork in the ceiling overhead. (The conversations you hear are taped, not floating up from the room of tourists below.)

Try to pace yourself, though, because there's still so much to see; and you can easily reach your limit before you get through the 68,000-square-foot museum. The next section covers the history of spying (the second-oldest profession) and tells about famous spy masters over time, from Moses; to Sun Tzu, the Chinese general, who wrote *The Art of War* in 400 B.C.; to George Washington, whose Revolutionary War letter of 1777 setting up a network of spies in New York is on view. Learn about the use of codes and code-breaking in spying, with one room of the museum devoted to the Enigma cipher machine used by the Germans (whose "unbreakable" codes the Allied cryptanalysts succeeded in deciphering) in World War II. An actual Enigma machine is displayed; interactive monitors allow you to simulate the experience of using an Enigma machine while learning more about its invention and inventor.

Much more follows: artifacts from all over (this is the largest collection of international espionage artifacts ever put on public display); a re-created tunnel beneath the divided city of Berlin during the Cold War; the intelligence-gathering stories of those behind enemy lines and of those involved in planning D-day in World War II; an exhibit on escape and evasion techniques in wartime; the tales of spies of recent times, told by the CIA and FBI agents involved in identifying them; and a mock-up of an intelligence agency's 21st-century operations center.

The museum's newest feature is **Operation Spy,** a 1-hour interactive immersion into espionage activities. Participants pretend to be intelligence officers and work in small teams as they conduct video surveillance of clandestine meetings, decrypt secret audio conversations, conduct polygraph tests, and so on, all in a day's work for a real-life spy. (You pay to play: a hefty $14 for those 12 and older, or $25 for combined admission to both the museum and this special feature.)

Note: Neither the main museum nor Operation Spy are recommended for children 11 and under.

You exit the museum directly to its gift shop, which leads to the Spy City Café.

While you may look with suspicion on everyone around you when you leave the museum, you can trust that what you've just learned at the museum is authoritative. The Spy Museum's executive director was with the CIA for 36 years, and his advisory board includes two former CIA directors, two former CIA disguise chiefs, and a retired KGB general.

Consider ordering advance tickets for next-day or future-date tours on the Spy Museum's website, which offers you the choice of printing your tickets at home or picking them up at the Will Call desk inside the museum. You can also purchase advance tickets, including those for tours later in the day, at the box office.

800 F St. NW (at 8th St. NW). ✆ **866/779-6873** or 202/393-7798. www.spymuseum.org. Admission $18 adults (ages 12–65), $17 for seniors, $15 for children ages 5–11. Operation Spy: $14 for ages 12 and up. Combined admission fee $25. Open daily, but hours vary; generally, the museum opens at 9am or 10am and closes most of the time at 6pm, but sometimes later, rarely earlier. Check website for details. Closed Thanksgiving, Dec 25, and Jan 1. Metro: Gallery Place/Chinatown (9th and G sts. exit) or National Archive/Navy Memorial.

Madame Tussauds Washington D.C. (Kids) Seven other Madame Tussauds exist, only two others are located in the U.S., and only one allows you the pleasure of sizing up George Washington, mingling with Beyoncé, helping Tiger Woods line up his putt, or discussing the state of the world up close and personal with Pres. Barack Obama and Michelle Obama. Madame Tussauds is a wax museum whose life-size wax figure replicas of famous Americans and historic icons appear in one of four sections: The Spirit of Washington, D.C.; Behind the Scenes; Glamour; and Sports. Interactive displays allow visitors to step into the pictures of historic, celebrity, and sports events, whether to attend George Washington's inauguration or to hang with Julia Roberts. You'll know you've found the museum when you spot Whoopi Goldberg's figure waiting to welcome you, just outside the museum. (During the celebration of Lincoln's bicentennial in 2009, Lincoln stood in for Whoopi.)

1025 F St. NW (btw. 10th and 11th sts.). ✆ **888/929-4632** or 202/942-7300. www.madametussaudsdc. com. Admission $20 adults, $15 children. Mid Apr–early Sep Sun–Fri 10am–6pm, Sat 10am–8pm; early Sep–mid Apr Sun–Thurs 10am–6pm, Fri–Sat 10am–8pm. Metro: Metro Center (11th and G sts. exit).

Marian Koshland Science Museum The National Academy of Sciences operates this small museum, which was conceived by molecular biologist Daniel Koshland, in memory of his wife, the immunologist and molecular biologist Marian Koshland, who died in 1997. The museum opened in April 2004 in the heart of downtown D.C. Recommended for children 14 and over, and especially for those with a scientific bent, the museum presents state-of-the-art exhibits that explore the complexities of science. (Do pay attention to the museum's age recommendation; I had a hard time wrapping my brain around the various exhibits, interesting though they were, and I'm a little bit older than 13.) Three exhibits currently on show are the Wonders of Science, which includes animations of groundbreaking research and an introductory film about the nature of science; Global Warming Facts and Our Future; and Infectious Disease, which covers the challenges to human health.

6th and E sts. NW. ✆ **202/334-1201.** www.koshlandsciencemuseum.org. Admission $5 adults, $3 ages 5–18 and seniors (65+). Wed–Mon 10am–6pm. Closed Thanksgiving, Dec. 25, and Jan 1. Metro: Gallery Place/Chinatown or Judiciary Square.

National Museum of Crime and Punishment No kidding, this museum has the feel of a haunted house, complete with dark passages, faux stone walls, a crawl space, and scary figures—mannequins dressed up as dangerous characters—placed here and there. Personally, I find it lame, but I am definitely in the minority, as you'll likely observe if you visit on a Saturday when the single-file line to get in extends out the door. Located in the heart of the Penn Quarter, the museum occupies three floors of a renovated town house, which limits the numbers of people who can shuffle through its five main chambers at any one time. Most of the museum offers a history of crime and punishment, along with tales of famous criminals, from the Middle Ages to the present.

Interactive exhibits allow visitors to place head and hands through a pillory, crack a safe, compare shooting skills to those of Old West outlaws, take a lie detector test, and simulate a police motorcycle chase. Exhibits display a hodgepodge of weapons, including hand irons and spiked chairs used to torture baddies during the Middle Ages. A replica **211** of Wild Bill Hickock's revolver joins other sundry artifacts and objects such as sample prison garb, a re-creation of Al Capone's jail cell, John Dillinger's brilliant red 1933 Essex Terraplane car, and the getaway car used in the 1964 film, *Bonnie and Clyde*.

The last section of the museum explores crime fighting and solving, encouraging one to channel his or her inner detective to solve a case using interactive kiosks within a replica crime-scene lab. On the lower level of the museum is the *America's Most Wanted* TV studio, from which John Walsh occasionally broadcasts the show. (John Walsh is a partner in the privately owned museum.) The museum operates a gift shop, the Cop Shop.

575 7th St. NW (at E St.). (✆) **202/393-1099.** www.crimemuseum.org. Order tickets online or by calling (✆) 202/621-5550. Adults $18 plus tax; seniors, military, and children $15 plus tax; free for children 5 and under. Walk-up ticket prices are $20 for adults, $17 for seniors and military, $15 for children. Daily Sept 1–Mar 19 10am–8pm; Mar 20–Aug 31 9am–9pm. Metro: Gallery Place/Verizon Center (7th and F sts./ Arena exit), or Archives/Navy Memorial.

National Museum of Women in the Arts Now in its 23rd year, this museum remains the world's foremost collection dedicated to celebrating "the contribution of women to the history of art." Founders Wilhelmina and Wallace Holladay, who donated the core of the permanent collection—more than 250 works by women from the 16th to the 20th century—became interested in women's art in the 1960s. After discovering that no women were included in H. W. Janson's *History of Art*, a standard text (which did not address this oversight until 1986!), the Holladays began collecting art by women, and the concept of a women's art museum soon evolved.

Since its opening, the collection has grown to more than 3,000 works by more than 800 artists, including Rosa Bonheur, Frida Kahlo, Helen Frankenthaler, Barbara Hepworth, Georgia O'Keeffe, Camille Claudel, Lila Cabot Perry, Mary Cassatt, Elaine de Kooning, Käthe Kollwitz, and many other lesser-known artists from earlier centuries. You will discover here, for instance, that the famed Peale family of 19th-century portrait painters included a talented sister, Sarah Miriam Peale. The collection is complemented by an ongoing series of changing exhibits. You should allow an hour for touring.

The museum is housed in a magnificent Renaissance Revival landmark building designed in 1907 as a Masonic temple by noted architect Waddy Wood. Its sweeping marble staircase and splendid interior make it a popular choice for wedding receptions. Lunch (weekdays only) in the Mezzanine Café (✆) **202/628-1068**), and you'll be surrounded by works from the museum's permanent collection.

1250 New York Ave. NW (at 13th St.). (✆) **800/222-7270** or 202/783-5000. www.nmwa.org. $10 adults, $8 students 18 and over with ID and seniors 60 and over, free for youth 18 and under. (These are general admission rates; special exhibition prices may be higher.) Mon–Sat 10am–5pm; Sun noon–5pm. Closed Thanksgiving, Dec 25, and Jan 1. Metro: Metro Center (13th St. exit).

Newseum ★★ Open since April 11, 2008, the Newseum is as much a fun house of participatory experiences and special-effects exhibits as it is a museum. In fact, the Newseum's tag line, "World's Most Interactive Museum," conveys its purpose in allowing the visitor to step into the picture: to play the reporter, TV journalist, researcher, or editor. The museum boasts 125 interactive game stations, 2 state-of-the-art broadcast studios, 14 galleries, and 15 theaters. At this particular time in history, with the business of journalism undergoing a world of change, the six-story Newseum manages to capture the magic of past, current, and future ways of covering the news.

First, take a look at the exterior, best viewed from across Pennsylvania Avenue. Covering the left side of the facade is a 75-foot-high tablet inscribed with words from the First Amendment ("Congress shall make no law . . . abridging the freedom of speech or of the press . . . "). Through its glass front, one can see (though much better at night) the huge high-definition screen hanging inside the atrium, spinning news story images. When you cross the street to enter the museum, you walk by a display of the day's front pages electronically obtained from newspapers across the country and around the world. Once inside, staff direct you first to the orientation film on the lower level (personally, I'd say skip this), then to the glass elevators that shoot you to the sixth floor. The outdoor promenade on its own is worth the price of admission, since it offers you a breathtaking view of Pennsylvania Avenue and the Capitol. Also take time to read the fascinating history of Pennsylvania Avenue and of the city, presented in an exhibit that runs the length of the terrace.

Fifth-floor exhibits cover history. A display of "Great Books" presents 20 books and documents (originals, not copies) that are widely considered our "cornerstones of freedom." These include the 1475 printing of Thomas Aquinas's "Summa Theologica" and a 1215 edition of the Magna Carta. Next to the display is a touch screen; touch the image of the book you'd like to examine and the screen presents that book, allowing you to scroll through the first few pages. Nearby, the History Gallery showcases the Newseum's extensive collection of historic newspapers and magazines, tracing 500 years of news. Several theaters on this floor continuously play short documentaries in which esteemed journalists talk about ethics, sources, "getting it right," and other topics.

On the fourth floor, the First Amendment Gallery explores the historical contexts of the five freedoms. The 9/11 Gallery displays items recovered at the World Trade Center, images and reporting from that day, and an 11-minute film featuring personal stories by journalists who covered the attacks. While at first glance it appears to be a modern sculpture, one artifact on display here is in fact a 360-foot piece of the antenna that had stood on top of the North Tower.

On the third floor, check out the display of *New Yorker* cartoons joshing the news. In the World News Gallery, you can tune in to a current news broadcast from one of many countries. (I listened briefly to a report from France on the Tour de France.) The "Dateline: Danger" exhibit displays artifacts from hazardous missions that journalists have undertaken—including the laptop computer used by *Wall Street Journal* reporter Daniel Pearl before he was killed and the bloodstained notebook of *TIME* magazine reporter Michael Weisskopf, who lost his hand in an explosion in Iraq. Following that exhibit is the Journalists Memorial, a sobering display of 1,843 names written in a glass tablet to mark the deaths of those journalists who have died in pursuit of the news between 1837 and 2007. Elsewhere on this floor are several studios used by news organizations—including NPR and ABC—to broadcast programs. Visitors can sit in the audience during broadcasts or take behind-the-scenes tours when the studios are not in use.

A veritable playground for news junkies of all ages awaits on the second floor. An interactive newsroom with 48 kiosks allows you to test your skills as a photojournalist, editor, reporter, or anchor. An ethics center tests your sense of ethics. And, for a price ($8.50), you can try your hand at news anchor, reading from a teleprompter as a staff person tapes you, then watching your performance on screen.

The first floor's gallery of Pulitzer Prize photographs leaves one speechless. The gallery's database of interviews with some of the photographers, a documentary, and vignettes accompanying the photos offer fascinating context to the craft and to the stories behind the photographs.

Last but not least, return to the concourse level to view the I-Witness, a 4-D film feature that makes you feel as if you're on the scene with legends Isaiah Thomas (radical printer, not basketball legend), Nellie Bly, and Edward R. Murrow. I'm not saying another word, except: Don't miss it.

The Newseum's on-site restaurant, the Source, is already a favorite of Washingtonians. The museum has several gift shops.

555 Pennsylvania Ave. NW (at 6th St.). © **888/NEWSEUM** (639-7386). www.newseum.org. $20 adults, $18 seniors 65 and older, $13 youth 7–12, free for children 6 and under. Daily 9am–5pm. (Closed Thanksgiving, Dec 25, and Jan 1. Metro: Judiciary Sq. (4th St. exit), Gallery Place/Verizon Center (7th and F sts./ Arena exit), or Archives/Navy Memorial.

Phillips Collection ★★   The centerpiece of this charming museum is its elegant 1890s Georgian Revival mansion, the gallery's anchor since the Phillips opened in 1921, making it America's first museum of modern art. Founders Duncan and Marjorie Phillips, avid collectors and proselytizers of modernism, once lived here; now Impressionist, modernist, and American master gems from the 2,500-work permanent collection reside here. Intimate galleries retain homey features: leaded- and stained-glass windows, oak paneling, plush chairs and sofas, and individually designed fireplaces. A new wing completed in 2006 doubled the original space and now houses the main entrance, as well as galleries devoted to special exhibits; a cafe run by the clever On the Fly folks (see the "Eating on the Fly" box, earlier in this chapter); a sculpture garden in the courtyard; and, most wonderfully, the Rothko Room, the small room devoted to four large, color-intense paintings by abstract expressionist Mark Rothko.

Best known for its Renoir masterpiece, *Luncheon of the Boating Party,* the Phillips boasts works by Daumier, Bonnard, Vuillard, van Gogh, Cézanne, Picasso, Degas, Klee, and Matisse. Ingres, Delacroix, Manet, El Greco, Goya, Corot, Constable, Courbet, Giorgione, and Chardin are among the premodernists represented. American notables, besides Rothko, include Dove, Hopper, Marin, Eakins, Homer, Lawrence, and O'Keeffe. You'll enjoy viewing the collection for an hour or so.

A full schedule of events includes temporary shows with loans from other museums and private collections, gallery talks, and concerts in the ornate music room. Concerts take place October to May on Sunday at 4pm; arrive early. On Thursday, the museum stays open until 8:30pm for **Phillips After Five,** evenings of live jazz, a cash bar, modern art and gallery talks.

Note: You may tour the permanent collection for free on weekdays, though a donation is welcome. Weekends, when there is no special exhibit, admission is $10 per adult, $8 for seniors and students 18 and older. When the museum is staging a special exhibit, you pay the special-exhibit admission price, usually $12 per adult, $10 per student or senior, which covers entry to both the permanent and special collections. The Phillips almost always has a special exhibition on view. You may order tickets in advance at the Phillips, or through Ticketmaster, online at www.ticketmaster.com, or by phone at © **800/551-SEAT** (7328).

1600 21st St. NW (at Q St.). © **202/387-2151.** www.phillipscollection.org. Admission: See information in the note, above. Tues–Sat 10am–5pm year-round (Thurs until 8:30pm); Sun 11am–6pm. Call ahead for information and admission prices on special exhibits. Closed federal holidays. Metro: Dupont Circle (Q St. exit).

John F. Kennedy Center for the Performing Arts ★   Opened in 1971, the Kennedy Center is both the national performing arts center and a memorial to John F. Kennedy. Set on 17 acres overlooking the Potomac and designed by noted architect Edward Durell Stone, the striking facility encompasses an opera house, a concert hall, two stage theaters, a theater lab, and a theater devoted exclusively to family productions.

The best way to experience the Kennedy Center is to attend a performance. Check the website or call the toll-free number below for information about Kennedy Center happenings and prices. See chapter 9 for specifics on theater, concert, and dance offerings, including highlights of the 2009–10 season. The Center also offers free 50-minute guided tours, which include some restricted areas.

Tours depart from the lower level, Level A, in the Hall of States. You tour the **Hall of Nations,** which displays the flags of all nations diplomatically recognized by the United States. Throughout the center you'll see gifts from more than 60 nations, including all the marble used in the building (3,700 tons), which Italy donated. First stop is the **Grand Foyer,** scene of many free concerts and programs and the reception area for all three theaters on the main level; the 18 crystal chandeliers are a gift from Sweden. You'll also visit the **Israeli Lounge** (where 40 painted and gilded panels depict musical scenes from the Old Testament); the **Concert Hall,** home of the National Symphony Orchestra; the **Opera House;** the **African Lounge** (decorated with beautiful tapestries and other artwork from African nations); the **Eisenhower Theater;** the **Hall of States,** where flags of the 50 states and four territories are hung in the order in which they joined the Union; the **Performing Arts Library;** and the **Terrace Theater,** a bicentennial gift from Japan. If there's a rehearsal going on, the tour skips the visits to the theaters.

Tours are offered in many languages, including French, German, Spanish, and Japanese, but you should contact the center in advance to arrange for a tour in a particular language. You can beat the crowds by writing in advance to a senator or congressperson for passes for a free congressional ("VIP") tour. Call ✆ **202/416-8340** for details.

Tours conclude on the roof terrace of the Kennedy Center, where you're invited to walk around the terrace perimeter, enjoying a panoramic view of Washington.

2700 F St. NW (at New Hampshire Ave. NW and Rock Creek Pkwy.). ✆ **800/444-1324,** or 202/467-4600 for information or tickets. www.kennedy-center.org. Free admission. Daily 10am–midnight. Free guided tours Mon–Fri 10am–5pm; Sat–Sun 10am–1pm. Metro: Foggy Bottom (free shuttle service btw. the station and the center, running every 15 min. 9:45am–midnight weekdays, 10am–midnight Sat, and noon–midnight Sun). Bus: 80 from Metro Center. Parking $17.

Library of Congress ★   You're inside the main public building of the Library of Congress, the magnificent, ornate Italian Renaissance–style **Thomas Jefferson Building.** Maybe you've arrived via the tunnel that connects the Capitol and the Library of Congress, or maybe you've entered through the First Street doors. In any case, you may be startled suddenly to find yourself inside a government structure whose every surface is covered in detailed embellishment. Before you line up for that tour or enmesh yourself in the library's literature, stroll around the building, from ground floor to the Great Hall, to the Main Reading Room Overlook, and just gape. Look up to admire the stained glass skylights overhead, glance down to notice the marble floors inlaid with brass and concentric medallions, gaze right, left, and all around to try and take in the gorgeous murals, paintings, stenciling, sculptures, and intricately carved architectural elements that make this building a visual treasure.

Now for the history lesson: Established in 1800 by an act of Congress, "for the purchase of such books as may be necessary for the use of Congress," the library today also serves the nation, with holdings for the visually impaired (for whom books are recorded on cassette and/or translated into Braille), scholars in every field, college students, journalists, teachers, and researchers of all kinds. Its first collection of books was destroyed in 1814 when the British burned the Capitol (where the library was then housed) during the War of 1812. Thomas Jefferson then sold the institution his personal library of 6,487 books as a replacement, and this became the foundation of what would grow to become the world's largest library.

Today, the collection contains a mind-boggling 142 million items. Its buildings house more than 32 million cataloged books; 62 million manuscripts; millions and millions of prints and photographs, audio holdings (discs, tapes, talking books, and so on), movies, and videotapes; musical instruments from the 1700s; and the letters and papers of everyone from George Washington to Groucho Marx. Its archives also include the letters, oral histories, photographs, and other documents of war veterans from World War I to the present, all part of its **Veterans History Project;** go to www.loc.gov/vets to listen to or read some of these stories, especially if you plan on visiting the National World War II Memorial.

The Jefferson Building was erected between 1888 and 1897 to hold the burgeoning collection and to establish America as a cultured nation with magnificent institutions equal to anything in Europe. Fifty-two painters and sculptors worked for 8 years on its interior. There are floor mosaics of Italian marble, allegorical paintings on the overhead vaults, more than 100 murals, and numerous ornamental cornucopias, ribbons, vines, and garlands. The building's exterior has 42 granite sculptures and yards of bas-reliefs. A 160-foot-high dome crowns the Main Reading Room. Originally intended to hold the fruits of at least 150 years of collecting, the Jefferson Building was, in fact, filled up in a mere 13 years. It is now supplemented by the **James Madison Memorial Building** and the **John Adams Building**.

The question most frequently asked by visitors to the Library of Congress is "Where are the books?" They are on the 650 miles of shelves located throughout the library's three buildings: the Thomas Jefferson, James Madison Memorial, and John Adams buildings.

In addition to its art and architecture, the Library displays ongoing exhibits of objects taken from its permanent collections; "Exploring the Early Americas" and "Creating the United States" are two shows that may still be going on, when you read this. The library also hosts a smorgasbord of events, including a free movie and concert series. Be sure to check the LOC website before you come. Concerts take place in the Jefferson Building's elegant **Coolidge Auditorium.** The concerts are free but require tickets, which you can obtain through Ticketmaster (© **800/551-7328**). Across Independence Avenue from the Jefferson Building is the **Madison Building,** which houses the Copyright Office and the **Mary Pickford Theater,** a venue for classic film screenings.

Anyone 18 and over may use the library's collections, but first you must obtain a user card with your photo on it. Go to Reader Registration in Room LM 140 (street level of the Madison Building) and present a driver's license or passport. Then head to the Information Desk in either the Jefferson or Madison buildings to find out about the research resources available to you and how to use them. Most likely, you will be directed to the Main Reading Room. All books must be used on-site.

101 Independence Ave. SE (at 1st St. SE). ✆ **202/707-8000.** www.loc.gov. Free admission. Madison Building Mon–Fri 8:30am–9:30pm; Sat 8:30am–5pm. Jefferson Building Mon–Sat 8:30am–4:30pm. Closed federal holidays. Stop at the information desk inside the Jefferson Building's west entrance on 1st St. for information. Docent-led tours are free, require no reservations nor tickets, and take place Mon–Fri at 10:30 and 11:30am, and 1:30, 2:30, and 3:30pm; Sat 10:30 and 11:30am, and 1:30 and 2:30pm. Contact your congressional representatives to obtain tickets for congressional, or "VIP," tours, a slightly more personal tour. Metro: Capitol South.

Union Station ★   When you visit Union Station, you're stepping into the heart (or at least into a major artery) of everyday Washington life. Located within walking distance and full view of the Capitol, the station is a vital crossroads for locals. You'll see Hill staffers who debark the Metro's Red Line at its stop here ("Union Station" is the station name, naturally); commuters who ride MARC and Amtrak trains from outlying cities such as Baltimore; residents who walk or Metro here to shop, work, dine, or dawdle; and travelers from all over who arrive and depart by train all day long. Paths collide, quite literally sometimes, as ambling visitors and people running to catch a train crisscross the same ground.

When it opened in 1907, this was the largest train station in the world. It was designed by noted architect Daniel H. Burnham, who modeled it after the Baths of Diocletian and Arch of Constantine in Rome. Its facade includes Ionic colonnades fashioned from white granite and 100 sculptured eagles. Graceful 50-foot Constantine arches mark the entryways, above which are poised six carved fixtures representing Fire, Electricity, Freedom, Imagination, Agriculture, and Mechanics. Inside is the **Main Hall,** a massive rectangular room with a 96-foot barrel-vaulted ceiling, an expanse of white-marble flooring, and a balcony adorned with 36 Augustus Saint-Gaudens sculptures of Roman legionnaires. Off the Main Hall is the **East Hall,** shimmering with scagliola marble walls and columns, a gorgeous hand-stenciled skylight ceiling, and stunning murals of classical scenes inspired by ancient Pompeian art. (Today this is the station's most pleasant shopping venue: less crowded and noisy, with small vendors selling pretty jewelry and other accessories.)

In its time, this "temple of transport" has witnessed many important events. President Wilson welcomed General Pershing here in 1918 on his return from France. South Pole explorer Rear Admiral Richard Byrd was also feted at Union Station on his homecoming. And Franklin D. Roosevelt's funeral train, bearing his casket, was met here in 1945 by thousands of mourners.

But after the 1960s, with the decline of rail travel, the station fell on hard times. Rain caused parts of the roof to cave in; and the entire building—with floors buckling, rats running about, and mushrooms sprouting in damp rooms—was sealed in 1981. That same year, Congress enacted legislation to preserve and restore this national treasure, to the tune of $160 million. The remarkable restoration involved hundreds of European and American artisans who were meticulous in returning the station to its original design.

At least 32 million people come through Union Station's doors yearly. About 120 retail and food shops on three levels offer a wide array of merchandise and dining options. The sky-lit **Main Concourse,** which extends the entire length of the station, is the primary shopping area as well as a ticketing and baggage facility. A nine-screen **cinema complex** lies on the lower level, across from the Food Court. You could spend half a day here shopping or about 20 minutes touring. Stop by the visitor kiosk in the Main Hall. See chapter 8 for information about Union Station **shops.**

Washington National Cathedral ★ Pierre L'Enfant's 1791 plan for the capital
city included "a great church for national purposes." Possibly because of early America's
fear of mingling church and state, more than a century elapsed before the foundation for
Washington National Cathedral was laid. Its actual name is the Cathedral Church of St.
Peter and St. Paul. The church is Episcopal, but it has no local congregation and seeks to
serve the entire nation as a house of prayer for all people. It has been the setting for every
kind of religious observance, from Jewish to Serbian Orthodox.

A church of this magnitude—it's the sixth-largest cathedral in the world, and the
second-largest in the U.S.—took a long time to build. Its principal (but not original)
architect, Philip Hubert Frohman, worked on the project from 1921 until his death in
1972. The foundation stone was laid in 1907 using the mallet with which George Washington set the Capitol cornerstone. Construction was interrupted by both world wars
and by periods of financial difficulty. The cathedral was completed with the placement
of the final stone on the west front towers on September 29, 1990, 83 years (to the day)
after it was begun.

English Gothic in style (with several distinctly 20th-c. innovations, such as a stained-
glass window commemorating the flight of *Apollo 11* and containing a piece of moon
rock), the cathedral is built in the shape of a cross, complete with flying buttresses and
110 gargoyles. Along with the Capitol and the Washington Monument, it is one of the
dominant structures on the Washington skyline. Its 57-acre landscaped grounds have two
lovely gardens (the lawn is ideal for picnicking), four schools, a greenhouse, and two gift
shops.

The cathedral is a truly historic place. Services to celebrate the end of World Wars I
and II were held here. It was the scene of President Wilson's funeral (he and his wife are
buried here), as well as President Eisenhower's. Helen Keller and her companion, Anne
Sullivan, were buried in the cathedral at her request. And during the Iranian crisis, a
round-the-clock prayer vigil was held in the Holy Spirit Chapel throughout the hostages'
captivity. When they were released, the hostages came to a service here. President Bush's
National Prayer and Remembrance service on September 14, 2001, following the cata-
clysm of September 11, was held here.

The best way to explore the cathedral is to take a 30-minute **guided tour;** the tours
leave continually from the west end of the nave. You can also walk through on your own,
using a self-guiding brochure available in several languages. Call about group and special-
interest tours, both of which require reservations and fees (© **202/537-5700**). Allow
additional time to tour the grounds or "close" and to visit the **Observation Gallery** ★,
where 70 windows provide panoramic views. Tuesday- and Wednesday-afternoon tours
are followed by a high tea in the Observation Gallery for $25 per person; reservations
required. Call © **202/537-8993** or book online at www.visit.cathedral.org/tea.

The cathedral hosts numerous events: organ recitals; choir performances; an annual
flower mart; calligraphy workshops; jazz, folk, and classical concerts; and the playing of
the 53-bell carillon. Check the cathedral's website for schedules.

EXPLORING WASHINGTON, D.C.

7

OTHER ATTRACTIONS

Massachusetts and Wisconsin aves. NW (entrance on Wisconsin Ave.). ℂ **202/537-6200.** www.national
cathedral.org. Donation $5 adults, $3 seniors, $15 families. Cathedral Mon–Fri 10am–5:30pm; Sat 10am–
4:30pm; Sun 8am–5pm; May 1 to Labor Day, the nave level stays open Mon–Fri until 8pm. Gardens daily
until dusk. Regular tours Mon–Fri 10–11:30am and 12:45–4pm; Sat 10–11:30am, 12:45–3:30pm; Sun
1–2:30pm. No tours on Palm Sunday, Easter, Thanksgiving, Dec 25, or during services. Services vary
throughout the year, but you can count on a weekday Evensong service at 5:30pm, a weekday noon
service, and an 11am service every Sun; call for other service times. Metro: Tenleytown, with a 20-min.
walk. Bus: Any N bus up Massachusetts Ave. from Dupont Circle or any 30-series bus along Wisconsin Ave.
This is a stop on the Old Town Trolley Tour. Parking garage free on Sun; flat rate of $6 on Sat; $4 per
hour/$16 maximum weekdays until 4pm and a flat rate of $5 after 4pm.

7 JUST ACROSS THE POTOMAC: ARLINGTON NATIONAL CEMETERY

The land that today comprises Arlington County originally was carved out of Virginia as part of the nation's new capital district. In 1847, the land was returned to the state of Virginia. It was known as Alexandria County until 1920, when the name was changed to avoid confusion with the city of Alexandria.

The county got its name from its famous estate, Arlington House, built by a descendant of Martha Washington, George Washington Parke Custis, whose daughter married Robert E. Lee. The Lees lived in Arlington House on and off until the onset of the Civil War in 1861. After the first Battle of Bull Run, at Manassas, several Union soldiers were buried here; the beginnings of Arlington National Cemetery date from that time. The Arlington Memorial Bridge leads directly from the Lincoln Memorial to the Robert E. Lee Memorial at Arlington House, symbolically joining these two figures into one Union after the Civil War.

Arlington has long been a residential community, with most people commuting into Washington to work and play. In recent years, however, the suburb has come into its own, booming with businesses, restaurants, and nightlife, giving residents reasons to stay put and tourists more incentive to visit (see "Electric Avenues for Live-Music Lovers," in chapter 9). Here are some sites worth seeing:

Arlington National Cemetery ★★   Upon arrival, head over to the **Visitor Center,** where you can view exhibits, pick up a detailed map, use the restrooms (there are no others until you get to Arlington House), and purchase a **Tourmobile ticket** ($7.50 per adult, $3.75 for children 3–11), which allows you to stop at all major sites in the cemetery and then reboard whenever you like. Service is continuous and the narrated commentary is informative; this is the only guided tour of the cemetery offered. If you've got plenty of stamina, consider doing part or all of the tour on foot. Remember as you go that this is a memorial frequented not just by tourists but also by those attending burial services or visiting the graves of beloved relatives and friends who are buried here.

This shrine occupies approximately 624 acres on the high hills overlooking the capital from the west side of the Memorial Bridge. It honors many national heroes and more than 300,000 war dead, veterans, and dependents. Many graves of the famous at Arlington bear nothing more than simple markers. Five-star General John J. Pershing's is one of those. Secretary of State John Foster Dulles is buried here. So are President William Howard Taft and Supreme Court Justices Thurgood Marshall and William Brennan. Cemetery highlights include:

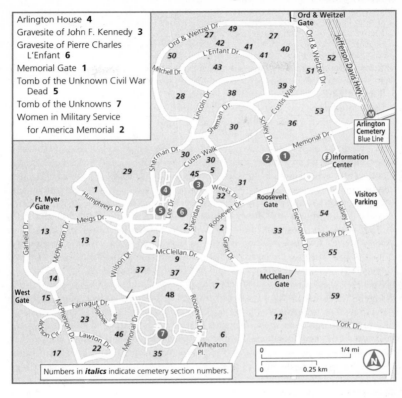

Arlington House **4**
Gravesite of John F. Kennedy **3**
Gravesite of Pierre Charles
    L'Enfant **6**
Memorial Gate **1**
Tomb of the Unknown Civil War
    Dead **5**
Tomb of the Unknowns **7**
Women in Military Service
    for America Memorial **2**

Numbers in *italics* indicate cemetery section numbers.

The **Tomb of the Unknowns,** containing the unidentified remains of service members from both world wars, the Korean War, and, until 1997, the Vietnam War. In 1997, the remains of the unknown soldier from Vietnam were identified as those of Air Force 1st Lt. Michael Blassie, whose A-37 was shot down in South Vietnam in 1962. Blassie's family, who had reason to believe that the body was their son's, had besought the Pentagon to exhume the soldier's remains and conduct DNA testing to determine if what the family suspected was true. Upon confirmation, the Blassies buried Michael in his hometown of St. Louis. The crypt honoring the dead but unidentified Vietnam War soldiers will remain empty. The entire tomb is an unembellished, massive white-marble block, moving in its simplicity. A 24-hour honor guard watches over the tomb, with the changing of the guard taking place every half-hour April to September, every hour on the hour October to March, and every hour at night year-round.

Within a 20-minute walk, all uphill, from the Visitor Center is **Arlington House** (© **703/235-1530;** www.nps.gov/arho), whose structure was begun in 1802, by Martha and George Washington's grandson, George Washington Parke Custis (actually, Custis was George Washington's adopted grandson). Custis's daughter, Mary Anna Randolph, inherited the estate; and she and her husband, Robert E. Lee, lived here between 1831 and 1861. When Lee headed up Virginia's army, Mary fled; and federal troops confiscated the property. A fine melding of the styles of the Greek Revival and the grand plantation houses of the early 1800s, the house has been administered by the National Park Service since 1933.

You tour the house on your own; park rangers are on-site to answer your questions. The house remains open but is likely to be unfurnished in 2010, as a renovation gets underway. Slave quarters and a small museum adjoin. Admission is free. It's open daily from 9:30am to 4:30pm, and until 5:30pm during the summer (closed Dec 25 and Jan 1).

Pierre Charles L'Enfant's grave was placed near Arlington House at a spot that is believed to offer the best view of Washington, the city he designed.

Below Arlington House is the **Gravesite of John Fitzgerald Kennedy.** John Carl Warnecke designed a low crescent wall embracing a marble terrace, inscribed with the 35th president's most famous utterance: "And so, my fellow Americans, ask not what your country can do for you; ask what you can do for your country." Jacqueline Kennedy Onassis rests next to her husband, and Robert Kennedy is buried close by. The Kennedy graves attract streams of visitors. Arrive close to 8am to contemplate the site quietly; otherwise, it's often crowded. Looking north, there's a spectacular view of Washington.

In 1997, the **Women in Military Service for America Memorial (𝄡 800/222-2294** or 703/533-1155; www.womensmemorial.org) was added to Arlington Cemetery to honor the more than two million women who have served in the armed forces from the American Revolution to the present. The impressive memorial lies just beyond the gated entrance to the cemetery, a 3-minute walk from the Visitor Center. As you approach the memorial, you see a large, circular reflecting pool, perfectly placed within the curve of the granite wall rising behind it. Arched passages within the 226-foot-long wall lead to an upper terrace and dramatic views of Arlington National Cemetery and the monuments of Washington; an arc of large glass panels (which form the roof of the memorial hall) contains etched quotations from famous people about contributions made by servicewomen. Behind the wall and completely underground is the **Education Center,** housing a **Hall of Honor,** a gallery of exhibits tracing the history of women in the military, a theater, and a computer register of servicewomen, which visitors may access for the stories and information about 250,000 individual military women, past and present. Hours are 8am to 5pm (until 7pm Apr–Sept). Stop at the reception desk for a brochure that details a self-guided tour through the memorial. The memorial is open every day but Christmas.

Plan to spend half a day at Arlington Cemetery and the Women in Military Service Memorial.

Just across the Memorial Bridge from the base of the Lincoln Memorial. 𝄡 **703/607-8000.** www.arlingtoncemetery.org. Free admission. Apr–Sept daily 8am–7pm; Oct–Mar daily 8am–5pm. Metro: Arlington National Cemetery. If you come by car, parking is $1.75 an hour for the 1st 3 hr., $2 an hour thereafter. The cemetery is also accessible via Tourmobile.

8 PARKS & GARDENS

Washington is extensively endowed with vast natural areas, all centrally located within the District. Included in all this greenery are thousands of parkland acres, two rivers, the mouth of a 185-mile-long tree-lined canalside trail, an untamed wilderness area, and a few thousand cherry trees. And there's much more just a stone's throw away.

Dumbarton Oaks (Finds)   This 19th-century Georgetown mansion named for a Scottish castle is a research center for studies in Byzantine and pre-Columbian art and history, as well as landscape architecture. Its magical yards, which wind gently down to Rock Creek Ravine, are modeled after European gardens. The pre-Columbian museum, designed by Philip Johnson, is a small gem; and the Byzantine collection is a rich one. The mansion's **formal gardens** are a favorite of Washingtonians. The gardens include an Orangery, a Rose Garden, wisteria-covered arbors, groves of cherry trees, and magnolias. You're likely to spend as much as an hour here when everything is in bloom, but expect to share the winding paths with like-minded wanderers. You can't picnic here; instead, exit at R Street, turn left, cross an honest-to-goodness Lovers' Lane, and proceed next door to Montrose Park to hold your picnic. There is parking on the street. See box "The Roads Less Traveled: A Back-Street Tour of Historic Georgetown, with Stops at Shops," in chapter 8, which points you here and to other nearby attractions, including shops and dining.

1703 32nd St. NW (garden entrance at 31st and R sts.). (🕐) **202/339-6401**. www.doaks.org. Gardens admission Mar 15–Oct 31 $8 adults, $5 children 12 and under and seniors; Nov–Mar 14 free. Museum admission free. Gardens Tues–Sun, year-round, weather permitting: 2–6pm Mar 15–Oct 31; 2–5pm Nov 1–Mar 14. Museum Tues–Sun 2–5pm. Museum and gardens are closed national holidays and Dec 24.

Enid A. Haupt Garden   Named for its donor, a noted supporter of horticultural projects, this stunning garden presents elaborate flower beds and borders, plant-filled turn-of-the-20th-century urns, 1870s cast-iron furnishings, and lush baskets hung from reproduction 19th-century lampposts. Although on ground level, the garden is actually on a $4^{1}/_{4}$-acre rooftop above the subterranean Ripley Center and the Sackler and African Art museums. An **"Island Garden"** near the Sackler Gallery, entered via a 9-foot moon gate, has benches backed by English boxwoods set under the canopy of weeping cherry trees.

A **"Fountain Garden"** outside the African Art Museum provides granite seating with walls overhung by hawthorn trees. Three small terraces, shaded by black sour-gum trees, are located near the Arts and Industries Building. And five majestic linden trees shade a seating area around the **Downing Urn**, a memorial to American landscapist Andrew Jackson Downing, who designed the National Mall. Downing's words are inscribed on the base of the urn: "Build halls where knowledge shall be freely diffused among men, and not shut up within the narrow walls of narrower institutions. Plant spacious parks in your cities and unclose their gates as wide as the gates of morning to the whole people." Elaborate cast-iron carriage gates made according to a 19th-century design by James Renwick, flanked by four red-sandstone pillars, are placed at the Independence Avenue entrance to the garden.

10th St. and Independence Ave. SW. (🕐) **202/633-1000**. Free admission. Late May to Aug daily 7am–9:15pm; Sept to mid-May daily 7am–5:45pm. Closed Dec 25. Metro: Smithsonian (12th St. and Independence Ave. exit).

United States Botanic Garden ★   For the feel of summer in the middle of winter, for the sight of lush, breathtakingly beautiful greenery and flowers year-round, stop in at the Botanic Garden, located at the foot of the Capitol next door to the National Museum of the American Indian. The grand conservatory devotes half of its space to exhibits that focus on the importance of plants to people, and half to exhibits that focus on ecology and the evolutionary biology of plants. But those finer points may escape you as you wander through the various chambers, outdoors and indoors, upstairs and down, gazing in stupefaction at so much flora. The conservatory holds 4,000 living species (about 26,000 plants); a high-walled enclosure, called "The Jungle," of palms, ferns, and vines; an Orchid Room; a meditation garden; a primeval garden; and gardens created especially with children in mind. And there are sounds—I swear I heard a frog or two. Just outside the conservatory is the National Garden, which includes the First Ladies Water Garden, a formal rose garden, a butterfly garden, and a lawn terrace. Ask at the front desk about tours. The USBG sometimes offers entertainment and periodically publishes calendars of events.

Also visit the garden annex across the street, **Bartholdi Park.** The park is about the size of a city block, with a stunning cast-iron classical fountain created by Frédéric Auguste Bartholdi, designer of the Statue of Liberty. Charming flower gardens bloom amid tall ornamental grasses, benches are sheltered by vine-covered bowers, and a touch and fragrance garden contains such herbs as pineapple-scented sage.

100 Maryland Ave. SW (btw. 1st and 3rd sts. SW, at the foot of the Capitol on the National Mall). ⓒ **202/225-8333.** www.usbg.gov. Free admission. Conservatory daily 10am–5pm, National Garden 10am–7pm in spring and summer, 10am–5pm fall and winter. Bartholdi Park dawn to dusk. Metro: Federal Center SW (Smithsonian Museums/Maryland Ave. exit).

PARKS
Potomac Park

West and East Potomac parks, their 720 riverside acres divided by the Tidal Basin, are most famous for their spring display of **cherry blossoms** and all the hoopla that goes with it. So much attention is lavished on Washington's cherry blossoms that the National Park Service devotes a home page to the subject: www.nps.gov/nama/planyourvisit/cherry-blossom-bloom.htm. (Also go to www.nationalcherryblossomfestival.org.) You can access the NPS site to find out forecasts for the blooms and assorted other details. You can also call the National Park Service (ⓒ **202/426-6841**) for information. In all, there are more than 3,700 cherry trees planted along the Tidal Basin in West Potomac Park, East Potomac Park, the Washington Monument grounds, and other pockets of the city.

To get to the Tidal Basin by car (*not* recommended in cherry-blossom season—actually, let me be clear: *impossible* in cherry-blossom season), you want to get on Independence Avenue and follow the signs posted near the Lincoln Memorial that show you where to turn to find parking and the FDR Memorial. If you're walking, you'll want to cross Independence Avenue where it intersects with West Basin Drive (there's a stoplight and crosswalk), and follow the path to the Tidal Basin. There is no convenient Metro stop near here.

West Potomac Park encompasses Constitution Gardens; the Vietnam, Korean, Lincoln, Jefferson, World War II, and FDR memorials; a small island where ducks live; and the Reflecting Pool (see "The National Mall & Memorial Parks," p. 176, for full listings

 Cherry Night

The National Park Service offers several kinds of cherry blossom tours, but the best is the lantern walk, which takes place at night. You bring your own flashlight and a park ranger guides you beneath the canopy of cherry blossoms for 1 1/2 miles around the Tidal Basin.

of the memorials). It has 1,678 cherry trees bordering the Tidal Basin, some of them Akebonos with delicate pink blossoms, but most Yoshinos with white, cloudlike flower clusters. The blossoming of the cherry trees is the focal point of a 2-week-long celebration, including the lighting of the 300-year-old Japanese Stone Lantern near Kutz Bridge, presented to the city by the governor of Tokyo in 1954. (This year's Cherry Blossom Festival is scheduled to run Mar 27–Apr 11, 2010.) The trees bloom for a little less than 2 weeks beginning sometime between March 20 and April 17; April 4 is the average date. Planning your trip around the blooming of the cherry blossoms is an iffy proposition, and I wouldn't advise it. All it takes is one good rain and those cherry blossoms are gone. The cherry blossoms are not illuminated at night.

East Potomac Park has 1,681 cherry trees in 10 varieties. The park also has picnic grounds, tennis courts, three golf courses, a large swimming pool, and biking and hiking paths by the water.

Rock Creek Park

Created in 1890, **Rock Creek Park** ★ (**www.nps.gov/rocr**) was purchased by Congress for its "pleasant valleys and ravines, primeval forests and open fields, its running waters, its rocks clothed with rich ferns and mosses, its repose and tranquillity, its light and shade, its ever-varying shrubbery, its beautiful and extensive views." A 1,750-acre valley within the District of Columbia, extending 12 miles from the Potomac River to the Maryland border, it's one of the biggest and finest city parks in the nation. Parts of it are still wild; coyotes have been sighted here, joining the red and gray foxes, raccoons, and beavers already resident. Most tourists encounter its southern tip, the section from the Kennedy Center to the National Zoo, but the park widens and travels much further from there.

The park's offerings include the Old Stone House in Georgetown (located on a busy street in Georgetown, outside the park but considered a park property, nonetheless), Carter Barron Amphitheater (see chapter 9), playgrounds, an extensive system of beautiful hiking and biking trails, sports facilities, remains of Civil War fortifications, and acres and acres of wooded parklands. See also p. 221 for a description of the formal gardens at **Dumbarton Oaks,** which border Rock Creek Park in upper Georgetown.

For full information on the wide range of park programs and activities, visit the **Rock Creek Nature Center and Planetarium,** 5200 Glover Rd. NW (© **202/895-6070**), Wednesday through Sunday from 9am to 5pm. To get to the Nature Center by public transportation, take the Metro to Friendship Heights and transfer to bus no. E2 to Military Road and Oregon Avenue/Glover Road, then walk up the hill about 100 yards to the Nature Center. Call © **202/895-6070** to request a brochure that provides details on picnic locations.

The Nature Center and Planetarium is the scene of numerous activities, including weekend planetarium shows for kids (minimum age 4) and adults; nature films; crafts demonstrations; live animal demonstrations; guided nature walks; plus a daily mix of lectures, films, and other events. Self-guided nature trails begin here. All activities are free, but for planetarium shows you need to pick up tickets a half-hour in advance. There are also nature exhibits on the premises. The Nature Center is closed on federal holidays.

Not far from the Nature Center is **Fort DeRussey,** one of 68 fortifications erected to defend the city of Washington during the Civil War. From the intersection of Military Road and Oregon Avenue, you walk a short trail through the woods to reach the fort, whose remains include high earth mounds with openings where guns were mounted, surrounded by a deep ditch/moat.

At Tilden Street and Beach Drive, you can see a water-powered 19th-century gristmill, used until not so long ago to grind corn and wheat into flour. It's called **Peirce Mill** (a man named Isaac Peirce built it), but it's currently closed for repairs.

Poetry readings and workshops are held during the summer at **Miller's Cabin,** the one-time residence of High Sierra poet Joaquin Miller, Beach Drive north of Military Road. Call ✆ **202/895-6070** for information.

You'll find convenient free **parking** throughout the park.

Theodore Roosevelt Island Park ★

A serene, 91-acre wilderness preserve, Theodore Roosevelt Island is a memorial to the nation's 26th president in recognition of his contributions to conservation. During his administration, Roosevelt, an outdoor enthusiast and expert field naturalist, set aside a total of 234 million acres of public lands for forests, national parks, wildlife and bird refuges, and monuments.

Native American tribes were here first, inhabiting the island for centuries until the arrival of English explorers in the 1600s. Over the years, the island passed through many owners before becoming what it is today—an island preserve of swamp, marsh, and upland forest that's a haven for rabbits, chipmunks, great owls, foxes, muskrats, turtles, and groundhogs. It's a complex ecosystem in which cattails, arrow arum, and pickerel-weed grow in the marshes, and willow, ash, and maple trees root on the mud flats. You can observe these flora and fauna in their natural environs on 2.5 miles of foot trails.

In the northern center of the island, overlooking a terrace encircled by a water-filled moat, stands a 17-foot bronze statue of Roosevelt. Four 21-foot granite tablets are inscribed with tenets of his conservation philosophy.

To drive to the island, take the George Washington Memorial Parkway exit north from the Theodore Roosevelt Bridge. The parking area is accessible only from the northbound lane; park there and cross the pedestrian bridge that connects the lot to the island. You can also rent a canoe at Thompson's Boat Center (p. 231) and paddle over, or take the pedestrian bridge at Rosslyn Circle, 2 blocks from the Rosslyn Metro station. You can picnic on the grounds near the memorial; if you do, allow about an hour here. Expect bugs in summer and muddy trails after a rain.

In the Potomac River, btw. Washington and Rosslyn, VA. See access information above. ✆ **703/289-2500.** www.nps.gov/this. Free admission. Daily dawn–dusk. Metro: Rosslyn, then walk 2 blocks to Rosslyn Circle and cross the pedestrian bridge to the island.

ACTIVITIES ON THE C&O CANAL

One of the great joys of living in Washington is the **C&O Canal** (**www.nps.gov/choh**) and its unspoiled 185-mile towpath. You leave urban cares and stresses behind while hiking, strolling, jogging, cycling, or boating in this lush, natural setting of ancient oaks and red maples, giant sycamores, willows, and wildflowers. But the canal wasn't always just a leisure spot for city people. It was built in the 1800s, when water routes were considered vital to transportation. Even before it was completed, though, the canal was being rendered obsolete by the B&O Railroad, which was constructed at about the same time and along the same route. Today, its role as an oasis from unrelenting urbanity is even more important.

A good source of information about the canal is the National Park Service office at **Great Falls Tavern Visitor Center,** 11710 MacArthur Blvd., Potomac, MD (✆ **301/767-3714**). At this 1831 tavern, you can see museum exhibits and a film about the canal;

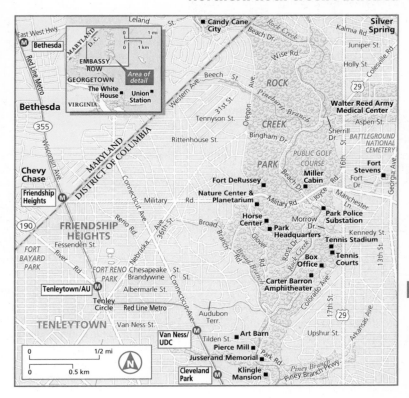

there's also a bookstore on the premises. The park charges an entrance fee, $5 per car, $3 per walker or cyclist.

In Georgetown, the **Georgetown Information Center,** 1057 Thomas Jefferson St. NW (② 202/653-5190), can also provide maps and information.

Hiking any section of the flat dirt towpath or its more rugged side paths is a pleasure (and it's free). There are picnic tables, some with barbecue grills, about every 5 miles on the way to Cumberland, beginning at the **Boat House at Fletcher's Cove** (② 202/244-0461; www.fletcherscove.com). It's about 3¼ miles out of Georgetown and is a good place to rent bikes or boats or to purchase bait, tackle, and a fishing license. Enter the towpath in Georgetown below M Street via Thomas Jefferson Street. If you hike 14 miles, you'll reach **Great Falls,** a point where the Potomac becomes a stunning waterfall plunging 76 feet. Or drive to Great Falls Park on the Virginia side of the Potomac.

Much less strenuous than hiking is a **mule-drawn 19th-century canalboat trip** led by Park Service rangers in period dress. They regale passengers with canal legend and lore and sing period songs. These boats depart from mid-April to mid-October. Both the Georgetown and Great Falls barge rides last about 1 hour and 10 minutes and cost $5

Finds **Albert Einstein Memorial, 22nd Street and Constitution Avenue NW**

In a grove of holly and elm trees at the southwest corner of the National Academy of Science grounds, you'll find this dear memorial displaying the slouching figure of brilliant scientist, great thinker, and peace activist Albert Einstein. He sits slightly bent and sideways, upon a granite bench, leaning on one hand and holding in the other a bronze sheet of paper on which are written mathematical equations for which he is famous. At his feet is a celestial map. His gaze looks worn and warm. The statue measures 12 feet in height and weighs 4 tons, yet children cannot resist crawling upon it and leaning up against this man.

for everyone except children 3 and under, who ride free. Check the website, www.nps.gov/choh, for the latest schedules.

Call any of the above information numbers for details on riding, rock climbing, fishing, bird-watching, concerts, ranger-guided tours, ice-skating, camping, and other canal activities.

9 ESPECIALLY FOR KIDS

As far as I know, Pierre L'Enfant and his successors were not thinking of children when they incorporated the long, open stretch of the Mall into their design for the city. But they may as well have. This 2-mile expanse of lawn running from the Lincoln Memorial to the Capitol is a playground, really, and a backyard to the Smithsonian museums and National Gallery which border it. You can visit any of these sites assured that if one of your little darlings starts to misbehave, you'll be able to head right out the door to the National Mall, where numerous distractions await. The Mall is always busy with walkers, joggers, and bikers. Vendors sell ice cream, soft pretzels, and sodas. Festivals of all sorts take place on a regular basis, whether it's the grand Smithsonian Folklife Festival for 10 days at the end of June into July (see "Washington, D.C., Calendar of Events," in chapter 3), or the Kite Festival in spring. Weather permitting, a 19th-century carousel operates in front of the Arts and Industries Building on the south side of the Mall. Right across the Mall from the carousel is the children-friendly National Gallery Sculpture Garden, whose shallow pool is good for splashing one's feet in summer and for ice-skating in winter.

You don't need the excuse of recalcitrant children to enjoy the Mall, of course, though it's always good to have an escape route. The truth is, many of Washington's attractions hold various enchantments for children of all ages. It might be easier to point out which ones are not recommended for your youngest: the Supreme Court, the chambers of Congress, the U.S. Holocaust Memorial Museum, and the Marian Koshland Science Museum. The International Spy Museum is now recommending that its museum is most suitable for children 12 and over. Generally speaking, the bigger and busier the museum, the better it is for kids. On the Mall, these would be the three top draws: the National Museum of Natural History, the National Air and Space Museum, and National

Favorite Children's Attractions

Check for special children's events at museum information desks when you enter. As noted within the listings for individual museums, some children's programs are also great fun for adults. I recommend the programs at the **Folger Shakespeare Library,** the **Phillips,** and the **Sackler Gallery** in particular. (The gift shops in most of these museums have wonderful toys and children's books.) Call ahead to find out which programs are running. Here's a rundown of big kid-pleasers in town (for details, see the full entries earlier in this chapter):

- **Madame Tussauds Washington D.C.** (p. 210): There are two kinds of people in this world: those who think wax museums are hokey, and children. Yeah, watch your offspring pretend to sing with Beyoncé, box with Evander Holyfield, stand tall next to George Washington, whoop it up with Whoopi. Maybe you'll find your inner child and start loving these wax figures, too.

- **National Museum of Crime and Punishment** (p. 210): Your little darlings can pretend to be little Dillingers and test their safecracking skills, or little Elliot Nesses as they learn how to take fingerprints and gather clues.

- **Newseum** (p. 211): Proceed directly to the interactive newsroom on the second floor, where your children will happily, endlessly play computer games while testing their news knowledge and journalism skills, and where they'll have the chance to play an on-camera reporter.

- **Lincoln Memorial** (p. 182): Kids know a lot about Lincoln and enjoy visiting his memorial. A special treat is visiting after dark.

- **National Air and Space Museum** (p. 189): Spectacular IMAX films (don't miss), thrilling flight simulators, planetarium shows, missiles, rockets, and a walk-through orbital workshop.

- **National Museum of the American Indian** (p. 194): Pick up a copy of the Family Guide for tips on enjoying this treasury of Native American history and culture with kids. Interesting multimedia and hands-on activities.

- **National Museum of Natural History** (p. 195): A Discovery Room just for youngsters, the new Butterfly Pavilion and exhibit, as well as the outdoor butterfly garden, an insect zoo, shrunken heads, dinosaurs, and the IMAX theater showing 2-D and 3-D films.

- **National Zoological Park** (p. 197): Pandas! Cheetahs! Kids always love a zoo, and this is an especially good one, with a Kids Farm.

- **Washington Monument** (p. 178): Spectacular 360-degree views from the center of Washington, D.C.

EXPLORING WASHINGTON, D.C.

7

ESPECIALLY FOR KIDS

Museum of American History, each of which has special areas and exhibits aimed specifically at children. D.C.'s newest attractions might have the rest beat: the **Newseum** (p. 211), **Madame Tussauds Washington D.C.** (p. 210), and the **National Museum of Crime and Punishment** (p. 210).

I have two daughters, ages 17 and 22; their favorite Washington activities over the years have included paddle-boating on the Tidal Basin (p. 232); shopping in Georgetown; attending plays at the Folger Theatre, the National Theatre, and the Kennedy Center; Wizards and Mystics basketball games at the Verizon Center (p. 256); ice-skating at the National Gallery; and visiting the National Zoo, the International Spy Museum, the National Postal Museum, the Albert Einstein Memorial (p. 226), and special exhibits at the National Gallery of Art, as long as we had something to eat at one of the cafes. (Parents, you will be happy to note that many of the museums offer food of some sort, or vendor carts at the curb.)

For more ideas, consult the online or print version of the Friday "Weekend" section of the *Washington Post,* which lists numerous activities (mostly free) for kids: special museum events, children's theater, storytelling programs, puppet shows, video-game competitions, and so forth. Call the Kennedy Center and the National Theatre to find out about children's shows; see chapter 9 for details.

I've noted "Family-Friendly Hotels" in chapter 5; a few, though not many, hotels have pools, and some offer little goodie packages at check-in. The "Organized Tours" and "Outdoor Activities" sections below may also be your saving grace when you've run out of steam or need a jump-start to your day.

10 ORGANIZED TOURS

Enterprising individuals and organizations keep coming up with new ways to introduce the city. Go to the **Cultural Tourism D.C.** website, **www.culturaltourismdc.org**, and click on "Tours and Trails" for a longer list of organized tours. Here's a sampling of what's available.

ON FOOT

A Tour de Force (© 703/525-2948; www.atourdeforce.com) is historian and raconteur Jeanne Fogel's 26-year-old company. She offers various modes of transport, from walking to bus, SUV, and limo tours. Fogel custom designs the route around the city per your request and size of group, from a romantic tour for a couple to a traditional sightseeing excursion for a convention crowd. Fogel (or her stand-in) peppers her narration with little-known anecdotes and facts about neighborhoods, historic figures, and the most visited sites. Call for rates.

Spies of Washington Walking Tours (© 703/569-1875; www.spiesofwashington tour.com) offers four walking tours that focus on espionage-related sites in Georgetown and around the White House, Pennsylvania Avenue, Capitol Hill, and the Russian Embassy areas. Carol Bessette, a retired Air Force intelligence officer, conducts the tours, which cost $12 per person. Private tours and bus tours are also available.

Anecdotal History Tours of Washington, D.C. ★ (© 301/294-9514; www.dcsight seeing.com) offers private and occasional public tours that take you on walks through the streets of Georgetown, Adams-Morgan, and other locations guided by author/historian Anthony S. Pitch. Inquire about rates.

Segway Tours (© 877/SEG-TOUR; www.citysegwaytours.com/washington) are available year-round, daily, at 10am, 2pm, and 6pm. Though technically they are "on foot," Segways are self-propelling scooters that operate based on "dynamic stabilization" technology, which uses your body movements. Tours last 3 hours, cost $70 per person, and include training; age 16 and up.

TOURMOBILE   Best-known and least expensive, **Tourmobile Sightseeing** (℡ 888/868-7707 or 202/554-5100; www.tourmobile.com) is a good choice if you're looking for an easy-on/easy-off tour of major sites, especially since security concerns have made the already limited parking nearly nonexistent. The comfortable red, white, and blue sightseeing trams travel to as many as 24 attractions (the company changes its schedule and number of stops depending on whether sites are open for public tours), including Arlington National Cemetery. Tourmobile is the only narrated sightseeing shuttle tour authorized by the National Park Service.

The company offers a number of different tours, but the most popular is the **American Heritage Tour,** which stops at 21 sites on or near the National Mall and at three sites in Arlington Cemetery. (Again, the number of stops may be fewer than 21, if regularly scheduled stops are not open for public tours due to increased security.) Normally, stops include the memorials and Washington Monument, Union Station, the National Gallery, most of the Smithsonian museums (National Air and Space, National Museum of Natural History, and the Arts and Industries Building/Hirshhorn Museum), the Capitol, the White House Visitor Center, and several other locations. In Arlington Cemetery, the bus stops at the Kennedy grave sites, the Tomb of the Unknowns, and Arlington House.

You can purchase tickets at the Union Station and Washington Monument booths, or inside the Arlington National Cemetery Visitor Center, or, for a small surcharge, order your ticket in advance from Ticketmaster at ℡ **800/551-7328** or www.ticketmaster.com. Or if you'd prefer, just pay your driver when you first get on the bus. Hop on a Tourmobile at any of the designated locations, then get off at any stop to visit monuments or buildings. When you finish exploring each area, just show your ticket and climb aboard the next Tourmobile that comes along. The buses travel in a loop, serving each stop about every 15 to 30 minutes. One fare allows you to use the buses all day. The charge for the American Heritage Tour is $27 for anyone 12 and older, $13 for children 3 to 11. For Arlington Cemetery only, those 12 and older pay $7.50, children $3.75. Children 2 and under ride free. Buses follow circuits from the Capitol to Arlington Cemetery and back. Well-trained and personable narrators give commentaries about sights along the route and answer questions.

The trams are heated in winter, but they're not air-conditioned in summer; and though the windows stay open, they can get hot and uncomfortable. Readers also report that Tourmobiles, being the largest trams, take a long time to load and unload passengers, which can be frustrating to those anxious to see the sights.

Tourmobiles operate 9:30am to 4:30pm, daily year-round, except Christmas. (In the busy tourist season, Tourmobile sometimes extends its hours.) Call Tourmobile or visit the website for further information about other tours and their rates.

OLD TOWN TROLLEY   Old Town Trolley tours (℡ **202/832-9800;** www.historictours.com) offer fixed-price, on-off service as you travel in three loops around the city, with a transfer point at the Lincoln Memorial stop to go on to Arlington Cemetery and a second transfer point at Ford's Theatre to get to Georgetown and to Washington National Cathedral. Many hotels sell tickets (see chapter 5); otherwise, you can purchase tickets online or at the Old Town Trolley Tour booths at Union Station, the D.C. Visitor Center in the Ronald Reagan Building, and many other places around town. Buses operate daily from 9am to 4:30pm, extended to 5:30pm in summer. The cost is $32 for adults, $16 for children 4 to 12, free for children 3 and under. You can buy tickets online in advance and at a discount, and use those e-tickets to board at any of the stops on the route. The full tour, which is narrated, takes 2 hours (if you don't get off and tour the sites, obviously), and trolleys come by every 30 minutes or so. Old Town Trolley tours cost more than Tourmobile tours, perhaps because the buses travel to neighborhoods and attractions away from the Mall.

BY BOAT

Since Washington is a river city, why not see it by boat? Potomac cruises allow sweeping vistas of the monuments and memorials, Georgetown, the Kennedy Center, and other Washington sights. Read the information below carefully, since not all boat cruises offer guided tours. Some of the following boats leave from the Washington waterfront and some from Old Town Alexandria:

Spirit of Washington Cruises, Pier 4 at 6th and Water streets SW (✆ **866/302-2469** or 202/554-8000; www.spiritcruises.com; Metro: Waterfront), offers a variety of trips daily, including evening dinner, lunch, brunch, and moonlight dance cruises, as well as a half-day excursion to Mount Vernon and back. Lunch and dinner cruises include a 40-minute musical revue.

The *Spirit of Washington* is a luxury climate-controlled harbor cruise ship with carpeted decks and huge panoramic windows designed for sightseeing. There are three well-stocked bars onboard.

Potomac Party Cruises (✆ **703/683-6076;** www.dandydinnerboat.com) operates the *Dandy* and *Nina's Dandy,* both climate-controlled, all-weather, glassed-in floating restaurants that run year-round. Lunch, evening dinner/dance, and special charter cruises are available daily. You board both vessels in Old Town Alexandria, at the Prince Street pier, between Duke and King streets. Trips range from a $2^{1}/_{2}$-hour weekday lunch cruise to a 3-hour Saturday dinner cruise.

Odyssey (✆ **866/306-2469;** www.odysseycruises.com) was designed specifically to glide under the bridges that cross the Potomac. The boat looks like a glass bullet, with its snub-nosed port and its streamlined 240-foot-long glass body. The wraparound see-through walls and ceiling allow for great views. You board the *Odyssey* at the Gangplank Marina, on Washington's waterfront at 6th and Water streets SW (Metro: Waterfront). Cruises available include lunch, Sunday brunch, and dinner excursions, with live entertainment provided during each cruise.

From April through October, the **Potomac Riverboat Company** ★ (✆ **877/511-2628** or 703/684-0580; www.potomacriverboatco.com), offers several 90-minute round-trip, narrated tours aboard sightseeing vessels that take you past Washington landmarks or along Old Town Alexandria's waterfront; certain cruises also travel to Mount Vernon, where you hop off and reboard after you've toured the estate. You board the boats at the pier behind the Torpedo Factory in Old Town Alexandria at the foot of King Street, or, for the Washington monuments and memorials tour, Georgetown's Washington Harbour. A concession stand selling light refreshments and beverages is open during the cruises.

The **Capitol River Cruise**'s *Nightingales* (✆ **800/405-5511** or 301/460-7447; www.capitolrivercruises.com) are historic 65-foot steel riverboats that can accommodate 90 people. The *Nightingales'* narrated jaunts depart Georgetown's Washington Harbour every hour on the hour, from noon to 9pm, April through October (the 9pm outing is offered in summer months only). The 45-minute narrated tour travels past the monuments and memorials to National Airport and back. A snack bar onboard sells light refreshments, beer, wine, and sodas; you're welcome to bring your own picnic aboard. To

get here, take Metro to Foggy Bottom and then walk into Georgetown, following Pennsylvania Avenue, which becomes M Street. Turn left on 31st Street NW and follow to the
Washington Harbour complex on the water.

A BOAT ON WHEELS   Old Town Trolley also operates **DC Ducks** (© 202/832-
9800; www.dcducks.com), which feature unique land and water tours of Washington
aboard the *DUKW,* an amphibious army vehicle (boat with wheels) from World War II
that accommodates 30 passengers. Ninety-minute guided tours aboard the open-air
canopied craft include a land portion taking in major sights—the Capitol, Lincoln
Memorial, Washington Monument, White House, and Smithsonian museums—and a
30-minute Potomac cruise. Purchase tickets inside Union Station at the information
desk; board the vehicle just outside the main entrance to Union Station. Hours vary, but
departures usually follow a daily 11am, 1pm, and 3pm schedule (Mar–Oct).

BY BIKE

Bike the Sites, Inc. ★ (© **202/842-2453;** www.bikethesites.com) offers a more active
way to see Washington, in season, from March to November. The company has designed
several different biking tours of the city, including the popular Capital Sites Ride, which
takes you past museums, memorials, the White House, Capitol, and Supreme Court.
The ride takes 3 hours, covers 7 to 8 miles, and costs $40 per adult, $30 per child 12 and
under. Bike the Sites provides you with a comfort mountain bicycle fitted to your size,
bike helmet, water bottle, light snack, and two guides to lead the ride. All tours start from
the rear plaza, 12th Street NW side of the Old Post Office Pavilion, which is located at
1100 Pennsylvania Ave. NW (Metro: Federal Triangle, on the Blue and Orange Line).
Guides impart historical and anecdotal information as you go. The company rents bikes
to those who want to go their own, unnarrated way for $7 an hour ($15 minimum) or
$45 a day, including helmet, bike, lock, and pump. It also customizes guided bike rides
to suit your tour specifications.

---

11 OUTDOOR ACTIVITIES

For information about spectator sports venues, including how to buy tickets and where
to go to watch **Washington Wizards** (men's) and **Mystics** (women's) basketball games,
the **Capitals** ice hockey meets, and **Nationals** baseball games, see chapter 9.

But if you prefer to work up your own honest sweat, Washington offers plenty of
pleasant opportunities in many lush surroundings. See "Parks & Gardens" earlier in this
chapter for complete coverage of the city's loveliest green spaces.

Joggers can enjoy a run on the Mall or along the path in Rock Creek Park.

As mentioned above, you can rent bikes from **Bike the Sites,** or from the **Boat House
at Fletcher's Cove,** Reservoir and Canal roads (© **202/244-0461;** www.fletcherscove.
com), or **Thompson's Boat Center,** 2900 Virginia Avenue at Rock Creek Parkway NW
(© **202/333-4861** or 333-9543; www.thompsonboatcenter.com; Metro: Foggy Bottom,
with a 10-min. walk); both Fletcher's and Thompson's rent bikes, weather permitting,
from about mid-March to mid-October. At **Big Wheel Bikes,** 1034 33rd St. NW, right
near the C&O Canal just below M Street (© **202/337-0254;** www.bigwheelbikes.com),
you can rent a bike year-round, Tuesday through Sunday. If you need suggested routes
or want company, check out Friday's *Washington Post* "Weekend" section, which lists
cycling trips. Rock Creek Park has an **11-mile paved bike route** ★ from the Lincoln

Memorial through the park into Maryland. Or you can follow the bike path from the Lincoln Memorial and go over the Memorial Bridge to pedal to Old Town Alexandria and to Mount Vernon (see chapter 10). On weekends and holidays, a large part of Rock Creek Parkway is closed to vehicular traffic. The C&O Canal and the Potomac parks, described earlier in "Parks & Gardens," also have extended bike paths. The **Capital Crescent Trail** takes you from Georgetown to the suburb of Bethesda, Maryland, following a former railroad track that parallels the Potomac River for part of the way and passes by old trestle bridges and pleasant residential neighborhoods.

Thompson's Boat Center and the **Boat House at Fletcher's Cove** (see above for both) rent boats following the same schedule as their bike-rental season, basically March to November. Thompson's has canoes, kayaks, and rowing shells (recreational and racing), and is open for boat and bike rentals daily in season from 8am to 5pm. Fletcher's is right on the C&O Canal, about 3$^{1}/_{4}$ miles from Georgetown. In addition to renting bikes, canoes, and kayaks, Fletcher's also sells fishing licenses, bait, and tackle. Open 7am to 7pm daily in season, Fletcher's is accessible by car (west on M St. to Canal Rd.) and has plenty of free parking.

From mid-March to mid-October, weather permitting, you can rent **paddle boats** ★ on the north end of the Tidal Basin off Independence Avenue (② 202/479-2426; www. tidalbasinpeddleboats.com). Four-seaters are $16 an hour; two-seaters are $8 an hour, 10am to 6pm daily mid-March to Labor Day and Wednesday to Sunday Labor Day to mid-October.

Washington has numerous **hiking paths.** The C&O Canal offers 185 miles stretching from D.C. to Cumberland, Maryland; Theodore Roosevelt Island has more than 88 wilderness acres to explore; and Rock Creek Park boasts 20 miles of hiking trails (maps are available at the Visitor Information Center or Park Headquarters).

If you're coming to Washington in winter, you can go **ice-skating** on the C&O Canal (call ② **301/299-3613** for information on ice conditions), as long as you bring your own skates. For a really fun experience, head to the **National Gallery Sculpture Garden Ice Rink** ★, on the Mall at 7th Street and Constitution Avenue NW (② **202/289-3360**), where you can rent skates, twirl in view of the sculptures, and enjoy hot chocolate and a sandwich in the Pavilion Café next to the rink.

If it's summer and your hotel doesn't have a pool, you might consider one of the neighborhood pools, including a large outdoor pool at 25th and N streets NW (② **202/ 727-3285**) and the Georgetown outdoor pool at 34th Street and Volta Place NW (② **202/282-0381**). Keep in mind that these are likely to be crowded.

Tennis lovers will have a hard time finding public courts in Washington. **East Potomac Park** (② **202/554-5962**) has 24 tennis courts (10 clay, 14 hard courts), three illuminated at night, and five indoor courts; the park rents rackets as well. Fees vary with court surface and time of play. **Montrose Park,** right next to Dumbarton Oaks (p. 221) in Georgetown, has several courts available free on a first-come, first-served basis; but they're often in use.

Shopping

The economic downturn and increasing popularity of online shopping notwithstanding, D.C.'s retail scene remains strong and buzz-worthy. Like everywhere else, of course, there have been casualties, notably, Olsson's bookstores, a beloved, local independent chain of nearly 40 years, with nine locations in its heyday; Olsson's was synonymous with high standards in literature and in staff—clerks knew what they were talking about.

But the city still has its crowded shopping districts; a thriving stable of longtime favorite stores, like The Phoenix (see "Crafts") and the Tiny Jewel Box (see "Jewelry"); and with each season, a flock of hot new arrivals, like the Penn Quarter's **Zola Wine and Kitchen** (see "Wine & Spirits"), where you can buy wine, take a cooking class, and attend a book signing by the latest top chef.

So read these pages to help you plan a shopping expedition. And if your wallet can't take it, why not visit one of our farmers' or flea markets, for more affordable finds? You're bound to stumble upon one in your travels here: D.C. has more farmers' markets per capita than any other locale except Honolulu.

1 THE SHOPPING SCENE

Most Washington-area stores are open from 10am to 5 or 6pm Monday through Saturday. Sunday hours tend to vary, with some stores opting not to open at all and others with shorter hours of noon to 5 or 6pm. Two neighborhoods prove the exception to these rules: Many stores in the Penn Quarter and in Georgetown keep later hours and are also open on Sunday. One example is the downtown Macy's department store (p. 249), in the heart of Penn Quarter, whose hours are noon to 6pm Sunday, 10am to 8pm Monday through Friday, and 9am to 9pm Saturday. Other exceptions include suburban shopping malls, which are open late nightly, and antiques stores and art galleries, which tend to keep their own hours. Be safe and call ahead if there's a store you really want to get to.

Sales tax on merchandise is 5.75% in the District, 5% in Maryland, and 4.5% in Virginia. Most gift, arts, and crafts stores, including those at the Smithsonian museums, will handle shipping for you; clothing stores generally do not.

2 GREAT SHOPPING AREAS

UNION STATION   It's a railroad station, a historic landmark, an architectural marvel, a Metro stop, and a shopping mall. Yes, the beauteous Union Station offers some fine shopping opportunities; it's certainly the best on Capitol Hill, with more than 100 clothes and specialty shops, and more than 40 eateries. **Metro:** Union Station.

PENN QUARTER   The area bounded east and west by 7th and 14th streets NW, and north and south by New York and Pennsylvania avenues NW, continues to develop as a central shopping area, despite the economic crisis. **Gallery Place,** a multiuse complex at

Finds   **The Roads Less Traveled: A Back-Street Tour of Historic Georgetown, with Stops at Shops**

Most people who visit Georgetown never get off the beaten track of the M Street/lower Wisconsin Avenue axis. Too bad for them, but good for you: While they bump into each other in the crowded bottom of Georgetown, you can tour the lovely, quiet streets in upper Georgetown, where a number of historic houses and beautiful gardens lie close to fun boutiques and delectable cafes. Consider this less traveled route. (See the color map on the last page of the color insert at the front of the book.)

Tudor Place, Dumbarton House, and the garden at Dumbarton Oaks are open for tours, but not every day, so call for hours if you want to incorporate house and garden tours in your back-street stroll; please note that all other houses on the tour are privately owned and not open to the public.

From the corner of Q Street and Wisconsin Avenue (a stop on the D.C. Circulator's Wisconsin Avenue line), walk east along Q Street to 31st Street and take a left on 31st Street to **Tudor Place** (© 202/965-0400), an 1816 mansion and gardens where Martha Washington's descendants lived until 1984. From Tudor Place, return to Q Street and walk farther east to no. 2715, **Dumbarton House** (© 202/337-2288), a Federal-style mansion built in 1805 and filled with 18th- and 19th-century furnishings and decorative arts.

Retrace your steps as far as 28th Street and proceed north on 28th Street, stopping to admire the 18th-century estate **Evermay,** built by a Scottish merchant, as you continue on your way to **Dumbarton Oaks Gardens** (p. 221; © 202/339-6401) at 31st and R streets. From the gardens, walk westward on R Street to Wisconsin Avenue, passing en route **3238 R St. NW,** an early-19th-century Federal brick building once used as a summer White House by President Ulysses S. Grant—its high elevation made it cooler than 1600 Pennsylvania Ave.

You have now reached Wisconsin Avenue, just a little farther north of the hustle-bustle, but a sweet spot for shopping at one-of-a-kind shops and for enjoying a scrumptious repast. Turn south on Wisconsin Avenue to find Italian

7th and H streets, in the heart of Chinatown, combines condominiums, offices, a bowling alley/bar, a 14-screen theater, stores that range from Urban Outfitters to Aveda, and several restaurants. Elsewhere in the neighborhood you'll find a long list of "name" stores, such as Banana Republic, Ann Taylor, H&M, and Jos. A. Bank Clothiers; and one-of-a-kind places, such as Apartment Zero and Mia Gemma. Look for the huge Borders at 14th and F streets NW, in the grand old Garfinckel's Building. Macy's (formerly known as "Hecht's"), at 12th and G streets, continues as the sole department store downtown. **Metro:** Metro Center, Chinatown/Gallery Place, or Archives/Navy Memorial.

ADAMS-MORGAN   Centered on 18th Street and Columbia Road NW, Adams-Morgan is a neighborhood of ethnic eateries and nightclubs interspersed with the odd secondhand bookshop and eclectic collectibles stores. It's a fun area for walking and

and French home and garden accessories at **A Mano** (no. 1677; ℭ **202/298-7200**), beautiful stationery at **Rooms with a View** (no. 1661; ℭ **202/625-0610**), and a variety of women's trendy clothing boutiques at **Sugar** (no. 1633; ℭ **202/333-5331**), **Sassanova** (no. 1641; ℭ **202/471-4400**), **Sherman Pickey** (no. 1647; ℭ **202/333-4212**), and, across the street, **Urban Chic** (no. 1626; ℭ **202/338-5398**). For refreshment, cross back to the other side to find (no. 1645): **Patisserie Poupon** (ℭ **202/342-3248**)—I highly recommend that you pause for a ham-and-cheese sandwich and, *absolument,* for a pastry dessert: Choose from tarts, éclairs, individual little cakes, and chocolate in all its forms.

Cross Wisconsin Avenue to continue your tour on the other side. Walk south on Wisconsin Avenue to N Street and turn right, following the street to **no. 3307,** the brick town house where John and Jacqueline Kennedy lived when Kennedy was a U.S. senator. In the same block, a few houses up at **nos. 3327–3339,** are five charming houses known collectively as **"Cox's Row,"** for owner John Cox, who built the dwellings in 1817. Cox, who was the first elected mayor of George-town, lived at no. 3339; Revolutionary War hero the Marquis de Lafayette stayed at no. 3337 on a visit in 1824. Follow N Street to 36th Street, and turn left and again left on Prospect Street to reach **Prospect House,** at no. 3508. This restored Georgian-style house was built in 1788 by Revolutionary War hero and wealthy tobacco merchant James McCubbin Lingan; the house, like the street, was named for the views one once had here of the Potomac River. From here, it's a short stroll to **Halcyon House,** at 3400 Prospect St., whose original owner, Benjamin Stoddert, was a Revolutionary War cavalry officer and first secretary of the navy. Two hundred years ago, the Potomac River lapped right up to Stoddert's terraced garden, designed by Pierre L'Enfant.

If you still have some energy left, finish the tour by visiting a Washington hot spot, the **Cafe Milano,** 3251 Prospect St. NW (ℭ **202/333-6183**). Then go home knowing that you've seen more of the "real" Georgetown than most Washingtonians.

shopping. Parking is possible during the day but impossible at night. For the closest **Metro,** you have a few choices: Woodley Park–Zoo/Adams-Morgan, then walk south on Connecticut Avenue NW until you reach Calvert Street, cross Connecticut Avenue, and follow Calvert Street across the Duke Ellington Memorial Bridge until you reach the junction of Columbia Road NW and 18th Street NW. Second choice: Dupont Circle; exit at Q Street NW and walk up Connecticut Avenue NW to Columbia Road NW. Best bet: the D.C. Circulator bus (see "Getting Around" in chapter 3), which runs between the McPherson Square and the Woodley Park-Zoo/Adams-Morgan Metro stations.

CONNECTICUT AVENUE/DUPONT CIRCLE Running from the mini–Wall Street that is K Street north to S Street, Connecticut Avenue NW is a main thoroughfare, where you'll find traditional clothing at Brooks Brothers, Talbots, Ann Taylor, and Burberry's;

casual duds at Gap; and haute couture at Rizik's. Closer to Dupont Circle are coffee bars and neighborhood restaurants, as well as art galleries; funky boutiques; gift, stationery, and book shops; and stores with a gay and lesbian slant. **Metro:** Farragut North at one end, Dupont Circle at the other.

U STREET CORRIDOR/14TH STREET   Urbanistas have been promoting this neighborhood for years, but now the number of cool shops, restaurants, and bars has hit the critical mass mark, winning the area widespread notice. If you shun brand names and box stores, you'll love the boutiques along U and 14th streets. Look for provocative handles, like Go Mama Go! and Pulp, then step inside to inspect their equally intriguing merchandise. **Metro:** U St./African-American Civil War Memorial/Cardozo.

GEORGETOWN   Georgetown is the city's main shopping area. In the heart of the neighborhood, stores line Wisconsin Avenue and M Street NW, and they also fan out along side streets. (For a tour of Georgetown that combines historic houses, shopping, and dining, see "The Roads Less Traveled" box on p. 234.) You'll find both chain and one-of-a-kind shops, chic as well as thrift. Sidewalks and streets are almost always crowded, and parking can be tough. Weekends, especially, bring out all kinds of yahoos, who are mainly here to drink. Visit Georgetown on a weekday morning, if you can. Weeknights are another good time to visit, for dinner and strolling afterward. **Metro:** Foggy Bottom, then catch the D.C. Circulator bus from Washington Circle (see chapter 4 for more information). Metro buses (the no. 30 series) travel through Georgetown from different parts of the city. Otherwise, consider taking a taxi. If you drive, you'll find parking lots expensive and tickets even more so, so be careful where you plant your car.

UPPER WISCONSIN AVENUE NORTHWEST   In a residential section of town known as Friendship Heights on the D.C. side and Chevy Chase on the Maryland side (7 miles north of Georgetown, straight up Wisconsin Ave.) is a quarter-mile shopping district that extends from Saks Fifth Avenue at one end to Sur La Table at the other. In between are Lord & Taylor, Neiman Marcus, Bloomingdale's, Banana Republic, Jimmy Choo, Christian Dior, Barney's Co-Op, Polo, Tiffany's, Versace, and two malls (the Mazza Gallerie and the Chevy Chase Pavilion). The street is too wide and traffic always too snarled to make this a pleasant place to stroll, although teenagers do love to loiter here. Drive if you want and park in the garages beneath the Mazza Gallerie or the Chevy Chase Pavilion. Or take the **Metro;** the strip is right on the Red Line, with the "Friendship Heights" exits leading directly into each of the malls.

OLD TOWN ALEXANDRIA   Old Town, a Virginia neighborhood beyond National Airport, resembles Georgetown in its picturesque location on the Potomac, historic-home lined streets, and plentiful shops and restaurants, as well as in its less desirable aspects: heavy traffic, crowded sidewalks, difficult parking. Old Town extends from the Potomac River in the east to the King Street Metro station in the west, and from about 1st Street in the north to Green Street in the south, but the best shopping is in the center, where King and Washington streets intersect. Weekdays are a lot tamer than weekends. It's always a nice place to visit, though; the drive alone is worth the trip. See chapter 10 for full coverage of Alexandria. **Metro:** King Street, then take a blue and gold DASH bus (the fare is $1.25) to reach the heart of Old Town.

3 SHOPPING A TO Z

ANTIQUES

A few miles north of the city is not too far to go for the good deal or true bonanza you're likely to discover on **Antique Row.** Some 40 antiques and collectible shops line Howard Avenue, on either side of Connecticut Avenue, in Kensington, Maryland, offering every sort of item in a wide variety of styles, periods, and prices. If you don't drive or taxi, you'll have to take the Metro and two buses. From Dupont Circle, board an L1, L2, or L4 bus and get a transfer from the driver. Ask him to tell you when you reach the transfer point for the L7/L8 bus. Once there, board an L7 or L8 bus and ask to be let off at Connecticut and Knowles avenues. Howard Avenue is one block north of Knowles. For antiques in D.C. and Alexandria, try these:

Brass Knob Architectural Antiques   When old homes and office buildings are demolished in the name of progress, these savvy salvage merchants spirit away salable treasures, from lots and lots of light fixtures and chandelier glass to wrought-iron fencing. 2311 18th St. NW. ✆ **202/332-3370.** www.thebrassknob.com. Metro: Woodley Park or Dupont Circle. A second location near Capitol Hill stocks old house parts: the Brass Knob's Back Doors Warehouse, 57 N St. NW (at 1st St. NW; ✆ **202/265-0587**).

Cherry   This is an antiques store, all right, but as its name suggests, a little offbeat. Expect affordable eclectic furnishings and decorative arts, and lots of mirrors and sconces. 1526 Wisconsin Ave. NW. ✆ **202/342-3600.** www.cherryantiques.com. Metro: Foggy Bottom, then walk or take the D.C. Circulator.

Cherub Antiques Gallery   The Cherub Antiques Gallery specializes in Art Nouveau and Art Deco; signed Tiffany, Steuben, Lalique, and Gallé pieces; Liberty arts and crafts; and Louis Icart etchings. Known for its collection of rare cocktail shakers and vintage barware. 2918 M St. NW. ✆ **202/337-2224.** www.trocadero.com/cherubgallery. Metro: Foggy Bottom, then take the D.C. Circulator.

Gore-Dean   This store's inventory runs from furnishings and fabrics (some American pieces, but mostly 18th- and 19th-century European furnishings) to decorative accessories, paintings, prints, and porcelains. 3214 O St. NW. ✆ **202/625-9199.** www.goredean.com. Metro: Foggy Bottom, then take the D.C. Circulator.

Marston-Luce   Stop in here at least to admire, if not buy, a beautiful 18th- or 19th-century French furnishing or two. 1651 Wisconsin Ave. NW. ✆ **202/333-6800.** www.marstonluce.bondandbowery.com. Metro: Foggy Bottom, then take the D.C. Circulator.

Millennium Decorative Arts   This is antiques shopping for the TV generation, where anything made between the 1930s and the 1970s is considered collectible. The shop works with nearly a score or so of dealers; stock changes weekly. Funky wares run from Bakelite to Heywood-Wakefield blond-wood beauties to toasters to used drinking glasses. Call for hours, since the shop tends to be open at select times on select weekdays, and on weekends. 1528 U St. NW. ✆ **202/483-1218.** www.millenniumdecorativearts.com. Metro: U St.–Cardozo (13th St. exit).

Old Print Gallery ★   Open since 1971, this gallery carries original American and European prints from the 17th to the 19th century, including political cartoons, maps, and historical documents. It's one of the largest antique print and map shops in the United States. Prices range from $45 to $10,000. 1220 31st St. NW. ✆ **202/965-1818.** www.oldprintgallery.com. Metro: Foggy Bottom, then take the D.C. Circulator.

Susquehanna Antiques ★ This is Georgetown's largest collection of fine American, English, and European furniture, paintings, and garden items of the late 18th and early 19th centuries. The shop is nearly 100 years old. 3216 O St. NW. ℂ 202/333-1511. www.susquehannaantiques.com. Metro: Foggy Bottom, then take the D.C. Circulator.

ART GALLERIES

Art galleries abound in Washington, D.C., but especially in the Dupont Circle, Georgetown, and Penn Quarter neighborhoods. For a complete listing of galleries throughout Washington, access the website, www.artlineplus.com/gallerymagazine/index.php.

Dupont Circle

For galleries listed below, the closest Metro stop is Dupont Circle. If you're in town the first Friday of the month, don't miss the Dupont Circle gallery walk, free and open to the public, 6 to 8pm. Many Dupont Circle galleries are located in old town houses on treelined streets, amidst foreign embassy buildings.

Burton Marinkovich Fine Art ★ One of the city's leading art galleries, this one showcases fine prints, drawings, and paintings by modern and contemporary international artists, including Jim Dine, Alexander Calder, and Helen Frankenthaler 1506 21st St. NW (P St.). ℂ 202/296-6563. www.burtonmarinkovich.com.

Foundry Gallery In business since 1971, this gallery is artist-owned and operated and features the works of local artists, who work in various media and styles, from abstract painting on silk, to mixed media collages. 1314 18th St. NW (Massachusetts Ave.). ℂ 202/463-0203. www.foundrygallery.org.

Studio Gallery This artist-owned gallery—the longest-running of its kind in the area—shows the works of some 30 local and professional artists, fine arts in all mediums. Don't miss the sculpture garden. Open Wednesday through Saturday. 2108 R St. NW (20th St.). ℂ 202/232-8734. www.studiogallerydc.com.

Georgetown

The closest Metro stop to the following galleries is Foggy Bottom; from there, you can walk, hop on the D.C. Circulator bus, or transfer to a Metrobus, any of the 30 series, to get you the rest of the way.

Addison/Ripley Fine Art This gallery represents internationally, nationally, and regionally recognized artists, from the 19th century to the present; works include paintings, sculpture, photography, and fine arts. 1670 Wisconsin Ave. NW (Reservoir Rd.). ℂ 202/338-5180. www.addisonripleyfineart.com.

Govinda Gallery This place, a block from the campus of Georgetown University, generates a lot of media coverage because it often shows artwork created by famous names and features photographs of celebrities, also pop and contemporary art. 1227 34th St. NW (Prospect St.). ℂ 202/333-1180. www.govindagallery.com.

Susan Calloway Fine Arts On display are antique European and American oil paintings; contemporary art by local, regional, and international artists; and a carefully chosen selection of 17th to 19th century prints. 1643 Wisconsin Ave. NW (Q St.). ℂ 202/965-4601. www.callowayart.com.

A couple of these galleries predate the renaissance taking place in this downtown neighborhood. To get here, take the Metro to either Archives/Navy Memorial (Blue–Orange Line) or Gallery Place/Chinatown/Verizon Center (Red–Yellow Line).

Flashpoint   Flashpoint is a dance studio, theater lab, office space, and art gallery all in one. Its art gallery is dedicated to nurturing emerging local artists, who tend to use a variety of mediums, including video, sculpture, photography, and drawings to tell their personal stories. 916 G St. NW (9th St.). 🕐 202/315-1305. www.flashpointdc.org.

Touchstone Gallery ★   The first floor of this historic building houses Apartment Zero, a stylish contemporary furniture and design store, well worth a visit on its own merits, especially since it hosts gallery-like events highlighting the ideas and products of up and coming "ware artists" from around the world. Then head upstairs to the second floor to find **Touchstone,** whose 16-foot-high ceilings and spacious rooms form the backdrop for a self-run co-op studio for 30 to 35 contemporary artists, each of whom has at least one work on display at all times. 406 7th St. NW (D St.). 🕐 202/347-2787. www. touchstonegallery.com.

BEAUTY

The city's best hair salons and cosmetic stores are in Georgetown, while spas are more evenly scattered throughout the city. Here's a sampling of recommended places to go for beauty treatments and products.

Beauty 360   CVS pharmacies are known as drugstores, mainly, where you can buy all your essentials, from candy to cold medicine to cheap cosmetics. With the launching of Beauty 360 (D.C.'s was the first to open), CVS ventures into the high-end cosmetics and skin treatment market. Trained and licensed professionals provide signature services including mini-manicures and express facials, while trying to interest you in buying, say, Juicy Couture fragrance, Paula Dorf makeup, or Payot skincare items. A regular old CVS lies just around the corner, if you need something not quite so chi-chi. 1350 Connecticut Ave. NW (Dupont Circle). 🕐 202/331-1725. www.beauty360.com. Metro: Dupont Circle (19th St. exit).

Blue Mercury   Half "apothecary," half spa, this chain's two D.C. locations offer a full selection of facial, massage, waxing, and makeup treatments, as well as a smorgasbord of high-end beauty products, from Acqua di Parma fragrances to Kiehl's skincare line. Very popular, so you might want to call in advance of your trip. Georgetown: 3059 M St. NW. 🕐 202/965-1300. www.bluemercury.com. Metro: Foggy Bottom, then take the D.C. Circulator. Dupont Circle: 1619 Connecticut Ave. NW 🕐 202/462-1300. Metro: Dupont Circle (Q St. exit).

The Grooming Lounge   Not your father's barbershop. Famous for its 30-minute "hot lather shave," The Grooming Lounge also dispenses treatments with names like "The Commander in Chief" and sells beauty accessories, um, I mean, grooming tools, from nail clippers to special shaving brushes. Or you can just get a haircut. 1745 L St. NW. 🕐 202/466-8900. www.groominglounge.com. Metro: Farragut North (L St. exit).

Okyo Beauty Salon   This is probably D.C.'s most popular hair salon, known as much for its celebrity clientele as for its fantastic cuts and coloring. Expect high prices and a tight schedule. 2903 M St. NW. 🕐 202/342-2675. www.okyosalon.com. Metro: Foggy Bottom, then take the D.C. Circulator.

SomaFit   If your hotel doesn't have a fitness center or spa, visit this ultracool, one-stop-spot for a workout, massage, yoga class, pedicure, facial—whatever your little body needs or desires. This is not a membership facility, so all you have to do is call or check online for a class schedule, and just show up (only a handful of classes require that you reserve a space in advance); or call to schedule a spa treatment. 2121 Wisconsin Ave. NW. © 202/965-2121. www.somafit.com. Metro: Foggy Bottom, then take the D.C. Circulator bus.

BOOKS

Real-live bookstores still have their fans. Here are some favorite shops in general, used, and special-interest categories.

General

Barnes & Noble   This three-story shop in Georgetown is well-stocked in all genres, including sizable software, travel-book, children's-title, and music sections. The store has a cafe on the second level. 3040 M St. NW. © 202/965-9880. www.bn.com. Metro: Foggy Bottom, then take the D.C. Circulator. Other area locations include 555 12th St. NW (© 202/347-0176) and 4801 Bethesda Ave., in Bethesda, MD (© 301/986-1761).

B. Dalton   This all-purpose bookstore is heavy on the bestsellers and carries magazines, too. Union Station. © 202/289-1724. www.bn.com. Metro: Union Station.

Borders   With its overwhelming array of books, records, videos, and magazines, Borders competes neck and neck with Barnes & Noble as well as Amazon.com and every other online bookseller. Many hardcover bestsellers are 30% off. 1801 K St. NW. © 202/466-4999. www.borders.com. Metro: Farragut North (L St. exit). Other Borders stores in the District include 600 14th St. NW #100. (© 202/737-1385) and 5333 Wisconsin Ave. NW (© 202/686-8270), in upper-northwest D.C.

Bridge Street Books   A small, serious shop specializing in politics, poetry, literature, history, philosophy, and publications you won't find elsewhere. Bestsellers and discounted books are not its specialty. 2814 Pennsylvania Ave. NW (next to the Four Seasons Hotel). © 202/965-5200. Metro: Foggy Bottom, then take the DC Circulator.

Kramerbooks & Afterwords Café ★ Finds   Opened in 1976, Kramer's was the first bookstore/cafe in Washington, maybe in this country, and has launched countless romances. It's jammed, is often noisy, stages live music Wednesday through Saturday evenings, and is open all night weekends. Paperback fiction takes up most of its inventory, but the store carries a little of everything. 1517 Connecticut Ave. NW. © 202/387-1400 or 387-3825 for information. www.kramers.com. Metro: Dupont Circle, Q St. exit.

Politics and Prose Bookstore ★   Located a few miles north of downtown in a residential area, this much-cherished two-story shop may be worth going out of your way for. It has vast offerings in literary fiction and nonfiction alike and an excellent children's department. The store has expanded again and again over the years to accommodate its clientele's love of books; its most recent enlargement added to the travel and children's sections. The shop hosts author readings nearly every night of the year. A warm, knowledgeable staff will help you find what you need. Downstairs is a cozy coffeehouse. 5015 Connecticut Ave. NW. © 202/364-1919. www.politics-prose.com. Metro: Van Ness–UDC, and walk, or transfer to an "L" bus to take you the ³/₄ mile from there.

Old & Used Books

Second Story Books   If it's old, out of print, custom bound, or a small-press publication, this is where to find it. The store also specializes in used CDs and vinyl and has an interesting collection of campaign posters. 2000 P St. NW. © 202/659-8884. www.second storybooks.com. Metro: Dupont Circle (South/19th St. exit).

Back Stage Books and Costumes Back Stage is headquarters for Washington's theatrical community, which buys its books, scripts, trades, and sheet music here. It's also a favorite costume-rental shop. 545 8th St. SE. © **202/544-5744.** http://backstagebooks.com. Metro: Eastern Market.

Lambda Rising This gay and lesbian bookstore in the heart of the Dupont Circle neighborhood is the unofficial headquarters for the GLBT community, carrying every gay, lesbian, bisexual, and transgender book in print, as well as videos, music, and gifts. 1625 Connecticut Ave. NW. © **202/462-6969.** www.lambdarising.com. Metro: Dupont Circle, Q St. exit.

Reiter's Bookstore Open since 1936, this is D.C.'s oldest independent bookstore. Located in the middle of the George Washington University campus, Reiter's is the go-to place for scientific, technical, medical, and professional books. The store is also known for its intriguing, sometimes amusing, mathematical and scientific toys in the children's section. 1990 K St. NW. (The entrance is on 20th St.) © **202/223-3327.** www.reiters.com. Metro: Foggy Bottom.

CAMERAS & FILM DEVELOPING

Penn Camera Exchange Penn Camera has been owned and operated by the Zweig family since 1953; its staff is quite knowledgeable, and its inventory wide-ranging. Their specialty is quality equipment and archival paper processing—not cheap, but worth it. 840 E St. NW. © **202/347-5777.** www.penncamera.com. Metro: Gallery Place (9th and G sts. exit). Also at 1015 18th St. NW (© **202/785-7366**).

Ritz Camera Center Ritz sells camera equipment for the average photographer and offers 1-hour film processing. Call for other locations; there are several in the area. 601 13th St. NW. © **202/628-0410.** www.ritzcamera.com. Metro: Metro Center (13th St. exit).

CRAFTS

A Mano Owner Adam Mahr frequently forages in Europe and returns with the unique handmade, imported French and Italian ceramics, linens, and other decorative accessories for home and garden that you'll covet here. 1677 Wisconsin Ave. NW. © **202/298-7200.** www.amano.bz. Metro: Foggy Bottom, then take the D.C. Circulator.

Appalachian Spring Country comes to Georgetown. This store sells pottery, jewelry, newly made pieced and appliqué quilts, stuffed dolls and animals, candles, rag rugs, handblown glassware, an incredible collection of kaleidoscopes, glorious weavings, and wooden kitchenware. Everything is made by hand in the United States. 1415 Wisconsin Ave. NW (at P St.). © **202/337-5780.** www.appalachianspring.com. Metro: Foggy Bottom, then take the D.C. Circulator. There's another branch in Union Station (© **202/682-0505**).

Go Mama Go! (Finds) Look here for Italian glassware, Dutch art, Pennsylvania tableware, Czech crystal, and original artwork. 1809 14th St. NW (S St.). © **202/299-0850.** www. gomamago.com. Metro: U St.–Cardozo (14th St. exit).

Indian Craft Shop ★ (Finds) The Indian Craft Shop has represented authentic Native American artisans since 1938, selling their hand-woven rugs and handcrafted baskets, jewelry, figurines, pottery, and other items. Since the shop is situated inside a federal government building, you must pass through security and show a photo ID to enter. Use the C Street entrance, which is the only one open to the public. The shop is open weekdays and the third Saturday of each month. Department of the Interior, 1849 C St. NW,

Room 1023. ℂ **202/208-4056.** www.indiancraftshop.com. Metro: Farragut West (17th St. exit), with a bit of a walk from the station.

The Phoenix Around since 1955, the Phoenix sells high-end Mexican folk and fine art; handcrafted sterling silver jewelry from Mexico and all over the world; clothing in natural fibers from Mexican and American designers like Eileen Fisher and Flax; collectors' quality masks; and decorative doodads in tin, brass, copper, and wood. Oaxaca folk and fine art are a specialty. 1514 Wisconsin Ave. NW. ℂ **202/338-4404.** www.thephoenixdc. com. Metro: Foggy Bottom, then take the D.C. Circulator.

Torpedo Factory Art Center Once a munitions factory, this three-story building built in 1918 now houses more than 82 working studios and the works of about 165 artists, who tend to their crafts before your very eyes, pausing to explain their techniques or to sell their pieces. Artworks include paintings, sculpture, ceramics, glasswork, and textiles. 105 N. Union St., Alexandria. ℂ **703/838-4565.** www.torpedofactory.org. Metro: King St., then take the DASH bus (AT2, AT5) eastbound to the waterfront.

FARMERS' & FLEA MARKETS

Alexandria Farmers' Market The oldest continuously operating farmers' market in the country (since 1752), this market offers locally grown fruits and vegetables, along with delectable baked goods, cut flowers, and plants. Open year-round, Saturday mornings from 5:30 to 11am. 301 King St. (at Market Sq. in front of the city hall), in Alexandria. ℂ **703/906-1481.** Metro: King St., then take the free-on-weekends DASH bus (AT2, AT5) eastbound to Market Sq.

Dupont Circle FreshFarm Market (Kids) At least 30 local farmers sell their flowers, produce, eggs, and cheeses here. The market also features kids' activities and guest appearances by chefs and owners of some of Washington's best restaurants: Vidalia, Zaytinya, Bis, and 1789. Held Sundays rain or shine, year-round, from 10am to 1pm January through March and 9am to 1pm, the rest of the year. The FreshFarm Market organization stages other farmers' markets on other days around town; go to the website for locations, dates, and times. On 20th St. NW (btw. Q St. and Massachusetts Ave.), and in the adjacent Riggs Bank parking lot. ℂ **202/362-8889.** www.freshfarmmarkets.org. Metro: Dupont Circle, Q St. exit.

Eastern Market ★ (Value) Finally re-opened in July 2009 after a devastating fire in April 2007 gutted this Capitol Hill institution, historic Eastern Market can still claim that it has been in continuous operation since 1873: the indoor vendors set up stands across the street in temporary quarters and the outdoor farmers' market stalls remained open throughout, selling fresh produce and other goods on Saturdays and flea market items on Sundays. Today Eastern Market's restored South Hall is once again a bustling bazaar Tuesday through Sunday, when greengrocers, butchers, bakers, farmers, artists, artisans, florists, and other merchants sell their wares. Best of all, the Saturday morning ritual of breakfasting on blueberry pancakes at the Market Lunch counter is back in play. The market is open 7am to 6pm, Sunday 9am to 4pm (call for other days and times of operations). 225 7th St. SE (North Carolina Ave.). ℂ **202/478-2429.** www.easternmarket.net. Metro: Eastern Market.

Montgomery County Farm Woman's Cooperative Market Vendors set up inside every Wednesday, Friday, and Saturday year-round from 8am to about 4pm to sell preserves, homegrown veggies, cut flowers, slabs of bacon and sausages, and mouthwatering pies, cookies, and breads; there's an abbreviated version on Wednesday. Outside, on

Saturday, Sunday, Wednesday, and Friday, from 8am to 4pm you'll find flea market vendors selling everything from rugs to tablecloths to furniture to sunglasses. 7155 Wisconsin Ave., in Bethesda. © **301/652-2291.** Metro: Bethesda.

FASHION

See also "Shoes," later in this section.

Children's Clothing

If your youngster has spilled grape juice all over his favorite outfit and you need a replacement, you can always head to the downtown **Macy's** (p. 249) or **H&M** (p. 245), or to the nearest **Gap Kids** in Georgetown (1267 Wisconsin Ave. NW; © **202/333-2411**). Chic moms undeterred by expense shop at the Georgetown store, while practical moms shop at the midtown Kid's Closet.

Kid's Closet (Kids) Now in its 28th year, Kid's Closet has seen numerous chi chi children's clothing stores come and go in D.C. The secret to its staying power lies in full view: Its storefront display of affordable and practical kids' clothes are cute enough for you to imagine your child in them, but not so precious as to make you worry in advance about how you're going to remove the inevitable stains. The store is easy to find, since it stands out among the bank and restaurant facades in this downtown block. 1226 Connecticut Ave. NW. © **202/429-9247.** www.kidsclosetdc.com. Metro: Dupont Circle or Farragut North.

Piccolo Piggies (Kids) Here you'll love the cutie-pie children's garb, Petit Bateau to Lilly Pulitzer, for newborns up to age 14 for girls and up to age 10 for boys, as well as shoes, toys, and accessories. 1533 Wisconsin Ave. NW. © **202/333-0123.** www.piccolo-piggies. com. Metro: Foggy Bottom, then take the Georgetown Metro Connection shuttle or the D.C. Circulator.

Men's Clothing

Local branches of **Banana Republic** are at Wisconsin and M streets in Georgetown (© **202/333-2554**) and F and 13th streets NW (© **202/638-2724**); **Gap** has several locations in Washington, including 1120 Connecticut Ave. NW (© **202/429-0691**) and 1258 Wisconsin Ave. NW (© **202/333-2657**). Also see "Vintage Shops" category.

Brooks Brothers Brooks sells traditional men's clothes, as well as the fine line of Peal & Company Collection shoes. This store made the news as the place where Monica Lewinsky bought a tie for President Clinton. It also sells an extensive line of women's clothes. 1201 Connecticut Ave. NW. © **202/659-4650.** www.brooksbrothers.com. Metro: Dupont Circle (19th St./Q St. exit) or Farragut North (L St. exit). Other locations are at National Airport (© **703/417-1071**), and at 5504 Wisconsin Ave., in Chevy Chase, MD (© **301/654-8202**).

Burberry's Here you'll find those plaid-lined trench coats, of course, along with well-tailored English clothing for men and women. Hot items include cashmere sweaters and camel's hair duffel coats for men. 1155 Connecticut Ave. NW. © **202/463-3000.** www.burberry. com. Metro: Farragut North (L St. exit).

Daddy & Son Camiceria Italiana This is the Italian men's store's sole retail location in the U.S. Expect to find exquisite Italian designs with fine touches, like mother-of-pearl buttons, hand-finished ties, shirts, and sweaters for boys and men. 1704 Connecticut Ave. NW (R St.). © **202/462-1324.** www.daddyesonusa.com. Metro: Dupont Circle (Q St. exit).

Jos. A. Bank Clothiers If you admire the Brooks Brothers line, but only wish it were more affordable, look here. This century-old clothier sells suits, corporate casual, weekend casual, and formal attire at great prices (lots of "buy one, get one free" offers). Union Station. © 202/289-9087. www.josbank.com. Metro: Union Station. Two other locations: Lincoln Square, 555 11th St. NW (© 202/393-5590) and 1200 19th St. NW (© 202/466-2282).

Sherman Pickey   Prep to the max is this store but also a little fey: Think red corduroys. Both men's and women's clothes are on sale here, including Bill's Khakis and Barbour Outerwear for men, embroidered capris and ribbon belts for women. It's not a chain, though, so it's different in that respect. 1647 Wisconsin Ave. NW. © 202/333-4212. www.shermanpickey.com. Metro: Foggy Bottom, then take the D.C. Circulator.

Thomas Pink   For those who like beautifully made, bright-colored shirts, this branch of the London-based high-end establishment should please. The store also sells ties, boxer shorts, women's shirts, cuff links, and other accessories. 1127 Connecticut Ave. NW (inside the Mayflower Hotel). © 202/223-5390. www.thomaspink.com. Metro: Farragut North (L St. exit).

Urban Outfitters   For the latest in casual attire, from fatigue pants to tube tops. The shop has a floor of women's clothes and a floor of men's clothes, as well as apartment wares, travel books and accessories, cards, and candles. 3111 M St. NW. © 202/342-1012. www.urbanoutfitters.com. Metro: Foggy Bottom, then take the D.C. Circulator. Second location: Gallery Place, 737 7th St. NW © 202/737-0259. Metro: Gallery Place (7th and H sts. exit).

Vintage Shops

Meeps Vintage Fashionette   This pioneer shop opened on U Street, but has since moved around the corner to lower Adams-Morgan; its clientele and inventory remain the same: men and women urbanistas attracted to local designer ware and vintage clothes, from 1930's gabardine suits to 1950's cocktail dresses to satiny lingerie. 2104 18th St. NW © 202/265-6546. www.meepsdc.com. Metro: U St.–Cardozo (13th St. exit) or Woodley Park–Zoo, with a bit of a walk from either station.

The Remix ★ Value   Locals know to shop here for sophisticated men's and women's clothes, including designer outfits, from the 1920s to the 1970s—think Fred Astaire-like smoking jackets, Grace Kellyish cocktail dresses. Jewelry and housewares are also available. 645 Pennsylvania Ave. SE (6th St.). © 202/547-0211. www.remixvintage.com. Metro: Eastern Market.

Secondhand Rose Value   This upscale second-floor consignment shop has been around for 30 years, specializing in designer merchandise. Creations by Chanel, Armani, Donna Karan, Calvin Klein, Yves Saint-Laurent, Ungaro, Ralph Lauren, and others are sold at about a third of the original price. Everything is in style, in season, and in excellent condition. Secondhand Rose is also a great place to shop for gorgeous furs, designer shoes and bags, and costume jewelry. 1516 Wisconsin Ave. NW (btw. P St. and Volta Place). © 202/337-3378. Metro: Foggy Bottom, then take the D.C. Circulator.

Secondi Inc. ★ Value   On the second floor of a building right above Starbucks is this high-style consignment shop that sells women's clothing and accessories, including designer suits, evening wear, and more casual items—everything from Kate Spade to Chanel. 1702 Connecticut Ave. NW (btw. R St. and Florida Ave.). © 202/667-1122. www.secondi. com. Metro: Dupont Circle (Q St. exit).

Women's Clothing

Washington women have many more clothing stores to choose from than men. Stores selling classic designs dominate, including **Ann Taylor,** at Union Station (© 202/371-8010), 1140 Connecticut Ave. NW (© 202/659-0120), 600 13th St. NW (© 202/737-0325), and Georgetown Park, 3222 M St. NW (© **202/337-0843**); and **Talbots,** at 1122 Connecticut Ave. NW (© **202/887-6973**). Beneath their modest apparel, however, Washington women like to wear racy **Victoria's Secret** lingerie—you'll find stores in Union Station (© **202/682-0686**) and Georgetown Park (© **202/965-5457**), as well as at Connecticut and L streets NW (© **202/293-7530**).

See "Men's Clothing," above, for locations of Banana Republic, Gap, Sherman Pickey, Brooks Brothers, and Urban Outfitters, all of which also sell women's clothes. See "Vintage Shops," above, for bargain shopping.

Hip boutiques and upscale shops proliferate as well:

Betsey Johnson   New York's flamboyant flower-child designer personally decorated the bubble-gum-pink walls in her Georgetown shop. Her sexy, offbeat, play-dress-up styles are great party and club clothes for the young and the still-skinny young at heart. This is the only Betsey Johnson store in D.C. 3029 M St. NW. © **202/338-4090.** www.betsey johnson.com. Metro: Foggy Bottom, then take the D.C. Circulator.

Betsy Fisher ★   A walk past the store is all it takes to know that this shop is a tad different. Its windows and racks show off whimsically feminine fashions by new American, French, and Italian designers. Access the website to find out about upcoming events; Betsy Fisher often hosts an evening cocktail hour to introduce a new line or inventory. 1224 Connecticut Ave. NW. © **202/785-1975.** www.betsyfisher.com. Metro: Dupont Circle (South/19th St. exit).

H&M   This Swedish-based store sells trendy clothes for the whole family at reasonable prices. Some designer knockoffs. 1025 F St. NW. © **202/347-3306.** www.hm.com. Metro: Metro Center (11th St. exit). A second location, in the Shops at Georgetown Park Mall, 3222 M St. NW ((© **202/298-6792**), sells only women's and youth lines.

Nana's   Owner Jackie Flanagan left the world of advertising and publishing to open this store a couple of years ago, naming it after her fashion-wise grandmother. The shop sells new creations from independent U.S. and Canadian designs, and a small rack of vintage styles of work and play clothes, the idea being to mix old and new for a fresh look. Handbags, gifts, and bath products also on sale. 1528 U St. NW (btw. 15th and 16th sts.). © **202/667-6955.** www.nanadc.com. Metro: U St.-Cardozo (13th St. exit).

Reiss Washington   This British import sells tailored but fun, fashion-forward but not simply trendy, clothes for both men and women. Best of all, for each design, the store sells only one item in each size, thereby narrowing the chances that you'll show up to an event wearing the same outfit as another. 1254 Wisconsin Ave. NW. © **202/944-8566.** www.reiss.co.uk.

Rizik Brothers   The year 2008 marked Rizik's centennial anniversary. This downtown high-fashion store sells bridal dresses and other high-toned fashions by European and American designers such as Carolina Herrera, Sylvia Heisel, and Lourdes Chavez. 1100 Connecticut Ave. NW. © **202/223-4050.** www.riziks.com. Metro: Farragut North (L St. exit).

Rue 14   If you like the latest looks in fashion but not the prices that usually go with them, shop here. Owners Andrew Nguyen and Jiwon Paik-Nguyen fill their second-story boutique with the affordable designs of Free People, BB Dakota, Plastic Island, and other trendsetters. 1803A 14th St. NW. © **202/462-6200.** www.rue14.com. Metro: U St.-Cardozo (13th St. exit).

Wink   Look for Wink beneath the Steve Madden store, and you'll discover Seven jeans and clothes by Diane von Furstenberg, Mystique, and Free People, and happy women of all ages sorting through the mix. 3109 M St. NW. Lower level. ✆ **202/338-9465.** www.shop winkdc.com. Metro: Foggy Bottom, then take the D.C. Circulator.

Zara   This cheery store is an outpost of a popular chain started in Spain. Clothes are both dressy and casual, but all trendy. A sprinkling of coats is also found here, when the season calls for it. 1238 Wisconsin Ave. NW. ✆ **202/944-9797.** www.zara.com. Metro: Foggy Bottom, then take the D.C. Circulator. Also at 1025 F St. NE. ✆ **202/393 2810.**

GIFTS/SOUVENIRS

See also "Crafts," earlier in this chapter. Museum gift shops are also full of possibilities. Also check out the online shop operated by the U.S. Secret Service Uniformed Division Benefit Fund (www.whitehousegiftshop.com) for sundry items, from sweatshirts to mugs, stamped with White House or Armed Forces logos.

America!   Stop here if you want to pick up a baseball cap with COMMANDER IN CHIEF printed across its bill, a T-shirt proclaiming I LOVE MY COUNTRY, IT'S THE GOVERNMENT I'M AFRAID OF, White House guest towels, Obama coasters, or other impress-the-folks-back-home items. Union Station. ✆ **202/842-0540.** www.americastore.com. Metro: Union Station. Or save your shopping for the airport; America! has at least one location at National (✆ **703/417-1782**), one at BWI (✆ **410/850-8373**) and several at Dulles (Terminal B: ✆ **703/572-2543**; Terminal C: ✆ **703/572-6033**; Terminal D: ✆ **703/572-6070**).

Chocolate Moose (Finds)   Its website welcomes browsers with the words "Serving weirdly sophisticated Washingtonians since 1978, but now attempting to reach out to the rest of you." I guess my family qualifies as weirdly sophisticated, since we're longtime fans. My husband endears himself to me and our daughters when he brings home gifts from this shop: a Wonder Woman daybook; chunky, transparent, red heart-shaped earrings; wacky cards; paperweight snow globes with figurines inside; candies; eccentric clothing; and other funny, lovely, and useful presents. 1743 L St. NW. ✆ **202/463-0992.** www.chocolatemoosedc.com. Metro: Farragut North (L St. exit).

Pulp Gifts   You'll find must-have items here that you never even knew existed: a deck of slang flashcards, "Dancin' in the Streets" T-shirts, and crazy greeting cards. 1803 14th St. NW. ✆ **202/462-7857.** www.pulpdc.com. Metro: U St.–Cardozo (13th St. exit).

GOURMET GOODIES TO GO

Demanding jobs and hectic schedules leave Washingtonians less and less time to prepare their own meals. Or so they say. At any rate, a number of fine-food shops and bakeries are happy to come to the rescue. Even the busiest bureaucrat can find the time to pop into one of these gourmet shops for a movable feast.

See also "Farmers' & Flea Markets," above.

Bread Line (Finds)   Bread Line is wildly popular and attracts the White House crowd for lunch, with favorite sandwiches like the roast pork bun or the muffuletta; tasty soups; and desserts such as bread puddings, pear tarts, and delicious cookies. Seating is available, but most people buy carryout. The shop also sells freshly baked loaves of wheat bread, flatbreads, baguettes, and more. Open weekdays 7:30am to 3:30pm. 1751 Pennsylvania Ave. NW. ✆ **202/822-8900.** www.breadlinedc.com. Metro: Farragut West or Farragut North.

Cowgirl Creamery (Finds)   I don't know how D.C. got so lucky as to have the only Cowgirl Creamery outside of California, but we can all be grateful. The creamery sells its own seven artisanal cheeses as well as those of the best 200 American and European cheese producers. Taste the brie here and you'll never be happy again with your local grocery store's brand. The creamery also sells freshly made sandwiches, salads, and soups, plus beer and wine. Open Monday through Saturday. 919 F St. NW. ℂ202/393-6880. www. cowgirlcreamery.com. Metro: Gallery Place/Verizon Center (9th St. exit).

Dean & Deluca   This famed New York store operates this fabulous emporium in a historic Georgetown building that was once an open-air market. Though it is now closed in, this huge space still feels airy, with its high ceiling and windows on all sides. You'll pay top prices, but the quality is impressive—charcuterie, fresh fish, produce, cheeses, prepared sandwiches and cold pasta salads, hot-ticket desserts, like crème brûlée and tiramisu, and California wines. Also on sale are housewares; on-site is an espresso bar/cafe. 3276 M St. NW. ℂ 202/342-2500. www.deandeluca.com. Metro: Foggy Bottom, then take the D.C. Circulator.

Firehook Bakery   Known for its sourdough baguettes, apple-walnut bread, fresh fruit tarts, red-iced elephant and blue-iced donkey cookies, and sandwiches like smoked chicken on sesame semolina bread, Firehook also runs the cafe at the National Building Museum (see "Museums of Special Interest," chapter 7). 1909 Q St. NW. ℂ 202/588-9296. www.firehook. com. Metro: Dupont Circle (Q St. exit). Also at 912 17th St. NW (ℂ 202/429-2253), 3411 Connecticut Ave. NW (ℂ 202/362-2253), 215 Pennsylvania Ave. SE (ℂ 202/544-7003), 555 13th St. NW (ℂ 202/393-0952), 441 4th St. NW (ℂ 202/347-1760), and at 2 locations in Alexandria, VA.

Marvelous Market   First there were the breads: sourdough, baguettes, olive, rosemary, croissants, scones. Now, there are things to spread on the bread, including smoked salmon mousse and tapenade; pastries to die for, from gingerbread to flourless chocolate cake; and prepared foods, such as soups, empanadas, and pasta salads. The breakfast spread on Sunday mornings is sinful, and individual items, like the croissants, are tastier and less expensive here than at other bakeries. The location is grand, with 18th-century chandeliers, an antique cedar bar, and a small number of tables. 1511 Connecticut Ave. NW. ℂ 202/332-3690. www.marvelousmarket.com. Metro: Dupont Circle (Q St. exit). Other locations include 3217 P St. NW (ℂ 202/333-2591), 1800 K St. NW (ℂ 202/828-0944), and 303 7th St. SE (ℂ 202/544-7127).

HOME FURNISHINGS

You may not have come to Washington to shop for furniture, but step inside these beguiling shops and you may change your mind.

Apartment Zero   Located on the first floor of a Penn Quarter historic building (its second floor is home to the Touchstone Gallery; see Art Galleries category, earlier in this chapter), this sophisticated store sells hot-off-the-design-floor furnishings: Eames sofas, Zanzibar stools, "orange slice" chairs, and "petits fours" benches. The clever designers are from around the world; the prices are out of this world. Besides furniture, Apartment Zero sells everything else you need for the home, from light fixtures to bed linens. 406 7th St. NW. ℂ 202/628-4067. www.apartmentzero.com. Metro: Gallery Place/Verizon Center (Arena/7th and F sts. exit) or Archives/Navy Memorial.

Cady's Alley ★   Cady's Alley refers not to a single store, but to the southwest pocket of Georgetown, where about 20 stores reside, in and around said alley, which dangles south of M Street. These are tony, big-name places, and include Waterworks, Thos. Moser Cabinetmakers, Baker Furniture, and European outposts, such as the high-concept designs of Ligne Roset and the hip kitchen furnishings of Bulthaup. 3318 M St. NW (btw. 33rd and 34th sts.). www.cadysalley.com. Metro: Foggy Bottom, then take the D.C. Circulator.

Home Rule (Value) Unique housewares; bath, kitchen, and office supplies; and gifts cram this tiny store. You'll see everything from French milled soap to martini glasses. 1807 14th St. NW (at S St.). *C* 202/797-5544. www.homerule.com. Metro: U St.–Cardozo (13th St. exit; check the website or call for specific directions from the station).

JEWELRY

Beadazzled The friendly staff demonstrates to you how to assemble your own afford-able jewelry from an eye-boggling array of beads and artifacts. The store also sells textiles, woodcarvings, and other crafts from around the world. There are also classes offered to those who prefer a more hands-on experience. 1507 Connecticut Ave. NW. *C* 202/265-BEAD (2323). www.beadazzled.net. Metro: Dupont Circle (Q St. exit).

Chas Schwartz & Son In business since 1888, Chas Schwartz specializes in dia-monds and sapphires, rubies and emeralds, and is one of the few distributors of Hidalgo jewelry (enameled rings and bracelets). The professional staff also repairs watches and jewelry. 1400 F St. NW, or enter through the Willard Hotel, at 1401 Pennsylvania Ave. NW. *C* 202/737-4757. www.chasschwartzjewelers.com. Metro: Metro Center (13th St. exit). There's another branch at the Mazza Gallerie (*C* 202/363-5432); Metro: Friendship Heights.

Keith Lipert Gallery This decorative-arts gallery sells Venetian glassware, high-end costume jewelry by designers such as Oscar de la Renta, and cute little old things, like Art Deco–style handbags. The owner shops in Europe for fashion jewelry and for exqui-site gifts suitable for giving to diplomats and international business executives. 2922 M St. NW. *C* 202/965-9736. www.keithlipertgallery.com. Metro: Foggy Bottom, then take the D.C. Circulator.

Mia Gemma ★ This pretty boutique sells the original designs of American and Euro-pean artists, including Judy Bettencourt, Sarah Richardson, and Randi Chervitz. All pieces are handcrafted, either of limited edition or one of a kind. If you'd like a custom-ized design, Mia Gemma can do that, too. 933 F St. NW. *C* 202/393-4367. www.miagemma. com. Metro: Gallery Place/Verizon Center (9th St. exit).

Tiffany & Co. Tiffany is known for exquisite diamonds and other jewelry that can cost hundreds of thousands of dollars. But you may not know that the store carries less expen-sive items as well, like $35 candlesticks. Tiffany will engrave, too. Other items include tabletop gifts and fancy glitz: china, crystal, flatware, and a bridal registry service. 5481 Wisconsin Ave., Chevy Chase, MD. *C* 301/657-8777. www.tiffany.com. Metro: Friendship Heights.

Tiny Jewel Box The first place Washingtonians go for estate and antique jewelry, but this six-story store next to the Mayflower Hotel also sells the pieces of many designers, from Links of London to Christian Tse, as well as crystal and other house gifts. In the month leading up to Mother's Day, the Tiny Jewel Box holds its Top-to-Bottom Sale, where you can save anywhere from 10% to 75% on most merchandise, including jewelry, handbags, and home accessories. 1147 Connecticut Ave. NW. *C* 202/393-2747. www.tiny jewelbox.com. Metro: Farragut North (L St. exit).

MALLS

If malls are your thing, the D.C. area has plenty for you to choose from: **Chevy Chase Pavilion,** 5335 Wisconsin Ave. NW (*C* 202/207-3887; www.ccpavilion.com; Metro: Friendship Heights); **Gallery Place,** 7th and H sts. NW (*C* 202/624-8627; www.galleryplace.com; Metro: Gallery Place/Verizon Center); **Mazza Gallerie,** 5300 Wisconsin

Emergency Shopping

You've just arrived in town, but your luggage hasn't—the airline lost it. Or you're about to depart for home or another destination and you notice that the zipper to your suitcase is broken. Or you've arrived at your hotel all in one piece, only to discover you've forgotten something essential: underwear, allergy medicine, an umbrella. What's a lonesome traveler to do? One of these suggestions might prove your salvation.

CVS: This is Washington's main pharmacy and essentials chain. Among the items sold at CVS stores are pantyhose, over-the-counter and prescription medicines, toys, greeting cards, wrapping paper and ribbon, magazines, film and 1-hour photo developing, batteries, candy, some refrigerated food such as milk and orange juice, and office supplies. The stores are ubiquitous, so chances are you'll find one near you. Two conveniently located 24-hour branches are at 2240 M St. NW (© **202/296-9877;** Metro: Foggy Bottom) and at 6-7 Dupont Circle NW (© **202/785-1466;** Metro: Dupont Circle); www.cvs.com.

Cobbler's Bench Shoe Repair: This shop on the lower (food court) level of Union Station is open daily, Monday to Friday from 7am to 8pm, Saturday 10am to 6pm, and Sunday noon to 6pm, to come to the rescue of travelers whose shoes or luggage need mending. The cobbler also cuts keys and sells repair items. Union Station, lower level. (© **202/898-9009**). Metro: Union Station.

Macy's: This former Hecht's remains an old reliable and the only department store located downtown. But though it's been around a while, the store continually updates its merchandise to keep up with the times. Run here if you need cosmetics, clothes (for men, women, and children), shoes (but not for children), electronics, appliances, lingerie, luggage, raincoats, and countless other need-immediately goods. Open daily: noon to 6pm Sunday; 10am to 8pm Monday to Saturday. 1201 G St. NW. (© **202/628-6661**). www.macys.com. Metro: Metro Center.

Metro Stations: If it starts raining and you're scrambling to find an umbrella, look no farther than your closest Metro station, where vendors are at the ready selling umbrellas and other handy things.

SHOPPING

8

SHOPPING A TO Z

Ave. NW (© **202/966-6114;** www.mazzagallerie.com; Metro: Friendship Heights); and the **Shops at Georgetown Park,** 3222 M St. NW (© **202/342-8190;** www.shopsat georgetownpark.com; Metro: Foggy Bottom, then take the Georgetown Metro Connection shuttle or D.C. Circulator). **Ronald Reagan Washington National Airport,** Arlington, VA (© **703/417-8600;** www.mwaa.com/national), has 100 stores to choose from, too, if you want to do some souvenir shopping on your way out of town.

Even if you aren't a mall rat, you might want to check out the following two establishments, which do double duty as both shopping centers and attractions:

Pavilion at the Old Post Office   Not so much a mall as a tourist trap with souvenir shops and a food court. But you can ride a pair of elevators to the clock tower for a stunning view of the city. 1100 Pennsylvania Ave. NW. ℂ **202/289-4224.** www.oldpostofficedc.com. Metro: Federal Triangle.

Union Station   One of the most popular tourist stops in Washington, Union Station boasts magnificent architecture and more than 100 shops, including Pendleton's and Appalachian Spring (p. 241). Among the places to eat are America, B. Smith, and an impressive food court. There's also a nine-screen movie-theater complex here. 50 Massachusetts Ave. NE. ℂ **202/371-9441** or 202/289-1908. www.unionstationdc.com. Metro: Union Station.

MISCELLANEOUS

Fahrneys Pens, Inc.   People come from all over to purchase the finest fountain pens, or to have them engraved or repaired. In business since 1929, Fahrneys is an institution, selling the best pens in the business, such as Montblanc, Cross, and Waterman, as well as stationery, desk accessories, and watches. 1317 F St. NW (btw. 13th and 14th sts.). ℂ **800/624-7367** or 202/628-9525. www.fahrneyspens.com. Metro: Metro Center (13th and G sts. exit).

Ginza, "for Things Japanese"   In business since 1955, Ginza sells everything Japanese, from incense to kimonos to futons to Zen rock gardens. 1721 Connecticut Ave. NW. ℂ **202/332-7000.** www.ginzaonline.com. Metro: Dupont Circle (Q St. exit).

Paper Source   If you're a stationery freak like I am, you'll have to stop here to revel in the beautiful writing and wrapping papers, supplies of notebooks, journals, albums, ribbons, folders, containers, and other essentials. This store is the chain's only mid-Atlantic location. I believe it's the best stationery store in D.C. 3019 M St. NW. ℂ **202/298-5545.** www.paper-source.com. Metro: Foggy Bottom, with a 25-min. walk, or ride the D.C. Circulator.

MUSIC

See also the listings for **Barnes & Noble,** p. 240 and **Borders,** p. 240.

Melody Record Shop   CDs, cassettes, and tapes, including new releases, are discounted here, plus the shop always has a table of unused but not newly released CDs that sell for about $10 each. Melody offers a wide variety of rock, classical, jazz, pop, show, and folk music, as well as a vast number of international selections. This is also a good place to shop for discounted portable electronic equipment, blank tapes, and cassettes. Its knowledgeable staff is a plus. 1623 Connecticut Ave. NW. ℂ **202/232-4002.** www.melody records.com. Metro: Dupont Circle (Q St. exit).

SHOES

For men's dress shoes, try **Brooks Brothers** (p. 243). For women, try the local outlets of **Nine West,** including locations at Union Station (ℂ **202/216-9490;** www.ninewest. com) and in Georgetown at 1227 Wisconsin Ave. NW (ℂ **202/337-7256**).

Carbon   "Changing D.C. from federal to funky" is this store's self-proclaimed purpose, and its merchandise is persuasive in this regard: Blackstones, Pikolinos, and Bronx are some of the names it carries in men's footwear. Carbon also carries women's shoes, and accessories and some clothes and furnishings for both sexes. 2643 Connecticut Ave. NW. ℂ **202/232-6645.** www.carbondc.com. Metro: Woodley Park–Zoo.

Comfort One Shoes   Despite its unhip name, this store sells a great selection of popular styles for both men and women, including Doc Martens, Birkenstocks, and Ecco. You can always find something that looks good and actually feels comfortable. 1630

Connecticut Ave. NW. © 202/328-3141. www.comfortoneshoes.com. Metro: Dupont Circle. Also at 1607 Connecticut Ave. NW (© 202/667-5300), 3222 M St. NW (© 202/333-4246), and many other locations.

Fleet Feet (Moments) Though part of a national chain, this store feels decidedly part of the community, an Adams-Morgan neighborhood fixture since 1984. The couple who owns the shop, Phil and Jan Fenty, are the parents of D.C. mayor Adrian Fenty, whose brothers, if not the mayor himself, you might find racing next to you during the weekly Sunday morning 5-mile fun run that Fleet Feet launches from its doorstep at 9am. (Just show up, if you're interested.) Merchandise-wise, the store sells sports and running shoes, apparel, and accessories, and is known for its friendly staff. 1841 Columbia Rd. NW. © 202/387-3888. www.fleetfeetdc.com. Metro: U St.–Cardozo (13th St. exit) or Woodley Park–Zoo, with a bit of a walk from either station.

WINE & SPIRITS

Barmy Wine and Liquor Located near the White House, this store sells it all, but with special emphasis on fine wines and rare cordials. 1912 L St. NW. © 202/833-8730. Metro: Farragut North (L St. exit).

Central Liquor (Value) This is like a clearinghouse for liquor: Its great volume allows the store to offer the best prices in town on wines and liquor. The store carries more than 250 single-malt scotches. 917 F St. NW. © 202/737-2800. www.centralliquors.com. Metro: Gallery Place (9th and F sts. exit).

Schneider's of Capitol Hill Two blocks south of Union Station is this family-run liquor store, in business for half a century. With a knowledgeable and enthusiastic staff, a 12,000-bottle inventory of wine, and a fine selection of spirits and beer, this shop is a find on Capitol Hill. 300 Massachusetts Ave. NE. © 202/543-9300. www.cellar.com. Metro: Union Station.

Zola Wine & Kitchen ★ Around the corner from Zola the restaurant (see p. 132) is its sibling, a wine shop and test kitchen, where you can browse for wines, peer through portholes in the wall to observe chef Bryan Moscatello experiment with recipes in his kitchen, and take an evening class on, say, how to prepare ceviche. Open daily, the shop also sells gourmet pre-packaged sandwiches and artisanal products in addition to its 400 varieties of international wines. 505 9th St. NW. © 202/639-9463. www.zolawinekitchen.com. Metro: Gallery Place/Verizon Center (9th St. exit).

9

Washington, D.C., After Dark

What to do during the day is usually uppermost in a traveler's mind, as plans for museum visits and landmark tours quickly consume a trip itinerary. What to do after dark is more often left to happenstance. And you know, in Washington, that's OK. The doors are always open at bars, after all, as well as at many clubs and lounges around town.

But if you really want to make the most of a trip to D.C., you owe it to yourself to check out all of your nightlife options ahead of time, especially since many of the city's best experiences, say, topnotch Shakespeare put on by the world-renowned Shakespeare Theatre Company, or the sounds of the latest indie band at D.C.'s best (some say the country's best) live music venue, the 9:30 Club, play to sold-out audiences.

So c'mon people, the night's forever young, and so are you. Start making plans. Read over the possibilities in this chapter and check these other sources: the Friday "Weekend" section of the *Washington Post,* online at **www.washingtonpost. com** or in print, to browse the *Post*'s nightlife information. Be sure to visit the *Post*'s "Going Out Gurus" blog, accessible from its Going Out Guide link; the "GOGs" answer questions about nightlife live online every Thursday at 1pm, and transcripts stay posted for a time. The *City Paper,* available free at restaurants, bookstores, and other places around town, and online at **www.washingtoncitypaper. com**, is another excellent source. Finally, check out the blog **www.dcist.com** for an irreverent inside look at what's going on around town.

1 THE PERFORMING ARTS

Washington's performing-arts scene has an international reputation. Almost anything on Broadway has either been previewed here or will eventually come here. Better yet, D.C. is home to truly excellent and renowned repertory theater troupes, and to fine ballet, opera, and symphony companies. Rock bands, headliner comedians, and jazz/folk/gospel/R&B/ alternative and other musical groups make Washington a must-stop on their tours.

THE TOP THEATERS

Arena Stage Founded by the brilliant Zelda Fichandler in 1950, the Arena Stage is home to one of the oldest acting ensembles in the nation. Several works nurtured here have moved to Broadway, and many graduates have gone on to commercial stardom, including Ned Beatty, James Earl Jones, Robert Prosky, and Jane Alexander. The excellence of Arena productions has brought the theater much success, to the extent that a major expansion is underway, with the opening targeted for the 2010-2011 season. During the construction of the new facility, Arena is staging its 10 productions at two locations: in Crystal City, Virginia, at 1800 S. Bell St.; and at the Lincoln Theatre, 1215 U St. NW, in the U Street NW Corridor of downtown D.C.

Getting Tickets

Most performing-arts and live-music venues mentioned in this chapter require admission by tickets, which you can purchase at the venue's box office or through one of the ticket vendors listed below.

TICKETplace, Washington's only discount ticket outlet, has one location: at 407 7th St. NW, between D and E streets (Metro: Gallery Place/Verizon Center or Archives/Navy Memorial). The TICKETplace booth displays a chalkboard listing of those performances that still have seats available, including opera, ballet, and events at major Washington-area theaters and concert halls. TICKETplace is open Wednesday through Friday from 11am to 6pm, Saturday from 10am to 5pm, and Sunday noon to 4pm. Otherwise, TICKETplace tickets are available online at **www.ticketplace.org** until 4pm for that day's performances. Whether you purchase tickets online or at the ticket outlet, you pay half-price, plus a 12% per-ticket service charge. TICKETplace accepts only American Express, MasterCard, and Visa. If you've ordered tickets online, you can pick them up at the "Will Call" booth of the venue you're attending; bring your credit card and confirmation of your purchase. TICKETplace is a program of the Cultural Alliance of Washington. For more information, including performances offered at the TICKETplace outlet, visit **www.culturecapital.com**. TICKETplace also sells Ticketmaster tickets—see below.

You can buy full-price tickets for most performances in town through **Ticketmaster** (© **800/551-7328;** www.ticketmaster.com); expect to pay taxes, plus a service charge, an order-processing fee, and a facility fee (if a particular venue tacks on that charge). Or you can visit one of Ticketmaster's numerous locations throughout the city, including TICKETplace (see information above; Macy's Department Store, at 12th and G sts. NW [Metro: Metro Center, 13th St. exit], and the Verizon Center, at 601 F St. NW [Metro: Gallery Place/Verizon Center]); you usually will not have to pay a convenience or order-processing fee when you purchase tickets in person.

Finally, check out **InstantSeats.Com**, which bills itself as the place to go for "online ticketing for the performing arts." (I see that the site also sells tickets for river cruises on the Potomac, so perhaps the company defines "performing arts" to cover a multitude of entertainment.) This is the site that handles sales of tickets to embassy events (see box later in this chapter, "The Best of D.C.'s International Scene," for more information).

The 2009–10 September-to-June season includes several musicals, *The Fantasticks* and *Duke Ellington's Sophisticated Ladies,* to name two; and a play bound for New York after its run here, Jane Anderson's *The Quality of Life,* starring JoBeth Williams.

The Arena Stage has always championed new plays and playwrights and is committed to producing works from America's diverse cultures, as well as to reinterpreting the works of past masters. Its mission during construction of its new theater is to celebrate "the rich mosaic of our nation's voices." Its main office, box office, phone number, and website remain the same: 1101 6th St. SW (at Maine Ave.). © **202/488-3300.** www.arenastage.org. Tickets

$47–$74; discounts available for students, people with disabilities, groups, and seniors. Metro at Crystal City location: Crystal City, exiting through the underground walkway marked CRYSTAL CITY SHOPS at 2100. Metro for Lincoln Theatre: U St./Cardozo, exiting at 13th St. exit.

John F. Kennedy Center for the Performing Arts

This 39-year-old theater complex strives to be not just the hub of Washington's cultural and entertainment scene, but a performing-arts theater for the nation. The center lies between the Potomac River and a crisscross of major roadways, which makes it sound like it's easily accessible when, in fact, the center remains just a bit west of the city's main action.

The Kennedy Center stages top-rated performances by the best ballet, opera, jazz, modern dance, musical, and theater companies in the world. Ticket prices vary from $15 for a family concert to $300 for a night at the opera, although most fall in the $30 to $75 range.

The Kennedy Center is committed to being a theater for the people, and toward that end, it continues to stage its **free concert series,** known as "Millennium Stage," which features daily performances by area musicians and sometimes national artists each evening at 6pm in the center's Grand Foyer. (You can check out broadcasts of the nightly performances on the Internet at www.kennedy-center.org/millennium.) The Kennedy Center is actually made up of six different national theaters: the Opera House, the Concert Hall, the Terrace Theater, the Eisenhower Theater, the Theater Lab, and the Family Theater.

The Kennedy Center's 2009–10 season includes two fabulous, week-long festivals: **Gospel Across America,** April 18–24, 2010, which hosts gospel groups from all over the country and national headliners, from Mavis Staples to the Fisk University Jubilee Singers; and the **Very Special Arts (VSA) International Festival,** June 6–12, 2010, a citywide, multicultural celebration that brings together artists with disabilities from around the world, including big name performers like Patti LaBelle and Marlee Matlin. For more information, check out the Kennedy Center's online information at www.kennedy-center. org. Other highlights of the Kennedy Center's 2009–10 season are:

- **Washington National Opera** (www.dc-opera.org) performances of Mozart's *The Marriage of Figaro* and the Gershwins' *Porgy and Bess,* under the artistic direction of Placido Domingo
- **National Symphony Orchestra** classical and pops concerts
- Performances by the **New York City Ballet,** the **American Ballet Theatre,** the **Suzanne Farrell Ballet,** and the **Bolshoi Ballet**
- **Musicals** *Mary Poppins* and *Young Frankenstein*
- **Kennedy Center jazz** performances by assorted masters, such as George Benson and Dianne Reeves
- **Family Theater** productions, like the **National Symphony Orchestra's Teddy Bear Concerts,** and
- Continuing performances of the comedy whodunit *Shear Madness,* now in its 23rd year at the Kennedy Center

2700 F St. NW (at New Hampshire Ave. NW and Rock Creek Pkwy.). (C) **800/444-1324** or 202/467-4600 for tickets and information. www.kennedy-center.org. 50% discounts are offered (for select performances) to students, seniors 65 and over, people with permanent disabilities, enlisted military personnel, and persons with fixed low incomes ((C) **202/416-8340** for details). Garage parking $17. Metro: Foggy Bottom (though it's a fairly short walk, there's a free shuttle btw. the station and the Kennedy Center, departing every 15 min. 9:45am–midnight Mon–Fri, 10am–midnight Sat, noon–midnight Sun). Bus: 80 from Metro Center.

Fun Facts **Longer Than the Washington Monument Is Tall**

Most Kennedy Center performances take place in theaters that lie off the Grand Foyer. But even if the one you're attending is on the Roof Terrace Level, one floor up, make sure you visit the Foyer anyway. The Grand Foyer is one of the largest rooms in the world. Measuring 630 feet long, 40 feet wide, and 60 feet high, the foyer is longer than the Washington Monument is tall (at 555⅝ ft.). Millennium Stage hosts free performances here nightly at 6pm, the famous Robert Berks sculpture of President John F. Kennedy is here, and just beyond the foyer's glass doors is the expansive terrace, which runs the length of the building and overlooks the Potomac River.

National Theatre   The splendid Federal-style National Theatre is the oldest continuously operating theater in Washington (since 1835) and the third oldest in the nation. It's exciting just to see the stage on which Sarah Bernhardt, John Barrymore, Helen Hayes, and so many other notables have performed. The 1,672-seat National is the closest thing Washington has to a Broadway-style playhouse. Past productions included the musicals *Mamma Mia* and *Jersey Boys,* which gives you a pretty good idea of the kinds of shows staged here.

One thing that has never flagged at the National is its commitment to offering free public-service programs: Saturday-morning children's theater (puppets, clowns, magicians, dancers, and singers) and Monday-night showcases of local groups and performers September through May, plus free summer films. Call 🕐 **202/783-3372** for details. 1321 Pennsylvania Ave. NW. 🕐 **800/447-7400** or 202/628-6161 to charge tickets. www.nationaltheatre.org. Tickets $47–$152 (most are in the $70–$90 range); discounts available for students, seniors, military personnel, and people with disabilities. Metro: Metro Center (13th and G sts. exit).

Shakespeare Theatre Company: at the Lansburgh Theatre and Sidney Harman Hall   This is top-level Shakespeare, with superb acting. Try your best to get tickets; the productions are reliably outstanding. Season subscriptions claim many of the seats, and the plays often sell out; so if you're interested in attending a play here, buy your tickets now. The Shakespeare Theatre Company's productions at the Lansburgh Theatre have long been so popular that the production company opened a second theater in 2008, the 775-seat Sidney Harman Hall, at 610 F St. NW, across the street from the Verizon Center and just around the corner from the 451-seat Lansburgh Theatre, on 7th St. NW. The 2009–10 season presents two plays at the Lansburgh, including a world premiere of Pierre Corneille's *The Liar* and Euripides's *The Bacchae;* and four plays at Harman Hall, including *As You Like It, Richard II,* and *Henry V.* Every year, for 2 weeks in late August, early September, the company stages a free-admission Shakespeare production, known as the "Free-For-All," in Harman Hall; *The Taming of the Shrew* was the feature in 2009. Lansburgh Theatre, 450 7th St. NW (btw. D and E sts.); Sidney Harman Hall, 650 F St. NW. 🕐 **202/547-1122.** www.shakespearetheatre.org. Tickets $24–$80, $10 for standing-room tickets sold 1 hr. before sold-out performances; discounts available for students, military, under-35 patrons, seniors, and groups. Metro: Archives/Navy Memorial or Verizon Center/Gallery Place (7th St./Arena exit).

Some of Washington's lesser-known theaters are gaining more recognition all the time. Their productions are consistently professional, and sometimes more contemporary and innovative than those you'll find in the more acclaimed theaters. These more intimate theaters have their own strong followings, which means their performances often sell out.

Studio Theatre, 1333 P St. NW, at 14th Street (📞 **202/332-3300;** www.studiotheatre. org), since its founding in 1978, has grown in leaps and bounds into a four-theater complex, helping to revitalize this downtown neighborhood in the process. Artistic director Joy Zinoman showcases interesting contemporary plays and nurtures Washington acting talent; the 2009–10 lineup marks the theater's 32nd season. The **Woolly Mammoth Theatre Company** (📞 **202/393-3939;** www.woollymammoth.net) offers as many as six productions each year, specializing in new, offbeat, and quirky plays, often world premieres. The Woolly resides in a 265-seat, state-of-the-art facility, 641 D St. NW, at 7th Street NW, in the heart of the Penn Quarter.

In addition, I highly recommend productions staged at the **Folger Shakespeare Library,** 201 E. Capitol St. SE (📞 **202/544-7077;** www.folger.edu), which celebrates its 78th anniversary in 2010. Plays take place in the library's Elizabethan Theatre, which is styled after the inn-yard theater of Shakespeare's time. The theater is intimate and charming, the theater company is remarkably good, and an evening spent here guarantees an absolutely marvelous experience. The 2009–10 season brings to the stage Shakespeare's *Much Ado About Nothing, Hamlet,* and Euripides's *Orestes.* The Elizabethan Theatre is also the setting for musical performances, lectures, readings, and other events.

INDOOR ARENAS & OUTDOOR PAVILIONS

When John Mayer, U2, or Beyoncé come to town, they usually play at one of the huge indoor or outdoor arenas. The 20,600-seat **Verizon Center,** 601 F St. NW, where it meets 7th Street (📞 **202/628-3200;** www.verizoncenter.com), in the center of downtown, hosts plenty of concerts and also is Washington's premier indoor sports arena (home to the NBA Wizards, the WNBA Mystics, the NHL Capitals, and Georgetown NCAA basketball). Less convenient and smaller is the 10,000-seat **Patriot Center** at George Mason University, 4500 Patriot Circle, Fairfax, Virginia (📞 **703/993-3000;** www.patriotcenter.com).

During the summer, there's quality entertainment almost nightly at the **Merriweather Post Pavilion,** 10475 Little Patuxent Parkway, just off Route 29 in Columbia, Maryland (📞 **410/715-5550** and www.merriweathermusic.com for general information; www. ticketmaster.com for tickets), about a 40-minute drive from downtown D.C. There's reserved seating in the open-air pavilion (overhead protection provided in case of rain) and general-admission seating on the lawn (no refunds for rain) to see such performers as Neil Young, Counting Crows, Diana Krall, the Killers, the Cure, or No Doubt. If you choose the lawn seating, bring blankets and picnic fare (beverages must be bought on the premises).

My favorite summer setting for music is the **Wolf Trap Farm Park for the Performing Arts,** 1551 Trap Rd., Vienna, Virginia (📞 **703/255-1868** for general information and tickets; www.wolftrap.org). The country's only national park devoted to the performing arts, Wolf Trap offers performances by the National Symphony Orchestra (it's their summer home), and has hosted Lucinda Williams, Shawn Colvin, Lyle Lovett, Sheryl Crow, Wilco, and many others. Performances take place in the 7,000-seat Filene Center, about half of which is under the open sky. You can also buy cheaper lawn seats on the

> **Fun Facts** **The Washington Nationals Score Their Own Stadium; Meanwhile Soccer's D.C. United Plays on at RFK**
>
> Washington, D.C.'s, Major League Baseball team, the **Washington Nationals,** arrived on the scene in 2005, but already have their own stadium: the newly built **Nationals Ballpark** (✆ 202/675-6287) opened on March 30, 2008. Located in southeast Washington, the 41,000-seat stadium is bounded by South Capitol Street, N Street, 1st Street, and Potomac Avenue. The closest Metro stop is the Green line's Navy Yard station (Navy Yard West exit). For tickets, go to the website, **www.nationals. com**; prices range from $10 to $335 (most are less than $70). Meanwhile, the 55,000-seat **Robert F. Kennedy Memorial Stadium,** 2400 E. Capitol St. SE (✆ 202/ 547-9077), where the Nationals played their first two seasons (the capital had been without a Major League Baseball team since 1971) remains the location for the men's soccer team, **D.C. United, www.dcunited.com,** at least until the team gets its own stadium. The **Washington Freedom** women's soccer team, **www.washington freedom.com**, plays its games at a suburban Maryland stadium.

hill, which is sometimes the nicest way to go. If you do, arrive early (the lawn opens 90 min. before the performance) and bring a blanket and a picnic dinner—it's a tradition. Wolf Trap also hosts a number of very popular festivals, including the Louisiana Swamp Romp Cajun Festival in June and the International Children's Festival each September. Wolf Trap is about a 30-minute drive from D.C.; the Wolf Trap Express Bus runs ($3.10 charge round-trip) between the West Falls Church Metro Station and the arts center.

The **Carter Barron Amphitheater,** 16th Street and Colorado Avenue NW (✆ 202/ 426-0486), way out 16th Street, is in Rock Creek Park, close to the Maryland border. This is the area's smallest outdoor venue, with 4,250 seats. Summer performances include a range of gospel, blues, and classical entertainment. The shows are usually free, but tickets are required.

SMALLER AUDITORIUMS

A handful of auditoriums in Washington are really fine places to catch a performance.

DAR Constitution Hall, on 18th Street NW, between C and D streets (✆ 202/628-4780; www.dar.org), is housed within a beautiful turn-of-the-20th-century Beaux Arts building and seats 3,746. Its excellent acoustics have supported an eclectic group of performers: Sting, the Buena Vista Social Club, John Hiatt, the Count Basie Orchestra, Tori Amos, Anita Baker, Bow Wow, Trisha Yearwood, and the Strokes.

In the heart of happening U Street, the **Lincoln Theatre,** 1215 U St. NW (✆ 202/ 328-6000; www.thelincolntheatre.org), was once a movie theater, vaudeville house, and nightclub featuring black stars like Louis Armstrong and Cab Calloway. The theater closed in the 1970s and reopened in 1994 after a renovation restored it to its former elegance. Today the theater books jazz, R&B, gospel, and comedy acts, and events like the D.C. Film Festival. The theater is also staging Arena Stage productions throughout 2010, while Arena's new theater is constructed.

The **Warner Theatre,** 513 13th St. NW, between E and F streets (✆ 202/783-4000; www.warnertheatre.com), opened in 1924 as the Earle Theatre (a movie/vaudeville palace) and was restored to its original, neoclassical-style appearance in 1992. It's worth coming by just to see its ornately detailed interior. The 2,000-seat auditorium offers year-round entertainment, alternating dance performances, like the Washington Ballet's Christmas performance of the *Nutcracker*, with comedy acts, like those of Steven Wright or Damon Wayans, with headliner entertainment (PJ Harvey, John Prine, Bob Dylan).

2 NIGHTCLUBS

If you're looking for a more interactive, tuneful night on the town, Washington offers hip jazz clubs, gay bars, warehouse ballrooms, places where you sit back and listen, places where you can get up and dance, even a roadhouse or two. If you're looking for comic relief, Washington can take care of that, too (the pickings are few but good).

Many nightspots wear multiple hats. For example, the Black Cat is a bar and a dance club, offering food and sometimes poetry readings. I've listed each nightspot according to the type of music it features. The details are in the description.

The best nightlife districts are Adams-Morgan; the U and 14th streets NW crossroads: U Street between 16th and 9th streets and 14th Street between P and V streets; north and south of Dupont Circle along Connecticut Avenue; the Penn Quarter, notably 7th and 8th streets and from Pennsylvania Avenue north as far as H Street; Georgetown; the area known as the Atlas District, which is H Street NE, between 12th and 14th streets; and D.C.'s newest bar-and-club scene, Columbia Heights, a neighborhood of mixed cultures and incomes. As a rule, while club-hopping—even in Georgetown—stick to the major thoroughfares and steer clear of deserted side streets. I should add that you should be especially careful in Adams-Morgan and Columbia Heights, where shootings have occurred recently. It seems that punks and criminals prey upon drunk and otherwise distracted partiers as they leave bars and clubs.

As stated in the introduction to this chapter, the best sources of information about what's doing at bars and clubs are the *Washington Post*'s "Weekend" edition, online at www.washingtonpost.com, and "Going Out Gurus" blog; the fat weekly, **City Paper,** available free at bookstores, movie theaters, drugstores, and other locations, and online at www.washingtoncitypaper.com; and the blog www.dcist.com. Also check out the monthly *On Tap,* another fat freebie found mostly in bars, but whose website, www.ontaponline.com, is essential reading for carefree 20-somethings. By the way, Thursday night is "College Night" at nearly every club.

Most of Washington's clubs and bars stay open until 1am or 2am Monday through Thursday and until 3am Friday and Saturday; what time they open varies. It's best to call ahead or check the website to make sure the place you're headed is open.

COMEDY

In addition to these two comedy venues, the **Warner Theatre** (see "Smaller Auditoriums," above) also features big-name comedians from time to time.

The Capitol Steps (Moments) This musical political satire troupe is made up of former Congressional staffers, equal-opportunity spoofers all, who poke endless fun through song and skits at politicians on both sides of the aisle and at government goings-on in general. Washingtonians have been fans since the Steps got started in 1981. Since then, the troupe has performed thousands of shows and released more than 29 albums, including the latest, "Obama Mia." Shows take place in the Amphitheater, on the concourse level of the Ronald Reagan Building and International Trade Center, at 7:30pm Friday

and Saturday. Order tickets from Ticketmaster (✆ **202/397-SEAT** [7328]), www.ticket
master.com, or in person at the Visitor Center of the Ronald Reagan Building. 1300
Pennsylvania Ave. NW (in the Ronald Reagan Building). ✆ **202/312-1555.** www.capsteps.com.
Tickets $35. Metro: Federal Triangle.

The Improv   The Improv features top performers on the national comedy club circuit
as well as comic plays and one-person shows. *Saturday Night Live* performers David
Spade, Chris Rock, and Adam Sandler have all played here, as have comedy bigs Ellen
DeGeneres, Jerry Seinfeld, and Robin Williams. Shows are about 1¹/₂ hours long and
include three comics (an emcee, a feature act, and a headliner). Showtimes are 8pm
Sunday, 8:30pm Tuesday through Thursday, 8 and 10:30pm on Friday and Saturday. The
best way to snag a good seat is to have dinner here (make reservations), which allows you
to enter the club as early as 7pm Tuesday through Thursday or after 6:30pm Friday
through Sunday. The Friday and Saturday 10:30pm show serves drinks and appetizers
only. Dinner entrees (nothing higher than $11) include sandwiches and Tex-Mex fare.
You must be 18 to get in. 1140 Connecticut Ave. NW (btw. L and M sts.). ✆ **202/296-7008.**
www.dcimprov.com. Tickets $15–$35, plus a 2-item minimum per person. Metro: Farragut
North (L St. exit).

ROCK/INDIE/ALTERNATIVE/HIP-HOP/DJ

This category is mostly about live-music clubs, but also includes a sprinkling of nightclubs known for their DJs and dance floors.

The Birchmere Music Hall and Bandstand   Worth the cab fare from downtown,
if you're a fan of live music by varied, stellar performers, such as Garth Brooks, Dave
Matthews, Jerry Jeff Walker, Crash Test Dummies, Shawn Colvin, Joe Sample, and John
Hiatt. The Birchmere is unique in the area for providing a comfortable and relatively
small (500-seat) setting, where you sit and listen to the music (there's not a bad seat in
the house) and order food and drinks. The Birchmere got started about 36 years ago,
when it booked mostly country singers. The place has expanded over the years and so has
its repertoire; there are still many country and bluegrass artists, but also folk, jazz, rock,
gospel, and alternative musicians. The menu tends toward American favorites, such as
nachos, burgers, and pulled-pork barbecue sandwiches. Purchase tickets at the box office
or online from www.ticketmaster.com. 3701 Mount Vernon Ave., Alexandria, VA. ✆ **703/549-
7500.** www.birchmere.com. Tickets $17–$60. Take a taxi or drive.

Black Cat   This comfortable, low-key, alternative rock club opened in 1993 and seems
likely to keep on kicking for all eternity. Every rocker who's anyone has played here over
the years, from Morphine in the early days to The Decemberists and Radiohead more
recently. The Black Cat has two stages: its main concert hall, which holds more than 600
people and hosts national, international, and local indie and alternative groups; and
Backstage, where soloists, smaller bands, and DJs hold court, and where film screenings
and poetry readings also take place. For quieter entertainment, the Red Room Bar is a
large, funky, red-walled living-roomy lounge with booths, tables, a red-leather sofa, pin-
ball machines, a pool table, and a jukebox stocked with a really eclectic collection. A
college crowd collects on weekends, but you can count on seeing a 20- to 30-something
bunch here most nights, including members of various bands who like to stop in for a
drink. Say hello to affable owner Dante Ferrando while you're here. Concerts take place
almost nightly, sometimes twice in a single night, on different stages. 1811 14th St. NW
(btw. S and T sts.). ✆ **202/667-4490.** www.blackcatdc.com. Cover $5–$20 for concerts; no cover
in the Red Room Bar. Metro: U St.–Cardozo (13th and U sts. exit).

DC9 This medium-size, 250-person capacity venue is open nightly, showcasing the music of indie rock bands and DJs, including a popular Liberation Party dance event Friday nights. The two-story club includes a bar downstairs with couches, booths, bar stools, and a digital jukebox of 130,000 tunes; and the hall upstairs reserved for music. 1940 9th St. NW. ℃ 202/483-5000. www.dcnine.com. No cover downstairs, $5–$15 cover upstairs, depending on show. Metro: U St.–Cardozo (African American Civil War Memorial/10th St. exit).

Eighteenth Street Lounge This place maintains its "hot" status. First you have to find it, and then you have to convince the bouncer to let you in. So here's what you need to know: Look for the mattress shop south of Dupont Circle, then look up. "ESL" (as those in the know call it) sits above the shop. Wear something exotic and sexy, anything but preppy or jock-ish. If you pass inspection, you may be surprised to find yourself in a restored, century-old mansion (Teddy Roosevelt once lived here) with fireplaces, high ceilings, and a deck out back. Or maybe you'll just get right out there on the hardwood floors to dance to acid jazz, hip-hop, reggae, or Latin jazz tunes spun by a DJ. 1212 18th St. NW. ℃ 202/466-3922. www.eighteenthstreetlounge.com. Cover $10–$20 Tues–Sat, after 9:30pm. Metro: Dupont Circle (South/19th St. exit) or Farragut North (L St. exit).

kstreet Lounge You pay for the privilege of partying here: $300 to $500 will reserve you a table and bottle service. (A full bottle of your favorite liquor is delivered to your table with juices, mixes, limes, and glasses, just to make sure that the alcohol flows steadily throughout the evening.) Exclusivity is the name of the game, and if that appeals, call days ahead to book your table, especially for a Saturday romp. Even with a reservation, you might find yourself standing in line for a time. Decor is white minimalist and high-tech, with plasma TVs broadcasting VIP arrivals. Dress code is simply minimal, the tighter and littler the dress, the better, in this beauty-competitive scene. Since there's no dedicated dance floor, dancers shimmy to the DJ beats wherever they find room. 1301 K St. NW. ℃ 202/962-3933. www.kstreetdc.com. Cover $10 women, $20 men. Metro: McPherson Square (Franklin Sq./14th St. exit).

9:30 Club Housed in a converted warehouse, this major live-music venue hosts frequent record-company parties and features a wide range of top performers. You might catch Simple Minds, the Clarks, Jakob Dylan, Jamie Lidell, Better Than Ezra, Sonic Youth, or even Tony Bennett. It's open only when there's a show on, which is almost every night (but call ahead), and, obviously, the crowd (as many as 1,200) varies with the performer. Best to buy tickets ($10–$50) in advance, whether at the box office or online. The sound system is state-of-the-art and the sightlines are excellent. There are four bars: two on the main dance-floor level, one in the upstairs VIP room (anyone is welcome here unless the room is being used for a private party), and another in the distressed-looking cellar. The 9:30 Club is a stand-up place, literally—there are few seats. 815 V St. NW (at Vermont Ave.). ℃ 202/393-0930. www.930.com. Metro: U St.–Cardozo (10th St. exit).

The Red & The Black Located along D.C.'s newest nightlife avenue, H Street NE, this club aims to offer an intimate setting for singer-songwriter acts, although louder indie rock bands frequently appear. The Red & The Black's owners also own the larger DC9 (see above), and it seems to catch that club's alternative sounds overflow. The two-story R&B features a New Orleans–style bar on its first level, with a tin ceiling and red-velvet drape decor, jambalaya on the menu, and Abitas listed among the beers. The music takes the stage nightly upstairs. 1212 H St. NE. ℃ 202/399-3201. www.redandblackbar.com. Cover $5–$8. Drive or take a taxi; or take the Metro to Verizon Center/Chinatown, then take the free H Street shuttle to the club. (The shuttle runs nightly from 5pm–until Metro closes.)

Washington is home to more than 180 embassies and international culture centers, which greatly contribute to the city's cosmopolitan flavor. There are a number of ways to soak up this international scene. First, access the website **www.embassy.org**, then click on "Embassies," which presents you with several options. If you click on "Embassy Row Tour," you'll see a detailed tour nicely outlined for you, leading you past embassies along Massachusetts and New Hampshire avenues, and including information about the neighborhoods, the embassies, and all that you see along the way. You can print the tour and take it with you as you walk.

By clicking on "Foreign Embassies of Washington, D.C.," you pull up a long list of all of the embassies in D.C., ordered alphabetically. Then click on the embassy you'd like to research and take it from there. Lots of embassies host events that are open to the public, sometimes for free, sometimes at minimal cost. In my opinion, **French Embassy's Maison Francaise** (www.la-maison-francaise.org) and the Swedish Embassy's **House of Sweden** (www.swedenabroad.com/Page____48067.aspx) have the funnest events. Here's an example: in June 2009, the embassies of Sweden, Denmark, Norway, Finland, and Iceland co-sponsored "Nordic Jazz Week," with jazz concerts staged on the roof of the House of Sweden building, located on the Georgetown waterfront overlooking the Potomac River. The cost was $25 per person per concert; the experience was priceless.

Finally, you can buy tickets for **Embassy Series** (✆ 202/625-2361, www.embassyseries.com) program events. These are world-class (literally), mostly classical music performances hosted by individual embassies, held at the embassy or at the ambassador's residence. Admission tends to be pricier for these events than for those staged separately by the embassy. For instance, a performance by a Portuguese pianist and guitar player in June 2009 took place at the Portuguese ambassador's residence and cost $100 per person, which also covered a lavish buffet and drinks. But so worth it!

Rock and Roll Hotel   On the same street as The Red & The Black, above, the R&R opened first, attracting devoted music lovers and night crawlers to come shoot pool in its second-floor pool hall, listen to live bands in its 400-person concert hall, or toss back shots in its bar. Washingtonians are loving the punk-rock decor of vintage furniture and flying guitars, but most especially the nightly acts, which range from local garage bands to national groups on tour. *FYI:* "Hotel" is just part of the name, no sleeping here. 1353 H St. NE. ✆ **202/388-7625.** www.rockandrollhoteldc.com. Cover $8–$15. Drive here or take a taxi; or take the Metro to Verizon Center/Chinatown, then take the free H Street shuttle to the club. (The shuttle runs nightly from 5pm–until Metro closes.)

JAZZ & BLUES

If you're a jazz fan and planning a trip to D.C. in early to mid June, check out the website, **www.dejazzfest.org**, for exact dates of the fabulous, weeklong **Duke Ellington Jazz Festival,** which showcases the talents of at least 100 musicians in various venues around town, including blowout, free concerts on the National Mall. And if you're a jazz and blues fan and you're coming to town at some other time of the year, check out the following venues.

Late-Night Bites

If your stomach is grumbling after the show is over, the dancing has ended, or the bar has closed, you can always get a meal at one of a growing number of late-night or all-night eateries.

In Georgetown, the **Bistro Francais,** 3128 M St. NW (✆ **202/338-3830**), has been feeding night owls for years; it even draws some of the area's top chefs after their own establishments close. Open until 4am Friday and Saturday, until 3am every other night, the Bistro is thoroughly French, serving steak frites, omelets, and pâtés.

On U Street, **Ben's Chili Bowl** (p. 144), 1213 U St. NW (✆ **202/667-0909**), serves up chili dogs, turkey subs, and cheese fries until 4am on Friday and Saturday nights.

In Adams-Morgan one all-night dining option is the **Diner,** 2453 18th St. NW (✆ **202/232-8800**), which serves some typical (eggs and coffee, grilled cheese) and not-so-typical (a grilled fresh salmon club sandwich) diner grub.

Finally, in Dupont Circle, stop in at **Kramerbooks & Afterwords Café,** 1517 Connecticut Ave. NW (✆ **202/387-1400**), for big servings of everything, from quesadillas to french fries to French toast. The bookstore stays open all night on weekends, and so does its kitchen.

Blues Alley   Blues Alley, in Georgetown, has been Washington's top jazz club since 1965, featuring such artists as Karrin Allyson, Ahmad Jamal, Sonny Rollins, Wynton Marsalis, Rachelle Ferrell, and Maynard Ferguson. There are usually two shows nightly at 8 and 10pm; some performers also do midnight shows on weekends. Reservations are essential (call after noon); since seating is on a first-come, first-served basis, it's best to arrive no later than 7pm and have dinner. Entrees on the steak and Creole seafood menu are in the $17 to $23 range, snacks and sandwiches are $5.25 to $10, and drinks are $5.35 to $9. The decor is "classic dive": exposed-brick walls; beamed ceiling; small, candlelit tables; and a very worn look about it. Sometimes well-known visiting musicians get up and jam with performers. 1073 Wisconsin Ave. NW (in an alley below M St.). ✆ 202/337-4141. www.bluesalley.com. Cover $16–$75 (most fall in the $20–$40 range), plus a $10 per person food or drink minimum, plus $2.50 per person surcharge. Metro: Foggy Bottom, then walk or take the D.C. Circulator.

Bohemian Caverns   Rising from the ashes on the very spot where jazz greats such as Duke Ellington, Billie Holiday, and so many others performed decades ago, Bohemian Caverns hopes to establish that same presence and host today's jazz stars, but remains a work in progress. The Caverns is actually three venues. Downstairs is the jazz club, whose decor is cavelike, as it was in the '20s. The club's performance schedule seems to fluctuate quite a bit, but when in full swing, hosts two performances nightly. At street level is Mahogany, the restaurant, whose entrees are named after jazz legends and start at about $19. The two upper floors comprise Liv, a nightclub, bar, and hip-hop lounge. 2001 11th St. NW (at U St.). ✆ 202/299-0800. www.bohemiancaverns.com. Cover $15–$22 weekends in the jazz club; $5 Fri, $20 Sat in the nightclub. Metro: U St.–Cardozo (U and 13th St. exit).

Habana Village This three-story nightclub has a bar/restaurant on the first floor, where a band plays Latin jazz (Fri–Sat); a bar/dance floor with DJ on the second level; and a salsa-playing combo on the third floor (Fri–Sat). Salsa and merengue lessons are given Wednesday through Saturday evenings, and on Sunday evenings in summer, $10 per lesson. 1834 Columbia Rd. NW. (C) 202/462-6310. www.habanavillage.com. Cover $6 Fri–Sat after 9pm (no cover for women and no cover if you've paid for dinner or dance classes). Metro: U St.–Cardozo or Woodley Park–Zoo/Adams-Morgan, and catch the D.C. Circulator.

HR-57 This cool club is named for the House Resolution passed in 1987 that designated jazz "a rare and valuable national American treasure." More than a club, HR-57 is also the Center for the Preservation of Jazz and Blues. Step inside Wednesday through Saturday evenings for a jazz jam session or star performance. 1610 14th St. NW. (C) 202/667-3700. www.hr57.org. Cover $8–$20. Metro: U St.–Cardozo (U and 13th St. exit).

Madam's Organ Restaurant and Bar (Finds) This beloved Adams-Morgan hang-out fulfills owner Bill Duggan's definition of a good bar: great sounds and sweaty people. The great sounds feature live music nightly: a funk/jazz/blues group on Sunday and Monday; Delta bluesman Ben Andrews on Tuesday; bluegrass with Bob Perilla & the Big Hillbilly Bluegrass Band on Wednesday; and the salsa sounds of Patrick Alban or Johnny Artis on Thursday, which is also Ladies' Night. On Friday and Saturday nights, regional blues groups pack the place—hope for Bobby Parker or Cathy Ponton King. The club includes a wide-open bar decorated eclectically with an antique gilded mirror, stuffed fish and animal heads, and paintings of nudes. The second-floor bar is called Big Daddy's Love Lounge & Pick-Up Joint, which tells you everything you need to know. Keep climbing the stairs to the rooftop deck, which is now open all year; you can't hear the music up there, but you'll discover an awesome view. *Other notes:* You can play darts here, and redheads pay half-price for Rolling Rock beer. Food is served, but I'd eat else-where. 2461 18th St. NW. (C) 202/667-5370. www.madamsorgan.com. Cover $3–$7. Metro: U St.–Cardozo or Woodley Park–Zoo/Adams-Morgan and catch the D.C. Circulator bus.

Twins Jazz This intimate, crowded, second-floor jazz club offers live music Wednesday and Thursday at 8pm and Friday and Saturday, at 9pm and 11pm. You're likely to hear local artists weeknights and bigger name, out-of-town acts, such as Bobby Watson and Gil Scott Heron, on weekends. Sunday night is a weekly jam session attended by musicians from all over town. The menu features American, Ethiopian, and Caribbean dishes. The age group of the crowd varies. 1344 U St. NW. (C) 202/234-0072. www.twinsjazz.com. Cover $10–$30, with a 2-drink-per-person minimum. Metro: U St.–Cardozo (13th St. exit).

U-topia Unlike most music bars, the arty New York/SoHo–style U-topia is serious about its restaurant operation. A moderately priced international menu ($12–$21 for entrees) features vegetable couscous curry and shrimp jambalaya, not to mention pastas and filet mignon with béarnaise sauce. There's also an interesting wine list and a large selection of beers and single-malt scotches. The setting is cozy and candlelit, with walls used for a changing art gallery show. The eclectic crowd here varies with the music, ranging from early 20s to about 35, for the most part, including South Americans and Euro-peans. There's live music Tuesday through Sunday, with Thursday always featuring live Brazilian jazz. 1418 U St. NW (at 14th St.). (C) 202/483-7669. www.utopiaindc.com. No cover, but $15 per person minimum for drink or food. Metro: U St.–Cardozo (13th St. exit)

Zoo Bar (Value) During the day, this establishment located across the street from, you guessed it, the zoo, caters to hungry families, but Thursday through Saturday nights after 10pm, it's a blues joint. Expect a divey setting and an eclectic crowd that skews older.

The quality of the music varies: Sometimes you'll stop in and find a serious bluesman from New Orleans, the next night it'll be a local boomer band fronted by a 20-something singer who can really belt it out. If you're looking for a hot club scene, this ain't it. But if you're a blues lover, the Zoo Bar's worth checking out. Plus, it's cheap—no cover—and conveniently located, right on Connecticut Avenue, a short walk from the Woodley Park–Zoo Metro stop on the Red Line. 3000 Connecticut Ave. NW (above Cathedral Ave. NW). ℂ 202/232-4225. www.zoobardc.com. No cover. Metro: Woodley Park–Zoo (Woodley and Connecticut Ave. exit).

GAY AND LESBIAN CLUBS

Dupont Circle is the gay and lesbian hub of Washington, D.C., with at least 10 gay or lesbian bars within easy walking distance of one another. Here are three from that neighborhood. (Also refer to Destination D.C.'s *GLBT Traveler's Guide,* available on the Destination D.C. website, www.destinationdc.org; see p. 55 for more information.)

Apex Apex (used to be called "Badlands") is an institution, holding the record in the city as the longest running gay dance club. It's still going strong. In addition to the parquet dance floor in the main room, the club has at least six bars throughout the first level. Upstairs is the Annex bar/lounge/pool hall, and a showroom where Miss Kristina Kelly and Company perform a popular drag show every Saturday night. 1415 22nd St. NW (at P St.). ℂ 202/296-0505. www.apex-dc.com. Sometimes a cover of $3–$12, depending on the event. Metro: Dupont Circle (South/19th St. exit).

Gazuza Actually, this second-story watering hole with its year-round deck overlooking Connecticut Avenue attracts straights as well as gays, couples as well as singles. Everyone wants to stand up there and survey the scene. The decor is upscale and industrial, but the glass-and-metal look is softened by candlelight and loungy sofas. D.C. doesn't offer lesbians an awful lot of club choices, but Gazuza's a good one. It's nearly right next door to the lesbian bookstore, **Lambda Rising** (p. 241), so if you meet someone there first, you can treat her to a drink just a few steps away at Gazuza. 1629 Connecticut Ave. NW (at Q St.). ℂ 202/667-5500. $100 minimum for a table of four on the weekends. www.latinconcepts.com/gazuza. Metro: Dupont Circle (Q St. exit).

J.R.'s Bar and Grill This casual and intimate all-male Dupont Circle club draws a crowd that is friendly, upscale, and very attractive. The interior—not that you'll be able to see much of it, because J.R.'s is always sardine-packed—has a 20-foot-high pressed-tin ceiling and exposed-brick walls hung with neon beer signs. The big screen over the bar area is used to air music videos, showbiz singalongs, and favorite TV shows. Every night offers a special something, like the Sunday $2 Skyy Highball all night long or Thursday's Retro night theme with free shots at midnight. The balcony, with pool tables, is a little more laid-back. Food is served daily, until 5pm Sunday and until 7pm all other days. 1519 17th St. NW (btw. P and Q sts.). ℂ 202/328-0090. www.jrswdc.com. Metro: Dupont Circle (Q St. exit).

3 BARS & LOUNGES

Washington has a thriving and varied bar scene. But just when you think you know all the hot spots, a spate of new ones pop up. See the introduction to the Nightclubs section, earlier in this chapter, for descriptions of the current favorite areas for revelry in the city. If you're up for a wild time that comes without transportation worries, consider reserving

a spot on the **Boomerang Bus** (www.ridetheboomerang.com), which travels to four or
five popular bars in different neighborhoods every Friday and Saturday night, picking
you up and dropping you off at the same bar location; the current price of $35 covers
the transportation and any charges for covers or specialty drinks, and allows you to
bypass any VIP lines.

Lounges are all the rage, so be sure to stop in at restaurants such as Sei, PS7's, and
Rasika. (See chapter 6 for details and more suggestions.) If you're in the mood for a
sophisticated setting, seek out a bar in one of the nicer hotels, like the **Willard,** the
Sofitel Lafayette Square, the **Ritz-Carlton Georgetown,** the **Hay-Adams,** and the **St.
Regis** (see chapter 5). Otherwise, here is a range of options, from upscale to low-key, but
each with its own character.

Big Hunt This casual and comfy Dupont Circle hangout for the 20- to 30-something
crowd bills itself as a "happy hunting ground for humans" (read: meat market). It has a
kind of *Raiders of the Lost Ark* jungle theme. A downstairs room (where music is the
loudest) is adorned with exotic travel posters and animal skins; another area has leopard
skin–patterned booths under canvas tenting. Amusing murals grace the balcony level,
which adjoins a room with pool tables. The candlelit basement is the spot for quiet
conversation. The menu offers typical bar food, and the bar offers close to 30 beers on
tap, most of them microbrews. An outdoor patio lies off the back poolroom.

Note: This place and the Lucky Bar might be the perfect antidotes to their exclusive
counterparts around town, including the nearby Eighteenth Street Lounge. If you're
rejected there, forget about it and come here. 1345 Connecticut Ave. NW (btw. N St. and
Dupont Circle). © 202/785-2333. www.thebighuntdc.com. Metro: Dupont Circle.

Bourbon (**Finds**) North of Georgetown, in the homey area known as Glover Park, is
this neighborhood bar that has a comfortable feel to it. The owners have invited their
regulars to bring in black-and-white family photos, which they use to adorn the walls.
Downstairs is a narrow room and long bar; upstairs is a dining room with leather booths.
Fifty bourbons are on offer, along with many fine wines and beers, and the usual complement of bar beverages. Bourbon has a second location in Adams-Morgan, at 2321 18th
St. NW (© **202/332-0800**). 2348 Wisconsin Ave. NW. © **202/625-7770**. www.bourbondc.
com. Take a taxi or hop the D.C. Circulator, which takes you almost all the way.

Brickskeller (**Value**) If you like beer and you like choices, head for the Brickskeller,
which has been around for about 50 years and offers more than 1,000 beers from around
the world. If you can't make up your mind, ask one of the waiters, who tend to be knowledgeable about the brews. The tavern draws students, college professors, embassy types,
and people from the neighborhood. Brickskeller is a series of interconnecting rooms
filled with gingham-tableclothed tables (upstairs rooms are open only weekend nights).
The food is generally okay; burgers are your best bet, especially the Brickburger, topped
with bacon, salami, onion, coleslaw, and cheese. 1523 22nd St. NW. © 202/293-1885. www.
lovethebeer.com/brickskeller.html. Metro: Dupont Circle (either exit) or Foggy Bottom.

Busboys and Poets Salon, bookstore, restaurant, performance space, lounge, bar,
political activist hangout: Busboys and Poets is all these things. The name pays tribute to
poet Langston Hughes, who worked as a busboy at the Wardman Park Hotel in the
1920s, writing poems on the side. Busboys has been popular right from the start, and a
diverse crowd collects here day and night to peck on their laptops, plan the revolution,
and listen to spoken-word performances, pausing only to take a sip of a preferred bever-
age, whether a Corona or champagne. Busboys' success has led owner Andy Shallal to

open locations in the Penn Quarter (1025 5th St. NW, ☎ **202/789-2227**), and in Arlington, Virginia (4251 Campbell Ave.; ☎ **703/379-9756**). In 2009, Shallal opened a restaurant called Eatonville (2121 14th St. NW; ☎ **202/332-9672**), named after the Florida town where Zora Neale Huston grew up, and located up the street from the original Busboys; it serves African-influenced low-country cuisine. 2021 14th St. NW (at V St.). ☎ **202/387-POET** (7638). www.busboysandpoets.com. Metro: U St/Cardozo (13th St. exit).

Chi-Cha Lounge (Finds)   At this popular neighborhood place, you can sit around on couches, eat Andean-inspired tapas, and smoke Arabic tobacco through a 3-foot-high hookah pipe. A DJ plays on the weekend. 1624 U St. NW. ☎ **202/234-8400**. (Call after 5pm.) www.latinconcepts.com/chicha. Metro: U St.–Cardozo (13th St. exit).

Clyde's of Gallery Place   This enormous new Clyde's, the latest in the local empire that includes a Georgetown branch (see chapter 6), looks like Las Vegas from the outside. Inside, the two-level, 23,000-square-foot salon is filled with eye-catching oil paintings of sailing and equestrian scenes, Tiffany glass, and burnished cherry-wood furnishings. Three bars anchor the place, which is pretty much hopping every night of the week. As big as Clyde's is, it still gets crowded, especially before and after sports events at the Verizon Center, which is in the same block. Late-night prowlers will be happy to know that Clyde's late-night menu is available daily until 1am. 707 7th St. NW (at H St.). ☎ **202/348-3700**. www.clydes.com. Metro: Gallery Place/Chinatown (H St./Chinatown exit).

CoCo. Sala   Chocolate is the watchword at this Penn Quarter lounge, where cocktails are infused with chocolate and small plates of both savory and sweet treats feature chocolate as an ingredient, too. Consider: malted milk martinis, CO Cojitos (chocolate-infused vodka, fresh mint and limes, topped with dark chocolate flakes), crabcakes with chocolate tomato glaze, and hot chocolate soufflés. Add sexy waiters and waitresses, a glass-enclosed chocolate room where confections are made, and a sultry clientele, and it all adds up to one of D.C.'s hot places of the moment. 929 F St. NW (at 9th St.). ☎ **202/347-4265**. www.cocosala.com. Metro: Gallery Place/Chinatown (9th St. exit).

The Dubliner   This is your typical old Irish pub, the port you can blow into in any storm, personal or weather-related. It's got the dark-wood paneling and tables, the etched and stained-glass windows, an Irish-accented staff from time to time, and, most importantly, the Auld Dubliner Amber Ale. Most come here to imbibe, but the Dubliner is open daily from breakfast until last call; so if you're hungry, consider the burgers, grilled-chicken sandwich, or fish and chips. The Dubliner is frequented by Capitol Hill staffers and journalists who cover the Hill. Irish music groups play nightly. In the Phoenix Park Hotel, 520 N. Capitol St. NW, with its own entrance on F St. NW. ☎ **202/737-3773**. www.dubliner dc.com. Metro: Union Station.

ESPN Zone   This is not a date place, unless your date happens to be Anna Kournikova. It's three levels of sports mania, in the form of interactive sports games, a restaurant, 200 televisions throughout the place tuned to sporting events, a bar area, and the most popular attraction, the Screening Room. This last venue offers a giant 16-foot video screen flanked by six 36-inch screens, each showing a different event. Seats with special headphones are arrayed in front of the screen, and you control what you listen to. ESPN Zone is also a sports bar/restaurant serving American staples: burgers, fries, huge salads, chicken tenders, and ribs. 555 12th St. NW. ☎ **202/783-3776**. www.espnzone.com/washingtondc. Metro: Metro Center (11th St. exit).

(Value) Cheap Eats: Happy Hours to Write Home About

Good-value promotions are often available at area bars and nightclubs, such as **Whitlow's on Wilson** in Arlington (see the "Electric Avenues for Live-Music Lovers" box on p. 268), where you can chow down on a half-price burger every Monday, good all day. A step above these are certain restaurants around town that set out tasty bites during happy hour, either free or for an astonishingly low price. Here are several you might like:

In the bar area only, **McCormick & Schmick's**, 1652 K St. NW, at the corner of 17th Street NW (☎ 202/861-2233), not far from the White House, order a drink costing $2.50 or more, and you may select from a $1.95, $2.95, or $3.95 bar menu with such tasty offerings as shrimp scampi, hummus, quesadillas, fish tacos, and more. The offer is good Monday through Friday from 3:30 to 7pm.

In Georgetown, **Morton's Steakhouse**, 3251 Prospect St. NW, just off Wisconsin Ave. NW (☎ 202/342-6258), serves up "Power Hour" bar bites, in its Bar 12-21, daily, 5 to 6:30pm and 9:30 to 11pm; and on the patio, Saturday from noon to 5pm. Drinks are normal price, but the bar bites menu features a variety: cheeseburger trio, four petite filet mignon sandwiches, blue cheese french fries, and so on, each priced at $5 per plate.

On Capitol Hill, **Johnny's Half Shell**, 400 N. Capitol St. NW (☎ 202/737-0400), pulls in young Hill staffers Monday through Friday, 4:30–7:30pm, not for its deals on drinks—$5 drafts, $7 to $9 cocktails—but for its delicious bites of mini burgers, shrimp, grits, and the like, priced from $2.50 to $6.

Finally, south of Dupont Circle, at 1990 M St. NW, upscale restaurant **Vidalia** (☎ 202/659-1990) hosts a wine tasting Monday to Friday, 5:30 to 6:30pm, during which the sommelier pours complimentary sips of three excellent wines, accompanied by plates of canapés whipped up by the chef.

Fadó Another Irish pub, but this one is Ireland as a theme park. The odd thing about it is its location: in the heart of Chinatown. Fadó was designed and built by the Irish Pub Company of Dublin, which shipped everything—the stone for the floors, the etched glass, the milled wood—from Ireland. The pub has separate areas, including an old Irish "bookstore" alcove and a country cottage bar. Authentic Irish food, like potato pancakes, is served with your Guinness. *Fadó*, Gaelic for "long ago," accepts reservations only for large groups. The pub sometimes hosts live music performances, and sometimes charges a cover, about $5, but sometimes not. 808 7th St. NW. ☎ 202/789-0066. www.fadoirishpub. com. Metro: Gallery Place/Chinatown (H and 7th sts. exit).

The Gibson Make a reservation for a seat in a bar? Yes, and I must say, it's worth it. The Gibson is a 21st-century speakeasy, hidden inside a nondescript, tenement-like, building. You usually have to ring a bell to be admitted. If you haven't made a reservation, you're probably not going to get in. The place is small, with room only for 48 people, and dimly lit. A mixologist at the bar concocts swell drinks, like a New Orleans Sazerac

Electric Avenues for Live-Music Lovers

Live-music venues are ever more popular in the capital, and one neighborhood is particularly noteworthy for the sheer amount and variety of fabulous music on tap on any given night: U Street NW, between 9th and 14th streets, and its side streets. Whether you're a fan of jazz, hip-hop, indie rock, or blues, you're bound to find something to please you just by strolling along the U and 14th street corridors, especially on a Friday or Saturday evening. Bohemian Caverns, HR-57, Twins Jazz, U-Topia, the 9:30 Club, DC9, and the Black Cat are among the clubs listed in this chapter. In another part of town that's come to be known as the "Atlas District," live-music venues also are springing up along H Street NE, between 12th and 14th streets (though it must be said that this locale, especially at night, is pretty iffy). Two Atlas District music clubs are reviewed in this chapter: The Red & The Black, p. 260, and the Rock and Roll Hotel, p. 261. For a less urban experience, you might also check out a stretch of suburban street in Arlington, Virginia: a section of Wilson Boulevard in the Clarendon neighborhood, roughly between Highland and Edgewood roads. Arlington Row is a lot tamer and tends to attract a crowd of all ages, usually dressed for comfort. And though it's outside the District, the area is easy to reach by Metro. Streets are safer and clubs front the streets with picture windows and aren't as exclusive.

The music is live, it's outstanding (most of the time), and it's here almost nightly. So take the Metro to the Clarendon stop and walk down Wilson, or drive up Wilson from Key Bridge, turn left on Edgewood Road or another side street, and park on the street. Check out these three spots, all within walking distance of each other; all serve food:

Galaxy Hut, 2711 Wilson Blvd. (© **703/525-8646;** www.galaxyhut.com), is a comfortable bar with far-out art on the walls and a patio in the alley. Look for live alternative rock Sunday and Monday nights; usually a $5 cover after 9pm

At **IOTA,** 2832 Wilson Blvd. (© **703/522-8340;** iotaclubandcafe.com), the best of the area's bands (if either Little Pink or Last Train Home is performing, go), as well as up-and-coming groups, take the stage nightly in a setting with minimal decor (cement floor, exposed-brick walls, and a wood-beamed ceiling) and a patio in back. Covers range $5 to $18.

Whitlow's on Wilson, 2854 Wilson Blvd. (© **703/276-9693;** www.whitlows.com), is the biggest spot on the block, spreading throughout four rooms, the first showcasing the music (anything from surfer music to hiphop), the other rooms holding coin-operated pool tables, dartboards, and air hockey. Two patios further enlarge Whitlow's. The place has the appearance of a diner, from Formica table-booths to a soda fountain, and serves a range of comfort food, including soul food, pastas, and hamburgers (Mondays are half-price burger nights—a good deal and very popular). Cover is $5; shows are Wednesday (acoustic), Friday and Saturday after 9pm.

or something called the Salad Days Sour (a pisco sour with hints of celery and cinnamon). Patrons sit at booths, tables, or at the bar, but when their allowed 2 hours are up, off they must go, so others can take their place. Cool. 2009 14th St. NW (at U St.). © 202/232-2156. Metro: U St/Carodozo (13th St. exit).

H Street Country Club   This playground for hipsters opened in June 2009, and not a moment too soon—the wait appears to have been excruciating for local gadabouts, judging from blog comments. Located in the Atlas District, the two-level club invites one and all to come play skee ball, shuffleboard, pool, and the jukebox, downstairs; or to head upstairs to play nine holes at D.C.'s only indoor miniature golf course. Libations abound, naturally. It is first and foremost a bar, after all. 1335 H St. NE (at 13th St.). © 202/399-4722. www.hstreetcountryclub.com. Metro: Verizon Center/Chinatown, then take the free H Street shuttle to the club. (The shuttle runs nightly from 5pm–until Metro closes.)

Lucky Bar   Lucky Bar is a good place to kick back and relax. But, in keeping with the times, it also features free salsa dance lessons on Monday night. Sometimes the music is live, but mostly it's courtesy of a DJ. Other times the jukebox plays, but never so loud that you can't carry on a conversation. The bar has a front room overlooking Connecticut Avenue and a back room decorated with good-luck signs, couches, hanging TVs, booths, and a pool table. Lucky Bar is known in the area as a "soccer bar," with its TVs turned to soccer matches going on around the world. Also: Lucky Bar's happy hour starts at 3pm and continues until 8pm! 1221 Connecticut Ave. NW. © 202/331-3733. www.luckybardc.com. Metro: Dupont Circle (South/19th St. exit) or Farragut North (L St. exit).

Lucky Strike Lanes   Drink up and bowl the night away at this bowling alley/lounge in the heart of the Penn Quarter, in the same block as the Verizon Center. Here you'll find a rambunctious crowd cheering, drinking, and giving the game their best shots, as a DJ plays loud hip-hop and R&B tunes. If you have to wait for a lane, which is likely if you haven't called ahead to reserve one, you can lounge on a sofa or banquette, play a game of pool, have a drink or a bite to eat at the 50-foot bar, or watch sports on one of the 10-foot projection screens. Ages 21 and older after 9pm. 701 7th St. NW. © 202/347-1021. www.bowlluckystrike.com. Metro: Gallery Place/Verizon Center (7th and H sts. exit).

Marvin   Marvin opened in late 2007 and the crowds came. Downstairs is a bistro that serves Belgian specialties, like steak frites and mussels in wine and beer, and American soul-food favorites, such as shrimp and grits and fried chicken atop a waffle. The split personality derives from namesake Marvin Gaye, the late soul singer and D.C. native, who lived in Belgium for a while. The split personality applies to Marvin's function, as well, for upstairs from the restaurant is a small lounge. Intended as a neighborhood hangout, the bar/lounge is really more like a scenemaker, especially on weekends. Both bistro and lounge are usually packed, although you can at least make reservations for the dining room. DJs play nightly upstairs, mixing Motown and R&B. Fortunately, an expansive patio extends the space and offers more seating and another bar. 2007 14th St. NW. © 202/797-7171. www.marvindc.com. Metro: U St/Carodozo (13th St. exit).

Park at 14th   This glass-fronted, four-level restaurant/lounge opened in late 2007, unabashedly promoting itself to celebrities, good-lookers, and for private parties. And it's working. Among those seen partying here have been Washington Wizards player Caron Butler, celebrating his 28th birthday, and comedian Chris Rock, who brought 10 friends with him after he finished his act at Constitution Hall. Luxury is on display, from the leather sofas, to arty glass chandeliers, to accents of mahogany and onyx. Balconies on

Wine Bars Woo the Capital

It isn't that Washington didn't have wine bars before now, it's just that, over-night, it seems, we have so many. Pioneers Bistrot Lepic, Mendocino Grille and Wine Bar, and Sonoma, restaurants all, deserve credit for being there first, whetting locals' appetite, perhaps, for the whole idea. Now the city is home to at least 10 wine bars, most of which serve food, while still focusing on the wine. The following list directs you to some of the best:

- **Bistrot Lepic and Wine Bar,** 1736 Wisconsin Ave. NW (✆ **202/333-0111;** www.bistrotlepic.com)   The Asian-accented, cozy wine bar and lounge on the second floor of its charming French restaurant offers complimentary tastings every Tuesday, 6 to 8pm. Open daily 5:30pm to midnight.
- **Veritas,** 2031 Florida Ave. NW (✆ **202/265-6270;** www.veritasdc.com) Located at the northern end of Dupont Circle, just off Connecticut Avenue, this tiny, exposed-brick-walled place holds no more than 50 people and serves 70 wines by the glass. A few nibbles are on the menu: small plates of cheeses and charcuterie, and some desserts. Open daily 5pm to closing.
- **Vinoteca Wine Bar and Bistro,** 1940 11th St. NW (✆ **202/332-WINE** [9463], www.vinotecadc.com)   Like many of its neighbors in the U Street neigh-borhood, Vinoteca is open late—until 3am on weekends, 2am all other nights. (It opens at 4:30pm.) Its town-house setting offers seating at a bar, on banquettes, in the upstairs lounge, or outside at sidewalk tables. Wine lovers can choose from 100 wines by the glass; a full menu of American cuisine is also available.
- **Cork,** 1720 14th St. NW (✆ **202/265-CORK** [2675], www.corkdc.com) Another cozy place, Cork features no American or Australian wines, choos-ing instead to highlight "Old World" wines. The bar offers 50 wines by the glass and a menu that serves small plates of light fare, meant for sharing (think french fries, olives, cheeses, and so on). Wine tastings and classes are also on tap. Open Sunday, Tuesday, and Wednesday 5pm to midnight; Thursday to Saturday 5pm to 1am.

the second and fourth floors overlook the interior action. Meanwhile, that four-story street-to-roof window front is not intended for those inside to look out, but rather to reveal the celebrating scene to wishful passersby outside. That feature and the velvet rope admission policy emphasize the exclusivity at work. The restaurant has been slow to get going, but that's all right, since for now, the Park is really about socializing. 920 14th St. NW. ✆ 202/737-7275. www.theparkatfourteenth.com. No cover. Metro: McPherson Sq. (Franklin Sq./14th St. exit).

P.O. V. Roof Terrace and Lounge   When it first opened in July 2009, this rooftop bar caused a stampede among the city's prime partiers. P.O.V. is located on the 11th floor of the trendy new hotel, the W Washington, D.C. (p. 91), holds only 104 people, and is accessed solely by an elevator. On opening night, a line formed in the lobby and a melee nearly ensued. Here's hoping that the frenzy has at last died down in time for your visit.

The big draw here is the unique view of the Washington Monument, the White House,
Pennsylvania Avenue, and the Lincoln Memorial—no other place in town serves it up in this kind of setting. The lounge accepts reservations, so call ahead for a spot. Then plunk yourself down on a couch, order up a mint julep, and take it all in. 515 15th St. NW, in the W Washington, D.C. Hotel. © **202/661-2400.** www.whotels.com/washingtondc. No cover. Metro: Metro Center (13th St. exit).

Pour House　This is three separate bars in one. The Pour House, on the first floor, plays on a Pittsburgh theme (honoring the owner's roots), displaying Steelers and Penguins paraphernalia, and drawing Iron City drafts from its tap and pirogi from the kitchen. Downstairs is the Scheisse Haus, a faux biergarten. The basement has pool tables, a bar, and a lounge area (behind beaded curtains); the street level has booths and a bar. On the top floor is "Top of the Hill," which is promoted as "hip and upscale," but it's not, really (although you will find leather chairs, art, and chandeliers here). 319 Pennsylvania Ave. SE. © **202/546-7782.** www.pourhouse-dc.com. Metro: Capitol South.

The Tombs　Housed in a converted 19th-century Federal-style home, the Tombs, which opened in 1962, is a favorite hangout for students and faculty of nearby Georgetown University. (Bill Clinton came here during his college years.) They tend to congregate at the central bar and surrounding tables, while local residents head for "the Sweeps," the room that lies down a few steps and has red-leather banquettes.

Directly below the upscale 1789 restaurant (p. 154), the Tombs has its own chef, who serves up the usual college fare of burgers, sandwiches, and salads, as well as more serious stuff. 1226 36th St. NW. © **202/337-6668.** www.tombs.com. Metro: Foggy Bottom, then take the D.C. Circulator to Wisconsin Ave. and walk from there.

Tryst　This is the most relaxed of Washington's lounge bars. The room is surprisingly large for Adams-Morgan, and it's jampacked with worn armchairs and couches, which are usually occupied, no matter what time of day. People come here to have coffee or a drink, get a bite to eat, read a book, or meet a friend. The place feels almost like a student lounge on a college campus, except alcohol is served. A bonus: Tryst offers free wireless Internet service. 2459 18th St. NW. © **202/232-5500.** www.trystdc.com. Metro: U St.–Cardozo or Woodley Park–Zoo/Adams-Morgan and catch the D.C. Circulator.

Tune Inn (Finds)　Capitol Hill has a number of bars that qualify as institutions, but the Tune Inn is probably the most popular. Capitol Hill staffers and their bosses, apparently at ease in dive surroundings, have been coming here for cheap beer and greasy burgers since it opened in 1955. (All the longtime Capitol Hillers know that Fri is crab-cake or, in season, soft-shell crab, day at the Tune Inn, and they all show up.) 331½ Pennsylvania Ave. SE. © **202/543-2725.** Metro: Capitol South.

WASHINGTON, D.C. AFTER DARK

9

BARS & LOUNGES

Side Trips from Washington, D.C.

Just across the Potomac River from Washington, D.C., within easy reach by car, bike, boat, or Metro, lie two historic sites you really should try to visit if you have the time: Old Town Alexandria, located just 8 miles outside the capital, and George Washington's estate, Mount Vernon, found another 8 miles further south. It's possible to visit both places in a single day, though I'd recommend taking 2, for a more leisurely experience.

Mount Vernon's 500-acre Potomac-front plantation includes orientation and education centers, the mansion that was Washington's home for 45 years, and the original outbuildings, gardens, and other points of interest, all of which offer a grand and fascinating introduction to America's first president. Old Town Alexandria enlightens us further, rounding out the historical picture of what life was like here in the late 18th century, when Washington came to town to attend church, to dine, and to train his troops; and in the years that followed Washington's era, up to the present. Founded in 1749, this compact, walkable, waterfront town contains cobblestone streets, Colonial and 19th-century architecture, and historic sites that are open for tours.

Old Town, you'll find, is also very much a modern town, full of of-the-moment eateries and fancy-soaps to fashion-nuts boutiques.

1 MOUNT VERNON

Only 16 miles south of the capital, George Washington's Southern plantation dates from a 1674 land grant to the president's great-grandfather.

ESSENTIALS

GETTING THERE If you're going by car, take any of the bridges over the Potomac River into Virginia and follow the signs pointing the way to National Airport/Mount Vernon/George Washington Memorial Parkway. Travel south on the George Washington Memorial Parkway, the river always to your left, and pass by National Airport on your right. Continue through Old Town Alexandria, where the parkway is renamed "Washington Street," and head 8 miles farther, until you reach the large circle that fronts Mount Vernon.

You might also take a bus or boat to Mount Vernon. **These bus and boat tour prices include the price of admission to Mount Vernon.**

Gray Line Buses (© 800/862-1400 or 301/386-8300; at Union Station 202/289-1995; www.graylinedc.com) offers two tours daily to Mount Vernon (except Christmas, Thanksgiving, and New Year's Day). The 4-hour tour travels past Old Town Alexandria to Mount Vernon; the 8-hour tour travels to Mount Vernon and includes stops in Old Town Alexandria and at Arlington National Cemetery on your return. Both tours depart

Though few people realize it, the George Washington Memorial Parkway is actually a national park. The first section was completed in 1932 to honor the bicentennial of George Washington's birth. The parkway follows the Potomac River, running from Mount Vernon, past Old Town and the nation's capital, ending at Great Falls, Virginia. Today, the parkway is a major commuter route leading into and out of the city. Even the most impatient driver, however, can't help but notice the beautiful scenery and views of the Jefferson and Lincoln memorials and the Washington Monument that you pass along the way.

at 8am from the bus terminal at Union Station, the shorter tour returning by 12:30pm, the longer tour returning by 4:30pm. The ticket kiosk is on the first level of the parking garage. The cost is $70 per adult, $45 per child for the 8-hour tour, and $55 per adult and $30 per child for the 4-hour tour. The tour is free for children 6 and under. (AAA members receive a 10% discount when they purchase tickets at the Union Station kiosk and show their membership card.) Gray Line offers several other tours, so call for further information.

Tourmobile Sightseeing (© 888/868-7707 or 202/554-5100; www.tourmobile. com; also see p. 229 for more information) offers daily bus tours to Mount Vernon during the summer, June 15 to Labor Day, departing from Arlington National Cemetery at 11am and returning there by 4pm. Tickets are $32 for adults, $16 for children, and must be purchased at the Arlington National Cemetery ticket booth.

The **Spirit of Washington Cruises'** (© 866/302-2469 or 202/554-8000; www. spiritcruises.com) *Spirit of Mount Vernon* leaves from Pier 4 (6th and Water sts. SW; 3 blocks from the Green Line Metro's Waterfront Station) at 8am, returning by 3pm, Friday through Sunday throughout March and from late August through October; and Tuesday through Sunday from April through late August. The cost is $45 per adult, $39 per child (ages 6–11; free for younger children).

The **Potomac Riverboat Company's** (© 877/511-2628 or 703/684-0580; www. potomacriverboatco.com) *Miss Christin* operates Tuesday through Sunday April through August, Friday to Sunday in September to mid-October, and Saturday to Sunday mid-October to November 1. It departs at 10:30am for Mount Vernon from the pier adjacent to the Torpedo Factory, where Union and Cameron streets intersect, at Old Town Alexandria's waterfront. The rate is $38 per adult, $20 per child (ages 6–11; free for children 5 and under). Arrive 30 minutes ahead of time at the pier to secure a place on the boat. The narrated trip takes 90 minutes each way, stopping at Gaylord's National Harbor to pick up and discharge passengers. The boat departs Mount Vernon at 4pm to return to Old Town via Gaylord's.

If you're in the mood for exercise in a pleasant setting, rent a **bike** (see "Biking to Old Town Alexandria & Mount Vernon," on p. 280, for rental locations and other information).

Finally, it is possible to take **public transportation** to Mount Vernon by riding the Metro to the Yellow Line's Huntington Station and proceeding to the lower level, where you catch the Fairfax Connector bus (no. 101) to Mount Vernon. The connector bus departs hourly on weekends, every 30 minutes weekdays; it's a 25-minute ride and costs $1.35. Call © 703/339-7200 or check www.fairfaxconnector.com for schedule information.

Mount Vernon Estate and Gardens ★★ If it's beautiful out and you have the time, you could easily spend half a day or more soaking in the life and times of George Washington at Mount Vernon. The centerpiece of a visit to this 500-acre estate is a tour through 14 rooms of the mansion, whose oldest part dates from the 1740s. The plantation was passed down from Washington's great-grandfather, who acquired the land in 1674, to George's half-brother, and eventually to George himself in 1754. Washington proceeded over the next 45 years to expand and fashion the home to his liking, though the American Revolution and his years as president kept Washington away from his beloved estate much of the time.

In fall 2006, the estate opened the Ford Orientation Center and the Donald W. Reynolds Museum and Education Center, which are located just inside the main gate. Much of the complex is built underground so as not to take away from the estate's pastoral setting. A 15-minute film in the orientation center fills you in on the life and character of George Washington. The education center's 25 galleries and theater presentations inform you further about Washington's military and presidential careers, rounding out the whole story of this heroic, larger-than-life man. It's especially helpful to absorb this information and gain some context for the life and times of Washington before setting off for the mansion, where tours are self-guided. Attendants stationed throughout the house and grounds do provide brief orientations and answer questions; when there's no line, a walk-through takes about 20 minutes. What you see today is a remarkable restoration of the mansion, displaying many original furnishings and objects used by the Washington family. The rooms have been repainted in the original colors favored by George and Martha.

After leaving the house, you can tour the outbuildings: the kitchen, slave quarters, storeroom, smokehouse, overseer's quarters, coach house, and stables. A 4-acre exhibit area called "George Washington, Pioneer Farmer" includes a replica of Washington's 16-sided barn and fields of crops that he grew (corn, wheat, oats, and so forth). Docents in period costumes demonstrate 18th-century farming methods. At its peak, Mount Vernon was an 8,000-acre working farm, reminding us that, more than anything, Washington considered himself first and foremost a farmer.

You'll want to walk around the grounds (especially in nice weather) and see the wharf (and take a 40-min. narrated excursion on the Potomac, offered several times a day, seasonally, Mar–Nov; $9 per adult, $5 per child ages 6–11), the slave burial ground, the greenhouse, the lawns and gardens, and the tomb containing George and Martha Washington's sarcophagi (24 other family members are also interred here). In spring 2007, Mount Vernon opened the restored distillery, located 3 miles south of the estate, next to the gristmill. Costumed staff demonstrate 18th-century techniques as they operate the gristmill and distillery, which is open April through October. Admission is $4 per adult and $2 per child, or, when combined with your Mount Vernon admission, $2 per adult and $1.50 per child (ages 6-11; kids 5 and under enter free). You'll have to get to the gristmill on your own or take the Fairfax Connector Bus #152 (✆ **703/339-7200;** www.fairfaxconnector.com).

Celebrations are held at the estate every year on the third Monday in February, the date commemorating Washington's birthday; admission is free to anyone who shares Washington's birthday, February 22.

Mount Vernon belongs to the Mount Vernon Ladies' Association, which purchased the estate for $200,000 in 1858 from John Augustine Washington, great-grandnephew

> **Tips** **Special Activities at Mount Vernon**
>
> Events at Mount Vernon, especially in the summer, include tours on 18th-century gardens, slave life, Colonial crafts, or archaeology; and, for children, hands-on history programs and treasure hunts. Call or check the website for schedule details.

of the first president. Without the group's purchase, the estate might have crumbled and disappeared, for neither the federal government nor the Commonwealth of Virginia had wanted to buy the property when it was earlier offered for sale.

Today more than a million people tour the property annually. The best time to visit is off season; during the heavy tourist months (especially in spring), avoid weekends and holidays if possible, and arrive early year-round to beat the crowds.

3200 Mount Vernon Memorial Highway. (mailing address: P.O. Box 110, Mount Vernon, VA 22121). ✆ 703/780-2000. www.mountvernon.org. Admission $15 adults, $14 seniors, $7 children 6–11, free for children 5 and under. Apr–Aug daily 8am–5pm; Mar and Sept–Oct daily 9am–5pm; Nov–Feb daily 9am–4pm.

DINING & SHOPPING

Mount Vernon's comprehensive **gift shop** offers a wide range of books, children's toys, holiday items, Mount Vernon private-labeled food and wine, and Mount Vernon licensed furnishings. A **food court** features indoor and outdoor seating and a menu of baked goods, deli sandwiches, coffee, grilled items, pizza, and Mrs. Fields cookies. Although you can't **picnic** on the grounds of Mount Vernon, you can drive a mile north on the parkway to Riverside Park, where there are tables and a lawn overlooking the Potomac. But the Mount Vernon Inn restaurant is the option I'd recommend.

Mount Vernon Inn AMERICAN TRADITIONAL   Lunch or dinner at the inn is an intrinsic part of the Mount Vernon experience. It's a quaint and charming Colonial-style restaurant, complete with period furnishings and three working fireplaces. The waiters are all in 18th-century costumes. Lunch entrees range from Colonial turkey "pye" (a sort of Early American stew served in a crock with garden vegetables and a puffed pastry top) to a pulled-pork barbecue sandwich. There's a full bar, and premium wines are offered by the glass. At dinner, tablecloths and candlelight make this a more elegant setting. Choose from soups, perhaps the homemade peanut and chestnut; entrees such as roasted duck served with George Washington's favorite apricot sauce or roast venison with peppercorn sauce; and dessert, such as whiskey cake or English trifle.

Near the entrance to Mount Vernon Estate and Gardens. ✆ 703/780-0011. www.mountvernon.org. Reservations recommended for dinner. Lunch main courses $6.95–$8.50; dinner main courses $16–$25. AE, DISC, MC, V. Daily 11am–3:30pm (11:30am–2:30pm weekdays in winter); Mon–Thurs 5–8:30pm, Fri–Sat 5–9pm.

2 ALEXANDRIA

Old Town Alexandria is about 8 miles S of Washington.

The city of Washington may be named for our first president, but he never lived there. No, he called this other side of the Potomac home from the age of 11, when he joined his half-brother Lawrence, who owned Mount Vernon. Washington came to Alexandria often, helping to survey its 60 acres when he was a lad of 17, training his militia in Market Square, worshiping at Christ Church, and dining and dancing at Gadsby's Tavern.

The town of Alexandria is actually named after John Alexander, the Scot who purchased the land of the present-day town from an English ship captain for "six thousand pounds of Tobacco and Cask." Incorporated in 1749, the town soon grew into a major trading center and port, known for its handsome houses.

Today, many of those handsome houses and the places frequented by George Washington stand at the heart of Old Town, a multimillion-dollar urban renewal historic district. Market Square is the site of the oldest continuously operating farmers' market in the country. (Go there on Sat btw. 5 and 11am, and you'll be participating in a 258-year-old tradition.) Christ Church and Gadsby's Tavern are still open and operating. Many Alexandria streets still bear their original Colonial names (King, Queen, Prince, Princess, Royal), while others, like Jefferson, Franklin, Lee, Patrick, and Henry, are obviously post-Revolutionary.

Twenty-first-century America thrives in Old Town's many shops, boutiques, art galleries, bars, and restaurants. But it's still easy to imagine yourself in Colonial times by listening for the rumbling of horse-drawn vehicles over cobblestone (portions of Prince and Oronoco streets are still paved with cobblestone); dining on Sally Lunn bread and other 18th-century grub in the centuries-old Gadsby's Tavern; and learning about the lives of the nation's forefathers during walking tours that take you in and out of their houses.

ESSENTIALS

GETTING THERE If you're driving from the District, take the Arlington Memorial or the 14th Street Bridge to the George Washington Memorial Parkway south, which becomes Washington Street in Old Town Alexandria. Washington Street intersects with King Street, Alexandria's main thoroughfare. Turn left from Washington Street onto one of the streets before or after King Street (southbound left turns are not permitted from Washington St. onto King St.), and you'll be heading toward the waterfront and the heart of Old Town. If you turn right from Washington Street onto King Street, you'll still be in Old Town, with King Street's long avenue of shops and restaurants awaiting you. You can obtain a free parking permit from the Visitors Center (see information about parking in the "Visitor Information" paragraph, below), or park at meters or in garages. The town is compact, so you won't need a car.

The easiest way to make the trip is by Metro, whose Yellow and Blue line trains travel to the King Street station. From the King Street station, you can catch the free King Street Trolley, which operates daily, 11:30am to 10pm, making frequent stops between the Metro station and the Potomac River. The eastbound AT2, AT5, or AT7 blue-and-gold DASH bus (© **703/370-DASH** [3274]; www.dashbus.com) marked either OLD TOWN or BRADDOCK METRO will also take you up King Street. Ask to be dropped at the corner of Fairfax and King streets, which will put you right across the street from Ramsay House Visitors Center. The fare is $1.25. Or you can walk into Old Town, although it's about a mile from the station into the center of Old Town.

VISITOR INFORMATION The **Alexandria Convention and Visitors Association**'s Ramsay House Visitors Center, 221 King St., at Fairfax Street (© **800/388-9119** or 703/746-3301; www.visitalexandriava.com), is open daily from 9am to 8pm (closed Thanksgiving, Dec 25, and Jan 1). Here you can obtain a map/self-guided walking tour and brochures about the area; learn about special events that might be scheduled during

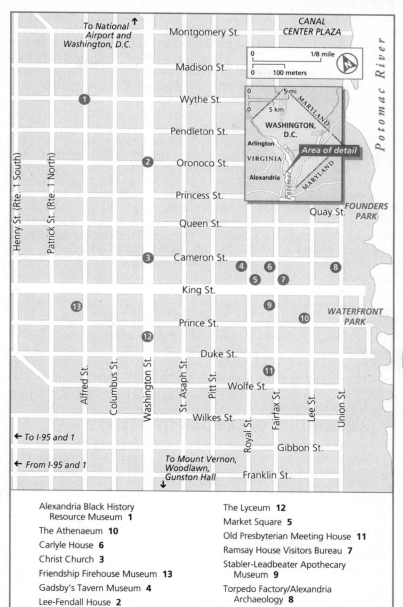

Alexandria Black History
  Resource Museum **1**

The Athenaeum **10**

Carlyle House **6**

Christ Church **3**

Friendship Firehouse Museum **13**

Gadsby's Tavern Museum **4**

Lee-Fendall House **2**

The Lyceum **12**

Market Square **5**

Old Presbyterian Meeting House **11**

Ramsay House Visitors Bureau **7**

Stabler-Leadbeater Apothecary
  Museum **9**

Torpedo Factory/Alexandria
  Archaeology **8**

your visit and get tickets for them; and receive answers to any questions you might have about accommodations, restaurants, sights, or shopping. The center supplies materials in five languages. You can also call ahead or go on the website to order a visitors guide and other information.

If you come by car, get a free 1-day parking permit here for any 2-hour meter for up to 24 hours. Make sure you put money in the meter to cover yourself until you get back outside with your permit, then head in to the Visitors Center and provide the staff person your license plate number to obtain your permit. The permit can be renewed for a second day.

ORGANIZED TOURS Though it's easy to see Alexandria on your own by putting yourself in the hands of Colonial-attired guides at individual attractions, you might consider taking a comprehensive walking tour of the town. Architectural and history tours leave from the Visitors Center garden, March through November, at least once a day, weather permitting. Tours depart at 10:30am Monday through Saturday and at 2pm on Sunday, with additional tours added during busy seasons. These walk-up tours (no reservations needed) take 1¹/₂ hours and cost $15 per person (free for age 6 and under). You pay the guide when you arrive at the Visitors Center.

Alexandria Colonial Tours (© 703/519-1749; www.alexcolonialtours.com) conducts a number of different tours. Its Ghosts and Graveyard Tour is offered March through November (weather permitting) at 7:30 and 9pm Friday and Saturday, and 7:30pm only on Sunday. A 7:30pm tour is offered Wednesday and Thursday evenings in the summer. This 1-hour tour departs from Ramsay House and costs $10 for adults, $5 for children ages 7 to 17, and is free for children 6 and under. Reservations are recommended, though not required, for these tours; or you can purchase tickets from the guide, who will be dressed in Colonial attire and standing in front of the Visitors Center.

CITY LAYOUT Old Town is very small and laid out in an easy grid. At the center is the intersection of Washington Street and King Street. Streets change from north to south when they cross King Street. For example, North Alfred Street is the part of Alfred north of King Street (closest to Washington, in other words). Guess where South Alfred Street is.

ALEXANDRIA CALENDAR OF EVENTS

The **Alexandria Convention and Visitors Association** (© 800/388-9119 or 703/746-3300; www.visitalexandriava.com) posts its calendar of events online and in its visitors guide, which you can order by phone or on its website. Event highlights include:

FEBRUARY

Alexandria celebrates **George Washington's Birthday** over the course of several days, including Presidents' Weekend, which precedes the federal holiday (usually the third Mon in Feb). Festivities typically include a Colonial costume or black-tie banquet, followed by a ball at Gadsby's Tavern, a 10-kilometer race, special tours, a Revolutionary War encampment at Fort Ward Park (complete with uniformed troops engaging in skirmishes), the nation's largest George Washington Birthday Parade (50,000–75,000 people attend each year), and 18th-century comic opera performances. Most events, such as the parade and historical reenactments, are free. The Birthnight Ball at Gadsby's Tavern requires tickets for both the banquet and the ball.

On the first Saturday in March, King Street is the site of a popular **St. Patrick's Day Parade.**

APRIL

Alexandria celebrates **Historic Garden Week in Virginia** with tours of privately owned local historic homes and gardens the third Saturday of the month. Call the Visitors Center (© **703/746-3300**) in early 2010 for more information about tickets and admission prices for the tour.

JUNE

The **Red Cross Waterfront Festival,** the second or third weekend in June, honors Alexandria's historical importance as a seaport and the vitality of its Potomac shoreline today with a display of historic tall ships, ship tours, boat rides and races, nautical art exhibits, waterfront walking tours, fireworks, children's games, an arts-and-crafts show, food booths, and entertainment. Entrance fee.

JULY

Alexandria's birthday (its 261st in 2010) is celebrated with a concert performance by the Alexandria Symphony Orchestra, fireworks, birthday cake, and other festivities. The Saturday following the Fourth of July. All events are free.

SEPTEMBER

Alexandria Festival of the Arts features the ceramics, sculpture, photography, and other works of more than 200 juried artists. On a Saturday and Sunday in early September. Free.

This year is the 68th Annual **Tour of Historic Alexandria Homes,** which takes you to some of the city's most beautifully restored and decorated private homes. Third Saturday in September. Tickets and information from the Visitors Center.

OCTOBER

Ghost tours take place year-round but pick up around **Halloween.** A lantern-carrying guide in 18th-century costume describes Alexandria's ghosts, graveyards, legends, myths, and folklore as you tour the town and graveyards. Call the Visitors Center for information.

NOVEMBER

There's a **Christmas Tree Lighting** in Market Square usually the Friday after Thanksgiving. The ceremony, which includes choir singing, puppet shows, dance performances, and an appearance by Santa and his elves, begins at 7pm. The night the tree is lit, thousands of tiny lights adorning King Street trees also go on.

DECEMBER

Holiday festivities continue with the **Annual Scottish Christmas Walk** on the first Saturday in December. Activities include kilted bagpipers, Highland dancers, a parade of Scottish clans (with horses and dogs), caroling, fashion shows, storytelling, booths (selling crafts, antiques, food, hot mulled punch, heather, fresh wreaths, and holly), and children's games. Admission is charged for some events.

The **Historic Alexandria Candlelight Tour,** the second week in December, visits seasonally decorated historic Alexandria homes and an 18th-century tavern. Colonial dancing, string quartets, madrigal and opera singers, and refreshments are part of the celebration. Purchase tickets at the Ramsay House Visitors Center.

There are so many **holiday-season activities** that the Visitors Association issues a special brochure about them each year. Pick one up to learn about decorations, workshops, walking tours, tree lightings, concerts, bazaars, bake sales, crafts fairs, and much more.

(Moments) **Biking to Old Town Alexandria & Mount Vernon**

One of the nicest ways to view the Washington skyline is from across the river while biking in Virginia. Rent a bike at Thompson's Boat Center, across from the Kennedy Center and right on the bike path, or from some other location listed under "Outdoor Activities," in chapter 7. Hop on the pathway that runs along the Potomac River and head toward the monuments and the Arlington Memorial Bridge. In Washington, this is the Rock Creek Park Trail; when you cross Memorial Bridge (near the Lincoln Memorial) into Virginia, the name changes to the Mount Vernon Trail, which is, not surprisingly, a straight shot to Mount Vernon.

As you tool along, you have a breathtaking view of the Potomac and of Washington's grand landmarks: the Kennedy Center, Washington Monument, Lincoln Memorial, Jefferson Memorial, and the National Cathedral off in one direction, and the Capitol off in the other.

Of course, this mode of transportation is also a great way to see Old Town Alexandria and Mount Vernon. The trail carries you past Reagan National Airport via two pedestrian bridges that take you safely through the airport's roadway system. Continue on to Old Town, where you should lock your bike to a lamppost, walk around, tour some of the historic properties listed in this chapter, and take in some refreshment from one of the many excellent restaurants before you proceed to Mount Vernon. The section from Memorial Bridge to Mount Vernon is about 19 miles in all.

WHAT TO SEE & DO

Colonial and post-Revolutionary buildings are Old Town Alexandria's main attractions. My favorites are the Carlyle House and Gadsby's Tavern Museum, but they're all worth a visit.

These sites are most easily accessible via the King Street Metro station, combined with a ride on the free King Street trolley to the center of Old Town. The exceptions are the Alexandria Black History and Resource Center, whose closest Metro stop is the Braddock Street station, and Fort Ward, to which you should drive or take a taxi.

Old Town is also known for its fine shopping opportunities. Brand-name stores, charming boutiques, antiques shops, art galleries, and gift shops sell everything you might desire. The Visitors Center offers brochures for specific stores as well as a general guide to shopping. Also see chapter 8, which includes some Alexandria shops.

Alexandria Black History Resource Museum In 1940, African Americans in Alexandria staged a sit-in to protest the segregation of blacks from Alexandria's main library. The black community built its own public library and it is this 1940s building that now serves as the Black History Resource Museum. The center exhibits historical objects, photographs, documents, and memorabilia relating to black citizens of Alexandria from the 18th century forward. In addition to the permanent collection, the museum presents rotating exhibits and other activities. If you're interested in further

to spend at the center.

The museum is actually on the outskirts of Old Town. From here, it makes sense to walk into Old Town, rather than taking the Metro or even a taxi. Have a staff person point you in the direction of Washington Street, east of the center; at Washington Street, turn right (or south) and walk 2 blocks or so to the Lee-Fendall House (p. 283) at Oronoco and Washington streets.

902 Wythe St. (at N. Alfred St.). ⓒ **703/838-4356.** www.alexblackhistory.org. Admission $2. Tues–Sat 10am–4pm. Metro: Braddock Rd. From the station, walk across the parking lot and bear right until you reach the corner of West and Wythe sts., where you'll proceed 5 blocks east along Wythe until you reach the center.

The Athenaeum This grand building, with its Greek Revival architectural style, stands out among the narrow old town houses on the cobblestone street. Built in 1851, the Athenaeum has been many things: the Bank of the Old Dominion, where Robert E. Lee kept his money prior to the Civil War; a commissary for the Union Army during the Civil War; a church; a triage center where wounded Union soldiers were treated; and a medicine warehouse. Now the hall serves as an art gallery and performance space for the Northern Virginia Fine Arts Association. Pop by to admire the Athenaeum's imposing exterior, including the four soaring Doric columns and its interior hall: 24-foot-high ceilings, enormous windows, and whatever contemporary art is on display. This won't take you more than 20 minutes, tops.

201 Prince St. (at S. Lee St.). ⓒ **703/548-0035.** www.nvfaa.org. Free admission (donations accepted). Thurs, Fri, and Sun noon–4pm; Sat 1–4pm. Closed major holidays.

Carlyle House Historic Park One of Virginia's most architecturally impressive 18th-century homes, Carlyle House also figured prominently in American history. In 1753, Scottish merchant John Carlyle completed the mansion for his bride, Sarah Fairfax of Belvoir, a daughter of one of Virginia's most prominent families. It was designed in the style of a Scottish/English manor house and lavishly furnished. Carlyle, a successful merchant, had the means to import the best furnishings and appointments available abroad for his new Alexandria home.

When it was built, Carlyle House was a waterfront property with its own wharf. A social and political center, the house was visited by the great men of the day, including George Washington. But its most important moment in history occurred in April 1755, when Maj. Gen. Edward Braddock, commander in chief of His Majesty's forces in North America, met with five Colonial governors here and asked them to tax colonists to finance a campaign against the French and Indians. Colonial legislatures refused to comply, one of the first instances of serious friction between America and Britain. Nevertheless, Braddock made Carlyle House his headquarters during the campaign, and Carlyle was less than impressed with him. He called the general "a man of weak understanding . . . very indolent . . . a slave to his passions, women and wine . . . as great an Epicure as could be in his eating, tho a brave man." Possibly these were the reasons his unfinanced campaign met with disaster. Braddock received, as Carlyle described it, "a most remarkable drubbing."

Tours are given on the hour and half-hour and take about 45 minutes; allow another 10 or 15 minutes if you plan to tour the tiered garden of brick walks and boxed parterres. Two of the original rooms, the large parlor and the dining room, have survived intact; the former, where Braddock met the governors, still retains its original fine woodwork, paneling, and pediments. The house is furnished in period pieces; however, only a few of

> **Tips   Planning Note**
>
> Many Alexandria attractions are closed on Monday.

Carlyle's possessions remain. In an upstairs room, an architecture exhibit depicts 18th-century construction methods with hand-hewn beams and hand-wrought nails.

121 N. Fairfax St. (btw. Cameron and King sts.). © **703/549-2997**. www.carlylehouse.org. Admission $4 adults, $2 children 12–17, free for children 10 and under. Tues–Sat 10am–4pm; Sun noon–4pm.

Christ Church   This sturdy red-brick Georgian-style church would be an important national landmark even if its two most distinguished members had not been Washington and Lee. It has been in continuous use since 1773; the town of Alexandria grew up around this building that was once known as the "Church in the Woods."

Over the years, the church has undergone many changes, adding the bell tower, church bell, galleries, and organ by the early 1800s, and the "wine-glass" pulpit in 1891. For the most part, the original structure remains, including the handblown glass in the windows.

Christ Church has had its historic moments. Washington and other early church members fomented revolution in the churchyard, and Robert E. Lee met here with Richmond representatives to discuss Lee's taking command of Virginia's military forces at the beginning of the Civil War. You can sit in the pew where George and Martha sat with her two Custis grandchildren or in the Lee family pew. You might also want to walk through the graveyard and note how old the tombstones are, including the oldest stone, dated March 20, 1791.

World dignitaries and U.S. presidents have visited the church over the years. One of the most memorable of these visits took place shortly after Pearl Harbor, when Franklin Delano Roosevelt attended services with Winston Churchill on the World Day of Prayer for Peace, January 1, 1942.

Of course, you're invited to attend a service (Sun at 8, 9, and 11:15am and 5pm; Wed at 7:15am and 12:05pm). There's no admission charge, but donations are appreciated. A guide gives brief lectures to visitors. A gift shop is open Tuesday through Saturday 10am to 4pm, and Sunday 8:45am to 1pm. Twenty minutes should do it here. Be sure to check out the website before you visit, since it offers a wealth of information about the history of the church and town.

118 N. Washington St. (at Cameron St.). © **703/549-1450**. www.historicchristchurch.org. Donations appreciated. Mon–Sat 9am–4pm; Sun 2–4pm. Closed all federal holidays.

Fort Ward Museum & Historic Site **Kids**   A short drive from Old Town is a 45-acre museum and park that transports you to Alexandria during the Civil War. The action here centers, as it did in the early 1860s, on an actual Union fort that Lincoln ordered erected. It was part of a system of Civil War forts called the "Defenses of Washington." About 90% of the fort's earthwork walls are preserved, and the Northwest Bastion has been restored with six mounted guns (originally there were 36). A model of 19th-century military engineering, the fort was never attacked by Confederate forces. Self-guided tours begin at the Fort Ward ceremonial gate.

Visitors can explore the fort and replicas of the ceremonial entrance gate and an officer's hut. A museum of Civil War artifacts on the premises features changing exhibits that focus on subjects such as Union arms and equipment, medical care of the wounded, and local war history.

There are picnic areas with barbecue grills in the park surrounding the fort. Living-history presentations take place throughout the year. This is a good stop if you have young children, in which case you could spend an hour or two here (especially if you bring a picnic).

4301 W. Braddock Rd. (btw. Rte. 7 and N. Van Dorn St.). ℂ **703/838-4848.** www.fortward.org. Free admission (donations welcome). Park daily 9am–sunset. Museum Tues–Sat 9am–5pm (Nov–Mar 10am–5pm); Sun noon–5pm. Call for information regarding special holiday closings. From Old Town, follow King St. west, go right on Kenwood Ave., then left on W. Braddock Rd.; continue for a mile to the entrance on the right.

Friendship Firehouse   Alexandria's first firefighting organization, the Friendship Fire Company, was established in 1774. In the early days, the company met in taverns and kept its firefighting equipment in a member's barn. Its present Italianate-style brick building dates from 1855; it was erected after an earlier building was, ironically, destroyed by fire. Local tradition holds that George Washington was involved with the firehouse as a founding member, active firefighter, and purchaser of its first fire engine, although research does not confirm these stories. The museum displays an 1851 fire engine, old hoses, buckets, and other firefighting apparatus. This is a tiny place that you can easily visit in 20 minutes.

107 S. Alfred St. (btw. King and Prince sts.). ℂ **703/838-3891.** www.oha.alexandriava.gov/friendship. Admission $2. Fri–Sat 10am–4pm; Sun 1–4pm.

Gadsby's Tavern Museum ★   Alexandria was once at the crossroads of 18th-century America. Its social center was Gadsby's Tavern, which consisted of two buildings, one Georgian, one Federal, dating from around 1785 and 1792, respectively. Innkeeper John Gadsby combined them to create "a gentleman's tavern," which he operated from 1796 to 1808; it was considered one of the finest in the country. George Washington was a frequent dinner guest; he and Martha danced in the second-floor ballroom, and it was here that Washington celebrated his last birthday. The tavern also welcomed Thomas Jefferson, James Madison, and the Marquis de Lafayette (the French soldier and statesman who served in the American army under Washington during the Revolutionary War and remained close to Washington). It was the scene of lavish parties, theatrical performances, small circuses, government meetings, and concerts. Itinerant merchants used the tavern to display their wares, and traveling doctors and dentists treated a hapless clientele (these were rudimentary professions in the 18th c.) on the premises.

The rooms have been restored to their 18th-century appearance. On the 30-minute tour, you'll get a good look at the Tap Room, a small dining room; the Assembly Room, the ballroom; typical bedrooms; and the underground icehouse, which was filled each winter from the icy river. Tours depart 15 minutes before and after the hour. Inquire about lantern tours, offered June through August on Friday nights from 7 to 10pm, admission $5, and about special living-history programs. Cap off the experience with a meal right next door, at the restored Colonial-style restaurant, **Gadsby's Tavern,** 138 N. Royal Street, at Cameron Street (ℂ **703/548-1288;** www.gadsbystavernrestaurant.com).

134 N. Royal St. (at Cameron St.). ℂ **703/838-4242.** www.gadsbystavern.org. Admission $4 adults, $2 children 11–17, free for children 10 and under. Tours Apr–Oct Tues–Sat 10am–5pm, Sun–Mon 1–5pm; Nov–Mar Wed–Sat 11am–4pm, Sun 1–4pm. Closed most federal holidays.

Lee-Fendall House Museum   This handsome Greek Revival–style house is a veritable Lee family museum of furniture, heirlooms, and documents. "Light Horse Harry"

SIDE TRIPS FROM WASHINGTON, D.C.

Lee never actually lived here, though he was a frequent visitor, as was his good friend George Washington. He did own the original lot but sold it to Philip Richard Fendall (himself a Lee on his mother's side), who built the house in 1785.

Thirty-seven Lees occupied the house over a period of 118 years (1785–1903), and it was in this house that Harry wrote Alexandria's farewell address to George Washington, delivered when he passed through town on his way to assume the presidency. (Harry also wrote and delivered the famous funeral oration to Washington that contained the words "First in war, first in peace, and first in the hearts of his countrymen.") During the Civil War, the house was seized and used as a Union hospital.

Thirty-minute guided tours interpret the 1850s era of the home and provide insight into Victorian family life. You'll also see the Colonial garden with its magnolia and chestnut trees, roses, and boxwood-lined paths. Much of the interior woodwork and glass is original.

614 Oronoco St. (at Washington St.). © **703/548-1789.** www.leefendallhouse.org. Admission $5 adults, $3 children 11–17, free for children 10 and under. Wed–Sat 10am–4pm; Sun 1–4pm. Call ahead to make sure the museum is open, since it often closes for special events. Tours on the hour 10am–3pm. Closed Thanksgiving and the month of Jan.

The Lyceum This Greek Revival building houses a museum depicting Alexandria's history from the 17th to the 20th century. It features changing exhibits and an ongoing series of lectures, concerts, and educational programs. You can obtain maps and brochures about Virginia state attractions, especially Alexandria attractions. The knowledgeable staff will be happy to answer questions.

The striking brick-and-stucco Lyceum also merits a visit. Built in 1839, it was designed in the Doric temple style to serve as a lecture, meeting, and concert hall. It was an important center of Alexandria's cultural life until the Civil War, when Union forces appropriated it for use as a hospital. After the war it became a private residence, and still later it was subdivided for office space. In 1969, however, the city council's use of eminent domain prevented the Lyceum from being demolished in favor of a parking lot. Allow about 20 minutes here.

201 S. Washington St. (off Prince St.). © **703/838-4994.** www.alexandriahistory.org. Admission $2. Mon–Sat 10am–5pm; Sun 1–5pm. Closed Thanksgiving, Dec 25, and Jan 1.

Old Presbyterian Meeting House Presbyterian congregations have worshiped in Virginia since the Rev. Alexander Whittaker converted Pocahontas in Jamestown in 1614. This brick church was built by Scottish pioneers in 1775. Although it wasn't George Washington's church, the Meeting House bell tolled continuously for 4 days after his death in December 1799, and memorial services were preached from the pulpit here by Presbyterian, Episcopal, and Methodist ministers. According to the Alexandria paper of the day, "The walking being bad to the Episcopal church the funeral sermon of George Washington will be preached at the Presbyterian Meeting House." Two months later, on Washington's birthday, Alexandria citizens marched from Market Square to the church to pay their respects.

Many famous Alexandrians are buried in the church graveyard, including John and Sarah Carlyle; Dr. James Craik (the surgeon who treated—some say killed—Washington, dressed Lafayette's wounds at Brandywine, and ministered to the dying Braddock at Monongahela); and William Hunter, Jr., founder of the St. Andrew's Society of Scottish descendants, to whom bagpipers pay homage on the first Saturday of December. It is also the site of a Tomb of an Unknown Revolutionary War Soldier. Dr. James Muir, minister between 1789 and 1820, lies beneath the sanctuary in his gown and bands.

The original Meeting House was gutted by a lightning fire in 1835, but parishioners restored it in the style of the day a few years later. The present bell, said to be recast from the metal of the old one, was hung in a newly constructed belfry in 1843; and a new organ was installed in 1849. The Meeting House closed its doors in 1889, and for 60 years was used sporadically. But in 1949 it was reborn as a living Presbyterian U.S.A. church, and today the Old Meeting House looks much as it did following its first restoration. The original parsonage, or manse, is still intact. There's no guided tour. Allow 20 minutes for touring.

321 S. Fairfax St. (btw. Duke and Wolfe sts.). ℂ **703/549-6670.** www.opmh.org. Free admission, but you must obtain a key from the office to tour the church. Sun services at 8:30 and 11am, except in summer, when a service is held at 10am.

Stabler-Leadbeater Apothecary Museum   When its doors closed in 1933, this landmark drugstore was the second oldest in continuous operation in America. Run for five generations by the same Quaker family (beginning in 1792), the store counted Robert E. Lee (who purchased the paint for Arlington House here), George Mason, Henry Clay, John C. Calhoun, and George Washington among its famous patrons. Gothic Revival decorative elements and Victorian-style doors were added in the 1840s. Today the apothecary looks much as it did in Colonial times, its shelves lined with original handblown gold leaf–labeled bottles (the most valuable collection of antique medicinal bottles in the country), old scales stamped with the royal crown, patent medicines, and equipment for bloodletting. The clock on the rear wall, the porcelain-handled mahogany drawers, and two mortars and pestles all date from about 1790. Among the shop's documentary records is this 1802 order from Mount Vernon: "Mrs. Washington desires Mr. Stabler to send by the bearer a quart bottle of his best Castor Oil and the bill for it."

105–107 S. Fairfax St. (near King St.). ℂ **703/838-3852.** www.apothecarymuseum.org. Admission $4 adults, $2 children 11–17, free for children 10 and under. Apr–Oct Tues–Sat 10am–5pm, Sun–Mon 1–5pm; Nov–Mar Wed–Sat 11am–4pm, Sun 1–4pm. Closed major holidays.

Torpedo Factory   This block-long, three-story building was built in 1918 as a torpedo shell-case factory but now accommodates some 82 artists' studios, where 165 professional artists and craftspeople create and sell their own works. Here you can see artists at work in their studios: potters, painters, printmakers, photographers, sculptors, and jewelers, as well as those who create stained-glass windows and fiber art.

On permanent display are exhibits on Alexandria history provided by Alexandria Archaeology (ℂ **703/838-4399;** www.alexandriaarchaeology.org), which is headquartered here and engages in extensive city research. A volunteer or staff member is on hand to answer questions. Art lovers may end up browsing for an hour or two.

105 N. Union St. (btw. King and Cameron sts. on the waterfront). ℂ **703/838-4565.** www.torpedofactory.org. Free admission. Daily 10am–6pm, open until 9pm Thurs; archaeology exhibit area Tues–Fri 10am–3pm, Sat 10am–5pm, Sun 1–5pm. Closed Easter, July 4, Thanksgiving, Dec 25, and Jan 1.

ACCOMMODATIONS

With a total of 4,200 hotel guest rooms throughout Alexandria, the city should have no trouble accommodating you, should you decide to stay overnight here. Hotels run the budget gamut, too, from Comfort Inns at the low end to the posh new Lorien Hotel and Spa at the luxe end. Two properties lie especially close to the heart of historic Old Town.

The **Hotel Monaco Alexandria,** at 480 King St. (© **703/549-6080** or 800/KIMP-TON; www.monaco-alexandria.com), is a former Holiday Inn, recently converted by boutique hotel group Kimpton Hotels into a luxury property with 241 stylish rooms, a pool, health club, and chef-driven restaurant. Rates vary by season and date, but expect to pay from $159 to $300 on the weekends, $229 to $370 weekdays, for a standard double room.

Another Kimpton property, **Morrison House,** 116 S. Alfred Street (© **800/367-0800** or 703/838-8000; www.morrisonhouse.com), is also a standout. Its 45 rooms are appointed in high style with canopied four-poster beds, mahogany armoires, decorative fireplaces, and the like. Rates can start at $175 for the smallest room off season on the weekend and at $289 for a standard room on a weekday in season. Morrison House is known for its restaurant, the **Grille,** which presents award-winning contemporary American cuisine.

For other recommendations, check the **Alexandria Convention and Visitors Association** website, **www.visitalexandriava.com,** where you can book an online reservation and also read about various promotions that hotels are offering.

DINING

There are so many fine restaurants in Alexandria that Washingtonians often drive over just to dine here. Below is a mix of restaurants to suit assorted budgets, tastes, and styles, but also consider additional suggestions listed below in the box, "More Alexandria Eats." All of these restaurants are easily accessible via the King Street Metro station, combined with a ride on the free King Street trolley to the center of Old Town.

Expensive

La Bergerie ★ FRENCH   This old-school French restaurant has been here forever and is ever popular. Waiters are tuxedoed and entrees are updated traditional: escargots sprinkled with hazelnuts, smoky foie gras, lobster bisque with lobster and its coral, tournedos of beef with wild mushrooms and béarnaise sauce. La Bergerie is known for its dessert soufflés, which you must request when you order your entrees. You'll want to dress up here. And be sure to order an Irish coffee, which is prepared at your table with flourishes and drama—and it tastes great, too.

218 N. Lee St. © **703/683-1007.** www.labergerie.com. Reservations required. Lunch (prix-fixe menu only) $22; dinner main courses $28–$34. AE, DC, DISC, MC, V. Mon–Sat 11:30am–2:30pm; Mon–Thurs 5:30–9:30pm; Fri–Sat 5:30–10:30pm; Sun 5–9pm.

Restaurant Eve ★★★ NEW AMERICAN   Named for the first child of owners Cathal (the chef) and Meshelle Armstrong, Eve is nationally recognized and locally beloved, which means it can be hard to score a reservation, so call way ahead. Dine in the casual bistro or in the elegant tasting room, where a five-course menu ($105 per person) and a nine-course menu ($145 per person) are offered. Bistro entrees might include bouillabaisse and sirloin of veal. Tasting-menu items range from butter-poached lobster with heirloom carrots to gnocchi with spring garlic and golden beets. Chef Armstrong has long been committed to seasonal cooking using the fresh produce of local farmers. Don't miss Eve's best dessert: an old-fashioned "birthday cake," which is a mouthwatering slice of white cake layered and iced with pink frosting and sprinkles. And be sure to read over the wine and cocktails list, since sommelier and "liquid savant" Todd Thrasher has gained such renown for his inventive concoctions—"Millions of Peaches" (peach vodka, champagne-vinegar-pickled peaches, and poached peaches), "Jose's Yin and Tonic" (made with house-made tonic)—that he's opened a nearby speakeasy lounge, PX, located just above Eamonn's A Dublin Chipper (see below), where he dispenses more fun drinks and good times.

110 S. Pitt St. (near King St.). ℂ **703/706-0450.** www.restauranteve.com. Reservations recommended. Jacket advised for men in bistro, jacket and tie advised for men in tasting room. Bistro: Lunch items $18–$25; dinner main courses $26–$34; tasting room fixed-price 5-course dinner $105, 9-course dinner $145. Lunch menu served at the bar weekdays 11:30am–4pm, $14 for any two items. AE, DC, DISC, MC, V. Bistro Mon–Fri 11:30am–2:30pm; Mon–Sat 5:30–10pm. Tasting Room Mon–Sat 5:30–9:30pm.

Moderate

Majestic Café ★ SOUTHERN   A lively bar fronts the narrow restaurant, making a dining experience here a little noisy; that can be either annoying or festive, depending on your mood. I promise, though, that you'll enjoy the grilled calamari salad, soft-shell crabs, artichoke and fontina cheese tart, spoon bread, hush puppies, and, for dessert, German chocolate cake. The Majestic was slated to close, until that dynamic couple Meshelle and Cathal Armstrong, of Restaurant Eve, rode to the rescue in 2007. The Majestic offers a bar

SIDE TRIPS FROM WASHINGTON, D.C.

10

ALEXANDRIA

More Alexandria Eats

If any of the above restaurants are booked or don't appeal, consider these other options, all of which win high marks from critics:

A La Lucia, 315 Madison St., ℂ **703/836-5123,** www.alalucia.com. Southern Italian cooking in a relaxed atmosphere. This is where area CEOs go when they want to dine anonymously and happily on pizza, veal scaloppini, and the like.

Bastille, 1201 N. Royal St., ℂ **703/519-3776,** www.bastillerestaurant.com. Couples especially savor the chic atmosphere, inventive wine cocktails, and delicious French fare, like the pan-seared foie gras with Calvados-sautéed apples, of this modern French bistro.

Brabo by Robert Wiedmaier, 1600 King St., ℂ **703/894-3440,** www.brabo restaurant.com. Not content with cheffing/owning two successful Belgian restaurants in the District (see Marcel's, p. 152, and Brasserie Beck, p. 142), Wiedmaier, in February 2009, opened his third, here in Alexandria, adjacent to the swank Lorien Hotel & Spa. Expect Wiedmaier's signature American-influenced Belgian cuisine served in a casual tasting room and in a more formal dining room, and, as always, a lively bar scene.

Overwood, 220 N. Lee St., ℂ **703/535-3340,** www.theoverwood.com. The wood-fired oven turns out fried ravioli, baby back ribs, and other good stuff for Overwood's family and sports fan clientele.

Vermilion, 1120 King St., ℂ **703/684-9669,** www.vermilionrestaurant.com. Downstairs appeals to an imbibing bar crowd. Upstairs, though also festive and relaxed, is better suited to conversation and enjoying the excellent American cuisine—try the Cobb salad, the braised lamb shank—prepared by chef Anthony Chittum.

lunch special Monday through Friday from 11:30am to 2:30pm: any lunch entree for $12; and a Sunday dinner special: $78 for four people and a set menu.

911 King St. (near Alfred St.). ⒞ **703/837-9117.** www.majesticcafe.com. Reservations recommended. Lunch $11–$21; dinner $19–$26. AE, DC, DISC, MC, V. Sun 11am–3pm; Mon–Sat 11:30am–2:30pm; Mon–Thurs 5:30–10pm; Fri–Sat 5:30–10:30pm; Sun 1–9pm.

Inexpensive

Eamonn's A Dublin Chipper ★ FISH AND CHIPS   Fish and chips and a few sides—onion rings, coleslaw—that's what we're talking here. But it's charming. Upstairs is PX, an exclusive lounge, where mixologist Todd Thrasher may be on hand to shake the drinks he's created. This is another in the priceless strand of rare restaurant experiences that Cathal and Meshelle Armstrong are perpetrating on this side of the Potomac. The Chipper is named after their son Eamonn, **Restaurant Eve** (see above) for their firstborn daughter. The Armstrongs have a following, so expect a crowd.

728 King St. ⒞ **703/299-8384.** www.eamonnsdublinchipper.com. Reservations not accepted. Main courses $5–$8. AE, DC, DISC, MC, V. Mon–Wed 11:30am–10pm; Thurs 11:30am–11pm; Fri 11:30am–midnight; Sat noon–midnight.

La Madeleine (Kids) FRENCH CAFE   It may be part of a self-service chain, but this place has its charms. Its French-country interior has a beamed ceiling, bare oak floors, a wood-burning stove, and maple hutches displaying crockery and pewter mugs. Also, the range of affordable menu items here makes this a good choice for families with finicky eaters in tow.

La Madeleine opens early—at 6:30am every day but Sunday, when it opens at 7am—so come for breakfast to feast on fresh-baked croissants, Danish, scones, muffins, and brioches, or a heartier bacon-and-eggs plate. Throughout the day, there are salads (such as roasted vegetables and rigatoni), sandwiches (including a traditional croque-monsieur), and hot dishes ranging from quiche and pizza to rotisserie chicken with a Caesar salad. After 5pm, additional choices include pastas and specials such as beef tenders *en merlot* or herb-crusted pork tenderloin, both served with garlic mashed potatoes and green beans almondine. Conclude with a fruit tart, or chocolate, vanilla, and praline triple-layer cheesecake with graham-cracker crust. Wine and beer are served.

500 King St. (at S. Pitt St.). ⒞ **703/739-2854.** www.lamadeleine.com. Reservations not accepted. Breakfast main courses $4.50–$9; lunch and dinner main courses $5–$13. AE, DISC, MC, V. Sun 7am–10pm; Mon–Sat 6:30am–11pm.

Fast Facts

1 FAST FACTS: WASHINGTON, D.C.

AMERICAN EXPRESS There's an American Express Travel Service office at 1501 K St. NW, entrance on 15th St. NW (© 202/457-1300).

AREA CODES Within the District of Columbia, it's 202. In Northern Virginia, it's 703. In D.C.'s Maryland suburbs, it's 301. You must use the area code when dialing any number, whether it's a local 202, 703, or 301 phone number.

AUTOMOBILE ORGANIZATIONS Motor clubs will supply maps, suggested routes, guidebooks, accident and bail-bond insurance, and emergency road service. The **American Automobile Association (AAA)** is the major auto club in the United States. If you belong to a motor club in your home country, inquire about AAA reciprocity before you leave. You may be able to join AAA even if you're not a member of a reciprocal club; to inquire, contact AAA (www.aaa.com). AAA has a nationwide emergency road service telephone number (© **800/AAA-HELP** [222-4357]). In Washington, AAA's downtown office is near the White House, at 1405 G St. NW, between 14th and 15th streets (© **202/481-6811**).

BUSINESS HOURS Offices are usually open weekdays from 9am to 5pm. Most banks are open from 9am to 3pm Monday through Thursday with some staying open until 5pm; 9am to 5pm on Friday; and sometimes Saturday mornings. Stores typically open between 9 and 10am and close between 5 and 6pm from Monday to Saturday. Stores in shopping complexes or malls tend to stay open late, until about 9pm on weekdays and weekends, and many malls and larger department stores are open on Sundays. (See chapter 8, p. 233, for more specific information about store hours.)

DRINKING LAWS The legal age for purchase and consumption of alcoholic beverages is 21; proof of age is required and often requested at bars, nightclubs, and restaurants, so it's always a good idea to bring ID when you go out. Liquor stores are closed on Sunday. District gourmet grocery stores, mom-and-pop grocery stores, and 7-Eleven convenience stores often sell beer and wine, even on Sunday.

Bars and nightclubs serve liquor until 2am Sunday through Thursday and until 3am Friday and Saturday.

Do not carry open containers of alcohol in your car or any public area that isn't zoned for alcohol consumption. The police can fine you on the spot. Don't even think about driving while intoxicated.

DRIVING RULES See "Getting There & Getting Around," p. 36.

ELECTRICITY Like Canada, the United States uses 110 to 120 volts AC (60 cycles), compared to 220 to 240 volts AC (50 cycles) in most of Europe, Australia, and New Zealand. Downward converters that change 220–240 volts to 110–120 volts are difficult to find in the United States, so bring one with you.

EMBASSIES & CONSULATES All embassies are located in the nation's capital, Washington, D.C. Some consulates are located in major U.S. cities, and most nations have a mission to the United Nations in New York City. If your country isn't listed below, call for directory information in Washington, D.C. (© **202/555-1212**) or check **www.embassy.org/embassies**.

The embassy of **Australia** is at 1601 Massachusetts Ave. NW, Washington, DC 20036 (© **202/797-3000**; usa.embassy. gov/au). Consulate locations include New York, Honolulu, Houston, Los Angeles, and San Francisco.

The embassy of **Canada** is at 501 Pennsylvania Ave. NW, Washington, DC 20001 (© **202/682-1740**; www.canadian embassy.org). Other Canadian consulates are in Buffalo (New York), Detroit, Los Angeles, New York, and Seattle.

The embassy of **Ireland** is at 2234 Massachusetts Ave. NW, Washington, DC 20008 (© **202/462-3939**; www.ireland emb.org). Irish consulates are in Boston, Chicago, New York, San Francisco, and other cities. See website for complete listing.

The embassy of **New Zealand** is at 37 Observatory Circle NW, Washington, DC 20008 (© **202/328-4800**; www.nz embassy.com). New Zealand consulates are in Los Angeles, Salt Lake City, San Francisco, and Seattle.

The embassy of the **United Kingdom** is at 3100 Massachusetts Ave. NW, Washington, DC 20008 (© **202/588-7800**; www.britainusa.com). Other British consulates are in Atlanta, Boston, Chicago, Cleveland, Houston, Los Angeles, New York, San Francisco, and Seattle.

EMERGENCIES Call © **911** for police, fire, and medical emergencies. This is a toll-free call. (No coins are required at public telephones.)

If you encounter serious problems, contact the **Travelers Aid Society International** (© **202/546-1127**; www.travelers aid.org.), a nationwide, nonprofit, social-service organization geared to helping travelers in difficult straits, from reuniting families separated while traveling, to providing food and/or shelter to people stranded without cash, to emotional counseling. Travelers Aid operates help desks at Washington Dulles International Airport (© 703/572-8296), Ronald Reagan Washington National Airport (© 703/417-3975), and Union Station (© 202/371-1937).

GASOLINE (PETROL) At press time, in the Washington region, the cost of gasoline (also known as gas, but never petrol), hovers around $2.40 a gallon. Taxes are already included in the printed price. One U.S. gallon equals 3.8 liters or .85 imperial gallons. Fill-up locations are known as gas or service stations.

HOLIDAYS Banks, government offices, post offices, and many stores, restaurants, and museums are closed on the following legal national holidays: January 1 (New Year's Day), the third Monday in January (Martin Luther King, Jr., Day), the third Monday in February (Presidents' Day), the last Monday in May (Memorial Day), July 4 (Independence Day), the first Monday in September (Labor Day), the second Monday in October (Columbus Day), November 11 (Veterans' Day/Armistice Day), the fourth Thursday in November (Thanksgiving Day), and December 25 (Christmas). The Tuesday after the first Monday in November is Election Day, a federal government holiday in presidential-election years (held every 4 years, and next in 2012).

For more information on holidays see "Calendar of Events," in chapter 3.

HOSPITALS If you don't require immediate ambulance transportation but still need emergency-room treatment, call one of the following hospitals (and be sure to get directions): Children's Hospital National Medical Center, 111 Michigan Ave. NW (© **202/476-5000**); George

Washington University Hospital, 900 23rd St. NW at Washington Circle (© 202/715-4000); Georgetown University Medical Center, 3800 Reservoir Rd. NW (© 202/444-2000); or Howard University Hospital, 2041 Georgia Ave. NW (© 202/865-6100).

HOT LINES To reach a 24-hour poison-control hot line, call © 800/222-1222; to reach a 24-hour crisis line, call © 202/561-7000; to reach a 24-hour rape crisis line, call © 202/333-7273 (RAPE).

INSURANCE For information on traveler's insurance, trip-cancellation insurance, and medical insurance while traveling please visit www.frommers.com/planning.

INTERNET ACCESS Washington, D.C., is lacking in Internet cafes, probably because everyone here carries her own personal connection with her, via Blackberry, laptop, iPhone, or some other form of PDA. I know of only one public Internet cafe: In Dupont Circle's **Kramerbooks and Afterwords** bookstore, 1517 Connecticut Ave. NW (© 202/387-1400), which has one computer available for free Internet access, with a 15-minute time limit. Also see "Staying Connected" in chapter 3.

LEGAL AID If you are "pulled over" for a minor infraction (such as speeding), never attempt to pay the fine directly to a police officer; this could be construed as attempted bribery, a much more serious crime. Pay fines by mail, or directly into the hands of the clerk of the court. If accused of a more serious offense, say and do nothing before consulting a lawyer. Here the burden is on the state to prove a person's guilt beyond a reasonable doubt, and everyone has the right to remain silent, whether he or she is suspected of a crime or actually arrested. Once arrested, a person can make one telephone call to a party of his or her choice. International visitors should call your embassy or consulate.

MAIL At press time, domestic postage rates were 28¢ for a postcard and 44¢ for a letter. For international mail, a first-class letter of up to 1 ounce costs 98¢ (75¢ to Canada and 79¢ to Mexico); a first-class postcard costs the same as a letter. For more information go to **www.usps.com**.

If you aren't sure what your address will be in the United States, mail can be sent to you, in your name, c/o General Delivery at the main post office of the city or region where you expect to be. (Call © 800/275-8777 for information on the nearest post office.) The addressee must pick up mail in person and must produce proof of identity (driver's license, passport, and so on). Most post offices will hold your mail for up to 1 month, and are open Monday to Friday from 8am to 6pm, and Saturday from 9am to 3pm.

Always include zip codes when mailing items in the U.S. If you don't know your zip code, visit www.usps.com/zip4.

NEWSPAPERS & MAGAZINES Washington's preeminent newspaper is the *Washington Post,* which is sold in bookstores, train and subway stations, drugstores, and sidewalk kiosks all over town. These are also the places to buy other newspapers, like *The New York Times,* and *Washingtonian* magazine, the city's popular monthly full of penetrating features, restaurant reviews, and nightlife calendars. For up-to-the-minute news, check out the websites of these publications: www.washingtonpost.com, www.nytimes.com, www.washingtonian.com.

Also be sure to pick up a copy of *Washington Flyer* magazine, available free at the airport or online at www.fly2dc.com, to find out about airport and airline news and interesting Washington happenings.

PASSPORTS See www.frommers.com/planning for information on how to obtain a passport. See "Embassies & Consulates," above, for whom to contact if you lose yours while traveling in the U.S. For other information, please contact the following agencies:

For Residents of Australia Contact the **Australian Passport Information Service** at ℂ **131-232,** or visit the government website at www.passports.gov.au.

For Residents of Canada Contact the central **Passport Office,** Department of Foreign Affairs and International Trade, Ottawa, ON K1A 0G3 (ℂ **800/567-6868;** www.ppt.gc.ca).

For Residents of Ireland Contact the **Passport Office,** Setanta Centre, Molesworth Street, Dublin 2 (ℂ **01/671-1633;** www.irlgov.ie/iveagh).

For Residents of New Zealand Contact the **Passports Office** at ℂ **0800/225-050** in New Zealand or 04/474-8100, or log on to www.passports.govt.nz.

For Residents of the United Kingdom Visit your nearest passport office, major post office, or travel agency or contact the **United Kingdom Passport Service** at ℂ **0870/521-0410** or search its website at www.ukpa.gov.uk.

For Residents of the United States To find your regional passport office, either check the U.S. State Department website or call the **National Passport Information Center** toll-free number (ℂ **877/487-2778**) for automated information.

POLICE In an emergency, dial ℂ **911.** For a nonemergency, call ℂ **202/727-1010.**

SMOKING The District is smoke-free, meaning that the city bans smoking in restaurants, bars, and other public buildings. Smoking is permitted outdoors, unless otherwise noted.

TAXES The United States has no value-added tax (VAT) or other indirect tax at the national level. Every state, county, and city may levy its own local tax on all purchases, including hotel and restaurant checks and airline tickets. These taxes will not appear on price tags.

The sales tax on merchandise is 5.75% in the District, 5% in Maryland, and 4.5% in Virginia. Restaurant tax is 10% in the District, 6% in Maryland, and varied in Virginia, depending on the city and county. Hotel tax is 14.5% in the District, varied 5% to 8% in Maryland, and averages about 9.75% in Virginia.

TIME The continental United States is divided into **four time zones:** Eastern Standard Time (EST; this is Washington's time zone), Central Standard Time (CST), Mountain Standard Time (MST), and Pacific Standard Time (PST). Alaska and Hawaii have their own zones. For example, when it's 9am in Los Angeles (PST), it's 7am in Honolulu (HST), 10am in Denver (MST), 11am in Chicago (CST), noon in Washington, D.C. (EST), 5pm in London (GMT), and 2am the next day in Sydney.

Daylight saving time is in effect from 1am on the second Sunday in March to 1am on the first Sunday in November, except in Arizona, Hawaii, the U.S. Virgin Islands, and Puerto Rico. Daylight saving time moves the clock 1 hour ahead of standard time.

TIPPING Tips are a very important part of certain workers' income, and gratuities are the standard way of showing appreciation for services provided. In hotels, tip **bellhops** at least $1 per bag ($2–$3 if you have a lot of luggage) and tip the **chamber staff** $1 to $2 per day (more if you've left a disaster area for him or her to clean up). Tip the **doorman** or **concierge** only if he or she has provided you with some specific service (for example, calling a cab for you or obtaining difficult-to-get theater tickets). Tip the **valet-parking attendant** $1 every time you get your car.

In restaurants, bars, and nightclubs, tip **service staff** and **bartenders** 15% to 20% of the check, tip **checkroom attendants** $1 per garment, and tip **valet-parking attendants** $1 per vehicle.

As for other service personnel, tip **cab drivers** 15% of the fare; tip **skycaps** at airports at least $1 per bag ($2–$3 if you have a lot of luggage); and tip **hairdressers** and **barbers** 15% to 20%.

TOILETS You won't find public toilets or "restrooms" on the streets in most U.S. cities but they can be found in hotel lobbies, bars, restaurants, museums, department stores, railway and bus stations, and service stations. Large hotels and fast-food restaurants are often the best bet for clean facilities. Restaurants and bars in resorts or heavily visited areas may reserve their restrooms for patrons.

VISAS For information about U.S. Visas go to **http://travel.state.gov** and click on "Visas." Or go to one of the following websites:

Australian citizens can obtain up-to-date visa information from the **U.S. Embassy Canberra,** Moonah Place, Yarralumla, ACT 2600 (© **02/6214-5600**) or by checking the U.S. Diplomatic Mission's website at **http://usembassy-australia. state.gov/consular.**

British subjects can obtain up-to-date visa information by calling the **U.S. Embassy Visa Information Line** (© **0891/ 200-290**) or by visiting the "Visas to the U.S." section of the American Embassy London's website at **www.usembassy. org.uk.**

Irish citizens can obtain up-to-date visa information through the **Embassy of the USA Dublin,** 42 Elgin Rd., Dublin 4, Ireland (© **353/1-668-8777;** or by checking the "Visas to the U.S." section of the website at **http://dublin.usembassy.gov.**

Citizens of **New Zealand** can obtain up-to-date visa information by contacting the **U.S. Embassy New Zealand,** 29 Fitzherbert Terrace, Thorndon, Wellington (© **644/472-2068**), or get the information directly from the website at **http:// wellington.usembassy.gov.**

VISITOR INFORMATION **Destination D.C.,** is the official tourism and convention corporation for Washington, D.C.,

901 7th St. NW, 4th Floor, Washington, DC 20001-3719 (© **800/422-8644** or 202/789-7000; www.destinationdc.org). Before you leave, order a free copy of the bureau's *Washington, D.C. Visitors Guide,* which covers hotels, restaurants, sights, shops, and more and is updated twice yearly. At the © **202/789-7000** number, you can speak directly to a staff "visitor services specialist" and get answers to your specific questions about the city.

Be sure to consult Destination D.C.'s website, where you can read and download the visitors guide, along with the latest travel information, including upcoming exhibits at the museums and anticipated closings of tourist attractions. The website is also an excellent source for maps, which you can download and print from the site or order for delivery by mail.

Once in D.C., you can stop by Destination D.C.'s offices on 7th Street NW (Metro: Gallery Place/Chinatown, H St. exit), to pick up the visitors guide and maps, and to talk to visitors services specialists. Office hours are Monday to Friday, 8:30am to 5pm.

If you're arriving by plane or train, you can think of your airport or the train station as visitor information centers; all three Washington-area airports and Union Station offer all sorts of visitor services. See chapter 3's "Getting There & Getting Around" section for details.

The **D.C. Chamber of Commerce Visitor Information Center** (© **866/324-7386** or 202/289-8317; www.dcchamber. org; click on "Visiting DC," then "Visitor Information Center") is a small bureau inside the immense Ronald Reagan International Trade Center Building, at 1300 Pennsylvania Ave. NW. To enter the federal building, you need to show a picture ID. The visitor center lies on the ground floor of the building, a little to your right as you enter from the Wilson Plaza, near the Federal Triangle Metro. From March

15 to Labor Day, the center is open Monday through Friday, 8:30am to 5:30pm, and on Saturday from 9am to 4pm; from Labor Day to March 14, the center is open Monday through Friday 9am to 4:30pm.

Also look for business improvement district (BID) offices and their patrolling "ambassadors," who dispense information, directions, and other assistance in their individual neighborhoods. Among the most established are: the **Downtown D.C. Business Improvement District (Downtown D.C. BID)**, 1250 H St. NW (© **202/ 638-3232;** www.downtowndc.org), the **Golden Triangle Business Improvement District (Golden Triangle BID)**, 1120 Connecticut Ave. NW (© **202/463-3400;** www.gtbid.com); and the **Capitol Hill Business Improvement District (Capitol Hill BID)**, 30 Massachusetts Ave. NE, inside Union Station's garage (© **202/842-3333;** www.capitolhillbid. org).

National Park Service information kiosks are located inside or near the Jefferson, Lincoln, FDR, Vietnam Veterans, Korean War, and World War II memorials and at the Washington Monument (© **202/ 426-6841** or 619-7222; www.nps.gov/ state/dc for all national parklands in D.C. or www.nps.gov/nama for National Mall and Memorials Park sites).

The **White House Visitor Center,** on the first floor of the Herbert Hoover Building, Department of Commerce, 1450 Pennsylvania Ave. NW (btw. 14th and 15th sts.; © **202/208-1631,** or 456-7041 for recorded information), is open daily (except for Christmas Day, Thanksgiving, and New Year's Day) from 7:30am to 4pm.

The **Smithsonian Information Center,** in "the Castle," 1000 Jefferson Dr. SW (© **202/633-1000,** or TTY [text telephone] 633-5285; www.si.edu), is open every day but Christmas from 8:30am to 5:30pm; knowledgeable staff answer questions and dispense maps and brochures.

Take a look at the D.C. government's website, **www.dc.gov,** and that of the nonprofit organization Cultural Tourism D.C., **www.culturaltourismdc.org,** for more information about the city. The Cultural Tourism D.C. site, in particular, provides helpful and interesting background knowledge of D.C.'s historic and cultural landmarks, especially in neighborhoods, or in parts of neighborhoods, not usually visited by tourists.

Check out the websites and blogs of www. washingtonpost.com, www.washingtonian. com, www.dcist.com and www.ontaponline. com for the latest commentary and information about Washington happenings. Refer to chapter 1's box of "Best Washington, D.C., Websites" for more sources.

2 AIRLINE, HOTEL & CAR-RENTAL WEBSITES

MAJOR AIRLINES

Air France
www.airfrance.com

Air Jamaica
www.airjamaica.com

Alaska Airlines/Horizon Air
www.alaskaair.com

American Airlines
www.aa.com

British Airways
www.british-airways.com

Continental Airlines
www.continental.com

Delta Air Lines
www.delta.com

Finnair
www.finnair.com

Frontier Airlines
www.frontierairlines.com

Hawaiian Airlines
www.hawaiianair.com

Iberia Airlines
www.iberia.com

JetBlue Airways
www.jetblue.com

Korean Air
www.koreanair.com

Lan Airlines
www.lanchile.com

Lufthansa
www.lufthansa.com

Midwest Airlines
www.midwestairlines.com

North American Airlines
www.flynaa.com

Northwest Airlines
www.nwa.com

Quantas Airways
www.quantas.com

South African Airways
www.flysaa.com

Swiss Air
www.swiss.com

TACA
www.taca.com

United Airlines
www.united.com

US Airways
www.usairways.com

Virgin America
www.virginamerica.com

Virgin Atlantic Airways
www.virgin-atlantic.com

BUDGET AIRLINES

AirTran Airways
www.airtran.com

Avolar
www.avolar.com.mx

easyJet
www.easyjet.com

Frontier Airlines
www.frontierairlines.com

Interjet
www.interjet.com.mx

JetBlue Airways
www.jetblue.com

Jetstar (Australia)
www.jetstar.com

Ryanair
www.ryanair.com

Southwest Airlines
www.southwest.com

Skybus
www.skybus.com

Spirit Airlines
www.spiritair.com

Ted (part of United Airlines)
www.flyted.com

MAJOR HOTEL & MOTEL CHAINS

Best Western International
www.bestwestern.com

Clarion Hotels
www.choicehotels.com

Comfort Inns
www.ComfortInn.com

Courtyard by Marriott
www.marriott.com/courtyard

Crowne Plaza Hotels
www.ichotelsgroup.com/crowneplaza

Days Inn
www.daysinn.com

Doubletree Hotels
www.doubletree.com

Econo Lodges
www.choicehotels.com

Embassy Suites
www.embassysuites.com

Farfield Inn by Marriott
www.farfieldinn.com

Four Seasons
www.fourseasons.com

Hampton Inn
www.hamptoninn1.hilton.com

Hilton Hotels
www.hilton.com

Holiday Inn
www.holidayinn.com

Howard Johnson
www.hojo.com

Hyatt
www.hyatt.com

InterContinental Hotels & Resorts
www.ichotelsgroup.com

La Quinta Inns and Suites
www.lq.com

Loews Hotels
www.loewshotels.com

Marriott
www.marriott.com

Motel 6
www.motel6.com

Omni Hotels
www.omnihotels.com

Quality
www.QualityInn.ChoiceHotels.com

Radisson Hotels & Resorts
www.radisson.com

Ramada Worldwide
www.ramada.com

Red Carpet Inns
www.bookroomsnow.com

Red Lion Hotels
www.redlion.rdln.com

Red Roof Inns
www.redroof.com

Renaissance
www.renaissancehotels.com

Residence Inn by Marriott
www.marriott.com/residenceinn

Rodeway Inns
www.RodewayInn.com

Sheraton Hotels & Resorts
www.starwoodhotels.com/sheraton

Super 8 Motels
www.super8.com

Travelodge
www.travelodge.com

Vagabond Inns
www.vagabondinn.com

Westin Hotels & Resorts
www.starwoodhotels.com/westin

Wyndham Hotels & Resorts
www.wyndham.com

CAR-RENTAL AGENCIES

Advantage
www.advantage.com

Alamo
www.alamo.com

Auto Europe
www.autoeurope.com

Avis
www.avis.com

Budget
www.budget.com

Dollar
www.dollar.com

Enterprise
www.enterprise.com

Hertz
www.hertz.com

Kemwel (KHA)
www.kemwel.com

National
www.nationalcar.com

Payless
www.paylesscarrental.com

Rent-A-Wreck
www.rentawreck.com

Thrifty
www.thrifty.com

INDEX

See also Accommodations and Restaurant indexes, below.